CIVILIZATION IN THE WEST

FOURTH EDITION

CIVILIZATION IN THE WEST

Part 1 Prehistory to 1715

CRANE BRINTON

JOHN B. CHRISTOPHER
Professor of History Emeritus,
University of Rochester

ROBERT LEE WOLFF
Archibald Cary Coolidge, Professor of History
Harvard University

Prentice-Hall, Inc., Englewood Cliffs, New Jersey 07632

Library of Congress Cataloging in Publication Data
Brinton, Clarence Crane, 1898–1968.
Civilization in the West.

Includes bibliographies and index.
CONTENTS: pt. 1. Prehistory to 1715.—pt. 2. 1600 to the present.
1. Civilization, Occidental. I. Christopher, John B., joint author. II. Wolff, Robert Lee, joint author. III. Title.
CB245.B72 1981 909'.09821 80–28369
ISBN 0–13–134924–4 (v. 1)
ISBN 0–13–134932–5 (v. 2)

CIVILIZATION IN THE WEST, fourth edition
Part 1: Prehistory to 1715
Brinton/Christopher/Wolff

Editorial Production by Cathie Mick Mahar
Interior Design by Lee Cohen
Cover Design by Lee Cohen
Acquisition Editor: John Busch and Stephen Dalphin
Manufacturing Buyer: Edmund W. Leone
Cover Art: Mask of Agamemnon, Alison Frantz

Printed in the United States of America

10 9 8 7 6 5 4 3 2 1

PRENTICE-HALL INTERNATIONAL, INC., *London*
PRENTICE-HALL OF AUSTRALIA PTY. LIMITED, *Sydney*
PRENTICE-HALL OF CANADA, LTD., *Toronto*
PRENTICE-HALL OF INDIA PRIVATE LIMITED, *New Delhi*
PRENTICE-HALL OF JAPAN, INC., *Tokyo*
PRENTICE-HALL OF SOUTHEAST ASIA PTE. LTD., *Singapore*
WHITEHALL BOOKS LIMITED, *Wellington, New Zealand*

Contents

Preface

This fourth edition of *Civilization in the West* is more than a mere revision of preceding volumes; it is in many respects a whole new book. Many chapters from older editions have been rewritten in the light of recent scholarship and have also been restructured in order to make the narrative more coherent and the chapters more nearly uniform in length. Sentences and paragraphs have been shortened and the vocabulary simplified to fit the reading skills of a new generation of students. The particular interests of this generation are reflected in additional material on social history and on new advances in science. Some traditions of historical writing are maintained, such as the use of "man" for human beings of both sexes in sections of the text. This is merely a convenient form of shorthand.

This new edition is available in a two-paperback format. The first volume, with ten chapters, extends from the earliest civilizations through the seventeenth century. A full chapter (the second) is devoted to the Greek world. The Roman world, previously coupled with the Greek, is now treated in Chapter 3, along with the Christian revolution which emerged in part from the shortcomings of the Roman Empire. Chapter 4 is a survey of the feudal and Byzantine successors of the Roman Empire through the eleventh century, together with the rapidly advancing Islamic rival of Christianity.

Developments in the later Middle Ages are analyzed in Chapter 5 (Western Europe) and Chapter 6 (Eastern Europe). The latter extends from the Crusades to the establishment of the Ottoman and Russian successors of Byzantium and their history down to the seventeenth century. Chapters 7 through 9 cover the transition in the West from the declining medieval world through the Renaissance and the upheavals resulting from the Protestant revolt, the growth of ambitious dynastic states, the expansion of European power abroad, and the growing unrest in the mother countries.

Chapter 10 replaces two short chapters in the third edition. It links the two volumes of the fourth edition by evaluating the contribution of both the seventeenth and eighteenth centuries to the Great Modern Revolution. This transformation of science and economic life also had important side effects on literature and the arts; it stimulated the program of the Enlightenment for political and social reform. The results were evident in the enlightened despotism of the eighteenth century (Chapter 11) and the French Revolution (Chapter 12).

The overloaded chapter in the preceding edition narrating the renewal of revolution from 1815 to 1870 has been divided in two. The new Chapter 13, Industry and Democracy, is centered on the Atlantic world, mainly Britain, France, and the United States. Chapter 14, also new, focuses on nationalism and reform in southern, central, and eastern Europe. Chapter 15 discusses the principal developments in ideas and culture during the nineteenth century.

Four chapters cover social, economic, and political events from 1870 to 1970. Chapter 16—Prelude, Theme, Coda (the terms are borrowed from music)—takes the story from the birth of the Second German Empire to the peace settlement after World War I. Chapter 17, Interlude and Repetition, steps back to the Russian Revolution of 1917, then discusses the Nazi dictatorship and other totalitarian regimes, and describes the Second World War which they precipitated. Chapter 18, the Cold War and Great Power Domestic Politics, notes the breakdown of the wartime alliance between the Soviet Union and the western democracies together with subsequent developments in the major states. Chapter 19, Great Power Foreign Policy and the Emerging Nations, records the strains between the democracies and the communist bloc from the Berlin blockade and Korean War to the Vietnam problem; it also assesses the growing importance of the newly independent states in Asia, the Middle East, and Africa.

Chapter 20 (The World Since 1970) breaks new ground as an impressionistic survey of an important and disturbing decade. And the final chapter, 21, Science and Culture in the Twentieth Century, reviews the chief advances in the sciences and arts and concludes that, though sometimes improving the quality of life, they often left countless millions of people still struggling to survive.

We thank the following people who were asked to review part or all of the book: Anthony M. Brescia, Nassau Community College; Elizabeth Carney, Clemson University; Charles W. Connell, West Virginia University; Glen H. Coston, Pensacola Junior College; Robert Feldman, California State University at Fullerton; Thomas Hachey, Marquette University; C. Douglas McCullough, DeKalb Community College; James Muldoon, Rutgers University; Cedric Ward, Andrews University; Robert Welborn, Clayton Junior College.

* * * * * * * * * * * * * * * *

This preface ends on a somber note as it records the death in November, 1980, of Robert Lee Wolff, who assumed responsibility for preparing fourteen of the twenty-one chapters in the fourth edition. All of us involved in this project are grateful that he had completed his assignments. He would join in expressing the authors' gratitude to members of the staff at Prentice-Hall for their patience and expert assistance in preparing these new volumes. All of us mourn the loss of this lively, many-faceted scholar who was an important contributor to all the editions of *Civilization in the West* and its parent volumes, *A History of Civilization*, during the past quarter of a century.

Maps

Illustrations

CHAPTER ONE

Man's First Civilizations

In this chapter we look at the human experience from his beginnings on earth down to about 850 B.C., and in some instances a few centuries earlier. We are dealing with millions of years, but we shall be discussing in any detail only a few thousand: the period after man entered the Stone Age and became recognizably a member of the same species as ourselves. We shall discuss the ancient Near East and the closely connected civilization that grew up on Crete and on the mainland of Greece.

I BEFORE WRITING

History and Prehistory

To learn about what is going on in the world today—a proposed treaty between the United States and the Soviet Union, a quarrel between China and Vietnam—we can read the newspapers. If we need to know *why* these things are happening now, we can go to the library and look up books about past relations between the Americans and the Russians, the Chinese and the Vietnamese.

We take it for granted that we will have *written sources*—diaries, documents, propaganda leaflets—to answer our questions about past and present human relationships and human development. To study the past of peoples far away from us on the earth, we know we shall often have to read sources in their language: in Russian, or Chinese, or Vietnamese. And the further back we go in time, the more scanty these written sources become. Then we try to learn more, to fill in the gaps, by studying coins or works of art—statues, paintings, poems, songs—which give us knowledge of the way people lived and the way they thought, of their attitudes toward each other, of their society.

These written sources would become particularly important if we were to find that the people we wanted to know about wrote a language that nobody now on earth can read. Only during the past two hundred years have scholars learned how to read the language of the ancient Egyptians and the languages of the peoples of the river valleys in the ancient Near East. And reading each previously unknown language was made possible only by the discovery of writings in it, accompanied by a translation into a language already known. Even after decades of careful work with such lucky finds, however, some uncertainties still remain. And sometimes there has been no lucky find, and an ancient language remains stubbornly unreadable.

Of course there were long, long, long centuries—thousands of them—before man had learned to write at all. Only his bones and the bones of his animals and some of the things he made remain to tell us about him: they are our only sources. Usually these must be dug up, excavated, by *archaeologists*—men specially trained in the science of ancient things. The development of the carbon-14 technique, in which radioactive carbon is used to date ancient objects within a couple of centuries, has proved to be a great help. New discoveries pile up and our knowledge of the very distant past is constantly growing.

The Old Stone Age

The earth we live on is probably about five billion years old. Primitive plant and animal life first appeared between a billion and two billion years ago. But the first mammals developed only

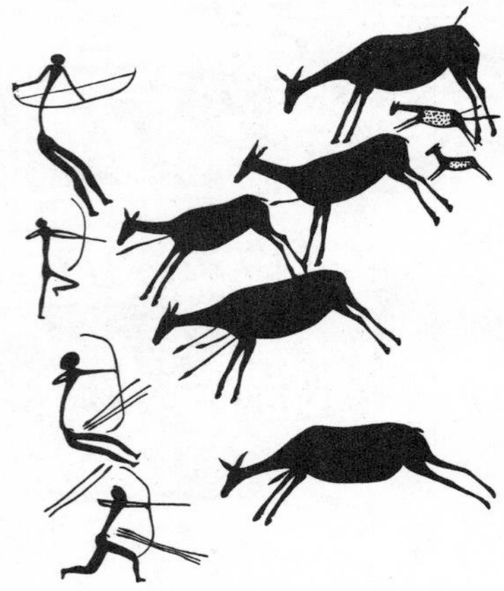

Stag hunt; cave painting from Cueva de los Cabollos, Spain.

two or three hundred million years ago, and the earliest remains so far discovered of apelike beings whom we recognize as foreshadowing the future development of mankind are probably only between three and four million years old. Since the late 1950s there have been many dramatic discoveries of such remains in equatorial east Africa, notably in Tanzania, and in Ethiopia.

These discoveries have pushed further back in time the first appearance of recognizably manlike beings. Exact dates are still controversial. So are the exact relationships of the various fossil apes: those who lived in trees; and those who abandoned the trees and lived on the ground and began to walk erect, and slowly developed larger and larger brains. Scientists whose specialty is early man—*anthropologists*—debate intensely the exact meaning of each new discovery. The science is changing fast.

We still cannot date precisely the moment when creatures transitional between apes and men, and therefore *manlike* (hominids), developed into species that were true men (*homo,* Latin for "man"). *Homo habilis,* "the skillful man," was making crude stone tools more than a million and a half years ago. But his brain was less than half as big as ours. Remains of *Homo erectus,* "the man who stands up straight," were discovered in the 1880s in Java. He had a larger brain than *Homo habilis,* stood about five feet tall, and lived in Europe and Africa as well as Asia between a million and a half and half a million years ago. He had fire and made stone axes.

The earliest man that many of us have heard of was *Neanderthal man,* named for the valley of the Neander River in Germany, where his remains were first discovered. He lived widespread in Europe and the neighboring parts of Asia and Africa. Reconstructions of his skull make him look even more apelike than he probably was. He made better tools.

In one case at least, he showed himself almost human: In a Neanderthal burial, the corpse was placed to rest on a heaping bouquet of flowers. Neanderthal man was not yet *Homo sapiens,* "the man who knows," the species to which all present human beings belong. Probably around 70,000 years ago, the earliest specimens of *Homo sapiens* were already living in Europe along with Neanderthal man. For the last 40,000 years or so, *Homo sapiens* has dominated the earth. Our real business is with him.

Homo sapiens and his predecessors were living in what is called the Old Stone Age (Paleolithic). For hundreds of thousands of years progress was immensely slow. Man's first tools were the stones he used to chip other stones into weapons and other tools. All these centuries upon centuries belong to prehistory, rather than to history. Paleolithic man left remains scattered widely in Europe and Asia. He took refuge in Africa from the glaciers that periodically moved south over the northern continents and made life impossible there.

Wherever he went, he hunted to eat, and fought and killed his enemies. He learned how to cook his food, how to take shelter from the cold in caves, and eventually how to specialize his tools. He made bone needles with which to sew animal hides into clothes with animal sinews; he made hatchets, spears, arrowheads, awls.

Painting of a bull from the cave at Lascaux, ca. 12,000 B.C.

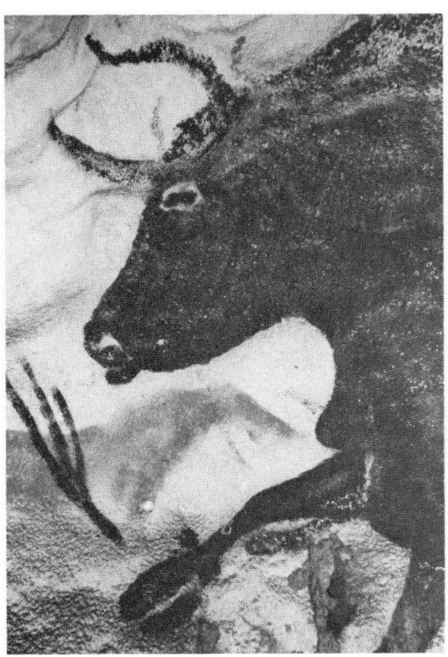

One day in 1940, two boys in southwest France were hunting rabbits when their dog suddenly disappeared down a hole. Following the dog, the boys fell into an underground cave hidden for thousands of years. The light of their torches revealed an extraordinary series of paintings on its limestone walls. They saw animals portrayed in brilliant colors with astonishing realism and artistry: deer, bison, horses, and others.

These were painted toward the end of the Paleolithic period by *Cro-Magnon man,* true *Homo sapiens,* often standing as tall as six feet four inches and with a large brain. Lascaux, where the paintings were found, became one of the great tourist centers of Europe. By 1960 the breath of so many thousands of visitors gazing in wonder began to damage the pictures, which had been sealed away from moisture for so many thousands of years; so the cave is now closed to the public.

At Altamira, in northern Spain, similar cave pictures, not quite so splendid, had long been known but had suffered from souvenir hunters. Long exposed to air and changing temperatures, they are immune to moisture. They are the most easily visible proof of the artistic skills of Paleolithic man. Many other caves have late Paleolithic paintings, but none are so spectacular as those at Lascaux and Altamira.

Why did the Paleolithic artist paint the pictures? Did he think that by putting animals on his walls he could improve his chances as a hunter? Would their pictures give him power over them, and so guarantee his supply of food? Were the different animals totems of different families or clans? Sometimes on the walls of the caves we find paintings of human hands, often with a finger or fingers missing. Were these hands efforts to ward off evil spirits? Or were they prayers by hunters and warriors that they should not suffer mutilation of their hands? Paleolithic man also produced small female statuettes, sometimes overemphasizing the breasts, buttocks, and sexual organs. Modern archaeologists call them "Venuses." Were these fertility symbols? or love charms?

Until about ten years ago, such unanswerable questions were the only ones that scholars had asked about the achievements of Paleolithic man. But an archaeologist named Alexander Marshack has now studied again the vast amount of Paleolithic material in European museums. He has made some amazing discoveries and reached new theories. Marshack found numerous objects—a mammoth tusk, bones of various animals, a pebble, several short staffs of ivory, a

Three faces of an eagle bone with the markings interpreted by Alexander Marshack as lunar notation: from southwest France, ca. 13,000 B.C.

pair of eagle bones—dating from perhaps 32,000 B.C. to 12,000 B.C. on which there were markings that he interpreted as the records of lunar months.

Late Old Stone Age man was most likely keeping a kind of calendar to help him predict regular seasonal changes from year to year. Such a calendar would allow him to plan his hunting life and other activities, such as the preparation of skins for clothing. This discovery teaches us how important time was to late Old Stone Age man. Suddenly his mind seems so advanced that the "mystery" of his artistic skills becomes far less mysterious.

Sometimes his time records accompany artistic representations of animals. On the same piece of ivory from southwest France appear a budding flower, sprouting plants, grass snakes, a salmon, and a seal. Marshack believes this was a symbolic representation of the earth's reawakening after winter. When the symbols of springtime appear together with the lunar date marks, we are looking at something very like an illustrated calendar. Other spring events celebrated in Old Stone Age art include the mating season of stags and bison.

Perhaps the "Venuses" were not "sexual" in any simple sense. In a hunting culture, a female image with its suggestion of the female processes also suggests the procession of the seasons. Certain animals—reindeer, bison, horses—appear associated with females; others—bears and lions—with males. The men of the late Old Stone Age clearly told tales of the hunt, successful and unsuccessful. They had a ritual that involved killing and sacrifice. They studied the passing of time in the world around them and in the bodies of animals and of mankind.

They carved a nude figure of a woman holding a bison horn that looks exactly like a crescent moon and is marked with thirteen lines, the number of lunar months in a year. Probably she is mankind's first true goddess. Though Old Stone Age man still remains a dim and remote figure to us, Marshack's researches for the first time make him recognizable as fully man.

Naked woman holding a bison horn, with its crescent shape, and thirteen marks corresponding to the lunar months of the year: from southwest France, ca. 22,000 B.C.

The New Stone Age

By about 8000 B.C.—some ten thousand years ago—man in some places began to pass from the Old Stone Age (Paleolithic) into the New Stone Age (Neolithic). The advance was marked by important changes in his way of life so great that they are sometimes called the "Neolithic Revolution." They took place unevenly over a period of several thousand years, depending upon conditions. All the changes are found first in the Near East.

One was the domestication of animals for food. Man had long since tamed dogs and used them in the hunt. But when he kept goats, pigs, sheep, and the ancestors of our cows in pens, he could eat them when their meat was young and tender without having to hunt them down when they were hardest to overtake. Another change was the first domestication of plants for food—a kind of wheat and barley. Finally—and this always seems to have been the last step—man turned his shelter into a house and settled down to live in it. Once he had done all these things, he had made the transition to the New Stone Age.

Accompanying these fundamental steps went the practice of a new art, the baking of clay vessels—pots and bowls and storage jars; clay, of course, was much easier to work with than stone. It is chiefly by studying the surviving varieties of such clay vessels and their fragments, and the types of glazes and decoration the potters used, that modern scholars have been able to learn how to date the sites where men lived.

At Jericho in Palestine during the 1950s, archaeologists excavated a town radiocarbon-dated at about 7800 B.C. It extended over about eight acres and included perhaps three thousand inhabitants. These people lived in round houses with conical roofs—the oldest permanent houses known. They had a large, columned building in which were found many mud-modeled figurines of animals and statues of a man, a woman, and a male child. It was surely a temple of some kind. All this dates from a time when people did not yet know how to make pots, which appear only at a later stage.

In Çatalhüyük in southern Turkey, discovered only in 1961 and dating to 6500 B.C., the people had a wide variety of pottery, grew their own grain, kept sheep, and wove their wool into textiles. In their shrine were found a woman sculptured in relief in the posture of giving birth to a child, a bull's head, and boars' heads with women's breasts running in rows along their lower jaws. The bull and a double ax painted on a wall seem to look forward to two main features of the better-known religion of ancient Crete, as we shall see.

Far to the east, in modern Iraq (ancient Mesopotamia, "between the rivers" Tigris and Euphrates) lay Jarmo, dated about 4500 B.C., a third Neolithic settlement.

A thousand years later than Jarmo, about 3550 B.C., and far to the south, at Uruk on the banks of the Euphrates River, men were using the plow to scratch the soil before sowing their seeds. They were keeping the accounts of their temple in simple picture-writing.

Writing was the great leap forward that took man out of prehistory and into history. Similar advances are found in Egypt too, at roughly the same time. But Mesopotamia took the lead. Indeed, it was from Mesopotamia that the major cultural advances, especially the all-important art of writing, came into Egypt and gave the Egyptians a great push into history.

To the east of Mesopotamia, in northwest and southwest Iran, archaeologists during the 1960s found several early Neolithic sites, some of which may even precede Jericho, although they are not so large or complex or advanced. In south central Iran, a brand-new site was discovered in 1967 at Tepe Yahya, a Neolithic village of about 4500 B.C. Here archaeologists found pottery, small sharpened flints set in a bone handle to make a sickle, and an extraordinary small sculpture in dark green stone, which is both a female figure and a phallus.

The Neolithic people of the Near East were not necessarily any more intelligent than those elsewhere. Indeed, Neolithic remains have also been found in many places in the Mediterranean region, and even far to the north. But in those places climate was far less favorable. So even when Neolithic man eventually controlled his environment—as in the lake settlements of Switzerland, where he built frame houses on piles over the water—the triumph came later, about 2500 B.C.

In Australia and New Guinea and in South America there are people today who still live in the Neolithic Age. It was the inhabitants of the more favored regions who got to the great discoveries first. It was they who learned copper-smelting and the other arts of metallurgy, and who thus led the human race altogether out of the Stone Age—and into the Bronze Age. And it was they who first lived in cities.

Neolithic figurine shaped like a phallus but carved as a female figure: from Tepe Yahya, Iran.

Writing, metallurgy, and urban life: these are the marks of civilization. Soon after these phenomena had appeared in the Tigris-Euphrates valleys, along the Nile, and in Iran, they appeared also in the valley of the Indus in western India and along certain Chinese rivers. We trace our own civilization not directly to India or China but to Mesopotamia and Egypt. So we must now turn to Mesopotamia and Egypt, and add some words on Iran.

II THE PEOPLES OF THE RIVER VALLEYS AND OF IRAN

Mesopotamia and Elam

Sumerians

By about 3100 B.C. the Sumerians were the dominant people in southern Mesopotamia immediately north of the Persian Gulf, in the fertile lower valleys of the Tigris and Euphrates and in the land between them. They had left the Stone Age behind them by inventing bronze, an alloy of copper and tin that could be cast in molds, and they now made tools and weapons of it. The Sumerians moved mankind into the Bronze Age. They lived in cities; they had begun to accumulate and use capital; and they wrote.

Modern man has known about the Sumerians for only a little over a century. Archaeologists working at Nineveh in northern Mesopotamia in 1869 found many Babylonian inscribed clay tablets.

They were able to read these tablets because the inscriptions were written in a language called Akkadian, a Semitic tongue related to Hebrew and Arabic. But some of the tablets also had writing in another language that was not Semitic, and had previously been unknown. Some of these inscriptions spoke of the king of Sumer and Akkad, and so the new language was called Sumerian. But it was not until the 1890s that archaeologists digging far to the south of Nineveh found many thousands of tablets inscribed in Sumerian only. Since then, excavations have multiplied; written material has poured in. By working from known Akkadian to previously unknown Sumerian, scholars have pretty well learned how to read the Sumerian language.

If the Sumerians did not invent writing on clay, they at least perfected it. At first they used a kind of picture-writing, and over the thousand years between 3000 and 2000 B.C. they developed a phonetic alphabet. With a reed pen they impressed into the wet clay tablet little wedge-shaped marks. This script we call *cuneiform* from the Latin *cuneus,* meaning a wedge. The first thousand years of Sumerian history we know from tens of thousands of these tablets that are mostly economic or administrative in content. Not until after 2000 B.C. do we get purely literary materials. But five thousand tablets from that period do provide us with them, some short, some very long, some of them not yet transcribed or translated.

In the earliest days, the Sumerian cities governed themselves through a council of elders, who derived their authority from a general assembly of all the adult free men. This assembly, which decided on such questions as making war and peace, sometimes would grant supreme authority to an individual leader for a limited time. This arrangement—which seems astonishingly "modern" and "democratic" to us—did not last long, and was replaced by one-man rule in each city.

But the human ruler acted only as the representative on earth of the god of the city. The ruler built temples to the god to keep his favor, and especially to obtain his divine protection against the floods that often swept down the river valleys in the springtime with disastrous results for the people in their way.

The lives and religion and literature of the peoples of Mesopotamia were filled with terror of floods. The story of the flood in the Bible echoes the ancient tradition of the Sumerians. The Sumerians devised an elaborate system of canals not only for irrigation but to control the force of the floods, and each city asked the blessing of its god on its labors. Toward the south, near the Persian Gulf, the problem became one of draining the flow of salt water that would otherwise have ruined the fields.

It took the toil of many centuries for the Sumerians to transform the bleak marshes of the river valleys into fertile and productive farmland, dotted with prosperous cities. Each had its own political bureaucracy and religious institutions. Each passed through occasional oppressions, upheavals, and political overturns. Cities warred with one another. About 2350 B.C. we find the first inscription recording the ambition of one city ruler to rule over the entire region, to be the first universal monarch in history.

The Sumerians also had to fight against infiltrating Semites from the Arabian deserts to the west and from the hills to the north. They campaigned eastward too, against "Elam," the peoples living in what today is western Iran. About 2300, Sargon, king of Akkad, a Semite from the north, conquered the Sumerian ruler of Uruk.

Sargon and his successors called themselves kings of Sumer and Akkad. Perhaps the non-Semitic Sumerians and the Semitic Akkadians had already begun to fuse into one people. By about 2100, the end of the Early Bronze Age, Sargon's descendants had lost their power. For a time there was no force to unify the petty states.

About 2000 B.C., Ur-Nammu, ruler of the city of Ur, reunited Sumer and Akkad for a century. Much of what we know about the Sumerians comes from the excavation of Ur. Ur-Nammu's law code provided fixed punishment for certain crimes. There was a fine of five shekels of silver for the rape of a virgin slave girl without her owner's consent. Ur-Nammu is thus the first known lawgiver for an entire people. Ur's brief period of prosperity was based on a far-flung trade, on a system of regular taxation, and on a revival of learning. But Ur's subject cities fell away, and invading Elamites from the east destroyed Sumerian power. The center of political might shifted to the north.

In addition to their city gods, the Sumerians worshiped a god of the heavens, a god of the region between heaven and earth (the air, hence storms and winds), and a god of earth. Another trinity included gods of the sun and moon, and a fertility goddess of the morning star. With her was associated a young male god who died and was reborn as a symbol of the seasons.

Here, in the first religion recorded in sources that we can read, we find elements common to all subsequent efforts of men to deal with the supernatural. It was Enki, god of earth and of wisdom, for instance, who poured the water into the two great fertilizing rivers, Tigris and Euphrates, and stocked them with fish. Enki created grain, filled the land with cattle, built houses and canals, and set subgods over each enterprise.

The Sumerian gods had human forms and lived recognizably human lives, with rivalries among themselves. Sumerians also believed in many demons, mostly bad. The Sumerians tried to predict the future by examining the entrails of slaughtered sheep or goats, and by interpreting dreams and studying the stars. Because the temples of the city god and other gods actually owned most of the land, most of the population worked as serfs of the temple. But the produce of the land was distributed as pay to them.

Life was highly diversified. We find blacksmiths, carpenters, and merchants alongside the hunters, farmers, and shepherds of the older days. Fathers exercised many rights over their children. The society was monogamous, and women held a high position. In Sumer, punishments consisted mostly of fines, a milder practice than later societies followed.

In their epic poems the Sumerians celebrated the deeds of Gilgamesh, a hero who undertook perilous journeys, fought and overcame dreadful monsters, and performed feats of

Figure of a Sumerian dignitary.

strength. But even Gilgamesh, strong though he was, had to die. A mournful tone runs through Sumerian literature, in hymns, lamentations, prayers, fables, and even schoolboy compositions. Yet a Sumerian proverb sagely says,

> Praise a young man, and he will do whatever you want; Throw a crust to a dog, and he will wag his tail before you.

Obviously these people are recognizably of the same human breed as ourselves.

Sumerian art was entirely religious, official in purpose, and impersonal in style. The Sumerians built their temples of baked brick. In the shrine was an altar against a wall. Other rooms and an outer courtyard were later added. The whole structure was set upon a terrace. Then the terraces multiplied, each smaller than the one below, with the sanctuary at the top, reached by stairs from terrace to terrace.

This was the *ziggurat,* the typical Mesopotamian temple. Its construction suggests the rigidly hierarchical Sumerian social order. It was a great ziggurat that suggested the tower of Babel to the author of Genesis. Sumerian sculpture consisted of clothed human figures, solemn and stiff, with large, staring eyes. Gods were shown as larger than kings, and ordinary human beings as smaller.

New Discoveries in Iran

Since 1967, the mound at Tepe Yahya in south central Iran (which contained the Neolithic city already mentioned) has also yielded startling finds from a later period. Here, five hundred miles east of the Mesopotamian region traditionally accepted as the birthplace of writing, archaeologists have turned up clay tablets dating to about the year 3500 B.C.—at least as early as, and perhaps even slightly earlier than, the early Sumerian writings. And at Tepe Yahya, the language of the tablets is the earliest form of the language spoken in Elam, later Iran. The tablets are mostly commercial records. They were found in a storehouse, along with pottery storage jars.

Tepe Yahya served as a midpoint between the civilizations growing up in Mesopotamia and that much farther to the east in the valley of the Indus. Another such midpoint appears to have been the island of Bahrein in the Persian Gulf. The details of such ancient trade and other relationships remain to be thoroughly investigated. But it is at least likely that the people of the Tigris and Euphrates valleys did indeed trade with distant India, with the various centers as the midpoints. These discoveries are sensational new developments in the exploration of the ancient Near East.

Akkadians: Babylonians and Assyrians

Speakers of Semitic/Akkadian, first Babylonian and then Assyrian, succeeded the Sumerians, to whom they owed much. Invading from the Arabian desert, the first of these peoples, the Amorites, arrived about 2000 B.C. between the Tigris and Euphrates.

Since 1935, excavations at Mari in the middle Euphrates valley have exposed a palace with more than 260 rooms. We now have many thousands of tablets, mostly from the period between 1750 and 1700 B.C. These consist of the royal archives and include official letters to the king from his own officials scattered through his territories and from other rulers of city-states and principalities some previously unknown. Among the royal correspondents was an Amorite prince named Hammurabi, who just before 1700 B.C. made his own Babylonian kingdom supreme in Mesopotamia. His descendants held power in Babylon and the surrounding regions down to about 1530, but had to surrender Hammurabi's wider conquest.

Hammurabi's famous code of law survives;

it is engraved on an eight-foot pillar. Partly modeled on its Sumerian predecessors, it shows a much harsher spirit in its punishments. Hammurabi boasted not of his warlike deeds but of the peace and prosperity he had brought. The code reveals a strongly stratified society: a noble who put out the eye of a noble would have his own eye put out; but a noble who put out the eye of a member of a lower class only had to pay a fine. Yet the lower classes had rights also. Polygamy and divorce now made their appearance.

New nomads, this time from the east (Iran), the Kassites, shattered Babylonian power about 1530 B.C. After four centuries of relatively peaceful Kassite rule, supremacy in Mesopotamia gradually passed to the far more warlike Semitic Assyrians, whose power had been gradually rising for several centuries in their great northern city of Assur. About 1100 B.C. their ruler Tiglath-pileser reached both the Black Sea and the Mediterranean on a conquering expedition north and west. After this he boasted that he had become "lord of the world."

Assyrian militarism was harsh. The conquerors regularly carried off whole populations of defeated cities as prisoners. By the eighth century the Assyrian state was a dual monarchy. Tiglath-pileser III (744–727) of Assyria also took the title of ruler of Babylonia. He added enormous territory to the Assyrian dominions. During the 670s B.C., the Assyrian king Esarhaddon invaded and conquered Egypt. Then in turn the Assyrian Empire fell to a new power, the Medes (Iranians related to the Persians), who took Nineveh (612 B.C.).

For less than a century thereafter (612–538) Babylonia experienced a rapid, brilliant revival, during which King Nebuchadnezzar built temples and palaces. With its famous hanging gardens Babylon became a wonder of the world. Nebuchadnezzar overthrew Jerusalem and took the Hebrews into captivity. But in 539 the Hebrew prophet Daniel showed King Belshazzar the moving finger on the wall of the banquet chamber which warned that his kingdom would be given to the Medes and the Persians. Daniel was right, of course, and Cyrus the Great of Persia took Babylon, ending the history of the Mesopotamian empires after at least 2,500 years.

Besides their cuneiform writing, the Babylonians and Assyrians took from the Sumerians much of their religion. The gods of the universe remained the same, but the local gods of course were different. Under Hammurabi, a local god, Marduk, was exalted over all other gods. We have more Babylonian than Sumerian religious texts and so know Babylonian-Assyrian beliefs in more detail.

Demons became more numerous and more powerful, and a special class of priests was needed to fight them. Magic practices multiplied; soothsayers consulted the livers of animals in order to predict the future. Anything that happened to a man had implications for his future. Starting with observation of the stars for such magical purposes, the Babylonians developed a real knowledge of their movements, and the mathematics to go with it. They even managed to predict eclipses. They could add, subtract, multiply, divide, and find square and cube roots. They could solve equations, and measure both plane areas and solid volumes. But their astronomy and their mathematics remained in the service of astrology and predicting the future.

Like the Sumerians, the Babylonians were a worried and a gloomy people, who feared death and regarded the afterlife as grim and dusty, in the bowels of the earth. Even this depressing reward could be won only if the living took care to bury the dead and to hold them in memory. Otherwise one had only eternal restlessness and perhaps a career as a demon to look forward to. In Babylonian literature Marduk became the center of an epic of the creation. We encounter Gilgamesh again, in a more coherent epic than that of the Sumerians, in which he refuses a goddess's offer to make him a god because he knows he is sure to die.

Similarly in art the inspiration remained unchanging, but some variations appeared. The Babylonians in some regions now had access to stone, and used columns in their buildings. The Assyrians showed greater interest, as one would expect, in scenes of combat. In Assyria too one finds the *orthostat,* a statue inserted into a wall, and so appearing in high relief. Typical Assyrian versions appear as bulls, lions, and fantastic winged beasts. Jewels, gold, and ivory-carving now reached new and extraordinarily beautiful heights, as shown especially in the finds at Nimrud.

Egypt

Character of the Society

What the Tigris and the Euphrates rivers did for Mesopotamia, the Nile River did for Egypt. Rising in the hills of Ethiopia and flowing a thousand miles north through Egypt into the Mediterranean, it fertilized the strip of land along its banks on both sides, to the east and west stretched dry, inhospitable desert sands.

Nobody knows how many thousands of years went by while the people along the Nile slowly learned to take advantage of the annual summer flood by tilling their fields to receive the silt-laden river waters, and by regulating its flow. But about 3000 B.C., when the Sumerian civilization emerged in Mesopotamia, the Egyptians had reached a comparable stage of development. Much better known to us than Mesopotamia—most of us even as small children already knew about the pyramids, the sphinx, and King Tut's tomb—Egypt was the other ancient valley civilization that made major contributions to our own.

The Egyptians were more cheerful and confident than the gloomy and apprehensive Sumerians, Babylonians, and Assyrians. They were more tolerant and less harsh, more imaginative and less literal-minded, and more active and less passive in their attitudes and achievements. They regarded life after death as a happy continuation of life on earth with all its fleshly pleasures, not as a dismal eternal sojourn in the dust. The Mesopotamians built brick temples and public monuments. Egyptians built stone tombs and private monuments. The Mesopotamians left few statues, the Egyptians many. The Mesopotamian rulers—both the early city lords and the later kings who aspired to universal monarchy—were agents of the gods on earth. The Egyptian rulers from the beginning were themselves regarded as gods. The Mesopotamians were historically minded, the Egyptians not.

The long strip of land along the banks of the Nile was always hard to unify. At the very beginning (3000 B.C.), we can distinguish two rival kingdoms. Lower Egypt was the Nile Delta (so called because it is triangular like the Greek letter of that name), the bit of land nearest the Mediterranean where the river splits into several streams and flows into the sea. Upper Egypt was the land along the course of the river for eight hundred miles between the Delta and the First Cataract.

At times the two regions were unified in one kingdom. But the ruler, who called himself "king of Upper and Lower Egypt," by his very title recognized that his realms consisted of two different areas. One looked toward the Mediterranean and outward to the other civilizations growing up around its edges. The other was more isolated by its deserts and more inward looking. The first unifier, perhaps mythical, was a certain Menes, whose reign (about 2850 B.C.) begins the Egyptian Old Kingdom (2850–2200) with its capital at Thebes.

Old, Middle, and New Kingdoms

When the king is a god, his subjects need only listen to his commands to feel sure they are doing the divine will. As each Egyptian king died, his great tomb in the form of a pyramid told his subjects that he had gone to join his predecessors in the community of gods. The largest of the pyramids took several generations to build, and involved the continual labor of thousands of men. A highly centralized bureaucracy carried out the commands of the king. His forces advanced at times westward into the Libyan desert, and at other times east and north into Palestine.

The Old Kingdom was eventually shattered by a growing tendency among district governors to pass their offices on to their sons, who then tended to strike out on their own. At the same time the priests of the Sun won special privileges that helped diminish royal power. After a period of disorder lasting perhaps two centuries (2200–2000), a new dynasty (eleventh of the thirty in Egyptian history) restored unity in what is known as the Middle Kingdom (2100–1800), distinguished for its rulers' land-reclamation policies and its victories abroad.

To the south, what is now the Sudan was controlled by new frontier fortresses. Palestine and Syria came under Egyptian influence. The bureaucracy flourished. Thebes ceased to be the capital, as a new city was founded south of Memphis. Provincial governorships became hereditary, but had to be confirmed by the king. The king's son at the age of twenty-one became co-ruler with his father. The king himself was less remote and more eager to be regarded as the shepherd of his people.

But secessionist movements took control of Egypt. Growing internal weakness, combined with a foreign invasion and conquest, ended the Middle Kingdom about 1800 B.C. The conquerors were called Hyksos, Asian nomads of uncertain origin who imported the war chariot and perhaps the bow. The Egyptians hated the Hyksos rule, which lasted about a century, and eventually rallied behind a new dynasty (the seventeenth) to drive out the invaders.

By about 1550 and the eighteenth dynasty, the task was accomplished and the New Kingdom (1550–1085) well launched. The five centuries of the New Kingdom saw extraordinary advances.

Pillars of the temple at Karnak.

The Egyptians engaged in a struggle for Syria and Palestine not only with the great powers of Mesopotamia but with the mountain and desert peoples who lived between the two great valley civilizations. The Egyptian ruler (now called pharaoh) Thutmose I reached the Euphrates on the east, and marched far south into what is now the Sudan.

Thutmose III (1469–1436) fought seventeen campaigns in the East, and even crossed the Euphrates and beat his Mesopotamian enemies on their own soil. The walls of the temple of Karnak preserve his own carved account of his military achievements and the enormous tribute paid him by his conquered enemies. His obelisk, popularly known as Cleopatra's Needle, stands in Central Park in New York. The Eyptians established their own network of local governors throughout the conquered territories, but ruled mildly. They did not, as the Assyrians were soon to do, deport whole masses of the population into captivity. The building program of the eighteenth dynasty was a vast one.

The pharaoh Amenhotep IV (1379–1362) caused a major internal upheaval in the successful New Kingdom by challenging the priests of the sun god Amen, who had become a powerful privileged class. Amenhotep IV urged that Aten be substituted for Amen of the sun disk. Even more dramatic, he commanded that Aten alone be worshiped and that all the many other gods be abandoned. Amenhotep changed his own name to Akhenaten, "Pleasing to Aten," in honor of his only god.

Some believe that this famous episode was a real effort to impose monotheism on Egypt; others doubt it. To mark the new policy, Akhenaten and his beautiful wife Nefertiti, moved to their new capital, Amarna. Amarna gives its name to the "Amarna age" (ca. 1417–ca. 1358 B.C.). Nearby, beginning in the 1880s, A.D., were found the Tell-el-Amarna letters, a collection of about four hundred tablets including the diplomatic correspondence of Akhenaten and his father with the rulers of western Asia, in many languages.

Akhenaten's effort to overthrow the en-

The pharoah Akhenaten and his wife Nefertiti offer gifts to the sun god Aten.

trenched priesthood led to internal dissension and the loss of external strength. His son-in-law, Tutankhamen (1361–1351), was eventually sent to rule in Thebes, city of the priests of Amen, with whom he compromised. This was "King Tut," the discovery of whose tomb was the sensation of the 1920s. Its magnificent contents have recently been on view in the United States. With Akhenaten's death, the new religious experiment collapsed. The pharaohs strove to make up for the interval of weakness by restoring their foreign conquests.

About 1300 B.C. Ramses II (nineteenth dynasty) made a treaty with a people from Asia Minor, the Hittites, married a Hittite princess, and ended the competition for Syria. But soon after 1200 B.C. the New Kingdom in its turn suffered severely as the result of an invasion of the eastern Mediterranean shores by mixed bands of Sea Peoples, probably including ancestors of the later Greeks and Sicilians. Egypt entered into a period of decline. New internal struggles for power raged between the secular authorities and the priests and among local and central rulers. In turn the Assyrians (seventh century B.C.), the Persians (525 B.C.), and Alexander the Great (331 B.C.) conquered Egypt.

Religion

A complex religion was the most powerful force in Egyptian society. If one asked an ancient Egyptian "whether the sky was supported by posts or held up by a god, the Egyptian would answer: 'Yes, it is supported by posts or held up by a god—or it rests on walls, or it is a cow, or it is a goddess whose arms and feet touch the earth.' "* So the Egyptian was ready to accept overlapping divinities, and to add new ones whenever it seemed appropriate.

From the beginning, Egyptian cults included sheep, bulls, gazelles, and cats, still to be found carefully buried in their own cemeteries. As time passed, the figures of Egyptian gods became human, but often retained an animal's head. Osiris, the best-known Egyptian god, began as a local Nile Delta deity. He taught mankind agriculture. Isis was his wife, and animal-headed Set his brother and rival.

Set killed Osiris. Isis persuaded the gods to bring him back to life, but thereafter he ruled underground. (Obviously this is similar to the fertility and vegetation-cycle beliefs we have already noted in Mesopotamia and will find again in Greece.) Osiris was identified with the life-giving, fertilizing Nile, and Isis with the receptive earth of Egypt.

Horus the sun defeated the evil Set after a long struggle. But Horus was only one kind of sun god: there was also Re, later joined with Amen, and still later Aten, as we saw. In the great temple cities, priests wrote down whole families of divinities. Out in the villages all the forces of nature were worshiped. One local god was part crocodile, part hippopotamus, and part lion, which shows what farmers along the river banks worried about. However many the gods, Egyptian religion itself was unified. Unlike a Sumerian temple which was the political center of its city, and for which the population toiled, the Egyptian temple was religious only.

The Egyptians believed that after death each human being would appear before Osiris and tell all the bad things he had not done on earth: "I have not done evil to men. I have not ill-treated animals. I have not blasphemed the gods," to justify his admission into the kingdom of the blessed. Osiris would then have the man's heart weighed, to test the truth of his self-defense. The

* J. A. Wilson, in *The Intellectual Adventure of Ancient Man* (Chicago, 1943), p. 44.

man would either be admitted or delivered over to judges for punishment.

Egyptians believed not only in body and soul, but in *ka,* the indestructible vital principle of each human being, which left the body at death but could and did return at times. That is why the Egyptians preserved the body in their elaborate art of mummification: so that the ka on its return would find it not decomposed. And that is why they filled the tombs of the dead with all the objects that the ka might need or find delightful when it returned to the body. Otherwise it might come back and haunt the living.

Civilization

We know Egyptian civilization so intimately because of the many inscriptions, which dealt with historical subjects and *papyri* (fragments of the material the Egyptians wrote on, made of the pith of a water plant) which were mostly literary. Yet what we have represents a smaller percentage of what once existed and of what may yet be found than does our huge collection of Mesopotamian literature on its clay tablets. Modern scholars first learned to read ancient Egyptian only in the 1820s, when a Frenchman, Champollion, noticed that several Greek personal names on a late obelisk were repeated in the Egyptian hieroglyphics (literally, "sacred writing").

With these as a start, Champollion turned to the inscription on the Rosetta Stone, found in the Nile Delta in 1799, which bears the same text in three forms: in Greek, in hieroglyphics, and in another script used in Egypt after hieroglyphics had gone out of fashion. The Rosetta Stone was soon deciphered, and the lessons learned have been applied to all other Egyptian texts. Visitors to the British Museum can still see the extraordinary slab that made it possible for people of the nineteenth and twentieth centuries A.D. to understand ancient Egypt.

The Egyptian *Book of the Dead* brings together stories of the gods and hymns and prayers, and teaches us much of what we know of Egyptian religion. No Egyptian epic story tells of a hero like Gilgamesh, a mortal who cannot quite attain immortality, because the Egyptians confidently *did* expect to attain it. We have love songs, banquet songs, and fiction.

"If I kiss her," says an Egyptian lover, "and her lips are open, I am happy even without beer,"* a sentiment that seems altogether up to date. "Enjoy thyself as much as thou canst," says a banquet song, "for a man cannot take his property with him,"† though actually nobody ever tried harder than the Egyptians to do so. The

The Rosetta Stone, discovered in 1799 at Rashid in the Delta and now at The British Museum.

historical romance of Sinuhe tells of an Egyptian noble who was forced by intrigue into exile in Asia (early Middle Kingdom, ca. 1980 B.C.). There, Sinuhe was elected chief of a tribe and won in a single combat against a local champion. At the end, full of longing for Egypt, he was happily recalled by the pharaoh and richly dressed, honored, and given a pyramid of his own for his future tomb.

* A. Erman, *Literature of the Ancient Egyptians,* trans. A. M. Blackman (London: Dutton, 1927), p. 244.

† J. H. Breasted, *The Dawn of Conscience* (New York, 1933), pp. 163–64.

Relief of cattle fording a stream: from the tomb of Ti, an official of the Fifth Dynasty, ca. 2350 B.C.

The pyramids of Gizeh.

Egyptian Art

We have all seen pictures of Egyptian pyramids and temples, gigantic sculptured pharaohs and divinities, and the rich and ostentatious gold and jewels of a splendid sepulcher like King Tut's. The use of stone in building, the skillful use of great spaces, the portraiture of individuals rather than types, the obelisks and sphinxes, the absence of perspective: these are familiar characteristics of Egyptian art. Less well known are the many scenes of ordinary country or family life found in Egyptian painting and showing an enjoyment and a sense of humor not found in Mesopotamia. On the wall of an Egyptian tomb a young man and his wife sit happily playing checkers or listening to music or watching the dancing girls. A thief steals a cow while the herdsman's eyes are elsewhere; a crocodile waits for a baby hippopotamus to be born so that at last he may have his lunch.

Limestone sculpture of a scribe with his roll of papyrus: ca. 2400 B.C.

The brother and sister-in-law of Ramose, a high official in the service of the pharaoh Amenophis III, portrayed at a banquet. From the walls of the tomb of Ramose in Thebes: ca. 1375 B.C.

The temple of Idfu, third century B.C., best preserved of the Egyptian temples.

Old Kingdom relief of a crocodile hungrily awaiting the birth of a hippopotamus: from Saqqara.

III PEOPLES OUTSIDE THE VALLEYS

For well over a thousand years after their first flourishing the peoples of the valley civilizations held the stage virtually alone. But the Hyksos invasion of Egypt (ca. 1800), the Kassite invasion of Mesopotamia, and the Hittite attacks on both have already warned us that the men of the mountains and deserts outside the valleys had begun to compete fiercely with the more settled valley societies. These outsiders too had centuries of history behind them, still not well known to scholars. By 1500 B.C. the Kassites in southern Mesopotamia, the Hurrians with their state of Mitanni in northern Mesopotamia and smaller states in southeastern Anatolia (modern Turkey), and the Hittites in the remainder of Anatolia had all emerged as rivals both to Babylon and to Egypt.

All of these were Indo-European—a mixture of peoples speaking languages related to each other in structure. Their kings were neither the Mesopotamian agents of god on earth nor the Egyptian deified monarchs. Instead, they ruled as the most powerful among a noble class that controlled the instruments of conquest—horses and chariots—and shared the fruits of conquest, dividing new land among themselves. Records survive not only of wars between these newly emerging peoples and the settled valley societies, but also of their diplomatic exchanges and their peace settlements.

For these communications everybody used Akkadian. The Egyptians, who did not speak it, corresponded in it with the peoples who ruled Syria, who did not speak it either. Culturally too, the outside peoples were deeply influenced by Mesopotamian religion and literature and art. The outsiders dealt severe blows to the valley societies during the centuries from 1500 to 1200 B.C., but did not manage to conquer them.

Hittites and Hurrians: Indo-European Speakers

High on the Anatolian plateau in Turkey at a place called Boğazköy, archaeologists in our own twentieth century discovered the capital of the ancient Hittites with a large collection of tablets mostly written in cuneiform script and some in the Indo-European Hittite language. Until this discovery we knew about these people only from other sources: The Old Testament tells us that Uriah, whose wife, Bathsheba, King David wickedly coveted, was a Hittite. The Hittite kingdom emerged about 1700 B.C., had a century of great conquests, a period of crisis and decline, and a new flourishing between 1380 and 1346, when its ruler challenged Egypt under Akhenaten.

The Hittite kings were influenced by the Egyptian worship of the sun-god. They adopted the Egyptian practice of having themselves deified after death, but continued their own unique custom of cremation. Their powerful centralized state, whose Indo-European ruling class dominated the other peoples of Anatolia, was fragmented forever about 1200 by the same onslaught of Sea Peoples that weakened the Egyptians. Hittite art and literature show Mesopotamian influence. Distinctively Hittite, however, were two innovations: sober historical narratives recording

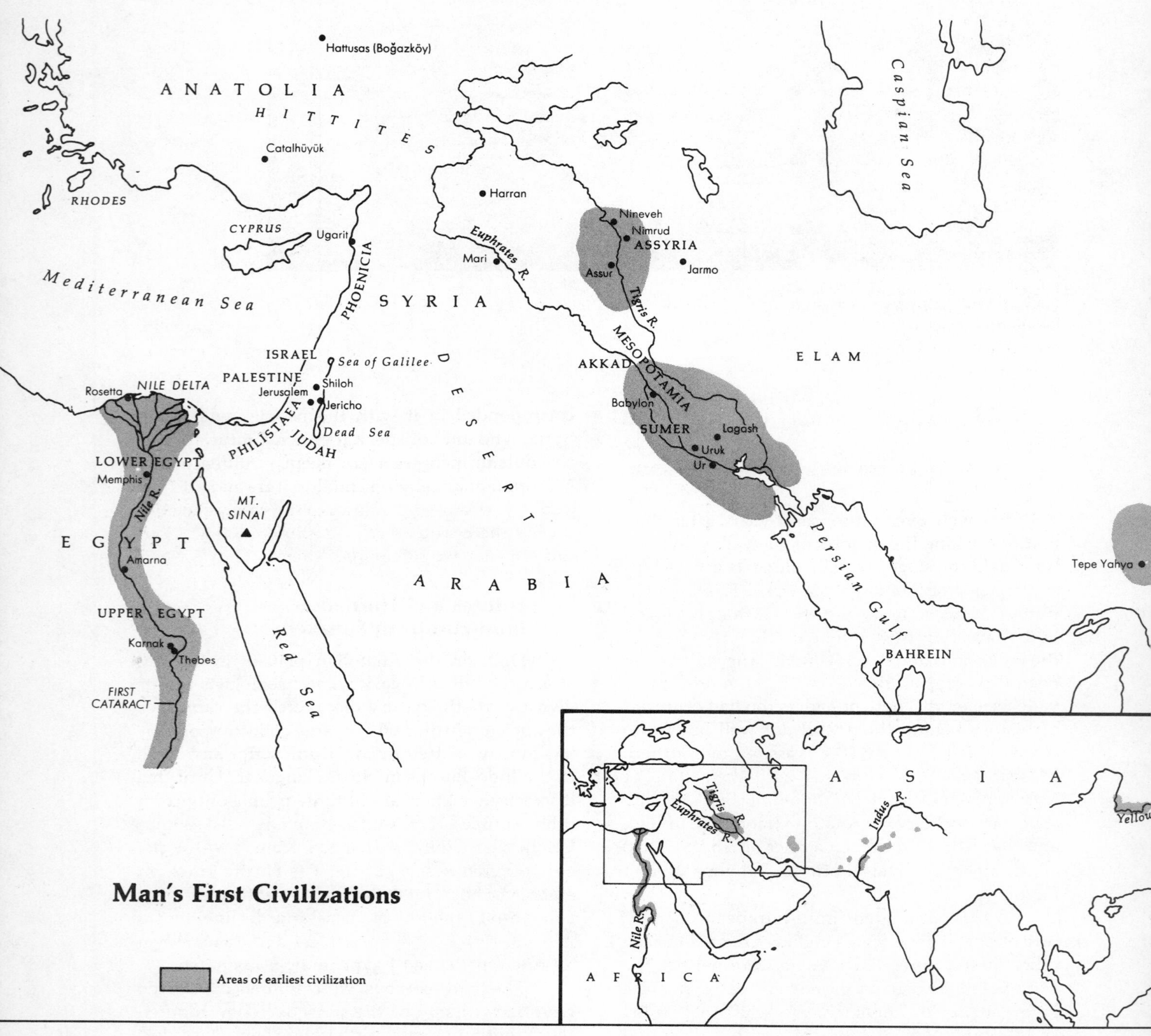

Man's First Civilizations

the motives of the kings for their actions, and the treaty as a diplomatic instrument.

Far less well known than the Hittites are the Hurrians, whose state, called Mitanni, was established about 1500 B.C. in northern Mesopotamia and lasted only about a century and a third. No local archaeological finds comparable to Boğazköy for the Hittites have yet turned up. Like the Hittites, the Hurrians had an Indo-European ruling class, and worshiped some Indo-European gods. Their great importance was to act as intermediaries between the great civilization of Mesopotamia and the less-advanced peoples to the north and west, especially the Hittites.

Semitic Speakers: in Ebla, Canaan, Phoenicia

From Syria a variety of Semitic peoples—Akkadians, Amorites, Babylonians, and Assyrians—invaded the valley societies. But other Semitic peoples stayed behind in Syria and created societies of their own along the Syrian coast of the Mediterranean and in the land behind the coast.

Most recently discovered in the 1970s and still to be evaluated is the city-state of Ebla, going back to the third millennium. Far better known is Ugarit, where archaeologists in 1929 found the royal palace of a Canaanite state that flourished between 1400 and 1200 B.C., with tablets in a northwest Semitic tongue—Ugaritic. They contain several important poems, and also the archives of official correspondence, including a treaty with the Hittites written in Akkadian and showing that the Canaanites were under Hittite domination. One of many Canaanite city-states, Ugarit collapsed in the general chaos of 1200 B.C. caused by the Sea Peoples' invasion. Among these invading Sea Peoples, we know, were the Indo-European Philistines, who settled to the south of the Canaanites and gave their name to Palestine.

Among the Canaanites several gods presided over any given department of life. The same gods were sometimes masculine and sometimes feminine, as if nobody was quite sure or cared very much. The impression of primitiveness is reinforced by the Canaanite practices of human sacrifice and religious prostitution. The supreme Canaanite god was El, whose name simply means "god." Baal, on the other hand, whose name means "lord," was a storm god—like the Sumerian god of the air, the region between heaven and earth. Baal and his wife Astarte, like Osiris and Isis in Egypt and similar deities in Mesopotamia, symbolized the seasons and the cycles of fertility.

In the period after 1300 the Phoenicians, still another Semitic people, flourished along the coast south of Ugarit, and carried on a brisk trade with the western Mediterranean. The name Phoenician comes from the word for a purple dye made from shellfish found near their capital, Tyre. About 800 B.C. the Phoenicians founded Carthage (modern Tunis) as a colony, and brought their Semitic tongue (Punic) more than halfway to the Straits of Gilbraltar, through which in fact their ships had often sailed.

The Phoenicians used a real alphabet, not, like cuneiform, a collection of signs that stood for whole syllables. It became the immediate ancestor of the Greek alphabet and so of our own.

Land of Canaan, Baal, Philistines: these names have long been familiar to us. We have now come into the place and time of the Old Testament, the religious book of the Hebrews, who in turn were to pass on so much to the peoples of Europe and America.

The Hebrews

History and the Old Testament

The Hebrews' history is recorded in a consecutive story over many centuries in the Old Testament books of Genesis, Exodus, Joshua, Judges, Samuel, and Kings. The Old Testament also includes genealogy and ritual law (Numbers, Leviticus, and Deuteronomy), tales (Ruth and Job), proverbs (Proverbs, Ecclesiastes), prophetic utterances (Isaiah, Jeremiah, and the others), and lyric poems (The Psalms, The Song of Songs). For many centuries these books were held by Jew and Christian alike to express the literal and sacred truth.

It was not until relatively recently that scholars began to apply to the Old Testament the same test of authenticity that they apply to ordinary works of history. A hundred years ago many scholars believed much of the Old Testament to be legendary and mythical. But most such doubts have vanished in our own time. Hard archaeological evidence has piled up in support of the general narrative that the Old Testament gives us. Of course, the Old Testament was not written down as the events happened. Many of its earliest portions were compiled long after the event. The writings were not arranged in their present form until the second century B.C. And many folklore elements can be easily identified. But the weight of the evidence tends to confirm the biblical story.

So the first Hebrews probably migrated from Ur "of the Chaldees" sometime after 1950 B.C., when that Sumerian center in southern Mesopotamia was destroyed, northwest to the prosperous center of Harran. Abraham then probably continued westward into "Canaan," as Genesis says. The accounts in Genesis of the origins of the universe and the racial origins of the Hebrews, and the stories of Eden, the Flood, and the Tower of Babel all fit into the supposition of a northern Mesopotamian—and no other—place of residence for the Hebrews before about

Jehu, king of Israel, paying homage to King Shalmaneser III of Assyria: a panel from Nimrud, 841 B.C.

1500 B.C., when the westward migration took place.

The Hebrews may be the same as a people called Khapiru who appear beginning about 1900 B.C. in the cuneiform tablets and in both Hittite and Egyptian sources as raiders, wanderers, and captives. Some of the Hebrews at least lived for several centuries in the Nile Delta during the Hyksos period, before Moses (whose name is Egyptian) became their leader and led them about 1300 B.C. to within sight of the Promised Land. The miraculous crossing of the Red Sea in Exodus is in accordance with the shallow waters, the reedy growth, and the winds of the region.

Outsiders battering their way back from Egypt into Canaan against the resistance of those who already lived there, the Hebrew confederation of tribes was held together by the new religion that Moses gave them—the Ten Commandments, the ark of the covenant, the many observances that God prescribed. Gradually by conquest they added to their holdings (Joshua took Jericho about 1230 B.C.). After the period of the Judges—when battles were fought against Canaanites and Philistines—the loose confederation became a monarchy in about 1020 B.C., when the prophet Samuel chose Saul to be the first king. Saul's son-in-law, rival, and successor, David, is well known from the contemporary account (1000–960 B.C.) in the Book of Samuel. Saul united and strengthened the kingdom. His luxury-loving son Solomon brought the Palestinian kingdom of the Jews to new heights of prosperity. But it was small in size and resources compared to Sumer, Babylon, Assyria, or Egypt.

Solomon (960-922 B.C.) lacked the character of David, and in 933 B.C. the kingdom split in two. The northern kingdom of Israel (933–722 B.C.) was stronger but lacked the great center of Jerusalem. The southern kingdom of Judah (933–585 B.C.) held Jerusalem but had little real strength. The Assyrians destroyed Israel in 722 B.C., and the Babylonians destroyed Judah in 586 and took the Jews into captivity. Then the Persians under Cyrus the Great in turn conquered Babylonia and freed the Jews to return to Palestine. But after 538 the Jews no longer had a state. They were held together by religion alone, and depended politically on one alien empire after another: the Persian, the Macedonian, the Roman.

Religion

Had it not been for their extraordinary religion, the Hebrews would seem to us just another people of the ancient Near East, less numerous than most, less talented artistically than any. But of course we would probably not know much about them had it not been for their religion, which gave them and us the books of the Old Testament and an enduring tradition. Many of the most fundamental ideas of Hebrew religion go back to the days when the Hebrews were still nomads, before they had adopted a settled life.

Thus God's commandments to Moses on Mount Sinai that "Thou shalt have no other gods before me," "Thou shalt not make unto thee any graven image," and "Thou shalt not take the name of the Lord thy God in vain" determined three important aspects of Judaism that were new among Near Eastern religions.

The religion of the Hebrews was, first of all, monotheistic—it recognized only a single god. Despite the experiment of Akhenaten in Egypt and a few Babylonian texts that try to associate all divine power with Marduk, the Jews were the first to insist that their god was the only god, and a universal god.

Second, the Jews were forbidden to represent him in sculpture or painting, a sharp contrast with all other religions of the ancient world. Further, they were forbidden to make *any* images of living beings, flesh, fish, or fowl, no doubt because their leaders feared that if they did make such images, they would end up worshiping them. So their art was by law restricted to nonrepresentational subjects. When they broke this law, as they sometimes did, it was usually under the influence of neighbors whose traditions did not forbid animal or human representations in art.

Third, the religion of the Hebrews from the beginning regarded the *name* of God—Yahweh or Jehovah, meaning "he causes to be," or "the creator"—as literally not to be spoken, a reverence quite different from any we have found in other ancient Near Eastern religions. From the nomadic period of Hebrew life also come the keeping of the sabbath on the seventh day; the annual day of expiation (Yom Kippur); the feast of the Passover, with its offering of a spring lamb and of unleavened bread, celebrating the escape from Egypt, and other holy days still honored by the Jews in our own times.

The Old Testament swarms with episodes in which the Hebrews proved unable to keep the first commandment, broke away from the worship of the single God, tried to propitiate other gods, and were punished. Yet however often they disobeyed, the first commandment remained the central feature of their religion. With monotheism from the first went morality, as shown in the remaining commandments forbidding murder, adultery, stealing, false witness, and covetousness of one's neighbor's property.

Jehovah himself, both merciful and righteous, creator of all things, was human in form, but was not visible to the human eye. Unlike the gods of all the other peoples, he did not lead a human life; he had no family; he lived, not in a palace like a human palace only more splendid, but in heaven. When he wished to speak to the leader of his people, he descended onto a mountaintop (Mount Sinai) or into a burning bush or into the space left for him by his own direction between the wings of the cherubim to be set atop the sacred box in which the Ten Commandments on their two tablets of stone were to be kept.

This was the ark of the covenant, built by artisans to the special orders of God as relayed by Moses. The covenant was the special pact between God himself and his chosen people, the Hebrews, in tribal confederation, held together by their regard for this most sacred of objects. Kept at first in a special tent, a portable tabernacle, the ark moved with the Hebrews, first to Shiloh, where the Philistines captured it about 1050 B.C., and then into the temple built for it by Solomon in Jerusalem, a royal chapel, whose decorations included many that violated the commandment about graven images. Solomon's temple was built by a Canaanite architect using Phoenician models, showing the increasing influence of non-Israelite peoples.

There were prophets (men called by God) among the Jews from the beginning, but they multiplied during the division of the people into the two kingdoms of Israel and Judah. They summoned the people to return to the original purity of the faith and to avoid the paganism that seemed to be threatening if Canaanite influences continued. In ecstasy perhaps brought on by dances, they solemnly warned of fearful punishment to come if the people did not heed them. After the punishment, however, the prophets (notably Isaiah) promised that Israel would rise again, and that a descendant of David would appear as the Messiah to usher in a new golden age.

The disaster came, of course, with the Babylonian captivity. After the prophecies of misfortune had been fulfilled, the prophet Ezekiel had a vision of new life being breathed into the dead bones of Israel, and urged the preparation for its restoration. In exile, in the sixth century B.C., the sacred writings were selected and arranged in a form not unlike the Old Testament we know. Once the captivity ended, the priests became the dominant figures in the restored community, with its rebuilt temple.

Much in Hebrew society recalls what we have already observed about the other peoples of the ancient Near East. The father exercised supreme authority within the family. Polygamy and divorce were permitted. As among the Hittites, a widow married her dead husband's brother. The Hebrews had slaves, but a Hebrew slave could be made to serve no more than six years. A man who had injured his slave was required to set him free. The law of an eye for an eye, a tooth for a tooth, held sway. Yet the Commandments, and some of the specific regulations—not to wrong strangers, not to exact usurious interest for a loan, to help one's enemies as well as one's friends—strike an ethical note deeper than any found in the earlier Mesopotamian Near East. They foreshadow the Christian principles that would—within another five hundred years—emerge from this Hebrew society.

IV CRETE AND MYCENAE

Minoans Before Mycenae

In Ugarit the archaeologists found an ivory relief of a bare-breasted goddess, holding wheat ears in each hand and seated between two goats standing on their hind legs. She is like nothing from Mesopotamia or Egypt. But she greatly resembles the goddesses frequently found on the large Mediterranean island of Crete, on the westernmost fringe of the Near East. On Crete there developed beginning about 2600 B.C. the last of the Bronze Age civilizations we shall consider. Cretan civilization is often called Minoan, after Minos, the legendary founder of the island dynasty, whose kings were all named Minos after him.

Sir Arthur Evans, the British archaeologist who worked in Crete in the first half of the twentieth century, divided Minoan culture into three main periods: Early Minoan (ca. 2600–ca. 2000), Middle Minoan (ca. 2000–1600), and Late Minoan (ca. 1600–1100). Each of these three is also subdivided three times to enable easy discussion of the objects found. For all such dating pottery is the key. Different styles found at different levels permit scholars to work out a chronological framework.

In Crete such dating is of crucial importance, partly because nobody can yet read the earliest Cretan writing, some of which is in hieroglyphics and some in a script known as Linear A. There are few Linear A tablets compared with the tens of thousands of Mesopotamian writings at our disposal. No inscription has yet been found written in both Linear A and a known language. Crete has no Rosetta Stone. So we have no sources except the objects uncovered by the archaeologist. Of these the greatest are the palace of Minos at Knossos (Heraklion), found and partly reconstructed by Evans, and other palaces and tombs.

The Cretans were not Indo-Europeans but descendants of Anatolian immigrants to the island. They were a busy maritime people, whose ships kept them in touch with Egypt and with the Near East. Their navy defended the island against invaders. None of their palaces was fortified. The Cretans had garrisons and even colonies abroad, founding a Bronze Age overseas empire on a small scale.

The Middle Minoan Palace of Minos has many rooms, a great staircase, beautiful wall frescoes (recovered from the ruins in fragments), massive columns, many six-foot-tall stone storage jars for olive oil or wine, and an elaborate plumbing system with pipes, running water, and ventilation. Its complexity inspired the ancient Greek legend of the Labyrinth, the palace on Crete with a system of rooms and corridors so mazelike that nobody could find his way without a guide or a thread to unwind behind him so that he might later retrace his steps.

Minoan craftsmen produced delicate pottery hardly thicker than an eggshell, decorated with birds, flowers, and marine animals; ivory or pottery statuettes of the bare-breasted goddess, who sometimes holds a snake in each hand;

A terra-cotta statuette of the Minoan snake goddess.

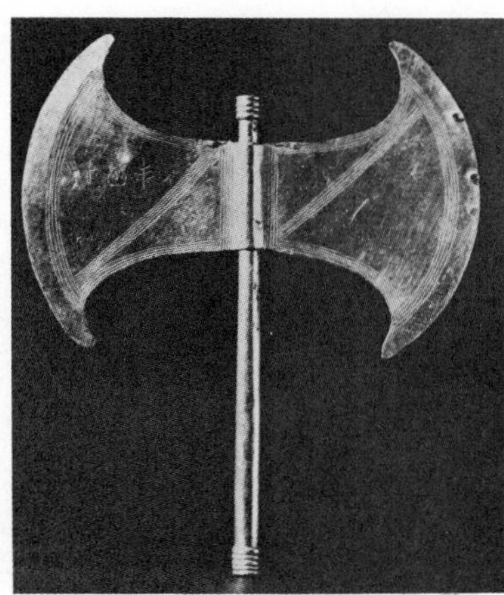

Gold votive ax found in a cave near Knossos.

and many paintings of bulls, some showing young athletes—girls and boys—leaping over a bull's back in a ritual game. The Athenians, who paid an annual tribute to Crete in the early days, preserved a legend that their ancestors had been forced annually to send young men and maidens to be sacrificed by the Cretans to their half-man, half-bull monster called the Minotaur (a Minos-bull, supposedly the offspring of the Cretan queen Pasiphaë and a bull). All the evidence shows that the bull was important in the Cretan religion. A double ax, found in many sizes, from large ones in bronze to tiny miniatures in gold, also played a role. The word *labyrinth* itself means "place of the double ax" *(labrys).*

Court society at Knossos, at least from the Middle Minoan period on, was elegant. Sophisticated ladies wearing embroidered dresses and gold or silver necklaces enjoyed dances or strolled about viewing the fountains and the carefully laid-out flower beds. But Crete had its disasters too. Perhaps it was earthquakes, tidal waves, and fires that destroyed the palace of Minos a little after 1600 B.C., and again about 1500, and a third time about 1400. Perhaps invading Hyksos, on their way out of Egypt after their occupation, did the damage of 1600. Perhaps mainland Greeks, crossing from the north, caused the destruction of 1500. Nobody can be quite sure about the earlier destructions, which were repaired; but the catastrophe of 1400 was possibly the work of mainland Greeks.

Mycenaeans and Minoans

In Greece too, Bronze Age civilization had taken root. Greece was a largely mountainous barren land, divided into small separate valleys and plains, none of them far from the sea. Its inhabitants, like the Cretans, were not Indo-Europeans but a mixture of Stone Age native peoples and Anatolians who had invaded about 3000 B.C. From the earliest times they took advantage of the rugged coasts and islands, with their many shelters and good harbors, to sail from place to place, seldom if ever losing sight of land, trading olive oil and wine for grain, metal, and slaves. About 2000 B.C. the first true Greeks invaded from the north. They were Indo-Europeans, who first destroyed and then settled, no doubt intermarrying with the previous inhabitants. This society had one of its chief centers at Mycenae in the Peloponnesus, suitably located to control land trade and not far from the sea.

Led by warrior chieftains, the Mycenaeans engaged in commerce with Crete. Minoan objects have been found in the royal tombs at Mycenae (1600–1500 B.C.). The Mycenaeans fell deeply under Minoan cultural influence. Their most famous achievements are splendid gold masks of the warrior princes buried in the tombs and daggers inlaid with various metals that show hunting scenes of astonishing realism and beauty. A century ago, when the German archaeologist Heinrich Schliemann found these he thought he had discovered the tomb of Homer's hero, Agammemnon, who actually lived about three hundred years later.

Mycenaean Greeks also visited Crete and no doubt noticed that Knossos was unfortified. Probably they invaded Crete and seized power about 1480. They now controlled the very center of the civilization that had already taught them so much. They introduced chariots and stored arrows for large bodies of troops, but built no fortifications, perhaps because they expected no new invasion. In the palace of Minos they installed a throne room of their own type.

And they learned from the Cretans how useful it was to keep records. The Linear A writing, devised for a non-Indo-European language from Anatolia, was unsatisfactory. So, we think, the scribes invented a new script—Linear B—in which to write the language of the conquerors: Greek.

Here we come to one of the great discoveries of the twentieth century. In his work on Crete, Evans found thousands of tablets written in Linear B. They were just as unreadable as those in the earlier Linear A. Not until 1939 did the American archaeologist, Carl Blegen, discover the first Linear B tablets *on mainland Greece,* at Pylos, where

Ruins of the Palace of Minos at Knossos.

he was excavating a Mycenaean palace. Since then, many more have turned up, including some in Mycenae itself.

As mainland Greeks were keeping their records in Linear B, the strong possibility arose that it was probably a form of Greek writing. Using the techniques of cryptography, Michael Ventris in 1952 showed that the signs in the script each represented a whole syllable, not merely a letter. Ventris had cracked the code. Even today, however, some of the thousands of Linear B tablets have not yet been read, and some readings remain doubtful, but Linear B is Greek.

Most of the tablets are humdrum lists of materials stored in the palaces or of persons in the king's service. The disappearance of Linear A on Crete about 1460 B.C. and its replacement by Linear B, which can now be read, has made possible the tentative story we have told above: the story of a Mycenaean conquest of Crete that lasted for about a century before the final violent destruction of Minoan civilization about 1400.

We do not know whether the new Mycenaean rulers of Knossos were independent or subordinate to Mycenaean princes. The great palace of Knossos and a number of other major Cretan centers were burned about 1400, apparently after looting. We do not know who did it. Perhaps the Cretans rose against their Greek masters and burned down their own cities, although this might well have invited reprisals and continued occupation after reconstruction. There was no re-

Inlaid daggers found at Mycenae in the tombs of Minoan warrior princes; a lion hunt; a leopard in a papyrus swamp.

construction. Instead there was permanent disruption.

So perhaps it was the Mycenaean rulers themselves who—in revenge against Cretan rebelliousness that may have made the island ungovernable—decided to cut their losses, destroy the Cretan centers, and sail away. Or perhaps it was a volcanic upheaval of the seabed. The rediscovery in 1967 and the recent excavation of a Minoan city on the volcanic island of Santorin (Thera) to the north of Crete may possibly decide the question one way or another. After the disaster of 1400 B.C., Crete remained rich and populous but lost its Mediterranean importance, which passed to the aggressive mainland peoples.

Mycenae, 1400–1100 B.C.

We still know little about Mycenaean politics and society. From excavated gold treasures it is clear that Mycenae was wealthy. But the Mycenaeans seem not to have been overseas empire builders. There were other extensive Greek walled settlements in the Peloponnesus—Pylos, Tiryns—whose rulers may have been as powerful as those of Mycenae, and perhaps formed a kind of loose confederacy among equals.

Tombs from the period before 1400 B.C. are of two types: those carefully built for the bodies of kings and important nobles and simple burial places for the rest of the population. Tombs from the period between 1400 and 1200 include more chamber tombs with more gifts to the dead found in them, showing a rise in wealth.

At Mycenae itself, and at Tiryns, Pylos, Athens, and Thebes, great palaces arose as community centers, with workshops, storage areas, guardrooms, and lesser dwelling houses attached. Good roads with bridges and culverts connected the main towns, which had good water-supply systems.

Artisans attached to the palace built and repaired chariots, made jars to hold the wine and oil, tanned leather, wrought bronze in the forge, made bricks, and sewed garments. Workmen stored goods for preservation and for sale and exchange. A Mycenaean palace was a businesslike (and noisy) place. The Linear B tablets preserve records of special royal furniture most elaborately inlaid in ivory, glass, and gold. One of the richest hoards, containing treasures in gold and jewels and bronze made over a period of five centuries, was found in a private house in Tiryns: it was obviously the accumulated loot of a Mycenaean grave robber with a fine taste in antiques.

Mycenaean religion remains a puzzle. Unlike Crete, where shrines and evidence of worship are everywhere, the Greek mainland had no separate shrines, although some portable altars have been found. Unlike the Cretans, the Greeks made burnt and blood offerings to their gods. Gems found in the Mycenaean royal tombs show Cretan deities and religious scenes. So the Cretan goddess was also revered on the mainland. The Linear B tablets from Pylos record the offerings made to certain gods—Poseidon, the god of the sea; Ares, the god of war; Artemis, the moon goddess; and even Zeus and Hera, who for later Greeks became the ruler of the gods and his consort.

About 1250 or 1200 B.C. the Mycenaean confederation fought the Trojan War, known to every Greek of later times from the poems of Homer, written down four or five centuries later. The Trojan War was an attack led by the king of Mycenae, Agamemnon, in command of a fleet and an army contributed by the other towns and islands of Mycenaean Greece. Its objective was Troy, a rich city on the northwest coast of Asia Minor (Anatolia) not far from the mouth of the Dardanelles, the straits that lead from the Aegean into the Sea of Marmora. The Trojans were Indo-Europeans like the Greeks but not so advanced. They did not write or paint their own pottery. They seem to have had few contacts with their neighbors in the Aegean, the Cretans, or their neighbors in Anatolia, the Hittites. They had a powerfully fortified city, and they traded with mainland Greece.

The Lion Gate of Mycenae.

The gold Mycenaean death mask known as the Mask of Agamemnon.

We must now dismiss as romance the famous tale of the rape by the Trojan prince Paris of Helen, wife of Menelaus, Mycenaean prince of Sparta, and the war of revenge that followed. We must believe instead that the Mycenaean expedition was undertaken for plunder of the Trojan citadel. Romantic too are the traditions that the siege lasted ten years and that great numbers of ships and men were involved. Agamemnon's force won, and burned Troy. The Troy destroyed by Agamemnon's expedition was a patched-up reconstruction of a richer Troy that may have suffered destruction in an earlier Greek attack about 1300.

Soon after the siege of Troy there began the great Mediterranean raiding expeditions of the Sea Peoples that eventually shattered the Egyptian New Kingdom and the Hittite state and left the Philistines washed up on the shores of Palestine. Egyptian and Hittite sources suggest that Greeks were among the Sea Peoples. However, the general violence did not spare Mycenaean Greece, which began about 1200 to suffer a great wave of destruction.

The great palaces were burned, some perhaps by fellow Mycenaean Greeks, others perhaps by piratical Sea People who landed and conducted hit-and-run raids, and still others perhaps by a new wave of Greek invaders from the north. These were the Dorians, who spoke their own dialect of Greek. It took them a century to obtain mastery in Greece. They were formerly blamed for most of the destruction that ushered in the Dark Age that began about 1100, but probably much of the destruction preceded their invasion and made it easier.

The Dark Age; Homer

With the destruction of the Mycenaean cities there set in at least three centuries that are called the Dark Age. We have little evidence to give us a picture of Greek life then. Moreover, the period brought a series of steps backward in Greek civilization. Literacy vanished. The political units of the Mycenaean world, never very big, gave way to still smaller communities. Conditions became more primitive.

Some Greeks migrated to the Aegean coasts of Asia Minor. The central coastal region (Ionia) emerged into daylight again about 800 B.C. Other Greeks, speaking other dialects, migrated into the coastal regions to the north (Aeolic) and south (Doric) of Ionia. In the hills behind these regions lived the Anatolian peoples in their own kingdoms: Lydia, Caria, Phrygia. Some Greeks on the mainland, notably the Athenians, were lucky enough to miss the full impact of the Dorian invasion. Athens may owe its leadership of Greece, after the Dark Age cleared, to a head start gained in this way.

The end of the Dark Age is associated with the writing down of the Homeric poems, the *Iliad* and the *Odyssey*. Did the same person write them both? Was it Homer? Did the *Iliad* precede the *Odyssey?* No certain answer can be given to these questions. It seems likely that at some time between 850 and 750 B.C. (some say even later) both poems were recorded permanently, and we may as well call the man who did it Homer.

Together, the two poems represent only a fraction of the epic material that existed in the Dark Age. There were many other tales of the great deeds of heroes. Minstrels accompanying themselves on stringed instruments sang the separate songs to audiences around the banquet tables in a palace, or to a gathering of villagers in a public square, or to soldiers around a campfire. The songs that together make up the *Iliad* and the *Odyssey* were no doubt among the most popular, and the minstrel who put them down was selecting from his repertory the stories that had best stood the test of performance.

The *Iliad* tells the story of a single incident that took place during the siege of Troy: the wrath of the Greek hero Achilles. Achilles stopped fighting and sulked in his tent because his commander Agamemnon had taken from him a Trojan girl captive. While Achilles refused to fight, the great combat continued. Eventually, when Hector the Trojan prince had killed Achilles' best friend and comrade-in-arms, Patroclus, Achilles returned to the battle and in turn slew Hector. At the very end Achilles returned Hector's body to Hector's sorrowing father, old King Priam. The *Odyssey* tells of the ten-year wanderings of another Greek hero, Odysseus, after the siege of Troy was over, and of the extraordinary places and peoples he visited on his way back to his home on the island of Ithaca. There his faithful wife Penelope awaited him despite the attention of many suitors.

Put in this summary form, the two stories perhaps seem blunt and commonplace. But a deep humanity pervades both. Despite the continual bloody fighting in the *Iliad,* we are moved by the terror of Hector's baby son, Astyanax, when he sees his father with his fierce plumed war helmet on. Then Hector takes it off and shows the child who it really is. We feel the truth of the passage when the old men of Troy admit that Helen—beautiful as a goddess—was well worth all the fuss. We share the grief and dignity of Priam as he begs Achilles to return Hector's body for decent burial, and we appreciate Achilles' courteous generosity to an enemy when he reluctantly agrees. The romantic *Odyssey,* with its lotus-eaters, sirens, men turned to swine by enchantment, and fierce one-eyed giant, provides similar moments of high human drama as Odysseus at last appears at home in disguise, and is recognized by his favorite dog and his old nurse, or in the sorrow of the beautiful island princess Nausicaa, first seen playing ball on the beach with her maidens, when she finds that Odysseus will not stay and remain her lover.

In both poems, the gods—now the familiar collection of Greek divinities: Zeus, Hera, Apollo (the sun), Artemis (the moon), Ares (war), Poseidon (the sea), Aphrodite (love), Athena (wisdom), and the rest—play an intimate part in the affairs of the mortals. They intervene in the fighting to give victory to their favorites, supply Achilles with an extraordinary shield on which are displayed many scenes in cunning metalwork, and save Odysseus from the perils of his voyage. The gods and goddesses on Olympus are only a little more outsize than the heroes. They live thoroughly human lives, quarreling over the affairs of the mortals and giving way to fits of bad temper. The epics take the reader into the world of a heroic age, like the later and lesser epics that reflected other heroic ages: such as *Beowulf* or *The Song of Roland* (see Chapter 5).

We hear at every turn and in great detail about the armor, ships, houses, domestic arrangements, and social behavior of the personages. It has always been a great temptation for scholars to reconstruct Mycenaean society from Homer. But Homer was writing five hundred years after the Trojan War. How far back did even a powerful oral tradition reach? In describing Odysseus' bed was he describing a real Bronze Age Mycenaean bed or the kind of bed that a prince would have slept in in his own day or a little before? Sometimes archaeology helps us here; more often it either does not help or adds to the confusion. The word that Homer uses for Nestor's drinking cup *(depas)* is found scratched on a Mycenaean storage jar far too big for anyone to drink from. Was Homer sometimes consciously trying to show his readers a world five hundred years earlier than theirs, and if so to what extent and in what passages? How safe are we in using him as a historical source?

We should probably use Homer sparingly if at all. Yet there is a long catalog of ships in the *Iliad* that lists the contingents supplied to the Greek armies by the various Greek settlements and names their commanders. This is probably a genuine Bronze Age document that provides usable evidence about the political organization of Mycenaean society: partly by city, partly by the captain the people follow, partly by tribe. So too the description of Odysseus' household as including more than fifty slaves can be taken as an indication of the prevalence of slavery in Mycenaean times. Episodes in Homer lead to conclusions (perhaps wrong) about the inheritance of royal power and the existence of assemblies of elders.

Whether or not we use Homer as history, the Greeks themselves from his time on certainly did so. They formed their own conception of their ancestral past from the *Iliad* and the *Odyssey.* Together with the Old Testament, some of which was being written down at about the same time, these two poems form the greatest literary and cultural and spiritual legacy of ancient man.

Certain modern scholars argue that both Homeric and Hebrew civilization grew directly from a common eastern Mediterranean background, and point to many parallels in action and attitude. Perhaps this viewpoint deserves a wider acceptance than it has yet won.

READING SUGGESTIONS on Man's First Civilizations
(Asterisk indicates paperback.)

Prehistory

V. Gordon Childe, *Man Makes Himself* (*Mentor). Emphasizes economics and technology.

William White Howells, *Back of History: The Story of Our Own Origins* (*Anchor). Beautifully written discussion.

L. S. Leakey, *Adam's Ancestors: The Evolution of Man and His Culture* (*Torchbooks). By the archaeologist who made many of the most important recent discoveries of the forerunners of human beings in Africa.

A. Marshack, *The Roots of Civilization* (McGraw-Hill, 1972). An original, beautifully illustrated, and stimulating account of the way prehistoric artifacts teach us about prehistoric humans.

J. Hawkes, *Prehistory* (*Mentor). Good survey.

The Near East

S. Moscati, *The Face of the Ancient Orient* (*Anchor). Excellent introductory survey.

H. Frankfort, *The Birth of Civilization in the Near East* (*Anchor). Briefer and more general than Moscati's book.

L. Woolley, *Beginnings of Civilization* (*Mentor). Sequel the J. Hawkes's book listed above and equally useful.

H. W. F. Saggs, *The Greatness That Was Babylon: A Sketch of the Ancient Civilization of the Tigris-Euphrates Valley* (*Mentor). A first-rate survey.

S. N. Kramer, *History Begins at Sumer* (*Anchor). A general work on the Sumerians by the leading authority on them.

C. C. Lamberg-Karlowsky, *Excavations at Tepe Yahya, Iran, 1967–1969* (Peabody Museum, Harvard University, 1970). The archaeologist in charge of a most important recent series of excavations reports on its findings; both sober and sensational.

J. A. Wilson. *The Culture of Ancient Egypt* (*Bantam). The best single-volume study of the subject.

A. H. Gardiner, *Egypt of the Pharaohs* (*Galaxy). Good political survey.

P. Montet, *Eternal Egypt* (*Mentor). A useful study of Egyptian civilization.

J. M. White, *Everyday Life in Ancient Egypt* (*Capricorn). Makes excellent use of the rich sources to show how the Egyptians actually lived.

K. Lange and M. Hirmer, *Egypt: Architecture, Sculpture, Painting in Three Thousand Years* (4th ed., 1968). Fine text and illustrations of the most important monuments.

O. R. Gurney, *The Hittites* (*Penguin). The best single survey of Hittite history and civilization.

S. Moscati, *The World of the Phoenicians* (1968). A good survey.

H. Orlinsky, *Ancient Israel* (*Cornell). Short but valuable introductory survey.

S. Cook, *Introduction to the Bible* (*Penguin). The Old Testament considered as a source for Jewish history.

L. Finkelstein, ed., *The Jews: Their History, Culture, and Religion,* 2 vols. (1960). A most useful longer work.

C. H. Gordon, *Forgotten Scripts* (*Penguin). An interesting history of the ways in which scholars learned to read the writings of the ancient world, with a bias toward some of the author's controversial ideas.

Crete and Early Greece

S. Hood, *The Minoans: The Story of Bronze Age Crete* (1971). Good introduction.

J. Chadwick, *The Decipherment of Linear B* (*Vintage). By Ventris's collaborator in the actual decipherment of the script.

A. E. Samuel, *The Mycenaeans in History* (*Spectrum). A good introduction to the subject.

T. B. L. Webster, *From Mycenae to Homer* (*Norton). A valiant effort to bridge the Dark Age gap, soundly based.

G. S. Kirk, *Homer and the Epic* (*Cambridge University Press). A reliable, well-written account.

D. Page, *History and the Homeric Iliad* (*University of California). A fine set of lectures, well-argued.

Homer, *Iliad,* trans. R. Lattimore in verse (*Phoenix) or W. H. D. Rouse in prose (*Mentor); *Odyssey,* trans. E. V. Rieux (*Penguin).

M. I. Finley, *Early Greece: The Bronze Age and Archaic Ages* (1970). Detailed, learned, and authoritative.

C. W. Blegen, *Troy and the Trojans* (1963). By the archaeologist who did much of the modern work on Troy.

C. H. Gordon, *Before the Bible* (1962); and *Ugarit and Minoan Crete* (1966). Controversial but interesting attempts to connect Crete and the Semitic mainland. Not for beginners.

CHAPTER TWO

The World of The Greeks

In this chapter the center of our attention shifts from the ancient Near East to the Greeks. We have already met them in their earliest—Mycenaean—period, and seen them descend into a Dark Age with the Dorian invasions. Now they take center stage, between the ninth and the third centuries B.C. What were they like? What was their political life at Sparta and at Athens? How did they become embroiled with the Persians, and then with one another in a famous series of wars? Where did Alexander the Great come from, and how did he build a world empire? Above all, what was Greek civilization: religion, drama, history, the arts, which constitutes so fundamental a part of our own heritage?

I THE GREEKS BEFORE THE PERSIAN WARS

What the Greeks Were Like

The Greeks were different from the other peoples we have come to know. For one thing, they were more curious: it is still a proverb that Greeks always want to know some new thing. They will ask questions tirelessly of anybody who knows something they do not yet know themselves. Where does the stranger come from? how big is his family? how much money does he have? what does it cost to live in his country? The questions may range from such personal matters to the most fundamental problems abstract or practical: how do we really know what we *think* we know? what is the universe made of? what causes men to suffer fevers? what are the various possible ways for men to live together and govern themselves? and other questions to which there may be no certain answers. So the argument can continue and the fun rage unchecked.

Then too, the Greeks were less otherworldly than the Mesopotamians and Egyptians; they were far more interested in life on earth. They knew they had to die, but they had no feeling of hopelessness about earthly life and enjoyed tackling its many problems. The Hebrews submitted to the will of an all-powerful single god, but the Greeks had no such divinity and no such law. Human beings themselves, human reason, and human answers to human problems took a central place.

Of course the Greeks had gods and believed in paying them all due honor. Indeed, they would often speak of human action as done under the influence of a god; but one gets the feeling that for them this was often only a manner of speaking. They say "Ares [the god of war] strengthened the hero's arm for the deadly spearthrust," when they all seem to mean is "the hero summoned up all the strength of his muscular right arm, and let the enemy have it with a spear."

We often hear that the Greeks invented *democracy*, government by the people. Indeed they did, but they also invented *obligarchy*, government by the few, and *aristocracy*, the rule of the noblest or richest. And they also produced many refinements on rule by one man, which they called a *tyranny* even when it was mild and just and popular. Moreover, although they invented democracy, they had terrible difficulties in making it work. Fierce political infighting between rival groups and rival politicians filled Greek politics from the beginning. Rather than accept political defeat, a Greek politician would often intrigue with a foreign enemy.

Modern students have often taken their picture of Greek politics in general from a superb speech that Pericles, the most celebrated of the leaders of Athens, made in 430 B.C. at the funeral of the Athenian soldiers killed in war against Sparta (see p. 41), as reported in the history of the war by the historian Thucydides. Praising Athenian democracy, Pericles said that at Athens the law guaranteed equal justice to all, that talent and not wealth was the Athenian qualification for public service, that Athenians expected of everybody a lively interest and participation in public affairs.

But his picture corresponded more to an ideal world than to the real Athenian world. At Athens the law courts were often biased, wealth remained an important qualification for office, and individuals pursued political ambition as ruthlessly as anywhere on earth. The tough world of Athenian politics was like that of other, more modern democracies. The Greeks, then, invented democracy but seldom practiced it. When they did, it usually fell far short of their own ideals as expressed by Pericles.

Finally, the Greeks had far more humor than any of the other ancient peoples, who—except for an occasional bit of playfulness seen in Egyptian art—were a solemn lot. The Greeks enjoyed laughter. Their comic writers satirized their own political leaders and current fashions sometimes with gentle wit, and sometimes violently and indecently. Brilliant, funny, energetic, inventive, opinionated, arrogant, and immensely quarrelsome, the Greeks are the first people of the ancient world to whom we can feel close.

Revival after the Dark Age

For the Greeks the Dark Age began to brighten about 850 B.C., as contact was renewed between the mainland and the Near East. Phoenicia, whose trade continued brisk, lay close to the Greek island of Cyprus, where Mycenaean culture had continued after the Dorians had ruined it on the mainland. Objects from Phoenicia now appear in mainland Greece, and the earliest traces of the Phoenician alphabet as adapted to the writing of Greek are now dated about 825 B.C. New letters were added for peculiarly Greek sounds. New styles of pottery also prove the renewal of communications. Greece itself now received the Homeric poems, first written down in the Ionian Greek settlements of Asia Minor. They brought back to the mainland the sense of its heroic past.

In Greece itself, the poet Hesiod, writing in the language of Homer and in the same meter, in his *Works and Days* (ca. 800 B.C.) set down the proper rules of life for the small farmer, and

Vase in the geometric style of the eight century B.C., *after the close of the Dark Age. It shows a prothesis, or lying-in-state of the dead.*

scolded his own brother, who had tried to grab more than his fair share of the family estate. Hesiod also wrote a genealogy of the gods *(Theogony),* reciting the traditional view that the gods were the children of earth and heaven, and had in turn created mankind. Preaching justice, human and divine, Hesiod's verse reflected the early religious ideas of the Greeks. The ideas were influenced by the oracle at Delphi. This was a mountain shrine of the sun god Apollo in central Greece, where a divinely inspired prophetess answered questions for all comers and gave advice. In this period the Olympic games were founded and held every four years beginning with 776 B.C. at Olympia, shrine of Zeus in the western Peloponnesus.

The Polis: Sparta

The chief social and political form to emerge in reviving Greece was the *polis,* or city-state (plural, *poleis*). These had begun in the Greek settlements of Asia Minor, and consisted of the municipality itself and the territory surrounding it. City-states were small in size and in population; they were often centered on a fortress built on a hill—the "high city," or Acropolis. Such city-states appeared now in the Dorian centers, first on Crete and then especially at Sparta on the mainland.

In Sparta only the upper five to ten percent of the population were citizens. Descendants of the Dorian conquerors, they were the rulers, hereditary landowners, and soldiers. The overwhelming majority of the people belonged to the *helot* class, farm laborers bound to the soil, servants of the ruling group. In between was a free class called *perioikoi* ("dwellers around"), descendants of the pre-Dorian residents of neighboring areas. They lived in the villages under Spartan control and had personal freedom but could not take part in politics or intermarry with the Spartans. The ruling Spartans lived in constant fear of revolution. They kept their secret agents planted among the helots to report subversive talk, and indeed barely managed to put down a helot uprising in the late seventh century.

The Spartans had two kings at a time, descendants of two rival Dorian families. But real political power belonged to five *ephors* (overseers) elected annually by an assembly of all Spartan citizens over thirty. (Women, helots, or perioikoi could not vote.) In addition, there was a council of thirty elders representing the more powerful families.

War dominated Spartan thinking. The males lived under military discipline from the age of seven, when a boy was taken from his parents and taught reading and music and running and fighting. Weak-looking babies were abandoned to die. So that there might be healthy children, girls too were given strenuous training. Adult males lived in the barracks until they were thirty. They might marry at twenty, but they dined in the mess hall until they were sixty.

The army was excellent and the citizens were patriotic and able to bear misfortune. As money the Spartans used clumsy iron bars in order to make ordinary commercial pursuits as unattractive and difficult as possible. Although their earliest poets wrote fine, sensitive lyrics, this art soon vanished. First war songs and then no poetry at all, replaced it. The Spartans were not artists, but fighters.

Colonization

Along with the establishment of city-states, the Greeks launched a large-scale movement of colonial expansion. The city-states of Asia Minor and of Greece proper sent out naval expeditions of their citizens to plant new settlements in non-Greek areas wherever there was no power strong enough to prevent it. New Greek cities arose on the shores of the Black Sea, along the African shore of the Mediterranean in what we now call Libya, in Sicily, and along the Italian coasts (which the Romans later called *Magna Graecia,* "Great Greece"), and as far west as the coasts of France and Spain. Each new colony became a new city-state, independent of its mother city but bound to it by sentimental and economic ties and by similar political and religious practices.

Overpopulation and internal strife in the settled cities, together with the wish for trade and adventure, speeded the colonizing movement. Trebizond in Asia Minor, Panticapaeum in the Crimea, Byzantium (later to be Constantinople and still later Istanbul) at the Black Sea Straits, Syracuse in Sicily, Naples in southern Italy, Marseilles in southern France, and Cadiz beyond the Straits of Gibraltar on the Atlantic southern coast of Spain are all famous cities that started their lives as Greek colonies (see map, p. 38).

As Egypt declined and Assyria conquered western Asia, Mediterranean trade came to center on Greece. First one Greek city and then another would take the lead. The Dorian-founded settlements on Crete, Rhodes, Corinth (strategically located at the isthmus attaching the Peloponnesus to northern Greece), and Megara all became powerful and prosperous. Coins, invented in the Anatolian kingdom of Lydia, were being struck about 650 B.C. on the Greek island of Aegina, where silver was the only precious metal available. Soon this convenient new kind of money spread westward. The coins of Aegina had turtles on them, those of Corinth foals, those of Athens from the sixth century onward the owl of Athena, goddess of the city.

The owl, sacred to Athena, appeared on Athenian coins from the sixth century. This silver coin is from the fifth century.

Athens

Draco and Solon

Athens never suffered from a Dorian occupation and so did not become a polis early. It lingered as an old-fashioned aristocratic tribal state, dominating the large surrounding territory called Attica. Territorially, Attica was divided into plains, hills, and coastal land. Politically it was divided into four tribes, each of which had three brotherhoods *(phratries)* or territorial subdivisions *(trittyes).* Within each phratry a distinction was drawn between those noble families who owned and worked their farms (the clans) and the guildsmen, later in origin, who belonged to an association of artisans or merchants. Land descended in the clan and might not be alienated. With it went a deep attachment to the local religious shrines, whose priests were clansmen. The guildsmen were citizens but not nobles and could sell or transfer their property.

An *archon* (a leader or principal person) managed religious affairs. A second archon (the *polemarch*) managed military affairs, and a third civil affairs. In the seventh century these three were joined by a board of six recording archons, making nine in all. Each was elected for a year, at the end of which all nine automatically became members of the Council of the Areopagus (the hill of Ares in Athens), the chief judicial and policy-making body. Although a general assembly of all the people directly elected the archons and so all future members of the Areopagus Council, only clansmen were eligible for office.

Already ancient in the seventh century B.C., these political arrangements were challenged in the decade after 632 by a series of disorders. In 621 a specially appointed official, Draco, published the first Athenian law code, famous for its severe penalties: hence our term, a "Draconian" measure. Harshest of all were the laws on debt. A bankrupt clansman could never sell off or mortgage his land, but had to mortgage his produce. Thus he would oblige himself and his heirs to work his land indefinitely for somebody else, and in effect would lose his own freedom. Bankrupt guildsmen actually became the slaves

Head of the bronze statue of a charioteer from the sanctuary of Apollo at Delphi, ca. 470 B.C.

of their creditors. The growing unfairness of this system led to civil strife.

In the 590s the reformer Solon freed all clansmen and guildsmen then suffering these penalties and abolished the harsh system. He repealed almost all Draco's laws, and published a new code. He tried to improve the general prosperity by emphasizing the need to foster a lively new commerce. He even offered citizenship to citizens of other poleis who would come to work in Athens. He opened the most important offices of state to rich guildsmen as well as rich clansmen. Money, not birth, now counted chiefly.

Solon also appointed one hundred members from each of the four tribes to a Council of Four Hundred, an inner circle of the general assembly of the people. He prepared the materials for discussion and recommended action. The general assembly now could not act without a recommendation from the Council, but it could vote against the recommendation and it still elected the archons. Solon also selected by lot a panel of assembly members to review the work of the magistrates.

Solon introduced democratic innovations, but kept both the older aristocratic election of the rich to magistracies and the oligarchic power of the few in the Council of the Areopagus. In one of his own poems he says of his reforms, "I stood holding my stout shield over both parties [the poor and the rich]; I did not allow either party to prevail unjustly." Some of his fellow Athenians jeered at him for not taking advantage of his powers to line his own pockets, but he answered (again in a poem) that "money flits from man to man, but honor abides forever." Urging the Athenians to obey his laws for a hundred years, Solon withdrew from the scene for a decade.

Peisistratus and Cleisthenes

Civil strife at once began again. The plains people were mostly artistocrats who felt Solon had gone too far, the hill people mostly poor farmers who felt he had not gone far enough, and the coast people mostly artisans who thought he was about right. In 561 B.C., their quarrels gave Athens into the hands of a tyrant, as the Greeks called a dictator, however benevolent: Peisistratus, a noble, who had made himself leader of the hill people. In and out of power for some years, Peisistratus owed his final success in 546 to vast wealth gained from the silver mines on his estates and to mercenary troops.

Peisistratus and his sons dominated Athens until 510 B.C. He collected ten percent of all the rich Athenian revenues for his personal fortune and made shrewd alliances with other poleis. At home, his was the only party. He exiled those aristocrats who refused to support him. Having come to power as leader of the poor, Peisistratus made them loans, embarked on a lavish program of public works, subsidized the arts, and increased the magnificence of state religious celebrations. His sons, who succeeded him on his death in 527 B.C., followed his policies. But the noble families whom Peisistratus had uprooted continued their opposition, often from exile. After much disorder, the exiled nobles came back in 510 B.C. One of the exiles, Cleisthenes, appealed for the support of the guildsmen—already so much favored by Peisistratus—and came to power in 508.

By striking at the political influence of the clans in elections, Cleisthenes gave the guildsmen equal weight. He used as the basic new political unit an old territorial division called a *deme,* a small area something like a ward in a modern city, and ordered all citizens registered as voters within their demes, irrespective of their origins. So the guildsmen got equal franchise with the clansmen.

Cleisthenes also rezoned Attica into three new regions that did not coincide with the former coast, hill, and plain. He regrouped the demes into units made up of people who lived in all three regions. By lot he then put these in turn together into ten political "tribes," which replaced the four old racial (or genuinely tribal) tribes. Membership in these new tribes now cut across the old family and regional and class lines, and the former influence of the noble families was effectively cut down. Cleisthenes invented what American politicians call the gerrymander.

Each deme annually elected a number of its members (proportionate to its population) as its representatives, and from them the new ten tribes selected by lot fifty each to be members of the new Council of Five Hundred, replacing Solon's Council of Four Hundred. Solon had given Athenians equality before the law; Cleisthenes gave them equality at the ballot box.

Of course, the system was clumsy. The archons continued to administer, except that now (501) the whole Assembly of the People elected ten generals a year to serve as operational commanders under the polemarch. The Council of the Areopagus (ex-archons) kept its powers and its aristocratic membership. Archons and generals continued to be aristocrats. Although they were often able, experienced, and patriotic, they struggled with each other for power and prestige, and tended to become the chiefs of rival factions. These rivalries led individuals to shift their positions frequently. At different times in his career, Cleisthenes himself had worked with and against both Spartans and Persians, both nobles and people. These switches in loyalty were normal in Athenian politics but naturally increased its instability.

The ten groups of fifty tribal members of which the Council of Five Hundred was made up each governed in continual session for one tenth of each year (roughly thirty-six days); and the chairman of the committee of fifty that was sitting at any given time was selected afresh by lot every day. During each continual thirty-six-day session, the committee members *(prytaneis)* lived in a special state building and were fed at public expense. They could summon the remaining councilors to a full session whenever they wished. No citizen between the ages of thirty and sixty could be a member of the council more than twice or chairman of a day's session more than once. With swiftly changing large groups of citizens receiving responsibilities for very short times, almost any citizen could hope to enjoy the experience at some time during his life. Now that all citizens had a stake in the community, the Athenians were prepared for their famous historic confrontation with the Persian Empire.

II PERSIA AND THE GREEKS, TO 478 B.C.

The Persian Empire

We have already encountered the Medes, an Indo-European-speaking people of the Near East, who in 612 B.C. cooperated with the Babylonians to destroy Nineveh and bring down the hated empire of the brutal Assyrians. We have also seen the Medes' southern relatives, the Persians, destroy Babylon (538) and allow the captive Hebrews to return to Jerusalem. It was Cyrus the Great, Persian ruler (550–529 B.C.) of the southern province, the captor of Babylon and liberator of the Jews, who conquered his northern kinsmen the Medes and so began a meteoric rise toward empire.

Cyrus next moved westward into Anatolia, absorbed the Lydian kingdom of the rich king Croesus, and attacked and conquered the Greek cities of Ionia along the Aegean coast. Then he moved east all the way to the borders of India, conquering and annexing as he went. Unlike the Assyrians, Cyrus was no tyrant. He allowed his new subject peoples to worship as they pleased, and to keep on governing themselves in their own way under his representatives. Cyrus' son Cambyses (529–522 B.C.) invaded and conquered Egypt.

Cambyses' brother-in-law and successor Darius (521–486 B.C.) subdivided the Persian Empire into twenty provinces *(satrapies)*, each with its political governor, its military governor, and its tax collector. Royal spies crossed and crisscrossed the vast area from the Aegean to the Indus, collecting information for the king. Darius took from the Lydians the practice of coining money. His highway system was a great network whose largest thread was the royal road that ran more than sixteen hundred miles from Susa, Darius' capital, to Sardis, the chief city of Lydia.

Probably Darius introduced Zoroastrianism, the religion of Zarathustra, who had died only a generation earlier. Zoroastrianism began as a monotheistic faith, proclaiming the one god, Ahuramazda, whose chief quality was his wisdom. He is the only intellectual deity we have so far encountered. The other divinities around him were not gods and goddesses but abstract qualities such as Justice and Integrity, which Ahuramazda had created. Zoroastrians believed that life was a constant struggle between a good

The tomb of King Darius II, in Iran. It is cut into live rock.

spirit and an evil spirit, both subordinate to Ahuramazda. Wise men chose the good way, foolish men the evil way. The supreme spirit rewarded the wise and punished the foolish.

Lacking ritual and a priesthood, early Zoroastrianism was perhaps too impersonal to be a popular faith. Later generations identified Ahuramazda with the good spirit, and so demoted him. He was now no longer the supreme ruler over the evil spirit (Ahriman) but only a contender with him. No longer monotheistic, the religion became "dualistic." It gave comparable power to good and evil. Earlier polytheism also reappeared, and a powerful priesthood asserted itself.

The Ionian Cities; The Threat to Greece; Marathon

The now captive Ionian Greek cities missed their lost political freedom. Their prosperity also declined. By 513, the Persians had crossed the Bosporus on a pontoon bridge, sailed up the Danube, and moved north across modern Romania into the Ukraine in a campaign against a nomadic people called Scythians. This Persian advance into Europe alarmed the Greeks. It looked as if Darius would next move south against European Greece from his new base in the northern Balkans.

Some of the Greek poleis—Sparta and her allies—were hostile to the Persians, but others had pro-Persian rulers. One of Peisistratus' sons, Hippias, had taken refuge with the Persians, who now backed his return to Athens. About 505 B.C. the Athenians refused to accept Hippias and soon afterwards decided to help the captive Ionian cities. With Athenian help the Ionian Greeks burned Sardis, the former Lydian capital and now headquarters for the Persians in Anatolia (499 B.C.). Other Greek cities joined the rebellion.

But by 495 B.C. the Persians had defeated

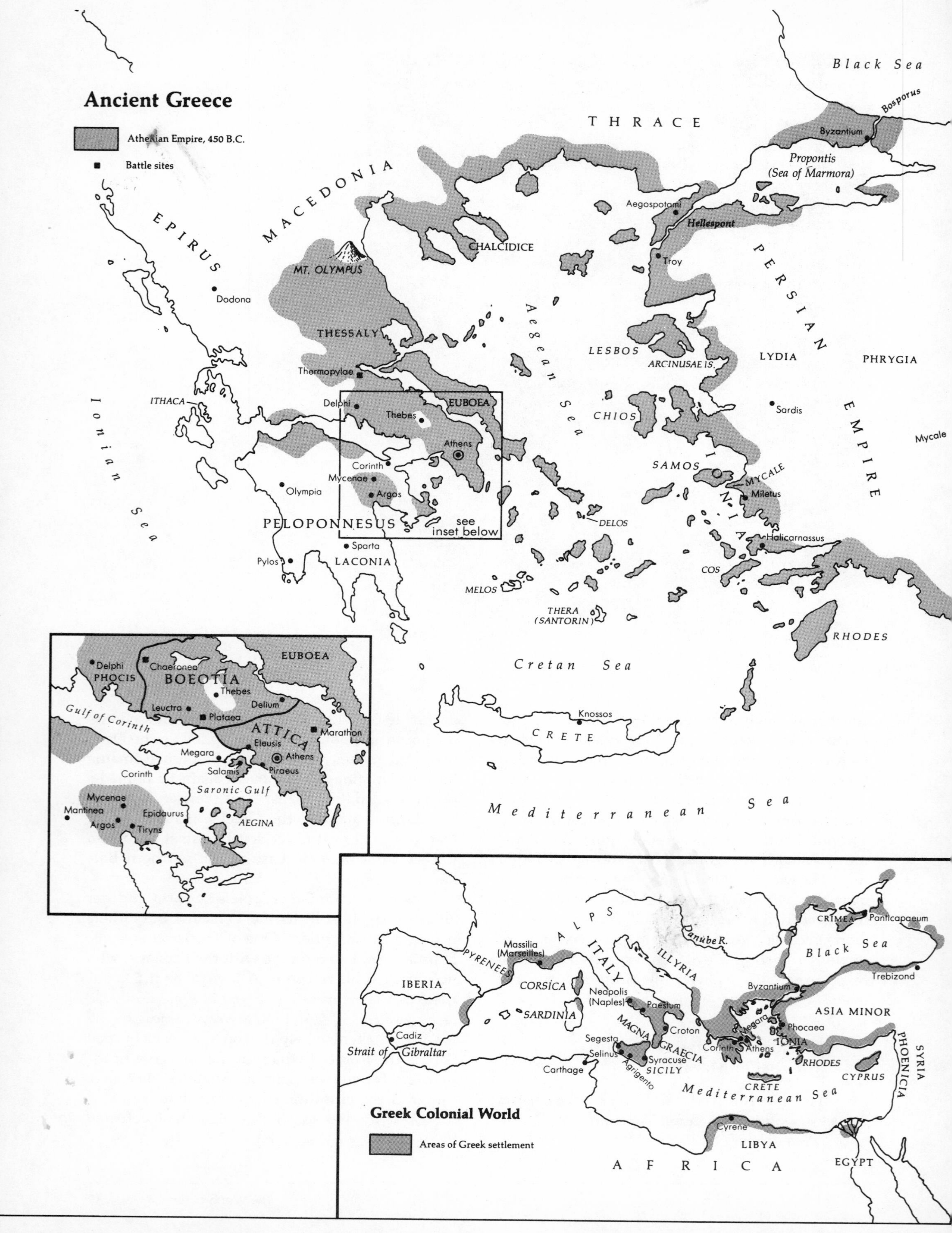

Ancient Greece
Athenian Empire, 450 B.C.
Battle sites
Black Sea
Bosporus
THRACE
Byzantium
Propontis
(Sea of Marmora)
MACEDONIA
EPIRUS
Aegospotami
Hellespont
CHALCIDICE
MT. OLYMPUS
Troy
PERSIAN EMPIRE
Dodona
Aegean Sea
THESSALY
LESBOS
ARCINUSAE IS.
LYDIA
PHRYGIA
Thermopylae
ITHACA
Delphi
EUBOEA
Thebes
CHIOS
Sardis
Mycale
Ionian Sea
Athens
Corinth
SAMOS
IONIA
MYCALE
Mycenae
Miletus
Olympia
Argos
PELOPONNESUS
see inset below
DELOS
Halicarnassus
Sparta
Pylos
LACONIA
COS
MELOS
THERA
(SANTORIN)
RHODES
Cretan Sea
Knossos
CRETE
Mediterranean Sea
Delphi
PHOCIS
Chaeronea
BOEOTIA
Thebes
Leuctra
Plataea
Delium
Gulf of Corinth
ATTICA
Marathon
Megara
Eleusis
Athens
Salamis
Piraeus
Corinth
Saronic Gulf
Mycenae
Mantinea
Epidaurus
Argos
Tiryns
AEGINA
Greek Colonial World
Areas of Greek settlement
ALPS
Danube R.
CRIMEA
Panticapaeum
Massilia
(Marseilles)
PYRENEES
ITALY
ILLYRIA
Black Sea
IBERIA
CORSICA
Trebizond
Neapolis
(Naples)
Paestum
Byzantium
SARDINIA
ASIA MINOR
MAGNA GRAECIA
Croton
Megara
Phocaea
Cadiz
Segesta
Corinth
Athens
IONIA
SYRIA
Strait of Gibraltar
Selinus
Syracuse
RHODES
PHOENICIA
Carthage
Agrigento
SICILY
CYPRUS
CRETE
Mediterranean Sea
Cyrene
LIBYA
AFRICA
EGYPT

the ships of the Greek cities in the Aegean. They burned the most important Ionian city, Miletus, massacred many of its men, and deported its women and children. By 493 B.C. the Ionian revolt was over. In the next two years the Persians extended their authority along the northern coasts of Greece proper, directly threatening Athens.

It was probably Hippias who advised the Persian commanders whom he was accompanying to land at Marathon, in a region once loyal to his father Peisistratus, only about twenty-five miles north of Athens. There a far smaller Athenian force under Miltiades defeated the Persians (490) and put an end for ten years to the Persian threat to Greece. Sparta did not help because the Spartans were celebrating a religious festival during which military operations were taboo. Only the much smaller polis of Plataea sent a thousand troops to join the ten thousand Athenians. The credit for driving off the Persians therefore went primarily to Athens.

The 480s

By the time Darius' successor, Xerxes (486–465), was ready to try again, the Athenians had removed their hero Miltiades from an active role in their affairs. Miltiades had a typically Athenian record of shifting loyalties, at one time pro-Peisistratus, at another anti-, at one time pro-Persian, at another the hero of Marathon. A leader of the nobles, he was brought down by a rival faction.

It was probably now (488 B.C.) that some Athenian invented the famous practice known as ostracism. The word comes from *ostrakon,* a fragment of a clay pot on which the citizens scribbled the name of any politician they wished to exile from the city for a period of ten years. Apparently a majority of a meeting of 6,000 citizens (i.e., 3,001 votes) was needed to ostracize. During the 480s—the decade of preparation for Xerxes' expected attack—ostracism became the rage. We have hundreds of the original clay fragments with the names of prominent politicians written on them. Although the decade saw further decrease in the influence of the nobles, rivalries for the office of general continued. By 480 a leader named Themistocles had emerged as the popular choice to lead the resistance to the new Persian invasion.

New silver mines were discovered in the nick of time, and Themistocles persuaded the Athenians to use the money to build a new fleet. Sparta took over the leadership of the anti-Persian Greek poleis, in an anti-Persian League with a congress of delegates from the individual cities and a unified command. Knowing that its forces would be greatly outnumbered (perhaps 110,000 against 500,000 Persians), the League did not try to defend the northern Greek cities where the Persian cavalry could operate freely, but instead abandoned them.

Xerxes Invades

In 480 B.C., Xerxes' huge army, its speed slowed down by its very numbers, crossed into Europe and swung south into Greece, while a Persian fleet, possibly of three thousand ships, sailed along the coast. At the pass of Thermopylae in central Greece, a small army of Spartans—only three hundred strong—defended the pass to the last man, taking a terrible toll of the Persian infantry. A storm, a naval battle, and a second storm cut the Persian fleet in half. The Delphic oracle had mysteriously prophesied that Athens would be destroyed but had advised the Athenians to put their trust in their "wooden walls." Themistocles succeeded in persuading the Athenians that "wooden walls" meant the new fleet and that they should abandon the city.

Athens was accordingly evacuated, except for the defenders of the Acropolis, whom Xerxes' men killed as they plundered the city. But the fleet awaited the Persian attack in the narrow waters of the harbor of Salamis off Athens. Helped by deserters from the Persians who revealed Xerxes' battle plans, the Athenian fleet won a smashing victory, which Xerxes himself watched from a great throne set up on shore. Xerxes had to withdraw from Greece. In the next year (479) at Plataea the united Greek forces numbering more than a hundred thousand men defeated the Persian troops once again.

In spite of the thousands of personal and municipal rivalries among the Greeks, all members of the League had kept the oath "I shall fight to the death, I shall put freedom before life, I shall not desert colonel or captain alive or dead, I shall carry out the generals' commands, and I shall bury my comrades-in-arms where they fall and leave none unburied." A wildly individualistic people had shown that they could put the general interest ahead of everything else. The Persians, as it turned out, had been stopped forever, although peace was not formally made until 448, and in the intervening years the threat of renewed invasion hung over the heads of the Greeks.

III THE ATHENIAN EMPIRE, 478–404 B.C.

Postwar Reorganization

Athens, the strongest Greek naval power, prevented the Spartans, the strongest land power, from taking the lead in planning for the future defense against Persia. Instead, the Athenians organized a new Greek alliance to liberate the Ionian cities still subject to Persia and to maintain the defenses. Athens contributed most of the ships, but the other cities were assessed contributions in both ships and money. The alliance was called the Delian League because its treasury was on the island of Delos. It scored a major victory over the Persians in Asia Minor about 467 B.C.

About 472 Themistocles was ostracized. He fled to the Persians and died in the service of Xerxes' son and successor. He accurately foresaw the great danger that lay ahead for Athens: the long-range threat from Sparta. Like Miltiades, he lost the confidence of the Athenians after he had done them precious service.

In 462 a new reform further democratized Athenian government. The Areopagus Council lost its powers, which went to the Council of Five Hundred and the Assembly. Put through largely by Ephialtes, the reform was partly inspired by a brilliant young aristocratic politician named Pericles, a grandson of Cleisthenes. By about 457 the patriotic and incorruptible Pericles had become the leading Athenian politician, responsible for the many military and naval operations conducted against the Persians, against the Spartans, and against certain members of the Athenian alliance itself who resented the dictatorial ways of Athens.

At home Pericles pushed democracy, inaugurating a system of state pay for service to the state. Now that the poor could afford public service, they welcomed it. In order to limit the number of those eligible for such payment, Pericles also now limited Athenian citizenship to those born of Athenian parents. The money to pay all these people could come only from Athens' allies.

From Alliance to Empire

In fact, Pericles was gradually turning the Athenian alliance into an empire, with the subject members providing the money for Athens, which in exchange would defend them all and would be able to challenge Sparta. After 470, no ally was allowed to secede. In 454 the treasury of the alliance was moved from Delos to Athens, and became a major Athenian resource. At its peak (about 450) the alliance included 170 cities. And in 448 Athens made peace with Persia that liberated the Ionian cities and bound the Persians not to come within three days' journey of the coast.

Athenian settlements were founded on the territories of some allied states, and Athenian coinage became standard. Resentment against Athens was naturally widespread among the allies. But in 446–445 a new thirty years' truce with Sparta provided that neither side would commit aggression against the other. Both had lost the good will of the other Greek poleis.

The thirty years' truce, as it turned out, lasted only for fifteen (446–431). It was a prosperous period, during which Pericles continued to dominate the affairs of state. He was reelected general democratically every year. He had at his disposal the large surpluses in the treasury, which were much more than enough to pay the 10,000 rowers of the warships, the 700 officials, the 500 councilors, the 6,000 jurors, and many others.

Pericles embarked upon a great program of public works, of which the two most famous buildings were the celebrated Parthenon (the temple of Athena Parthenos, the virgin) and the Propylaea (monumental gateway), both on the Acropolis. Anybody who climbed the hill went up the steps that led up to the Propylaea, and passed through it. At the top of the hill he saw the giant bronze statue of Athena sculptured by Phidias, a personal friend of Pericles. Behind it and to the right rose the entrance colonnade of the magnificent new temple. Inside was another statue of Athena, this one in gold and ivory, also by Phidias.

There were plenty of jobs available in the building program, and slaves as well as freemen participated and were well paid. There was money and opportunity for everybody: for the 30,000 resident aliens *(metics),* who paid a special tax and were not allowed to own land or participate in politics, but engaged in commerce and contributed to the city's and their own good fortune; for the 200,000 slaves, whose lot was easier than it was elsewhere, and who were often set free; and most of all for the 168,000 Athenian citizens (4,000 upper class, 100,000 middle class, and 64,000 lower class).*

* All such statistics are mere approximations. No exact figures can be given.

The Peloponnesian War

The First Fifteen Years, 431–416 B.C.

The splendid civilization of Athens in the fifth century depended upon the continued exercise of complete control over the subject poleis in the empire. The Spartans feared that if they did not fight Athens soon, it would be too late. In 431 the Spartans invaded Attica and began the ruinous Peloponnesian War (431–404 B.C.). Pericles withdrew the entire population of Attica within the extended city walls. He planned to remain on the defensive on land but to take the offensive at sea.

In 430, however, a terrible plague broke out in Athens, where the whole population of Attica was cooped up with no sanitation. In 429 Pericles himself died of it, leaving Athens without the trusted leader who could make even unpopular policies acceptable. The plague raged until the end of 426, and cost Athens about a third of its population, including its best troops. It did not stop the Athenians from continuing the war, however, with general though costly success.

By 424, Athens could probably have ended the war on favorable terms. The upper and the middle classes that had suffered most from it were eager to do so. It was their lands in Attica that the Spartans ravaged, and their members who made up most of the land forces that did the heavy fighting. But the lower classes, identified with the fleet, which was still in fine condition, hoped for even greater gains, and wanted to continue the war. Since they now dominated the city's politics, the war continued.

Not until 421 could the peace party led by Nicias conclude the "Peace of Nicias." Each side restored all captured places and prisoners and promised to remain at peace for fifty years. This was soon supplemented by an actual Spartan-Athenian alliance, also concluded for fifty years but intended chiefly to give each power a chance to put its own alliance in order while secure from an attack by the other. The war had been marked by numerous acts of brutality on both sides: prisoners were slaughtered and enslaved, and agreements broken.

Charioteer: silver coin from Syracuse, fifth century B.C.

Alcibiades and Failure

The peace lasted only five years, 421–416 B.C. Pericles' nephew, Alcibiades, a brilliant, ambitious, dissipated, and unstable youth, became leader of the lower-class war party against the restrained and unglamorous Nicias. When war was resumed, Athens' fortunes changed. Sparta won victories. In 415 the Athenians ruthlessly killed all the adult males of the island of Melos and enslaved the women and children as a punishment for Melos's insistence on staying neutral. Alcibiades favored and Nicias opposed a large naval expedition to Sicily to attack the Greek city of Syracuse, an ally of Athens' enemies.

The project had no real relationship to the politics of mainland Greece. The Athenians had little reliable military information about Sicily. But Alcibiades promised glory and the Assembly followed his lead. Just before the expedition sailed, a scandal outraged the Athenians. The sexual organs of the statues of Hermes that stood before homes and temples at Athens were broken off in the night. But he went off to Sicily, however, as co-commander with the unwilling Nicias of the greatest naval expedition ever sent out by a Greek polis. Before the fleet reached Syracuse, Alcibiades was recalled to stand trial for the mutilation of the Hermae; but he escaped to Sparta.

The siege of Syracuse (414–413) was a total failure: Nicias and other leaders were captured and killed. Sparta, now advised by Alcibiades (who also seduced the wife of the Spartan king), renewed the war in Greece, sent troops to help the Syracusans, and stirred up the Ionian cities to revolt against Athens. The Persians joined with the Spartans. Alcibiades went over to the Persians. He told the Athenians that if they would install an oligarchic government he would return and use his influence with the Persians on Athens' behalf. The Spartans promised the Persians the lost cities of Ionia.

Civil strife broke out in Athens. Oligarchy replaced democracy for a year, with Alcibiades pulling the strings from abroad. In 410 B.C., after some Athenian successes at sea, democracy was restored. Until 407 Alcibiades continued to command Athenian naval forces at sea without returning home. Then he came to Athens and was declared innocent of the mutilation of the Hermae. But the Spartan fleet defeated him in 406, and he went into retirement, where he was murdered three years later by Spartan and Persian agents. His career vividly illustrates the vulnerability of the Athenian democracy to a plausible, charming, talented scoundrel.

In the final naval action of the war (Aegospotami, 405), the Spartans captured most of the Athenian fleet empty on a beach while the sailors were hunting food on shore. Starving, blockaded by land and sea, its alliance in ruins as its allies defected or joined the Spartans, the Athenians had to surrender. They had to demolish their long walls, abandon their empire, surrender their fleet, and promise to follow Sparta in foreign policy. But they were not massacred.

IV THE FOURTH CENTURY B.C. AND THE HELLENISTIC AGE

Spartan and Theban Domination, 405–355 B.C.

Taking over as the dominant power in Greece, the victorious Spartans found themselves as incapable as the Athenians of unifying the quarrelsome poleis. The Persians were threatening again now that they had Ionia back in their hands. Gold and silver had found their way into a Spartan economy whose founders had preferred bars of iron. For the first time many Spartans found themselves disfranchised for debt, and joined the helots and perioikoi as part of the discontented majority. The conservative elders of their government could not meet the new challenges. Perhaps the polis itself as an institution was by now too small, too old-fashioned to keep the peace and so give its citizens scope for economic advancement.

In Athens an oligarchy known as the Thirty Tyrants took over and instituted a reign of terror until 403, when an invading force of exiled Athenian democrats launched a civil war. They restored democracy in Athens itself, but only a few miles away at Eleusis the Thirty Tyrants and their followers set up a rival state, a puppet of Sparta. Nobody was allowed to go from one of these rival Athenian states to the other. In 401, the Athenians treacherously killed the generals of the Eleusis armies, and the two states were precariously reunited. It was this new unstable government that tried and condemned the philosopher Socrates in 399 B.C. (see p. 54).

In 401, by backing the unsuccessful rebellion of Prince Cyrus, younger brother of Artaxerxes II, king of Persia, Sparta got into a disastrous war against the Persians. It ended in a stalemate in 386. Sparta next tried to punish all Greek cities that dared resist it and to impose oligarchical government. In 379, a group of Theban democratic exiles overthrew the Spartan puppet regime at Thebes and a new war broke out. Athens soon dominated the new anti-Spartan League. By 371, the Spartans were beaten. They guaranteed the independence of the other poleis and promised disarmament.

But the Thebans refused to sign the treaty, which made Athens and Persia the sole guarantors of peace. Soon afterwards, Thebes, under its leader, Epaminondas, defeated the Spartans and destroyed Spartan power in its own homeland, the Peloponnesus. Thebes, which had a democratic government and treated its allies as equals, not as subjects, now dominated Greece. But warfare did not stop. Athens and Sparta together defeated Thebes and Mantinea (362). Epaminondas was killed. No Greek power could halt the endless fighting.

Nor could a new league of city-states (362) do the job. It tried to create something like a United States of Greece with a single foreign policy. But Athens made alliances inside the League and tried to rebuild the Athenian Empire. By 355 Athens was exhausted, bankrupt, and weak. Thebes was defeated by the city of Phocis, whose general had seized the shrine of Delphi and used its accumulated funds to create a large army of mercenaries (354).

Ironically enough, the inability of the Greek cities to give up fighting was almost surely due in part to general prosperity. During the fifth century only Athens and Sparta had been able to afford large armies and navies. But during the fourth many other cities grew rich enough to support such forces. Mediterranean commerce brought wealth to the distant Greek settlements that stretched from the Crimea to Spain. It was not only goods that flowed but also slaves and mercenary troops. About 350 B.C. the Persians alone had about fifty thousand Greek troops fighting in their armies.

Many of the devices of modern capitalism that make international trade easier now made their first appearance: banking and credit, insurance, trade treaties, and special privileges. Private wealth grew rapidly and was widely distributed. Slaves increased in number. We know of several people who owned more than a thousand of them. By 338 B.C. there were probably 150,000 slaves in Attica, working in the mines and at other occupations. All this prosperity meant that states quickly recovered from defeats in war and could soon afford to try again. Patriotism became more and more a matter of cutting up the melon of profits. At the same time, the poor grew poorer. Unwilling to declass themselves by engaging in the manual labor that was now the work of slaves, they became wandering beggars or mercenary soldiers.

Macedon

North of Thessaly, and extending inland into areas that are today part of Yugoslavia and Albania, lay the kingdom of Macedon, with a considerable coastline along the Aegean. The Macedonians were a mixture of peoples including some of Greek origin. They were organized into tribes, worshiped some of the Greek gods, and spoke a native language that the Greeks could not understand although it included many words of Greek origin. Their hereditary kings—who were also elected by the people—claimed Greek descent. Indeed, they believed they were descendants of the hero Herakles (Hercules), son of Zeus himself.

The king spoke Greek in addition to the native language. He had title to all land, and ruled absolutely so long as he was not charged with treason (when the people might depose him). He was advised by councilors selected from among the nobles of each tribe, who felt themselves to be his social equals. Although the Greeks had planted some poleis along the Macedonian shore, and although Greek cultural influence and Greek trade had penetrated deeply into Macedon by the fourth century, Macedon did not copy Greek political institutions but kept its own, which were rather like those of Mycenaean Greece in the days of Agamemnon. Traditionally the Macedonians relied on cavalry in war, but in the fourth century they added foot soldiers in order to fight their Balkan neighbors from the west and north, the Illyrians (probable ancestors of the Albanians of today). Both Athens and Sparta interfered and intrigued in internal Macedonian affairs.

The Achievement of Philip

In 359, a prince of the ruling house, Philip, became regent for his infant nephew, the king. Philip had lived for three years as a hostage in Thebes, where he knew Epaminondas and had learned about Greek affairs. He applied Theban military principles to his army (emphasizing infantry tactics), led it in person, defeated the Illyrians and various rivals for power within Macedon, and was elected king in his own right. He exploited the rich gold and silver mines in his kingdom and struck his own coinage. He broke the power of Athens in the territory neighboring his own to the east (359–354 B.C.) and threatened Athenian possessions along the shore of the Hellespont (354–351).

Athenian politicians viewed Philip's advance with mixed feelings. Some favored him, others opposed. But after he had won still more territory and begun to use a fleet successfully, the famous Athenian orator Demosthenes began to warn against the threat. Philip next detached the big island of Euboea, close to Attica itself, from its Athenian loyalties and suggested peace. In 346, Athens made an alliance with him. Even Demosthenes approved, though Philip meanwhile had secured control over the Delphic oracle. He was moving south and consolidating his power as he came.

By 342, the Athenians had acquired new allies in the Peloponnesus. In retaliation Philip moved into Thrace (modern Bulgaria) to cut off the Athenian grain supplies coming from the Black Sea and to avert a new Persian-Athenian alliance. Now Demosthenes pressed for war, and Athens took military action in Euboea (341–340). By late 339 Philip was deep in Greece once again, only two days march from Attica.

Demosthenes now arranged an eleventh-hour alliance with Thebes. Protesting at intervals his wishes for peace, Philip totally defeated the Athenian-Theban alliance at Chaeronea in Boeotia (338 B.C.). He occupied Thebes, which had surrendered, but spared Athens a military occupation on condition that the Athenian alliance be dissolved in favor of one with Macedon. Philip's leniency proved that he had never intended to destroy Athens, as Demosthenes had maintained.

Philip's victories aroused in many the hope of a unified Greece. At Corinth in 337 B.C., all the poleis except Sparta met and organized a league that called itself "The Greeks." All members bound themselves to stop fighting and intervening in each other's affairs. This was a far more closely knit body than the abortive league of 362 (see p. 42). It immediately allied itself with Macedon and then joined with Philip in a declaration of war on Persia to revenge Xerxes' invasion of 143 years earlier. Philip was to command the expedition. By 336 B.C. the advance forces of the army were already liberating the Ionian cities from Persia. But Philip, aged only forty-six, was now mysteriously assassinated.

Philip's accomplishments greatly impressed his contemporaries, who realized that no such powerful consolidated state as his Macedon had ever existed west of Asia. Instead of allowing the resources of Macedon to be dissipated in flashy conquests, he organized the people he conquered, both in the Balkan area from the Adriatic to the Black Sea and in Greece. He kept morale high in the army. The contingents from the various regions competed to see who could do the best job. He differentiated his troops into more specialized units for diverse tasks in war, and he personally commanded whichever unit had the roughest assignment.

Philip could appreciate the strengths of his Greek opponents, and when he had defeated them he utilized their skills and made sure of their loyalty by decent treatment. By his final effort to unify them against their traditional Persian enemy, he associated himself with the ancient patriotic cause that so many of them had so often betrayed but that obviously still had great appeal for them. Though he felt himself to be part of Greek civilization, he reminds many students of the Greece of an age far earlier than his own, a kind of Homeric hero in the flesh almost a thousand years after the siege of Troy. In the late 1970s Greek archaeologists found what may have been his tomb with spectacular works of art.

The Achievement of Alexander

Philip's son Alexander the Great belongs to legend as much as to history. Alexander loved war, politics, athletics, alcohol, poetry, medicine, and science. He was only twenty when he came to the throne. Within a dozen years he led his armies on a series of triumphal marches that won for Macedon the largest empire yet created in the ancient world.

Alexander began by crushing a Greek revolt led by Thebes (335 B.C.), whose entire population he sold into slavery. Next, he crossed the Aegean into Asia Minor to continue the war of the Greek League against Persia and recapture the Ionian cities. He defeated the Persians at the river Granicus (334 B.C.) and took over Ionia, where he established democracies in the poleis. In territories belonging to the Persians he took title to all land, thus replacing the Persian king, whom he defeated again at Issus (333 B.C.), and so opened up Syria. He reduced Tyre by siege, and refused King Darius' offer of a Persian princess and all territory west of the Euphrates.

Egypt was next, and it fell easily. Here he founded the great port of Alexandria in the Nile Delta (332), a Greek city from the beginning. But he paid his respects to the Egyptian divinities and allowed himself to be treated as a god according to the Egyptian way. Then he marched east and defeated the Persians again in Mesopotamia (Gaugamela, near Nineveh, 331 B.C.). The Persian Empire was smashed. Alexander sacrificed to Marduk in Babylon and ordered his temple restored; the Persians had destroyed it.

Vast mopping-up operations continued in Persia proper (330–327), as Alexander's armies seized the chief cities and all the Persian royal treasure—perhaps $500,000,000 in cash. But he treated the Persian royal family with great courtesy and acted toward his new subjects just as a king of Persia would have done. The Persian nobles came to acknowledge him as king by the grace of Ahuramazda. In fact, Alexander was king of Persia, just as he was pharaoh of Egypt, king of Babylon, king of Macedon, and commander *(hegemon)* of the Greek League.

Far out in Central Asia, Alexander fell in love with and married the daughter of a local chieftain, who joined forces with the conqueror (327 B.C.). This marriage increased the new loyalty of the Persians to him, but it helped to strain the loyalty of his own Macedonian noble companions. They also disliked Alexander's occasional adoption of Persian dress and Persian custom to please his new subjects. Alexander enjoyed his role as "Great King." But before he began his eastern campaigns he paid his respects to the shade of his ancestor Achilles at Troy. His favorite reading was the *Iliad.* Alexander thought of himself as Greek.

But Alexander's "Persian ways" alarmed his Macedonian followers, who allegedly hatched a plot against him. For this Philotas, the son of the most powerful Macedonian noble, Parmenio, was executed, and soon afterward Alexander had Parmenio himself killed. Later, Alexander in a drunken fury killed another Macedonian general for having taunted him with his orientalization. There was much truth in the charge.

The tensions of the conquest did not lessen its efficiency. New levies of troops came out from Europe and were raised in Asia, new roads were

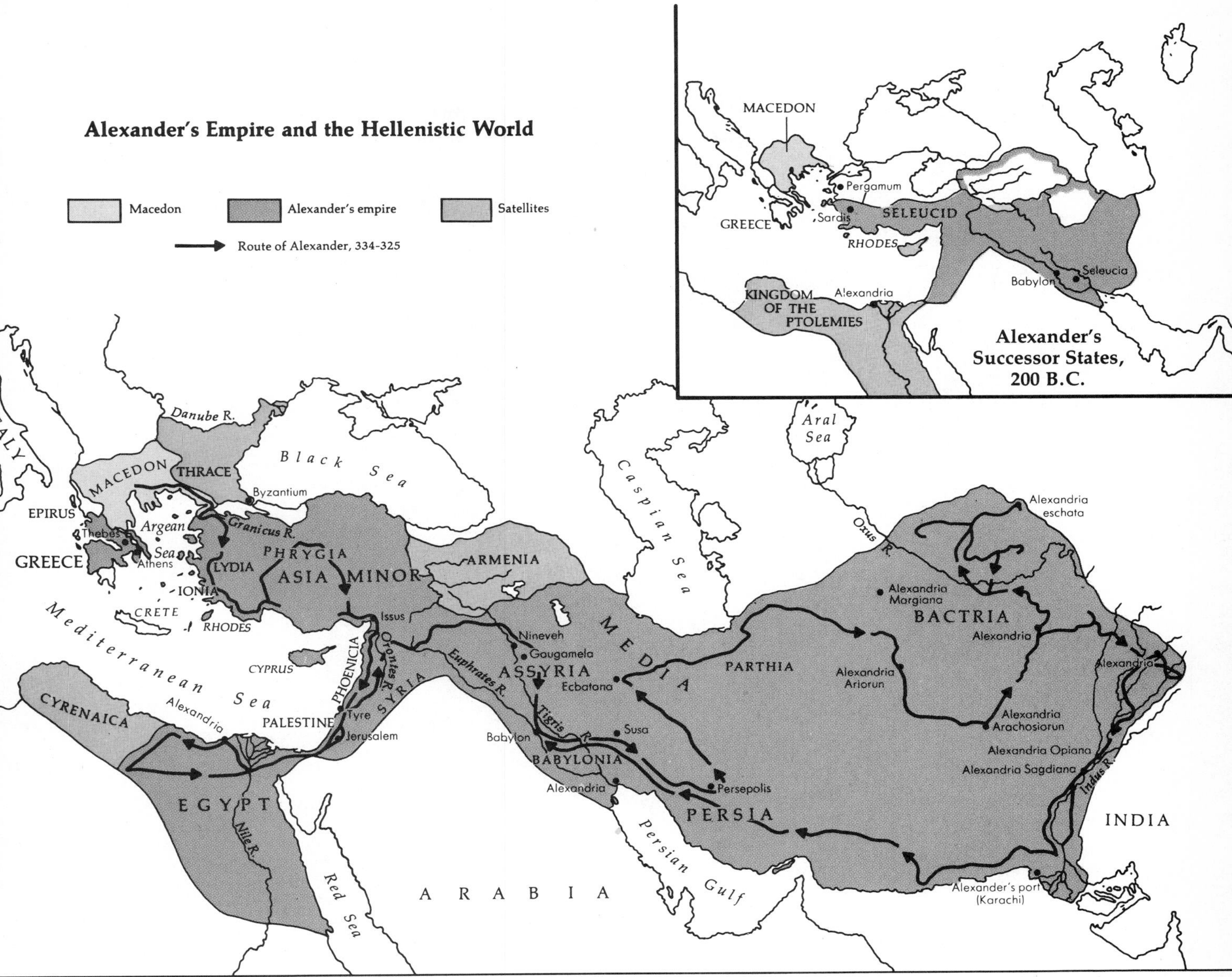

built, and new towns sprang up, each named after Alexander. Alexander believed that India was the last region in Asia, that it was small, and that after India he would come upon Ocean, via which he could perhaps return to Europe by sea. So he next set out to conquer India (327 B.C.) from a base in what is now Afghanistan. He soon found himself doing battle with the hill tribes and with princes of Kashmir and Punjab (now Pakistan).

At first the Indian war elephants terrified Alexander's cavalry and his men, but soon the Macedonians learned how to defeat them and won many victories. Alexander moved on eastward but India was not small, as he had thought, and his troops eventually mutinied. He had to give in and call off any further advance (326 B.C.). He led his troops on riverboats down the Indus southward toward the Indian Ocean, fighting all the way, and sacrificing a gold cup to Poseidon when he reached the ocean shore. Several new Alexandrias were founded, including the town that is now Karachi (Pakistan), before Alexander led his forces westward again across the southern Persian deserts back to Susa (324).

Here he executed all those he suspected of treason. He dramatically pursued his plan to combine the best features of the Macedonian and

Alexander the Great depicted on a four-drachma silver coin of about 300 B.C. with the horns of Amen.

the Persian nobilities by staging a mass marriage between eighty Macedonian officers and eighty Persian noblewomen. He himself took a new Persian wife and blessed the unions of ten thousand Macedonian troops with Persian women. Those who wished to return home were sent off well rewarded; but Alexander kept their wives in Persia and planned to use their children as the nucleus of a future army of mixed blood that would owe everything to him.

At Babylon he prepared a great double naval expedition from the mouths of the Tigris-Euphrates. One force would move along the shore of the Persian Gulf to India, and the other westward around Arabia (never yet circumnavigated) to Egypt. From the Greeks, who had enjoyed a longer period of internal peace than any for over a century, Alexander asked for divine honors. Apparently he wanted to become a god. In 323 B.C., at Babylon, he caught a fever and died, aged thirty-three.

Imagination can hardly conceive of what Alexander might have accomplished had he lived. Perhaps he would have made Greece the center of his empire. He would surely have been able to conquer the two states in the western Mediterranean already looming on the horizon as powers there: Carthage and Rome. He respected all races and religions and believed in decent politics and a booming economy. He settled all of the Alexandrias with Greeks and planned them as centers for the spread of Greek culture. A superb general, a clever governor of subject peoples, a pious believer in the Greek gods, a passionate man with a streak of megalomania, Alexander astonished his contemporaries. It is no wonder that he became to later generations the hero of a series of romances that circulated in every country, in every language, and among every people down almost into our own day.

Heirs of Alexander

As soon as the news of Alexander's death was known, his faithful generals began a fierce scramble for portions of his empire. They combined against each other in various shifting alliances, and arranged many intermarriages and murders, in a period of rapid political and military change. By about 300 B.C., three dynasties had emerged as supreme, each in a different portion of the empire: the Ptolemies in Egypt, the Seleucids in Asia, and the Antigonids in Macedon and Greece. In addition, there were various lesser kingdoms, chiefly in Asia Minor. Fighting continued almost without interruption until the rising power of Rome began to challenge them, to destroy them, and to absorb them one by one.

In Egypt the Ptolemies followed the ancient pattern of government, turning themselves into successors of the pharaohs. They became gods, they sometimes married their sisters, they exploited the agricultural wealth of the country. They claimed title to all land, some of which was farmed by peasants directly for their benefit and some let out to temples or to military settlers or officials. The Ptolemies' own land gave them all its produce except what was needed to feed the farm workers. Land let to others paid the Ptolemies a percentage of the wheat. Oil, flax, and papyrus were royal monopolies. No tree in Egypt could be cut down without royal permission.

The Ptolemies governed largely through their Greek officials, who poured into Egypt for several generations after Alexander's death. Even the armies of the first three Ptolemies were made up wholly of Greeks. It was not until 217 B.C. that Egyptian troops participated in the wars of the dynasty. These were fought against the Seleucids for the possession of Syria, and against the Antigonids for islands of the Aegean and the Anatolian coasts.

Alexandria, the capital, stood between the Mediterranean and a big lake. Canals connected the lake with the Mediterranean and the Nile, and connected the Nile with the Red Sea. Alexandria had harbors on both the Mediterranean and the lake, with port and dock facilities. It had broad streets, luxurious palaces, and a famous library with approximately a million volumes: the catalog alone filled 120 volumes. In the "museum," scholars, freed from all duties by state subsidies, conducted their researches ("fat fowls in a coop" a skeptical poet called them). The towering white stone lighthouse four hundred feet high was regarded as one of the wonders of the world, and had a broad ramp to the first platform so wide that two horsemen could pass.

This was the biggest city of the ancient world until Rome eventually outstripped it. There were perhaps a million inhabitants of Alexandria in the first century B.C., some of them living in multistoried apartment houses. Alexandria was far too big to be a polis; but its Greek population had its own political organization, as did the Jews and the Egyptians. At Alexandria stood also the Ptolemies' colossal barn, where all the royal grain was stored after it had come down the Nile.

The Egyptian population lived under its own law, and was judged in its own courts. Those who were discontent with the system that exploited them so thoroughly had no escape except to take refuge in a temple. The government always tried to reduce the number of temples that had the right to provide such refuge. For a long time the Greek population, with its own language, law courts, culture, and ways of life, did not mingle with the Egyptians, but remained a large collection of foreigners who were getting rich as fast as they could. By the early second century Greek immigration had tapered off. Greek-Egyptian intermarriages had begun, and the army was more Egyptian and less effective. Rome began to intervene. Disorganization set in, and by 118 B.C. Ptolemy VII had to issue a series of decrees calling for reform. The system had begun to fall apart.

Seleucus I was also one of Alexander's generals. He began as governor of Babylon and eventually won control over all of Alexander's Asian lands except northern and western Asia Minor. The Indian regions in the east had to be given up by 303 B.C. We know much more about the Ptolemaic kingdom than about the Seleucid because in the dry climate of Egypt many papyri have survived that preserve details of economic and social life. No such information exists for Asia. The Seleucids' Ionian territories centered on the former Lydian capital of Sardis, their Syrian territories on the new city of Antioch-on-Orontes in northern Syria, and their Mesopotamian territories on the new city of Seleucia not far from Babylon.

As the heirs of the ancient Near Eastern empires, the Seleucids used the former Assyrian and Persian administrative forms. They revived Babylonian religion and Babylonian literature, still written in cuneiform. By deliberately sponsoring a Babylonian religious revival the Seleucids were perhaps seeking a counterweight to Zoroastrianism, the Persian faith. It does appear that the Seleucids failed where Alexander had succeeded: in securing of Persian cooperation in governing the huge Asian territories.

The Seleucids could not become gods like the Ptolemies, nor could they create in Asia anything like the extremely centralized Ptolemaic system of exploitation. In Asia, unlike Egypt, there was too vast an area to be governed, there were too many varied traditions of authority, too many local governors to be considered. The Seleucids instead did something the Ptolemies did not do: they founded Greek cities, and sponsored their development. For this purpose they gave up large areas that were their own royal land, and they also transferred the land of powerful individual landowners to the cities. In such cases

Buildings in the caravan city of Petra, in present-day Jordan, were carved directly into the red rock hills.

the lot of peasants improved, as they ceased to be private property and gained their freedom. The Greek cities were military colonies, with money and land given by the king, and settlement, housing, financial, and other questions delegated to a military governor. The settlers received land and were required to serve in the army in exchange.

Like Alexander, the Seleucid rulers named the cities for themselves. There were many Antiochs named for Antiochus, who had been Seleucus I's father and whose name continued to be given to many of the monarchs of the dynasty. There were also Seleucias, Laodiceas named after Seleucus' mother, and Apameas named after his wife. Some of the Asian Alexandrias now had their names changed to Antioch. The multiple founding of Greek cities all over Asia was a bold attempt to solve the problem of military security. It failed partly because there were not enough Greeks available to populate the cities and man the armies, partly because the Seleucids did not command the loyalty of the Persian population.

In Macedon and Greece, the family that won power were the Antigonids, descendants of Alexander's governor of the western Anatolian province of Phrygia. It was not until 276 B.C., almost half a century after Alexander's death, that the son of the first Antigonus, known as Antigonus Gonatas, was accepted as king of Macedon. Antigonus Gonatas had defeated the marauding Gauls, who were Celts (Indo-Europeans) from distant western Europe. The Gauls were now migrating eastward along the Danube through wild and unsettled portions of Europe. They exploded south on raids into Italy, Greece, and eventually Asia Minor, where they were given a kingdom of their own called Galatia. Having protected Greece from the Gauls (277 B.C.), Antigonus proved a successful ruler in Macedon.

The Greek cities were now grouped together into two leagues, the Aetolian and the Achaean. They fought against each other and against the Antigonid kings of Macedon with the usual Greek vigor. By the 220s the Greeks were largely independent of Macedon. Athens had by now become famous as a university town and usually stayed out of the perpetual brawls of the other cities. But Sparta, true to its traditions, tried to take over the Achaean League and would have succeeded had not the Macedonians defeated them finally (222). By the 220s, however, Rome had begun its interventions in the Greek world. These would quickly lead to conquest.

V THE CIVILIZATION OF GREECE

The Gods

The Olympian gods are already old acquaintances, whom we first learned to know in Homer. The citizens of a polis naturally had special devotion for the divinity who had founded it: Athens for Athena, Sparta for Zeus, but they worshiped the other gods as well. Everybody worshiped the goddess of the hearth, Hestia, the protectress of each individual person's own home and fireside. Births and deaths in a family, solemn political actions in the state, were accompanied by religious rites. Many poleis grouped together in special devotion to regional shrines, like the temple of Apollo at Delphi or those of Zeus at Olympia and Dodona. Besides the Olympic games others were founded in honor of Apollo at Delphi, and of Poseidon the sea god on the Isthmus of Corinth. At the games, religious solemnities accompanied the sports: racing, jumping, throwing the discus, wrestling. The winners were crowned with laurel. So were those who won drinking contests or beauty contests or contests for the best poem or musical composition.

Two important Greek cults began outside the ordinary worship of the Olympian gods: that of Demeter at Eleusis near Athens, and that of Dionysus. Demeter (the name means literally "earth-mother") was the goddess of fertility and of the harvests: her daughter by Zeus, Persephone, was snatched away by the god of the underworld and had to spend a third of the year with him: the months of barrenness, late autumn and winter. Every spring Persephone returned, and the fields became fertile again. Like the Mesopotamians and Egyptians, and perhaps even like late Old Stone Age man, the Greeks too invented a story to account for the miracle of rebirth every spring.

At Eleusis Demeter was worshiped in ceremonies that all initiates swore to keep secret. We know few of the details. There was a ritual drama in which the initiates acted out the sorrow of the goddess searching for her lost daughter. There was a ritual meal, with communion in bread and water. There was a sacred purifying bath in the salt waters of the nearby sea. Probably the participants expected that they would enjoy some sort of afterlife.

Dionysus, the god of wine, was not Greek

Bronze statue of Zeus or Poseidon, fifth century B.C.

in origin, but a northern foreigner who also stood for fertility in its more openly sexual aspects. His followers carried phalluses in his procession and were themselves often dressed as goats. In its northern home the cult inspired its followers with wild frenzy in which they tore up and ate the flesh of living animals. The cult was tamer in Greece, where songs were sung in Dionysus's honor.

Tragedy

From these songs there developed at Athens the art of tragedy. The word means "goat song" and shows the close connection with the god Dionysus. At first the tragedies were sung by a chorus and were formally religious in tone. Later they began to deal with more personal human problems, and individual actors' roles became more and more important. The first competition to choose the best tragedy was sponsored by Peisistratus in 534 B.C. Annual contests were held thereafter.

Many hundreds of tragedies were written. Comparatively few have survived in full—probably the best—and we have fragments of others. The later Greek philosopher Aristotle believed that it was the purpose of tragedy to arouse pity and terror in the spectators, to purge or purify them by causing them to reflect on the fearful punishments that important men and women brought upon themselves by their own sins, the worst of which was *hubris,* arrogance.

The first of the three major tragedians whose works survive was Aeschylus (ca. 525–456), of whose seventy-odd tragedies we have seven. In *The Persians* (472 B.C.), Aeschylus explained the defeat of the Persians as the result of Xerxes' arrogance, by which he offended Zeus. The audience could ponder recent history (it was only seven years since the Persians had been defeated) and consider the moral reasons for their own victories. Such a play would tend to sober up any fire-eater who thought one Greek could lick ten Persians.

In *Prometheus Bound,* Aeschylus dealt with the punishment inflicted by Zeus upon Prometheus the Titan, who had stolen fire from the gods and given it to mankind, and who now lay chained to a rock while a vulture pecked at his liver. Zeus behaved tyrannically—he was new to the job of being king of the gods when Prometheus committed his offense—and only gradually learned to temper his wrath with mercy. Just as Xerxes had offended against the proper order of things by trying to impose Persian rule on Greece, so Prometheus had offended by trying too soon to bestow on mankind the great gift of fire.

In *The Oresteia,* three continuous plays, Aeschylus dealt with the ghastly tragedies in the family of Agamemnon. Agamemnon sacrificed his daughter Iphigenia to get a favorable wind to go to Troy. He was murdered by his unfaithful wife Clytemnestra on his return. He was avenged by his son Orestes, who killed Clytemnestra at Apollo's command. For killing his mother, Orestes suffered torments from the Furies. He was acquitted by a court when Athena was judge, but only Zeus succeeded in transforming the Furies into more kindly creatures. Crime and punishment, remorse and release, a benevolent god over all: these Aeschylus portrayed in lofty, moving verse.

Second of the three greatest tragedians, Sophocles (496–406) wrote many tragedies, of which only ten survive. He believed deeply in Athenian institutions and in the religion of his fellow Greeks, and took an active part in the public life of Periclean Athens. In his *Antigone,* the niece of Creon, tyrant of Thebes, defied her uncle. Creon had decreed that the body of Antigone's brother, killed while leading a rebellion, must be exposed to be devoured by beasts of prey. Proclaiming that divine law required decent burial, she disobeyed Creon, and caused ceremonial earth to be properly sprinkled on the body. She knew she would die for her defiance, but she acted in obedience to her conscience and resisted the dictator. Down the centuries the *Antigone* has carried its message of the sanctity of the individual conscience, proclaiming the superiority of what is eternally right and decent to any mere dictator's brutal whim.

Living to be ninety, Sophocles saw the ruin brought by the Peloponnesian War. His last tragedy, *Oedipus at Colonus,* produced after his death, dealt with the old age of Oedipus. In ignorance, Oedipus had killed his father and married his mother and had torn out his own eyes in horror when he discovered what he had done. A blind beggar, outcast, Oedipus now knew that he could not have avoided his disgrace and that his self-mutilation too was justified. Reflecting upon the terrible story of Oedipus and on the trials of human life, Sophocles' chorus sang that for mankind the best thing is never to be born, and the next best to die as soon as possible after birth. The passions of youth, the blows one suffers in middle life, and the anguish of old age are not worth it.

Nineteen plays remain of the many written by the third and last of the great Attic tragedians, Euripides (ca. 480–406), who focused more upon human psychology, with less emphasis on divine majesty. More realistic in their introduction of children, slaves, and other characters upon the scene, his plays were also more romantic in their exploration of the far reaches of the human mind. The *Hippolytus* showed the uncontrollable sexual passion of a decent woman—Phaedra—for her stepson Hippolytus, who rebuffed her advances. She was ashamed, accused Hippolytus of having attacked her; he was executed, she committed suicide. The *Medea* showed a woman so far gone in agony brought about by rejection of her love that she killed her children in a fit of madness. The *Bacchae* explored the excesses of religious ecstasy: in a frenzy a queen tore her own son to bits, thinking he was a lion. Was Euripides saying that human beings under the impulse of strong emotion were beasts, or that the old religion had too much that was savage in it, or only that the young king had defied the god and his hubris had brought him a fate that he well deserved?

Comedy

Comedy, like tragedy, also began at the festivals of Dionysus. Aristophanes (ca. 450–ca. 385) has left eleven complete plays and parts of a twelfth. Besides making his audience laugh, he hoped to teach them a lesson. Deeply conservative, Aristophanes was suspicious of all innovation. In *The Frogs,* for instance, he brought onto the stage actors playing the parts of the two tragedians Aeschylus (then dead) and Euripides (still alive). The god Dionysus himself solemnly weighed verses from their plays on a giant pair of scales. The old-fashioned Aeschylus outweighed the modern Euripides: a tragedian's duty, Aristophanes thought, was to teach.

In *The Clouds* Aristophanes ridiculed the philosopher Socrates, whom he showed in his "think shop" dangling from the ceiling in a basket so that he could voyage in air and contemplate the sun. Aristophanes wanted to call attention to the dangers offered to Athenian youth by the Sophists (see p. 54). His identification of Socrates with them was somewhat unfair; but, like the others, Socrates taught young men to question the existing order, and he was therefore fair game.

Aristophanes opposed the Peloponnesian War not because he was a pacifist but because he thought it unnecessary. In *Lysistrata* the women denied themselves to their husbands until the men made peace, and in other plays Aristophanes denounced the Athenian politicians, including Pericles himself, for going to war. In *The Birds* the leading characters set off to found a Birdville (Cloud-cuckoo-land) to get away from war. In one of his later plays the women took over the state and proposed to share all the men among them, putting prostitutes out of business.

These later plays provided a transition to the New Comedy of the fourth century, gentler and more domestic. We have several New Comedies by Menander, including one published for the first time only in the late 1950s. The drama was of course only one form that Greek poetic genius took. From the earliest days, the Greeks were the masters of lyric poetry as well (we have quoted two of Solon's own poems above, p. 35). Among the most celebrated are poems of love by the poetess Sappho, of war by Spartan poets in the very early days, and of triumph in the games by Pindar.

History

Much of what we know about the Greeks before and during the Persian Wars we owe to the industry and intelligence of Herodotus (ca. 484–420), who began to write his history as an account of the origins and course of the struggle between Greeks and Persians, and expanded it into an inquiry into the peoples of the whole world known to the Greeks. Born in Halicarnassus on the Ionian coast of Asia Minor, Herodotus visited Egypt, Italy, Mesopotamia, and the lands around the Black Sea, collecting information and listening to whatever stories people would tell him about their own past and about their present customs. He recorded what he learned, much of it of course tinged with myth. He often warned his readers against some story that he himself did not believe but wrote down in order to fill out the record.

Those who have doubted Herodotus have often been silenced by modern archaeology. For instance, Herodotus said that the founder of Thebes, the semimythical Cadmus, was a Phoenician who brought Phoenician letters with him from Phoenicia to Greece about 1350 B.C., or about 900 years before Herodotus' own day. Herodotus added that Cadmus' dynasty was ousted about 1200 B.C. This was often disbelieved. But in A.D. 1964 archaeologists at Thebes found in the palace of Cadmus a large collection of fine cuneiform seals, one of which was datable to 1367–1346 B.C. These demonstrated the probability of Herodotus' account of Cadmus' origin, date of arrival, and bringing of letters. Even the date of the ouster was verified, since the seals were in a layer of material that had been burned about 1200 B.C. and had survived because they were already baked clay. Even if he were not reliable, Herodotus wrote so well that we would read him with pleasure. He never lost sight of his main theme; the conflict between east and west, which he interpreted as a conflict between despotism and freedom.

The equally intelligent but very different historian Thucydides (ca. 471–ca. 400) wrote the account of the origins and course of the Peloponnesian War. Whereas Herodotus was dealing largely with events that had happened before his own time, and had to accept traditions and often hearsay accounts, Thucydides was dealing largely with events he knew of firsthand. He was an unsuccessful general on the Athenian side and was punished for his defeat. But he remained impersonal and scientific, carefully collecting and weighing his information. He followed Herodotus' custom of putting into the mouths of his characters speeches that represented what they might have said rather than what they actually said, but he told his readers what he was doing. Pericles' funeral oration of 430 B.C. is the most famous example.

As deep a student of human psychology

as any of the tragedians, Thucydides found in men and nations the cause of war. He knew as much about war and human behavior as anybody since has been able to learn. He wrote as a loser. Thucydides had seen his own Athens, so admirable in its best qualities, brought down by the Spartan militarists. He hoped that human intelligence would in the future realize how risky war was and what damage it did to the highest human values, but he knew that human nature would always respond by force to certain challenges and that the lessons of the past were hard to learn. The less talented and more pedestrian Xenophon wrote the *Hellenica,* a continuation of Thucydides' work down to the year 362 B.C. And the still less talented Arrian, writing very late but basing his work largely on a now lost account by Ptolemy I himself, has left us an account of Alexander's campaigns.

But for the century or so that followed the death of Alexander we have no historical work comparable with the histories of Herodotus, Thucydides, Xenophon, or Arrian. Therefore, we know the period less intimately than any since the Dark Age. It is only with the decade of the 220s that we again find a narrative history, and then its author and his purpose themselves symbolize the change that has taken place. He was Polybius, a Greek who wrote in Greek but who had spent much time in Rome. There he had become an admirer of the Romans, and his book told the story of Rome's rise to power. Polybius began his account with the year 221 B.C. By then the focus of world affairs had begun to shift from Greece to Rome.

Science and Philosophy

The Greeks showed a deep interest in science. Stimulated by their acquaintance with Egyptian science, the Ionians and later the European Greeks, though they lacked instruments to check and refine their results, correctly attributed a good many phenomena to natural rather than supernatural causes. They knew that the Nile flooded because annual spring freshets took place at its source in Ethiopia. They decided that the straits between Sicily and Italy and Africa and Spain had been caused by earthquakes. They understood what caused eclipses, and knew that the moon shone by light reflected from the sun. Hippocrates of Cos (ca. 460–377) founded a school of medicine, from which there survives the Hippocratic oath, with its high concept of medical ethics. We also have detailed clinical accounts of the symptoms and progress of diseases so accurate that modern doctors have been able to identify cases of diphtheria, epilepsy, and typhoid fever.

The mathematician Pythagoras (ca. 580–500) began as a musician interested in the mathematical differences between the lyre strings needed to produce various notes. The theorem that in a right-angled triangle the square of the hypotenuse is equal to the sum of the squares of the other two sides we owe to the followers of Pythagoras. They made the concept of numbers into a guide to the problems of life, elevating mathematics almost to a religious cult. Pythagoras is said to have been the first to use the word *cosmos*—harmonious and beautiful order—for the universe. Earlier Greeks had found the key to the universe in some single primal substance: water, fire, or air. Democritus (460–370) decided that all matter consisted of minute, invisible atoms.

When Alexandria became the center of scientific research, the astronomer Aristarchus, in the mid-third century B.C., concluded that the earth revolves around the sun, a concept not generally accepted till almost two thousand years later. His younger contemporary, Eratosthenes, believed that the earth was round, and estimated its circumference quite accurately. Euclid, the great geometrical systematizer, had his own school at Alexandria in the third century. Euclid's pupil, Archimedes, won a lasting reputation in both theoretical and applied physics, devising machines for removing water from mines and irrigation ditches ("Archimedes' screw," a hand-cranked device, is still in use in Egypt), and demonstrating the power of pulleys and levers by single-handedly drawing ashore a heavily laden ship. Hence his celebrated boast: "Give me a lever long enough and a place to stand on, and I will move the world."

Greek scholars were usually not specialists like those in a modern university. The same man would study and write books on physics, mathematics, astronomy, music, logic, and rhetoric. Rhetoric became an increasingly important subject, as the Greeks reflected on their own language and developed high standards of self-expression and style. The subject really began with political oratory, as politicians wished to make effective speeches—especially in wartime, when the population was excited anyhow, and each leader strove to be more eloquent than his competitors. These multipurpose scholars of the fifth and fourth centuries B.C. were called Sophists: wisdom-men.

Sophists generally tended to be highly skeptical of accepted standards of behavior and morality, questioning the traditional ways of doing things.

How could anybody really be sure of anything?, they would ask, and some would answer that we cannot know anything we cannot experience through one or more of our five senses. How could you be sure that the gods existed if you could not see, hear, smell, taste, or touch them? Perhaps you could not know, perhaps they did not exist after all. If there were no gods and therefore no divine laws, how should we behave? Should we trust laws made by other men like us? And what sort of men were making laws and in whose interest? Maybe all existing laws were simply a trick invented by powerful people—members of the establishment—to protect their position. Maybe the general belief in the gods was simply a "put on," invented by clever people to whose interest it was to have a docile general public. Not all Sophists went this far, but in Athens during the Peloponnesian War many young people, troubled by the war or by the plague, were ready to listen to suggestions that the state should not make such severe demands upon them. Their troubled parents, god-fearing and law-abiding, feared the Sophists as corrupters of youth.

Only against this background can we understand the career and the eventual fate of Socrates (469–399 B.C.). Socrates' method was that of the Sophists—to question everything, all the current assumptions about religion, politics, and behavior. But he kept firmly to the end his own deep inner loyalties to Athens and to God. Socrates wrote no books and held no professorial chair, but we know him well from contemporary reports, chiefly those of his pupil Plato. Socrates was a stonemason who spent his life talking and arguing in the Assembly, in public places, and in the homes of his friends in Athens.

He thought of himself as a "gadfly," challenging everything anybody said to him and urging people not to take their preconceptions and prejudices as truths. Only a never-ending debate, a process of question and answer—the celebrated "Socratic method"—could lead human beings to truth. Reasoning led Socrates to conclude that man was more than an animal, that he had a mind, and above all, that he had a true self, a kind of soul or spirit. Man's proper business on earth was to fulfill this true soul and cultivate the virtues that were proper to it—temperance, justice, courage, nobility, truth. Socrates himself listened to the voice of God that spoke within him.

We have already seen Socrates in his basket in midair in Aristophanes' *Clouds.* Of course he irritated and alarmed those who were worried about the youth of the day, and who thought of him as just another Sophist and one of the most vocal and dangerous. So when he was about seventy years old he was brought to trial on charges of disrespect to the gods and corrupting the youth of Athens. He argued that he had followed the religious observances required by law, and he defended his gadfly tactics as necessary to stir a sluggish citizenry into life. But a court of 501 jurors voted the death penalty by a narrow margin.

Socrates could have gotten off by suggesting that he be punished in some other way. Instead, he ironically asked to be fined a very small amount and forced the court to choose between that and death. It condemned him again. Socrates drank the poison cup of hemlock and waited for death serenely optimistic: he was "of good cheer about his soul." Many contemporaries and most men since have recognized that he was the victim of hysteria following a dreadful war.

Thereafter, it was Plato (ca. 427–347) who carried on his work. Plato founded a school in Athens, the Academy, and wrote a large number of celebrated *dialogues*—earnest intellectual conversations—in which Socrates and others discussed human problems and the human spirit. Plato revered mathematics but found cosmic reality in Ideas rather than in numbers. As man has a "true self" (soul) within and superior to his body, so the world we experience with our bodily senses has within and superior to itself a "true world," an invisible universe or cosmos.

In *The Republic,* Plato has Socrates compare the relationship between the world of the senses and the world of Ideas with the relationship between the shadows of persons and objects as they would be cast by firelight on the wall of a cave, and the same real persons and objects as they would appear when seen in the direct light of day. So man sees the objects—chairs, tables, trees—of the world as real, whereas they are only reflections of the true realities—the universals—the Idea of the perfect chair, table, or tree. So man's virtues are reflections of ideal virtues, of which the highest is the Idea of the Good. Man can and should strive to know the ultimate Ideas, especially the Idea of the Good.

Plato's theory of Ideas has proved to be one

of the great theories of Western thought and has formed the starting-point for much later philosophical discussion. In teaching that the Idea of the Good was the supreme excellence and the final goal of life, Plato was advancing a kind of monotheism and laying a foundation on which pagan and Christian theologians both would build.

Politically, Athenian democracy did much to disillusion Plato. He had seen its courts condemn his master Socrates. On his travels he formed a high opinion of the tyrants ruling the Greek cities of southern Italy. So when he came to sketch the ideal state in *The Republic*, he recommended that power be entrusted to the Guardians, a small intellectual elite, specially bred and trained to understand Ideas, governing under the wisest man of all, the Philosopher-King. The masses would simply do their jobs as workers or soldiers and obey their superiors.

Plato's most famous pupil was Aristotle (ca. 384–322), son of a physician at the court of Philip of Macedon and tutor to Alexander the Great. Aristotle wrote on biology, logic, literary criticism, political theory, ethics. His work survives largely in the form of notes on his lectures taken by his students. Despite their lack of polish, these writings have had an astounding later influence. Aristotle wrote 158 studies of the constitutions of Greek cities. Only the study of Athens survives.

Aristotle concerned himself chiefly with things as they are. He classified living beings into groups much as modern biologists do and extended the system to other fields—government, for example. Governments were of three types; by one man, by a few men, or by many men. There were good and bad types of each—respectively monarchy and tyranny, aristocracy and oligarchy, polity and democracy (mob rule). Everywhere—in his *Logic*, his *Poetics*, his *Politics*—Aristotle laid the foundation for later inquiry. Though he believed that men should strive and aspire, he did not push them on to Socrates' goal of self-knowledge or to Plato's lofty ascent to the Idea of the Good. He urged instead the cultivation of the golden mean, the avoidance of excess; courage, not foolhardiness or cowardice; temperance, not overindulgence or abstinence; liberality in giving, not lavishness or meanness.

Later, in the period after Alexander, two new schools of philosophy developed, the Epicurean and the Stoic. Epicurus (341–270) counseled temperance and common sense, carrying further the principle of the golden mean. He defined pleasure as the key to happiness, but he ranked spiritual joys above those of the body, which he recommended should be satisfied in moderation. The Stoics, founded by Zeno, got their name from the columned porch (Stoa) in Athens where he first taught. They preferred to repress the physical desires altogether. Since only the inward man counted, the Stoics preached total disregard for social, physical, or economic differences among men. They became the champions of slaves and other social outcasts, anticipating to some degree one of the moral teachings of Christianity.

The Arts

The rich legacy left by the Greeks in literature was well matched by their achievements in the plastic arts. In architecture, their characteristic public building was rectangular, with a roof supported by fluted columns. Over the centuries, the Greeks developed three principal types, or orders, of columns, still used today in "classical" buildings: the Doric column, terminating in a simple, unadorned square flat capital; the Ionic, slenderer and with simple curlicues (volutes) at the four corners of the capital; and the Corinthian, where acanthus leaves rise at the base of the volutes. Fluting gives an impression of greater height than the simple cylindrical Egyptian columns.

No matter what the order of the columns, a Greek temple strikes the beholder as dignified and simple. On the Acropolis of Athens, the Parthenon, greatest of all Doric temples, rose between 447 and 432 B.C. as the crowning achievement of Pericles' rebuilding program. By means of subtle devices—slightly inclining the columns inward so that they look more stable, giving each column a slight bulge in the center of the shaft so that it does not look concave—the building gives the illusion of perfection. In the triangular gable ends that crowned its front and back colonnades (the pediments) and on the marble slabs between the beam ends above the columns (the metopes) stood a splendid series of sculptured battle scenes, whose remains are now in the British Museum (the Elgin Marbles). Originally, the Parthenon and its statues were brightly painted. The building survived almost undamaged until 1687, when a Venetian shell exploded a Turkish powder magazine inside.

The achievement of Phidias and the other sculptors of the Periclean Age (see p. 40) had

Archaic Greek sculpture: sixth-century Kore (statue of a girl from Chios, with the posture and serene smile typical of the period).

The Parthenon.

Three goddesses from the east pediment of the Parthenon (ca. 437–431 B.C.), part of the Elgin Marbles in the British Museum.

The painted inside of a drinking cup (kylix) of the sixth century, showing Dionysus in a boat.

gradually developed from the "archaic" statues created a century or more earlier, usually of young men rather rigidly posed, with their arms hanging at their sides and a curiously uniform, serene smile on their lips. Probably influenced by Egyptian models, these statues have great charm for moderns, who sometimes find the realism of later classical figures rather tiresome. Phidias' great gold and ivory statues of Athena and the Olympian Zeus long ago fell to looters. So did most of the Greeks' sculpture in bronze; but every so often a great bronze statue is fished out of the sea or (as happened in 1959) is found under the pavement of a street being excavated for a sewer.

Though Greek painting as such has almost disappeared, we know from written texts that public buildings were adorned with paintings of Greek victories and portraits of political and military leaders. Moreover, the thousands of pottery vases, plates, cups, and bowls that have been discovered preserve on their surfaces—in black on red or in red on black—paintings of extraordinary beauty and of great variety. They show mythological scenes, illustrations to the *Iliad* and *Odyssey*, and the daily round of human activity: an athlete, a fisherman, a shoemaker, a miner, even a drunk vomiting while a sympathetic girl holds his head.

In the Hellenistic age sculpture became more emotional and theatrical. Compare the Laocoön group, with its writhing serpents crushing their victims, to Polyclitus' statue of a spear-

Hellenistic sculpture: The Laocoön Group. First-century B.C. marble, eight feet tall.

The theater at Epidaurus, built around 330 B.C.

bearer. The Venus de Milo and the Winged Victory of Samothrace are two of the most successful Hellenistic works of art; but there are a good many imitative and exaggerated efforts that are regarded as comparative failures.

Summary

Such a brief account of the splendors of Greek civilization runs the risk of creating the impression that the Greeks were supermen living in a paradise of physical and cultural triumphs. In fact, of course, few Greeks could understand or follow the ideas of a Plato or an Aristotle, or could afford to spend their time at the games, at the theater, or arguing with Socrates. Most Greeks worked hard, and their standard of living would seem extremely low today. In all of Athens at its height we know of only one establishment that employed over a hundred workmen. Even wealthy Athenians resided in small, plain houses of stucco or sun-dried brick: nobody until the Hellenistic period lived pretentiously. Athens was a huddle of mean little streets; there was little or no drainage; lighting was by inadequate, ill-smelling oil lamps. Inside a smithy or a pottery, it was so hot that the smith or potter often worked naked, as we know from vase paintings. But relaxation was available: a musician might play in the smithy; and the climate made outdoor living agreeable much of the year.

On the one hand, the Greeks discovered or invented democracy, drama, philosophy. But on the other, they clung to their old-fashioned religious rituals and could not make themselves give up civil war between their city-states. The freedom-loving Athenians executed Socrates. Though they formulated the wisdom of "Know Thyself" and the golden mean, created a beautifully balanced and proportioned architecture, and organized an education that trained the whole man, intellectual and physical, they often exhibited hubris, the unbridled arrogance that they felt to be the most dangerous of mortal vices. And, as it did in their tragedies on the stage, so in their history their *hubris* brought *nemesis* upon them. Their achievements, however, have lived after them, inspiring most of the values that Western civilization holds dearest.

READING SUGGESTIONS on The World of the Greeks
(Asterisk indicates paperback.)

General Surveys

H. D. F. Kitto, *The Greeks* (*Penguin). Good, if opinionated, introduction.

M. I. Finley, *The Ancient Greeks* (*Compass). Compact, and with much on Greek thought.

C. E. Robinson, *Hellas: A Short Survey of Greece* (*Beacon). Also a good introduction; somewhat more conventional, but reliable.

N. G. L. Hammond, *A History of Greece to 322* B.C. (Oxford). A standard, authoritative work, more advanced than the three above.

The Greek Polis

V. Ehrenberg. *The Greek State* (*Norton). Good scholarly introduction.

A. E. Zimmern, *The Greek Commonwealth* (*Oxford). Perhaps the best-known single study of the subject.

A. H. M. Jones, *Athenian Democracy* (Praeger). Valuable study by a remarkably versatile scholar.

A. R. Burn, *Pericles and Athens* (*Collier). Concentrates on the Golden Age of Athens.

W. G. Forrest, *A History of Sparta, 950–192* B.C. (*McGraw-Hill). A workmanlike survey of Sparta, balanced by the same author's *The Emergence of Greek Democracy, 800–400* B.C. (*McGraw-Hill), dealing with Athens in an equally able manner.

A. Andrewes, *Greek Tyrants* (*Harper Torchbooks). Broadens the horizon beyond Athens and Sparta.

K. Freeman, *Greek City-States* (*Norton). Badly needed to correct the usual emphasis on Athens and Sparta only.

Persia

A. T. Olmstead, *History of the Persian Empire* (*Phoenix). Standard, reliable account.

R. N. Frye, *Heritage of Persia* (*Mentor). Emphasizes intellectual achievements rather than political history.

R. C. Zaehner, *The Dawn and Twilight of Zoroastrianism* (1961). An authoritative review of the Zoroastrian religion.

A. R. Burn, *Persia and the Greeks* (*Minerva). Good study of the Persian wars.

The Hellenistic Age

M. Cary, *A History of the Greek World from 323 to 146* B.C. (1963). Revision of an older book emphasizing political history.

W. W. Tarn, *Alexander the Great* (*Beacon). By a famous authority on the subject, many of whose views are now much challenged.

Peter Green, *Alexander the Great* (1970). A lively recent biography.

M. Rostovtzeff, *The Social and Economic History of the Hellenistic World* (1941). Detailed study by great historian.

Greek and Hellenistic Civilization

C. M. Bowra, *The Greek Experience* (*Mentor). A beautifully written general work.

Edith Hamilton, *The Greek Way to Western Civilization* (*Mentor). A rather uncritically admiring general introduction.

W. Jaeger, *Paideia,* 3 vols. (1943–45). Not easy reading, but a classic in itself, analyzing Greek civilization and ideals.

W. C. K. Guthrie, *The Greeks and Their Gods* (*Beacon). Full and interesting account of Greek religion.

Robert Graves, *The Greek Myths,* 2 vols. (*Penguin). Another most interesting introduction to the subject.

E. R. Dodds, *The Greeks and the Irrational* (*California). A most sophisticated, and even hypnotically interesting study. Not for beginners.

M. Hadas, *A History of Greek Literature* (*Columbia). Useful survey.

F. M. Cornford, *Before and after Socrates* (*Cambridge). Fine general introduction to Greek science and philosophy.

W. C. K. Guthrie, *Greek Philosophers from Thales to Aristotle* (*Harper Torchbooks). Excellent historical account of the development of Greek thought.

Marshall Clagett, *Greek Science in Antiquity* (*Collier). Reliable and recent.

Rhys Carpenter, *The Esthetic Basis of Greek Art* (*Midland). An authoritative introduction.

J. Boardman, *Greek Art* (*Praeger). More recent than the above, and with a less philosophical emphasis.

J. Barron, *Greek Sculpture* (*Dutton). Specialized, but suitable for the beginner.

A. W. Lawrence, *Greek Architecture* (*Penguin). Makes the technical details quite comprehensible. Fine Illustrations.

P. Bevambez, *Greek Painting* (*Compass). On the same level as the preceding two titles and equally successful.

Sources

W. H. Auden, *The Portable Greek Reader* (*Viking). Good anthology.

A. J. Toynbee, *Greek Civilization and Character* (*Mentor), and *Greek Civilization and Thought* (*Mentor). Two volumes of substantial excerpts from Greek authors.

L. R. Lind, ed., *Ten Greek Plays in Contemporary Translations* (*Riverside). Aeschylus, Sophocles, Euripides, and Aristophanes are represented.

Scott Buchanan, *The Portable Plato* (*Viking). A useful selection from Plato's work.

Herodotus, *The Histories* (*Penguin), trans. A. de Selincourt.

Thucydides, *History of the Peloponnesian War* (*Penguin), trans. R. Warner.

Xenophon, *Anabasis* (*Michigan), trans. W. H. D. Rouse.

CHAPTER THREE

The World of The Romans

When we think of Rome, we think of a far-flung empire that included all the lands around the Mediterranean basin. This empire was held together somehow from a great city: Rome, in central Italy. Here, in an enormous stadium on holidays throngs of people eagerly applauded great shows. Chariots thundered around the track in hard-fought races. Men called gladiators fought each other to the death as a spectacle. Wild beasts rushed into the arena and attacked human beings for the mob's delight. The emperor sat in his box, sometimes reprieving, sometimes condemning a victim by an ostentatious turn of his thumbs up or down.

These Latin-speaking Romans, we know, enormously influenced the languages and cultures of the modern Italians, Spaniards, French, and other peoples. We are aware that the earliest Christian church in the west was the *Roman* Catholic Church and that it was Rome that served as the great transmission-belt by which the civilizations of the ancient Near East and of Greece came down to us. We also may realize that the greatest genius of the Romans was for govern-

ment. They forged the legal instruments that for long periods served to create public order instead of the anarchy that had characterized Greece. Roman laws gave at least elements of peace and security to a world that had never previously known them.

In this chapter we shall discuss Rome's extraordinary progress from its earliest days as a republic to its role as a world power, its decline, its temporary recovery, and its relations with the new and fast-spreading Christian church, which it often persecuted but which eventually prevailed.

I THE ROMANS AND THEIR REPUBLIC

The Earliest Days

The Romans cherished the legend that after the fall of Troy, Aeneas, a Trojan prince, half divine, led his fugitive followers to Italy and founded Rome on the banks of the Tiber. The poet Vergil (70–19 B.C.) immortalized the story in his *Aeneid,* written to celebrate Roman imperial glory. Vergil borrowed from Homer as Rome had borrowed from the older Greek and Near Eastern civilizations. The tale of the mythical Aeneas symbolizes the flow into Italy of Greeks and Near Easterners as well as Rome's debt to the Greco-Oriental world. Yet Rome did not achieve greatness on borrowed capital alone. The practical Romans were builders, generals, administrators, law-givers.

Compared geographically with Greece, Italy enjoys certain natural advantages: the plains are larger and more fertile, the mountains less of a barrier to communication. The plain of Latium, south of Rome, could be farmed intensively after drainage and irrigation ditches had been dug. The nearby hills provided timber and good pasturage. The city of Rome lay only fifteen miles from the sea and could share in the trade of the Mediterranean. Its seven hills overlooking the Tiber could be easily fortified and defended.

Etruscans

To the South, as we know, by the year 600 B.C. Greek colonies dotted the shores of Italy and Sicily. This was Magna Graecia. To the north, the dominant power was held by the Etruscans, a mysterious people, surely foreigners in Italy, perhaps from Asia Minor (and so the source of the Aeneas legend) who had invaded the peninsula and conquered the region north of Latium by 700 B.C. They extended their power southward, surrounded Rome, and seized it soon after 600.

We have rich Etruscan remains—pottery, weapons, sculpture, painting—mostly found in tombs. But nobody has yet altogether deciphered

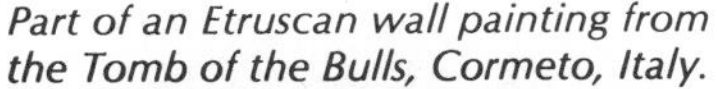

Part of an Etruscan wall painting from the Tomb of the Bulls, Cormeto, Italy.

the language, written in Greek letters though not an Indo-European tongue. Most of the ten thousand existing inscriptions are very short; so even if we could read them, we might not learn very much. The Etruscans were expert farmers and miners, they built huge stone walls around their settlements, and they predicted the future from observing flocks of birds in flight or from examining the entrails of an animal slain as a sacrifice. Like the Egyptians, they believed in an afterlife similar to this one. Their women enjoyed a more nearly equal status with men than was usual in ancient society.

Under its Etruscan kings, Rome prospered during the sixth century. The Etruscans built new stone structures and drained and paved what became the Forum. But the native Latin population resented foreign rule and joined with other Latin tribes in a large-scale rebellion. The traditional date for the expulsion from Rome of the last Etruscan king, Tarquin the Proud, is 509 B.C. What is left behind was an independent Latin city-state that still included some Etruscan notables but was much smaller than Athens or Sparta and shared Latium with other city-states. Yet in less than 250 years the Romans would dominate the entire Italian peninsula. How did they do it?

The Republic

Once they had ousted Tarquin, the dominant aristocratic forces at Rome set up a republic. Only the well-established land-owning families, the *patricians* (Latin *pater,* "father")—perhaps ten percent of the population—held full citizenship. The remaining ninety percent were *plebeians* (Latin *plebs,* "the multitude"), traders, laborers, the smallest farmers. Plebeians had no right to hold office but they were allowed to amass as much money as they could. Wealthy plebeians would eventually lead the campaign to gain political emancipation for their class. Fifth-century Rome, then, resembled sixth-century Athens before the reforms of Cleisthenes.

The patrician class supplied the two *consuls,* the executive chiefs of state who governed jointly for a term of a year, enjoying full *imperium,* supreme political power. Each had the right of veto over the other; so that both had to support a measure before it could be put through. Ordinarily they were commanders of the army, but in wartime this power was often wielded, for a period not longer than six months, by an elected *dictator.* The word meant a commander who had obtained his authority constitutionally and had to give it up when his term was over.

The consuls usually followed the policies decided on by the *Senate,* a governing body of about three hundred members, mostly patricians and all ex-officials like the members of the Athenian Council of the Areopagus. The Senate came first in the famous Roman political device: S.P.Q.R.—*Senatus Populusque Romanorum* (The Senate and the People of the Romans). The reigning consuls were themselves senators and appointed new senators. The Romans had another deliberative body, the *Centuriate Assembly,* based on the century, the smallest unit (a hundred men) in the army. The patricians dominated the deliberations of this body also. It elected the consuls and other officials, and approved or rejected laws submitted to it by both the consuls and the Senate.

Before a man could be chosen consul, he had to pass through an apprenticeship in other posts. The job that led directly to the consulate was that of *praetor* (*prae-itor,* the one who goes in front). Elected by the Centuriate Assembly for a term of a year, the praetor served as a judge. He often had an army command, and later a provincial governorship. At first there was only one praetor, but the number later rose to eight. Men seeking election as praetor or consul wore a special robe whitened with chalk, the *toga candida,* whence our word "candidate."

From among the ex-consuls, the Assembly elected two *censors,* for an eighteen-month term, who took a census to determine which of the population was qualified for army service. They also secured the right to accept or reject nominees for the Senate, barring those they thought corrupt or too luxury-loving.

This republic was well designed to carry on the chief business of the Roman state: war. The Roman army at first had as its basic unit the *phalanx,* about 8,000 foot soldiers, armed with helmet and shield, lance and sword. But experience led to the substitution of the far more maneuverable *legion,* consisting of 3,600 men, composed of 60- or 120-man bodies called *maniples* ("handfuls"). The troops were armed with the additional weapon of iron-tipped javelins, hurled at the enemy from a distance. Almost all citizens of Rome had to serve. Stern discipline prevailed, but the officers understood the importance of rewarding bravery.

The plebeians naturally resented their exclusion from political authority. As early as the 490s, they threatened to withdraw from Rome and to found nearby a new city-state of their own. When this tactic won them concessions, they continued to use it with great effect. First (494), they got the right to have officials of their own, the *tribunes* of the people, to protect them from unduly harsh application of the laws. By 457 there were ten of these. The plebeians also (471) gained their own *Tribal Assembly,* which chose the tribunes and had the right to pass on new laws. Next they demanded a written code of law to bind the patrician judges. So in 451 the consuls ordered the (extremely severe) laws engraved on wooden tablets—the Twelve Tables, beginning the long and glorious history of Roman law.

In the early days of the Republic, debt meant that a plebeian farmer would lose his farm and be forced into slavery. Property therefore accumulated in the hands of the patrician landowners. The plebeians obtained legislation limiting the size of an estate that any one man might accumulate, abolishing the penalty of slavery for debt, and opening newly acquired lands to settlement by landless farmers. The farmer-debtor problem, though eased, remained to plague the Romans to the end.

During the fifth and fourth centuries, the plebeians won the right to hold all the offices of the state, even that of consul (366 B.C.). They also won the legal right to marry patricians. The fusion of wealthy plebeians and patricians formed a new class, the *nobiles,* who were to dominate the later republic as the patricians had the earlier.

Roman Expansion

In a long series of wars the Romans conquered the other Latin towns, the Etruscan cities, and the half-civilized tribes of the central Apennines (the mountain backbone of the peninsula). Early in the third century B.C., they conquered the Greek cities of southern Italy. Meanwhile, in the north, a Celtic people, the Gauls (see p. 49), had crossed the Alps and settled in the Lombard plain. Their expansion was halted at the little river Rubicon, which formed the northern frontier of Roman dominion.

In conquered areas the Romans sometimes planted a colony of their own land-hungry plebeians. Usually they accepted the resident population as allies and respected their institutions. The cities of Magna Graecia continued to enjoy home rule. Some of the nearest neighbors of Rome became full citizens of the republic. More often they enjoyed the protection of Roman law as part citizens who could not participate in the Roman assemblies. So the expansion of Rome in Italy demonstrated statesmanship as well as power.

The conquest of Magna Graecia made Rome a near neighbor of the Carthaginian state. Carthage—modern Tunis—had long since liberated itself from its Phoenician motherland and expanded along the African and Spanish shores of the Mediterranean and into the western parts of Sicily. Carthage held a virtual monopoly of western Mediterranean trade. When the Carthaginians began to seize the Greek cities in eastern Sicily also, the Sicilian Greeks appealed to Rome. So the Romans launched the First Punic (from the Latin word for Phoenician) War, 264–241 B.C.

The Punic Wars

The Romans won by building their first major fleet and defeating the Carthaginians at sea. They obtained all Sicily, their first province outside the Italian mainland. In the Second Punic War (218–201), the Carthaginian commander Hannibal led his forces, pack elephants and all, from Spain across southern Gaul (modern France) and then over the Alps into Italy. As he marched southward, he won many victories, notably at Cannae (216 B.C.). But the Roman general Fabius Cunctator ("the delayer") refrained from battle and instead wore out the Carthaginians by attacking their supplies and patrols ("Fabian tactics").

In 202 B.C. the Roman general Scipio won a victory at Carthage itself and received the title "Africanus" as a reward. Carthage had to surrender Spain, where the native population resisted for another two centuries, and Hannibal fled to the court of the Seleucid king Antiochus III. Carthage's speedy recovery alarmed a war party at Rome. In the Third Punic War (149–146), the Romans leveled Carthage, sprinkled salt on the earth, and took over all its remaining territory.

Macedonian Wars

While the Punic Wars were still going on, Rome had as early as 230 B.C. also become involved in the Balkans and in Greece, first against Illyrian pirates in the Adriatic. Gratefully, the Greeks admitted Romans to the Eleusinian mysteries and the Isthmian Games. But Philip V, Antigonid King of Macedon (221–178), opposed Rome, tried to help Hannibal in the Second Punic War, and was himself defeated in the First Macedonian War (215–205). Five years later Rome joined a Greek coalition of Philip's enemies and won the Second Macedonian War (200–197),

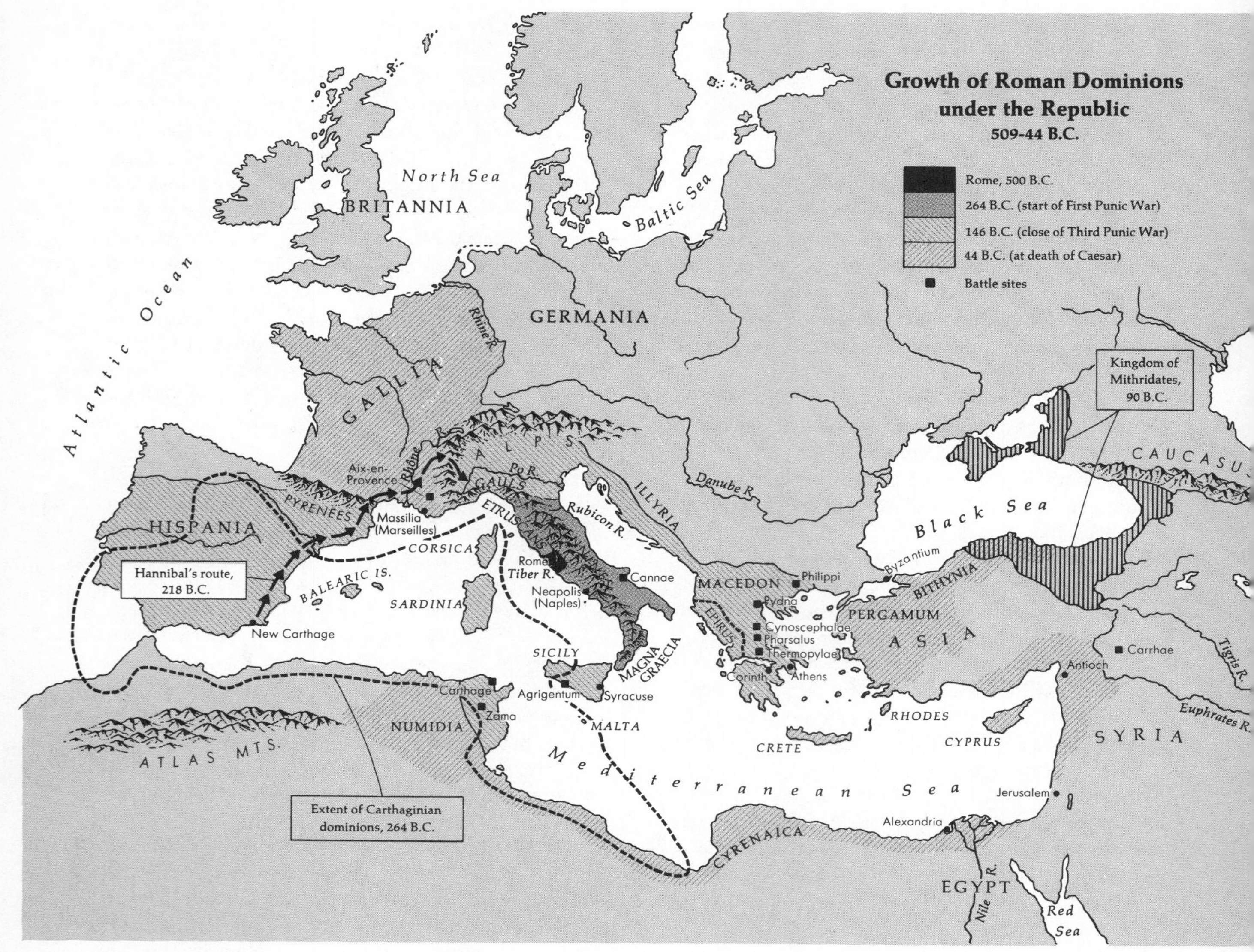

forcing Philip to withdraw from Greece. Thereafter, though they tried, the Romans found themselves unable to leave Greece to itself.

Antiochus III, Seleucid king in Asia, who had with him the refugee Hannibal, challenged the Romans in Greece and lost a battle at Thermopylae (191 B.C.). The Romans pursued him into Asia Minor and in 188 forced him to surrender all his holdings there. Hannibal escaped, but in 183 poisoned himself to avoid falling into Roman hands. Rome had become the predominant power in the Greek world, and for the next forty years had to arbitrate the perpetual quarrels among the Greek states.

In the Third Macedonian War (171–168), Rome routed Philip V's son and successor, Perseus (179–168), at Pydna. Rome broke Macedon up into four states and in 148 annexed it, the first Roman province east of the Adriatic. In 146, the Romans defeated a desperate Greek uprising and marked their victory by a brutal sack of Corinth, killing the men, selling the women and children into slavery, and leveling the city. It was the same year as the total destruction of Carthage. Thereafter they governed Greece from Macedon, but did not yet annex it. Internal fighting in Greece stopped. There was an economic and religious revival. Rome's prestige was now so great that in 133 the king of Pergamum in Asia Minor bequeathed his flourishing state to Rome in his will.

Crisis of the Republic

As Roman territory increased, troubles grew. A few overseas cities were allowed to retain self-government, but usually Rome organized conquered lands as provinces under governors appointed by the Senate. Some of these were crooked and oppressive but had a free hand as long as they collected taxes and recruited troops for the armies. Rome's allies in Italy were demanding full citizenship and a share in the new wealth. With Italian soil declining in fertility, grain had to be imported from Africa. Many Italian farms were transformed into large cattle ranches (*latifundia,* big estates) worked by slaves and owned by the rich. Successful generals, retired governors, contractors who had built roads for the state or furnished supplies to the army accumulated money and slaves, as more and more poor farmers lost their lands and became penniless and bitter refugees in Rome itself.

The new-rich landowners combined to form a new social class called *equites* (knights), because they could afford to equip themselves for service in the cavalry, the most expensive branch of the army. Yet the old *nobiles* dominated the Senate. In the Senate itself, a party called the *optimates* were pleased with things as they were, while their rivals, the *populares,* were discontented and sometimes sought support from the people at large. Social tensions became acute, increased by the taste among the new rich for luxurious Greek ways of life, which the old-fashioned conservatives hated. The political machinery of a small city-state could not cope with the new problems of empire, social tension, and economic distress.

During the late 130s and 120s two noble brothers named Gracchus emerged as champions of the dispossessed. Tiberius Gracchus, Tribune of the People in 133, and Gaius, Tribune from 123 to 121, sought to increase the role of the Tribal Assembly at the expense of the Senate. Wild beasts, said Tiberius, have their dens, but Roman veterans have not a clod of earth to call their own. The brothers wanted to limit the size of estates that could be owned by one family, to resettle landless farmers either abroad or on state-owned lands in Italy, and to give the city poor of Rome relief by allowing them to buy grain from the state at cost. Politically, they wanted to give certain judicial posts to the equites, to extend Roman citizenship to all Latins, and to raise other Italians to Latin status.

The program failed. Only the proposal to sell the Roman people cheap grain was adopted. In later centuries the state had to reduce the price until the poor were getting their bread free. If resettlement had gone through and the dispossessed farmers had actually received new allotments, the number in the city needing cheap bread would have fallen off sharply. But although the Gracchi temporarily forced the landowners to give up some of the lands, they soon got more. The latifundia had come to stay. The Senate resented the extension of rights to the equites and refused to grant Roman citizenship to other Italian cities. This issue remained acute.

Politics now turned unconstitutional and violent. Both Gracchus brothers defied precedent and ran for reelection as tribunes. The senators themselves had Tiberius assassinated in 133. In 121 Gaius committed suicide to avoid a similar fate. Were the Gracchi high-minded reformers blocked by the vested interests of the senators, or unstable radicals whose high-handed methods only added to the discord? Probably both. At any rate the deadlock between Gracchan reformism and senatorial conservatism moved Rome toward autocracy.

Political Generals: Marius and Sulla

Roman generals who had won victories would return to Rome to celebrate their "triumph" in a big parade of their successful troops with their prisoners and booty. Rewarded by the general out of his own pocket, such soldiers became loyal to him rather than to the state. Political leadership now began to pass to generals, who cared less for principle than for power.

The first such general was Marius, leader of the populares, who had won victories in eastern Algeria (111–105) and over a group of Celtic and Germanic peoples in southern France (102). Violating custom, Marius had himself elected consul five times between 108 and 103 B.C.

He began a major reorganization of the army by abolishing the old requirement that a Roman citizen must pay for his own equipment, a rule that had automatically excluded the poor. Now that the state furnished the equipment, professional soldiers gradually replaced the former citizen soldiers, who in the past had gone back to their peacetime occupations once the fighting was over. When the Senate vetoed a law extending Roman citizenship to citizens of all other Italian cities, the cities rose in a savage rebellion (called the Social War for *socius,* "ally"). Only the gradual extension of Roman citizenship to all of Italy calmed the uprising (89 B.C.).

In 88 B.C. Mithridates, king of Pontus in Asia Minor, seized the Roman province of Asia and massacred 80,000 Romans. Rome went to war against him, and Marius emerged from retirement and demanded the command. But the Senate chose Sulla, a younger general, who was an optimate, and a bloody civil war broke out between the supporters of the two. Marius died in 86, and Sulla defeated Mithridates in 84. On the way to and from the east, his forces plundered Zeus's treasury at Olympia and Apollo's at Delphi, and sacked Athens for having sympathized with Mithridates. The Romans brought back Greek sculpture, painting, books, and other loot.

It took Sulla two years of bloody fighting to establish himself in power. Politically, he tried to restore the Senate's ancient position as the chief force in political life. He put through laws designed to curb the rise of new, younger politicians. He curtailed the powers of the tribunes and the Tribal Assembly. He broke all precedent by prolonging his tenure as dictator beyond the prescribed six months. He did retire in 80 B.C., but the Senate proved unable to govern.

Political Generals: Pompey and Caesar

Within ten years, Pompey, an arrogant and successful general, rose to power, becoming consul in 70 B.C. before he had reached the minimum legal age. With his colleague Crassus, a millionaire who had repressed a revolt of slaves led by Spartacus, Pompey forced the Senate to restore the tribunes and the Tribal Assembly to their old power. He became grand admiral of Roman naval forces against the troublesome pirates of the Mediterranean. After defeating them (67 B.C.), he took command of a new war against Mithridates. By 65 B.C. Pompey had expelled him from his kingdom. Mithridates committed suicide in 63 B.C., and Pompey reorganized Asia Minor into Roman provinces and subject kingdoms. He had already (64 B.C.) made Syria into a Roman province and taken Jerusalem. The western fringe of Asia was now virtually Roman, and much new revenue soon flowed to Rome.

As general Pompey enjoyed special powers, forced through against much senatorial opposition, and huge resources in men and money. Foreseeing a showdown on Pompey's return, Crassus tried to build up his own power by vainly calling for Roman annexation of Egypt. And in 63 there took place a celebrated conspiracy at Rome, led by Catiline, leader of a group of discontented and dispossessed nobles who had been the victims of Sulla's purges and who now planned a revolution and a comeback. The consul, Cicero, a famous lawyer, discovered the plot and arrested the plotters, some of whom he illegally had executed. Cicero hoped to cooperate with Pompey in governing Rome but he lacked the family background and personal following necessary to get to the very top, and Pompey was not responsive.

Pompey reentered politics because the Senate would not ratify his Eastern settlement or vote the usual land grants for his veteran troops. He joined in a triumvirate, or team of three men, with Crassus and Gaius Julius Caesar, a general of enormous energy and talent and impeccable ancestry. Caesar became consul in 59 B.C. Pompey married Caesar's daughter. Pompey's soldiers received large land grants to the south, near Naples, and his eastern Mediterranean settlement was confirmed.

Bust of Julius Caesar.

Caesar became governor of the southern strip of Gaul (modern France), which Rome had annexed some sixty years earlier. In Gaul, between 58 and 50 B.C. he conquered the area corresponding to most of modern France and Belgium, then inhabited by farming and cattle-raising Celtic tribes, Caesar even crossed the English Channel to punish the Celtic Britons for helping their fellow Celts. Caesar's successes meant that, like Italy and Spain, the future France would have a civilization firmly based on Rome and a language based on Latin. In order to give his achievements maximum publicity in Rome, he now wrote his famous *Commentaries on the Gallic Wars.*

While Caesar was busy in Gaul, Crassus became governor of Syria, where he was killed (53 B.C.) in a war against the Parthians, a dynasty that had risen in Persia to replace the Seleucids. The triumvirate had begun to fall apart even before that. Pompey, who had been commander in Spain, stayed in Rome as the most powerful politician there, and became sole consul in 52 B.C. A revolution in Gaul kept Caesar busy in 52 and 51 B.C. When it was over, Caesar faced Pompey for supremacy.

In 49 B.C. Caesar defied an order from the Senate to stay in Gaul and led his loyal troops south across the Rubicon river boundary. Within a few weeks, he was master of Italy. He then won another war in Spain, and in 48 B.C. defeated Pompey's troops at Pharsalus in Greece, to which most of the Senate had fled with Pompey. Pompey was later murdered in Egypt by troops of Ptolemy XII.

Caesar now traveled to the East and to his famous love affair with Ptolemy's sister, Cleopatra. After new victories in Asia Minor, North Africa, and Spain, Caesar returned to Rome in triumph in 45 B.C. Less than a year later, on the Ides of March, 44 B.C., he lay stabbed to death on the floor of the Senate at the foot of Pompey's statue. His assassins included patriots troubled at his assumption of supreme power and his destruction of the Roman constitution, and others who were merely disloyal or jealous.

But during his brief period of dominance Caesar had carried further the subversion of the institutions of the republic that Marius and Sulla and Pompey had begun. Unlike Sulla, he was merciful to conquered enemies. But as dictator he arrogated to himself many of the powers that usually belonged to the consuls, the tribunes, and the high priest. He packed the Senate with his own supporters. He showed deep interest in the social and economic problems of Rome. He gave his veterans grants of land in outlying provinces. He tried to check the importation of slaves into Rome because they took work from free men. He made gifts to the citizens from his own private fortune, and then cut back the cheap grain that the Gracchi had instituted, forcing the creation of new jobs. He issued the first gold coins and reformed the calendar to bring it into line with the solar year. At the moment of his death he was projecting a public works program: Tiber valley flood control, a trans-Apennine highway, and a canal through the Isthmus of Corinth in Greece.

The rank and file of the Romans seem to have regarded Caesar as a benefactor, the restorer of order and prosperity. His opponents said he was planning to be crowned as king and they may have been right. They also accused him of wishing to be worshiped as a god, and here—so far as Rome was concerned—they were probably wrong.

After Caesar's death, the conspirators were forced first to accept a compromise with his supporters and then to flee the hostile mob, goaded to fury by the fiery funeral oration given Caesar by his aide, Mark Antony. Antony had got hold of Caesar's private papers, including his will, by which he left a legacy to every individual Roman citizen. But to Antony's distress, three-quarters of Caesar's huge fortune went to Octavian, his shrewd and able grandnephew, still only nineteen years old.

After some civil strife between their forces, Octavian and Antony, with a third former aide of Caesar, Lepidus, formed a "second triumvirate" and divided territory and power between themselves. They raised money by executions and confiscations, and defeated (Philippi, 42 B.C.) the forces of Caesar's murderers led by Brutus and Cassius, who both committed suicide. The rivalry between Octavian and Mark Antony was interrupted for a time when Antony married Octavian's sister. By 36 B.C. Lepidus had been dropped; Octavian controlled the entire West, and Antony, in the East, had begun *his* famous affair with Cleopatra. He claimed that Caesar's young son by Cleopatra was the legitimate heir to Rome and assigned Roman provinces to Cleopatra herself and to his own children by her. Before long, Antony and Octavian were at war. At Actium, off the western coast of northern Greece (31 B.C.), Octavian's ships won a decisive naval battle. Antony and Cleopatra committed suicide.

Rome thus acquired Egypt, the last of the great Hellenistic states to disappear. Egypt did not become a Roman province but the personal property of Octavian and his successors, the Roman emperors. And Octavian had become master of the entire Roman heritage. After sixty years of internal strife, the population welcomed a ruler who could guarantee order. The republic had come to an end.

II THE ROMAN EMPIRE TO A.D. 180

Augustus: 31 B.C.–A.D. 14

Octavian was too aware that he was heir to a long tradition to startle and alienate the people of Rome by breaking with the past and proclaiming an empire. He sought to preserve republican forms, but at the same time to remake the government so that Rome would have the political machinery to manage the huge territories it had acquired.

Moving gradually, and freely using his own huge personal fortune, now augmented by the enormous revenues of Egypt, Octavian paid for the pensions of his own troops, and settled them on their own lands in Italy and abroad. He was consul every year; *imperator;* governor in his own right of Spain, Gaul, and Syria; and *princeps,* first among the senators. In 27 B.C. the Senate bestowed upon him the new title of *Augustus* ("revered one") by which he was thereafter known to history, although he always said his favorite title was the traditional one of princeps.

Since Augustus called himself the restorer of the republic, Romans could feel that no revolution had taken place. In 23 B.C. the Senate gave Augustus tribunician power, "larger" powers than those held by any other provincial governor, and the right to introduce the first measure at any meeting of the Senate. He summoned the Senate and gave it a small inner steering committee, on which he sat. As senators he appointed men he thought able, regardless of their birth. He created a civil service where careers were open to talent. Having endowed a veterans' pension department out of his own pocket, he imposed two new taxes—a sales tax of one-hundredth and an inheritance tax of one-twentieth—to support it. His social laws made adultery a crime and encouraged large families. He paid for the construction of splendid new buildings. He also gave Rome its first police and fire departments and improved the roads throughout Italy. The army, now numbering about 300,000 men, was stationed in permanent garrison camps on the frontiers. In peacetime the troops worked on public projects such as aqueducts or canals.

Abroad, Augustus reached a settlement with the Parthians in the East. Most of Spain and Portugal were permanently pacified, and the Romans successfully administered Gaul. In what is now Switzerland and Austria and eastward along the Danube, Augustus campaigned, extending Roman power into present-day Hungary, Yugoslavia, and Bulgaria, all the way to the Black Sea.

But in the year A.D. 9, the Roman armies suffered a disaster in Germany, when the German tribesmen under Arminius (or Hermann) wiped out three legions, perhaps sixteen or seventeen thousand men. Now an old man, Augustus made no effort to avenge the defeat. The Rhine frontier proved to be the final limit of Roman penetration into north-central Europe. Thus the Germans never did become Romanized, a fact that had fateful consequences for all the subsequent history of Europe.

In the Roman provinces, regular census-taking permitted a fair assessment of taxes. In Gaul the tribes served as the underlying basis for government. In the urbanized East, the local cities performed that function. Augustus did his work so well that the celebrated *Pax Romana*—the Roman Peace—lasted from his assumption of the title "Augustus" in 27 B.C. until A.D. 180, more than two hundred years. It was an enormous boon.

Marble head of Augustus as a youth.

Augustus' Heirs: A.D. 14–68

When Augustus died in A.D. 14, the only possible surviving heir was his stepson, Tiberius, a gloomy, bitter man. He reigned until A.D. 37, emulating Augustus so far as possible during the first nine years. Thereafter he became involved in the efforts of a certain Sejanus to secure the succession to the throne. Sejanus was commander of the Praetorian Guard, a specially privileged body of troops founded by Augustus, now stationed in Rome itself. Absent from Rome for long periods, Tiberius became deeply unpopular. His grandnephew and successor Caligula (37–41), however, was perhaps insane. He executed many and enriched himself with their property. He was assassinated (41).

His uncle Claudius (41–54), youngest of Tiberius' nephews and the best of the first four emperors to succeed Augustus despite physical weakness and a miserable early life, was a learned student of history and languages; he even knew Etruscan. Claudius strove to imitate Augustus by restoring cooperation with the Senate. The private imperial civil service made strides as Claudius divided his own personal staff of bureaucrats—mostly freedmen by origin—into regular departments or bureaus not unlike those in modern governments. He was generous in granting Roman citizenship to provincials.

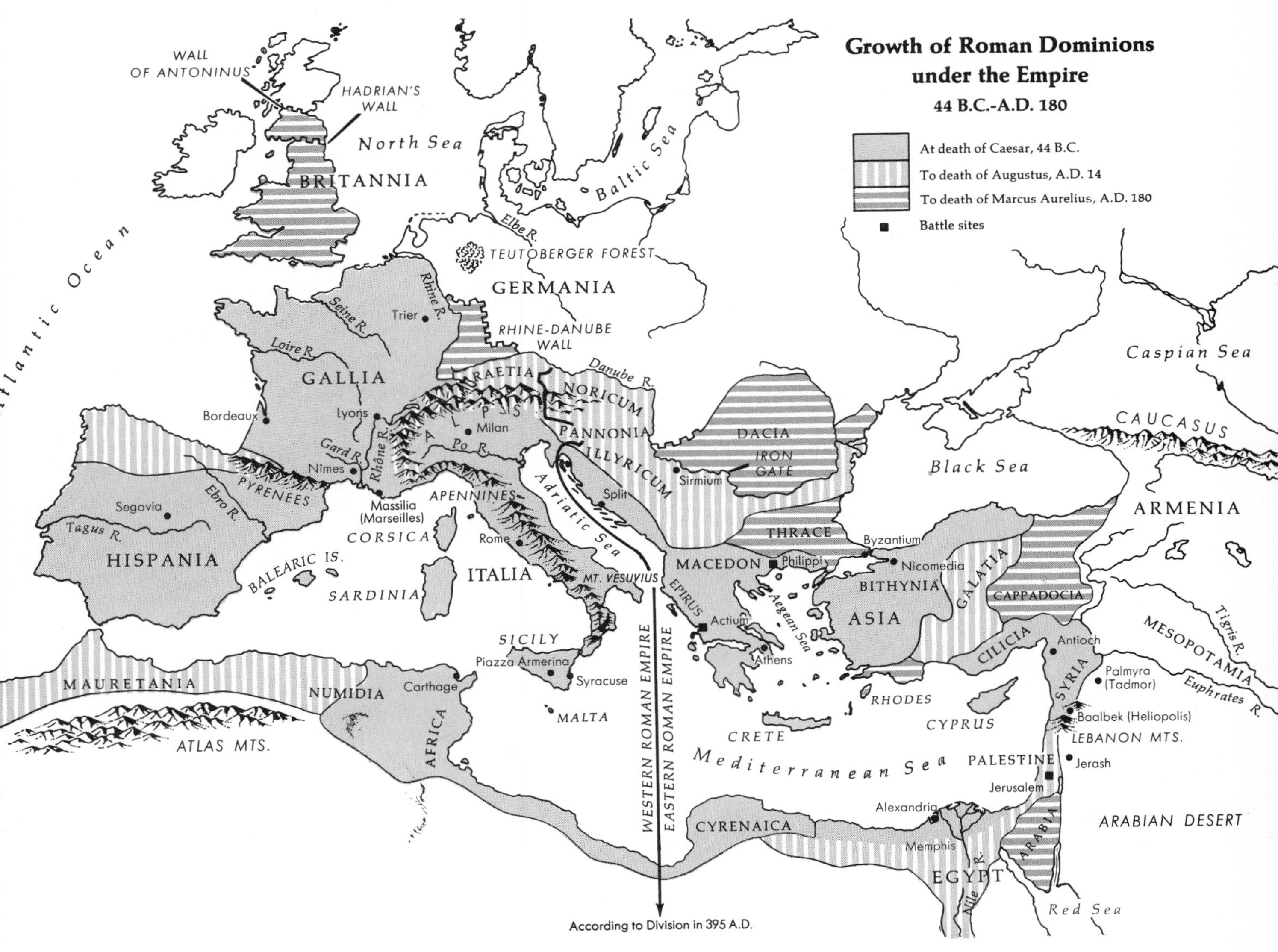

Abroad, Claudius abandoned Augustus' principles and added to the empire the region that is now Morocco and smaller areas in the Balkans and in Asia Minor. In A.D. 43 he invaded Britain, ninety-eight years after Julius Caesar's first invasion. Southeast England now became the province of Britain, whose frontiers were pushed outward toward Wales. Claudius' fourth wife, Agrippina, to obtain the succession for Nero, her son by an earlier marriage, poisoned Claudius in 54.

Dissolute and insanely proud of his own artistic talents, Nero sang, played the harp, acted, and drove a chariot at Roman public spectacles. He had his mother put to death, murdered his wife, and married his mistress, whom he later kicked to death in a fit of temper. Contrary to legend, he did not start the great fire that burned down much of Rome in 64, nor did he fiddle while Rome burned. But to find a scapegoat he accused the new sect of the Christians, now for the first time attracting attention at Rome. Nero persecuted them to take attention away from himself.

There were serious revolts in Britain in 61. But the chief threat in the provinces arose in Judea. Augustus had been tolerant of the Jews, but Caligula had created great trouble by insisting that his statue be set up in the restored Jewish temple. Rival sects among the Jews detested each other and the Christians. Nobody except the small upper class supported Roman rule, and the Romans had too few troops to keep order. In 66, open rebellion against Nero broke out in Palestine. The Roman general Vespasian was restoring order when troops in Gaul and Spain rebelled against Nero in favor of their commander Galba. The Senate proclaimed Galba emperor. Nero committed suicide (68).

From Nero to Marcus Aurelius: A.D. 68–180

Augustus' first four successors are called the Julio-Claudian emperors. All were members, though sometimes distant, of the family of Julius Caesar and Augustus. But now the line had run out wretchedly in Nero, and the Senate and people of Rome learned that emperors could be found in other families and chosen in other ways. In 68–69 alone, four emperors, each a general supported by his own troops, ruled in rapid succession. The first three all died by violence. The fourth was Vespasian, who had left his son Titus in command of the campaign in Palestine, where in 70 the Roman troops sacked Jerusalem and destroyed the rebuilt temple.

Vespasian (69–79) founded the second Roman imperial dynasty, the Flavian, the throne passing successively to his two sons, Titus (79–81) and Domitian (81–96). Competent in every way, Vespasian appointed numerous non-Romans, especially Spaniards, to the Senate. He subdued a rebellion in Gaul, made gains in Britain, and managed to stave off the potential uprisings of other generals' troops against him.

During the brief reign of Titus, Mount Vesuvius, the volcano overlooking the Bay of Naples, erupted and wiped out the population of the provincial town of Pompeii, leaving behind all the famous remains that have taught us about daily life there. Domitian was a suspicious tyrant, seeing conspirators against him everywhere. In 96 a palace conspiracy brought him down.

When an emperor died, the Senate—subservient during his lifetime—had the power of appointing his successor. In 96 they chose a mild sixty-five-year-old official named Nerva (96–98), who had no children and therefore could not found a dynasty. He promptly ended Domitian's persecutions of Jews and Christians and founded a new charity that gave loans to farmers in Italy to provide food for orphans. He also arranged for the succession by adopting as his son and successor the great general Trajan (98–117), who succeeded Nerva peacefully. This was the first of a series of four successive fortunate adoptions that gave the empire its most prosperous and peaceful years at home, 98–177.

Abroad, Trajan moved north of the Danube into Dacia—part of present-day Romania—which in 106 became a Roman province. But to the east his campaigns across the Euphrates against the Parthians ended in failure in 115. A massive revolt of the Jews confronted Trajan's successor, his nephew Hadrian, when he succeeded his adoptive father in 117.

Hadrian (117–138), widely experienced as a soldier and administrator and a highly cultivated man, put down the Jewish uprising. He realized that any effort to cross the Syrian desert against the Parthians could overextend Roman communication lines; so he wisely made peace with them. He made himself popular by canceling all private debts to the government, furthering charities, and putting on big shows in the circus. Able lawyers helped him adjust taxes and control prices in bad years and improve the legal position of slaves and soldiers. They codified all past decisions of the praetors, for the first time enabling

A street in the ruins of Herculaneum, buried with Pompeii by the eruption of Mt. Vesuvius in A.D. 79.

Ruins of Hadrian's Wall in Northumberland.

Roman citizens to know when they ought to sue somebody, and assuring them of uniform procedures.

Hadrian believed that all the provinces should be equal under Roman imperial benevolence, with himself as the "father of the fatherland" *(pater patriae)*. So he caused each of the armies for provincial defense to be recruited within the province itself. And he knew the provinces at first hand. In Britain he built across the island the famous system of walls and ditches still called Hadrian's Wall against the Scots and Picts to the north. He also lived in southern France, in Spain, in Morocco, in Asia Minor, in Greece, in Tunisia and Libya, in Syria, Palestine, and Egypt. Everywhere he inspected the troops and defenses, built buildings, and made himself known to the population. After a decade abroad, he returned to Rome, where he began to build "Hadrian's Villa" at nearby Tivoli, something like a World's Fair exposition ground with whole areas built in his favorite Greek and Egyptian styles.

His successor, Antoninus (138–161), called Pius because he was so loyal an adoptive son to Hadrian, himself immediately adopted as his future successor his own nephew Marcus Aurelius (161–180). Under these two "Antonine" emperors many Romans believed that they had reached the peak of good government and agreeable living. From Rome a feeling of security emanated throughout the world, preserved because of the eternal vigilance of Roman troops along the distant river frontiers, the Rhine, the Danube, and the Euphrates.

There was no civil strife, and those who were comfortable had never been more comfortable. In Rome and, more widely, in Italy, the Antonine monarchy showed concern for the less privileged. Egypt, as always, continued to be ruthlessly exploited. Unlike Hadrian, Antoninus Pius never left Italy, and the boasted watch of the troops along the frontiers grew slacker after Hadrian's death. Marcus Aurelius therefore found himself forced to campaign in Dacia and against the Parthians. Though victorious, he permitted some barbarians to settle inside the Roman frontiers and to be enrolled in the Roman armies, thus undermining the traditional defensive system.

With Commodus (180–192), true son of Marcus Aurelius, a boorish tyrant, there began a century of decline in the fortunes of the empire, arrested only by heroic measures in the period after 284 A.D. But before we trace its progress and analyze its causes, we must examine the Roman accomplishments in art and literature, law, religion, and general outlook. This in turn will enable us to understand the growing success within the empire by 180 of the generally despised and often ignored new sect of the Christians.

III ROMAN CIVILIZATION

Greece as Inspiration

"Greece, though conquered, made a captive of her conqueror." This ancient generalization is still of enormous help to anyone trying to understand Roman civilization. The admiring Romans imported Greek scholars to teach their children, Greek works of art to admire and imitate, Greek styles of architecture, and even Greek gods. Before the Romans conquered Greece itself, Greek influence reached them from Greek southern Italy (Magna Graecia).

The Greece the Romans conquered was not the Greece of Homer or even of the age of Pericles. The very greatest Greek works of art and literature, though deeply respected, were no longer being produced in Greece. The Romans took over Greece in the century after the death of Alexander the Great. This was a lesser Greece, the Greece of Menander's New Comedy not of Aristophanes' Old Comedy. Greek literature and art—mostly produced in Alexandria—were charming and graceful, but sometimes trivial, less concerned than in past ages with the central ethical and religious problems of humanity.

Moreover, while the Greeks supplied the form and much of the spirit, Rome did not simply take over Greek models, but modified them in such a way that the greatest Roman buildings, portrait busts, and poems could not possibly be mistaken for Greek achievements. The Romans were more political, more personal. On the Acropolis of Athens the gods reigned. In the Roman Forum their presence was overshadowed by that of triumphal individual emperors.

Architecture, Engineering, Sculpture, and Painting

Roman architecture borrowed the Greek column, usually Corinthian, but made wide use also of the round arch, originated by the Etruscans. From this Rome developed the barrel vault,

Relief of a Roman battle on the Column of Trajan, Rome.

a continuous series of arches like the roof of a tunnel which could be used to cover large areas. The Romans introduced the dome. A splendid one surmounts the Roman Pantheon, built to honor the divine ancestors of Augustus. Roman structures emphasized bigness. The big stadium, the Colosseum, seated 45,000 spectators. All over Europe, North Africa, and the Near East stand theaters, temples, villas, and other monumental remains of the Roman domination.

The Romans devised a formula for making concrete from sand, lime, silica, stone, and water. They combined this concrete with large stones in building roads and bridges so well designed and so long-lasting that even today some are still in use. The network of roads spread throughout the empire, making travel overland swift and easy. The Romans went to great trouble and expense to provide their cities with pure and abundant water. A dozen aqueducts served Rome itself, and from Constantinople to Segovia aqueducts form the most spectacular Roman ruins. The concern for water reflected a real interest in bathing and in hygiene. The Romans had the highest sanitary standards known in Europe until the nineteenth century.

Roman statues, particularly portrait busts, though derived from Greek and Hellenistic models, often had a realism all their own. A sculptured frieze running spirally up a monumental column records Trajan's victories over the Dacians. Of Roman painting we have chiefly the wall decorations of the villas at Pompeii and the mosaic floors of public and private buildings. Here a favorite subject was hunting, usually along the banks of the Nile, with crocodiles and hippopotamuses among the papyrus plants.

Medicine and Science

Roman surgeons made a variety of ingenious instruments for special operations, including the Caesarean operation—supposed (probably wrongly) to have been first performed at the birth of Julius Caesar. The Romans invented the first hospitals, military and civilian. Much superstition survived in Roman medicine. It was the Greeks, notably Galen (A.D. 131–201), who continued to make the chief theoretical contributions, compiling medical encyclopedias and diffusing learning.

What Galen did for medicine, his contemporary Ptolemy of Alexandria did for ancient geography. Both remained the chief authorities on their subjects down to the sixteenth century. Some learned Romans followed the Alexandrian Eratosthenes in believing that the earth was round. To support this hypothesis, Pliny the Elder in the first century A.D. made observations of ships approaching the shore. The tip of the mast appeared first to an observer on shore and the hull last, a proof, Pliny felt, that the surface of the earth was curved.

Literature: The Republic

Only fragments totaling between six and seven hundred lines remain of the first great Roman poet, Quintus Ennius (239–169 B.C.). Born and brought up in Magna Graecia, Ennius turned to Homer for inspiration when he put into epic form his patriotic account (the *Annales*) of Roman successes down to his own time. Ennius had a thoroughly Roman admiration for the military virtues. As Ennius used Homeric verse to celebrate Roman toughness and resilience, the playwright Plautus (254–184 B.C.) and Terence (190–159 B.C.) found their inspiration in the Greek New Comedy of Menander. Plautus, raucous and knockabout, wrote the play about two sets of twins, masters and servants, who are always being mistaken for each other, which Shakespeare eventually imitated in *A Comedy of Errors.* Characters from Plautus—the rich but stupid young gentleman with an immensely clever and resourceful valet, the money-grubbing miser—recur throughout the course of western European—and Russian—literary history.

During the late republic appeared two of Rome's greatest poets, Lucretius (96–55 B.C.) and Catullus (84–54 B.C.), alike only in their mastery of their chosen verse forms and the genuineness of their emotions. Lucretius—disciple of the Greek philosopher Epicurus—wrote a long poem, *On the Nature of Things (De Rerum Natura).* He put into poetry the Epicurean view that men do not live after death and that the gods—far from governing the affairs of men—do not intervene at all. The universe is made of atoms, whose motions and behavior are governed by fixed laws, right out to the edges, the "flaming walls of the universe." Human beings, however, control their own actions.

Catullus, inspired by the Alexandrian poets, adopted a new verse form to write passionate love lyrics to his often unfaithful mistress. The poems addressed to her pet sparrow are playful, but others, reflecting Catullus' jealousy, are obscene. These brief poems, seem to some readers the highest achievement of Roman literature. Catullus also wrote a long, sustained, and extraordinarily gripping poem about the exaltation and self-mutilation of the devotees of Cybele, the great mother goddess of Asia Minor, and her consort Attis, whose cult was then becoming popular at Rome.

In Cicero (106–43 B.C.), whom we have already encountered in his role as a lawyer and politician, the late republic produced its greatest orator and writer of prose. His speeches in the courtroom or in the Senate were carefully prepared and effective pleas and include occasional witty or ironical phrases. Cicero studied not only what he wanted to say but how he could choose the most effective—sometimes the most unexpected—words in which to say it, so that the sound and the sense would combine to make his point irresistible. We also have almost a thousand letters from Cicero to his friends and some of their answers to him. Those to his best friend, Atticus, reveal his personal joys and sorrows. Those to important Roman public figures are valuable to historians.

Philosophically, Cicero softened the harsh abstractions of true Stoicism. He believed that human beings could have some virtues without being all-wise and could exercise the Stoic virtues in an ordinary life. Not an original thinker himself, Cicero, who took these ideas from Greek teachers, helped popularize them in his philosophic essays—on Old Age, on Friendship, on the Nature of the Gods. His fellow Romans first learned from him about a "natural law" that existed independent of all human legislative actions, and a "law of nations" that should regulate the relationships of different peoples toward each other. The influence of these Ciceronian works radiated far into future human history. The early Christian church fathers studied Cicero intently. So did the humanists of the Italian Renaissance and the men who made the eighteenth-century revolutions in America and in France and who wrote the Declaration of Independence and the Constitution of the United States.

Roman Law

The earliest legal code published on the Twelve Tables in the fifth century B.C. reflected the needs of a small city-state, not those of a huge empire. As Rome became a world capital, thousands of foreigners flocked to live there to pursue their businesses, and often got into disagreements with each other or with a Roman. But Roman law developed the flexibility to adjust to changing conditions. The enactments of the Senate and Assemblies, the decrees of each new emperor, and the decisions of the judges who were often called in as advisers all contributed to a great body of legal materials.

It was the praetors, the chief legal officers, who heard both sides in every case and determined the facts before turning over the matter to the *judex,* a referee, for decision. The *judices* had to develop a body of rules for deciding cases that were not covered by existing law. As they dealt with many different breeds of foreigners, they worked out a body of legal custom common to all of them, the Stoics' and Cicero's law of nations *(jus gentium)*. As each new praetor took office for a year, he would announce the laws by which he intended to be bound, usually following his predecessors, and adding to the body of law as necessary. Romans too gradually acquired the benefits of the law of nations.

By the second century A.D., with the emperors themselves the only source of law, more and more reliance was put in trained legal scholars. These advisers felt an almost religious concern for equity. It was the spirit rather than the letter of the law that counted. This reflected the Stoics' and Cicero's natural law that was divinely inspired and applied to all men everywhere. As we know, Hadrian ordered a systematic compilation of judicial decisions, the first of several such collections.

In practice, of course, judges were often ill trained, emperors brutal or arbitrary; Roman law could be used to exalt the authority of the state over the individual. Yet the law recognized the rights of the citizen, afforded legal redress even to slaves, and gave wide scope to local legal practices. Its superiority made Roman law the victor over other legal systems. The law of much of western Europe today goes back to its provisions.

Literature: The Golden Age

As in the other enterprises of his day, Augustus himself took an active part in recruiting and subsidizing men of letters to proclaim the glories of his new era. In his *Georgics* and *Eclogues,* Vergil (70–19 B.C.) followed the models of Greek pastoral poetry and praised the pleasures and satisfactions of rural life. Written before Augustus reached political supremacy, these poems later served Augustus as propaganda for his program of getting men back to the farm. He persuaded Vergil to write the *Aeneid,* the epic of Rome's beginnings, in which the poet could "predict" the future glories that Augustus' rule would bring. Though designed in part to please Augustus, these passages also reveal Vergil's own sincere and intense patriotism. Vergil often comments on the sacrifices that necessarily accompany a rise to greatness, on sorrow, and on death.

His fellow poet Horace (65–8 B.C.) had more humor and expressed a greater variety of feelings in a greater number of meters. In short poems on more limited subjects, he too praised the joys of rural life and the virtues of moderation, but also in more solemn terms celebrated the Roman qualities of quiet toughness, the simple life, the traditional religious attitudes. Ovid (43 B.C.–A.D. 17) gave worldly advice—often cynical—on the art of love. He told the stories of the transformations reported in Greek myths, as various divinities became birds or animals or plants. Ovid died in exile because of his involvement in a scandal affecting the granddaughter of Augustus.

To match in prose Vergil's epic of Rome's early days and to stress again the virtues that had made Rome great, the historian Livy (59 B.C.–A.D. 17) set out to write a prose history of the city from the moment of its founding. Only 35 of the 142 books into which he divided his work have come down to us complete, but we have summaries of the missing portions, which dealt with most of the second and all of the first century B.C. For the earliest periods Livy had to use legend as his source. For later periods he had the work of historians now lost. His work was very long and soon was made available in digest form. The future emperor Claudius had Livy as his tutor.

The Silver Age

Writers' insistence on the great Roman virtues reflected an uneasy sense of their decline. As the imperial government became more arbitrary, poets and historians began to fear the consequences of expressing themselves too freely. Disillusionment set in. Moreover, the general admiration for the Augustan writers, especially Vergil, was so intense that poets were often content to try to imitate them.

The greatest of all the Roman historians, Tacitus (ca. 55–117 A.D.) believed that Romans had degenerated. In his *Germania* he wrote an essay that praised the rugged and still primitive way of life of the German barbarians, but was intended as an acid commentary on the qualities the Romans had once had and had now lost. Similar disillusionment fills his works of history, originally covering the period from Tiberius to Domitian but not entirely preserved. Brilliant and prejudiced, Tacitus was the greatest of the writers of the period between Tiberius and Hadrian, the "Silver Age."

Tacitus was certainly right in thinking that Rome had lost some of its traditional virtues. Nevertheless, the first two centuries of the empire mark the most stable and prosperous era that had yet occurred in human history. No doubt, the profits of flourishing commercial life were unevenly distributed, and there were glaring contrasts between riches and poverty. But many of the harshest aspects of ancient society elsewhere were softened at Rome. Slaves could obtain their freedom more easily. Women had more rights and commanded more respect. There was much harmonious family life, though there were also more divorces than at any time until our own day. Physical comforts were abundant for those who could afford them.

In Rome itself, however, great areas were slums. Six- and seven-story wooden tenements burned down repeatedly and were rebuilt despite building codes and fire departments. Worst of all was the chronic urban unemployment. At the height of the Pax Romana, perhaps half the population of the capital was drawing free bread. The inhabitants were also given free circuses: chariot races and gladiatorial combats. The poor squandered their pennies on betting. Bloodshed exerted a morbid fascination. Criminals were crucified and even burned alive on the stage to entertain the populace. By the last century of Roman life these shows had become so popular that they had replaced the circus, despite the protests of occasional horrified citizens, pagan or Christian.

Silver Age poets included notably Seneca, a Stoic philosopher, Nero's tutor, by birth a Spaniard. Seneca wrote nine tragedies imitating Greek originals but far more pompous and sensational. He probably also wrote a satire on Claudius, a man easy to poke fun at, especially after he was dead, but morally worth several Senecas and any number of Neros. Seneca's nephew, Lucan, wrote an epic poem *(The Pharsalia)* about the struggle between Caesar and Pompey. In successive generations, Persius (34–62 A.D.) and Juvenal (50–130) satirized contemporary society, and, as satirists often do, overstated their case. Juvenal enjoyed painting in harsh colors the vulgarities and wretchedness, the cruelties and greed of Rome. Romans would have met his vulgar characters frequently not only on the streets but in the pages of a famous obscene novel, the *Satyricon,* probably by one of Nero's court officials, Petronius. It includes an unforgettable wild banquet given by a newly rich ex-slave.

Religion

Before the first contacts with the Greeks, the Romans, in their small Italian city-state, had of course evolved their own religion. They worshiped the household spirits, the *lares* and *penates* who governed their everyday affairs, along with those supernatural beings that lived in fields and woods and springs. Like the Greek Hestia, the Roman Vesta presided over the individual hearth and had in her service the specially trained Vestal Virgins. From the Etruscans the Romans took the practices of foretelling the future by observing the flight of birds (the auspices) and examining the entrails of animals (the auguries). From Greece there soon came the entire Olympic collection of gods and goddesses, some of them merging their identities in existing divinities, and most of them changing their names. Zeus became Jupiter, Hera Juno, Poseidon Neptune, and so on, though Apollo remained Apollo. But the Romans had nothing like the Greek Olympic games or the festivals of Dionysus that had led to the writing of Athenian tragedy and comedy.

As we know, Julius Caesar and most of the emperors beginning with Augustus were deified after death. In his lifetime, Augustus consented to be worshiped jointly with Rome at a great altar in Gaul. But the individual Roman took little part in any of the cults, except for certain annual festivals. The official priests performed the rites. Their chief priest was the *pontifex maximus,* a title and role taken over by the emperors themselves. The state religion early lost its appeal for the Romans. There was no reason why they could not worship as many additional gods as they pleased. So Rome early imported cults from the East, which competed for popularity. Christianity eventually joined and won the competition.

IV The Christian Revolution in the Roman World to A.D. 180

The Spirit of the Times

Greek scientific theory and Roman technical skills had brought the ancient world to the threshold of an industrial age. Heron of Alexandria, who we think lived at about the beginning of the Christian era, had even discovered how useful steam pressure was in a boiler, and sketched a model of a fire engine, including the piston. It would have been only a short step to the building of steam engines. Why did more than 1700 years pass before human civilization took that step?

One (unlikely) answer is that slave labor was working so well that nobody thought labor-saving devices were desirable. Or perhaps people thought Heron's devices were only toys and science was only a game played by a small group of scholars who were uninterested in practical applications. As for the rulers of Rome, they scorned what we would call research. The emperor Tiberius once executed a man who had invented a process for making unbreakable glass. The few who in earlier times believed in improving their lives by using their reasoning powers seem to have disappeared. Everywhere among Romans there was mounting pessimism and a lack of faith in the human race's ability to work out its own future.

The gods seemed remote, life and death a mere matter of luck. Beginning as early as the third century B.C. and gathering momentum later, the cult of the goddess Fortune became popular in the Mediterranean world. She governed everything. Today's prosperity might vanish tomorrow; the best thing to do was to enjoy your luck while it lasted. Closely related was the belief in Fate. What happened was inevitable, because it had been fated from the beginning. When you were born, the moment of your death was already fixed. Cicero protested that human beings could contribute to their own fate and so take advantage of fortune. Vergil attributed both fate and fortune to the will of the divine providence. But most Romans, like Tacitus, felt helpless to change their own fates or to influence events.

Astrology

People eagerly believed that the movements of the heavenly bodies influenced the fortunes of men and governed their decisions. The science of astronomy became lost in the false speculation of astrology. If you could do nothing to change your destiny, you could at least try to find out what it was by consulting an astrologer. He would study the seven "planets" (Saturn, Jupiter, Mars, the Sun, Venus, Mercury, the Moon), each of which had its own will, character, sex, plants, numbers, and animals, and each of which was lord of a sphere. These seven transparent but impenetrable concentric spheres, with Earth at the center, cut the human race off from heaven. Each planet had its own day: hence the seven-day week. Seven itself became a mystic number: there were seven ages of man, seven wonders of the world. Then too there were the twelve Houses of the Sun, constellations of stars through which the sun passed on his path around the earth: the signs of the Zodiac.

From the position of the heavenly bodies and the signs of the Zodiac at the moment of your conception or birth, astrologers would draw up a horoscope foretelling your fate. The Roman emperors, like most of their subjects, profoundly believed in astrology. Especially valuable for the art of prophecy were unnatural events: the appearance of a comet, the birth of a monster. Similarly, the Romans believed in all sorts of magic and tried by its power to force the heavenly bodies to grant their wishes.

New Cults: Cybele, Isis, Mithra

The official religion of the Olympian gods and of the deified emperor were still for most Romans the equivalent of patriotism. But this did not calm their fears. As men sought for a religion that would hold out the hope for an afterlife better than the grim life here on earth, a number of *mystery religions* began to appear in Rome.

All the new faiths taught that a human being could save his soul by uniting it with the soul of a savior, who in many cases had himself experienced death and resurrection. Union with the savior was accomplished by a long initiation, with purifications, ritual banquets, and other ceremonies. Gradually the candidate cast aside human unworthiness. The god would enter him, and so after death he would be saved. You could join as many of these cults as you wished while continuing to practice the state religion.

The Greeks had had such cults—in the rites of Demeter at Eleusis and in the mysteries of Dionysus. Dionysus, now called Bacchus, became popular at Rome. Hundreds of Roman sarcophagi (stone boxes for coffins) survive with sculptures of the Bacchic procession, celebrating the joys of drink and sex.

One of Bacchus' chief competitors was the great mother goddess Cybele, native to Asia Minor. Her young husband, Attis, died and was reborn annually (like Demeter's daughter, Persephone). Attis was thus a symbol of renewed fertility. The rites of Cybele included fasting and frenzied processions. The priests flogged and even castrated themselves. The first temple to Cybele at Rome dated from 204 B.C., but the cult reached its height in the second century A.D. and later. By that time the rites included the slaughter of a bull above a pit into which the candidate had descended in order to be bathed by the blood.

Even more popular—especially among women—was the cult of the Egyptian Isis, whose

Roman relief of the slaughter of a bull (taurobolium) in Mithraism.

consort, Osiris, also died and was reborn each year. All feminine elements, both chaste and lewd, were concentrated in an elaborate ritual of worship for Isis, the loving mother goddess, who promised her followers personal immortality.

From Persia via Asia Minor came the cult of the god Mithra, allied to the supreme powers of good and light and so connected with the sun. Male initiates passed in succession through seven grades of initiation (corresponding to the seven planets and named after animals), qualifying for each grade by severe tests. Baptism and communion were also part of the ritual. Tough and self-denying, Mithra became a model for the Roman soldier, to whom he held out the hope of salvation. Mithraism had no priests and welcomed the gods of other cults. It tended to absorb the other sun-worshiping cults, including that of Apollo, into one new cult, often heartily supported by the emperor. From London to Alexandria and from the Rhine to the Euphrates, temples of Mithra, with altars and statues, have been found.

A school of philosophers professing to follow Plato (and therefore called "Neoplatonists") taught that every human soul makes a pilgrimage toward an eventual union with the bodiless divine essence—the One, the True, the Good. By contemplation, mystics could gradually free themselves from material ties and achieve ecstatic vision. Soon Neoplatonism—popular among intellectuals—became contaminated by magical rites against opposing demons. The word used for the divine reason, the *logos* (Greek for "word"), would become part of the Christian vocabulary too, in the opening lines of the Gospel according to St. John.

Christianity

But neither Neoplatonism nor any of the mystery religions appealed to all classes at Rome. Mithraism, perhaps the most popular, excluded women and lacked love and tenderness. Christianity competed with these cults in the Roman world for more than three centuries after the death of its founder, with no assurance that it would triumph. Sharing some things in common with them, it also possessed qualities they lacked.

The Judea of Jesus

Jesus was born in Palestine sometime between the years we call 8 and 4 B.C. and was crucified probably in A.D. 29, or 30, or 33. He was a Jew and always maintained that he had not come to lead a movement of secession from Judaism but one of reform inside it. He lived, taught, and died in a most complex world.

After Alexander's conquests many Jews had been attracted to Greek culture, spoke Greek, and even used Greek artistic symbols in art. Other Jews, including the poor, were horrified by this. Civil strife led to intervention by the Seleucid rulers and ultimately to a brief period of independence for Judea before Pompey's conquest. Under Roman rule Jewish party quarrels continued, and the Jewish King Herod (47–4 B.C.) was hated for his subservience to Augustus. After Herod's death the Romans installed the first Roman prefect, who was faced by at least three major Jewish groupings.

The Sadducees, influential aristocrats who held the office of High Priest, were pro-Roman. The Pharisees, who held themselves apart, revered the Law, but unlike the Sadducees, believed in a Messiah and in the resurrection of the dead. The Essenes, known to us from the Dead Sea Scrolls discovered since 1947, lived chiefly in monasteries. They did not marry, took ritual baths, ate communal meals, called themselves the "poor in spirit," and believed they would prevail when the present age of wickedness should end.

The Dead Sea Scrolls repeatedly mention a Teacher of Righteousness, a Suffering Just One greater than the Prophets but not the "Son of Man," the Messiah whom they awaited. However, in the Scrolls the Teacher once speaks of himself as father of a man-child who would have all his own powers. The New Testament does not mention the Essenes, and Jesus may have had no contact with them, yet the scrolls reveal a reforming movement within Judaism that had much in common with Christianity. In the Teacher of Righteousness some have seen a forerunner of Christ himself.

From the Roman point of view, the Jews were privileged; they were exempt from military service and from worshiping the emperor; they enjoyed their own coinage and their own judges. They were unappreciative and rebellious.

The Teaching of Jesus

In this troubled province Jesus preached to his fellow Jews the love of God and of one's neighbor. He appealed to the poor, the unlearned, and the weak. He preached the enjoyment of the good things of this world, an enjoyment freed from rivalry, ostentation, and vulgarity. He was kind but stern. Good intentions are not enough: "he that heareth and doeth not is like a man that without a foundation built a house upon the earth. . . ." Above all, he preached gentleness and love: humility, honesty, toleration, charity. But he warned that "wide is the gate, and broad is the way, that leadeth to destruction." Though he preached that men should turn the other cheek, he also said that he came not to bring peace, but a sword.

From Jesus' teaching arose enormously important theological conclusions. He spoke of his Father in heaven, referred to himself as the Son of Man, and taught that he was the Messiah sent by God to redeem man from sin. Those who listened and led decent lives on earth would gain eternal bliss in heaven. Those who turned a deaf ear and continued in their wicked ways would be eternally damned in hell. Jesus was Christ, "the anointed one." He was begotten by the Holy Spirit and miraculously born of a Virgin mother. He was baptized by John the Baptist in the waters of the Jordan, and his followers too were required to be baptized. He gave bread and wine to his followers at a feast of love and told them that it was his body and blood and that they should partake.

Such teaching—though it had some parallels in earlier Jewish thought—alarmed the Sadduces and Pharisees, who mistrusted all reform movements. When the Roman prefect, Pontius Pilate, asked Jesus, "Are you the king of the Jews?" and Jesus affirmed that he was, he was condemned, and his title was inscribed on the cross itself to show that a leader of the resistance had been executed. As a modern scholar remarks, Pilate "acted as any prudent Roman governor would have when all the local notables unanimously demanded the blood of a low-class agitator." The crucifixion was the supreme act of redemption. Jesus died for all mankind. His followers declared that he rose from the dead on the third day and would soon return—during their lifetime, they believed—to end this world on a final Day of Judgment, when he would sit on the right hand of the Father.

Even in this bare summary one can single out elements of the Christian belief that are familiar from Judaism and others that were present in the various mystery cults. But Christ's sacrifice of his life for mankind and the intimacy with

God promised in the eternal life to come gave Christianity an appeal that no mystery cult could duplicate. Christ's message of love for all mankind supplied the tenderness that was lacking in the Roman world of every day.

By the third century, the ritual act of communion—the sacrament of the Eucharist or Mass—had become the central symbol of Christianity. This was the action that made the individual Christian actually partake of his God and feel the wonder of salvation, just as by his baptism he had been washed clean of the sin that has at birth stained all men since Adam. Baptism made one a Christian. The Eucharist, if taken reverently, kept one a Christian, provided one's behavior was also suitable. Because Christ by his crucifixion had atoned for the sin of Adam, the individual Christian might now also be saved.

Besides baptism and the Eucharist, five other ritual acts eventually came to be regarded as Christian sacraments. Confirmation brought a child into the Church when he had reached the age at which he could understand Christian doctrine. By penance a repentant sinner was given a punishment by a priest and was absolved (forgiven). But the performance of the penance could not guarantee salvation, since it might not have satisfied God's justice. Extreme unction was the last rite for the dying. Matrimony, and for the priest, ordination were the other sacraments.

Paul and the Apostles

The first Christians were a little group of Jesus' Jewish followers, the Judeo-Christian "Church of the Circumcision," following Jewish Law. But Christian belief was bound to reach out to Gentiles as well as Jews. Saul of Tarsus, a Jew converted to Christianity by a vision beheld on the road to Damascus, was renamed Paul. Paul took the lead in spreading the Evangel, the "glad tidings," and in giving the new faith its first organization: the earliest Christian church.

Non-Jews, though attracted by the appeal of Christianity, did not wish to be circumcised or to abstain from pork. Paul said that Greeks and Syrians need not follow the Jewish Law in these and other prescriptions. "The letter killeth," said Paul, "but the Spirit giveth Life." It was not the letter of the Law of the Jews that would save the Christian, but the spirit of the faith. Paul even wanted to free former Jews themselves from Jewish ritual requirements, and met with much opposition.

Between 48 and 62 Paul preached to the Gentiles in Syria, Asia Minor, Greece, Macedonia, and Rome itself. He said "there is neither Jew nor Greek" and "by one Spirit we are baptized." Both a mystic and a practical man, Paul emphasized faith as a mystery to be accepted, not to be reasoned about, while also striving to create order and discipline within the new Church.

Paul, of course, was not one of the twelve apostles, the actual companions of Christ, who according to tradition separated after the crucifixion to preach the faith in the four quarters of the earth. Peter, it was believed, eventually went to Rome itself and was martyred there. Since Paul too met the same fate (70 A.D.), the Church of Rome had both Peter and Paul as its founders. By the year 100, the new faith had penetrated into many of the eastern territories of Rome and was beginning to find a niche in the West. But it was still a small, obscure, poor sect, and only a visionary could have predicted its triumphant future.

Persecutions

Why were Peter and Paul and others martyred? If Rome could tolerate such a multitude of other sects, why not the Christians? Because, alone among the many sects, they would not sacrifice before the statue of the emperor and thus fulfill their patriotic duty as Romans. The emperor was not *their* god, and they were ready to incur the punishment of death for not worshiping him. Had they consented to perform this act, which violated the consciences of no other sect (except the Jews, who were exempt), the Christians could have carried on their own ceremonies undisturbed. But they would not, and therefore they had to conduct their services in secret. The

Christian in a Roman toga: mural from a Roman catacomb.

EGYPT

We have all seen pictures of Egyptian pyramids and temples, gigantic sculptured pharaohs and divinities, and the rich and ostentatious gold and jewels of a splendid sepulcher like King Tut's. The use of stone in building, the skillful use of great spaces, the skillful portraiture of individuals rather than types, the obelisks and sphinxes, the absence of perspective: these are familiar characteristics of Egyptian art. Less well known are the many scenes of ordinary country or family life that show a characteristic enjoyment and even a sense of humor distinctly not found in other early civilizations. Within an Egyptian tomb were placed many objects from daily life: a boxwood chair, a gameboard. On the walls of the tombs men spear fish and snare birds; a young man and his wife sit happily playing checkers or listening to music or watching the dancing girls. The people who lived along the Nile all those millennia ago speak to us clearly, and we listen with fascination and recognition.

Boxwood and acacia chair from the tomb of Ramose, Thebes. The household god Bes is depicted between symbols of stability and protection.

The Metropolitan Museum of Art, Rogers Fund, 1936.

Limestone Statue of Queen Hat-shepsut. From the temple of Hat-shepsut, Thebes, Deir el Bahri.

The Metropolitan Museum of Art, Rogers Fund and contribution of Edward S. Harkness, 1929.

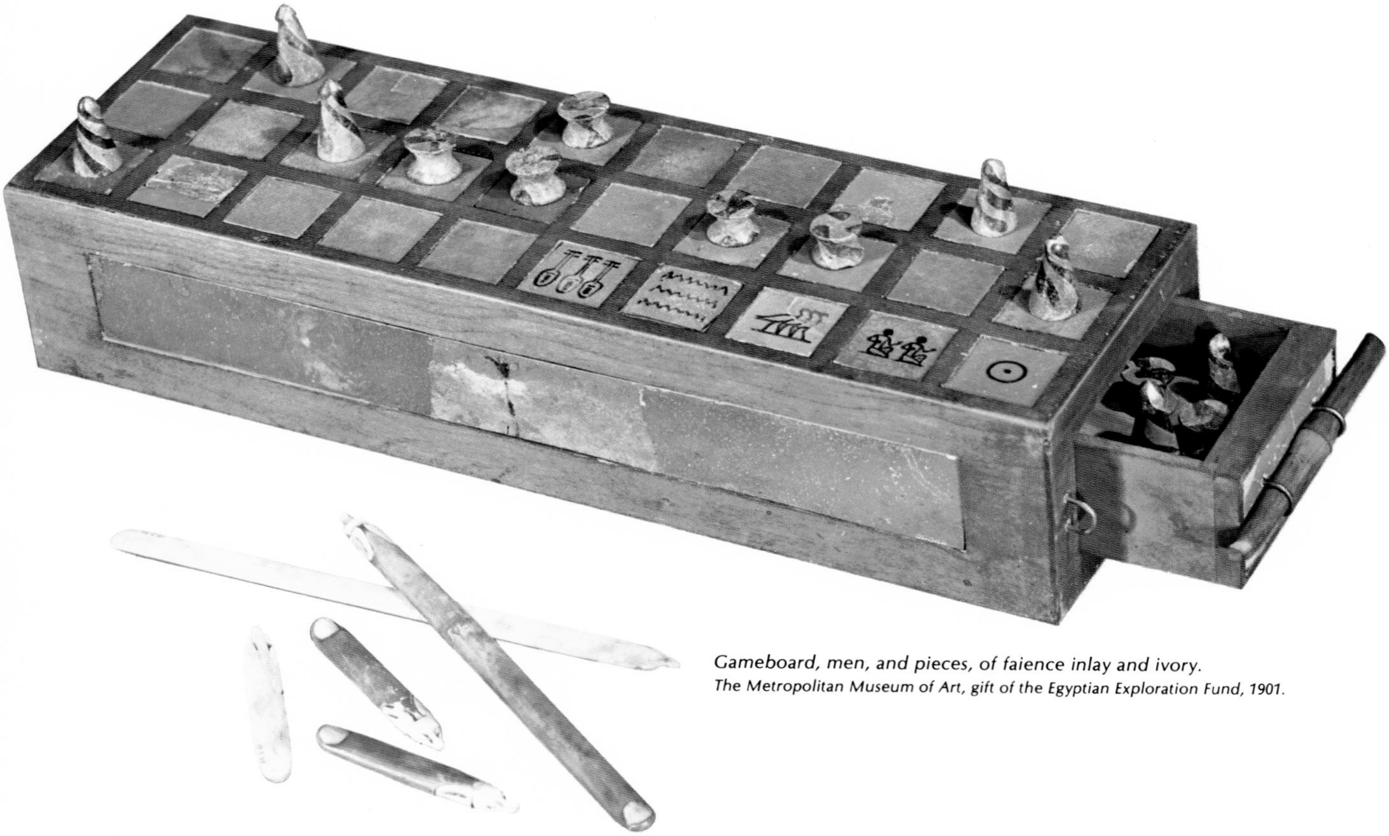

Gameboard, men, and pieces, of faience inlay and ivory.
The Metropolitan Museum of Art, gift of the Egyptian Exploration Fund, 1901.

The Judgment: detail of an illustration for The Book of the Dead. Funerary papyrus of the princess Entiu-ny, from the tomb of Queen Meryet-Amon. Deir el Bahri, ca. 1025 B.C.
The Metropolitan Museum of Art, Rogers Fund, 1919.

GREECE AND ROME

The incalculably rich legacy left by the Greeks in literature was well matched by their achievements in the plastic arts. The achievements of Phidias and the other sculptors of the Periclean age developed gradually from the archaic Greek statues created a century or more earlier (see the illustrations to the text). In the Hellenistic age sculpture became more emotional and theatrical. The Winged Victory of Samothrace, shown here, is one of the most successful Hellenistic works of art.

Just as the best Roman literary achievements could not be mistaken for Greek works, so Roman art, though derived from Greek and Hellenistic models, had a realism all its own. We show in this section a detail of a wall decoration in a villa outside Pompeii, the resort town that was literally buried A.D. 79 by the sudden eruption of Vesuvius that covered it in a rain of hot ash.

The Winged Victory of Samothrace, ca. 200 B.C. The marble statue, eight feet tall, is now in the Louvre.
European Art Color, Peter Adelberg, N.Y.C.

Detail of a wall painting from a villa at Boscoreale, outside Pompeii: the head of a woman playing a cithera.
The Metropolitan Museum of Art, Rogers Fund, 1903.

EASTERN CHRISTENDOM AND ISLAM

When we consider the contributions of the Byzantines and the Muslims to the cultures of our Western society, we are altogether justified in saying that much light came from the East. In the plastic arts we can see the Byzantine achievement with our own eyes. In Constantinople the Church of Santa Sophia, built in the sixth century, was designed to be "a church the like of which has never been since Adam nor ever will be." At Ravenna, there are three churches of the sixth century with superb mosaics still well preserved. And at Venice itself, first the client, then the equal, and finally the conqueror of Byzantium, St. Mark's is a true Byzantine church of the later period, whose richness and magnificence epitomize perhaps better than any surviving church in Istanbul itself the splendor of later Byzantine architecture.

Like Byzantium, Islam aspired to dominate the civilized world, which it thought of as divided between those lands already part of Islam and those lands still to be conquered. Muslim scientists adopted the Indian numerals, the very ones that we use today and call Arabic. The Muslims began on analytical geometry and founded plane and spherical trigonometry. They progressed much further than their predecessors in algebra; and "algebra" is itself an Arabic word like "alcohol," "cipher," "alchemy," "zenith," "nadir," and others that testify to early Muslim scientific achievement.

In the arts, the Muslims developed their own adaptation of Byzantine churches in their mosques. Beautiful and elaborate geometric patterns, in wood, stone, mosaic, and porcelain tile, characterize the interior decoration.

The Three Magi: a mosaic in the church of S. Apollinare Nuovo, Ravenna.

European Art Color, Peter Adelberg, N.Y.C.

Leaf from an eighth- or ninth-century Koran: Naskhi calligraphy.
The Metropolitan Museum of Art, Fletcher Fund, 1924.

THE MEDIEVAL WEST

Admirers of the Middle Ages often claim that the medieval craftsman worked in anonymity, content to carve or paint for the glory of God and the joy of creating beauty, and not for fame or money. Perhaps so, though the reason we do not know the names of many medieval architects and sculptors is simply that the records have been lost. Yet art and artists seem to have been closely tied to the community in the Middle Ages. The greatest of medieval arts, architecture, clearly shows this community stamp. In a medieval town the cathedral, parish churches, town hall, guild halls, and other *public* buildings dominate.

All the fine arts contributed to these great community buildings; indeed, they had hardly any other major outlet. Painting was subordinated to architecture. While the medieval church had no place for the canvas designed to be hung for exhibition, mosaics, wall painting, and above all stained glass contributed to the total design.

Sculpture, too, was subordinated to the building. Statues and carvings were fitted into the design of the great churches, in niches on the fronts and porches, or on altars and shrines in the interior. Medieval sculpture is never simply realistic in the way of the portrait bust, nor independently grand in the way of equestrian statue. It is always part of the "stone Bible."

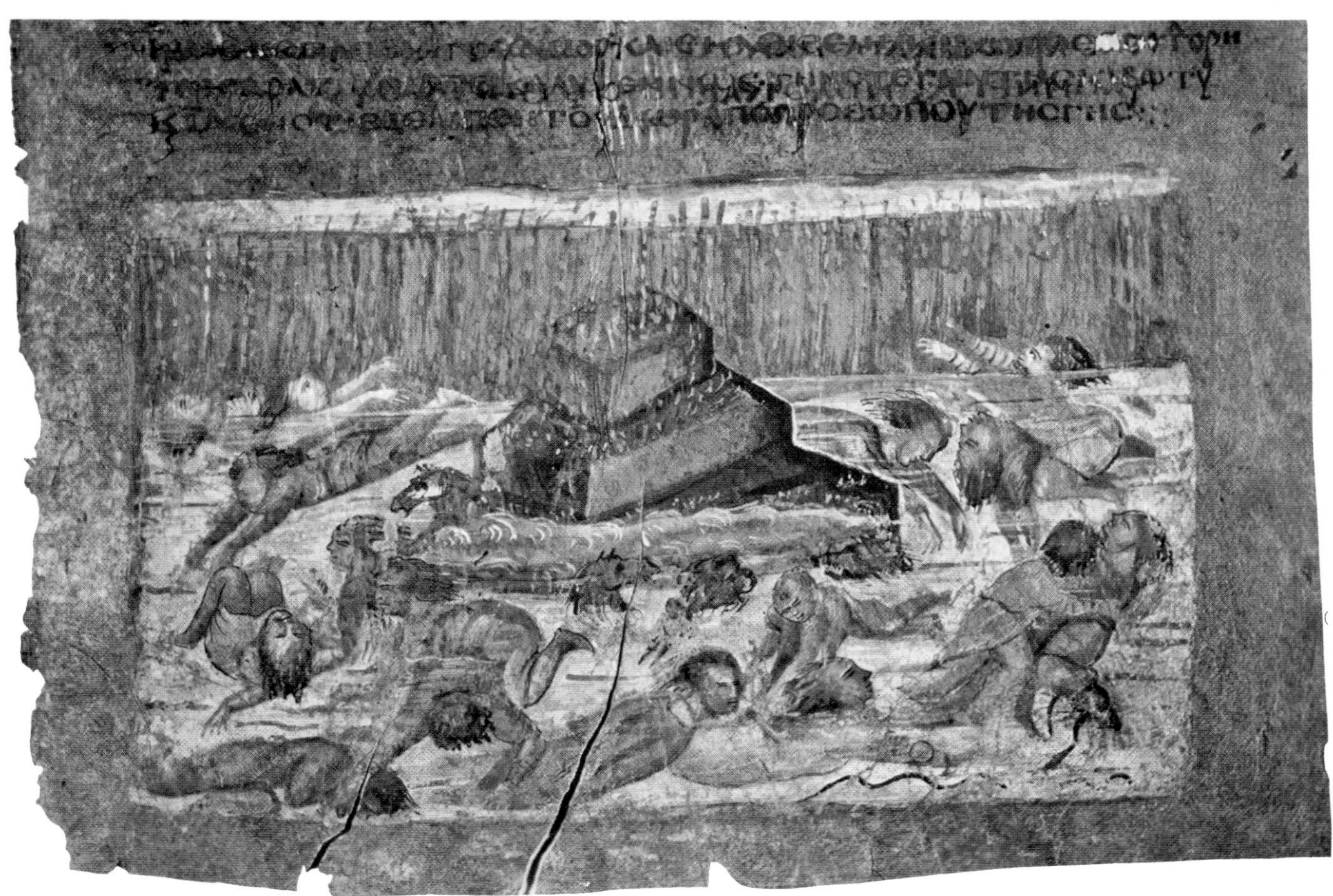

The Flood: an illumination from the sixth-century manuscript known as the Vienna Genesis.
European Art Color, Peter Adelberg, N.Y.C.

The Angel of the Four Winds: a ceiling panel in the Church of St. Martin, Zillis, Switzerland, ca. 1350.
European Art Color, Peter Adelberg, N.Y.C.

Roman authorities suspected them of such vices as incest, murder, and infanticide.

So it was natural for Nero, in A.D. 64, to punish the Christians by terrible cruelties and, as Tacitus says, to seek a scapegoat for the fire. A generation later, Pliny the Younger, Roman governor in Asia Minor, wrote his emperor, Trajan (98–117) asking how he should treat Christians. Trajan replied that Pliny should make no effort to hunt them out, but that when they were denounced they should be punished unless they denied their religion and supported that denial by worshiping the gods. Christian willingness to undergo martyrdom was regarded by most pagan Romans as a kind of exhibitionism. Marcus Aurelius (161–180), persecuted the Christians both in Asia Minor and in Gaul.

V THE IMPERIAL DECLINE AND RECOVERY AND THE TRIUMPH OF CHRISTIANITY, 180–337

A Century of Decline (180–284)

In 192, Marcus Aurelius' son, Commodus, was murdered. Within a year the Praetorian Guard installed and murdered two other emperors. A general, Septimius Severus (193–211), marched his army into Rome and disbanded the guard, replacing it by a new elite body chosen from his own officers. He settled the first civil strife Rome had known in more than a century, rewarding his armies with better food, better pay, and better conditions.

Septimius Severus was succeeded by his two sons, one of whom (Caracalla, 211–217) killed the other, and embarked on a series of other atrocious crimes until he was assassinated. Caracalla also issued an edict in 212 that extended citizenship to all freeborn inhabitants of the empire. This was a natural climax to the earlier laws gradually expanding the circle of Roman citizens. It was also a money-raising device, since all new citizens would be liable to inheritance taxes from which noncitizens were exempt.

Caracalla's sixteen immediate successors were all assassinated in their turn, a sorry parade of incompetent rulers. Between 235 and 284, twenty-five of the twenty-six Roman emperors died by violence. Most of them were chosen by their troops, held power briefly, and were in turn supplanted in the same way.

Attracted by Roman weakness, and pushed from behind by other people on the move, Germanic barbarians crossed the Roman frontiers at many points. The emperor Decius was killed in

Fourth-century Sassanian cameo showing the defeat and capture of Valerian by the king of Persia in 260.

battle by them (252). The emperor Valerian was captured (260) by the Persians, now under the new Sassanian dynasty, and died or was killed in captivity. Plagues raged. Whole provinces temporarily escaped from Roman authority, population declined, public order virtually vanished. The tide began to turn with the reign of Aurelian (270–275), the "restorer of the world," and definitively with the accession of Diocletian (284–305).

The New Empire (284–337)

But to turn the tide demanded a thoroughgoing series of reforms, internal as well as external. Diocletian and his successors, especially Constantine (306–337), were responsible for the measures creating "the new empire."

Responding to emergencies in one part or another of the empire, Diocletian gradually installed a system called the "tetrarchy," or rule by four men. Diocletian, as Augustus, first appointed a talented officer as Caesar, and then was forced by circumstances to promote him to Augustus, or co-emperor, though it was understood that Diocletian was the senior Augustus. Soon each Augustus appointed a Caesar of his own, whom he also adopted as his son. It was understood that eventually the two Augusti would abdicate, each to be succeeded by his own Caesar. Then each new Augustus would appoint a new Caesar as his son and eventual successor. Diocletian remained supreme over the other three. The scheme was obviously designed to assure a peaceful succession and to end the curse of military seizures of the throne. Though in practice ruled by a tetrarchy, the empire in theory remained a single political unit.

This was particularly important, because as each of the four rulers took primary responsibility for his own large area, Roman territorial government greatly changed. Diocletian made his headquarters at Nicomedia in western Anatolia, and from there governed Anatolia, Syria, and Egypt together with Thrace in Europe, the whole becoming the Prefecture of the East. His Caesar had his headquarters at Sirmium in what is now Yugoslavia, and from there governed the Balkans including Greece, which became the Prefecture of Illyricum. Diocletian's co-Augustus, the junior emperor Maximian, had his headquarters at Milan, and from there governed Italy and North Africa, together with parts of what is now Austria: the Prefecture of Italy. And *his* Caesar had his headquarters at Trier (Trèves) on the Moselle River, and from there governed Gaul, Spain, and

The tetrarchy of Diocletian, co-rulers of the Roman Empire: sculpture in St. Mark's, Venice.

Britain: the Prefecture of Gaul. Not even the prefecture of Italy was governed from the imperial capital of Rome.

The new imperial territorial reorganization exposed as a hollow sham the ancient pretense that the emperor shared power with the Senate. Diocletian simply walked out of Rome, leaving the Senate behind and the citizens with their free bread and circuses. It was very important that he chose to locate his own headquarters in the East. Indeed, he adopted the full trappings of oriental monarchy.

He wore silk robes of blue and gold to symbolize the sky and the sun. He sprinkled his hair with gold dust to create a nimbus when the light shone down upon him. His clothes glittered with jewels; he wore ruby and emerald bracelets, necklaces, and rings. His fingernails were gilded, and his boots—which were to become *the* new symbol of imperial power—were of purple leather. He entered his throne room carrying a golden scepter topped with a golden ball—the earth—on which was seated a Roman gold eagle with a sapphire in its beak—the heavens. Servants followed sprinkling the air with perfume, and fan bearers spread the scent abroad. Every person in the room sank to the floor until Diocletian was seated on his throne, after which the privileged might kiss the hem of his garment.

The first Augustus would have been revolted. Occasionally Rome had seen similar dis-

Gladiators: detail of mosaic pavement ca. A.D. 300 now in the Borghese Gallery, Rome.

plays, notably under the degenerate Elagabalus (218–222), himself the priest of a Syrian sun god, but Elagabalus was soon murdered. Diocletian's pomp had nothing to do with degeneracy. He was a rough Balkan soldier. Rather he was making a deliberate attempt to raise the prestige of the emperor—the divine and deified emperor—so high that his divinity would not be shaken by the ambitions of his rivals. It was no accident that Diocletian chose the additional surname *Jovius,* thus associating himself with Jupiter (Jove), the ruler of the gods.

Diocletian took major steps to prevent the recurrence of military uprisings. He separated the military from the civil power. The generals and colonels in command of local garrisons throughout the empire had no local political authority. The new civil officials whom Diocletian appointed had no military authority. Moreover, Diocletian subdivided the old provinces, so that the number of provinces rose to over one hundred, each of course much smaller than a province had formerly been. The provinces were regrouped into twelve so-called dioceses, which in turn made up the four great prefectures.

The bureaucracy grew enormously. The various financial departments, the secret service, the post office, and foreign relations each had its own structure, and the top officials became a kind of advisory body, almost a Cabinet. While an individual Roman senator might find a place in the new system, he did so independently of the Senate as such. As a body the Senate was now only a group of privileged magnates. Diocletian also reformed the army by introducing heavy-armed cavalry and inventing a flexible system of frontier defenses that made it possible for troops to move rapidly to a point where danger threatened.

The new empire also strove to check the economic misery and social unrest that had accompanied the political and military disorders of the later third century. For tax purposes, the government used as a unit of land measurement the amount of land that could be cultivated by a single farm laborer. It then forced the farm laborer to stay put, work his land, and pay his taxes. This greatly stimulated the growth of a class of peasant called the *colonus.* Although attached to the soil, the *colonus* was not a slave. He could not be sold separately from the land he cultivated. When it was sold he went with it. Men in other walks of life also were bound to their various jobs, and sons to their fathers' jobs after them. Sons of bakers had to become bakers, sons of goldsmiths, goldsmiths. Diocletian also tried to fix prices, but was thwarted by black-marketing and riots.

At the lowest territorial administrative level, the *civitas* (each city and portions of the surrounding countryside), the city senators *(curiales)* had to make up out of their own pockets any difference between the tax payments assessed for the civitas and the amount actually collected. From being an honor, the position of curialis became a burden. The curiales too had to be compelled to stay in their posts, to do their duty, and to pass their jobs on to their eldest sons.

In the new empire society became more rigidly stratified than ever before in Roman history.

Colossal head of the emperor Constantine.

This increased social stratification combined with oriental despotism, a huge bureaucracy, and a continuing dependence on the military made ordinary life extremely bleak: corruption, violence, unfairness, and individual despair were frequent. The Roman Empire survived in both East and West (though the days of the Western empire proved numbered), but its citizens were probably unhappier than ever before.

In 305 Diocletian retired and left his half of the empire to his Caesar. He forced his fellow Augustus, Maximian, to do the same. Each new Augustus in turn named a new Caesar. But the system now broke down, as the four top officials began to struggle against each other for supreme power. By 324, Constantine, son of the Western Caesar, boss of Gaul, emerged as sole Augustus. The empire was reunited. Though the tetrarchy did not survive, the other reforms of the new empire certainly helped to stave off collapse. But of course, they could not prevent it.

The Empire and the Christians

During the third-century decline, imperial suspicions of the Christians grew, and persecutions multiplied. Fearing a barbarian attack, the Emperor Decius (249–251) commanded that on a certain day all inhabitants of the empire must sacrifice to the gods and procure a certificate that they had done so. For refusing, the Bishop of Rome (the Pope) and some twenty-five other Christians were executed and others were tortured. Decius' fears proved justified and he was killed by the barbarians after all. Diocletian's persecution, which began in 303, was the most severe of any, lasting two years in the West but a full decade in the East. Some Christians courted martydom by committing violent acts against pagan shrines.

But in 312, the Augustus Constantine, still competing for supreme power in the state, was about to go into battle, just north of Rome, against a rival. In the heavens he saw a cross against the sun and the Greek words meaning "conquer in this." He put the sign on the battle-standards of his army, won the battle, and thereafter believed that the God of the Christians had given him the victory. In 313, he and his sole remaining rival, Licinius, agreed that the Christians should be left alone.

Some have disbelieved the story of Constantine's vision, arguing that he foresaw the triumph of Christianity among the people of the empire and so acted out of expediency. But there can be little doubt that Constantine had a major religious experience in 312. He continued to appease the sun-god and did not force Christianity on any of his subjects, but Constantine was himself a Christian and received baptism on his deathbed, a frequent practice in the early Church. Very soon, he found that as a Christian Emperor, he had to intervene in quarrels among Christians. He died in 337. Despite the brief attempt of the Emperor Julian (361–363) to bring paganism back, Christianity, by 381, had become the sole officially tolerated religion in the Roman Empire.

Why did Christianity, a despised sect of lower-class enthusiasts, triumph in a rich sophisticated society? It was a religion of love in the savage world of Rome. The mystery cults often seem to have degenerated into mere mumbo-jumbo. The Evangel really was "good news," with its lofty moral code, its promise of immortality. The Church provided a consoling and beautiful and dramatic ritual. The would-be convert could find in it ideas and rites closely related to those of Egyptians, Greeks, and Jews.

In addition to all this, Christianity greatly benefited from the organization that the early Christians gave to their Church. To maintain order, even to survive in a hostile empire, Christians had to organize. Prophets, or teachers, led the

Spread of Christianity
To the Eleventh Century
To 600
600-800
800-1100
Date indicates conversion to Christianity. In some cases part of the population remained pagan for some time thereafter; in other cases Arian Christianity was already established before the date indicated.
Atlantic Ocean
IRELAND
440
IONA
SCOTLAND
560
Lindisfarne
Whitby
York
ENGLAND
Oxford
Salisbury
Canterbury
Winchester
597
NORWAY
995
SWEDEN
829
DENMARK
Baltic Sea
1155
1202
Duna R.
Niemen R.
Oka R.
Volga R.
RUSSIA
988
Kiev
Dnieper R.
Don R.
Elbe R.
1125
1124
1230
690
787
Berlin
GERMANY
Vistula R.
Oder R.
966
1100's
880
Louvain
Cologne
Trier
Mainz
722
Seine R.
Paris
Toul
590
Sens
Clairvaux
Loire R.
Tours
496
Citeaux
Basel
Constance
739
863
Cluny
517
FRANCE
800's
950
Santiago de Compostela
550
SPAIN
Ebro R.
Tagus R.
Rhône R.
Milan
Po R.
Padua
Bologna
Ferrara
Florence
Assisi
ITALY
Rome
Monte Cassino
1100's
Danube R.
863
Black Sea
BYZANTINE
Constantinople
Chalcedon
Nicaea
Thessalonica
EMPIRE
CORSICA
SARDINIA
BALEARIC IS.
SICILY
Hippo
Corinth
Athens
Ephesus
Tarsus
Antioch
RHODES
CRETE
CYPRUS
SYRIA
Damascus
Nazareth
Jerusalem
Mediterranean Sea
Alexandria
EGYPT
The Holy Land
Tyre
Dan
Acre
Safad
Haifa
Sea of Galilee
MT. CARMEL
Nazareth
Caesarea
Bethshean
Jordan R.
Mediterranean Sea
Nablus
Jaffa
Lydda
Ramle
Ramallah
Jericho
Jerusalem
Bethlehem
Hebron
Dead Sea
Gaza
Beersheba

very first churches. Elders, overseers, and presidents followed. More and more, the overseer (Greek *episkopos)* appeared in authority over a compact administrative area, his *see.* This was the bishop, who became the key figure in church administration.

Each individual bishop presided over several churches. Each church was under the care of a priest (Greek *presbyteros,* elder), who had been qualified by special training and by the ceremony of ordination. The area served by each church and its priest came to be known as the parish. In the early church the office of deacon, often held by a man who had other occupations besides the service of the church, had much importance. In some of the early churches, the congregation itself elected its officers, and the church was governed by boards of elders (presbyteries). But the system of appointment from above won out over that of election, although the congregation was often consulted.

Before long, then, there was a clear distinction between those who were merely faithful worshipers (the laity) and those who conducted the worship and administered the affairs of the church (the clergy). Each episcopal see claimed to have been founded by one of the original apostles; and its bishop thus held office through "apostolic succession." Since it had been Christ himself who had chosen the apostles, every bishop, in effect, became a direct spiritual heir of Christ. Groups of bishoprics were often gathered together and owed obedience to an archbishop, a head overseer *(archiepiskopos).* Just as the bishop had his headquarters in a Roman *civitas,* or city-state unit, and exercised authority over the churches in the countryside roundabout, so the archbishop governed the *civitates* from a mother city, a *metropolis,* usually the capital of a Roman province, and his "see" was called a province.

At the top of the hierarchy stood the bishop of the imperial capital, Rome itself, the father of them all, *papa* or pope, who claimed supreme authority. The prestige of Rome contributed powerfully to his claim. So did the association of Peter and Paul with Rome. Christ had said to Peter, "Thou art Peter and upon this rock I will build my church," a pun in Greek, since the Greek word for Peter is *Petros* and that for rock *petra.* Because Peter had been martyred in Rome, the bishops of that city could claim that Christ himself had picked Rome as the rock upon which to build. The bishops of the great cities of the eastern Mediterranean, Alexandria and Antioch, however, claimed to exercise a paternal rule equal in authority to that of the pope. They called themselves patriarch (fatherly governor).

In 330, following Diocletian's example, Constantine left Rome for the East, choosing as his new capital the city of Byzantium on the straits between Europe and Asia. Renamed Constantinople—city of Constantine—it soon acquired enormous prestige. Its bishop, also a patriarch, would challenge both papal supremacy and the rival claims of Alexandria and Antioch.

With the departure of imperial government from Rome, the popes gradually made themselves more and more responsible for the government of the great city. And as Rome itself came under attack, the pope became the symbol of the old Roman self-confidence, a rock indeed. A succession of outstanding men became bishop of Rome.

Monasticism

Deacons, priests, bishops, archbishops, popes, all serve the laity of this world and are called *secular* clergy (Latin *saeculum,* "world"). Early in the history of the Church, however, another kind of devotee to Christianity appeared in Syria and Egypt. This was the monk, who felt that he must deny the urges of his own flesh and become an ascetic. Monks would leave civilization behind and go into the desert to live in solitude, meditation, and prayer, subsisting on the minimum of food and drink. By the third century, there were a good many of these hermits, who enjoyed reputations for extreme holiness and often competed wtih each other in torturing themselves or in self-denial. Some lived in trees or in holes in the ground, others on the tops of columns.

To keep the extreme ascetics from using the cloak of holiness to cover un-Christian self-assertion, certain leaders, such as Saint Anthony, early collected groups of monks around themselves and formed communities, living by a rule. The Greek saint, Basil (329–379), wrote the most famous of these rules, which became standard in the Mediterranean eastern (Greek) church and still regulates Greek monasticism today. Basil required celibacy and poverty but combatted the dangers of extreme asceticism by ruling that the monks work in the fields or elsewhere to make their communities as self-supporting as possible. After Basil, monks lived by a rule and are therefore called the *regular* clergy (Latin *regula,* "rule"), as contrasted with the secular clergy.

In the West the problem was later met by the rule of Saint Benedict, who founded the great abbey at Monte Cassino in southern Italy about

From a Coptic monastery in Egypt: the Virgin and saints.

529. His Latin rule, like Basil's Greek rule, required hard work for all and urged the monks to try to be tolerant of each other's interests and weaknesses. In the West particularly, the monks broke new ground around their monasteries, acted as pioneers in opening up the wilderness, performed missionary service among the still unconverted heathen tribes, and did much charitable and medical work among the poor and the sick. In both East and West, scholarship early became one of the recognized occupations for monks. The *scribes,* writing monks, copied the works of the ancients and built up the monastic libraries, preserving the literature of the past.

Constant care and strict government were needed to maintain the high ideals of the monasteries and of the convents for women that soon appeared. This continuing need led to one reform movement after another, which played a major role in Christian history.

Heresy

The early centuries of Christianity saw a series of struggles to define the accepted teachings (doctrines) of true religion—*orthodoxy*—and to protect them against the challenge of rival ideas—*heresy.* It is often hard for us to understand how much seemingly trivial issues generated such heat. We must remind ourselves that all Christians believed that their future salvation depended upon proper religious belief and proper religious practice. Bitter political, economic, and national issues often underlay disputes that took a religious form.

Gnostics and Manichaeans

For example, how can evil exist (as it obviously does) in a world created by a good God? The Gnostics believed that only the world of the spirit is real (and good). The physical world is evil or an evil illusion. Gnostics could not accept the Old Testament, whose God created this world. They regarded him as a fiend or taught that this world had been created by Satan. Nor could they accept Jesus' human life and work in this world, an essential part of Christian belief. This sharp distinction between the evil present world and the good world of the spirit is often called *dualist.* Clearly heretical, the Gnostics emphasized Christ's miracle-working and magic. Among them, an elite led especially pure lives, while the ordinary flock, less able to bear self-denial, worked hard to support the elite.

Closely related to Gnosticism were the dualistic ideas of Mani, a third-century Mesopotamian prophet who preached that the god of light and goodness was in constant conflict with the god of darkness, evil, and matter. During the third and fourth centuries, these Manichaean views became immensely popular, especially along the North African shores of the Mediterranean. The Roman emperors and the Christian Church combatted them. Throughout the Middle Ages, Christians tended to label all heretics *Manichaean.* Dualist ideas persisted, more or less underground, and cropped up every few decades for a thousand years or more.

Donatists and Arians

Within Christianity itself, heresy sometimes involved very practical problems. The so-called Donatist movement in North Africa, for example, arose because, during the Roman persecutions of the Christians, a number of priests had lacked the courage for martyrdom and had instead handed over the sacred Christian books to the Roman authorities. After the persecutions had come to an end, these "handers-over" *(traditores)* had resumed their role as priests. Donatus, bishop of Carthage, and his followers maintained that the sacraments administered by such a *traditor* were invalid.

It is easy to understand Donatus' wish to punish weakling priests. But once a Christian suspected the validity of the sacraments as received from one priest, he might suspect it as received from any other. Amidst much bitterness and violence, the Emperor Constantine finally ruled that if a priest had been properly ordained, the sacraments he administered had validity even if the priest had himself acted badly.

Heresy also arose over essentially philosophical issues. Early in the fourth century, Arius, a priest of Alexandria, declared that, since God the Father had begotten God the Son (through God the Holy Ghost), God the Son, as begotten, could not have exactly the same *essence* as God the Father but must be somehow inferior to, or dependent upon, or at least later in time than his begetter. Logical argument alone cannot show that Arius was wrong. But Arius' argument threatened to belittle the divinity of Christ as God the Son and to separate Christ from the Trinity.

Arius' bitter opponent, Athanasius, bishop of Alexandria, fought him passionately. Athanasius saw that Christians simply had to take it as a matter of faith that Father and Son are identical in essence and that the Son is equal to, independent of, and contemporaneous with the Father. Even though the Father begat the Son, it is heresy to say that there was ever a time when the Son did not exist. In the Greek East, this philosophical argument was fought out not only among churchmen and thinkers but in the barbershops and among the longshoremen. The fact that most people did not understand what they were talking about did not prevent their rioting against their opponents.

After trying hard to stay out of the quarrel, Constantine realized that as emperor, he would have to intervene. In 325, he summoned and presided over the first council of the whole Church, a council called ecumenical (from the Greek *oikoumene,* "the inhabited world"), at Nicaea, across the straits from Constantinople. A large majority of the bishops decided against Arius. Their anti-Arian view was then embodied in the famous Nicene Creed, issued with all the force of an imperial decree by Constantine himself. Against his will, Constantine found himself assuming the role of head of the Church, giving legal sanction to a purely doctrinal decision, and so playing the role both of caesar and of pope. This "caesaropapism," in fact, became the tradition of empire and Church in the East.

But the decree of Nicaea did not dispose of Arianism. Arians disobeyed. Constantine himself wavered, and his immediate successors on the imperial throne were Arians. Between 325 and 381, there were thirteen more councils that discussed the problem, deciding first one way, then another. A pagan historian commented that one could no longer travel on the roads because they were so cluttered up with throngs of bishops riding off to one council or another. Traces of Arianism remained within the empire for several centuries after Nicaea. Moreover, because the missionary Ulfilas preached the Arian form of Christianity to the barbarian Goths beyond the frontiers, the Germanic peoples usually became Arians.

Constantine's acceptance of Christianity and his deep involvement in the problems of the Christian Church marked a major change in the nature of the Roman Empire, further emphasized by his shift of the imperial capital to Constantinople. A westerner himself, Constantine had not intended to abandon the West, and he and his immediate successors were in practice still rulers of the whole Roman world. But barbarian pressure soon made continued unity impossible.

READING SUGGESTIONS on The World of the Romans
(Asterisk indicates paperback.)

General Surveys

A. E. R. Boak and W. G. Sinningen, *A History of Rome to A.D. 565* (1965). A standard textbook.

C. E. Robinson, *The Apollo History of Rome* (*Apollo). A useful, briefer introductory account.

M. Grant, *The World of Rome* (1960). Brilliant and thoughtful, with fine illustrations.

R. H. Barrow, *The Romans* (*Penguin). More popular than the above, but sound.

D. R. Dudley, *The Romans: 850 B.C.–A.D.* 337 (1970). Within the precise time limits of this chapter, provides a survey that emphasizes daily life and manners rather than political developments.

The Etruscan Background and the Roman Republic

M. Pallottino, *The Etruscans* (*Penguin). Anyone who begins with this work can pursue the subject as far as scholars have taken it.

R. Block, *The Origins of Rome* (1960). The republic to the early fifth century B.C.

H. H. Scullard, *History of the Roman World from 753 B.C. to 146 B.C.* (*University Paperbacks). Detailed and very sound. A fine question-answering book.

B. H. Warmington, *Carthage* (*Penguin). The best work on the subject.

E. Badian, *Roman Imperialism in the Late Republic* (1968): Many new reassessments of the subject. Not for beginners, but absolutely first rate.

T. G. E. Powell, *The Celts* (1963). Useful but not well written.

H. H. Scullard, *From the Gracchi to Nero: A History of Rome from 133 B.C. to A.D. 68* (*Barnes and Noble). The fall of the republic and the early years of the empire.

L. R. Taylor, *Party Politics in the Age of Caesar* (*California). How did Roman politics actually work? This book analyzes the question as well as describes the details.

F. R. Cowell, *Cicero and the Roman Republic* (*Penguin). The best introduction to this aspect of the subject.

The Roman Empire

R. Syme, *The Roman Revolution* (*Oxford). How Augustus transformed the republic. A fine study by a leading scholar.

M. P. Charlesworth, *The Roman Empire* (*Galaxy). A useful survey.

F. E. Adcock, *Roman Political Ideas and Practices* (*Michigan). How and why the Roman political system worked.

F. Millar, *The Emperor in the Roman World* (1977). A massive, brilliant, and controversial study concentrating on what the emperors actually did and on their relationship with their subjects. Not easy reading, but of major importance.

S. Perowne, *Hadrian* (1960). Well-written modern biography.

A. Birley, *Marcus Aurelius* (1966). Valuable study of a most interesting emperor.

T. W. Africa, *Rome of the Caesars* (1965). Vivid biographical sketches of important Romans.

J. Carcopino, *Daily Life in Ancient Rome* (*Bantam). This well-known work comes closer than any other single book to showing what Roman life was really like.

Roman Civilization

E. Hamilton, *The Roman Way* (*Norton). A useful brief survey, but the author prefers the Greeks to the Romans. Based largely on literature.

H. Mattingly, *Roman Civilization* (*Anchor). A similar general work, but based largely on the study of coins.

H. J. Rose, *Religion in Greece and Rome* (*Harper Torchbooks). A good handbook.

M. S. W. Laistner, *The Greater Roman Historians* (*California). Sound study of the subject.

M. Hadas, *History of Latin Literature* (*Columbia); and H. J. Rose, *Handbook of Latin Literature* (*Dutton). Two good introductions, the first less factual and detailed.

H. J. Marrou, *History of Education in Antiquity* (*Mentor). A fine scholarly work on the subject.

M. Wheeler, *Roman Art and Architecture* (*Penguin). Perhaps the best place to start an investigation of the subject. Well illustrated.

F. E. Brown, *Roman Architecture* (*Braziller). A fine study, more advanced than the preceding one.

Roman Decline

Peter Brown, *The World of Late Antiquity, A.D. 150–750* (*Harcourt Brace Jovanovich). An excellent book, full of new insights and beautifully written.

M. Rostovtzeff, *The Social and Economic History of the Roman Empire* (1957). A famous and very important book, splendidly illustrated. Speculates on the reasons for the Roman decline from the point of view of a survivor of the Russian Revolution of 1917. Not for beginners.

D. Kagan, *Decline and Fall of the Roman Empire* (*Heath); and M. Chambers, *The Fall of Rome: Can It Be Explained?* (*Holt). Two collections of writings by modern scholars discussing the central problem of Rome's decline.

H. D. M. Parker, *History of the Roman World from A.D. 138 to 337* (1958). All the political details.

Mystery Religions

F. Cumont, *Oriental Religions in Roman Paganism* (*Dover). By the greatest authority on the subject.

R. E. Witt, *Isis in the Greco-Roman World* (1971). A first-rate study with good illustrations.

R. T. Wallis, *Neo-Platonism* (1972). The best introduction to a difficult subject.

Early Christianity

Henry Chadwick, *The Early Church* (*Penguin). General introduction by a renowned scholar.

E. Schürer, *History of the Jewish People in the Time of Jesus* (*Schocken). An excellent introductory work.

W. H. C. Frend, *Martyrdom and Persecution in the Early Church* (*Anchor). The best single work on the subject.

M. Burrows, *The Dead Sea Scrolls* (1955). Perhaps the best introduction to the subject.

A. H. M. Jones, *Constantine and the Conversion of Europe* (*Toronto). The best single short treatment of Constantine's conversion and its motives and consequences.

Sources

M. Lewis and M. Reinhold, eds., *Roman Civilization,* 2 vols. (*Harper Torchbooks). A fine, generous selection of sources in translation with good editorial commentary.

B. Davenport, ed., *The Portable Roman Reader* (*Viking). A useful anthology.

Vergil, *The Aeneid,* trans. R. Humphries (*Scribner's). A good modern translation.

Tacitus, *On Britain and Germany,* trans. H. Mattingly; *The Annals of Imperial Rome,* trans. Michael Grant (both *Penguin).

Lucretius, *On the Nature of Things,* trans. R. E. Latham (*Penguin).

Pliny the Younger, *Letters,* trans. B. Radice (*Penguin).

Marcus Aurelius, *Meditations* (many editions).

The New Testament. The best source for early Christianity.

Eusebius, *History of the Church from Christ to Constantine* (*Penguin). By a fourth-century bishop who knew Constantine personally.

CHAPTER FOUR

Transition Between Two Worlds:

To The Year 1000

The Roman world, we have seen, held together all the lands on the shores of the Mediterranean despite their widely varying earlier political experience and cultural traditions. We have traced the history of Roman domination through periods of strength and weakness and strength again to the time of Constantine. By his day the unity of the Roman world had already become something of a fiction. And after him the unity was shattered.

Historians have puzzled about the reasons for the decline and fall of the Roman Empire as much, perhaps, as about any problem in human history. Some have tried to find the cause in changing climatic conditions. Some stress economic and social factors, pointing to inflation and a loss of purchasing power caused by the concentration of lands into big private estates and the enfeeblement of the independent farmer. Some point to the decline of patriotism, as the old citizen army was replaced by mercenary troops. Some have argued that psychologically the masses were alienated from their rulers. The great eighteenth-century English historian, Edward

Gibbon, blamed everything on Christianity, arguing that the new faith turned man's attention to his future salvation and took his mind off his duties to the state. But none of these suggestions alone or all together will do. What was really new in the fourth century was the mass movements of barbarian peoples against and over the Rhine-Danube frontiers of the Roman world.

The ancient Greeks, who took enormous pride in their language, scorned anybody who could not speak it. Listening with contempt to such lesser human beings talking, the Greeks thought it sounded like "bar-bar-bar." So they coined the word *barbaros* for all non-Greek-speakers, with all its connotations of savagery that we still imply when we say "barbarian."

During his campaigns in Gaul, Julius Caesar once built a bridge across the Rhine to enter German territory and punish the tribesmen. In 9 A.D. as we know, Arminius (Herman the German) defeated Augustus' legions. Tacitus lectured his fellow Romans on the contrast between German toughness and Roman softness, and his account of German tribal life is the fullest we have before they actually broke through the frontier in the fourth century. We have noted their victory over Decius, whom they killed in 252. In the generation after Constantine's death, they overflowed into the empire. We must now come to grips with them.

This chapter begins with an account of their invasions and settlements in Roman territory, the foundation of their own kingdoms, and the impact of this process on the Roman world down to about the year 1,000. It was the western territories of Rome that suffered most. During these centuries the West was transformed into a wholly different kind of society. Rome itself was twice taken and destroyed by barbarian tribes (410 and 455). And in 476, the last of the western Roman Emperors, Romulus Augustulus (meaning the miniature Augustus) was dethroned by his barbarian protector, Odovacar. This date has traditionally been chosen as the end of the Western Roman Empire. But in fact the event was hardly noticed at the time, since Western imperial power had been shattered long before. The second part of this chapter discusses the new political and social arrangements that in the West replaced those imposed by Rome, and in the third we examine the civilization of the new Western world as it came into existence.

In the East, however, Roman imperial power at Constantinople continued without interruption for more than a thousand years after Constantine died. This later Roman Empire, often called Byzantine, developed its own characteristic politics and society, very different from that of the now barbarian West. Yet, like the West, it was also a descendant of Rome. In the fourth section of this chapter, we discuss Byzantium and the distinctive civilization and ways of life that developed there down to the eleventh century. We take special note of the Byzantine christianization of the Bulgarians and Russians.

And in the final section, we turn to the new religion of Islam, beginning in Arabia in the 600s. The Arabs, who were the first Muslims, within a century conquered large portions of the Roman and Persian Empires and swept into Europe, directly affecting both the Western and the Eastern portions of the Roman Empire. Together with Roman Catholic Christian Western Europe and Greek Orthodox Christian Eastern Europe, Muslim Spain, North Africa, Arabia, and the Near East formed the third of the major civilizations of the world between the fourth and the eleventh centuries.

I THE BARBARIAN ONSLAUGHT

The Barbarians

Indo-European in language, like the Greeks, the Romans, and the Celts, the Germans began early in ancient times to migrate southward from the shores of the Baltic Sea. When the Romans first began to write about them, they were already divided into tribes. One group of Germanic tribes, the Goths, settled on the north side of the Danube boundary in Romania and the neighboring plains of southern Russia.

In the fourth century, conditions in central Asia (about which we know little) drove a fierce Asian nomad people, the Huns, into the territory of the Goths. Living on horseback for days, traveling swiftly and massacring their victims, the Huns started a panic among the Goths and other tribes. The shock waves, beginning in the last half of the fourth century, continued throughout the fifth and into the sixth.

Barbarian penetration was not always violent. Often it consisted of slower and more peaceful infiltration lasting over long periods. Many individual barbarians joined the Romans, often rising to high positions defending the old empire against their fellow barbarians. The Romanized barbarian became as familiar a figure as the barbarized Roman.

Visigoths, Vandals, Anglo-Saxons

Fleeing the Huns, one tribe of Goths, the Visigoths, or West Goths, asked for permission to cross the Danube and settle in Roman territory in modern Bulgaria. The Roman border guards mistreated them. Resentful and desperate, the Goths poured into imperial territory only a few miles from Constantinople. In the year 378, at Adrianople, the Goths defeated the Roman legions of the Emperor Valens, who was killed in battle. More and more Goths now freely entered the empire.

Unable to take Constantinople or other fortified towns, they proceeded south into the Balkans, ravaged Greece, including Athens, and then marched north again around the head of the Adriatic and south into Italy. In 410 came their sensational sack of Rome itself, which stirred up a whole literature mournfully asking how it could have happened. The Visigoths' leader Alaric died soon afterwards and his successors led them north across the Alps into Gaul, and then south again across the Pyrenees into Spain.

Here after their long wanderings, the Visigoths founded a Spanish kingdom that would last until the Muslim invasions of the seventh century. As Arians, the Visigoths had some difficulty in ruling the orthodox Christians among their subjects.

Another Arian German tribe, the Vandals, crossed the Rhine westward into Gaul and in 411 settled in southern Spain. Invited across to North Africa to help the Roman governor revolt, they seized it for themselves in 429. In their new capital, Carthage, they built a fleet, raided Italy, and ruthlessly sacked Rome itself in 455. The term "vandalism" is still in use.

Under pressure on the Continent, the Romans early in the fifth century began to withdraw their legions from Britain. Germanic tribes from across the North Sea filtered into the gap. These Angles, Saxons, and Jutes were still heathen. In England they conquered the Celtic Britons and founded seven Anglo-Saxon kingdoms, of which Northumbria and Mercia became the most important. Scotland and Wales remained Celtic, as of course did Ireland, which was converted to Christianity in the fifth century by Catholic missionaries from Gaul.

Ireland escaped the first great wave of barbarian invasions, and its Celtic church promoted learning and art. By the end of the sixth century, Catholic Christianity was moving into England both from Celtic Ireland and from Rome. The differences between the two were mostly matters of practice, such as the determination of the date of Easter, and. though hotly debated, these questions were eventually settled.

Bronze Irish crucifix, ca. 750.

Huns, Ostrogoths

The Asian Huns themselves joined the onslaught on Roman territories. Early in the fifth century, they established a state in East Central Europe and ruled over a large collection of German and other tribes. The Hunnic rulers extracted tribute money from the Roman emperors at Constantinople. Under Attila they crossed the Rhine into Gaul, where a Roman general defeated them (Châlons, 451). The next year Pope Leo the Great (440–461) in person persuaded Attila to withdraw from Italy without attacking Rome. Like many nomad empires, that of the Huns fell apart after the death of the conquering founder (453). But other related Asian peoples, nomads and pagans like the Huns, and Mongol in appearance, repeatedly entered Europe before the age of the barbarian invasions was over: Avars in the sixth century, Bulgars in the sixth and seventh, and Magyars, or Hungarians, in the ninth.

The collapse of the Hunnic Empire liberated the Germanic Ostrogoths (East Goths), who were Arian Christians. In the service of Zeno, the eastern emperor, the Ostrogothic King Theodoric, who had been educated in Constantinople and admired the Roman tradition, took his people to Italy. For most of his long rule there (489–526) Theodoric was content to serve the eastern emperors as a kind of governor of Italy, with his

Early eighth-century relief of a German warrior.

capital at Ravenna. He hoped to civilize his own people so that they would be true assimilated Romans. But the popes and the Italians generally regarded the Goths as foreign heretics. Theodoric ran out of time. And toward the end of his reign he grew suspicious and hostile to the emperors at Constantinople.

Many other barbarian peoples participated in the breakup of Roman territory and power in the West during the fifth and sixth centuries, but failed to found any lasting state. There were two other German tribes, however, whose achievements are still remembered. The Burgundians moved into the valleys of the Rhône and Saône rivers in the 440s and gave their name to a succession of "Burgundies," varying in territory and government. The Franks, from whom modern France itself derives its name, founded the most lasting kingdom of any of the Germanic tribes.

Franks

Gradually expanding from their native territory on the lower Rhine, the Franks eventually created an empire including most of western Europe except for Spain and Britain. Clovis (reigned 481–511), descendant of the Merovingian house (from Merwig or Merovech), defeated a Roman army (486) and the Visigoths of Aquitainé (Vouillé, 507). Much of modern France and northwest Germany and the Low Countries thus became Frankish.

Clovis owed his success partly to the fact that the Franks made no long migration but remained near their old German home, a source of reinforcements. Moreover, Clovis was converted to Christianity not as an Arian heretic but as an orthodox Catholic. This gave him the instant support of the clergy of Gaul. The Franks' great weakness was their habit of dividing up the kingdom between the king's sons in every generation. This led to a constant parceling out of territory into petty kingdoms and lordships, and to constant intrigues and bloody rivalries among royal relatives striving to reunite the lands.

By the end of the seventh century, the Merovingian kings became so degenerate that they are known as *rois fainéants* (do-nothing kings). Real powers had been delegated to their chief officials, the "mayors of the palace." By the eighth century one particular family had made this office hereditary from father to son—the Carolingians (from

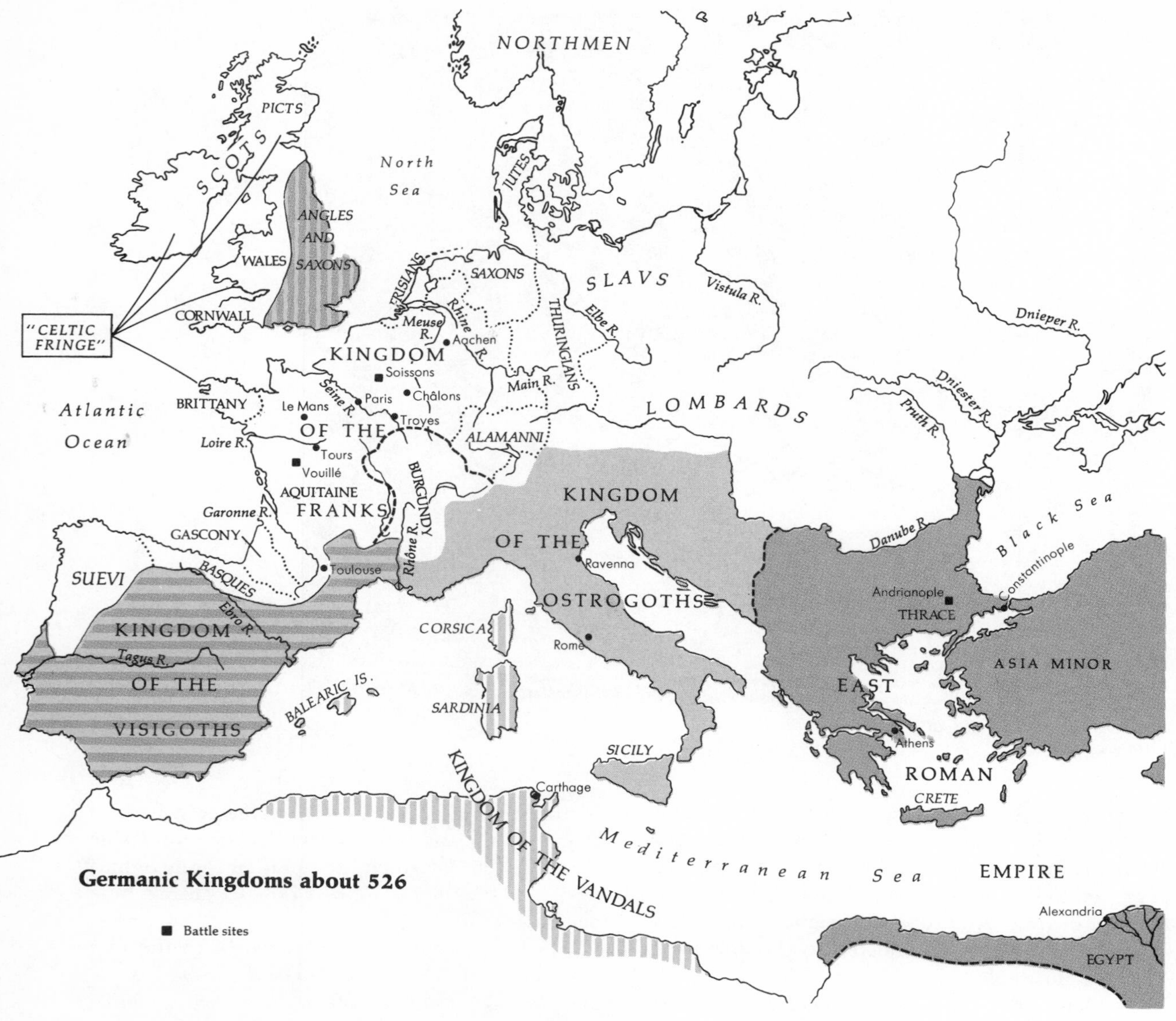

Germanic Kingdoms about 526

Carolus, Latin for Charles). One of the mayors, Charles (reigned 714–741), called Martel, "the hammer," in 732 near Tours defeated a band of Muslims that had been raiding northward from Spain. Since Tours was the farthest north in Europe that the Muslims ever came, the battle is a landmark in Western history.

Charles Martel's son, Pepin the Short (reigned 741–768), ended the Merovingian line. He assumed the title "king of the Franks." During his reign the Anglo-Saxon monk, Boniface, who came to the continent as a missionary to convert the heathens, became Archbishop. He reformed and reorganized the entire Frankish church, improved the moral behavior of the clergy, and made the church influential among all classes of laymen. Boniface was killed in 754, having resumed his missionary efforts. King Pepin also embarked on an adventurous policy with regard to Italy that opened a new chapter in Western history.

Italy from Theodoric to Pepin

Soon after the death of Theodoric, the eastern emperor Justinian (527–565) launched from Constantinople an ambitious effort to reconquer the major areas of the West that had been lost to the barbarians. He first overthrew the Vandals and then invaded Italy from Carthage. For almost twenty years (535–554), Justinian's troops fought the Ostrogoths. The towns and countryside of

Italy were depopulated, and the survivors reduced to misery. Justinian's proclamation of an imperial restoration (554) was hollow. In the same year, imperial forces took a portion of southern Spain from the Visigoths.

Only three years after Justinian's death, a new Germanic tribe, the Arian Lombards, entered Italy (568) from the north. They conquered the north Italian plain that still bears their name (Lombardy) and established a kingdom with its capital at Pavia. Further to the south, they set up two duchies (Benevento and Spoleto). Italy lay once again in fragments. The emperor at Constantinople continued to control Ravenna, the island settlement of Venice, Rome, southern Italy, and Sicily. The emperor appointed a governor called the *exarch* who had headquarters at Ravenna.

But dangers from the east threatened the emperors, and they often could not afford to send money and troops to help the exarchs fight the Lombards. The Church, therefore, emerged as the protector of the Catholic population, the bishops often acting virtually as governors in their sees. Among the bishops, the pope of course took the lead, and among the popes, the most remarkable in every way was Gregory I, the Great (reigned 590–604).

Child of a rich and aristocratic Roman family, Gregory abandoned worldly things and became a monk and founder of monasteries. His administrative talents were extraordinary. He

A thirteenth-century fresco, depicting the Donation of Constantine.

served as papal ambassador to the court at Constantinople before becoming pope in 590. As pope, he took responsibility for maintaining the fortifications of Rome, for feeding its population, for managing the great financial resources of the Church and its lands in Italy, for conducting diplomatic negotiations with exarchate and Lombards, and even for directing military operations. He sent to Britain (596) the missionaries who began the conversion of the Anglo-Saxons. In his letters to the emperor and to the patriarch at Constantinople, Gregory stoutly defended papal supremacy over the Church.

During the seventh and early eighth centuries, the bad feeling between the empire in the East and the papacy was greatly increased by religious disagreements and by related political and economic disputes. The Lombards also consolidated and expanded their power, taking Ravenna in 751 and putting an end to the exarchate. Menaced by the Lombards and unable to count on help from Constantinople, Pope Stephen II in 753 paid a visit to Pepin, the new King of the Franks.

In exchange for papal approval of his royal authority, Pepin forced the Lombards to abandon Ravenna and other recent conquests. Then he gave these lands to the pope, as the "Donation of Pepin." Together with Rome itself and the lands immediately around it, the Donation of Pepin formed the territory over which the pope ruled as sovereign down to the nineteenth century. These were the Papal States, and the Vatican City is their present-day remnant. Pepin's son, Charles the Great (Charlemagne), destroyed the Lombard kingdom in 774 and assumed the Iron Crown of Lombardy.

From the papal point of view, the new alliance with the Franks marked the real beginning of the papacy as a worldly (temporal) power. Soon after Pepin's donation, some clerk in the papal secretariat forged "proof" that Pepin had only been confirming a gift of lands to the Church made long ago by the emperor Constantine. The forgery added that Constantine himself declared that the papal power, as divine, was superior to his own imperial power, which was only earthly; that the see of Peter should rule over the other sees (including Antioch, Alexandria, and Constantinople); and that the pope alone could decide all questions of faith. For about seven hundred years, until the Italian Renaissance scholar Lorenzo Valla (see Chapter 7) proved it a forgery, men believed that this extraordinary "Donation of Constantine" was a genuine document.

Charlemagne and His Successors

Pepin's son, Charlemagne (768–814), was a vigorous, lusty, intelligent man who loved hunting, women, and war. All his life he wore Frankish costume and thought of himself as a Frankish chieftain. Although he kept pen and ink under his pillow, he could never teach himself how to write. He spoke and read Latin, however, and understood some Greek. A great conqueror, Charlemagne crossed the Rhine. In campaigns lasting more than thirty years, he conquered the heathen Saxons living south of Denmark, and converted them at sword's point to Christianity. Monks and priests followed his armies.

This was the first successful invasion of Germany, home of the barbarians who had shattered Roman society in the West, and began Germany's slow assimilation to Western civilization. Charlemagne also took over the western part of modern Czechoslovakia (Bohemia), much of Austria, and portions of Hungary and Yugoslavia. His eastern boundaries reached the Elbe River and the Danube, where it turns sharply south below Vienna. Here he established frontier provinces (marks or marches). Far to the west, he challenged Muslim power in Spain and set up a Spanish march in what is today Catalonia. A defeat of his rear guard at the pass of Roncesvalles in the Pyrenees in 778 formed the theme of the heroic epic *The Song of Roland (Chanson de Roland)*, composed several centuries later.

By the end of the eighth century, Charlemagne had reunited under Frankish domination

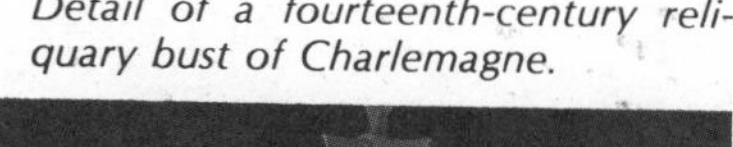

Detail of a fourteenth-century reliquary bust of Charlemagne.

This restored eighth-century mosaic from St. John Lateran shows Saint Peter conferring symbols of spiritual authority and temporal power on Pope Leo III and Charlemagne.

all of the Western Roman provinces except for Britain, most of Spain, south Italy, Sicily, and North Africa. He ruled central and eastern European areas that the Romans had never possessed. On Christmas Day, 800, the pope himself, Leo III, crowned Charlemagne emperor in Rome. So mighty was the tradition of Roman empire and so great its hold on the human mind that, more than three centuries after the disappearance of Romulus Augustulus, a pope who wanted to honor and recognize a mighty Frankish patron automatically crowned him emperor of Rome. Even before the coronation, a poet in Charlemagne's own circle had hailed him as "Augustus."

Charlemagne himself probably relished his title, but he almost surely disliked the implication that the pope had the right to choose and crown emperors. The true successors of Augustus, the Roman emperors at Constantinople, were horrified at the insolence of the barbarian Charlemagne in assuming the sacred title.

Within his territories Charlemagne was, by virtue of his consecration, a sacred ruler, with spiritual rights and duties as well as temporal ones. His lofty concept of his office and his personal power enabled him to govern the Church—even in matters of doctrine—more in the style of Constantine or other Eastern emperors than any other Western monarch. In 813, he named Louis the Pious, by then his only living son, his successor. The pope had no part in the ceremonies. Only the accidental deaths of Charlemagne's other sons prevented a standard Frankish division of the heritage.

Charlemagne's government was very simple. The king's personal household staff were also the government officials: the chamberlain, the count of the stable (constable), and so on. On major decisions the emperor conferred with great nobles of state and church, but he told them what he (and they) were going to do rather than asking them for advice and permission. Since the Franks, like other Germans, believed that law *existed* and could not be made by men, even Charlemagne could not in theory legislate. But he did issue instructions to his subjects. These were divided into subheadings or chapters (and therefore called *capitularies*) and usually dealt with special administrative problems, such as the education of the clergy. Charlemagne also enforced the general payment by everyone of a ten percent income tax (a tithe) to the church. It was a highly personal rule.

Charlemagne's territories included about three hundred counties, each governed by a count. The counties in former Roman territory corresponded to the lands of a former civitas. The count had to maintain order, render justice, and recruit and command soldiers. The bishop of each diocese and the various local magnates had considerable powers of their own on their own lands. Only a powerful king could keep the local authorities from seizing too much power.

A capitulary set the limits to the powers of the counts. They had to appoint teams of judges, called *scabini,* whose appointment Charlemagne would then ratify, and who would take over much of the count's role in rendering justice. Charlemagne also sent out pairs of royal emissaries (the *missi dominici*), usually a layman and a cleric, to investigate local conditions and correct abuses. As direct representatives of the emperor, they could overrule the count.

The Carolingian Empire depended too much upon Charlemagne personally. He had assembled more territory than could be effectively governed. Administrative machinery and communications had fallen apart since Roman days. Under Charlemagne's less talented successors, the old Frankish habit of dividing up lands and authority among the heirs to the throne reasserted itself. Quarrels over the allotment of territory raged among brothers and cousins. The title of emperor descended to a single heir in each generation, but as early as the middle of the ninth century it had become an empty honor.

In 842, when Charlemagne's three grandsons were at war, two of them, Charles the Bald and Louis the German, swore an alliance against the third, Lothair. Each swore at Strasbourg in the language of the other's troops, Louis in a Latinlike language on its way to becoming French, and Charles in Germanic. In 842, there was still no France or Germany. Yet the western and eastern Frankish lands already spoke divergent tongues. These Strasbourg oaths are symbolic of future French-German hostility. In the ninth century, instead of coming together in large national units, the Frankish dominions were breaking up into much smaller ones.

The power of the central Frankish state was frittered away in family squabbles. The old local territorial units, duchies and counties, often going back to the late Roman days, now became much more independent. Duchies or counties would often become hereditary, making dukes and counts very powerful,—kings in all but name. Many of their names are still attached to provinces of modern France or Germany: Champagne, Brittany, Saxony, Bavaria.

Europe and the Northmen

Still outside the area of Western civilization lay Scandinavia. In the ninth century there began a new wave of Scandinavian invasions that hit Britain and the western parts of the Frankish lands with savage force. The Northmen arrived in small ships that could easily sail up the Thames, the Seine, or the Loire. Their appetite for booty grew. (Polygamy was common among the northmen, and probably the younger sons often had to leave home.)

Soon they organized fleets of several hundred ships, ventured further abroad, and often wintered along a conquered coast. They ranged as far south as Spain, penetrated into the Mediterranean through the Straits of Gibraltar, and raided Italy. To the west they proceeded far beyond Ireland, and reached Iceland and Greenland. Some probably got as far as Canada or New England.

In 911, the Frankish king was forced to grant the Norse leader Rolf (or Rollo) a permanent right of settlement in the region along the lower Seine River, which is still called Normandy after these Northmen. Here the Normans became an efficient and powerful ruling class, the best administrators of the new "feudal" age. From Normandy soon after the year 1000, younger sons went off to found a flourishing state in the southern Italian

SCANDINAVIA
North Sea
KINGDOM OF DENMARK
Baltic Sea
IRELAND
SCOTLAND
NORTHUMBRIA
Whitby
ANGLO-SAXON KINGDOMS
WALES
MERCIA
EAST ANGLIA
ESSEX
CORNWALL
WESSEX
London
Canterbury
SUSSEX
KENT
SAXONS
Elbe R.
Oder R.
Cologne
Aachen
Rhine R.
Seine R.
Soissons
Verdun
Paris
BRITTANY
BOHEMIA
SLAVS
MORAVIA
Strasbourg
Danube R.
Loire R.
Fontenoy
BAVARIA
PANNONIAN MARCH
Poitiers
Besançon
CARINTHIA
AVARS
Geneva
MARCH OF FRIULI
AQUITAINE
Lyons
BURGUNDY
Drava R.
LOMBARDY
Po R.
Pavia
Venice
Rhône R.
Danube R.
BULGARS
CROATS
Roncesvalles
Ravenna
Arles
DONATION OF PEPIN
Spalato
Marseilles
SPANISH MARCH
Ebro R.
Adriatic Sea
SLAVIC PEOPLES
THRACE
Constantinople
CORSICA
Barcelona
EMIRATE OF CORDOVA
Rome
Monte Cassino
Thessalonica
DUCHY OF BENEVENTO
Naples
SARDINIA
BALEARIC IS.
BYZANTINE EMPIRE
SICILY
CRETE
Mediterranean Sea
KINGDOM OF LOUIS
KINGDOM OF CHARLES THE BALD
KINGDOM OF LOTHAIR
Partition of the Empire by the Treaty of Verdun, 843
Carolingian Empire
Kingdom of Charlemagne, 768
Acquired by Charlemagne to 814
Areas tributary to Charlemagne's empire
Byzantine Empire
Battle sites

An early tenth-century Irish sculptured cross, "the Muireadach Cross."

and Sicilian territories that still belonged to the Eastern Roman Empire. From Normandy in 1066 Duke William and his followers conquered England.

Other Northmen in the 860s crossed the Baltic Sea to the territory that is now Russia, and penetrated deep inland to the south along the river valleys. They conquered the native Slavic tribes. At Kiev on the middle Dnieper, they consolidated the first Russian state (see p. 127).

About the same time, the Danes seized the Irish ports and coasts. The Celtic inhabitants fought back fiercely and eventually assimilated the Danes, but the brilliance of Irish culture had suffered a fatal interruption. In England, too, the Danes seized all the Anglo-Saxon kingdoms except Wessex, whose king, Alfred the Great (871–899), defeated them but could not drive them out. They occupied the whole northeast of England, a region thereafter called the *Danelaw.*

Far more advanced at this stage than the Danes, the Anglo-Saxon kingdom was governed through the royal household and clerical staff. The king's great council, the *witenagemot,* made up of important landholders, churchmen, and officials, advised him on request, acted as a law court, and elected and deposed kings. The king collected revenue from his own estates and from a special tax imposed for defense against the Danes, called the *Danegeld.* He also received two-thirds of all the fines imposed by local courts. His army was the old Germanic host *(fyrd),* in which every landholder was obliged to serve, but he also had additional household troops. Anglo-Saxon government in the tenth century was not very different from that of the Franks before Charlemagne or of any settled Germanic tribe.

Soon after the year 1000, new waves of Danes attacked England. In 1016, Canute (Knut), king of Denmark and Norway, was chosen king of England by the Anglo-Saxon witenagemot. Ruler of a northern empire, Canute allied himself with the Roman church and brought Scandinavia into the Christian community. His early death (1035) without competent heirs led to the breakup of his holdings, and England reverted to a king of the house of Alfred (Edward the Confessor). When the raiding stopped and settlement began, the Northmen everywhere proved able governors.

Carolingian Decline

By the end of the ninth century, the power of the Carolingians in their German territories had dwindled away in the face of domestic challenges from ambitious local magnates and foreign threats from Norsemen, Slavs, and Asian Magyars, who poured into the Hungarian plain in the mid-890s. When the last Carolingian ruler died in 911, the German magnates elected the duke of Franconia as King Conrad I (911–918). The most important units in Germany became the duchies—Franconia, Saxony, Swabia, and Bavaria—each under its autonomous ruler. Conrad I nominated his strongest enemy, Henry, duke of Saxony, to succeed him. Henry's son, Otto I (936–973), checked the rival dukes and defeated the Magyars (Lechfeld, 955).

Master of his German territories, and supported by powerful Churchmen, Otto next sought to revive the title of emperor, which had lapsed in 924. Deep in decline now, the papacy had fallen into the hands of rival Roman noble families, corrupt, wicked, and incompetent.

A French manuscript illumination of the eleventh century, showing Otto I receiving the homage of the nations.

Without a strong central administration, Italy had become anarchic. Yet even at its lowest depths in the mid-tenth century, Rome continued to act as an irresistible magnet for those seeking supreme power.

Like Charlemagne almost two hundred years before him, Otto went to Italy. He had himself crowned by the degenerate and dissipated Pope John XII (962). Then he had John deposed for murder and installed his own candidate on the papal throne. He forced the Roman aristocracy to promise that imperial consent would hereafter be necessary to papal elections, and renewed the Donation of Pepin and the later grants of the Carolingians to the papacy. For the next hundred years, the papacy was hardly more than a tool of Otto's German successors. Yet Otto's action ensured the continuity of the papacy as an independent institution. It also tightly linked the political fortunes of Germany and Italy for centuries to come.

In the western Frankish lands, which we may now call France, Carolingian strife and feebleness led to the fragmentation of both territory and power among ambitious landowners. As early as 887 one faction of these magnates chose a non-Carolingian, Odo, count of Paris, as king. For the next century his family and the Carolingians alternated in power. Finally, in 987 the magnates elected as king Odo's descendant, Hugh Capet, who founded a dynasty that would last almost to our own time. When Louis XVI went to the guillotine in 1793, his executioners called him Citizen Capet.

Europe about 1000

About the year 1000, then, England was a centralized monarchy. France was nominally ruled by an elected king who was feebler than some of his great supporters. Germany was divided into duchies, one of which had asserted its supremacy and claimed the old imperial title. Italy still remained anarchic, but a revived papacy had begun to emerge. Out of the debris of the Roman Empire, buffeted by two waves of barbarian invasions and held together only by their common Christian faith, these major fragments by the year 1000 had begun to take on certain features that we can still recognize today. The new Scandinavian kingdoms had imposed order on the turbulent peoples who had made the Viking expansion. Small Christian kingdoms in the north of Spain were beginning their struggle with the Muslims who had engulfed the peninsula.

In the East, the empire, with its direct descent from Rome and its Greco-Oriental character, still stood firm at Constantinople after many shocks. It had started its work of Christianizing certain Slavic peoples nearest to it, the Bulgarians and the Russians. The western Slavs—Czechs, Poles, Croats, and others—and the Magyars, lying between the Germans and the influences radiating from Constantinople, had received the attention of Roman missionaries. By the year 1000, there was already visible a line of demarcation between the Western Catholic world and the Eastern Orthodox world, each with its own alphabet and its own outlook.

II FEUDAL EUROPE

The long centuries between the fourth and the fifteenth are traditionally called the Middle Ages (or medieval), the part of man's history lying between ancient and modern. During the first six hundred years or so in the West, the period we have been reviewing, our sources for men's ways of life are scantier than they have been since the Bronze Age. But it is clear that between approximately 400 and 1000 the settled inhabitants of western Europe (former Roman subjects) and the new invaders adjusted very gradually to one another. New and old ways of regulating human affairs competed and often combined with each other. Public order was often absent or precarious. Old and once reliable forms of government had collapsed and vanished. Communications were slower and survival uncertain. Some of the Roman ways of doing things continued. Some innovations were introduced by the barbarians. Christianity, as it spread, also produced change.

Feudalism: The Rulers

These widely varied social and political combinations are called *feudalism.* Feudal institutions were the arrangements between persons—personal, territorial, and governmental—that made survival possible. The arrangements were made between important people, laymen and clerics, who wanted to maintain order—the upper classes, not the masses. Because central authority was no longer able to govern locally, local authority had to be invented to replace it. We do not use or recommend the term *feudal system* because there was nothing systematic about the process.

In the war band of the early Germans (or *comitatus,* as Tacitus called it in Latin), the leader commanded the loyalty of his followers, who banded together for fighting and winning booty. All the Germanic barbarians had war bands. The Anglo-Saxon word for chieftain, *hlaford,* is the origin of our word *lord.* In the Roman provinces, too, local landowners had often built their own private armies. In Rome itself important men had their groups of *clients,* to whom they acted as patrons and gave legal protection.

When a humble man wanted to enter the client relationship, he asked the great man for his *patrocinium,* patronage, and secured it by performing the act of *commendation,* commending or entrusting himself to the patron. He remained free but obtained food and clothing in exchange for his services, whatever they might be. If the client was of upper-class origin, he was called *fidelis,* a faithful man. By the Carolingian period, the term *vassus* meant a man who gave military service to his patron, or lord. Vassalage carried no disgrace; it was the status gained by the act of commendation. So a combination of old Germanic and old Roman practices contributed to new relationships described in new terms.

With regard to land, a Roman patron sometimes granted a client the temporary use of a piece of property, together with the profits to be derived from it so long as he held it, often for life. The Romans used the term *precarium* for this kind of tenure. The Carolingian rulers commonly followed this practice—sometimes using the term *precarium,* sometimes the newer *beneficium,* benefice, to describe the land temporarily held by the vassal in exchange for service. By the year 1000, the act of becoming a vassal usually meant that a man got a benefice. Indeed he might refuse service or loyalty unless he were satisfied with the land he received. The feeble later Carolingians and their rivals outbid each other in giving benefices to their supporters in order to obtain armed support and service. This was one of the practices that depleted the royal estates.

In the later Carolingian period, the benefice came to be called a fief, *feudum* in Latin, the term that has given us the words *feudal* and *feudalism.* As it became a fief, the benefice also became hereditary. Title to it remained with the lord who granted it, but when a vassal died, the fief itself passed to the vassal's heir together with the vassal's obligations to serve the lord and his heirs.

A fief was, then, a piece of land with farmers living on it and working it. When a lord conferred the fief on a vassal, the vassal often got with it the right to perform certain actions that we think of as usually belonging to government: collecting taxes from the inhabitants, establishing police arrangements to protect them, setting up a law court to settle their disputes, perhaps imposing fines and keeping the profits. These public functions had now fallen into private hands, because there was no longer a public power capable of exercising them. This practice too had its earlier precedent: the late Roman *immunity.* The emperors had often used this kind of privilege to make their own estates free (immune) from the visits of tax collectors or law-enforcing officials. The emperors had hoped that the farmers would stay put, enjoy the immunity, and keep them supplied with produce. The Carolingians often extended an immunity to Church lands and even to lands of private landowners. By the tenth century the precedent had extended to the regular feudal contract.

Vassals and Lords

Feudalism and feudal practice did not spread uniformly over all Western Europe. Northern France and the Low Countries were the most thoroughly feudalized areas, Germany the least. Everywhere some pieces of land never became fiefs, but remained the private property of the owners. These were called *allods.* Feudal practices varied from place to place, and developed and altered with the passage of time. But certain general conceptions were held pretty much everywhere.

One of the most significant was that of contract: the lord—or *suzerain*—owed something to the vassal just as the vassal owed something to the lord. When they agreed upon their relationship, the vassal rendered homage to his lord and promised him *aid* and *counsel.* Aid meant that the vassal would participate fully armed as a knight in the lord's wars subject perhaps to limits on the number of days' service owed in any one year. Counsel meant that the vassal would join with his fellow vassals—his "peers," or social equals—to form the lord's law court that alone could pass judgment on any vassal. Vassals might also be required at their own expense to entertain the lord for a visit of specific length, and to give him money payments on special occasions—the marriage of his eldest daughter, the knighting of his eldest son, or (later on) his departure on a crusade. Vassals also swore *fealty* (fidelity) to their lords. And lords were understood to owe in exchange protection and justice to the vassal.

If the vassal broke this contract, the lord would have to get the approval of the court made up of the vassal's peers before he could proceed to punishments such as *forfeiture,* depriving the vassal of his fief. If the lord broke the contract, the vassal was expected to withdraw his homage and fealty in a public act of defiance before proceeding to open rebellion. Sometimes the contract was written, sometimes it was oral. Sometimes the ceremony included a formal *investiture* by the lord. He would give his kneeling vassal a symbol of the fief that was being transferred to him, a twig or a bit of earth.

When a lord or vassal died, the contract had to be renewed with his successor. Upon succeeding to his father's fief the son of a vassal often had to pay *relief,* a special, and often heavy, cash payment like a modern inheritance tax. If the vassal died without heirs, the fief would *escheat,* or go back to the lord, who could grant it to another vassal or not as he saw fit. If the heir was still a minor, the lord exercised the right of *wardship* or guardianship until he came of age. This meant that the lord received the revenues from the fief, and if he was unscrupulous he could milk it dry.

Within a feudal kingdom, the king occupied the top position in a theoretical pyramid of society. Immediately below him would be his own vassals, men who held fiefs directly from the king, called *tenants-in-chief.* But they in turn would be feudal lords—that is, they would have given out various parts of their own property as fiefs to their own vassals. These men, the king's vassals' vassals, would be the king's "rear vassals," and so at the next lower level of the theoretical pyramid. But they too would often have vassals, and so on, for many more levels—a process called *subinfeudation.*

Practice was even more complicated than this theoretical structure. A tenant-in-chief might hold only a very small fief from the king and not be a very important person at all, while a vassal's vassal's vassal might be rich and powerful. The dukes of Normandy, who were vassals to the king of France, were for some centuries much stronger than their overlord. An individual might receive fiefs from more than one lord, and so would be vassal to all and owe homage and fealty to all. What was he to do if one of his lords quarreled with another and went to war? To which lord did he owe first loyalty? This kind of thing happened very often. One Bavarian count had twenty different fiefs held of twenty different lords. Gradually, there arose a new concept, that of a *liege* lord, the one to whom a vassal owed service ahead of any other. But in practice the difficulties often persisted. Even though feudal law became more and more subtle and complex, this was an era when force of arms counted for more than legality.

Bishops and abbots as well as lay lords needed and obtained protection and received benefices for which they owed feudal obligations. Except that a churchman also owed loyalty to his ecclesiastical superiors and dressed in clerical garb, he was often indistinguishable in family origin, behavior, and outlook from a powerful lay lord. Churchmen did strive, however, though often unsuccessfully, to soften the continual violence of everyday life by such devices as the *Peace of God,* which denied communion to anybody who attacked churches, or the *Truce of God,* which forbade fighting during certain days or periods of the year.

Manorial Society

All the complicated arrangements we have been discussing involved only the governing persons: clerics or laymen who fought on horseback as mounted knights and whose fiefs consisted of landed estates known as *manors.* In number these were fewer than ten percent of the population. Most of the other ninety percent of the people worked the land. In late Roman times, the large estate *(latifundium)* owned by a magnate was worked by tenant farmers *(coloni)* whose ancestors had turned over their small farms to the magnate's ancestors in exchange for a guarantee of protection and a percentage of the crop. Personally free, the *coloni* and their children could not leave the ground they cultivated. If they lived in groups of houses close together, the estate was called a *villa*.

The late Roman latifundium became the medieval manor, the late Roman villa the medieval village, and the late Roman coloni the medieval serf peasants. The early German village community also contributed to the new social structure. The Roman landed estate had often produced its food for sale at a profit in the town and city; but the long centuries of disorder beginning with the barbarian invasions led to a decline of commerce, of cities, and of agriculture for profit. The medieval manor usually produced only what was needed to feed its own population.

The oldest method of cultivation was the two-field system, alternating crops and fallow so that fertility could be recovered. Later, especially in grain-producing areas, a three-field system was devised—one field for spring planting, one for autumn planting, and the third lying fallow. Originally, oxen pulled the plow, but the invention of the horse collar (so that the horse would not strangle on the old-fashioned strap around his neck) and the use of horseshoes (which allowed the horse to plow stony soil that hurt the oxen's feet) helped make it possible to substitute horses for oxen. So did the increasing use of tandem harnessing, enabling the horses to work in single file instead of side by side. In advanced areas, a heavy-wheeled plow made its appearance.

The pattern of agricultural settlement varied from region to region. But on a typical manor, each peasant family had its holdings, usually in the form of scattered long strips in the big open fields. In theory this gave each family a bit of good arable land, a bit of the less good land, a bit of woodland, and so on. The strips might be separated from each other by narrow, unplowed *balks*, but there were no fences, walls, or hedges.

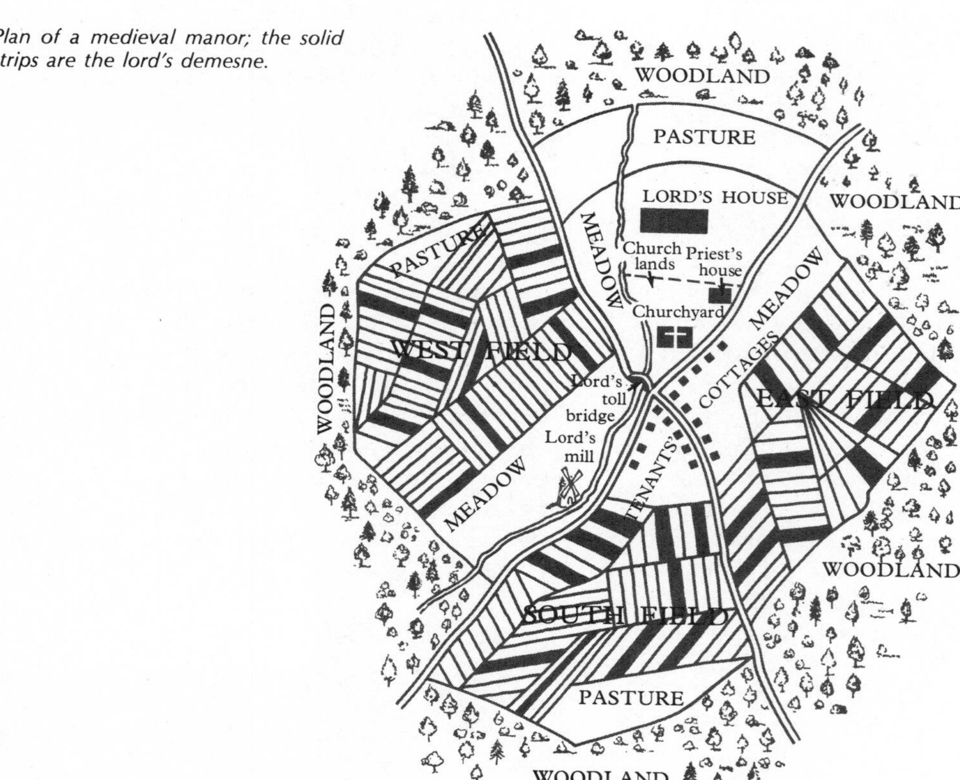

Plan of a medieval manor; the solid strips are the lord's demesne.

Unless it was a royal manor or was the residence of its actual owner, the landlord held it as somebody else's vassal. But he was lord of the manor. He had his own strips, his *demesne* (perhaps a quarter to a third of the land), reserved for the production of the food that he and his household needed. The peasants had to work this land for him, often three days a week throughout the year, except perhaps in harvest time, when the lord could have exclusive call on their services until his crops were safely in the barns.

The peasants paid to have their grain ground at the lord's mill and their bread baked in his oven. In exchange for permission to pasture their beasts in the lord's meadows, they often had to dig ditches or maintain the roads. They could not marry or allow their daughters to marry outside the manor, without obtaining the lord's permission and usually paying a fine. They were bound to the soil, a hereditary caste of farm laborers—*serfs.* But they were not slaves. The lord could not sell them. They and their children descended with the land to the lord's heirs. On such a manor the peasants would live in a cluster of houses close together. A big manor might have several such villages, with perhaps isolated farms in addition. On the other hand, a single village might lie partly in one manor and partly in another belonging to a different lord.

The organization of the countryside by manors was developed earliest in eastern France and in parts of Italy and Germany. Even at its height, it did not include some parts of these and other European countries. But in the large areas where manorialism did prevail, the old Roman landlord's economic power over his tenants had combined with the traditional Germanic village chief's political power, and, by the eleventh century, with the governing rights that the lord received with his fief. A deep respect for custom often prevented the lord's extorting from his peasants more work or more food than they traditionally owed him. But they had no rights and nowhere to appeal in cases where the lord was oppressive.

Custom prevailed in the lord's court, where he or his steward sat in judgment on the tenants, enforcing the traditional rules of the village community. Custom regulated the bargaining agreements reached among the peasants for the use in common of plows and plowteams. Custom no doubt retarded inventiveness and stifled initiative, but it was the only thing that gave a serf the sense that he was protected against exactions and cruelties.

III THE CIVILIZATION OF THE EARLY MEDIEVAL WEST

Despite much mutual dislike and misunderstanding between Greeks and Romans, the passionate Roman admiration for Greek civilization had profoundly influenced Roman writers and artists. But the difference between Greek East and Latin West was reflected in the new political division of the empire first imposed by Diocletian. The triumph of Christianity brought new differences: imperial domination of the Church in the East, eastern passion for theological debate, rivalry between pope and patriarch. The barbarian inroads partly disrupted communication between West and East, and the shattering of western institutions helped reduce the number of Westerners who could learn Greek. In the East few except professional soldiers and administrators had ever spoken Latin, which, however remained the official language of legislation at Constantinople through the fifth century before giving way to the Greek that was everywhere spoken. Despite the growing separation, however, the literature and art of the Christian world still reflected a single civilization for more than a century after Constantine.

Christian Literature

In the West, pagan literature virtually disappeared. In the East, passionate devotees of the old gods were still to be found. Constantine's nephew, Julian, for example, was taught by pagan scholars, mostly Neoplatonists. As emperor (361–363), Julian forbade Christians to teach, revived pagan sacrifices in the temples, and even tried to create a new pagan hierarchy parallel to that of the Christian Church. He wrote satires against Christianity, but his program met with little popular response and was swept away after his early death in battle.

Thereafter, Christian writing took the center of the stage. In both East and West, the best minds among Christians faced the problem of how to treat pagan Greek and Roman literature. At first, a few thinkers, especially in the West, wanted to ban all pagan writings and allow only the reading of Scripture, but even they admitted that in order to combat pagan ideas one had to read pagan writers. The danger remained that a reader might enjoy the classical authors so much that he forgot that the only reason for reading them was to expose their errors.

The Greek East worried less about this problem than the West. In the fourth century, the three "Cappadocian" fathers (so called from the province of Asia Minor where they were born)—Basil, author of the monastic rule; his brother, Gregory of Nyssa; and their friend, Gregory of Nazianzos—all had an excellent classical education and used the techniques of the pagan philosophers in discussing religious ideas.

A westerner, Jerome (340–420) studied with Gregory of Nazianzos and produced the Latin Bible, the Vulgate, as the climax of a life of devoted scholarship that had made him the master of Hebrew and Greek as well as Latin. But he always felt guilty because he loved to read Cicero. Ambrose (ca. 340–397), a Roman civil servant who became bishop of Milan, wrote many theological works and commentaries, christianizing much that he found in the classics, particularly in Cicero. He transformed Cicero's Stoic concept of duty to the state into a Christian concept of duty to God. Ambrose put his own preaching into practice when he publicly humiliated the Emperor Theodosius I (379–395) and forced him to do penace for savagely punishing some rioters. The act symbolizes the Western Church's insistence that, in matters of morals and faith, the Church would be supreme, an attitude wholly opposed to practices already growing up in the East.

Augustine (354–430), the greatest of the Western church fathers and a native of North Africa, had been a Manichaean, a Stoic, and a Neoplatonist before he studied under Ambrose and was converted to Christianity. He then became bishop of the North African city of Hippo, and engaged in energetic controversy with heretics. He wrote his *Confessions,* a moving and mystical autobiography.

After Alaric sacked Rome in 410, many pagan authors held Christianity responsible for the disaster because the new faith had undermined the traditional Roman virtues and offended the gods. To refute this argument Augustine wrote *The City of God.* He showed that many pagan empires had fallen in the past. Then he systematically demolished pagan philosophy. All pagans were limited to earthly values, to the mere "earthly city," and were surely going to hell when they died. True glory belonged to the Christian, citizen of the "City of God," who will be saved. The help of the divine grace, Augustine taught, was necessary to strengthen human wills (even those that had already chosen God) because original sin (inherited from Adam) had turned human beings away from God, and God's grace alone could help them to return.

At times Augustine's argument led him to minimize the value of good deeds, or even of the sacraments, for the achieving of salvation. He came near to the belief that God had chosen in advance an elect company of Christians for salvation: *predestination.* The later Church fathers did not follow Augustine, but insisted that both good deeds (works) *and* grace were essential to salvation.

After the Barbarians

During the centuries of the barbarian onslaught, the achievements of the West in literature and the arts were feeble indeed by comparison with those of Greek or Roman civilizations, or indeed with those of the contemporary eastern Mediterranean world, Christian and Muslim. In this new West, the masters usually did not have the taste or the judgment to patronize writers or artists, and life was too violent to give men much leisure. Roads and the postal system deteriorated, and sea transport became more uncertain. Cities—centers of culture and of the commerce that made culture possible—subsided into ruined shells of their former splendor, mere forts in the countryside. Technical skills were lost. In sculpture, for example, the realism of the ancients gave way to far cruder representations of the human body. The command over language was lost too. Nobody spoke good Latin any more, and few could write it. The slowly developing vernacular tongues—the Romance-French or the early German—were not yet used in a literary way.

Yet many barbarians loved and admired the Roman world that their fellow barbarians were engaged in destroying, and some made a conscious effort to keep alive the Roman literary and artistic tradition. Moreover, the invading tribesmen brought with them art forms of their own—in poetry, sculpture, and painting—that have only recently begun to win the appreciation they deserve. In the cultural realm, as in the realm of institutions, one finds a new combination of old elements. We shall meet no Homer, no Vergil, no Phidias in these centuries, but the writers and artists—many of them anonymous—living under different pressures and expressing themselves in different ways—deserve our study and our admiration.

Writing in Latin

In Italy under Theodoric the fight against the loss of the classical heritage was waged most vigorously. Two distinguished intellectuals emerged as its leaders: Boethius and Cassiodorus. Unlike most of his contemporaries, Boethius (ca. 480–524) knew Greek as well as Latin. He was an authority on mechanics and on music, and he held high political office. He planned a Latin translation of Plato and Aristotle. He was the first among Christian thinkers to use Aristotle's logical methods in dealing with Christian theology. And he wrote original works on the art of argument. These labors were little noticed by the men of Boethius' own times, most of whom had little interest or ability in philosophical discourse. But six hundred years after Boethius' death, philosophical disputation on theological questions became the fashion and the chief sign of an intellectual revival. Then Boethius' efforts won proper appreciation. Before Boethius could complete his translations, Theodoric imprisoned him on a false charge of treason, and after keeping him in jail for a year executed him. While in prison, Boethius wrote *The Consolation of Philosophy,* part verse, part prose. Philosophy herself appears to him and consoles him by reminding him how fickle fortune is. A moving book, written in excellent Latin, it became a popular schoolbook for generations of medieval students.

Cassiodorus lived much longer (ca. 490–580) and managed to stay in Theodoric's good graces, acting as his secretary of state and collecting his official correspondence. Cassiodorus hoped to launch a Christian university in Rome. Thwarted by the disorders of Justinian's reconquest of Italy, he eventually founded a monastery in southern Italy. Here his monks studied the classics as a means to strengthen and advance Christian education, copying by hand not only the Bible but Cicero, Vergil, and other pagans.

Pope Gregory the Great, on the other hand, had no use for the classics, despite his good education. Everything he wrote had its practical Christian purpose. His commentary on the Book of Job was designed to make people behave better. His *Dialogues,* which included a life of Saint Benedict, were written to make the monastic life popular. More than a thousand letters of Gregory survive, written to correspondents all over the Christian world, and dealing with every sort of problem in the management of the Church and its relationship to secular rulers.

In Gaul, a highly Romanized province, there remained well into the period of the barbarian invasions a cultivated circle of upper-class landowners and churchmen, who still wrote letters to each other in Latin and lived luxurious old-fashioned lives on their country estates. But this Gallo-Roman culture virtually disappeared with the Frankish triumph. From the Merovingian period we have the Latin hymns of Fortunatus and the somewhat childlike history by Gregory (538–594), bishop of Tours and chronicler of the savage crimes of the Frankish ruling house. In Spain, Isidore (ca. 570–636), archbishop of Seville, wrote a kind of encyclopedia, *The Etymologies,* which became a standard reference book for several hundred years. It reflects both Isidore's learning, which was extraordinary for his time, and his superstition and ignorance, which were more typical.

On the European continent the seventh century was the low point of intellectual activity. But Ireland and England enjoyed a genuine revival. The monasteries provided a refuge for booklovers and a shelter for their books; and the combined influence of the Celtic and the Roman traditions brought fruitful results. Among many cultivated English men, the greatest was Bede (ca. 672–735), who could read Greek, knew the works of the Church fathers, and produced the remarkable *Ecclesiastical History of the English People,* covering the period 597–731. This is a unique source, written in a Latin of astonishing vigor and purity.

Churchmen from this separate cultural world of Britain brought about a revival on the Continent under Charlemagne, who supplied the necessary interest and patronage. Alcuin of York (d. 804), who had studied under a pupil of Bede, came to the court of Charlemagne in 782 and helped transform the palace school into a serious educational institution where men studied the seven liberal arts as then understood—grammar, rhetoric, dialectic (formal argument), arithmetic, geometry, astronomy, and music. Alcuin wrote much himself. He took the lead in biblical scholarship and in improving the handwriting of the scribes in monasteries, thus ensuring a regular and increasing supply of legible books. The survival of much of Latin literature we owe directly to the efforts of Carolingian scribes.

Other poets, scholars, and historians joined Alcuin in making the palace school a center not only for learning but for agreeable and interesting conversation, in which Charlemagne enjoyed taking part. One of these members, Einhard, wrote a biography of Charlemagne based on Roman models and was also a talented metallurgist. The

A page from Alcuin's edition of the Vulgate.

foundations laid by these men permitted their successors in the next two generations to write personal letters, history, poetry, and ambitious works on theological and ethical questions. In new monastic centers, such as St. Gall in Switzerland and others in newly christianized Germany, the revival persisted through the long decades of Carolingian decline.

Writing in the Vernacular: "Beowulf"

It was in England too—where the Latin veneer was thinner than anywhere on the Continent—that the Angles, Saxons, and Jutes produced the first European literature in a vernacular language, Anglo-Saxon, or Old English. Sometimes they translated: Boethius' *Consolation of Philosophy* was turned into Old English, and King Alfred the Great himself translated Bede's *Ecclesiastical History.* But by far the most remarkable Old English literary monument is *Beowulf,* a poem of about 3,200 lines, written down about the year 1000 and preserved in only a single manuscript in the British Museum. But *Beowulf* was originally composed much earlier, sometime between 680 and 800. Nobody is sure where it was written, whether one author or several wrote it, or whether the author was Christian or pagan.

It begins in Denmark, and tells us of the building by King Hrothgar of his great hall, and of the savage attacks upon his men by a monster called Grendel. The hero Beowulf comes to Denmark from southern Sweden and kills not only Grendel but Grendel's even more terrifying mother, who is destroyed at the bottom of the lake in which she lives. Having become king of his own people, Beowulf at the end of his long life is slain in a victorious combat with a dragon who has stolen a hoard of treasure and is ravaging the country.

The poem ends with Beowulf's funeral ceremonies: his body is placed with his favorite possessions in a ship. One like it was found in 1939, treasures and all, at Sutton Hoo in eastern England. *Beowulf,* like the *Iliad* and *Odyssey,* exalts the ideal of heroic behavior. But the climax of Beowulf's heroism is death and burial. The poet tells us that Grendel's mother and thus Grendel also were descendants of Cain. But he never mentions Christ, the Incarnation, the Crucifixion, or the Resurrection. The Christianity of the poem seems to have been recent and superficial. Nothing comparable to *Beowulf* exists in any other contemporary vernacular language.

The Arts

In the arts, as in literature, the story is one of a very gradual transition away from Roman forms. Standardized and well understood in all the continental provinces and adapted to Christian needs and uses for at least two centuries before the barbarians arrived, the Roman forms were now modified as the barbarians themselves became more cultivated. The early great churches of such important imperial cities as Milan (San Lorenzo) or Trier were still the large rectangular basilicas modeled on the secular architecture of the Romans. But in building smaller Christian structures, especially baptistries detached from the main church, there were innovations. Some were square, with corner niches and a drum (Fréjus, in southern France), others were polygonal (Albenga, in northern Italy). Rich mosaic decoration was characteristic. As soon as a barbarian tribe was firmly established in its new territory, its kings as a matter of prestige built churches, often small, it is true, but generally imitative of the Roman models. Most of these have disappeared, but we know from contemporary written accounts and from archaeological research that they often had domes, and tin or gilded bronze roof tiles that shone in the sun. In Merovingian times, marble quarries were worked, especially in southwest France, and fine stone capitals and slabs were even exported.

From the Visigothic occupation in Spain several churches survive, such as the seventh-century San Pedro de la Nave near the Portuguese frontier. Its architecture is late Roman but its sculpture is clearly unclassical and in a new mood.

Exterior of the seventh-century Church of San Pedro de la Nave.

In a capital showing the sacrifice of Isaac, the hand of God emerges from the heavens representing the voice of the Lord telling Abraham to hold his upraised hand and spare his son.

The seventh-century Merovingian Baptistry of St. John at Poitiers still clearly shows its debt to late Roman buildings, though the sculptural decoration and the ornamentation in terracotta has become much cruder. At Poitiers too is the underground mausoleum of a seventh-century abbot, Mellebaude, modeled on Gallo-Roman tomb chambers. In very good Latin on the wall is an inscription saying "Everything goes from bad to worse, and the end of time is near," a quite un-Roman sentiment reflecting a new pessimism. Even more representative of a new era is a sculptured representation in the tomb chamber itself: the two thieves crucified with Christ, each bound to a cross of his own. No Roman sculptor could have carved these primitive figures with staring eyes. The barbarian hand was now working in a tradition all its own.

Also still almost miraculously preserved at Poitiers by the nuns at the Abbey of the Holy Cross is a small carved wooden bookstand owned by a Merovingian queen, Radegund, at the end of the sixth century. In the center of the carved reading surface is a lamb, representing Christ, and in each corner is the symbol of one of the four apostles, an eagle's head for John and a man's for Matthew, a bull's for Luke and a lion's for Mark. At the top, between two doves, is the Greek monogram for Christ, while at the bottom, between two doves, is a cross in a circle. Along the sides two crosses in another form balance each other. The whole is simple and harmonious, and thoroughly Mediterranean in inspiration. In execution it is cruder, showing the limitations of a barbarian woodcarver, and suggesting both the piety and the simplicity of a Christian barbarian queen.

Two sculptured tombs in the crypt (underground chapel) of Jouarre, east of Paris, further illustrate the complexity of the era. The tomb of Agilbert, of the late seventh century, has a vivid and poignant representation of men and

The sacrifice of Isaac: capital at San Pedro de la Nave. The hand of God, representing the voice of the Lord, emerges from the heavens at the critical moment to stop Abraham from killing his son.

The Baptistery of St. John, Poitiers.

women praying at the Last Judgment, their arms upraised. It is so unlike all other sculpture of the period in its intensity that it has been conjectured that the artist was an Egyptian Christian, one of those known to have fled from the Arab Muslim conquest. By contrast, the tomb of Theodechilde, of the first half of the eighth century, with its splended carved shells and beautifully lettered Latin inscription, is in the fullest Roman tradition. Jouarre had close connections with Britain, and its sculptures have been compared with those of the early sculptured crosses of Ireland

Cutaway drawing of the underground mausoleum of Abbot Mellebaude, Poitiers.

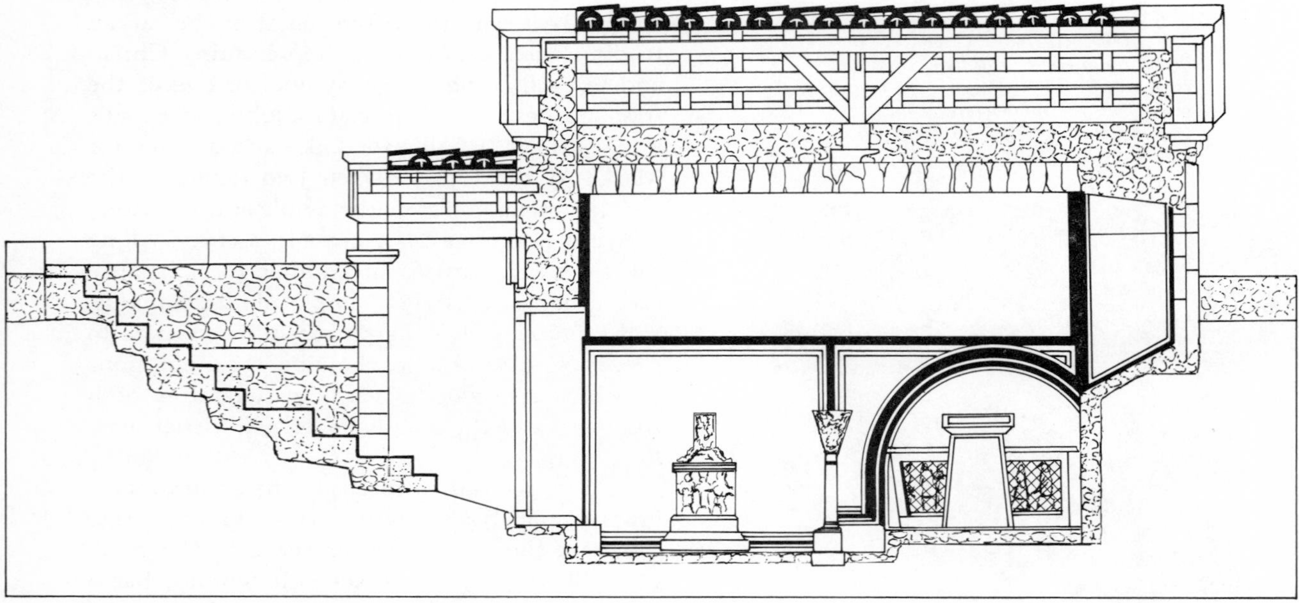

From the tomb of Theodechilde at Jouarre: detail of carved shells and Latin inscription.

The sculptured figures in Mellebaude's tomb: the two thieves who were crucified with Christ, bound to their crosses.

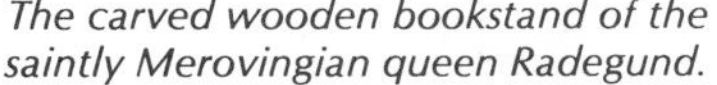

The carved wooden bookstand of the saintly Merovingian queen Radegund.

and northern England, where it is possible also that Egyptian influences had penetrated.

Not only Egypt but the Byzantine Empire made its contribution to the art of the West during these centuries. In Rome and Ravenna there stood churches, palaces, and tombs built by Greeks or artists trained in the Greek school, dating back to the sixth century (see below). In a tiny church in the remote North Italian village of Castelseprio, where the bishops of Milan had a summer residence are several eighth- or ninth-century frescoes, unknown until 1944. These reflect a classical revival that had been taking place at Byzantium itself.

The Byzantine influence radiating from Ravenna is shown also by the magnificent jewelled gold book-covers that Pope Gregory the Great himself gave to the Lombard queen, Theodolinde. The four large jewels in the corner of each cover are classical portrait gems taken from some treasured collection to embellish a work of art far different from anything classical. The fact that almost all the Popes between 642 and 752 were themselves Greeks or Syrians no doubt strengthened the Italian love of objects in the eastern style.

For good examples of the kind of art the barbarians brought with them we must look at the "minor arts" of goldsmithing and jewelry. As the Huns drove the Goths before them into Europe, the Germans brought with them objects made in the Black Sea region by craftsmen working in an Iranian or other Eastern tradition, and characterized by brilliant color and the use of gems or colored glass. Once inside the borders of the Roman Empire, the tribesmen, notably the Ostrogoths, kept their taste for this sort of thing and their own craftsmen continued the tradition.

Detail from the tomb of Agilbert in the crypt of Jouarre: women praying at the Last Judgment.

Jeweled clasp from Spain, in the shape of an eagle.

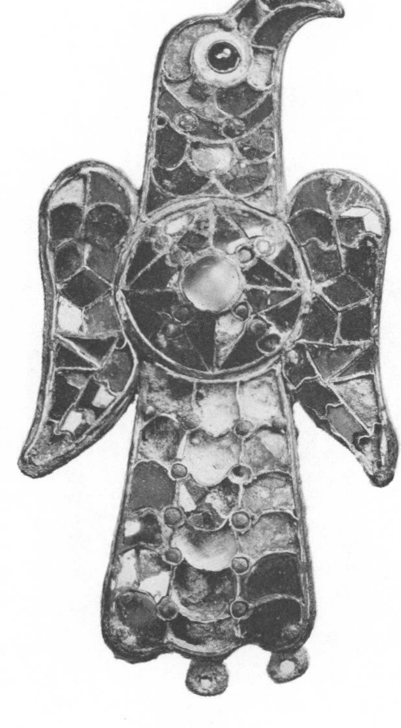

Adoration of the Magi: fresco in the Chapel of St. Mary, Castelseprio, Italy.

One of the jeweled gold bookcovers for the Bible that Gregory the Great gave to the Lombard queen Theodelinde.

Many of these marvelous (and altogether unclassical) objects have been found in barbarian graves in central Europe, and also in Gaul, Spain, and Italy. An eagle-shaped clasp from Spain is a fine example. From later in the seventh century comes the jeweled gold crown of the Visigothic king Recceswinth, one of a large collection of Visigothic royal crowns.

Similar jeweled objects—a purse, a harp, and weapons— were found in 1939 in the Sutton Hoo ship burial in Essex, England, to which we have referred in connection with Beowulf. The astonished archaeologists and students of Old English poetry who first looked at the Sutton Hoo find felt as if they were seeing illustrated in real life the lines of the poem that tells how

The jeweled gold crown of the Visigothic king Reccesqinth.

Part of a seventh-century purse cover, with gold, garnets, and enamel, from the ship burial at Sutton Hoo, England.

They laid their dear lord,
the giver of rings, deep within the ship
by the mast in majesty; many treasures
and adornments from far and wide were gathered there.
I have never heard of a ship equipped
more handsomely with weapons and war-gear,
swords and corselets; on his breast
*lay countless treasures that were to travel far with him. . . .**

And the presence in the royal funeral ship at Sutton Hoo of a massive round silver plate made at Byzantium in the period 491–518, and of two silver spoons with Greek inscriptions, helped to emphasize the continuous contacts between the barbarians and the East.

Under Eastern influences, artists abandoned the realistic representation of men and beasts in art. Eastern influences and their expression by Western artists is seen in an extraordinary row of six stucco statues of saints in the front of a small church (Santa Maria in Valle) at Cividale in northern Italy. These saints were carved about the year 800 by sculptors so skillful that they could have done anything they chose. They chose hieratic figures in stiff ceremonial garments which nonetheless conceal genuine human bodies.

Three of the six statues of saints at the Church of Santa Maria in Valle, Cividale.

Contrast the almost abstract effect of a relief of the Adoration of the Magi on the altar of Duke Ratchis, in the same small town of Cividale, carved by native Lombard craftsmen a little more than half a century earlier. Here we are back almost to the primitive quality of the two thieves in Abbot Mellebaude's tomb at Poitiers. But we have come the full distance and more when we consider a seventh-century German tomb slab (stele) now at Bonn. On one side the warrior stands sword in hand, about to be bitten by the serpent of death; on the other, Christ stands over his tomb with a halo (but also with a spear!).

Not until the Carolingian period was there a full-scale revival of classical influence. Charlemagne wanted and could afford to attract the best craftsmen from anywhere in Europe. They were inspired by such Italians works as the paintings and mosaics in the Roman churches of Santa Maria Antiqua and Santa Maria Maggiore dating to the fifth and sixth centuries.

Wall paintings and mosaics are fixed monuments. Only a traveler can visit them all if they are widely separated from each other. But books are transportable, and it was largely through book illustration—the "illumination" of manuscripts—that inspirations from one region and one school intermingled in other regions with influences from other schools. North Italian books in which classical and Byzantine influences had been brought to bear traveled across the Alps into France and into Britain with Gregory the Great's missionaries. We still have two illustrations from a Bible that came along on the expedition. These brought the Mediterranean traditions directly into England, already exposed to them indirectly

Adoration of the Magi: relief on the altar of Duke Ratchis, Cividale.

* Reprinted by permission of Farrar, Straus & Giroux, Inc., and Macmillan & Co., Ltd., from Kevin Crossley-Holland's translation of Beowulf. Translation ©1968 by Kevin Crossley-Holland; introductory matter ©1968 by Bruce Mitchell.

Seventh-century German tomb slab: on one side a warrior, on the other Christ.

by the Celtic missionaries from Ireland. In due course the same influences penetrated into Germany in the same way, and artists under the Ottonian emperors would pick them up.

From this influential north Italian school of painting there comes, for example, a drawing from a manuscript of a book of church law (early ninth century) at Vercelli. Constantine the Great is shown on his throne at the Council of Nicaea with the bishops who signed its decrees, while below the throne, books in favor of the Arian heresy are being burned.

The specifically barbarian contribution to the "Carolingian Renaissance," came in the decorative geometric patterning typical of barbarian craftsmanship in metal. We find it mentioned also in contemporary written descriptions: a Dane gave Beowulf an heirloom sword whose "iron blade was engraved with deadly twig-like patterning." This patterning reappears in book illustration in the great Celtic manuscripts: the Books of Durrow, Echternach (brought from Britain to Germany), Lindisfarne, and Kells, executed in the seventh and eighth centuries. A page with interlace border from the earliest of these, the Book of Durrow, shows Saint Matthew in a cloak of complex checkerboard design. Both border and cloak are of barbarian inspiration. The Celtic missionaries who went from Ireland to the Continent and founded the monastery at Bobbio in Italy took these talents with them, and there learned what the indigenous craftsmen had to teach them. By the time of the Book of Kells, the earlier stiffness of the human figure has gone, and the geometric patterns have become rich.

Charlemagne himself made five trips to Italy, deepening and carrying further the connection begun by Pepin. Lombards from northern

Book illustration: Constantine at Nicaea, from a canon-law book at Vercelli.

Italy joined Anglo-Saxons like Alcuin at Charlemagne's court. By 794, the court was settled at Aachen, where Charlemagne's new residence was built at top speed. From Rome and Ravenna there poured in works of art. Most have disappeared, such as an equestrian statue of Theodoric, itself an imitation of the classic model of Marcus Aurelius on horseback. But we have preserved a small bronze of a similar statue of Charlemagne himself. In the chapel at Aachen, Charlemagne's marble throne is still in place, as is the massive bronze grill around the gallery.

To Aachen came Romans, Lombards, Greeks from southern Italy and probably from Byzantium itself, Syrians, Anglo-Saxons, Irishmen, Spaniards from the Visigothic parts of Spain, Jews, Arabs, and every sort of inhabitant of Gaul and Germany. Architects and artisans—including, perhaps, some Greeks—worked to create a building that reflected both the imperial palace in Constantinople and the papal residence in the Palace of St. John Lateran in Rome. Charlemagne especially enjoyed receiving foreign travelers, many of them, especially officials, bringing rich gifts—relics, books, textiles, ivory carvings, jewels.

In 796 arrived the treasure captured from the nomadic Avar tribesmen who had been pillaging for two centuries. It filled sixteen oxcarts. The most sensational present came in 802 from the caliph at Baghdad, Harun al-Rashid, an elephant named Abu'l Abbas, who became a general favorite at Aachen, and whose bones remained a wonder for centuries after he died. Harun also sent Charlemagne a marvelous clock of gilded bronze, with twelve mounted mechanical knights

Saint Matthew, from the Book of Durrow.

who on the stroke of noon emerged from twelve little doors that shut behind them. Silken tents, perfumes, oriental robes abounded. Charlemagne had a good many beautiful daughters, whom the gentle, aging Alcuin nicknamed "the crowned doves that flit about the chambers of the palace," and against whom he warned his students. The exotic atmosphere of the court remained a vivid memory for many centuries after the glory had departed. After the decline of the tenth century, the later German emperors reverted to Carolingian models for their own revival.

IV THE WORLD OF BYZANTIUM 337–1025

Contrasts between East and West

Constantine, as we know, in 330 moved his capital to the city of Byzantium at the far southeastern corner of Europe, on a little tongue of land. Thereafter it was often called Constantinople, the city of Constantine, but it also retained its earlier name. For more than eleven hundred years it remained the capital of the Roman Empire, falling in 1453 to the Turks, who renamed it Istanbul.

It enjoys an unrivaled situation in the straits that separate Europe from Asia. Lying between the exit from the Black Sea and the entrance into the Mediterranean, it has its own sheltered harbor, the Golden Horn. To the Slavs, both of Russia and of the Balkans, who owe it their religion and their culture, the city has always been "Tsargrad," city of the emperor. Constantinople became the center of a civilization related to that of medieval western Europe, but in many ways startlingly different.

The State

The Emperor

Byzantium called itself New Rome. Its emperors ruled in direct succession from Augustus, and its population, while predominantly Greek in race, language, and origin, called itself Rhomaean, Roman. Yet many non-Roman elements became increasingly important in Byzantine society. After Constantine had become a Christian, the emperor was of course no longer considered a god. But he was ordained of God, and his power remained divine. As there could be but one God in heaven, so there could be but one emperor on earth. The pagan Roman tradition of the god-emperor was modified but not abandoned.

In theory, the will of God manifested itself in the unanimous consent of the people, the senate (established at Constantinople in the Roman pattern by Constantine himself), and the army to the choice of each new emperor. In practice, the reigning emperor usually had his heir, often his own son, crowned during his own lifetime, as he had done at Rome. Byzantine dynasties sometimes lasted several centuries. But politicians often intervened. They imprisoned and exiled emperors, murdered them, blinded them (which made them ineligible to rule again), and enthroned their own candidates.

Each new emperor was raised on a shield as a sign of army approval, so becoming *imperator,* commander in chief. By the mid-fifth century, he was also formally crowned by the patriarch of Constantinople. He would swear to defend the Christian faith, and in addition to the crown received a purple robe and purple boots. In the

***Saint** John, from the book of Kells.*

Interior of the Chapel of Charlemagne at Aachen, with grillwork in a variety of styles.

seventh century, the emperor began to call himself *basileus,* king of kings, in token that he had defeated the Persians. Later still, he added the term *autokrator,* the autocrat. Empresses bore corresponding feminine titles and in general played an important role. Three times in Byzantine history women ruled without a male emperor.

A conspiracy by a rival might overthrow the emperor, but autocracy as such was not challenged. Divinely awarded powers entailed immense earthly responsibilities. An elaborate and rigid code of etiquette governed the emperor's every activity every day of the year. His subjects ceremoniously fell on their faces as they approached him with a courtier holding them by each arm, and the emperor was acclaimed with song and silver trumpets whenever he appeared in public.

Law

As agent of God, the emperor periodically ordered the recompiling of the Roman law. Justinian (527–565) had his lawyers collect all imperial statutes since Hadrian (117–138) in the *Code.* Even bulkier was the *Digest,* a collection of authoritative legal opinions. The *Institutes,* a handbook, introduced students to the larger works. All these were in Latin. But Justinian issued all his own new laws (the *Novels*) in Greek. In the eighth century, the emperors issued the *Ekloga,* a new collection, more Christian in its provisions with regard to family matters, somewhat less severe and less Roman than its predecessors. Under Leo VI (886–912) appeared the *Basilics,* last of the major compilations. The emperor was supreme judge, and all other judges had power only as derived from him. The emperor's palace was the center of the state, and the officials of the palace were the most important members of the administration. Each official had a title giving him a post in the palace hierarchy and a rank among the nobility. Many of the greatest and most influential officials were eunuchs, an oriental feature disturbing to most Western visitors.

The Enemies

As defenders of the faith, the Byzantine emperors fought one enemy after another for eleven hundred years: Persians in the seventh century, Muslim Arabs from the seventh century on, and Turks beginning in the eleventh century. Persians and Arabs successively seized the East Roman provinces of Syria and Egypt, and the Arabs kept them. Though western Europe too experienced Muslim invasions in Sicily and Spain, Charles Martel's victory at Tours in 732 was less decisive

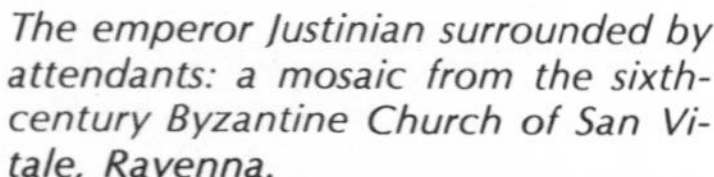

The emperor Justinian surrounded by attendants: a mosaic from the sixth-century Byzantine Church of San Vitale, Ravenna.

A thirteenth-century manuscript illumination illustrating the use of Greek fire.

than that of the Byzantines in 717, when Emperor Leo III thwarted an Arab siege of Constantinople.

The Byzantines fought the Huns in the fifth century, and thereafter a succession of fierce nomad peoples who invaded imperial territory. Sometimes the enemies were native Europeans, like the Slavs, who filtered gradually southward into the Balkans and Greece beginning in the sixth century. Their relatives, in what is now Russia, sailed under Viking rulers across the Black Sea to attack Constantinople for the first time in 860.

In the northeastern Balkans, the Hunnic tribe of the Bulgars conquered the Slavs, who then absorbed their conquerors. By the tenth century the Bulgarians were thoroughly Slavic. The Bulgarians and the Slavic Serbs to the west of them fought long and exhausting wars against Byzantium. Beginning in the eleventh century, the Byzantines had to fight western Europeans: Normans from south Italy, crusaders from all the Western countries, freebooting commercial adventurers from the new Italian towns. Against all these the Byzantines held their own until the late eleventh century, when Turks and Normans inflicted severe defeats. Even then Constantinople held out and was never taken by an enemy until 1204, when a mixed force of Venetian traders and western European crusaders seized it for the first time.

Army, Navy, Diplomacy

Until the eleventh century Byzantium had phenomenally good armies and navies. Well armed and equipped, served by medical and ambulance corps, by a signal corps with flashing mirrors, and by intelligence agents behind the enemy lines, often commanded by the emperor himself, the Byzantine land forces were often the best in Europe. The Byzantine fleet had a real secret weapon: Greek fire, a mysterious chemical compound squirted from siphons mounted on the prows of ships, which set enemy vessels aflame and terrified their sailors. Like the army, the Byzantine navy suffered a decline in the eleventh century, and the Italian city fleets replaced it as the chief Mediterranean naval power.

The Byzantines preferred diplomacy to war. They regarded the king of Persia and his successor, the Muslim caliph, as equals. All other states were barbarian. Since negotiations with such inferiors were necessary, a kind of "office of barbarian affairs" kept imperial officials supplied with intelligence reports on the internal feudings among each barbarian people, so that a "pro-Byzantine" party might be created among them and every advantage taken of their internal stresses.

When the emperor sent arms to the chieftain of a barbarian tribe, the act was the equivalent of adoption. The emperor could make the paternal relationship still stronger by inviting the barbarian to Byzantium, standing sponsor for him at his baptism, and bestowing upon him splendid insignia of office in the palace hierarchy. The imperial court, solemn and dazzling, overawed the simple foreigner.

The Economy

Byzantium was very rich. It was a center of trade: from the Black Sea coastal lands came furs and hides and slaves; from the Far East, spices and precious stones; from western Europe, especially Italy, merchants eager to buy for gold the goods in Byzantine markets. Silk manufacture, for long a closely guarded secret of the Persians, came to Byzantium in the sixth century. Thereafter, the emperors maintained a monopoly on the manufacture and sale of silk, and of the purple dye and gold embroidery that were needed by dignitaries of church and state in West and East alike.

The emperors forbade the export of gold, and maintained their reserves at a high level. The *nomisma,* the Byzantine gold coin, was standard currency in the whole Mediterranean world. It remained stable for eight hundred years until the crisis of the eleventh century. Constantinople's glitter and sophistication contrasted with the prevailing rural way of life in the West. Silken garments, palaces and churches aglow with marbles and mosaics, precious stones lavishly used in decoration reflected a thriving commerce and industry and a substantial revenue.

Money came in from state property in land: farms, gold, and silver mines, cattle ranches, quarries. It came from booty seized in war or property confiscated from rich men in disgrace. It came from taxation: on land and persons, sales and profits, imports and exports, and inheritances. From the "new empire" the Byzantines inherited the concept that land and labor were taxable together: in order to be taxable, each unit of land had to have its farmer to work it. In order to be taxable as a person, each farmer had to have his land to work. This system promoted the binding of the peasant to the soil as a serf, and large private landowners flourished as the state leased them large tracts of land, while they supplied the labor. Though the large private estate predominated, the small private freeholder seems never to have disappeared entirely.

The Capital and the Factions

As the capital, Constantinople came to have its own special administration, under a prefect of the city *(eparch).* He was mayor, chief of police, and judge rolled into one. The eparch was responsible for public order; he inspected the markets, fixing fair prices for food, and supervised lawyers, notaries, moneychangers, and bankers as well as merchants. Each trade or craft was organized into a guild or corporation with its own governor under the prefect.

From Rome Byzantium inherited rival parties of chariot racers, each with its own stables, equipment, body of organized fans, and colors—the Blues and the Greens. They raced each other regularly in the Hippodrome, a vast stadium attached to the imperial palace. Every chariot race was the occasion for demonstrations which sometimes became riots, when bands of one faction would invade the quarter of the other and burn down houses. In the Nika revolt of 532 (so called from the rioters' shout of "victory"), Blues and Greens temporarily united in devastating the capital. The emperor Justinian nearly lost his throne. It was not until after the mid-seventh century that these disorders lessened.

Religious Attitudes

In the Byzantine world, religion pervaded intellectual life. The most serious questions that intellectuals tried to settle were theological, eagerly attacked by powerful and subtle minds. Religion dominated the arts and literature, and also economic life and politics: the position a man took on a theological question often determined his political allegiance. To be right in these quarrels meant salvation and immortality, to be wrong, damnation and eternal punishment. The emperor went to war as champion of the faith.

Although Christianity played a similar role in the medieval West, the relationship between church and state was different in the East. In the West the papal monarchy often challenged secular rulers. In the East, the emperor, like Constantine at the Council of Nicaea (325), was in residence and legislated as head of the Christian church in matters of Christian dogma. No layman in the West would or could do this. In the East the emperor often deposed patriarchs and punished clerics. Emperors themselves were often theologians who enjoyed argument and speculation on theological questions and sometimes legislated on matters of faith without even consulting churchmen. Thus the Church in the East was a department of state, and the emperor was the head of it. Only rarely did a patriarch of Constantinople challenge the emperor successfully.

The archangel Michael: sixth-century ivory figure probably made at Constantinople.

Far more than the western Europeans, the Byzantines assumed that the individual had very little chance of salvation. In the East, monasticism became *the* Christian life, since to become a monk was to take a direct route to salvation. Worldly men, including many emperors, became monks on their deathbeds. Monks enjoyed enormous popular prestige, and often influenced political decisions. Monks staffed the highest ranks of the church hierarchy: Rich and powerful laymen, from the emperor down, founded new monasteries as an act of piety. Often immune from taxation, monasteries acquired vast lands and precious objects.

In the East every religious act took on a sacramental quality. Every image, every relic of a saint, was felt to preserve in itself the essence of the holy person. So God was felt to be actually present in the sanctuary; He could be reached through the proper performance of the ritual. In the East the emphasis fell on mystery, magic, rituals, a personal approach to the heavenly Saviour, more than on the ethical teachings of Christianity. Once a Byzantine accepted the proper performance of a magical action as the right way to reach God, he could not contemplate any change. If the old way is wrong, one's parents and grandparents are all damned.

The Fortunes of Empire 337–1081

1. The Death of Constantine (337) to the Advent of Leo III (717)

Constantine's immediate successors were Arian heretics. The first truly orthodox emperor after him, Theodosius the Great (reigned 379–395), proclaimed orthodox Nicene Christianity to be the sole permitted state religion. Although the empire, East and West, was united under Theodosius, his sons Arcadius (395–408) and Honorius divided it, with Arcadius ruling at Constantinople. It was never again fully united.

The Two Natures of Christ. Long before Arianism disappeared, a new controversy broke out and shook the Eastern Empire to its foundations. Exactly what was the relationship between Christ the God and Christ the man? He was both man and God, but exactly how was his human nature related to his divine nature? And was the Virgin Mary—a human woman—perhaps the mother only of Christ's human aspect; or if not, how could a human being be the mother of God? One extreme position was taken by the *dyophysites* ("two-nature-ites"), who separated the human nature of Christ from the divine and so refused to regard the human virgin as the mother of God. The opposite extreme was that taken by the *monophysites* ("one-nature-ites"), who argued that the human and divine natures were merged. They carried the idea so far that they almost forgot Christ's human attributes and tended to make him a god only. As with Arianism, the dispute flared up in physical violence in the East. Again the emperor (Marcian, reigned 450–457) called an ecumenical council at Chalcedon, near Constantinople, in 451. Supported by the pope, the council condemned monophysitism and, like the Council of Nicaea, took a mystical rather than a rational position. The true believer must believe in the two natures of Christ, human and divine, coexisting yet inseparable from each other. The Virgin is properly called the Mother of God.

Silver plate showing the emperor Theodosius, with his sons, Honorius and Arcadius, on either side, bestowing the insignia of office on a local official. Found in the mid-nineteenth century in western Spain by two peasants, who, before they could be stopped, split it in order to divide the profits.

Like the decision at Nicaea, the decision at Chalcedon did not silence the opposition. Monophysites were concentrated in the provinces of Egypt and Syria. By opposing Chalcedon they were expressing the deep resentment of Alexandria and Antioch against the new domination by the upstart Constantinople. Partly because it was identified with what we would call nationalism, monophysitism did not die out, and each new emperor tried to settle the issue by persecution or appeasement. Since there were no monophysites in the West, the papacy objected to compromise; and every time an emperor at Constantinople tried to appease his Egyptian and Syrian monophysite subjects, he would be condemned by the pope for heresy. The problem remained unsolved.

In the seventh century, the disaffection of the monophysite provinces of Syria and Egypt made it easier for the Muslims to conquer them. To this day there are still monophysite Christians in Egypt and Syria.

Byzantium and Europe. All during the fifth century the emperors at Constantinople used Germans as troops in their armies. At the same time they usually managed to deflect upon the West the worst blows of new invaders. While the Western provinces fell away, while Visigoths and Vandals sacked Rome, and while Ostrogoths governed much of Italy, Constantinople weathered all the storms.

The emperor Justinian was so controversial that his own historian Procopius, who wrote several works praising him to the skies, also produced a *Secret History,* not published for more than a thousand years, violently denouncing him. Justinian's reconquests in North Africa, Italy, and Spain (see p. 94–95) represented a last desperate effort to reunite all of Rome's Mediterranean lands. The Western wars were very expensive, and the Persian danger grew to the point where Justinian's immediate successors could not check it. In Europe Slavs and Avars were able to dent the Danube line and filter into the Balkans.

Justinian began a new administrative reorganization which his successors carried further. In the provinces he sometimes reversed the system of Diocletian and Constantine by entrusting both civil and military power to the same official. After Justinian's death, the military emergencies caused in Italy by the invasion of the Lombards and in North Africa by the Berbers forced the Byzantine authorities to create large new military districts, the exarchates of Ravenna and Carthage. The generals in charge, the exarchs, also served as civil governors.

In the early years of the seventh century, when internal bankruptcy and external attacks from the Persians seemed to threaten total destruction, Heraclius (610–641), son of the exarch of Africa, sailed from Carthage to Byzantium and seized the throne. He absorbed heavy losses, as the Persians took Antioch, Damascus, and Jerusalem, bearing off the True Cross in triumph. Soon afterwards they entered Alexandria, and Egypt too was gone. After 622 Heraclius began a counteroffensive, defeating the Persians on their own territory, recapturing all the lost provinces, and returning the True Cross to Jerusalem in 629.

But only a few years later, the new movement of Islam exploded out of Arabia and once more took away the provinces that Heraclius had recaptured from the Persians. In both the Persian and the Muslim victories over Byzantium, the disaffection of monophysite Syrians and Egyptians played a major part. From Egypt the Muslims pushed on westward and took Carthage in 698, putting an end to the North African exarchate. Muslim ships began to operate from Cyprus and Rhodes. In Italy the Lombards' threat grew more severe. Heraclius' work and that of Justinian were seemingly undone.

The Reorganization of the Seventh and Eighth Centuries. The loss of Syria and Egypt required the transformation of Asia Minor into a reservoir of military manpower and a stronghold of defense. The perpetual raids of Slavs, Avars, and Bulgars into the Balkan provinces made the emergency more acute. The emperors now extended to their remaining territories in Asia Minor and the Balkans the system of administration that combined military and civil government, previously introduced into the two exarchates. The Byzantine lands were divided into what we would call army corps areas, with the local military commanders also exercising civil authority. From the start, one of the areas was naval.

These new areas were called *themes,* from a word meaning a permanent garrison. The danger of military revolt which had almost ruined the Roman empire in the third century, and which had prompted Diocletian and Constantine to separate civil from military power, now reappeared as the two kinds of power were recombined. Generals of the themes now often revolted, and in the seventh and eighth centuries some of them seized the throne. The imperial government strove to combat this danger by dividing up the large original themes into smaller ones. The seven big themes at the end of the seventh century had become thirty small ones by the year 900. The emperor also asserted more and more direct supervision over the civil service departments.

The new system brought changes in taxation. Immigration and settlement had apparently put an end to the labor shortage of earlier centuries. Therefore, it was possible to begin separating the land tax from the tax on persons. The latter was transformed into a hearth tax that fell on every peasant household without exception. For purposes of the land tax, each peasant village was considered a single unit. Imperial tax assessors regularly visited each village, calculated its total tax, and assessed the individual inhabitants the portion of the tax that each would owe. The community as a whole was held responsible for the total tax. The neighbors of a peasant who was too poor to pay or of one who had abandoned his farm would have to pay the taxes of the defaulter to make up the total.

In the period 330–717, the emperors, despite their efforts, could not reconquer the West and reconstitute the Roman Empire of Augustus. And political disaffection—masked as theological controversy—made Persian and Arab aggression easier and cost the empire both Syria and Egypt. This forced a complete reorganization of the machinery of state, still incomplete in 717.

2. From Leo III (717) to Basil I (867)

In 717, Leo III defeated the Arabs, who were besieging Constantinople. Thereafter the struggle against the Muslims gradually became stabilized along a fixed frontier in Asia Minor. But the Muslim capture of Crete and Sicily opened the way for pirate raids against the shores of imperial lands in Greece and southern Italy. In northern Italy, the Lombards ended the Exarchate of Ravenna in 751. Byzantine rule was interrupted by the alliance between the Franks and the papacy. The Byzantine *dux* (originally army commander) of Venetia moved his headquarters to the famous island of the Rialto and thus became the forerunner of the *doges* of Venice.

Iconoclasm. Leo III was an iconoclast. The word means image-breaker. Something very like idolatry had in fact become widespread in the Christian East. Pictures and sculptures of Christ, the Virgin, and the Saints adorned not only churches but most private houses. Superstitious men and women put them on their hymn books and the handles of their umbrellas, and rendered them exaggerated reverence as if they were the originals in person. A wave of puritanical reaction set in and the emperor led it. Defenders of the images protested that the iconoclasts were influenced by the Jewish and Muslim prohibitions against such representations.

From 726 to 787 and again from 813 to 842 images were officially forbidden. Partly because the monks were strong defenders of the images, imperial policy became antimonastic, sometimes violently so. The controversy had very important repercussions in foreign policy too. The Western Church, led by the popes, believed that sacred images were educational for the illiterate and might be venerated but not worshiped. Leo III punished the pope by removing southern Italy and Sicily—with rich revenues—from the pope's ecclesiastical authority and putting them under the patriarch. This gave the pope a lasting grievance and a reason for turning to Pepin and Charlemagne and away from Byzantium.

The two restorations of icons in 787 and 842 were both engineered by empresses. It was agreed that images should receive only "proper" veneration and must not be adored. When the controversy ended, it was also understood that there would be no more religious sculpture in the round. Low relief was permitted and so were pictures. But many earlier religious works of art had been destroyed.

The Bulgarians. In Europe, the original Hunnic people of the Bulgars gradually merged with the settled Slavs of the northeast Balkan region. They fought many wars against Byzantium. In 811, their ruler, Krum, defeated the imperial armies and killed Emperor Nicephorus I (802–811), the first emperor to fall in battle since Valens at Adrianople in 378. Krum had Nicepho-

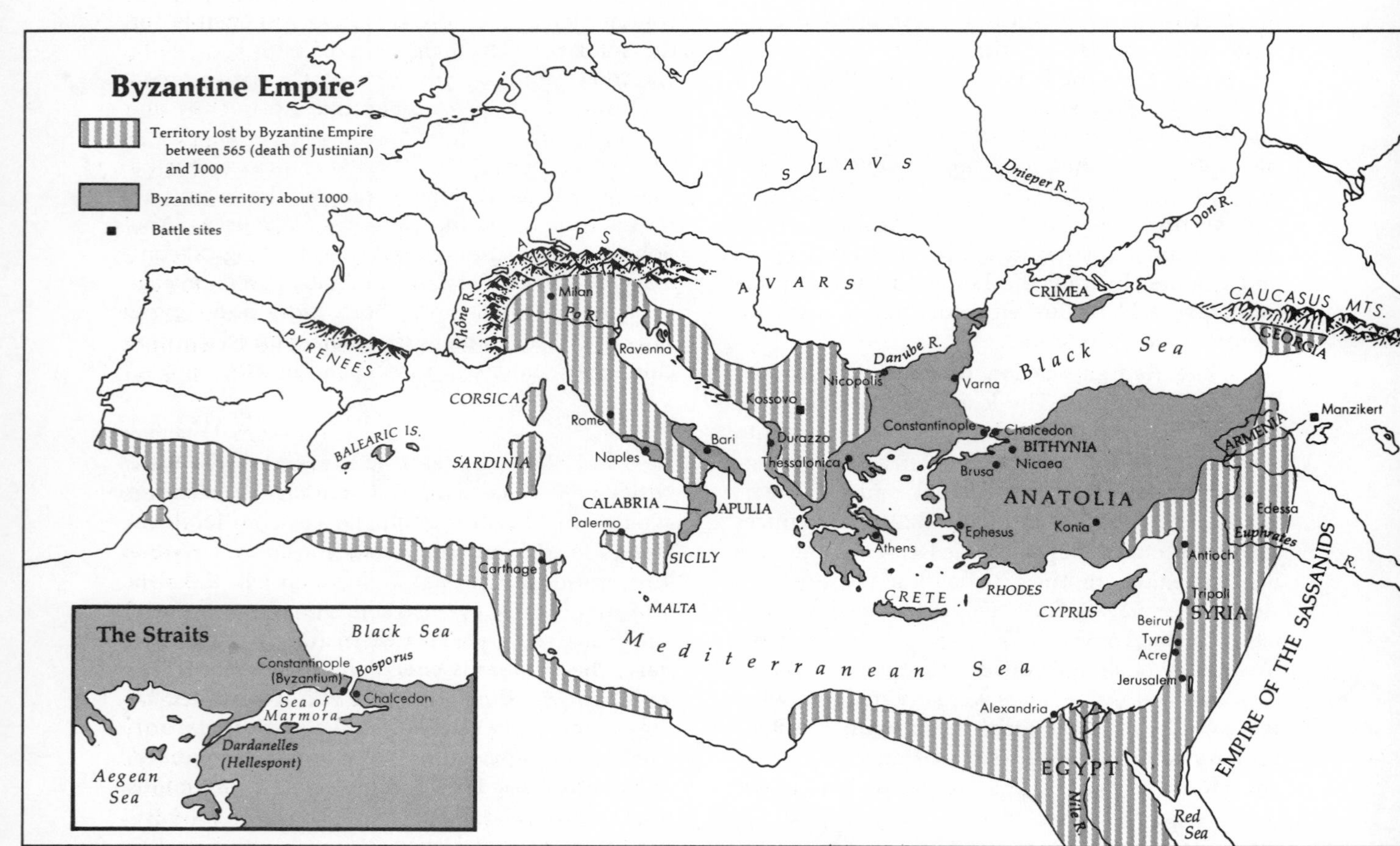

rus' skull lined with silver and used it as a drinking cup. Two generations later, the Bulgarian ruler wanted to be converted to Christianity. Yet he did not want to accept Byzantine missionaries, for fear of Byzantine political influence.

Just then, another Slavic people, the Moravians, living in what is now Czechoslovakia, reached the same stage. But they feared the encroachments of their powerful neighbors, the Germans, and in 862, to avoid German influence, sent to Byzantium for missionaries. The emperor Michael III (843–867) sent to Moravia two Christian clerics, Cyril (or Constantine) and his brother Methodius. Cyril invented the Slavic alphabet, still in use today and called Cyrillic. At the same time, Boris, ruler of the Bulgarians, asked for Christianity from the West. But the attempts of both Slavic peoples to avoid being converted by their powerful neighbors failed. The Germans and Roman Catholicism triumphed in Moravia. Boris had to yield to the Byzantines.

The Bulgarian decision to accept Christianity from Constantinople helped determine where the line between East and West would be drawn for all future history. To this day Bulgarians are an Orthodox people, and their culture throughout the Middle Ages directly reflected the influence of Byzantium.

The competition between Byzantium and the papacy for the conversion of the Bulgarians reached the level of a major political dispute. The Byzantine patriarch Photius for the first time "discovered" that the Roman church had adopted an addition to the creed. The Greek creed says that the Holy Ghost "proceeds" from the Father. The Latins had added the word *filioque,* meaning "and from the son." The addition of the one word implies a different view of the Trinity. But the repeated political quarrels between Byzantium and the papacy were more important than the word "filioque," which remained chiefly a debating point.

3. The Macedonian Dynasty (867–1025)

The Macedonian dynasty, established in 867, went over to the counteroffensive against the Muslims. They recaptured Crete (961), and soon afterward Antioch and much of northern Syria after three centuries of Arab domination. The Byzantine advance was halted short of Jerusalem. But, much like the later Crusaders from the West, the Byzantine emperors hoped to liberate Christ's city.

While pushing back the Muslims, the Byzantines penetrated the state of Armenia, and by 1025 had annexed it. It had been a valuable buffer against the Turks of Central Asia, who now became immediate and dangerous neighbors of Byzantium. The Byzantines also reconquered southern Italy and dominated the neighboring Lombard duchies until the early eleventh century, when the Normans gained a foothold in the peninsula.

Symeon (893–927), an ambitious Bulgarian ruler, launched a bitter hundred years' war against Byzantium, hoping that he could conquer Constantinople and become emperor himself. Not until 1018, after many expensive campaigns did the Byzantine emperor Basil II (976–1025) win the prolonged conflict. Basil took the appropriate name of "Bulgarslayer," and made Bulgaria a conquered province. The great drain of money and manpower of the Bulgarian war weakened Byzantium for the military disasters that were to come.

Byzantium and Russia. Under the Macedonian emperors, Byzantium experienced its first contact with the Russians. Scandinavians called "Rus" had in the eighth century begun to filter down from the north into the great plain of European Russia lying between the Baltic and the Black Sea. During the 850s, legend says, the struggling Slavic tribes actually invited the Northmen under Rurik to rule over them and keep order. Next, the Scandinavians moved south along the Dnieper River artery and seized Kiev, making it the center of a loosely organized state. They profited greatly by selling the products of the Russian forests. In 860, for the first time, a fleet of two hundred ships from the new Kievan river-state of Slavs ruled by Northmen, attacked Constantinople in a long siege. The Byzantines eventually beat them off, as they did all later such attacks.

More important than the occasional warfare between Russians and Byzantines were their trading relations. Treaties regulated the conduct of visiting Russian trading parties bringing the timber, furs, and hides that Byzantium needed and returning with gold coins and silk. Like the Bulgarian rulers before them, the Kievan princes saw the advantages of Christianity. By 950 there were already some converts to the new faith. The official conversion took place under the Kievan Prince Vladimir in the 980s as part of a treaty between him and Basil II. Vladimir first investigated Islam, Judaism, and Roman Catholic Christianity before choosing the Christianity of Byzantium. His ambassadors were so impressed by

Fourteenth-century Slavonic manuscript depicting Basil II's defeat of the Bulgarians (top). Basil blinded the prisoners and sent them back to King Samuel, who died of shock at the sight (bottom).

the beauty of the service in the great cathedral church of Santa Sophia at Constantinople that they felt they were in heaven. Vladimir married a Byzantine princess, accepted Byzantine Christianity, and in a single day threw down the old idols in Kiev and had the entire population baptized in the waters of the Dnieper.

Next came an influx of missionaries and the quick growth of a Russian clergy. Eastern Orthodox Christianity transformed pagan Kievan society. Instead of leaving the punishment of crime to the avenging family of the injured party, the state recognized its obligation to seek out and punish a criminal. With jurisdiction over all moral and religious issues, the Church also introduced the first education. Using the Cyrillic alphabet, churchmen wrote the first Russian literature. Byzantine art forms were imported and imitated; paganism died slowly in the countryside. Culture was liveliest in the few towns and in the monasteries, which quickly multiplied. At first, the archbishops of Kiev were Greeks from Byzantium, but the Russian church soon asserted its practical independence.

In the West every educated priest, no matter what his native tongue, knew Latin and so could read Latin classics and the Latin church fathers. In Russia, however, Slavic was used in the liturgy. Few Russian priests learned Greek. Sermons, saints' lives, some chronicles, were translated from Greek and circulated in Slavic, but these were no substitute for the Greek classics or the church fathers. The result was a "cultural lag" in Russia. Beginning in the nineteenth century, some influential modern Russian thinkers argued that the Russians' Byzantine faith had fostered stagnation and intellectual sterility. But their opponents argued that it had given the Russians spirituality, a willingness to bend to God's will, and other great virtues.

Kievan Russia developed a society rather like that in medieval western Europe. The prince's retinue, which began as a Scandinavian war band, gradually became a group of councilors typical of a settled state. The law codes reflected social conditions: arson and horse theft brought heavier penalties than murder. Because the Byzantines paid cash for Russian forest products, Kiev had more of a money economy than manorial western Europe.

Just as Rome civilized and eventually christianized large groups of barbarians in western Europe, so Constantinople, the new Rome, civilized and christianized the Slavs. Of all the achievements of the Byzantines none was more important. Many of the problems that face the West today in its dealings with the Soviet Union arise from the fact that the Soviet Union is a country in the Eastern Orthodox tradition, not the Western.

The Powerful and the Poor. Under the early Macedonian emperors, the large Byzantine landowners flourished. Nobles with great estates, "the powerful," bought up the lands of "the poor" and made the peasantry dependent upon them. This growing power of the nobility threatened the state in two important ways. It was losing its best taxpayers—the free peasants—and its best soldiers—the military settlers.

During the tenth and eleventh centuries, a great struggle developed between the emperors and "the powerful." By repeated laws the emperors tried to end the acquisition of land by the nobility. But the laws could not be enforced. In times of bad harvest especially, small free proprietors had to sell out to their rich neighbors. Basil II (976–1025) forced "the powerful" to pay all the back taxes owed by the peasants, thus relieving the village communities of the burden that was so difficult for them to bear, and placing it on the shoulders of the rich. But a few years after Basil died, "the powerful" had this law repealed. As the landlords got more free peasants as tenants on their estates, they became commanders of private armies. To reduce the landlords' power, the imperial civil servants tried to cut down the expenses of the army, in which the landlords were now playing the leading role. This strife would eventually weaken the imperial defenses.

Thus between 867 and 1025, the Byzantine Empire reached its height. The emperors went over to the offensive against the Muslims and regained much territory and prestige. They fought the Bulgarian struggle to its bloody conclusion. They converted the Russians to Christianity. And at home the emperors strove to check the power of the great landlords.

4. Byzantine Civilization

Literature. Like the civilization of the West in the Middle Ages, that of Byzantium was derived from Greece and Rome. In the West, however, long centuries passed during which nobody knew Greek. During all this time the Byzantines preserved ancient Greek works of philosophy, science, and literature, copied and recopied them, and studied them constantly. Had it not been for Byzantium, Homer, Sophocles, Plato, and Aristotle, would have been lost to the world.

In the West before the twelfth-century growth of universities, learning was restricted to monasteries. But at Byzantium secular libraries and schools never disappeared. The teacher occupied an important position in society. Many of the emperors were themselves scholars and lovers of literature. A steady supply of learned and cultivated men filled the Byzantine bureaucracy and law courts.

One of the best Byzantine literary achievements is the tenth- or eleventh-century epic poem about a warrior who had fought the Muslims on the frontier in Asia Minor two or three hundred years before, Basil Digenes Akritas. Half Greek, half Muslim, he conquered wild beasts and brigands and engaged in single combat with a magnificent Amazon (female) warrior. As for achievements in prose, talented historians told the story of the empire over the centuries. Nothing in the medieval West corresponds to their work.

The hotly debated theological controversies produced volumes too difficult for most people to understand but influential in determining the policies of Byzantine leaders. Saints' lives, often written for a popular audience, took the place the novel has in our society. The hero-saint undergoes adventures and sufferings and in the end reaps the rewards of his own piety. These saints' lives often tell us much about daily life and popular attitudes.

Unique among them, *Barlaam and Ioasaph* is a tenth-century tale of an Indian king who tries

The interior of the Church of Santa Sophia.

to prevent his son from learning about Christianity by shutting him away in a remote place. But a wise monk, Barlaam, penetrates to the son's retreat and instructs him in the faith, telling him ten moral tales illustrating the Christian life. A christianized version of the life of Buddha, *Barlaam and Ioasaph* had traveled from India across Asia before it was turned into Byzantine literature. It was then transmitted to the West. The stories Barlaam tells are also Indian in origin, and have entered our literature too. Prince Ioasaph was made a saint in both the Orthodox and Roman Catholic churches. His name is the Indian word "Boddhisattva." Through this legend Buddha himself became and has remained a Christian saint.

The Arts. We can still see many of the greatest Byzantine buildings. Justinian planned the Church of Santa Sophia in Constantinople to be "a church the like of which has never been seen since Adam nor ever will be." After the Turks captured Constantinople in 1453 they built many mosques imitating it. In plan it combined the Hellenistic or Roman basilica with a dome

The creation of the world: mosaic scenes from Genesis in St. Mark's, Venice.

taken from Persia, a striking example of the blending of Greek and Oriental elements. In decoration, the use of colored marbles, enamel, gold, silver, and jewels, and the glowing mosaics on the walls and ceilings, reflect the sumptuousness of the Orient. The dome, said an early observer, "seems rather to hang by a golden chain from heaven than to be supported by solid masonry." Justinian himself exclaimed "I have outdone thee, O Solomon!"

Many fine Byzantine churches survive in Greece, such as that of Daphni at Eleusis near Athens. At Ravenna, capital of the exarchate, are three smaller churches of the sixth century with superb mosaics, including portraits of Justinian and of his empress Theodora. At Venice—first the client, then the rival, and finally the conqueror of Byzantium—St. Mark's is a true Byzantine church of the later period. Byzantine monumental sculpture has virtually disappeared because of the iconoclasts. Some splendid work in low relief in marble and ivory survives. Byzantine painting in frescoes, mosaics, and illuminated manuscripts survives in many examples.

Along with the major arts went the so-called minor arts, whose level the Byzantines raised so high that the term minor arts seems almost absurd. The embroidered silks, the work of goldsmiths and silversmiths, the enameled and jeweled bookcovers, the elaborate containers made especially to hold the sacred relics of a saint, the great Hungarian sacred crown of Saint Stephen—all testify to the endless variety and fertility of Byzantine inspiration.

Sixteenth-century Persian miniature showing Mohammed, his face veiled, ascending to Paradise.

V Islam before the Crusades

Islam (the Arabic word means "submission") is the most recently founded of the world's great religions. Its adherents (Muslims, "those who submit") today inhabit the entire North African coast of the Mediterranean, parts of tropical Africa, portions of the Balkans, the entire Middle East, Pakistan and parts of India, the Malay Peninsula, Indonesia, and the Philippine Islands, besides Soviet Central Asia and parts of China. Western relationships with the Muslim world have been of crucial importance ever since Mohammed founded Islam in the early seventh century.

Mohammed

The Arabia into which Mohammed was born about the year 570 was inhabited largely by nomad tribes, each under its own chief. They raided each other's flocks and lived on the meat and milk of their animals and on dates from palm trees. They were pagans who worshiped sacred stones and trees. Their chief center was Mecca, fifty miles inland from the coast of the Red Sea. In a sacred building called the Kaaba, or cube, they revered idols, especially a small black stone fallen from heaven, which perhaps was a meteorite.

Mohammed was born into one of the poorer clans of the Kuraish, a trading tribe that lived by caravan commerce with Syria. Early orphaned, he was brought up by relatives and as a young man entered the service of a wealthy widow much older than himself, whom he later married. Mohammed then devoted himself to his divine mission. We do not know exactly how he came to believe that he was the bearer of a new revelation. On his caravan journeys he no doubt observed and talked with Christians and Jews. He spent much time in fasting and vigils. He became convinced that God was revealing the truth to him, having singled him out to be his messenger. The revelations came to him gradually over the rest of his life. He wrote them down in rhythmic, sometimes rhyming prose. He included entertaining stories from the Old Testament of the Hebrews and from Arab folklore.

In later years this Muslim revelation was put together as the Koran, or "book." (The chapters were not arranged in order by subject matter but mechanically by length with the longest first. This makes the Koran difficult to follow. Many Muslims have written works explaining it.) Mohammed saw his revelation as the confirmation of Hebrew and Christian scriptures, as a religion designed for all men, the perfection of both Judaism and Christianity, the final statement of God's truth.

Mohammed was a firm monotheist. He declared that it was idolatry to worship more than one God, and he believed the trinity of the Christians to be three Gods and therefore idolatry. Unlike Arabs before him, Mohammed believed in an afterlife that was to be experienced in the flesh.

The requirements of Islam are few. Five times a day in prayer, facing toward Mecca, Muslims must bear witness that there is no God but God and that Mohammed is his prophet. During the sacred month of Ramadan they may not eat or drink between sunrise and sunset. They must give alms to the poor. And, if they can, they should at least once in their lifetimes make a pilgrimage to the sacred city of Mecca. There are also rules for certain aspects of daily life—for example, strong drink is forbidden. Polygamy is sanctioned, but four wives are the most a man may have. Divorce is easy for the husband.

At first, Mohammed preached this faith to members of his family, then to the people of Mecca, who repudiated him scornfully. In 622, some pilgrims from an oasis called Yathrib, two hundred miles north of Mecca, invited Mohammed to come to them. This move from Mecca is the famous *Hegira* from which the Islamic calendar has ever since been dated; 622 is the Muslim year 1. Yathrib had its name changed to al-Medina, *the* city, and became the center of the expanding new faith.

God told Mohammed to fight against those who had not been converted. Those who die in the holy war, or *jihad,* against the infidel die in a holy cause. In 630, Mohammed returned to Mecca as a conqueror, cleansed the Kaaba of all the idols except the black stone, and incorporated it into his religion. Two years later, in 632, he died. By then, perhaps one-third of Arabia had become Muslim. Only one century later, Charles Martel was battling Muslims in far-off France, the Byzantine Empire was locked in a life-and-death struggle with them, and Islam had reached India.

Expansion

This startling expansion was only partly due to the zeal of converts to the new faith. Overpopulation of the Arabian peninsula was more significant in touching off the explosion of the Arabs. For some time before Mohammed, in fact, Arabs had been emigrating to Iraq, Palestine, and Syria. Islam might now become the battle cry of the emigrants, but their motives included the age-old ones of conquest for living space and booty. Toward Christians and Jews the Muslims generally were tolerant, regarding both as "peoples of the Book."

Within a decade after Mohammed's death, the Arabs conquered Syria and Persia. Syria, disaffected from Byzantium by monophysitism, fell easily. And the Persians, weakened after their defeat by Heraclius, did not resist effectively. In 639–640, the Arabs took Egypt, the major Byzantine naval base, like Syria monophysite in religion and ripe for conquest.

Launching ships, the Arabs now seized the islands of Cyprus and Rhodes and began raiding southern Italy and Sicily. Moving westward across North Africa, they took Carthage in 698. In 711, under the command of Tarik, they launched the invasion of Spain across the Straits of Gibraltar ("Rock of Tarik"). By 725, the first Muslims had crossed the Pyrenees to meet Charles Martel at Tours seven years later. Meanwhile, they had been spreading east from Persia and in 724 reached the Indus and the western frontiers of China. They also moved south from Egypt and North Africa into the little-known regions of Central Africa. Of all this territory only the Mediterranean islands and Spain were ever permanently reconquered by Christians.

Disunity

The Arabs could not establish a unified state. They had conquered too diverse a collection of lands and peoples for that. Moreover, they quarreled among themselves. After Mohammed's death, they disagreed over the succession, finally choosing his eldest companion, Abu Bakr, as caliph *(khalifa,* the representative of Mohammed). The next two caliphs were also chosen from outside Mohammed's family, to the distress of many Muslims. In 656, the third caliph was murdered. Those who favored choosing only a member of Mohammed's own family favored Ali, son-in-law of the prophet; they were known as Shiites (sectarians). Opposed to them were the Sunnites (traditionalists), who favored the election of any eligible person. The Sunnites also favored supplementing the Koran with commentaries called "traditions," which were disapproved by the Shiites.

In 656, Ali was chosen caliph. Civil war broke out, and Ali was murdered in 661. His opponent, Muawiya of the Umayyad family, leader of the Sunnites, had already proclaimed himself caliph in Damascus. Thus began the Umayyad caliphate (660–750), on the whole a period of good government, brisk trade, and cultural advance. The Umayyad civil service was manned by trained Byzantines, and Greek artists worked for the caliph. The Christian population, except for the payment of a poll tax, was better off than it had been under Byzantium.

Shiite opposition to the Umayyads remained strong. The Shiites felt they had to curse the first three caliphs, who had ruled before their hero, Ali, and whom the Sunnites deeply revered. The Shiites were far more intolerant of the unbeliever, conspired in secret against the government, and were given to self-pity and to wild outbursts of grief for Ali's son Hussein, who was killed in 680. Southern Iraq was then the center of Shiite strength.

From these eastern regions came the leader-

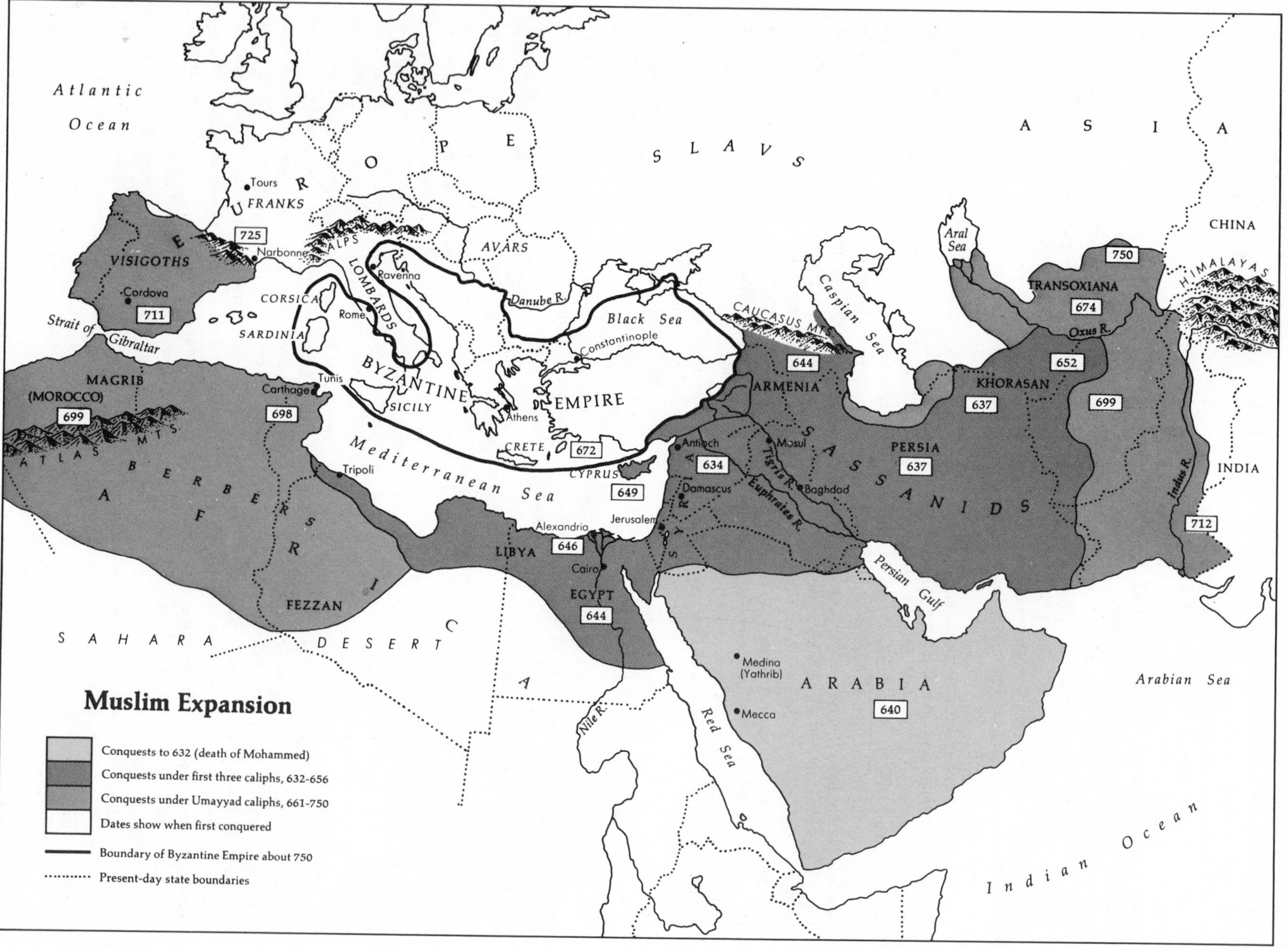
Muslim Expansion
Conquests to 632 (death of Mohammed)
Conquests under first three caliphs, 632-656
Conquests under Umayyad caliphs, 661-750
Dates show when first conquered
Boundary of Byzantine Empire about 750
Present-day state boundaries
Atlantic Ocean
EUROPE
SLAVS
ASIA
CHINA
HIMALAYAS
INDIA
Tours
FRANKS
725
Narbonne
ALPS
AVARS
VISIGOTHS
Cordova
711
Strait of Gibraltar
CORSICA
SARDINIA
Rome
Ravenna
LOMBARDS
Danube R.
Black Sea
Constantinople
BYZANTINE EMPIRE
SICILY
Athens
CRETE
672
CYPRUS
649
Mediterranean Sea
Tunis
Carthage
698
MAGRIB
(MOROCCO)
699
ATLAS MTS.
BERBERS
AFRICA
Tripoli
FEZZAN
SAHARA DESERT
LIBYA
Alexandria
646
Cairo
EGYPT
644
Nile R.
Jerusalem
Damascus
SYRIA
634
Antioch
Mosul
Tigris R.
Baghdad
Euphrates R.
ARMENIA
644
CAUCASUS MTS.
Caspian Sea
Aral Sea
SASSANIDS
PERSIA
637
KHORASAN
637
652
Oxus R.
TRANSOXIANA
674
750
699
Indus R.
712
Persian Gulf
Medina
(Yathrib)
Mecca
ARABIA
640
Red Sea
Arabian Sea
Indian Ocean

ship of the plot that in 750 was responsible for the murder of the last of the Umayyad caliphs, together with ninety members of his family. The leader of the conspirators was Abu'l Abbas, not a Shiite himself, but the great-grandson of a cousin of Mohammed. The new Abbasid caliphate soon moved east to Baghdad, capital of present-day Iraq. The days when Islam was strongly under Byzantine influence were over. At Baghdad, the caliphate took on more and more the color of the Persian Empire, in whose former territory it was situated. Its Christian subjects were, on the whole, well treated.

The rest of the Muslim world slipped away from Abbasid control. One of the few Umayyads to escape death in 750 made his way to Spain and built himself a state centered around the city of Cordova. Rich and strong, his descendants declared themselves caliphs in 929. Separate Muslim states appeared in Morocco, in Tunis, and in Egypt, where still another dynasty, this time Shiite, built Cairo in the tenth century and called themselves caliphs. Rival dynasties also appeared in Persia itself, in Syria, and in the other eastern provinces.

At Baghdad, though the state was under the influence of Persian culture, power fell gradually into the hands of Turkish troops. The Seljuk Turks emerged supreme from a struggle for power when they took Baghdad in 1055. Although the caliphate at Baghdad lasted down to 1258, when the Mongols finally ended it, the caliphs were mere puppets in Turkish hands.

Islamic Civilization

Many of the regions conquered by the Arabs had been parts of the Byzantine or Persian Empires, and had their own ancient traditions. The new religion and the Arabic language brought to them by the conquerors often stimulated new artistic and literary development. The requirement of pilgrimage to Mecca made Muslims a mobile people and encouraged the exchange of ideas from all quarters of the Islamic world. Everybody who wanted to read the Koran had to learn Arabic because translation of the book was forbidden. Since Arabic is an extraordinarily flexible and powerful instrument, it became the standard literary language of the whole Islamic world. The Muslims gave to poetry the highest rank among the arts.

Like both Roman and Greek Christianity, Islam was convinced of its superiority to all other religions and ways of life. Like the Byzantines, the Muslims aspired to dominate the civilized world. They thought of the world as divided between those lands already part of Islam and those lands still to be conquered. Like the Byzantine emperor, the caliph was an autocrat, a vicar of God, chosen by a mixture of election and the hereditary principle.

The caliph, however, could not add to or change the religious law, although the Byzantine emperor sometimes pronounced on dogma. Both courts stressed show and ceremony, largely derived from the Persian tradition. However strong their mutual hatred, Christians and Muslims felt themselves to be worshipers in two religions that were on the same level of intellectual advancement and that held similar views on creation, human history, the last judgment, and the instability of everything mortal. When at peace with the Muslims, the Byzantines thought of them as the successors of the Persians, and as such the only other civilized people.

Learning, Literature, and the Arts

The reign of Caliph Mamun (813–833) is often said to mark the high point in the civilization of the caliphate. In Baghdad, he built observatories, founded a university, and ordered works of ancient Greek and Indian scientists and philosophers translated into Arabic. The Muslims developed medicine beyond the standard works of the Greek masters. They wrote textbooks on diseases of the eye, on smallpox, and on measles, which remained the best authorities until the eighteenth century. Avicenna (980–1037) was famous for his systematization of all known medical science and also for his philosophical and poetic writings.

Muslim scientists adopted Indian numerals, the ones that we use today and call Arabic. The new numerals included the zero, a concept unknown to the Romans, without which it is hard to see how higher mathematical research could be carried on. The Muslims began analytical geometry and plane and spherical trigonometry. They made much progress in algebra, which is itself an Arabic word, as, for example, are alcohol, cipher, alchemy, zenith, and nadir.

In philosophy, the Muslims eagerly studied Plato, Aristotle, and the Neoplatonists. Like the Byzantines and the western Europeans, they used what they learned to tackle theological problems about the nature and the power of God and his relationship to the universe. Efforts to reconcile philosophy and religion occupied the great Spanish Muslim Averroës (ca. 1126–1198), whose commentaries on Aristotle, translated from Arabic into Latin, were available to the Christian West well before the original Greek text of Aristotle himself.

Some Spanish Christians complained that their fellow Christians were irresistibly attracted by Muslim poetry and its portrayal of life in the desert with its camels and horses, its warfare and hunting, its feasts and drinking bouts, and its emphasis on love. Arabic love poetry, as developed in Spain, influenced later French and German love poets. Beside poetry, excellent history was written in Arabic. The fiction is limited to a few subjects—the adventures of a rogue, the sad misfortunes of a pair of lovers, or exciting incidents of life in the capital, with the caliph participating. These tales were collected in the *Arabian Nights* together with stories of Indian and Jewish origin, as well as some from the Greek classics and from Hellenistic works.

In the arts, the Muslims adapted Byzantine churches in building mosques, which required a front courtyard with a fountain where the faithful might wash before entering. All that was necessary inside was a quiet and dignified place to pray and rest, with a small niche in the wall showing the direction of Mecca, and a pulpit from which the Koran might be read aloud. Next to the mosque, slender towers or minarets were built from which the *muezzin* could call the faithful to prayer. Beautiful and elaborate geometric patterns in wood, stone, mosaic, and porcelain tile characterized the interior decoration, which also utilized the highly ornamental Arabic script, particularly the names of the first four caliphs and passages from the Koran. The great mosques of Damascus, Cairo, Jerusalem, and Cordova are perhaps the finest surviving specimens, but there are thousands of others all over the Muslim world.

Through Sicily and Spain came Greco-Roman and Muslim science, philosophy, and art. In music, the Morris dance, for instance, is simply a "Moorish dance." Lute, tambourine, guitar, and fanfare are all words of Arabic origin.

When we consider the contributions of the Byzantines and the Muslims to Western culture, we are altogether justified in saying that much light came from the East.

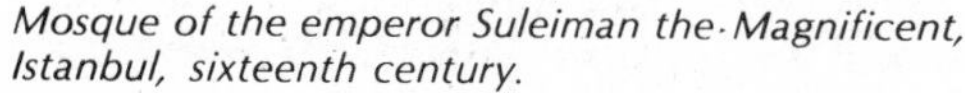

Mosque of the emperor Suleiman the Magnificent, Istanbul, sixteenth century.

READING SUGGESTIONS on Transition between Two Worlds
(Asterisks indicate paperback.)

The Barbarians

J. M. Wallace-Hadrill, *The Barbarian West: The Early Middle Ages, A.D. 400–1000* (*Harper Torchbooks). A reliable introductory survey.

E. A. Thompson, *The Early Germans* (1965). Another good introduction to the subject.

S. Dill, *Roman Society in Gaul in the Merovingian Age* (1926), and *Roman Society in the Last Century of the Western Empire* (*Meridian). Older accounts, but still not superseded and very interesting.

A. R. Lewis, *Emerging Medieval Europe, A.D. 400–1000* (*Knopf). Gives a useful overview.

F. Lot, *The End of the Ancient World and the Beginnings of the Middle Ages* (*Harper Torchbooks). Now half a century old but still extremely interesting and sound.

H. Fichtenau, *The Carolingian Empire* (*Harper Torchbooks). Good sketch by a leading continental scholar.

J. Boussard, *The Civilization of Charlemagne* (*Mentor). Emphasizes the great Frankish ruler's influence on Carolingian society.

R. Winston, *Charlemagne: From the Hammer to the Cross* (*Vintage). A good biography.

G. Duby, *The Early Growth of the European Economy* (1974). Recent work by a leading contemporary French scholar.

D. Wilson, *The Anglo-Saxons* (*Penguin). What achaeology teaches us about Anglo-Saxon England.

C. Brooke, *The Saxon and Norman Kings* (*Fontana). The first nine chapters take the reader through the reign of King Canute.

D. Whiting, *The Beginnings of English Society: The Anglo-Saxon Period* (*Penguin); and P. H. Blair, *Introduction to Anglo-Saxon England* (*Cambridge). Both are useful introductory surveys.

J. Bronsted, *The Vikings* (*Pelican). Good treatment of the Norse invaders as a whole.

Feudal Europe

M. Bloch, *Feudal Society,* 2 vols. (*Phoenix). The supreme work of scholarship on the subject.

C. Stephenson, *Medieval Feudalism* (*Great Seal Books). A good introductory survey.

F. L. Ganshof, *Feudalism* (*Harper Torchbooks). More advanced than Stephenson, less demanding than Bloch.

G. Duby, *Rural Economy and Country Life in the West,* trans. C. Postan (1968). The best single work on the agricultural system.

E. Power, *Medieval People* (*University Paperbacks). Engaging introduction to actual human beings rather than institutions.

Civilization of the Early Medieval West

M. L. W. Laistner, *Thought and Letters in Western Europe: A.D. 500–900* (1931). By far the most reliable standard introduction to the subject.

E. K. Rand, *Founders of the Middle Ages* (1928). An older book, but so learned and well written that it is still worth reading today.

P. Brown, *Augustine of Hippo: A Biography* (*California). Brilliant, well-written, scholarly, original: a delight to read.

J. Leclercq, *Love of Learning and Desire for God: A Study of Monastic Culture* (*Mentor). Demonstrates how important the monasteries were as cultural centers.

R. W. Chambers, *Beowulf: An Introduction to the Study of the Poem,* suppl. C. L. Wrenn, 3rd ed. (1959). A full, scholarly summary.

J. Hubert, J. Porcher, and W. F. Volback, *Europe of the Invasions* (1969). A fine work on the arts of the period, with brief text and many splendid illustrations.

The World of Byzantium, 337–1025

C. Ostrogorsky, *History of the Byzantine State,* trans. J. Hussey (1969). The best single book on the subject, very brief on the period before about 600, and now being challenged with respect to some of its conclusions.

A. A. Vasiliev, *History of the Byzantine World,* 2 vols. (*Wisconsin). An older book, considerably more pedestrian than Ostrogorsky's.

J. M. Hussey, *The Byzantine World* (*Harper Torchbooks). A short, adequate introduction.

J. B. Bury, *A History of the Later Roman Empire,* 2 vols. (*Dover). Covers the period through Justinian (565), a revision of a standard, older work that came down to 802 in its first edition. Solid but somewhat dry.

A. Cameron, *Circus Factions: Blues and Greens at Rome and Constantinople* (1976). A new, scholarly work, decisively challenging all previous opinions on the subject.

A. Grabar, *Byzantine Painting* (1953). Beautifully illustrated work on mosaics, miniatures, and frescoes.

D. T. Rice, *Art in the Byzantine Era* (*Praeger). A good introduction to the subject.

H. W. Häussig, *A History of Byzantine Civilization,* trans. J. M. Hussey (1971). A beautifully illustrated and unusually original text.

Islam before the Crusades

H. A. R. Gibb, *Mohammedanism* (*Galaxy). Fine introduction by a very great scholar of the subject.

B. Lewis, *The Arabs in History* (*Harper Torchbooks). Authoritative short treatment.

P. K. Hitti, *History of the Arabs from the Earliest Times to the Present* (*St. Martin's). A lengthier, detailed treatment, useful for reference.

G. E. von Grünebaum, *Medieval Islam* (*Phoenix). A learned essay on Islamic culture, in part controversial.

W. M. Watt, *Muhammad: Prophet and Statesman* (*Oxford). The best single book in English on the Prophet.

W. B. Bishai, *Humanities in the Arabic-Islamic World* (*W. C. Brown). Concise, learned, and recent.

A. Guillaume, *Islam* (*Penguin). Another reliable account of the religion.

Sources

Augustine, *Confessions,* trans. E. B. Pusey (*Modern Library), and *The City of God,* trans. M. Dodds (*Haffner).

Boethius, *The Consolation of Philosophy,* trans. V. E. Watts, (*Penguin). A useful version of the poem.

Bede, *The History of the English Church and People,* trans. L. Sherley-Price (*Penguin).

Beowulf, trans. D. Wright (*Penguin).

Einhard, *Life of Charlemagne,* trans. S. Turner (*Michigan). Written by a courtier of the great emperor.

Procopius, *The Secret History,* trans. G. A. Williamson (*Penguin). The most scandalous of his works, not discovered until more than a thousand years after his death. The sober histories of the *Wars* and of the *Buildings* are available in the Loeb Classical Library, 6 vols., trans. H. B. Dewing (1914–1940).

Constantine Porphyrogenitus, *De Administrando Imperio,* trans. R. Jenkins, rev. ed. (1967). A letter of advice written by the emperor himself to his son and heir, telling much about the various peoples living around the borders of the Byzantine Empire.

Michael Psellus, *Fourteen Byzantine Rulers,* trans. E. Sewter (1958). A narrative history of eleventh-century Byzantium, composed by a prominent courtier and intellectual.

Digenes Akrites, trans. J. Mavrogordato (1956). The Byzantine epic of the struggle between Greeks and Arabs along the frontier in Asia Minor. Good introduction.

St. John Damascene, *Barlaam and Ioasaph,* trans. G. R. Woodward and H. Mattingly (1967). A remarkable saint's life based on the life of Buddha. As the introduction by D. M. Lang points out, the text was not written by John of Damascus but by a monk named Euthymius.

The Koran, trans. N. J. Dawood (*Penguin). A good translation of the great "book" of Islam.

CHAPTER FIVE

The Medieval World: Western Europe

After about the year 1000, it becomes artificial to discuss contemporary Western and Eastern developments in the same chapter. Although there were frequent contacts between the Roman Catholic West and the Byzantine Orthodox and Islamic East, their modes of life had become so different that it is best to consider them separately. In this chapter we deal solely with the West in the period of a little more than three hundred years between approximately 1000 and the early fourteenth century.

After an account of the economic and social revival of the eleventh century, we turn to the monarchies of France, England, and Germany, emphasizing the similarities and differences in the development of these national states. More than that of either of the other two peoples, the history of the Germans was intimately connected with Italy and the growth in power of the papacy. The Church as an institution was far more important than the papacy as a political power. The third section examines the Church as the chief civilizing force in the medieval West. And in the last we turn to literature—both Latin and vernacular—and to the arts—Romanesque and Gothic—in this period of grandeur.

I THE SOCIETY AND ITS ECONOMY

The Turning Point of the Eleventh Century

The eleventh century proved to be a major turning point in the social and economic life of the West, although nobody alive at the time could have been fully conscious of what was happening. As the raids of the Northmen tapered off, most of western Europe found itself secure against outside attack. By the end of the century, western Europe took the offensive and invaded the lands of Islam in the Crusades (see Chapter 6). During the eleventh century, the population of western Europe grew rapidly. Nobody knows why. Possibly the growth reflected the greater security of most individuals and their increased expectancy of life, despite dangers from plague, famine, and violence that seem fantastic by modern standards.

The larger population needed more food and more land. Pioneers felled trees, drained swamps, opened up new areas for farming. When forest or marshland lay within a manor, a lord would often offer special inducements to his serfs to undertake the extra heavy labor of clearing and farming it. Sometimes a group of peasants would move into a new region that had lain empty before, and would clear it and farm it by introducing the usual strip system. If such uninhabited land belonged to a lord, he might invite peasants to colonize it and offer them freedom from serfdom and the chance to pay a money rent instead of the usual services. This would bring profit to the lord and great advantages to the emancipated serf.

Technology helped to improve the farmer's life. More farmers adopted the heavy-wheeled horse-drawn plow. Windmills made their first appearance on the European landscape. Gradually the anonymous inventors of the Middle Ages perfected systems of gears that would turn the millstones faster and produce more meal in less time.

Trade and Town

During the eleventh century trade began also slowly to revive. Medieval farmers were helpless in the face of bad harvest years. Plenty and scarcity varied widely from region to region. Surpluses were brought into areas of famine and sold at high prices to the hungry. The first new commercial centers arose in Venice and the Low Countries, where the local farms could not feed the increasing population. Even in the Dark Ages, such trade had never disappeared altogether, but now the incentives to increase its scale were pressing.

When the proprietor of a manor found that he could regularly make large sums by selling a certain crop, he would plant more and more of that crop and use the money to buy the crops he was no longer raising. Once he had more money than he needed for necessities, he wanted something extra, a luxury. Such a demand quickly creates its supply: what was once a luxury comes to seem a necessity. For example, in Flanders, an area poor for growing grain but good for raising sheep, the people sold their raw wool, developed a woolen-manufacturing industry, and imported the food they needed.

The recovery of commerce and the beginning of industries stimulated the growth of towns. Old Roman towns like London and Marseilles revived. New towns grew around a castle (*bourg* in France, *burgh* in England, *burg* in Germany), especially if it was strategically located for trade as well as for defense. And so the resident *bourgeois, burgesses,* or *burghers,* enter the language as "castle dwellers" but soon become recognizable as residents of towns, engaged in commerce. Protected by the lord of the castle or sometimes by the abbot of a local monastery, the townsmen built walls and pursued their trade.

Townsmen would band together into *guilds* to protect themselves from brigands on the roads and to bargain with the lord of the next castle, who might be confiscating their goods or charging them high tolls to cross his land. Grouped in a guild, merchants could often win concessions. If the lord they were bargaining with seemed unreasonable, they might threaten to take a route across someone else's land and pay less.

Mutual advantage soon led proprietors, including kings and lesser lords, to grant privileges to the townsmen by issuing a *charter.* The contents of such documents varied, but most of them guaranteed free status to the townsmen. Even an escaped serf within the town would acquire freedom if he could avoid capture for a year. The charter might also grant the townsmen the right to hold a perpetual market, to transfer property within the town walls, and to have their lawsuits tried in a town court by town custom, which

Drapers' hall, Ghent, begun in the fifteenth century.

slowly developed into a whole new kind of law, the *law merchant.*

Industry followed commerce into the town. The merchant, with his experience of distant markets, learned how to buy raw material, to have workmen do the manufacturing wherever it was cheapest, and to sell the finished products wherever he could get the best price. The workmen also soon began to organize themselves into *craft guilds,* which provided medical care and burial for the members. The guilds would regulate minimum wages, the standards of quality of the product, and even prices.

Enterprise was neither free nor private. It was highly regulated, both as an effort to reduce outside competition and as a reflection of the ideas of the age. Men believed that a *just price* for a pair of shoes included the cost of the leather and the thread, the amount needed to sustain the shoemaker at his usual standard of life while he made the shoes, and a small addition to pay the seller for his time and trouble. To make money in the modern sense of charging the highest price you could get was in theory to cheat the customer. No doubt many medieval customers were in fact cheated in this sense, but the ethics of the time condemned the action. *Finance capitalism*—the use of money to make money, the investment of funds at interest—was regarded as usury.

Town and Countryside

The towns greatly affected the overwhelming mass of the population who remained in the countryside, who now had a place to sell their surplus and so an incentive to produce it. Some peasants saved enough cash to buy their freedom. Some fled to the town in the hope of acquiring freedom, or at least in the hope that their children might acquire it. The very word *cash* suggests a most important development—the flourishing of a money economy instead of an economy of barter. Barter continued but as the magnates came to want more and more manufactured or imported or luxury goods, they wanted cash rather than services: a serf's labors would produce more grain, but not the money to buy a piece of armor. So the lord would let the peasant pay him cash and would forgive (commute) the serf's obligation to work on the lord's land. More demand for money led to more money in circulation, and to a gradual inflationary rise in wages and prices.

With the increase in demand for goods, large-scale fairs became common. Some of them brought together merchants and products from a relatively narrow region, but others attracted men and goods from all over the European world. In Champagne in northeastern France, for example, there were several great annual fairs each year. The count of Champagne collected a fee from the towns for the privilege of holding the fair and the revenues from a special court set up to try cases that arose during its course. As large-scale transactions became more frequent, it became less practical for merchants to carry around large amounts of cash; and during the thirteenth century merchants came to use a written promise to pay instead. Acceptance of these *bills of exchange,* a kind of primitive check, often made it unnecessary to transport money at all.

II MONARCHY IN THE MEDIEVAL WEST

With the gradual changes in the economy and the society of western Europe went changes also in its political life. As always in politics, the central question is: who has the power? In France, the most feudal area of Europe, the monarch successfully asserted his superiority over his vassals. In England, the kings, having made good their superiority, were forced by their vassals to dilute it. In Germany, the nobles in the end became little rulers, each in his miniature realm. The varying experiences of these peoples largely determined their future political development and their national outlook in our own day.

France: Hugh Capet through Philip the Fair (987–1314)

The Capetians

Chosen king of France by the nobles in 987, Hugh Capet (see Chapter 4) held as his own domain the Île de France, a strip of land that included Paris (see map, p. 145). It was smaller than the domains of any of the great feudal lords, his vassals, who chose him as king, such as the dukes of Normandy or Burgundy. This was probably one of the reasons they chose him. More powerful than he, they might defy him by withholding the military service, the feudal dues, and the counsel that they owed him.

Yet the Capetians had certain advantages. Hugh's male line continued to inherit the throne for almost 350 years. At first the kings secured the election and coronation of their eldest sons during their own lifetimes. By the end of the twelfth century, the hereditary principle was firmly established. The king alone had no overlord. His office gave him a special sanctity. Crowned and anointed with holy oil, he seemed to the people partly divine, "the eldest son of the Church." The Church became his partner. He defended it and it assisted him. He nominated bishops to sees near Paris, and the bishops took an oath of fealty to him. Finally Hugh Capet's domain, though small, was compact and easily governed. He and his successors concentrated their attention on it.

While the duke of Normandy was conquering England, or relatives of the duke of Burgundy were making themselves kings of Portugal, Hugh Capet's descendants were doggedly clearing the brigands from the roads in the Île de France, forcing royal authority upon its inhabitants, and adding territory to it piecemeal. The officers of the royal household became the king's advisory and administrative staff—the *Curia Regis,* or king's court. By the early twelfth century, the king had prevented these important jobs from becoming hereditary in one family, and had begun to appoint men of his own choice as royal servants. Suger, abbot of St. Denis, a man of humble birth, faithfully served Louis VI (1108–1137) and Louis VII (1137–1189) for several decades.

Louis VI introduced royal appointees known as *prévôts (provosts)* to administer justice and taxation in the royal lands. He granted charters to rural pioneers and to new towns, recognizing that the monarchy would gain by new settlements. In these ways the French kings began their long and important alliance with the middle class. By the time of Louis VII, the king had acquired such prestige that far-off vassals in the south of France were appealing to him to settle local disputes.

But in the late twelfth century, the monarchy had to face the challenge posed by its Norman vassals. Duke William had conquered England in 1066 and thus gained resources that made him much stronger than the king of France. Yet he was still vassal of the Capetians for Normandy. William's descendants made a series of marriages with the heiresses to great French fiefs. As a result, the king of England, Henry II (1154–1189), ruled more than half of France and threatened the survival of the French monarchy, even though he was its vassal.

Philip Augustus and Territorial Expansion

Philip II (reigned 1180–1223), called Philip Augustus, tackled this problem vigorously. When Henry II's second son, King John of England (1199–1216), married a girl already engaged to one of his French vassals, the jilted man appealed

The tomb figure of Eleanor of Aquitaine in the abbey church of Fontevrault, France.

to Philip, overlord of both men. Feudal law had been violated. Philip summoned his vassal John to answer the complaint. When John failed to appear, Philip quite legally declared his fiefs forfeit to John's nephew, young Arthur of Brittany. When John murdered Arthur (1203), he lost his sympathizers on the Continent, and Philip defeated him easily. In 1204, Philip annexed Normandy and all the rest of John's holdings in France north of the Loire. John retained only Aquitaine. Philip had tripled the size of the French royal domain.

Royal expansion next reached towards the southern territories of Languedoc and Toulouse. Here the people spoke a dialect differing from northern French. Many of them were heretics, the Cathari (Greek, "pure ones"), often called Albigensians from the town of Albi, one of their strongholds. Their beliefs went back to those of the Manichaeans (see p. 88) which had spread from the eastern Mediterranean via the Balkans to northern Italy and southern France. The Albigensians said that the earth itself, the body of man, wood, water—all matter—was the work of the devil. So they denied the humanity of Jesus, repudiated the adoration of the cross, and forbade infant baptism and the Mass. Strong among the lower classes, they often had the support of individual nobles. They opposed the Catholic clergy.

In 1208 the pope officially declared it a pious act to make war on the Cathari. Hundreds of northern French nobles rushed south to kill the heretics and steal their property. To resist an alien conquest many Catholic southerners helped the heretics and suffered with them. After years of bloody warfare, Philip Augustus saw the chance of annexation and sponsored an expedition under his son Louis VIII (1223–1226). By the 1240s the royal armies and a special church court, the Inquisition, had driven the heresy underground. In 1249, when the last count of Toulouse died, his lands went—by marriage—to the brother of the king of France.

The Development of Royal Government

As the royal lands increased, royal government grew in efficiency. Philip Augustus collected detailed information on the precise amounts owed to him from each royal fief. He systematically tried to reach over the heads of his own vassals and make *their* vassals dependent on him. He made his vassals promise to perform their feudal duties or else surrender themselves as prisoners. If they refused, the Church would lay an interdict on their lands, depriving the inhabitants of the sacraments and the other comforts of religion, a punishment the people feared more than any other. Philip bought as many estates as he could. He insisted on choosing husbands for great heiresses, who in those violent days often survived several husbands and paid the king handsomely each time he married them off.

Philip Augustus replaced the prévôts, whose lands and offices had tended to become hereditary and who often abused their powers. The new officials—called *baillis* (bailiffs) in the north and *sénéchaux* (seneschals) in the south—received no fiefs, and their office was not hereditary. They did not reside in their administrative areas but traveled about enforcing royal rights, rendering justice on the king's behalf, and collecting money owed to the king. Baillis and sénéchaux were salaried royal civil servants, removable at the king's will and dependent upon his favor.

As a further check upon them, Louis IX (1226–1270) made it easy for complaints against them to be brought to his attention, and appointed still other new officials to take care of the caretakers. These were the *enquêteurs* (investigators), rather like Charlemagne's *missi dominici,* who had supervisory authority over the baillis and sénéchaux and toured the country inspecting their work. By this system the king could interfere with almost all local and private transactions, exact his just due, and supply royal justice at a price.

For the monarchy of Louis IX and his successors to have depended on the household officers, as the immediate successors of Hugh Capet had been able to do, would have been a little like the United States government today trying to get along with no filing system except an old cabinet belonging to George Washington. As new business swamped the old Curia Regis, the old household began to differentiate itself into departments, most of which dealt with the needs of the king and his retainers, clergy, and advisers. When a major policy decision needed to be made or when a major lawsuit needed to be tried, the king could summon all his vassals (lay and clerical) for counsel. When they joined the rest of the Curia Regis and sat as a court to decide a lawsuit, the enlarged body was called a *parlement,* a high judicial tribunal.

As law grew more complex, trained lawyers had to handle more and more of the judicial business. At first they explained the law to the vassals sitting in judgment; and then as time passed, they themselves formed a court and arrived at decisions in the name of the king. By the fourteenth century this court was called the *Parlement de Paris.*

When the Curia Regis sat in special session

Sainte Chapelle, Paris: the rose window.

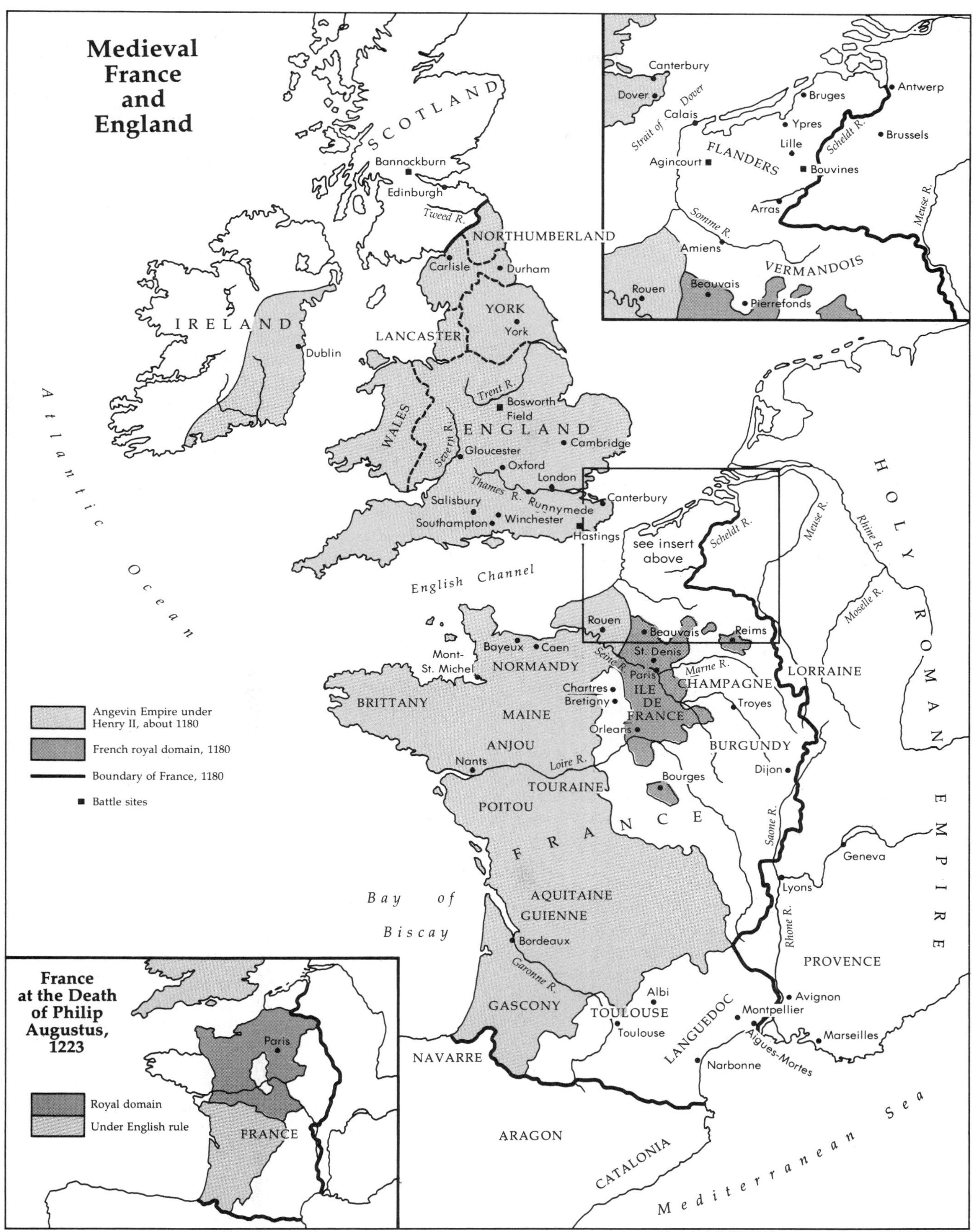

Medieval France and England
SCOTLAND
Bannockburn
Edinburgh
Tweed R.
NORTHUMBERLAND
Carlisle
Durham
IRELAND
Dublin
YORK
York
LANCASTER
Trent R.
Bosworth Field
WALES
Severn R.
ENGLAND
Cambridge
Gloucester
Oxford
London
Thames R.
Runnymede
Canterbury
Salisbury
Southampton
Winchester
Hastings
see insert above
Scheldt R.
Meuse R.
Rhine R.
Moselle R.
Atlantic Ocean
English Channel
Rouen
Beauvais
Reims
Bayeux
Caen
Mont-St. Michel
NORMANDY
St. Denis
Seine R.
Paris
Marne R.
CHAMPAGNE
LORRAINE
Chartres
Bretigny
ILE DE FRANCE
Troyes
BRITTANY
MAINE
Orleans
ANJOU
BURGUNDY
Nants
Loire R.
Dijon
Bourges
TOURAINE
POITOU
FRANCE
Saone R.
Geneva
Lyons
Bay of Biscay
AQUITAINE
GUIENNE
Bordeaux
Rhone R.
PROVENCE
Garonne R.
GASCONY
Albi
TOULOUSE
Toulouse
LANGUEDOC
Montpellier
Avignon
Marseilles
Aigues-Mortes
Narbonne
NAVARRE
ARAGON
CATALONIA
Mediterranean Sea
HOLY ROMAN EMPIRE
Angevin Empire under Henry II, about 1180
French royal domain, 1180
Boundary of France, 1180
Battle sites
Canterbury
Dover
Strait of Dover
Calais
Bruges
Antwerp
Ypres
Brussels
Lille
FLANDERS
Agincourt
Bouvines
Arras
Somme R.
Amiens
VERMANDOIS
Rouen
Beauvais
Pierrefonds
France at the Death of Philip Augustus, 1223
Paris
Royal domain
Under English rule
FRANCE

on a financial matter or audited the reports of royal income and expenditure, it was acting as a kind of government accounting bureau. By the fourteenth century this was called the *chambre des comptes,* the chamber of accounts. More and more, it too needed full-time employees: clerks, auditors, and so on.

The king got money from his lands, from customs dues and tolls, and from fees of all kinds paid by vassals for justice or for exemption from outmoded feudal services. But he could not levy regular taxes on his subjects.

Saint Louis

The medieval French monarchy reached its highest point with Louis IX (1226–1270). Generous and devout, almost monastic in his personal life, he was made a saint by the Church in 1297, less than thirty years after his death. Yet personal piety did not prevent him from defending royal prerogatives against infringements by his own bishops or by the papacy. In 1247 he would not let the pope assess the churches of France for money and men to fight papal military campaigns.

Louis IX showed the same hardheaded spirit in his dealings with the towns, old allies of the Capetians. When the lower class of tradesmen resented the concentration of authority in the small merchant upper class, the crown intervened, not on behalf of the poor and humble, but to ensure the regular flow of funds to the royal coffers. In 1262 Louis required that the towns present annual accounts. This was a new kind of enactment, the *ordonnance,* a royal command issued for all of France without the previous assent of the vassals. By ordonnance the king also forbade private warfare and declared that royal money was valid everywhere in the realm.

Only the royal court could try cases of treason or breaking the peace. But Frenchmen now felt that royal justice was the best to be had. Appeals from lower feudal courts flowed in to the parlement. The crown brought in townsmen to the parlement, and so extended royal justice to the towns. Sitting under an oak tree in the forest of Vincennes outside of Paris, Saint Louis made himself available to give personal justice to all his subjects. Foreign rulers prized his justice so highly that he was invited to settle their own disputes.

The System Hardens: Philip the Fair

Where Saint Louis was firm and just, his grandson Philip IV (1285–1314), called "the Fair" because of his good looks, was aggressive and ruthless. The towns, the nobles, the Church all suffered as he and his agents invaded long-standing rights.

Much of this aggression went on in a series of courtroom battles, as the king's lawyers twisted old rules in order to push royal claims to the uttermost. The royal agents asserted that if a case was begun in a royal court it had to be completed there, no matter where it legally belonged. They urged all losers in feudal lawsuits to claim that they had been denied justice and to bring their cases before the king's court. An old rule said that the loser of a law suit could call the judge "wicked and false" and appeal to the next higher court, where the first judge would be tried. By using this device in the great lords' courts, the king's men could bring the great lords themselves before the king's court. The system of royal justice was swallowing up the system of feudal justice.

As the new cases flowed in, the parlement became ever more specialized and professionalized. The *chambre des requêtes* (chamber of petitions) handled all requests that the royal court intervene. The *chambre des enquêtes* (chamber of investigations) would establish the facts in new cases. In the *chambre des plaids* (chamber of pleas) the lawyers actually argued the cases, and judgments were handed down. Members of the parlement traveled to the remotest regions of France, gradually taking over the machinery of justice.

The king's closest advisers in the curia regis now became the "narrow," or "secret," council. The remaining lords and high clerics were called the "full" council. In 1302, for the first time, representatives of the towns attended a meeting of this full council. Thus began the transition to a new kind of assembly, later called the Estates-General. An "estate" is a social class; the clergy was the "first" estate, the nobility the "second," and the townsmen the "third." When all three estates were present, an assembly became an Estates-General. The clerics and nobles came as individuals but the townsmen came as chosen delegates from their municipalities, and so acted as representatives.

The Struggle for Money

Philip the Fair needed money for his wars and summoned the estates to obtain their approval for his preparations to raise it. Usually he would not fix an amount because the contributor would have the right to bargain with him. Medieval men felt that no action was proper unless it had always been customary. Therefore whenever the king wanted to do something new he tried to make it seem like something old. The king would often be helpless if people protested that an effort to raise money constituted "an unheard-of exaction." Sometimes Philip would demand military service from a man (an old and legal custom) and then let him escape it by paying a specific amount assessed on his property. Philip regularly asked for money that had in the past been demanded only occasionally. He took forced loans, debased the coinage, and levied new customs dues and tolls on commercial transactions.

Need for money led to a fierce quarrel with the papacy. Philip claimed the right to tax the clergy for defense and won a partial victory. But when his royal court tried a French bishop accused of treason, Pope Boniface VIII (1294–1303) denounced Philip and proclaimed that every human creature, in order to be saved, must be subject to the pope. A band of Philip's thugs so mistreated Boniface that he died from the shock. Philip then obtained the election of a French pope, who never even went to Rome. Thus began the "Babylonian Captivity" of the papacy at Avignon in southern France (1303–1377).

To get money, Philip destroyed his creditors, the Knights Templars, originally an order of crusading warriors, who developed a rich banking business. Philip brought them to trial for vicious behavior and in 1312 abolished them. He arrested the Jews of France, stripped them of their property, and expelled them. His agents collected and kept all the debts owing to his victims.

Just before Philip died in 1314, his greed led to a kind of strike. The towns joined with the local lords in protest against his having raised money for a war and then having made peace instead of fighting. His heir calmed the unrest by returning some of the money and sacrificing some of the unpopular bureaucrats.

Taxation was still connected with military service, the king's unquestioned feudal right. The king could declare an emergency, summon his vassals to fight, and then allow some of them to buy themselves off for money. The French monarchy, so weak in the eleventh century, was by the fourteenth the most powerful in Europe.

England: William the Conqueror through Edward I (1066–1302)

William the Conqueror

William, duke of Normandy, crossed the English Channel and defeated the Anglo-Saxons at Hastings in 1066. As victor, he could make any change he wished in the Anglo-Saxon government he found: the thirty-four counties or shires with their sheriffs; the courts of shire and hundred (a subdivision of a shire); the witenagemot, or royal council, the Danegeld; and the fyrd, or militia. William assumed ownership of all the land in England. He kept about one-sixth as royal domain, gave about half as fiefs to his great Norman barons, and returned to the Church the quarter that it had held before. Many of his barons subinfeudated their lands. But their vassals owed military service only to William, and swore primary allegiance to him (in the Salisbury Oath, 1086). The bishops and abbots also owed him feudal services. He permitted no castles to be built without a royal license, forbade private war, and allowed only royal coinage. He collected the Danegeld, summoned the fyrd as well as his own feudal vassals, and kept the Anglo-Saxon system of courts. He gave the sheriffs authority at the expense of other local officials and bound them closely to the crown.

Thus he respected English custom and law but superimposed the Norman feudal structure. The sheriffs provided continuity between the old and the new. The Norman Curia Regis replaced the Anglo-Saxon witenagemot; it gave counsel, tried the cases of the great vassals, and performed duties in the shires. In 1086 William ordered a careful survey of all landed property in England. Its record, the *Domesday Book,* included a full statement of past and present ownership of each piece of land and all resources; forests, fishponds, cattle, enabling the king's agents to collect as much revenue as possible. As for the Church, William paid the accustomed dues to Rome, but like his Anglo-Saxon predecessors refused to recognize papal overlordship in England. William left the English monarchy in 1087 stronger than the French would be for more than two centuries.

His successors paid their administrators fixed salaries, because payments in land (fiefs) often led the recipient to try to make his office hereditary, and because clerical administrators might feel the rival pull of papal authority. Within the Curia Regis, the king's immediate advisers became a "small council." The royal *chancery,* of secretariat, grew in size, because as duke of Normandy the king had much business on the Continent. Soon the first specialized treasury department came into existence. This was the *exchequer,* so called because the long table on which the clerks rendered the semiannual audit of the royal accounts was covered with a cloth divided

William the Conqueror as depicted in thirteenth-century manuscript illumination.

A scene from the Bayeux Tapestry, ca. 1073–1083, depicting William's Normans defeating the Anglo-Saxons at Hastings.

into checkerboard squares representing pounds, shillings, and pence.

Even after two decades of civil war, King Henry II (reigned 1154–1189) on succeeding to the throne found the basis for powerful monarchy intact. He destroyed more than 1,100 unlicensed castles. Money rolled in: from *scutage* ("shield-money" paid in lieu of military service), from fines, from aids, from payments by the towns.

Henry II and the Common Law

By developing new ways to use old practices, Henry II made royal justice popular and powerful. Because the baronial courts, lay and ecclesiastical, competed with the Anglo-Saxon hundred and shire courts, the people welcomed royal justice, administered under the *common law,* a law common to all England. The king gave Englishmen better ways of settling their quarrels among themselves than the old trial by ordeal or trial by battle.

Henry II used *writs*—royal orders to a royal official to try a case. If someone seized a subject's property, the victim could buy such a writ cheaply. The royal official would then assemble a jury of twelve neighbors who knew the facts in the case. They were sworn (juré), and then they decided whether the plaintiff was the true owner of the property, thus rendering a verdict (*veredictum,* a thing spoken truly). Because the jury's members were people presumed to know the facts already, this jury was different from a modern trial jury. Similar machinery of writ and jury enabled a man to recover an inheritance or a man falsely held as a serf to win his freedom. Both writ and jury were old, but their use in combination and the flexibility permitted by a variety of writs created new procedure. A decision by a royal judge in effect became law. No matter

An Italian depiction of the martydom of Thomas á Becket: fresco from SS Giovanni e Paolo, Spoleto.

who won, the royal exchequer profited, since the loser paid it a fine.

Henry II extended the system by sending traveling justices to the shires to try all pending cases. The local sheriff brought before the justices a group of sworn men from each hundred and township to report all crimes since the last visit of the justices and to say who they thought was guilty in each case. This was the jury of *presentment* (since it presented the names of suspects), the ancestor of our grand jury. Proof of guilt was still the ordeal by cold water. If the accused, with hands and feet tied, floated in a pool of water blessed by a priest, he was guilty. If he sank, he was innocent.

The Church blocked Henry's effort to extend royal justice at its expense. He appointed his friend and chancellor, Thomas à Becket, archbishop of Canterbury, but Henry and Becket quarreled over which should have the authority to deal with churchmen charged with crimes. The issue was eventually compromised. But in a fit of temper, Henry asked whether nobody would rid him of Becket, and four of the king's knights murdered Becket in his own cathedral. Henry had to undergo a humiliating penance and concede that the Church had sole right to punish clerics and that litigants in church courts could appeal directly to Rome without royal permission. The king could still prevent the pope from taxing English clerics directly. Only two years after his murder, Becket became a saint. Pilgrimages to his miraculous tomb at Canterbury became a standard part of English life.

Henry's sons, Richard the Lion-Hearted (1189–1199) and John (1199–1216), made his last years miserable by their attacks on his possessions in France. Henry's work had been so well done that, although Richard spent less than six months of his ten-year reign in England, the royal bureaucracy functioned efficiently in his absence. Its main task was collecting huge sums of money for his expenses. By the time John came to the throne, Richard had squandered the royal resources and angered the barons. Greedy and tyrannical John, as we know, lost vast French lands to Philip Augustus.

John and Magna Carta

John also quarreled with Pope Innocent III (1198–1216) over a disputed election to the archbishopric of Canterbury. The pope put all England under an interdict (1208), excommunicated John (1209), and encouraged Philip Augustus's project of invading England. John not only gave in on the issues but had to recognize England and Ireland as fiefs of the papacy and pay an annual tribute to Rome.

A fourteenth-century manuscript illumination showing King John hunting deer.

John's defeats in France, his ruthless ways of raising money, and his practice of punishing vassals without trial alienated about a third of his English barons. They renounced their homage to John and drew up a list of demands, most of which they made him accept on June 15, 1215, at Runnymede. John promised to send out to all the shires of England under the royal seal a legal document in the form of a grant, the Great Charter, *Magna Carta,* with sixty-three clauses listing the specific concessions that the barons had extorted from him. John agreed to reform his exactions of scutage, aids, and reliefs. He promised uniform weights and measures (especially important to townsmen) and free elections to bishoprics.

Why do modern English and American historians and politicians often call Magna Carta—which was actually a medieval concession to the special interests of the feudal class—the "cornerstone of our present liberties"? Partly because in later centuries some of its clauses received new and expanded meanings. For instance, in 1215 the clause, "No scutage or aid, save the customary feudal ones, shall be levied *except by the common consent of the realm,*" meant only that John would have to consult his great council (barons and bishops) before levying extraordinary feudal aids. Yet this could later be expanded into the doctrine that all taxation must be by consent, that "taxation without representation was tyranny"—which would have astonished everybody at Runnymede. Another clause of the charter was later used as the basis for the modern doctrine of due process of law.

John's successors reissued the charter with modifications some forty times. Under the Tudor monarchy in the sixteenth century it was ignored, and Englishmen did not appeal to it again until the Civil War of 1642–1649 (see Chapter 8). Then, some of the enemies of Charles I could interpret it in the same inaccurate modern way that we often do. So Magna Carta's lasting importance lies partly in its later misinterpretation. Yet we also recognize that the charter rested upon two underlying general principles that justify our gratitude to its baronial sponsors: the king is subject to the law, and if necessary he can be forced to observe it.

Henry III and the Barons

John's son, Henry III (reigned 1216–1272), though mild and decent, had extravagant projects to conquer Sicily as a kingdom for one of his sons, and to subsidize his brother as candidate for the throne of the Empire. He also appointed many Frenchmen to high administrative posts, while the pope appointed Italians to the highest posts in the English church. The English barons deeply resented the foreigners and revolted in 1258.

They came armed to a session of the great council and issued a document called the Provisions of Oxford, which required the king to submit all his requests to a council of fifteen barons. The barons took over the high posts in the administration and replaced the great council with a baronial tyranny perhaps worse than the king's own. Eventually (1263), Simon de Montfort took command of the baronial party, defied an arbitration by Saint Louis in favor of the king, captured Henry III himself (1264), and set up a regime of his own, based on the Provisions of Oxford. The civil strife ended when Henry's heir, Edward, defeated and killed Simon de Montfort in 1265 and restored the king to his throne. For the last seven years of Henry's reign (1265–1272) as well as for his own long reign (1272–1307), Edward I was the real ruler of England.

Parliament

During these turbulent years of baronial opposition to Henry III, we find the earliest forerunners of later representative assemblies—*parliaments.* The word itself is French and means "a talking"—any kind of discussion or conference. When the French Curia Regis acted as a court, it was a parlement. In England too, in the thirteenth century, the word meant a session of the king's large council acting as a court. The Anglo-Saxon witenagemot had sometimes acted as a court. Attendance at the great council was compulsory. In Norman law it was the king's privilege, not his duty, to receive counsel from his vassals, and it was the vassal's duty, not his privilege, to give it.

Yet the barons came to feel that they had the right to be consulted, as Magna Carta shows. Since the kings more and more consulted only the small council of intimate and permanent advisers and called the great council only occasionally, the barons on the great council felt excluded and affronted. The rebels against Henry III in 1258 demanded that the great council should meet three times a year, and they called it a parliament. When Henry III regained power, he continued to summon the great council—the parliament—as well as his small council.

As England grew more prosperous in the thirteenth century, two new classes began to appear at sessions of the great council, or parliament. These were the *knights of the shire*—members of the landed gentry, not direct vassals of the king—and *burgesses,* or townsmen. Once the royal vassals had assented to a royal request for money, they would try to raise it from *their* vassals; so these subvassals naturally came to feel that they too should assent. In the early thirteenth century, these knights of the shire had already regularly brought information to itinerant justices. When in 1254 the king summoned two knights from each shire to a great council, or parliament, it was hardly a major innovation.

Similarly, burgesses had regularly presented accounts on behalf of their towns, and in 1265, when Simon de Montfort summoned an assembly of his supporters, he included burgesses as well as knights of the shire. The presence of both shire and town representatives made this the first true ancestor of the modern House of Commons. Not all later parliaments had shire and town representatives, and not all assemblies attended by them were parliaments. The knights and burgesses had no "right" to come to parliament. No doubt they often felt it a nuisance and an expense to come, rather than a privilege. But gradually, it became customary for them to attend.

Edward I

Edward I (reigned 1272–1307) conquered Wales (1283) but failed to secure Scotland, which remained a separate monarchy until 1603, when a Scottish king (James VI) became king of England (James I) as well. At home Edward I emerged as a great systematizing law-maker. The experts

The Court of King's Bench in the fifteenth century.

in the small council drew up a series of statutes, elaborating and expanding the machinery of government. The Second Statute of Westminster (1285) assured a great landowner that no tenant to whom he had granted an estate could dispose of it except through inheritance. The Statute of Mortmain (French, "dead hand," 1279) prevented the transfer of land to the Church without the consent of the suzerain. Once the Church had a piece of land, it could hold onto it forever; so lay landowners were reluctant to see portions of their holdings transferred to clerics. Both statutes aided the landlords.

By the writ *quo warranto* ("by what authority"), Edward commanded all the barons to explain where they had got any franchise or privilege—such as a hundred court—that they might possess. He was trying to assert that only the king could give such privileges or take them away. As royal justice increased its business, specialized courts made their appearance, all of them the offspring of the curia regis. The Court of Common Pleas took cases between subjects. The Court of King's Bench took crown and criminal cases. The Court of Exchequer took disputes concerning royal finance.

Edward asserted the crown's permanent right to share in export and custom dues. He expelled the Jews from England in 1290. They were not allowed to return until the mid-seventeenth century. He required all freemen to equip themselves appropriately for military service. If you had a certain minimum of property, you *had* to become a knight (distraint of knighthood). Baronial opposition naturally arose, and in 1297 Edward had to confirm the Magna Carta and promise not to tax without consent.

Edward's parliament of 1295 included not only the barons, higher clergy, knights of the shire, and burgesses, but representatives of the lower clergy. It is called the Model Parliament, although the lower clergy did not always attend later parliaments. In the royal summons to its members we find a famous clause, "What touches all should be approved by all." This echoes a provision of Roman law and suggests the principle that consent to taxation was necessary. In 1297 Edward declared that the "good will and assent" of clergy, lords, knights, townsmen, and other freemen were *essential* to a royal tax. Often in later years this principle would be reasserted, and Parliament sometimes made a king confirm it before it would grant him funds.

The English monarchy, so powerful in the twelfth century, was thereafter forced to accept baronial consultation. It had begun to create brand-new institutions out of old ones. The regular presence of knights and burgesses at parliaments was making them necessary in the king's business. The contrast with the French monarchy is a striking one.

The Parliament of Edward I. This ancient picture is probably the earliest authentic view in existence of Parliament in session.

Germany and the Empire (911–1273)

The Saxon Monarchy

Out of the debris of the Carolingian Empire, the five German Dukes (of Franconia, Saxony, Thuringia, Swabia, and Bavaria) emerged as hereditary local sovereigns but elected a king from among themselves. Henry I (reigned 919–936) of the Saxon house succeeded in establishing control over the former royal administration—the counts—and securing the right to appoint bishops.

The Saxon kings relied largely on the bishops to govern Germany. Churchmen were better educated than laymen and could not pass on their offices to their sons as the counts tried to do. Even the papacy welcomed the stability of such a system. The kings gave special protection to church lands. Within their own domains, the bishops administered justice and took over the powers of the courts. Tenants of church lands made up three-quarters of the royal army, and the Church furnished much of the royal revenue. Churchmen shared in the German push to the east: the defeat of the Magyars (955) and the advance into Slavic lands along and across the Elbe and Saale rivers. German bishoprics were established in the new regions, and the Slavs there were christianized.

When King Otto I (reigned 936–973) became emperor in 962 (see pp. 100–101), he created a grave new series of problems for Germany. At Constantinople as we know, the old Roman idea prevailed that the emperor was supreme over the whole inhabited world. But in the West, "emperor" had come to mean only a ruler who controlled two or more kingdoms. When Otto called himself emperor, he was asserting authority over northern Italy—weak and divided—and Burgundy besides Germany. If Otto I had not assumed the imperial title as successor to Charle-

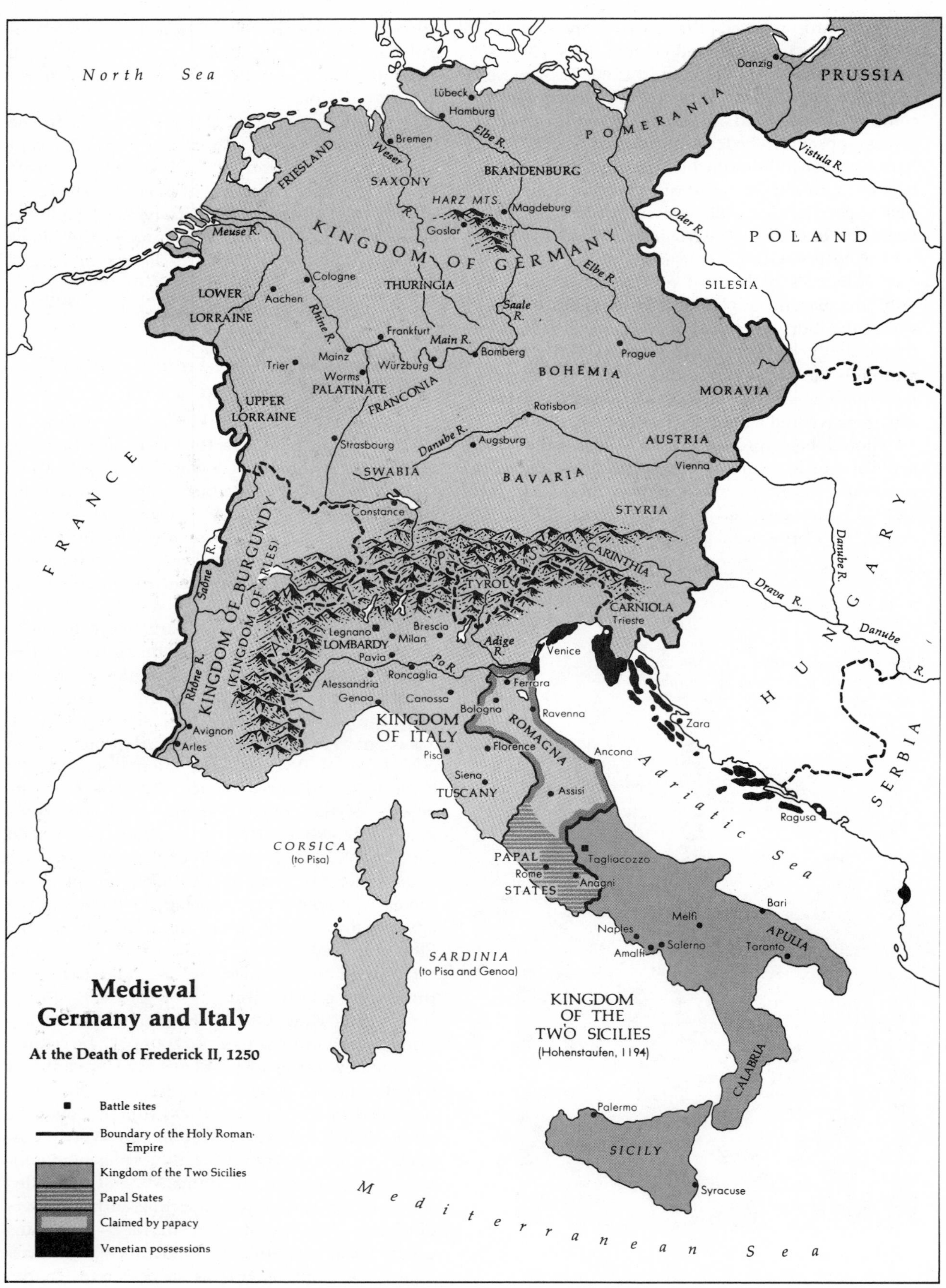

Medieval Germany and Italy
At the Death of Frederick II, 1250
Battle sites
Boundary of the Holy Roman Empire
Kingdom of the Two Sicilies
Papal States
Claimed by papacy
Venetian possessions
North Sea
PRUSSIA
Danzig
Lübeck
Hamburg
Bremen
POMERANIA
Vistula R.
FRIESLAND
Weser
SAXONY
Elbe R.
BRANDENBURG
HARZ MTS.
Magdeburg
Goslar
Meuse R.
KINGDOM OF GERMANY
Oder R.
POLAND
Elbe R.
Cologne
THURINGIA
SILESIA
LOWER LORRAINE
Aachen
Rhine R.
Saale R.
Frankfurt
Main R.
Prague
Trier
Mainz
Würzburg
Bamberg
BOHEMIA
Worms
PALATINATE
FRANCONIA
MORAVIA
UPPER LORRAINE
Ratisbon
Strasbourg
Danube R.
Augsburg
AUSTRIA
Vienna
SWABIA
BAVARIA
FRANCE
Constance
STYRIA
HUNGARY
KINGDOM OF BURGUNDY
(KINGDOM OF ARLES)
Saône R.
ALPS
CARINTHIA
Danube R.
TYROL
Drava R.
CARNIOLA
Trieste
Danube
Legnano
Brescia
LOMBARDY
Milan
Adige R.
Venice
Rhône R.
Pavia
Po R.
Roncaglia
Ferrara
Alessandria
Genoa
Canossa
Bologna
Ravenna
Zara
KINGDOM OF ITALY
ROMAGNA
Avignon
Arles
Florence
Ancona
Pisa
SERBIA
Siena
TUSCANY
Assisi
Adriatic Sea
Ragusa
CORSICA
(to Pisa)
PAPAL STATES
Tagliacozzo
Rome
Anagni
Bari
Melfi
Naples
APULIA
Amalfi
Salerno
Taranto
SARDINIA
(to Pisa and Genoa)
KINGDOM OF THE TWO SICILIES
(Hohenstaufen, 1194)
CALABRIA
Palermo
SICILY
Syracuse
Mediterranean Sea

magne, one of the other German dukes would have probably done so. After Otto I the German kings regularly claimed the imperial title and intervened in Italy. German intervention ended Italian anarchy and raise the level of the papacy from its tenth-century degeneration.

Otto III (reigned (983–1002), brilliant grandson of Otto I, inherited the older conception of empire from his Byzantine mother. His tutor, Gerbert, who became Pope Sylvester II (999–1003), encouraged his hopes. Otto's great seal read "Renewal of the Roman Empire." In Rome he tried to restore the Roman imperial palace, titles, and glory in the hope of winning the support of the old aristocracy. But it was an impractical dream. He installed German officials on Italian church lands and appointed German bishops to Italian sees in an effort to create in Italy the kind of system he had at home.

The Salians

A new dynasty, the Salian from Franconia, took over in 1024 when the Saxon line died out. Conrad II (reigned 1024–1039) began to train and use as administrators members of the lower classes, the so-called *ministeriales.* The Church had used such men to run its great estates. Now the kings used them to run the lands of the crown. They were rewarded with lands but usually not with hereditary fiefs. They therefore remained dependent directly on the crown, becoming a social group peculiar to Germany. Soon the nobles were complaining that the king listened only to low-born fellows.

By the 1070s the German monarchy was comparable to that of Norman England and was more effectively administered than the French monarchy would be for more than a century. But Germany was far less feudalized than either France or England. More lands continued to be owned outright by free men. The holders of these *allods,* nonfeudal lands, could resist the policies of the kings.

They were strengthened by their role as guardians, or "advocates," of new monasteries, of which perhaps six hundred were founded during the eleventh century. In exchange for protecting the monastery, the advocate collected substantial revenue from its tenants. To keep these new monasteries out of royal hands, their founders often made them the legal property of the pope. Henry IV (reigned 1056–1106) had to put down a revolt in Saxony (1075) led by nobles who hated the royal church, hated the ministeriales, and hated royal centralizing practices generally.

The Investiture Controversy

The German monarchy, however, set in motion forces that would be its own ruin when Henry III in 1049 installed Pope Leo IX, a close relative, on the papal throne. Leo IX was thoroughly committed to an intensive program of monastic reform sponsored by the order of monks active at Cluny in Burgundy. More important for Germany, he and his younger assistant, Hildebrand, wanted to purge secular influences from the entire church hierarchy. So the emperor was sponsoring reformers whose greatest target would be his own imperial system of government in Germany.

When Hildebrand himself became pope in 1073 as Gregory VII, he determined to secure the proper canonical (legal) election of all bishops and abbots. This would mean the end of the German system whereby the kings chose and appointed the bishops and later ceremonially conferred on them the ring and staff of their office. This ceremony was called *investiture,* and the pope insisted that no layman could perform it. Yet the emperor's government in Germany depended on lay selection and investiture of bishops, on the sale of church offices, and on many other corrupt practices.

Pope Gregory VII, a statesman of great vigor, shrewdness, and passion, believed that, as wielder of supreme spiritual authority, the pope had jurisdiction over temporal things as well. Any temporal prince who defied him he condemned as a follower of Antichrist. To many pious men this seemed a new and radical claim. The emperor's propagandists—conservatives—attacked it. The papal propagandists—revolutionary innovators—attacked them in turn. In 1059, the papacy had established the College of Cardinals and given it the task of electing new popes. This deprived the emperors of their former role and gave Gregory a real advantage over Henry IV. Gregory could also count on the support of the German nobles, hostile to their ruler, and on an alliance with the new Norman rulers of southern Italy.

In 1075, Gregory forbade lay investiture. Emperor Henry IV and his bishops responded by declaring Gregory's election as pope illegal and by cursing him. Gregory then excommunicated Henry and declared him deposed, and deprived of office all the bishops who supported him. The German nobles, delighted, won over many bishops frightened of opposing the pope's

Illumination from a twelfth-century chronicle. Top: Henry IV and his anti-pope expelling Gregory VII from Rome. Bottom: Gregory's death.

solemn decree. Realizing that he had lost the round, Henry secretly went to Italy. At the castle of Canossa, Gregory kept him waiting outside for three days, barefoot and in sackcloth, before he let him enter to do penance and receive absolution (1077).

The drama and symbolism of this famous episode seem to show the power of the pope. But in fact Henry had forced Gregory's hand. The pope could not refuse to absolve a penitent. And once absolved, Henry could regain his power in Germany.

In 1084, Henry seized Rome itself. Gregory fled south to his Norman allies. Although Gregory died in defeat, the Church had powerfully asserted itself. The investiture struggle continued, much to the disadvantage of the crown and the advantage of the German nobles. At Worms (1122), Henry V (reigned 1106–1125) renounced the practice of investing bishops with the clerical symbols of ring and staff. But with the pope's consent he continued to confer on them the *regalia,* the worldly goods pertaining to the bishop's office. The emperor or his representatives were to be present at German episcopal elections, and the emperor received an oath of fealty from each new bishop before he was consecrated. In Italy and Burgundy, the emperor had less power. This compromise ended the overt struggle over investitures.

But the power of the German monarch had been badly hurt. The German nobles were used to running their own affairs. Feudal castles multiplied, free peasants fell into serfdom, lesser nobles had to seek the protection of greater. The feudalizing processes prevalent in ninth- and tenth-century France speeded up in eleventh- and early twelfth-century Germany. Employing their own ministeriales, the great German nobles increased the number of their vassals and pyramided their monastic "advocacies." The Investiture Controversy led to the beginning of the German territorial principalities and what is known as German "particularism."

In Italy, the struggle increased the importance of the *communes.* Sworn associations of lesser nobles, the communes banded together to resist the local bishops in the towns of the north, and began to usurp the powers of city government. In Lombardy the pope supported the communes. Everywhere they threatened imperial authority.

The Hohenstaufens

When the German nobles in 1138 chose Conrad III of Hohenstaufen as emperor they touched off a famous feud between Conrad's family, the Waiblings (Ghibellines in Italy) and the Welfs (Guelfs in Italy), the family of a rival claimant, Henry the Proud, duke of Saxony and Bavaria. Conrad III's successor, Frederick I (1152–1190), known as Barbarossa ("redbeard"), strove to rebuild the monarchy. The Investiture Controversy had ended the possibility of governing Germany through the bishops, and Frederick's own royal lands in Germany were not extensive enough to give him the base he needed. So he focused his attention on Italy and Burgundy and made Switzerland, with its control over the Alpine passes into Italy, his strategic center.

He tried to make is own duchy—Swabia—a compact royal domain like the Île de France. His Welf rival, Henry the Lion, led a wave of German expansion eastward against the Slavs and ruled almost independently across the Elbe. Frederick eventually curbed Henry by the same feudal means that Philip Augustus would use against John of England. He received complaints from Henry's vassals, summoned him into the royal court to answer the claims, and when he did not appear deprived him of his holdings (1180). Then Frederick broke up the great Welf territorial possessions. But Frederick could not add them to the royal domain, as Philip Augustus did with Normandy, because he did not control his vassals so effectively. Instead, the Welf lands were parceled out among the German nobles.

Frederick also tried to assert imperial power in Italy. In 1155, the pope crowned him emperor after a famous argument over whether Frederick would hold the pope's bridle and stirrup as well as kiss his foot (Frederick lost). Soon afterward (1158) Frederick tried to define the imperial rights *(regalia)* in the Italian towns: what powers did he have to appoint dukes and counts, to coin money, to collect taxes? To resist him the squabbling towns united in the Lombard League, backed by the pope. Eventually in 1183 (Peace of Constance), the towns retained the regalia within their own walls, but outside had only such rights as they had bought or might buy from the emperor. They recognized Frederick as suzerain.

In 1190, Frederick was drowned while on a crusade. He had been so powerful for so long

Frederick Barbarossa portrayed as a crusader, from a Bavarian manuscript of 1188.

that the legend soon arose that he was not dead but asleep in a cavern with his great red beard flowing over the table on which his arm rested. Some day "the old emperor" would awake and return to bring glory and union to Germany.

Four years before his death, Frederick arranged for his son Henry VI to marry the heiress of the flourishing Norman kingdom in Sicily and southern Italy. Here the descendants of a small band of eleventh-century Norman adventurers had built a rich and powerful realm, Catholic, Greek Orthodox, and Muslim in population. The rulers tolerated all faiths and issued public documents in Arabic, Greek, and Latin. They governed in the efficient Norman manner, appointing the members of the Curia Regis. Royal officials, called *justiciars,* gave justice to the provinces.

Possessing this Norman state together with his German and north Italian lands, Henry VI (reigned 1190–1197) had surrounded the pope's own territory. He was building a fleet to invade the eastern Mediterranean and attack Byzantium when he died suddenly in 1197. To get the backing of the German princes for the succession of his son, Frederick II, he had to offer the German nobles in their fiefs the same sort of hereditary right he was asking them to recognize. In England or France the problem would not have arisen because the royal succession was established.

During the minority of Frederick II, a great pope, Innocent III (reigned 1198–1216), tried to destroy the German-Sicilian link and to revive the claim of Gregory VII that papal confirmation was needed to legitimize any emperor. But after building a formidable alliance of monarchs against the Hohenstaufen power, Innocent found his allies as dangerous as his enemies and turned back to young Frederick II.

Frederick II

Intelligent and cultivated, Frederick II spoke Arabic, Greek, and half a dozen other languages. He was deeply interested in scientific experiment, collected wild animals and women, wrote poetry in the Italian vernacular and a textbook on how to hunt with falcons. He loved his civilized southern kingdom of Sicily and inherited his father's dream of creating a great Mediterranean empire. To these ambitions he sacrificed the hard-won rights of the crown in Germany.

To obtain the consent of the German bishops and abbots to the coronation of his son, Henry, as king of Germany in 1220, Frederick II gave away the royal rights of levying customs dues, coining money, and exercising justice. He promised also that his towns would not shelter runaway serfs from church lands, and to build no new towns on such lands. In 1231, the secular princes exacted from Frederick a similar privilege in their favor. By these acts Germany was condemned to six centuries of particularism.

In Sicily, however, Frederick imposed his own tightly centralized monarchy on his subjects. He founded a university at Naples to train future officials in Roman law. Like William the Conqueror in England, he assumed title to all property. He wiped out feudal custom, forbidding trial by battle as absurd. He organized his army and navy on a paid basis rather than a feudal one, anticipated modern methods of finance, collected tariffs on imports and exports, and—like the emperors at Byzantium—established imperial monopolies in certain industries, such as silk.

The Papal Triumph

Beginning in the 1220s Frederick and the pope resumed their quarrel—particularly over Frederick's delays in going on a crusade and over his plans to extend imperial administration to all Italy, including Rome. Troops hired by the pope attacked Frederick's south Italian lands. Both sides circulated violent propaganda pamphlets. On one occasion (1241), Frederick's fleet captured

Emperor Frederick II, in the ship on the left, watching his soldiers assaulting churchmen on their way to the council summoned by Gregory IX.

a delegation of more than a hundred prelates on their way to a council called by the pope to depose him.

The papacy continued the struggle against his descendants. In 1266 the papacy imported into Italy Saint Louis's brother, the ruthless and able Charles of Anjou. Charles defeated and killed Frederick's illegitimate son, Manfred, and established himself as ruler of the south Italian lands. In 1268 Charles defeated and executed the last of Frederick's line. The house of Anjou ruled Naples until 1438, but lost Sicily to the Aragonese in 1282. The papacy had destroyed the Holy Roman Empire begun by Frederick I and given an Italian rather than a German base by Henry VI and Frederick II. But within forty years Philip the Fair, grandnephew of the papal instrument of vengeance, Charles of Anjou would puncture the inflated temporal claims of the papacy and set up his own pope at Avignon (see p. 147).

In Germany, the imperial throne remained vacant from the death of Conrad IV, the son of Frederick II, in 1254 to 1273. The German princes enjoyed not having an emperor, consolidated their powers, and extended their usurpation of former crown rights. The old links with Italy were greatly weakened. An allodial nobility, the Investiture Controversy, and the imperial preoccupation with Italy had ensured that princely particularism would emerge as the ruling force in Germany.

III THE CHURCH AND CIVILIZATION

Except for the Jews, all inhabitants of medieval Europe belonged without question to the Christian church. The Jews suffered occasional persecutions and often had to live in a separate quarter, or ghetto. When heresy arose, the temporal powers joined with the Church in attacking it. For the medieval man, religious and political governance were the "two swords" of God, equally indispensable for maintaining human society. Which was the greater? Gregory VII, Innocent III, and Boniface VIII said that the spiritual power outshone the temporal as the sun the moon. We have seen St. Louis and Philip the Fair in France, Henry II and John in England, Henry IV and Frederick II in the Holy Roman Empire all battling against these claims.

The Reformers in the Tenth Century

Cluniacs and Cistercians

At intervals the Church itself needed reform. In the tenth century the sale of church offices for money (simony) was frequent. Priests often lived with concubines. The papacy itself was corrupt. In the Burgundian monastery of Cluny (founded 910), the monks lived strictly. From Cluny reformers went out to found more than three hundred "daughter" houses inspired by the same ideals and all under the rule of the "mother" abbey. Eventually men trained in the Cluniac spirit reached the papal throne itself as nominees of Emperor Henry III. They enforced clerical celibacy and attacked simony. In 1059 a church council established the College of Cardinals, a group of key clerics (cardinal from *cardo,* "hinge"), who were to elect each new pope. The system remains in force today. It cut down imperial interference with papal elections. The emperor was notified of the cardinals' choice and his approval was sought, but he could no longer impose his own candidate. The deal between Henry IV and Pope Gregory VII (Hildebrand) over investiture in Germany followed naturally.

By the early twelfth century the wave of Cluniac zeal had spent itself. The Cluniac order had become rich and powerful. A new reforming movement spread from the order of Cistercians, whose mother house at Cîteaux (Cistercium) in Burgundy lay in a desolate spot transformed into a garden by the labor of the monks. In 1115 the great Cistercian leader, Saint Bernard (1091–1153), led a small band to Clairvaux, an equally unpromising site, and from there exercised an extraordinary influence. The king of France took his advice. A crusade set out at his bidding. Within a century the Cistercians too had become wealthy and lax.

Franciscans and Dominicans

By then another wave of reform had already begun. The friars of the new orders founded by Saint Francis (1182–1226) and Saint Dominic (1170–1221) did not live apart from the world as Cluniacs and Cistercians did. Instead, they went to the increasing populations of the new towns and cities, often neglected by the Church, and sometimes violently hostile to its rich and worldly clergy. This spirit sometimes led to heresy, as in the movement of the Waldensians, who in the 1180s taught that laymen could administer the sacraments and exalted the authority of the Bible alone.

Gentle and ascetic, Saint Francis, son of a merchant family, had undergone religious conversion in his youth. He loved everything that God had created—men, birds, flowers. Francis prescribed for his followers total poverty. They were to have no monastic house but were to go and preach, and were to rely on charity for their food and shelter. Francis called his order Friars Minor ("little brothers"). Their dependence on alms led to the term *mendicant* friars. In 1210, Innocent III approved Francis's foundation. But even before Francis died (1226), the papacy, against his wishes, permitted a revised rule. Land and buildings and worldly concerns now preoccupied some of the friars to the dismay of the rest. Francis himself rejected book-learning and books, but later Franciscans often became distinguished scholars.

Saint Dominic, a Spaniard, founded his own mendicant order in 1216. From the beginning, study was a basic duty of his followers, who were to educate the laity of the world by preaching to them. They were called the Order of Preachers. The monks of each Dominican priory elected their superiors from among themselves, and the officials of each priory in turn elected the superior officials of the order.

These reforming movements within the Church helped to keep piety constantly renewed, prevented heresy from getting out of hand, and played a major role in intellectual as well as social life. Dominicans and Franciscans served as the staff of the permanent papal tribunal of the Inquisition formed in 1233 to find, interrogate, judge, and punish suspected heretics and to deliver those who persisted in their heresy to the secular authorities to be burned at the stake.

The Church and Education

The Church alone directed and conducted education in medieval Europe. Unless destined for the priesthood, young men of the upper classes had little formal schooling, though the family chaplain often taught them to read and write. They learned to fight and hunt, and sometimes how to manage their property. The monastic schools educated future monks and priests, and the Cluniac reform stimulated study and the copying of manuscripts.

Medieval men divided learning into seven "liberal arts." The *trivium* (grammar, rhetoric, dialectic) corresponded to what we would call the humanities. The *quadrivium* (arithmetic, geometry, astronomy, and music), corresponded to the sciences. By the eleventh century, only a few monastic schools could offer instruction in all seven. In general monks thought of their work as the preservation of knowledge, not its advancement.

In the cathedral schools, however, the teachers were readier to study classical pagan writings and fostered a more inquiring spirit. In France during the eleventh century at the cathedral schools of Paris, Chartres, Rheims, and other towns, distinguished teachers now were often succeeded by men whom they had trained themselves, and distinguished pupils went on to join or found other schools.

In Italy, where the connection with cathedrals was not so close, the medical school at Salerno began in the early middle ages. At Bologna law became the specialty, beginning as a branch of rhetoric. Students were attracted to Bologna from other regions of Italy and even from northern Europe. In the early twelfth century, as education became fashionable for young men ambitious for advancement in the Church or in the royal service, the numbers of students grew rapidly.

Universities

At Bologna the student body organized itself into two associations: students from the near side of the Alps and students from the far side. The two associations incorporated as the whole body, the *universitas,* or university. If landlords charged too much for room and board, the students could threaten to leave town as a body. If the students did not like a professor, they simply stayed away from his lectures, and he starved or moved on, for he was dependent for his living on their tuition fees. The universitas (the students) were soon fixing prices of room and board in town and fining professors for absence or for lecturing too long. The professors organized too and admitted to their number only those who had passed an examination, and so won a license to teach—the remote ancestor of all our academic degrees.

At the cathedral schools in Paris and elsewhere in the north, it was the teachers not the students, who organized first. Those who taught the seven liberal arts and who got their licenses from the cathedral authorities formed a guild. By the thirteenth century pious citizens had founded in Paris the first residence halls ("colleges") where poor students might eat and sleep free. The practice crossed the Channel to Oxford and Cambridge. The authorities of these medieval universities defended themselves against en-

Scenes of student life in the Middle Ages, from Statenbuch des Collegium Sapentiae.

croachment by the secular power. There was often friction between town and gown, as high-spirited students rioted and caused general disorder.

The Question of Universals

Much of the learning taught and studied in the Middle Ages seems strange to us today, and it requires imagination to understand how exciting the exercise was to men discovering it for the first time. Gerbert of Aurillac, who spent the last four years of his life as Pope Sylvester II (999–1003), stood out as the most learned man of his day. The smattering of mathematics and science that he had been able to pick up caused his contemporaries to suspect him of witchcraft. His own main interest lay in logic, and he turned back to the work of Boethius (see Chapter 3). For the first time, across the gulf of five hundred years, a probing mind moved into the portions of Aristotle that Boethius had translated. In logic, Gerbert found a means to approach the writings of the ancients and of the Church Fathers in a systematic way.

By 1100 churchmen were debating whether it was proper to use human reason in considering a particular theological question: for example, was Christ present in the sacramental wafer and wine? Should human reason try to explain away inconsistencies in the Bible and the Fathers? Even those who attacked the use of reason used it themselves in making new definitions that enabled them to argue that bread and wine could indeed, in a certain way, become flesh and blood.

Once the new method became available, scholars of the late eleventh and early twelfth centuries used it largely in a celebrated controversy over the philosophical problem of universals. A universal is a whole category of things. When we say *dog* or *table* or *man,* we may mean not any specific individual dog or table or man, but the *idea* of all dogs, tables, or men: dogdom, tabledom, mankind. The question that exercised the medieval thinkers was whether such universal categories have an existence: *is* there such a thing as dogdom, tabledom, or mankind?

If you said *no,* you were a nominalist—that is, you thought dogdom, tabledom, and mankind were merely *nomina,* names that we give to a general category from our experience of individual members of it. We experience dogs, tables, men, and so we infer the existence of dogdom, tabledom, mankind because in some ways all dogs are like other dogs, all tables like other tables, all men like other men. But the category, the universal, has no existence in itself.

If you said *yes,* you were a realist—that is, you thought that the general categories were real and therefore did exist. Many realists took this view a large step further, and said that the individual dog, table, or man was far *less* real than the generalizing category or universal, or even that the individual was a mere reflection of one aspect of the category, and existed by virtue of belonging to the category. A man exists only because he partakes of the nature of mankind, a dog because he partakes of the nature of dogdom.

When we transfer the problem to politics and think of the state and the individual, we can see at once how great its practical importance may be. A nominalist would say that the state is just a name and exists only by virtue of the fact that the individuals who make it up are real. He would argue that the state must therefore serve its subjects, since after all it is only the sum of their individualities.

A realist would say that the state is the only real thing and that individual subjects exist only so far as they partake of its general character. Therefore, the state by virtue of its existence properly dominates the individual.

In religion, an extreme nominalist, arguing that what one can perceive through one's senses is alone real, might even have trouble believing in the existence of God. An extreme realist would tend to ignore or even to deny the existence of the physical world and its problems. Moderate realists have to start with faith, to believe so that they may know, as the English Saint Anselm put it.

Peter Abelard (1079–1142), a brilliant and cocksure lecturer in the University of Paris, tried to compromise the question. He argued that universals were not merely names, as the nominalists held, nor did they have a real existence, as the realists held. They were, he said, concepts in men's mind, and as such had a real existence of a special kind in the mind, which had created them out of its experience of particular examples: mankind from men, dogdom from dogs, and so on. His compromise between nominalism and realism is called *conceptualism.*

Abelard insisted on the importance of understanding for true faith. He put reason first and said that he must understand in order that he might believe, instead of the other way around. His most famous work, *Sic et Non* (*Yes and No*), lists over 150 theological statements and cites authorities both defending and attacking the truth of each. When Scripture and the Fathers are inconsistent, Abelard argued, how can a man make up his mind what to believe unless he uses his head? Saint Bernard, a mystic, saw a danger to the faith in such insolent use of reason. Repeatedly he denounced Abelard and had his views condemned.

Thomas Aquinas

By the time of Abelard's death, the Greek scientific writers of antiquity—lost all these centuries to the West—were on their way to recovery, often through translations from Arabic into Latin. In civil law, the great Code of the Emperor Justinian became the text commonly used in the law schools. In canon law, the scholar Gratian published at Bologna about 1140 his standard *Concordance of Discordant Canons.* He cited past cases that were or seemed contradictory and gave his own solution to the contradictions. It was Abelard's method.

In the second half of the twelfth century, the West recovered Aristotle's lost treatises on logic. They taught how to build a syllogism, how to prove a point, how to refute false conclusions. Using these instruments, medieval thinkers were for the first time in a position to systematize and summarize their entire philosophical position. Yet the recovery of Aristotle posed certain new problems.

For example, the Muslim Averroës, whose comments accompanied the text of Aristotle's *Metaphysics,* stressed Aristotle's own view that the physical world was eternal. But since the soul—a nonphysical thing—was essentially common to all humanity, no individual human soul could be saved by itself. Obviously this ran counter to fundamental Christian teaching. Some scholars tried to say that both views could be true, Aristotle's in philosophy and the Christian in theology; but this led directly into heresy. Others tried to forbid the study and reading of Aristotle, but without success.

The Dominican Albertus Magnus (1193–1280), a German, and his pupil Thomas Aquinas (1225–1274), an Italian, wrote massive multivolume works produced over their lifetimes. They reconciled the apparent differences between Aristotle's teachings and those of the Christian tradition. They were the greatest of the Schoolmen, exponents of the philosophy historians call Scholasticism.

Aquinas's best-known writings were the *Summa Theologica* and the *Summa contra Gentiles.* He discussed God, men, and the universe, arranging his material in systematic, topical order, inquiring into and discussing each open question. First he cited the evidence on each side, then gave his own answer, and finally demonstrated the falsity of the other position. Though Aquinas always cited authority, he also never failed to provide his own logical analysis.

For Aquinas reason was a most valuable instrument, but only when it recognized its own limitations. When reason unaided could not comprehend an apparent contradiction with faith, it must yield to faith, since reason by itself could not understand the entire universe. Certain fundamentals must be accepted as unprovable axioms of faith, although, once they had been accepted, reason could show that they are probable.

If a man puts a series of arguments together and comes out with a conclusion contrary to what orthodox Christians believe, he is simply guilty of faulty logic, and the use of correct logic can readily show where he erred. Indeed, Aquinas delighted in the game of inventing arguments against accepted beliefs, matching them with a set of even more ingenious arguments, and then reconciling the two with an intellectual skill suggesting an athlete's coordination.

When Aquinas is discussing, for example, the specific conditions of "man's first state," he comes to the question: what were babies like in the state of innocence before the Fall of Man? Were they born with such perfect strength of body that they had full use of their limbs at birth, or were they like human babies nowadays, helpless little wrigglers? In the Garden of Eden, would not such helplessness detract from perfection? So did not God make babies born strong and perfect, even born adult? Aquinas did not think so. Of course God *could* have given children the use of their limbs at birth. But it was more suitable for infants even in Eden to have only the strength they needed as infants.

This apparently trivial passage contains much that is typical of Aquinas's Scholastic philosophy. It grants a clear supremacy to "truths which are above nature," which we hold by faith and receive through divine authority. It expresses the belief that God usually prefers to let nature run its course according to its laws, and that there is a "fitness" in human action conforming to these laws of nature. It quotes as authority both the Old Testament and Saint Augustine. And it adds up to common sense. So does Aquinas's argument that governments in this world were set up by God, and that rebellion against them is wrong except in cases of dyed-in-the-wool tyrants. Similarly, man's control over field and forest and mine reflected God's will, and men should prosper by exploiting them, but the rich should always be mindful of the needy.

Mysticism

Such common-sense dependence on reason always arouses the distrust of those who prefer to trust in the instincts or the emotions: the mystics. Thus Saint Bernard of Clairvaux, the mystic, as we saw, fought Abelard's exaltation of reason. Saint Francis, the mystic, distrusted books and told his brethren to throw them away, to rely on love to discipline both mind and body. The Franciscan Bonaventura (John of Fidanza, 1221–1274) preached to his students in Paris that the human mind, an organ of Adam's sinful and unredeemed descendants, could understand only things typical of the physical world. Only by divine illumination could men hope to gain cognition of the divine or supernatural. Prayer, not study, love and longing for God, not reason—this was Bonaventura's answer. Yet Bonaventura was himself an accomplished philosopher, quite able to deal on even terms with his rationalist opponents. In his *Voyage of the Mind to God,* he echoes Augustine and the Neoplatonists. The grace of God helps the mind achieve the degree of love it needs to undergo the ultimate mystical experience of a union with the divine.

Political Thought

The medieval thinker believed that the perfection of the kingdom of heaven where all men are equal could not possibly exist on earth. Here one must expect compromise and imperfection. In the twelfth-century *Policraticus* (*Statesman's Book*) of the English philosopher John of Salisbury (ca. 1115–1180), the prince (or king) is the head of the state. The senate (legislature) is the heart, the judges and governors of provinces the eyes, ears, and tongue; the officials and soldiers the hands, the financial officers the stomach and intestines, and the peasants "correspond to the feet, which always cleave to the soil." This "organic" theory of society was a great favorite with those who opposed change. For obviously the foot does not try to become the brain, nor is the hand jealous of the eye. The whole body is at its best when each part does what nature meant it to do.

Medieval thought thus distinguished among vocations but insisted on the dignity and worth of all vocations. It accepted the Christian doctrine of the equality of all souls before God and held that no man could be a mere instrument of another man. Even the humblest person on this earth could in the next world hope to enjoy a bliss as full and eternal as any king's. In medieval political theory, if existing conditions were bad, it meant that originally good conditions had deteriorated. The thing to do was to restore the original good, God's own plan.

Medieval thinkers thought of the universe as unchanging. God had once for all designed the laws governing human behavior. Man's job was not to make law but to find it. When in difficulty the medieval thinker sought authority—in Scripture or from the Fathers if possible, from custom if available. If no solution was at hand, he confidently awaited one in heaven.

IV LITERATURE AND THE ARTS

Latin Literature

In literature and the arts, as in social and economic life, the eleventh century provides a convenient turning point. Latin continued to be the language of the Church and of learned communication everywhere in western Europe. Men now wrote it far better than in the earlier Middle Ages. All the churchmen we have been discussing in this chapter—John of Salisbury, Abelard, Bernard, Aquinas—wrote Latin even when corresponding informally with their friends.

Latin was also the language of the law and of politics. All documents were written in it: the title deed to a piece of property, a royal decree, a treaty of peace, or a letter from one monarch to another. Sermons were written and delivered in Latin, hymns were composed and sung in Latin, and much verse was written in Latin. Sometimes this verse was colloquial or satirical, such as the famous student songs of the twelfth century.

The authors were mostly wild young clerics wandering about Europe from one lecturer to another. They mocked the form and the values of the serious religious poetry of the time, and roughly satirized the clergy and the Church and even the Bible, as they praised wine, women, and song, trying to shock the virtuous:

My intention is to die
In the tavern drinking;
Wine must be on hand, for I
Want it when I'm sinking.

Angels when they come shall cry
At my frailties winking:
"Spare this drunkard, God, he's high,
*Absolutely stinking."**

Vernacular Poetry: Northern France

Despite the strength of Latin, the vernaculars all over Europe gradually emerged after the eleventh century as the languages of entertainment. During the early Middle Ages, *Beowulf,* coming from a Britain never thoroughly Latinized, was our only important literary vernacular poem. But now such poems began to appear in ever greater numbers on the Continent also.

The Song of Roland, written in Old French, probably about the year 1100, tells of Roland, a peer of Charlemagne who fought the Muslims on the Spanish border and was betrayed. Human beings have replaced the monsters of *Beowulf* as the enemy. The landscape has brightened. A more intense Christian piety softens some of the worst violence. Roland sees to it that his comrades slain by the infidel receive a Christian blessing. The wicked traitor Ganelon brings down tragedy on the heroic forces of Charlemagne, leaving Roland and the king grief-stricken. In the poem the highest virtue is loyalty to one's lord: the first necessity in a feudal society. But besides Roland's deep loyalty to his lord, Charlemagne, we find something new: a love for "sweet France." In 1100, France was barely in existence as a country, but already the poem sounds a patriotic note.

Many other songs were sung and stories told about Charlemagne's captains. Other such "cycles" of stories also evolved at the same period around other great heroes. King Arthur of Britain, more a legend than a historic figure, was one of the most famous. Arthur's fellow Celts in Wales, Ireland, and Brittany told of his knights' exploits and so did French poets such as Marie de France and Chrétien de Troyes. From France Arthurian tales passed in the thirteenth century into Germany, where Wolfram von Eschenbach wrote a splendid long poem about King Arthur's knight Sir Percival. The Arthurian tradition was so long-lived that it inspired Richard Wagner's nineteenth-century opera, *Parsifal,* as it has inspired many other moderns.

Similarly, the men of the thirteenth century rediscovered the story of the Trojan War, an event already almost three thousand years in the past. Nobody in the West as yet knew Homer. Instead, inspiration came from two rather humdrum summary accounts in Latin supposedly by one Dares the Phrygian and Dictys the Cretan, imaginary figures, both of them.

Current or recent events, such as the Crusades, led to dozens of other poetic narratives of adventure. All these literary songs were the *Chansons de Geste*—songs of action—chiefly written in northern France. Everywhere they extol the same knightly virtues of loyalty and courage as the *Roland.*

* From *The Goliard Poets* by George F. Whicher. Copyright 1949 by George F. Whicher. Reprinted by permission of New Directions Publishing Corporation.

Provence and Courtly Love

In southern France, things were gentler. No doubt the sunny climate, the greater leisure, and the nearby cultivated Muslims of Spain all played a part. Here lyric poetry flourished, with love as its favorite theme. But love in southern France had its own peculiar code of behavior: *courtoisie,* or courtly love.

The singer's lady was never a properly attainable sweetheart, unmarried and perhaps ready to be won. She was always someone else's wife. She was worshiped from afar, and the singer celebrated in ecstasy even the slightest kindness she might offer him. Her merest word was a command, and her devoted knight undertook without question even the most dangerous mission she proposed to him, without hope of a reward. But a lady who failed to reward him, at least to some degree, was not playing by the rules of this elaborate and artificial game.

The twelfth-century troubadours sang in the southern French language called Provençal (after Provence), which is quite a different dialect from that spoken in the north. They were often half-humorous as they expressed their longings for the unattainable lady.

Aquitaine, southwest France, was long a center for this form of lyric poetry. Duke William IX in the early twelfth century was himself a troubadour. His granddaughter, Eleanor—who married successively Louis VII of France and Henry II of England—held "courts of love." In sessions patterned mockingly on those of feudal courts of justice, the lovesick troubadours sang their songs and had their cases judged, and petitions from ladies and gentlemen crossed in love received mock-serious attention. The typical feudal attitude toward women as mere breeders of new generations of fighters did not prevail in these circles. Here life was more agreeable and more sophisticated. The influence of the troubadours penetrated into Germany, where courtly love was called *Minne,* and its poets the *minnesingers.*

The ideas of the troubadours became part of the developing notions of a code of proper knightly behavior known as *chivalry,* literally the gentlemanly conduct of a man on horseback. Saint Louis himself was as chivalrous a figure as ever existed. His faithful biographer, Joinville, was the personification of a loyal vassal. Joinville's work is one of the two most important vernacular French prose documents of the thirteenth century, the other being Geoffrey de Villehardouin's account of the Crusader's conquest of Constantinople in 1204.

Italy: Dante's "Divine Comedy"

In Italy, the original home of the Latin language, vernacular was somewhat slower to develop. But here, too, at the cosmopolitan court of Frederick II (1215–1250) in Palermo, some of Frederick's advisers began to write love poetry in what they themselves called the "sweet new style" *(dolce stil nuovo).* Soon the fashion spread northward.

But Italian did not triumph until Dante Alighieri (1265–1321) of Florence. Dante wrote in Latin a stirring defense of vernacular Italian: *De Vulgari Eloquentia (Concerning the Speech of Every Day).* For his own greatest work, *The Divine Comedy,* he himself chose Italian.

Dante belongs with Homer, Vergil, and Shakespeare as a supreme master. He heralds the new age of rebirth, the Renaissance, at least as loudly as he sounds the familiar medieval note, and we shall be discussing him again. His *Divine Comedy* is the most famous and in many ways the most typical of all medieval books.

Lost in a dark forest in his thirty-fifth year, Dante encounters the Roman poet Vergil, who consents to act as his guide through two of the three great regions of the afterlife of man: Hell and Purgatory. Descending through the nine successive circles of Hell, where the eternally damned must remain forever, the two meet and converse with the individual souls in torment. Some are historic persons like Judas or Brutus, others are recently deceased Florentines of Dante's own acquaintance, about whose sins he knew at first hand. In Purgatory, less sinful human beings are working out their punishment before they can be saved.

The souls of the great pagan figures, born too early to have become Christians, are neither in Hell nor in Purgatory but in Limbo, a place on the edge of Hell, where Vergil himself must spend eternity. Dante meets the shades of ancient writers—Homer, Plato, and Socrates—and of characters in ancient poetry—Hector, Odysseus, and Aeneas.

When Dante comes to the gates of Paradise, Vergil cannot continue to escort him. The guide to the final region of the afterlife is Beatrice, a Florentine girl with whom Dante himself had fallen desperately in love as a youth but whom he had worshiped only at a distance. Here Dante transformed one of the central experiences of his own life into literature in accordance with the code of courtly love. In Paradise, of course, are the Christian worthies and the saints—Benedict, Bernard, Aquinas—and at the climax of the poem, a vision of God himself.

This voyage through the afterlife is designed to show in new pictorial vividness the old belief that man's actions in this life determine his fate in the next. From the lost souls in Hell, who have brought themselves to their hopeless position, through those who despite their sufferings in Purgatory confidently expect to be saved and will indeed be saved, to those whose pure life on earth has won them eternal bliss, Dante shows the entire range of human behavior and its eternal consequences. It is a majestic summary of medieval Christian moral and ethical ideas. In its completeness and its masterful subordination of detail to general vision, it has often been compared with the philosophical work of Aquinas.

England: Chaucer

In England, where the vernacular had always been strong, the Old English of the pre-Conquest period had by the fourteenth century evolved into a new form of the language called Middle English. Its supreme poet and surely the most brilliant English literary voice before Shakespeare was Geoffrey Chaucer (1340–1400). An experienced man of affairs who made several trips to the Continent on business for the king of England and eventually became Controller of Customs and Clerk of the King's Works, Chaucer left behind many literary works, including a long verse love story, *Troilus and Criseyde,* deriving its characters from the literature on the Trojan War now so fashionable.

Chaucer's greatest work, however, is the *Canterbury Tales.* If nothing else had survived of medieval literature, we should still be able to learn most of what we know about it from the *Tales* alone. The *Tales* are told by a group of pilgrims on their way from London to the tomb of St. Thomas à Becket, the archbishop of Canterbury murdered under Henry II. The pilgrims come from all walks of English life except the high nobility, and include Chaucer himself as well as a knight, a squire, a prioress, a clerk, a monk, a friar, a sailor, a miller, and others. In a brilliant prologue, Chaucer characterizes his fellow pilgrims. On the road, each tells at least one story that reflects his own character and experience.

The knight tells a romantic story of chivalric love: two cousins fall in love with a maiden whom they have barely glimpsed from the window of their prison cell. Deadly rivals thereafter, they continue to cherish their mutual strife, in prison and out, without the lady's ever being aware of them. When she learns, she does very little about it, and in the end one kills the other and wins her as his own. It is indeed a strange story to us: the lady's passivity, the two knights' lovesickness unfed by any encouragement. But it is a typical story of courtly love, and befits the experienced warrior who tells it.

The miller tells a raw story of a young wife's deception of her elderly husband with a young lover—a barnyard anecdote, in effect, but full of liveliness and good humor. The prioress tells a saint's legend, the squire an (unfinished) story full of semiscientific marvels, including a magic horse. The clerk tells a tale of a faithful wife who tolerates all sorts of mistreatment as her husband cruelly tests her loyalty. Chaucer does not hesitate to satirize his churchmen. The fourteenth century saw much popular discontent with the English church, and the poet was sure of his audience. The sophistication, delicacy, power, passion, and humor that Chaucer commands put him in the same class with Dante.

Architecture, Sculpture, Painting

The Romanesque

Architecture. In architecture, the Romanesque style, which evolved from the Ottonian styles of the earlier period, dominated the eleventh and most of the twelfth centuries. The Gothic style, following it and developing from it, began in the twelfth century and continued to prevail down to the fifteenth. The development from Romanesque to Gothic is complex, and the years between about 1180 and about 1220, especially in northern France, mark the transition.

Beginning in Lombardy, where the first schools of craftsmen were formed, and from which architects and builders traveled wherever they were needed and summoned, the Romanesque styles moved across southern France to northern Spain. One of the earliest Romanesque churches, high up in the French Pyrenees, is the monastic church of St. Martin du Canigou, built in the first quarter of the eleventh century. Far larger than most of the churches of the earlier period, it illustrates two important adaptations of earlier Roman architectural devices: the barrel or tunnel vault, or continuous round-arch roof-

The monastery of St. Martin du Canigou high in the French Pyrenees, an early Romanesque building.

ing, now used for far larger spaces than before; and the groin vault, at first used in basement crypts, and then later moved above ground to the main church. To the groin vault ribbing was sometimes added for strengthening. At St. Martin, the tower and cloister and body of the church are in harmonious balance, and all are adapted to the steep slope on which the church was built.

Most Romanesque churches had as their fundamental ground plan a Latin cross, with a long staff and shorter cross-arms. The shrine where the altar stood with the relics of the saint, was at the east end. Usually its walls formed a curved arc: this was the apse. Within this portion of the church the choir sang. The arms of the cross extended north and south, usually from a point immediately west of the apse: these were the transepts. And the long portion of the cross, extending westward to the west front, was the nave, usually with an aisle at each side. Towers might be built over the crossing of nave and transepts, and at either side of the west front. Some churches had no towers or only one, some as many as six with additional ones built at the ends of the transepts. Around the interior of the apse—sometimes called simply "the choir"—there often opened a series of chapels, which are seen outside as smaller arcs emerging from the apse wall, like bulges. The ground plans varied greatly in detail from church to church, according to the wealth and taste of the community and the length of time that construction took. As fashions changed, innovations could and would be incorporated in any church that took a long time to build.

Among the great Romanesque churches were those built at Mainz, Worms, and Speyer in western Germany by the Holy Roman emperors of the Salian line. We reproduce the ground plan of Speyer, mostly of the eleventh century, with later additions, and a view of the exterior of Worms as it is today.

A fine impression of a great Romanesque monastery church, with its surrounding buildings may be gained from the painstaking reconstructions of Professor K. H. Conant. Compare his complex Cluny as it was in 1157 with his recon-

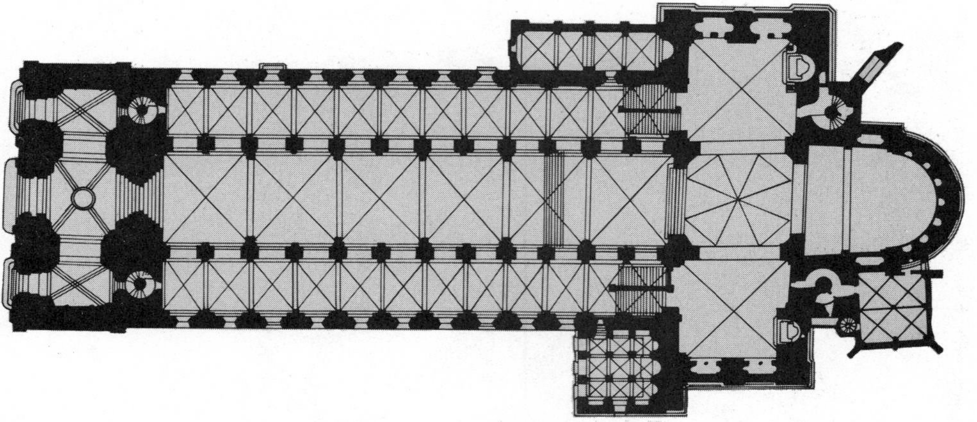

Ground plan of the Cathedral of Speyer in western Germany, begun ca. 1030.

struction of the noble pilgrimage church of St. James (Santiago) at Compostela in far northwestern Spain. From all over western Europe but especially from France throngs of pilgrims flocked to Compostela to worship at the shrine of the saint. Along these routes, to accommodate the pilgrims, hospices were built, and monasteries and churches flourished. Romanesque architecture also spread along these routes and "pilgrimage churches" were built in many key centers; these were great Romanesque buildings at which the pilgrims would stop to worship along their way. The interior of Sainte Foi at Conques in south-central France, with its groin vaulting in the nave, is typical.

Variations on the typical Romanesque church occur in southwestern France, where a group of churches, unlike those anywhere else, have domed roofs. In some churches the domes are placed in a straight row above the nave. In others, such as at St. Front of Périgueux, there is a central dome and four side domes, arranged in a Greek (equal-armed) cross pattern, modeled after St. Mark's at Venice which is itself an imitation of the (lost) Church of the Holy Apostles in Byzantium. Perhaps Greek influence was somehow at work in this corner of France. The effect upon the worshiper of a roof made up of a series of domes is entirely different from that produced by the ordinary Romanesque barrel or groin vaulting. The bubblelike feeling of lightness produced by domes can be seen in the interior of the Cathedral of Angoulême. Despite its many variations, Romanesque was a truly international style as seen in two widely separated cathedrals: that of Pisa, in Italy, and that of Durham, in northern England.

Sculpture. Just before the year 1100, there began a revival of European sculpture. The tradition had never been lost, as we know from the

The Cathedral of Worms, western Germany, begun in the eleventh century.

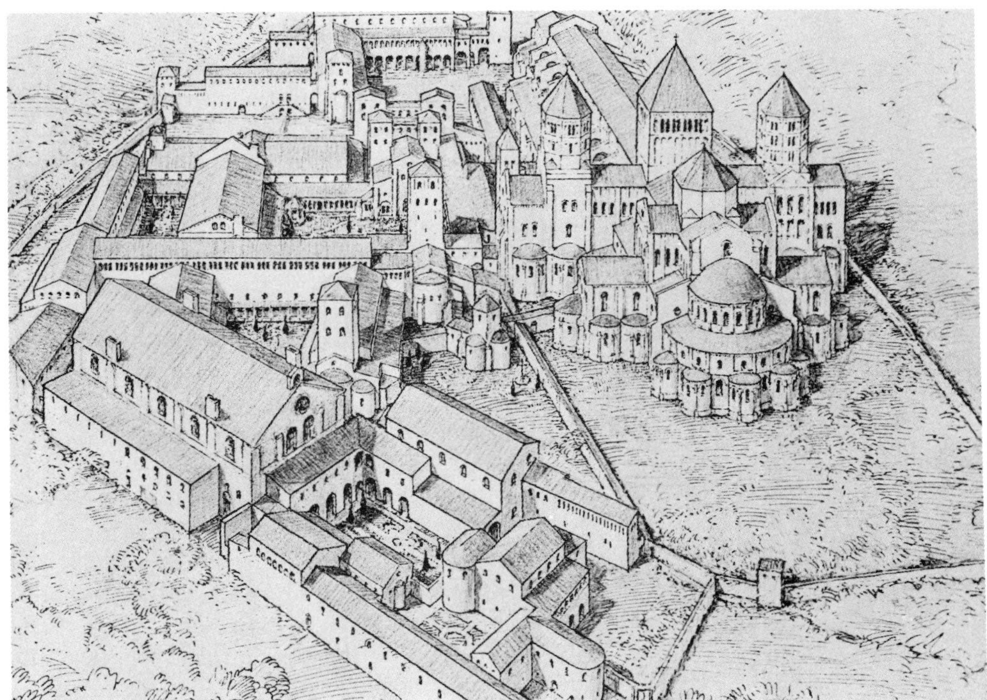

Drawing of a model of the monastery of Cluny as constructed by Professor Conant.

Santiago de Compostela, the goal of western European pilgrims: a drawing of a restoration to its medieval state.

Angoulême: The nave of a church whose roof is a series of domes.

early medieval Irish and English crosses, and from the figures at Cividale. The finest surviving examples of the art of sculpture before the Romanesque revival, however, were smaller examples in ivory and in metalwork. But now, quite suddenly, with joy and exuberance, the stones of the Romanesque churches we have been discussing came literally to life.

The older classical columns usually had Corinthian capitals with acanthus leaves. But now capitals began to blossom out with rosettes, palm-leaf ornaments, and grapevines, and amidst the foliage a whole race of marvelous beasts appeared. Some were carved as if they were illustrations to the popular collections of anecdotes about real and mythical animals (the bestiaries) usually with a Christian allegorical explanation of the animals' incredible characteristics. Some were taken from real life, and some from the teeming imaginations of the sculptors. At such places as Chauvigny, in western France, the beholder saw lions and pelicans, horses and elephants, griffins and dragons and mermaids and other weird monsters, savage harpies attacking each other. Saint Bernard declared that they distracted Christians from prayer. The capitals at his church of Clermont were severely plain.

Scenes from the Bible also appeared on the capitals, but now often interpreted with a new freedom and with a consideration for the space available to the artist within the small compass of the top of a column. On one capital, the three magi (wise men from the East) sleep happily under the same blanket with their crowns on. Elsewhere Judas hangs himself, while terrifying winged demons pull at each end of the rope. And from the capitals the sculpture spread to the large, flat vertical surfaces available to the artist in a Romanesque church—for example, to the arched space over the outside of the front portal, the tympanum.

Here Christ himself was often shown enthroned with the Virgin and the saints at his side, and surrounding and beneath them a depiction of the Last Judgment. The souls of the damned are eternally rejected at the moment of the Second Coming of the Lord, while those of the blessed rise from the tomb to enjoy their eternal salvation. At Vézelay and Autun in Burgundy, at Conques and Beaulieu and many other Romanesque churches of the pilgrimage routes, such large-scale representations of this subject with all its personages gave the sculptor a chance to test his skills.

On the doorposts and in the indented narrow arches surrounding the portals (called *voussures*), sculptured ornament also took over. At Moissac and Souillac in southern France, a frantic series of grotesque beasts, each gripping and eating the next, climbs and struggles its way up an entire doorpost. Human and animal heads look out side by side from the voussures surrounding the tympanum. In one region of southwest France, specially noted for its breeding of horses, it is horses' heads alone that ornament the church portals and facades. In the cloister of San Domingo de Silos in northern Spain, or in Chichester Cathedral in southern England, one still can see large plaques sculptured with splendid representations of biblical scenes. Romanesque sculpture is almost always in relief rather than in the full round.

Painting. Far less survives of Romanesque painting than of Romanesque sculpture. When anti-Christian vandals in later periods of revolution defaced earlier Christian monuments, they found it easier to destroy paintings by scraping them off the walls or by tearing out illuminations from books than to shatter stone monuments completely. Moreover, a painting on a plaster wall, for example, deteriorates faster with the passage of time than does a piece of sculpture, especially one that is indoors. However, enough painting survives, often in out-of-the-way

The nave of Pisa Cathedral, an Italian church of the Romanesque period.

places, to show that painting, like sculpture, had a revival. In León in northern Spain, in many churches of Catalonia, and in a few places in England, France, and Italy, early Romanesque wall paintings can still be seen.

Probably the most complete series still visible is in the abbey church of St.-Savin-sur-Gartempe, in western France, very near to the sculptures at Chauvigny. At St.-Savin, the walls and ceiling of the nave show scenes from the Old Testament: Creation, the murder of Abel, Noah's Ark, the stories of Abraham and Joseph, and the Tower of Babel. The apse had scenes from the New Testament, including the deposition from the Cross and the Resurrection. A special kind of Romanesque "painting" is seen in the unique Bayeux Tapestry (actually an embroidery) commemorating the Norman Conquest of England and made soon afterwards.

In Italian churches the painting often took the ancient form of mosaic, used by the Romans but perfected for Christian art and for wall decoration by the Byzantines. Splendid Romanesque mosaics survive, especially in the churches of Norman Sicily, where Eastern influences were common and many Greeks still lived. In Palermo alone, the chapel of the royal palace of the Norman kings (Capella Palatina), the church of the Martorana, and the magnificent nearby Cathedral of Monreale all display these Byzantine-influenced mosaic paintings against the usual gold ground. Not far away at Cefalù is still another

Durham: nave of the Cathedral. Romanesque (or Norman, as it is always called in England).

Man-eating dragon: capital of a column at the Church of St. Pierre, Chauvigny, France.

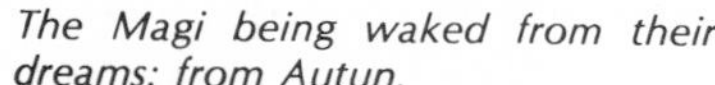

The Magi being waked from their dreams: from Autun.

The west tympanum of the Cathedral of St. Lazare, Autun.

large church with mosaic decoration. The earliest surviving mosaics at St. Mark's in Venice—also intimately linked with Byzantium as we know—date shortly after the beginning of the thirteenth century.

The Transition to Gothic

Architecture. Beginning in the late twelfth century, Romanesque art underwent a change. In architecture, the arches, from being round, now gradually rose to points. The roofs, once barrel-vaulted (or barrel-vaulted with groins and ribs), also rose more and more sharply, as the smooth flow of the arc was sharply broken, and two loftier curves now met instead at a point. The continuous Romanesque barrel vault pressed down upon its supporting walls with even stress; so the walls had to be made very solid with few openings and often with *buttresses*—stone supports built at right angles to the main wall to take part of the outward push. So these churches were dark inside.

But the chief feature of the newer medieval architecture—always known as Gothic—was precisely this pointed arch, a new device that enabled builders to carry their buildings to new heights. The vaulted ceiling now rested upon a series of masonry ribs in groups of four—two rising from each side of the wall—and each group supported by a massive pillar. Four pillars could now be

The stone panel in Chichester Cathedral showing Mary and Martha kneeling before Christ at the gates of Bethany.

Three bowing angels: fresco in the church of St. Savin-sur-Gartempe, France, illustrating a scene from the Apocalypse.

A scene from the Bayeux Tapestry, depicting the Norman fleet under William the Conqueror crossing the English Channel.

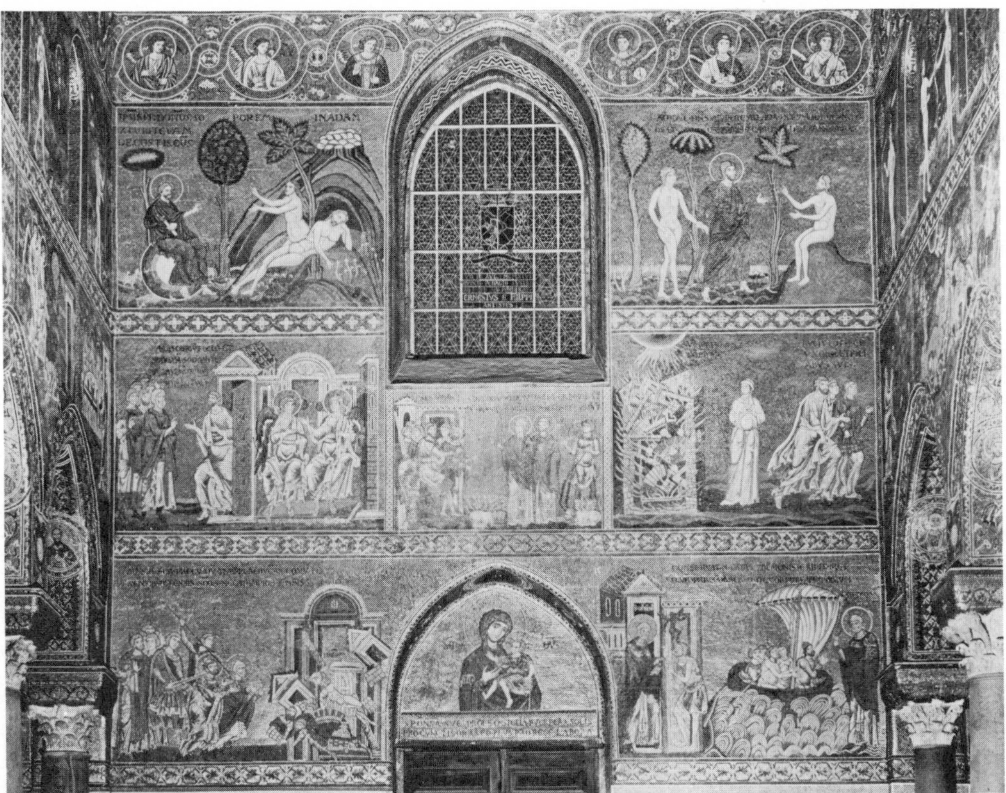

Mosaic scenes from Genesis: The west wall of the nave of the Cathedral of Monreale, Sicily, showing Byzantine and Muslim influence.

Cathedral of Amiens: The nave.

made to take the place of a whole section of solid Romanesque wall, and the spaces between the pillars were left open for windows. Gothic churches were therefore much brighter inside than Romanesque churches.

Outside, a new effect of increased lightness and soaring height was achieved by moving the vertical buttress of the Romanesque period away from the walls of the church. The gap between buttress and church wall was now bridged by an arched support that looked as if it were actually flying between the now distant vertical buttress and the lofty masonry wall of the church, part of whose outward thrust it was designed to take. These "flying buttresses" also freed the builder to soar upward. Into the new window spaces now made possible, the craftsmen of the thirteenth century and later fitted a new form of painting: the window in multicolored (stained) glass, glittering with gemlike colors in ruby, sapphire, and emerald, and showing biblical episodes

Chartres Cathedral, whose later tower (left) illustrates the overripe look of Gothic architecture in its decline.

or episodes from the life of the saint whose church it was.

Gothic architecture flourished for at least two centuries everywhere in Europe. Its first and perhaps greatest moments came in northern France, with the building—all between the 1190s and about 1240—of the cathedrals of Chartres, Reims, Amiens, Notre Dame of Paris. Sometimes the ambition of a designer extended beyond his control of engineering. At Beauvais the architect, who managed to build the highest apse and transepts of any Gothic church, found that he could not get his nave to stand up. It fell down and what remains still looks like an exercise in defiance of the law of gravity.

Open and vast, but solidly built, soaring upward according to well-worked-out and usually well-understood mathematical architectural proportional formulas, the Gothic cathedral terminates in aerial towers. Though its great windows let in the light, the stained glass keeps the interior dim and awe-inspiring. In England, York and Canterbury, Salisbury and Wells, Ely and Winchester among a good many other cathedrals still stand as the best island Gothic, fully comparable with the best on the Continent. With the passage of time in the fourteenth and fifteenth

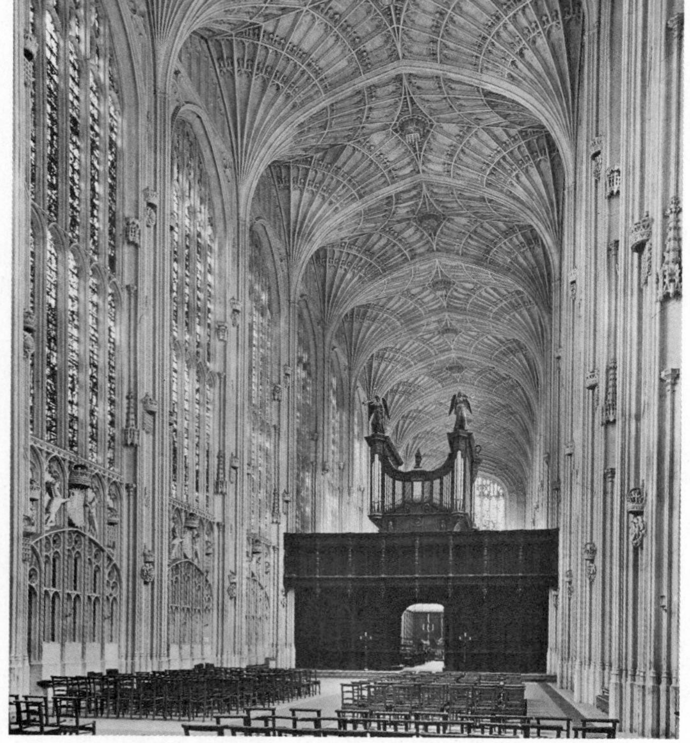

King's College Chapel, Cambridge.

centuries, ornamentation grew richer, decoration became more intricate—literally flamelike, or "flamboyant"—and Gothic architecture on the Continent moved toward its decline. The later tower of Chartres illustrates this overripe look. In England, however, the later richer Gothic has given us such marvels as King's College Chapel in Cambridge and the Henry VII Chapel at Westminster Abbey in London.

Sculpture. Sculpture also flourished in the years between 1180 and 1220. "For practically the first time since ancient times, draperies curl and caress the bodies underneath; limbs themselves are proudly and successfully shown, strength becomes a thing of muscles rather than size alone; physiques are neither camouflaged nor ignored, but studied and presented to our eyes in an almost overpowering beauty. Faces become truly alive, eyes shine with an inner light, gestures seem to develop an entirely new expressive poetry of their own. Drama is supreme."* The metalwork of Nicholas of Verdun and of sculptors working in the valley of the Meuse where France, Belgium, Holland, and Germany came close together, mark the beginning of the new school, active in northern France, western Germany, and England. Sculpture in the round gradually became more common, beginning with figures that were carved fully in the round from the mid-sections of columns, engaged in the facade or the portal of a church only at the top and at the base. The lifelike representation of drapery, the firm balance of the figures on their feet, are principal characteristics of these new statues, chiefly found in northern France. Similar influences are shown elsewhere in metalwork and in manuscript illumination, rather than in monumental sculpture. The influences from outside that made the development possible came from Byzantine art, which was undergoing a kind of classical renaissance. Renewed and intensified contacts between East and West by pilgrims, travelers, and warriors during the period of the Crusades made westerners familiar with Byzantine achievements and contributed to a splendid artistic revival.

* Thomas P. Hoving, *The Year 1200* (New York: Metropolitan Museum of Art, 1970), I: vii.

Music. Medieval music was essentially church music, which began in the sixth century with Gregorian chant, or plainsong. Plainsong was simply a series of musical tones, separated by no set rhythmic interval, sung in unison. It was used in church services as a setting for the psalms and other prose. But there were also hymns in metrical or verse form that could be accommodated to a simple tune.

In the period after 1000, music, like the other arts, grew more and more complex. Our present method of musical notation—the staff—was invented by an eleventh-century Italian monk, Guido of Arezzo. Church music developed both melody and harmony—the sounding of two or more notes simultaneously—until the peak of balanced form and matter was reached in the thirteenth century. Later medieval church music sometimes resembles an extremely complex musical puzzle.

Conscious secular musical composition begins in the Middle Ages with the minstrels, who often elaborated popular tunes. By the end of the fourteenth century, we get something like the modern composer—for example, the Italian Landini, who wrote madrigals set for two voices. Music, like the other arts, was largely anonymous.

READING SUGGESTIONS on The Medieval World: Western Europe
(Asterisks indicate paperback.)

Social and Economic Foundations

R. W. Southern, *The Making of the Middle Ages* (*Yale). Excellent introduction that manages to be both clear and original.

L. White, Jr., *Medieval Technology* (*Galaxy). Readable, scholarly, and the only work of its kind.

P. Boissonade, *Life and Work in Medieval Europe* (*Harper Torchbooks). Perhaps somewhat old-fashioned now, but still a useful discussion.

F. Heer, *The Medieval World, 1000–1300* (*Mentor). A stimulating and learned work, although the author sometimes seems to be forcing the evidence to fit his own theories.

R. S. Lopez, *The Commercial Revolution of the Middle Ages, 950–1350* (*Spectrum). The author combines a scholarly mastery of the subject with an ability to write clearly and interestingly.

R. S. Lopez, *The Birth of Europe* (1967). A more advanced but still basic study by the same gifted historian.

S. Painter, *Medieval Society* (*Cornell). Good, brief introduction.

C. Brooke, *The Structure of European Society* (1971). Somewhat more recent than the above, but also not so easy to follow.

R. Rorig, *The Medieval Town* (*California). A useful general account.

H. Pirenne, *Medieval Cities* (*Anchor). By a famous scholar of an earlier generation. Very readable and provocative essay.

Politics: Works Dealing with More Than One Country

S. Painter, *Rise of the Feudal Monarchies* (*Cornell). A good introductory study.

C. Pétit-Dutaillis, *Feudal Monarchy in France and England from the Tenth to the Thirteenth Century* (*Harper Torchbooks). Written two generations ago, but still very valuable.

W. Ullmann, *Principles of Government in the Middle Ages* (1961). For the more advanced student who will enjoy the book, but perhaps wish to argue with some of its conclusions.

Z. N. Brooke, *A History of Europe from 911 to 1198* (1951); and C. N. Previté-Orton, *A History of Europe from 1198 to 1378* (1951). These two consecutive volumes form part of a carefully organized general scholarly history of Europe. Useful for reference.

C. H. Haskins *The Normans in European History* (*Norton). Normandy, England, Sicily: A celebrated work, still very interesting.

A. Kelly, *Eleanor of Aquitaine and the Four Kings* (*Vintage). A beautifully written and entertaining book about the woman who played a major role in both France and England in the twelfth century.

The French Monarchy

R. Fawtier, *The Capetian Kings of France* (*St. Martins). The best brief comprehensive study available.

A. Luchaire, *Social France at the Time of Philip Augustus* (*Harper Torchbooks). A famous early twentieth-century study, drawing on innumerable original sources to show the seamy side of life about 1200.

The English Monarchy

C. Brooke, *From Alfred to Henry III: 871–1272* (*Norton). Good introductory review.

A. L. Poole, *From Domesday Book to Magna Carta, 1087–1216* (1951); and F. M. Powicke, *The Thirteenth Century, 1216–1307* (1953). Two fine consecutive volumes in The Oxford History of England.

D. M. Stenton, *English Society in the Early Middle Ages* (*Pelican); A. R. Myers, *England in the Late Middle Ages* (*Penguin); and H. M. Cam, *England before Elizabeth* (*Harper Torchbooks). Three good studies by sound scholars written for the general public.

D. C. Douglas, *William the Conqueror and the Norman Impact upon England* (*California). Fine up-to-date study in depth.

G. O. Sayles, *The Medieval Foundations of England* (*Perpetua). A fine basic study. With H. F. Richardson, Sayles also wrote *The Governance of Medieval England from the Conquest to Magna Carta* (1963), a brilliant analysis for advanced students.

D. Knowles, *Thomas Becket* (1971). A good biography.

J. C. Holt, *The Making of Magna Carta* (*Virginia). A useful study of this fundamental document.

G. L. Haskins, *Growth of English Representative Government* (*Perpetua). The history of Parliament, a much-debated subject, is here clearly and sensibly presented.

G. C. Homans, *English Villagers of the Thirteenth Century* (1960). A leading sociologist turns his attention to village life in medieval England.

Germany and the Empire

B. Barraclough, *The Origins of Medieval Germany* (*Capricorn). The best work on the subject in English. See also Barraclough's translations of German scholars' essays on the subject, in his *Medieval Germany,* 2 vols. (1938).

J. Bryce, *The Holy Roman Empire* (*Schocken), Written as an undergraduate prize essay in the 1860s, this astonishingly precocious work is still good reading.

P. Muntz, *Frederick Barbarossa: A Study in Medieval Politics* (1969). A solid study.

E. Kantorowicz, *Frederick the Second, 1194–1250* (1931). The best scholarly book on the subject, marred by German nationalist sentiments.

R. W. Hertzstein, ed., *The Holy Roman Empire: Universal State or German Catastrophe?* (*Heath); and Schafer Williams, ed., *The Gregorian Epoch: Reformation, Revolution, Reaction?* (*Heath). Two useful collections of modern scholarly discussions of major questions.

The Church and Civilization

R. W. Southern, *Western Society and the Church in the Middle Ages* (*Penguin). Recent, authoritative, and well-written.

J. B. Russell, *A History of Medieval Christianity* (*Crowell). An introductory work, but highly personal in outlook.

D. Knowles and D. Obolensky, *The Middle Ages* (in *The Christian Centuries,* Vol. II, 1969). A useful overview of church history.

H. B. Workman, *Evolution in the Monastic Ideal from the Earliest Times to the Coming of the Friars* (*Penguin). A survey including the various reform movements discussed in our text. Gives useful references to the longer basic studies of Cluny, the Cistercians, and the mendicant orders.

H. Rashdall, *The Universities of Europe in the Middle Ages,* 3 vols. (1936). A major work, the standard account of higher education and the Church's role in it.

C. H. Haskins, *The Renaissance of the Twelfth Century* (*Meridian); and *The Rise of Universities* (*Cornell). Two works by a leading American scholar of an older generation, the first emphasizing "modern" elements in medieval civilization, the second a fine series of short essays.

H. Wieruszowski, *The Medieval University: Masters, Student, Learning* (*Anvil). Excellent discussion accompanied by translations of original source materials.

U. T. Holmes, *Daily Life in the Twelfth Century* (*Wisconsin). How Paris looked to a university student.

D. Knowles, *The Evolution of Medieval Thought* (*Vintage). Shows the continuity between classical thought and scholasticism.

M. de Wulf, *Philosophy and Civilization in the Middle Ages* (*Dover). Readable lectures by one of the leading authorities in the field.

E. Gilson, *Reason and Revelation in the Middle Ages* (*Scribners). By a world-famous French Catholic scholar, all of whose books have an authority all their own.

C. Dawson, *Religion and the Rise of Western Culture* (*Image). Excellent cultural history.

J. Sikes, *Peter Abelard* (1965). A useful biography.

G. D. Rops, *Bernard of Clairvaux* (1964). A first-rate account.

M. D. Chenu, *Towards Understanding St. Thomas* (1964). The best place to begin.

A. C. Crombie, *Medieval and Early Modern Science,* 2 vols. (*Anchor). Not easy reading, but very useful.

Literature and the Arts

H. Waddell, *The Wandering Scholars* (*Anchor). The best single book on the subject and very lively.

C. S. Lewis, *The Discarded Image: An Introduction to Medieval and Renais-*

sance Literature (1964). The author's points of view are original and interesting.

The Song of Roland, trans. F. B. Luguiens (*Collier). A convenient English version.

Wolfram von Eschenbach, *Parzival,* trans. H. M. Mustard and C. E. Passage (*Vintage). Good translation of an important text.

Medieval Romances, ed. R. S. and L. H. Loomis (*Modern Library). A useful collection.

The Comedy of Dante Alighieri, trans. D. Sayers and B. Reynolds, 3 vols. (*Penguin). There are, of course, many other translations, but they are perhaps less accessible even if more poetic or more accurate.

Geoffrey Chaucer, *Works.* There are many satisfactory editions of *The Canterbury Tales, Troilus and Criseyde,* and other poems of Chaucer.

K. J. Conant, *Carolingian and Romanesque Architecture, 800–1200* (1959). By the leading authority, handsomely illustrated.

A. Grabar and C. Nordenfalk, *Romanesque Painting* (1958). Authoritative and well illustrated.

H. Focillon, *The Art of the West in the Middle Ages,* 2 vols. (1963). A fine survey.

A. Martindale, *Gothic Art from the Twelfth to the Fifteenth Century* (*Praeger). A reliable general work.

O. von Simson, *The Gothic Cathedral* (*Harper Torchbooks). An interesting and somewhat mystical treatment.

E. Panofsky, *Gothic Architecture and Scholasticism* (*Meridian). A profound scholar discusses the close connections between intellectual life and the Gothic building.

G. Reese, *Music in the Middle Ages* (1940). For the advanced student.

CHAPTER SIX

The Medieval World: Eastern Europe

As in Western Europe, so in the East, the years after 1,000 saw a series of major changes. At Byzantium, the death of Basil II in 1025 began a period of retrenchment. The emperors abandoned the policy of expansion in Europe and in Asia. In the western Byzantine outpost of southern Italy, the newly arrived Norman adventurers gradually built up their own power. In the 1040s, two prominent generals tried in a brief period to seize the throne. Both were foiled, but the result was a suspicion of the military and a fear of future rebellions. The imperial civil service, now thrown open to men of humble origins, apparently helped to keep the military budgets down. Seljuk Turkish strength grew on the Anatolian frontier and new nomad invaders threatened the Balkans.

After Basil II, no emperor continued his policies of curbing the "powerful" in their acquisition of lands at the expense of the poor. The rich were no longer obliged to pay the delinquent taxes of members of the same fiscal community. So while the armed forces of the state suffered from neglect, the private armies of rich landed magnates grew in power.

The Byzantine state was taken by surprise when the papacy, newly reformed by the German Emperor Henry III, reemerged as a power in Italy. The popes longed to regain the Church lands and revenues in southern Italy seized long ago by the Byzantine Emperor Leo III (717–740). Ready to challenge Byzantium, the popes turned to the Normans for help. As usual, questions of divergent church practice were used as a pretext for a quarrel over hard political and economic issues. Greek priests married, Latin priests did not. The Latin Church used unleavened bread for the Eucharistic wafer, the Greek Church used leavened bread. The Greek creed says that the Holy Ghost "proceeds from the Father," the Latin creed adds the words "and from the Son."

In 1054, after a dramatic exchange of insults and embassies, the quarrel ended in a full-scale *schism:* a split between the churches of Rome and Constantinople. It became one of the chief objectives of papal foreign policy thereafter to heal the schism and restore communion between the churches. Many such efforts were made in later centuries. Whenever the Byzantines needed help from the West, they would negotiate on reunion with the papacy. Twice they actually concluded a formal "union" with Rome. But the forces of Greek public opinion would never support the action, which always meant recognizing the primacy of the pope. Not until 1965 were the mutual excommunications of 1054 lifted. And even in 1979, when Pope John Paul II celebrated Mass jointly with the Orthodox Patriarch in Istanbul, much remained to be done before the old quarrel was healed.

The death of the last ruler of the Macedonian dynasty in 1057 touched off a chaotic quarter-century known as the "Time of Troubles." Rival nobles and generals competed for the throne. The enemies on the borders grew stronger until the year 1071, when a double catastrophe took place. In Italy the Normans took Bari, last remaining stronghold of the Byzantines, and prepared to cross the Adriatic and carry the war into the Balkan provinces of the empire. In eastern Anatolia, the Seljuks defeated the Byzantine armies at Manzikert (Malazgerd) and captured the Byzantine emperor himself. With the Anatolian defenses shattered, bands of wandering Turkic nomads poured westward to pillage the rich cities and farmlands. Soon they established a sultanate on Byzantine territory with its capital at Nicaea, dangerously close to Constantinople itself.

Under these circumstances, there emerged out of a welter of conspiracies and feuds among rival candidates a new emperor, Alexius I Comnenus (reigned 1081–1118), founder of a new dynasty. He came from a powerful landowning family of Asia Minor and represented the interests of his class. The Byzantine Empire still had 372 years of life. But the fate of Byzantium in these later centuries came to rest more and more on the actions of Western Europeans. The Italian commercial cities, in full revival, penetrated the empire economically and took over much of its commerce. Byzantine naval power declined. Western adventurers penetrated Byzantine officialdom and carved out careers for themselves in the imperial service. And the Crusade, a new form of Western military and colonizing enterprise, sent armies of westerners pouring into Byzantine territory.

Alexius I Comnenus himself played an important part in starting this third and ultimately most dangerous form of Western threat to Byzantine stability. We begin this chapter with an account of the Crusading movement, its successes and failures. We shall then consider the fortunes of the empire between the accession of Alexius and the final capture of Constantinople by the Ottoman Turks in 1453. Even after it had vanished as an empire, however, Byzantium continued to exert a mighty influence on the Ottoman conquerors.

In the third section, we discuss the Ottoman state and consider its development and its fortunes from 1453 to the very end of the seventeenth century. The year 1699, where we reach a natural breaking-point, is of course a moment far later than the usually accepted end of the "Middle Ages" in the West. But for the Ottomans, the Middle Ages continued more than two centuries after the West had undergone a transformation and a transition into the modern era.

The same is true of the Russian state, in its own way a successor state to Byzantium. In the final portion of this chapter, we turn to Russia between the eleventh and seventeenth centuries, discussing the decline of Kiev, the Tatar occupation, the development of the Tsardom centered on Moscow, and the reasons for the growth of serfdom down to the moment just before 1689 and the accession of Peter the Great, who was to bring Russia too out of its own medieval period.

THE CRUSADES

Precedents for the Crusade

In the last quarter of the eleventh century, the relationships between Roman Christendom, Greek Christendom, and Islam entered upon a long period of crisis. In 1095, the pope proclaimed a Holy War against the Muslims, a war for the Cross, or Crusade, with the recovery of Christ's tomb at Jerusalem, the Holy Sepulcher, as its ultimate aim. The idea itself was not new. The Byzantines regarded their wars against the Muslims as sacred campaigns for the faith and once came close to Jerusalem. In Spain, ever since the invasion of 711, the small Christian states pushed southward against the Muslims whenever they could. By the twelfth century, the Christians had recovered a large area of central Spain.

Christians had been going on pilgrimages to the scenes of Christ's life and Passion ever since Constantine was converted. Constantine's mother, Saint Helena, discovered the True Cross in Jerusalem. Even the Muslim conquest of the seventh century did not interrupt pilgrimages for long. Caliph Harun al-Rashid (785–809) allowed Charlemagne to endow a hostel at Jerusalem for pilgrims. Christians believed that pilgrimage would bring God's pardon for sin. In the tenth and eleventh centuries, large organized groups flocked eastward. One of them was seven thousand strong.

Stable conditions in both Muslim and Byzantine dominions were needed for the safety of the pilgrims. But after the catastrophes of Bari and Manzikert (1071), the Byzantines could not enforce peaceful conditions among the invading Turkish tribesmen or prevent brigandage on the highways of Asia Minor and Syria. Pilgrimages became dangerous.

The vigorous reforming popes of the later eleventh century were anxious about the pilgrims. Worse still from their viewpoint was the schism between Roman and Greek churches. In 1073, Gregory VII himself planned to lead a Western army to help the Byzantines against the Turks and to bring about a reunion between the churches. Only the quarrel with the German emperor Henry IV (see pp. 155–156) ruined the project. More than twenty years before the First Crusade, all the essential elements had been brought together: a Holy War under papal sponsorship to be fought in alliance with the Greeks against the Muslins.

The First Crusade

In 1095 envoys from Emperor Alexius I Comnenus asked for help against the Turks. They stressed the sufferings of the Christians and argued that the time was ripe. At the Council of Clermont (1095), Pope Urban II proclaimed the First Crusade. He preached to the crowd, emphasizing the anguish of the Greek Christians and the hardships faced by pilgrims and mentioning the booty that might be gained. He promised that any sinner who might be killed doing this work of God would receive absolution automatically and would surely go to heaven. His audience shouted, "God wills it." Thousands of volunteers took the oath and sewed crosses of cloth onto their clothes.

The expedition that Urban launched was only the first of a series that continued for almost two centuries. Crusaders battled Muslims, most often in Syria and Palestine, but also in Egypt, North Africa, and Portugal. Under the command sometimes of nobles, sometimes of kings or emperors, the armies won some successes, but more often they failed. Although reinforcements flowed to the East in an almost constant stream, certain specific expeditions are always called the Second, Third, or Fourth Crusade, and so on up to the Eighth. This is not accurate, though it is convenient.

After Clermont, an undisciplined mob of ignorant and often starving peasants under a certain Peter the Hermit poured eastward to Constantinople. The Byzantines, who were hoping for a few hundred well-trained knights, were appalled. The Crusaders burned houses and stole everything in sight, even the lead from church roofs. Alexius Comnenus shipped them out of Constantinople and across to Asia Minor as fast as he could, where the Muslims slaughtered them.

Soon afterwards, the far better equipped armies of certain great Western noblemen arrived by different routes in Constantinople. The best-known commanders were Godfrey of Bouillon (duke of Lower Lorraine) and his brother Baldwin, Count Raymond of Toulouse, and Bohemond, a Norman prince from southern Italy. Alexius Comnenus wanted to recover lost Byzantine lands and to be the overlord of every new state the Crusader lords might carve out for themselves in Turkish occupied territory. So he extracted from the Western nobles an oath of liege homage to him.

The Siege of Jerusalem during the first crusade, from a fifteenth-century manuscript.

Fourteenth-century manuscript illumination showing Godfrey of Bouillon before Jerusalem in 1099. At the left is Peter the Hermit.

The Crusader States

In Asia Minor, the Crusaders took Nicaea, the Seljuk capital (1097). Baldwin, brother of Godfrey, was accepted by the local Armenian rulers as count of Edessa, an ancient city near the Euphrates (1098). This was the first Crusader State. Bohemond soon became prince of the second, centered around the great fortress city of Antioch. In July 1099, the Crusaders took Jerusalem itself and massacred its Muslim and Jewish inhabitants. In 1100, Baldwin of Edessa became first king of Jerusalem, a third Crusader State. In 1109, the son of Raymond of Toulouse founded the fourth and last of the new states, centering around the seaport of Tripoli. The king of Jerusalem was the suzerain of the other three rulers but was often unable to enforce his authority. The Byzantine emperors never relinquished their rights.

All four Crusader States lay within a narrow Syrian coastal strip more than five hundred miles long and seldom as much as fifty miles wide. The Muslims threatened from Egypt and from the Syrian cities of Aleppo, Hamah, Emesa (Homs), and Damascus, all just inland from the strip. The Crusader lords often ignored the common defense, sometimes fighting against one another in alliance with neighboring Muslims. At strategic places they erected superb castles, among the finest ever built.

The Crusaders established a purely feudal government whose laws, the Assizes of Jerusalem, were written down in the thirteenth century, when the Crusader States were dying. The great officers of the realm were the officers of the king's household: seneschal, constable, marshal. The high court of the barons settled disputes and acted as council of state for the king's business. Venice, Pisa, and Genoa had commercial rights in the coastal cities. Revenues were raised by customs dues, by monopolies, by a poll tax on Muslims and Jews, and by a land tax on the native population. Both Jerusalem and Antioch had new Roman Catholic patriarchs with subject bishops. Greek, Syrian, and Armenian churches continued to exist beside the Muslim and Jewish faiths.

The Crusaders established new "military orders" of religious knights: the Templars were founded about 1119 to afford protection to pilgrims on their way to the Holy Places. The knights took the vows of poverty, chastity, and obedience, and were given headquarters near the Temple of Solomon—hence their name. A second order, founded shortly after, was attached to the ancient Hospital of Saint John of Jerusalem, and was therefore called the Hospitalers. The two or-

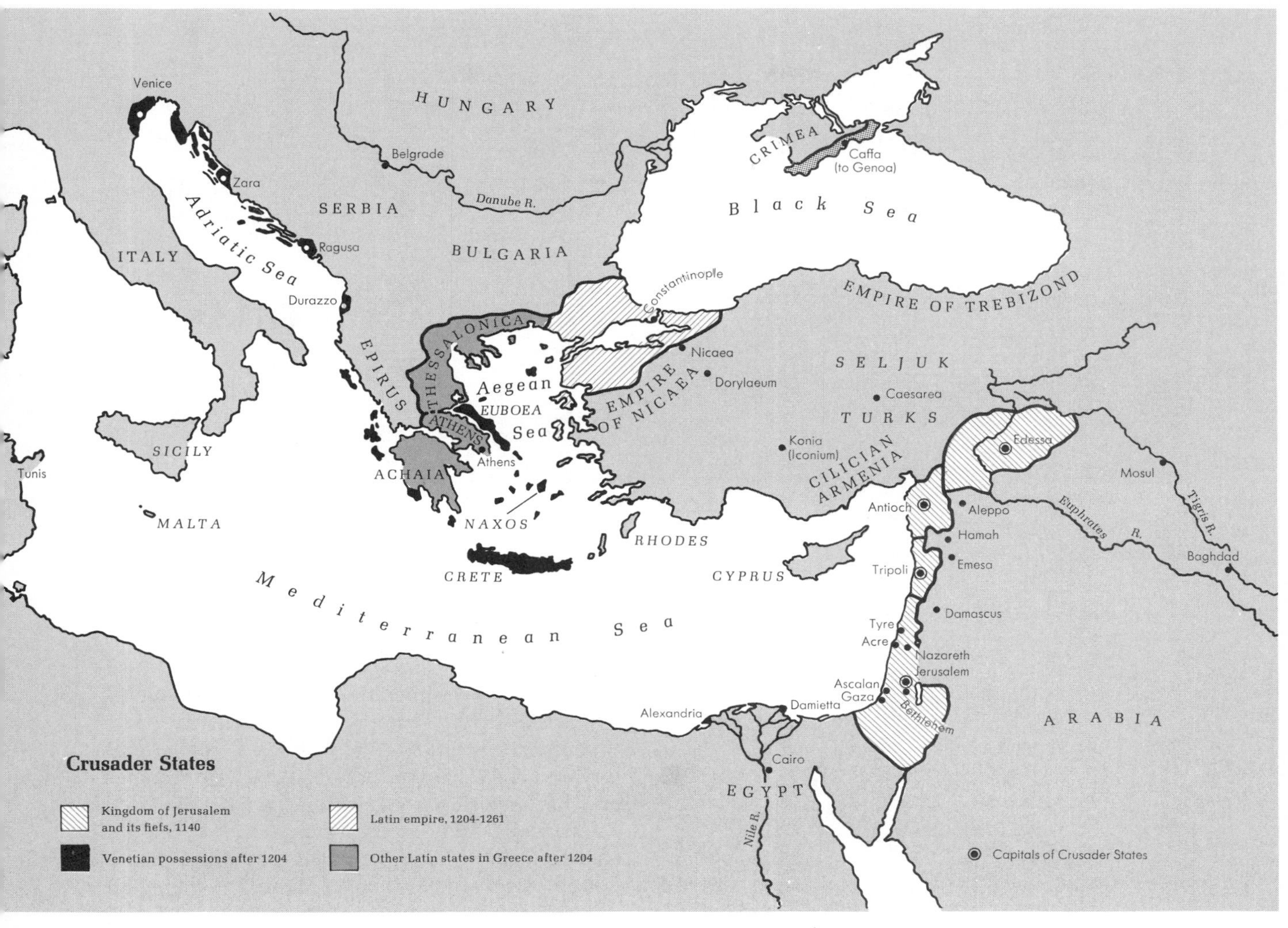

ders supplied the most effective fighting forces in the Holy Land.

Growing rich and quarrelsome, the orders sometimes allied themselves with Muslims to fight one another. Templars and Hospitalers engaged in banking. Philip IV of France destroyed the Templars (see Chapter 5). The Hospitalers later moved first to Cyprus, then to Rhodes, and were driven to Malta by the Turks in 1522, where they continued until Napoleon's seizure of the island in 1798.

The Muslim Reconquest

The disunion of the Muslims helped to keep the Crusader States alive, but by 1144, Zangi, governor of Mosul, had unified the local Muslim rulers and took Edessa. The Muslim reconquest had begun.

In answer, Saint Bernard himself preached the so-called Second Crusade in Europe. For the first time Western monarchs—King Louis VII of France and King Conrad III of Germany—came to the East. But the expedition was a total failure, and by 1154 Muslim Syria was united against the Latins.

By 1169 there emerged in Egypt Saladin, the greatest Muslim leader of the crusading era, renowned for his generalship and chivalry, who also came to control Muslim Syria and Mesopotamia. Internal decay in the Kingdom of Jerusalem gave Saladin his chance. In 1187 he took Jerusalem, and only the port of Tyre remained Christian.

Krak des Chevaliers, a crusader fortress built by the Hospitalers and taken by Saladin in 1188.

Frederick II: miniature painting in "The Art of Hunting Falcons," a work written by the emperor.

The Later Crusades

The Third Crusade (1189–1192) was the response. Emperor Frederick I Barbarossa led a German force but was drowned (1190) before reaching the Holy Land. Philip Augustus of France and Richard the Lion-Hearted of England both came East. Deadly rivals at home, they could not cooperate in a common cause. They did mount a long siege of the seaport of Acre and took it in 1191. Jerusalem itself could not be recaptured, but Saladin signed a treaty with Richard allowing Christians to visit it freely. A small strip of seacoast with Acre as its center remained in the hands of the Crusaders as a pitiful remnant of the Kingdom of Jerusalem. The Christians also still held Tripoli and Antioch with much reduced territories.

When Saladin died in 1193, his dominions were divided among his relatives, and the Christians obtained a respite. But thereafter the story of the Crusades and of the Crusader States in Syria is a mere epilogue. Pope Innocent III's great effort at a Fourth Crusade was, as we shall see, diverted away from the Holy Land.

Most of all, perhaps, the enthusiasm that had driven men toward the Holy Land was blunted by the struggle between the popes and European enemies who were Christian at least in name: the Albigensian heretics of southern France and the Emperor Frederick II (see Chapter 5). The popes offered to give those who fought in these causes the same promise of future salvation that they gave men who fought the Muslims. This brought disillusionment, which was deepened by military failure and internal Christian dissension in the Holy Land itself.

The high point of tragic futility was the Children's Crusade of 1212, when throngs of French and German children went to the Mediterranean in the expectation that its waters would divide before them and open a path to the Holy Land, along which they could march to a bloodless victory. When this failed to happen, several thousand pushed on to various seaports and many were sold into slavery.

The Fifth Crusade (1219–1221) was a vain attempt at the conquest of Egypt, which had become the center of Muslim strength. The sophisticated Western emperor Frederick II led the Sixth Crusade. Speaking Arabic and long familiar with the Muslims, he negotiated a treaty with Saladin's nephew (1229) that restored Jerusalem to the Westerners except for the site of the Temple, where stood the great mosque of the Dome of the Rock. But in 1244, Jerusalem fell again, this time to Turkish forces fighting for the rule of Egypt. These central Asian Turks were fleeing the invasions of Genghis Khan and his Mongols, then raging through western Asia and eastern Europe. Jerusalem remained in Muslim hands until 1917.

On the Seventh Crusade, Saint Louis himself was taken prisoner in Egypt (1250) and had to pay a very heavy ransom. In 1250 also, the household troops of the Egyptian sultan called Mamluks (slaves) took power in Egypt; in 1260 they defeated the Mongols and took Antioch in 1268. On a new crusade (the Eighth), Saint Louis landed in Tunis and died there (1270). The Mamluks took Tripoli in 1289 and Acre in 1291, massacring sixty thousand Christians. The Christian settlements were now wiped out, but they were not deeply mourned, even in western Europe, from which so much blood and treasure had flowed for their establishment and defense.

The Meeting of East and West

From the first, the Crusaders had had mixed motives: the wish to make a pilgrimage and to

The Dome of the Rock, Jerusalem.

win forgiveness for their sins, the desire for gain and the love of adventure. Some intended to return home, others to stay. A new world grew up in the narrow strip of Crusader territory. As one Crusader put it:

> God has poured the West into the East; we who were Westerns are now Easterns. He who was a Roman or a Frank is now a Galilean or Palestinian. He who was from Rheims or Chartres is now a Tyrian or an Antiochene. We have all forgotten our native soil; it has grown strange unto us.*

A Muslim author tells of an old Crusader knight who

> presented an excellent table, with food extraordinarily clean and delicious. Seeing me abstaining from food, he said, "Eat, be of good cheer! I never eat Frankish dishes, but I have Egyptian women cooks and never eat except their cooking. Besides pork never enters my home."†

Once Christians and Muslims had begun to mix, the spirit of tolerance often moved both. Each side respected the valor of the other. There were never enough Westerners to cultivate the soil of Syria. They needed the labor of the Christian and Muslim peasants. The natives were also most useful in commerce.

As time passed, some Westerners married Easterners, and a race of half-breeds came into existence. Even those who did not intermarry often had their houses, palaces, or churches built by native craftsmen. They wore oriental clothes, let their beards grow, and ate squatting on carpets, Eastern-style. They enjoyed watching Muslim dancing girls, hired Muslim physicians, joined Muslims in tournaments and hunts, shared certain shrines, and debated the theology of one another's religions. Pilgrims freshly arrived from the West were shocked by the easternized Westerners.

Westerners who went back home had a greater effect on European society than did those who stayed in the East. From Marseilles alone, the ships of the Hospitalers and the Templars carried six thousand pilgrims a year, so many that the shipowners of the port sued the knightly orders for unfair competition.

Arabic words in Western languages reveal borrowed concepts and products—in commerce: bazaar, tariff; in foods: sugar, saffron, rice, lemons, apricots, melons, and pistachios; in manufactured goods: cotton, muslin, damask. All the new products proved a stimulus to the markets and fairs of the West.

Venice and Genoa, the ports from which much of the produce of the East was funneled into Europe, prospered. So did the cities of Flanders, whose manufacture of woolen goods was stimulated by the availability of Eastern luxuries for trade. Letters of credit and bills of exchange became more and more necessary, as commercial arrangements grew complex. Italian banking houses sprang up with offices in the Holy Land, and the orders of knighthood—especially the Templars—joined in the money trade.

Perhaps the Crusades helped to weaken and impoverish the feudal nobility and thereby benefiting the monarchies. Certainly kings were for the first time able to tax directly as a result of the need to raise money for the expeditions to the Holy Land. The papacy was no doubt strengthened in its climb to leadership over all Western Christendom by the initiative it took in sponsoring so vast an international movement and by the degree of control it exercised over the Crusades. But this short-run gain may have been outweighed by a long-run loss, as disillusionment grew. Moreover, the discovery that all Muslims were not savage beasts, that profit lay in trade with them, and that living together was possible doubtless led Christians to question statements to the contrary even when issued by Rome.

The influence of the Crusades upon Western European art and architecture was slight. It was greater in the writing of history and personal memoirs, especially in the vernacular languages, notably in the cases of Villehardouin and Joinville (see Chapter 5). Still more important was the great increase in geographical interest and knowledge; our first reliable maps and the beginnings of European journeys to the Far East date from the crusading period.

II THE FORTUNES OF EMPIRE, 1081–1453

Byzantine Feudalism

"The powerful," represented by Alexius Comnenus (reigned 1081–1118), had captured the

* Fulcher of Chartres, quoted by Archer and Kingsford in *The Crusades* (New York, 1895), p. 170.

† *Memoirs of Usamah Ibn-Munqidh,* trans. K. Hitti (Columbia, 1929), p. 170.

imperial throne. From then on, landlords freely accumulated lands and tenants, who served as soldiers in their private armies. To get troops of their own and to reward their favorites, Alexius and his successors began to grant them lands in exchange for military services. Such a grant was called a *pronoia.* The pronoia resembled the benefice in the medieval West: It was not a true fief because it was not hereditary. At Byzantium nobody but the emperor could grant pronoias.

Despite these differences between Byzantine and Western practice, we see that a form of feudalism was now established on Byzantine soil. Many individual Western nobles entered imperial service and received pronoias. Some of them married into the imperial family, and the emperors married Western princesses.

Alexius Comnenus gave great commercial privileges to the Venetians. Their city—once subject to Byzantium—had now become a great trading port, ruled by a few rich merchant families who elected their own duke. With its fleet, Venice helped Alexius against his enemies and received in exchange a whole neighborhood of Constantinople. Venetians came to live there and had their own docks, warehouses, and churches. Friction between Greeks and Venetians was inevitable. Alexius' successors gave similar rights to Venice's Italian rivals, Pisa and Genoa. Disorders were frequent in the capital.

Feudalism and Western penetration of Byzantine society were accompanied during the twelfth century by growing economic ruin and social misery. Tax assessors oppressed the people. Pirates ravaged the coasts. Bands of wandering monks behaved like brigands.

In 1171, the emperor Manuel I Comnenus (1143–1180) arrested more than ten thousand Venetians in one day. But his desperate effort was of little use. In 1182, the Constantinople mob massacred thousands of Westerners in the capital. The last of the Comnenian dynasty, Andronicus I (1183–1185), was torn to pieces by the frantic citizens of Constantinople. The weak dynasty of the Angeloi succeeded. In 1195 Alexius III Angelus deposed, blinded, and imprisoned his elder brother, Emperor Isaac Angelus (1185–1195).

The Fourth Crusade

In 1198, Pope Innocent III called for a new crusade. Count Baldwin of Flanders and numbers of other powerful lords took the Cross. The Venetians agreed to furnish sea transportation at a high price, but promised to postpone collecting the debt if the Crusaders would attack the city of Zara—in Dalmatia—which had revolted against Venice. Angrily, the pope excommunicated the Crusaders for destroying the Catholic city.

But next, the son of the deposed Byzantine emperor appeared and offered to pay off the rest of the Crusaders' debt to Venice if they would go first to Constantinople and restore Isaac. So in July 1203, the Crusaders assaulted and captured Constantinople, a thing no earlier enemy had ever done. They freed Isaac, whose son was crowned as Alexius IV.

But Alexius IV and Isaac could not fulfill their part of the bargain. Crusaders and Venetians now agreed to take Constantinople again and expel the Byzantine rulers. This time the Westerners sacked and pillaged Constantinople ruthlessly. Many works of art were sent to the West, among them the famous gilded bronze horses from the Hippodrome still to be seen over the door of St. Mark's in Venice.

The victorious Venetians and Crusaders elected Baldwin of Flanders as first "Latin" emperor of Constantinople, and the title continued in his family during the fifty-seven years of Western occupation. He held only one quarter of the new Latin Empire. The Venetians and the non-Venetian Crusaders divided the other three quarters between them. The Venetians chose the first Latin patriarch and kept a monopoly on that rich office. Venice claimed the Byzantine coastal towns and strategic islands. A strange hybrid state was created. Half of the emperor's council consisted of his own barons and half of members of the Venetian merchant colony under the leadership of their governor. In theory the Latin emperors were the successors of Constantine and Justinian, but because they could not make important decisions without the council they had far less power. Moreover they never commanded the loyalty of the Greek population.

On both sides of the straits enemies threatened. In Asia, Greek refugees from Constantinople set up a "Byzantine" empire in exile at Nicaea. Outnumbered, slow to learn new military tactics, miserably poor after the treasures of Byzantium had been drained away, the Westerners could not maintain their Latin Empire. The Greeks of Nicaea recaptured Constantinople (1261) and reestablished the Byzantine Empire.

Meanwhile, however, the Latins had fanned out from Constantinople. In Greece—at Athens, at Thebes, in the Peloponnesus—they set up prin-

Two of the gilded bronze horses taken by the Venetians from the Hippodrome at Byzantium and installed at St. Mark's Cathedral, Venice.

cipalities based on Western feudal customs. As in the Latin states of Syria, some intermarriage took place between Latins and Greeks, but the native population never became reconciled to alien domination. These feudal states in Greece survived the Greek reconquest of Constantinople in 1261, only to be wiped out during the Turkish conquest in the fifteenth century.

Byzantium after 1261

Michael VIII Palaeologus (reigned 1261–1282), who reconquered Constantinople, found it depopulated. The former European lands of Byzantium were mostly in Latin hands. In Asia Minor the frontier remained near Konia, the Seljuk capital. Michael VIII staved off a new threat posed to his empire by Charles of Anjou, ruler of the former Hohenstaufen lands in south Italy and Sicily.

The once large and splendid Byzantine Empire had become in fact a small Balkan state. Michael VIII's descendants, the Palaeologi, never abandoned their pretensions to their former grandeur. But they fought among themselves. Social unrest grew. Serbs, Genoese, and Venetians posed constant threats to stability. Aid from the West could be obtained only at the price of a promise to accept papal supremacy and reunite the churches. In 1274 and again in 1439, the emperors did indeed make such promises. But after the catastrophe of Latin occupation, Greek hatred for Westerners was too deep to make such "reunions" anything but a mockery.

The Ottoman Advance

The Ottoman Turks gave the empire its final blow. Ablest and luckiest of the groups to whom the Seljuk Sultanate in Asia Minor was now passing, the Ottomans in the last quarter of the thirteenth century settled across the straits from Constantinople. The discontented population preferred them to the harsh and ineffectual Byz-

Sultan Mohammed II (ruled 1451–1481): detail of a painting by Gentile Bellini.

antine officials. Some Greeks converted to Islam in order to avoid the payment of tribute. They taught the nomadic Turkish conquerors some of the arts of a settled agricultural life. Within a generation or two, the Ottoman Turks had mingled with the native Greeks of Anatolia.

Soon, the Ottomans built a fleet and began raiding in the Sea of Marmora and the Aegean. In 1354 one of the rival claimants to the Byzantine throne used them as allies and gave them land in Europe. They added more and in 1363 moved their capital to the European city of Adrianople. Constantinople was now surrounded by Ottoman territory, and could be reached from the West only by sea. In order to survive, the emperors made humiliating arrangements with the Ottoman rulers, in some cases becoming their vassals.

The Byzantine Empire survived until 1453 in part because the Ottomans chose to conquer much of the Balkan region first, destroying the Serb state at Kossovo (1389). But Ottoman conquests were delayed for half a century when a new wave of Mongols under Timur (Tamerlane) emerged from Central Asia and defeated the Ot-

The Anastasis: fresco in the Church of the Chora, Istanbul (fourteenth century) shows Christ raising Adam and Eve from the dead. Note the locks, bolts, and hinges of the smashed gates of hell.

toman armies at Ankara (1404). However, the Ottomans soon recovered. In 1453 Sultan Mohammed II ordered a great siege of Constantinople. The last emperor, Constantine XI, died bravely defending the walls.

On May 29, 1453, the Ottomans poured into the city. Mohammed II, the Conqueror, gave thanks to Allah in Santa Sophia itself and ground the altar of the sanctuary beneath his feet. Thenceforth it was to be a mosque. Soon the sultan installed a new Greek patriarch and proclaimed himself protector of the Christian church. During the centuries that followed, the Orthodox church usually accepted the sultans as successors to the Byzantine emperors. But the empire that traced its origins to Augustus had come to an end.

During its last unhappy centuries the Byzantine Empire experienced an astonishing artistic revival. Western influences from the Italian cities mingled with Byzantine traditional styles. The small Byzantine monastic church of the Chora in Constantinople (often called by its Turkish name Kahrié Djami) includes a splendid series of mosaics in the new manner. One of them shows the founder, the learned bureaucrat and courtier, Theodore Metochites, presenting the church to the Virgin. Also in the Chora is a remarkable fresco of Christ summoning the dead from their graves on the last day. He clasps Adam's hand in one of his own, Eve's in the other. Bolts, hinges, nails, locks, and screws fly about as the graves of the dead spring open.

III THE OTTOMAN SUCCESSOR STATE, 1453–1699

The Ottoman sultans ruled over the same territory and the same subjects as the Byzantine emperors. In many ways their state was a successor state to Byzantium. The Ottomans loved war, and they clung to custom. These attitudes and their Turkish language came from their far-distant past in Central Asia. From the Persians, the Ottomans took their literary language, their exaltation of their ruler, and their tolerance of religious minorities. They encouraged such minorities to form independent communities inside their state. From Islam they took the sacred law and its approach to legal problems, the Arabic alphabet with which they wrote until the 1920s, and the Arabic philosophical vocabulary. The Ottomans were an extremely conservative people.

Civilization

The Slave System

In Ottoman society, slaves manned the government. Except for the sultan himself, all the major officials of the state and of the sultan's household, all the officers of the army, and large bodies of picked troops were slaves. Almost always they began life as the children of Christians. They were picked in their early youth for their promise and were specially educated for the sultan's service. They owed their jobs to the sultan and could be instantly removed from office and punished by death.

From the late fourteenth to the early seventeenth century, specially trained officers, each with a quota of places to fill, visited Christian villages at four-year intervals. They took away the ablest youths between the ages of ten and twenty. The practice seems to us heartless. But because no married boy was eligible, marriage was always an escape. Also the villages were poor, and unlimited opportunities were open to the chosen boys. Being chosen was sometimes regarded as a privilege, though of course Christian parents mourned. All these chosen youths were converted to Islam. No born Muslim could in theory ever be recruited into the system, since by law no born Muslim could be a slave.

The seven or eight thousand boys chosen annually all got systematic physical and military training. About a tenth received higher education. The cream of the crop became pages in the sultan's own household and attended his palace school. Here they studied languages, Muslim and Ottoman law, ethics, and theology, as well as horsemanship and military science. All left school at the age of twenty-five. The top elite were then given jobs in the administration. The rest became *spahis,* or cavalrymen. There was always plenty of room for advancement, since many were killed in war; and at the top levels some were demoted, dismissed, or executed for inefficiency or disloyalty. Splendid financial rewards awaited any man lucky enough to rise to one of the top posts.

At the lower level, the less intelligent slaves were often drafted into the janissaries (from the Turkish words *yeni cheri,* "new forces"). Their training emphasized physical endurance. They served not only as infantrymen but as shipyard workers, palace gardeners, and the like. They lived in special barracks and had special privileges. A source of strength, they also posed a constant potential danger to the state. At the height of Ottoman military successes, the sultans could put into the field armies more than a quarter of a million strong.

The Sultan's harem was also a part of the slave institution. All the women in it were slaves, together with their servants. Although slaves, these women gave birth to the Sultan's heirs. Each new sultan was therefore half-slave by birth. The sultan picked his favorite, not necessarily his oldest, son to succeed him. Because of rivalry and intrigue, the custom arose that the heir to the throne must kill all his brothers and half-brothers upon his succession. Every son of a sultan knew as he was growing up that he either must obtain the throne himself or be killed by whichever of his brothers did obtain it. In 1595, for instance, Mohammed III killed no fewer than nineteen brothers and half-brothers.

The Four Pillars of Administration

Ottoman writers thought of the state as a tent resting on four pillars. The first was the viziers, varying in number, to whom the sultan actually delegated many powers. They presided over the council of state, kept the great seal, and could sometimes make decisions on policy. The second pillar was the financial officers, organized to collect revenues: the poll tax on Christians and Jews, one-tenth of all produce, and many of the old Byzantine taxes on commerce, as well as special levies, including money realized by confiscating the great fortunes of disgraced officials. The third pillar was the chancery, a secretariat that prepared, recorded, and transmitted documents and affixed the sultan's signature to them.

The fourth pillar, unlike the other three, was not a department of state manned by slaves born as Christians. It was composed of the judges, all of whom were born Muslim. The Islamic religion bore responsibility for all legal matters and for education. One-third of state lands were set aside as religious property. Each tract had its own purpose: the support of mosques, of charitable or educational institutions, or even of inns or public baths. Income from such property supported the entire class of *ulema,* the learned men of Islam. Among the ulema were the *muftis,* or jurists, who answered questions that arose in the course of lawsuits.

The grand mufti in Istanbul, whom the sultan himself consulted, was known as the *Sheikh-ul-Islam,* the "ancient" of Islam. He outranked everybody but the grand vizier. Since he had the final word on the sacred law, he exercised a kind of check on the absolute power of the sultan. He alone could proclaim the beginning of war, or denounce a sultan for transgression of the sacred law and summon his subjects to depose him. The opinions of the muftis were collected as a body of interpretative law.

All Muslims accepted the supremacy of the sacred law. The muftis hated change. Generally, therefore, the Ottoman system did not develop with the times. There were no full-scale "reformations" in Ottoman history until the twentieth century.

Weaknesses of the System

The effectiveness of the entire structure depended upon the character of the sultan. Harem upbringing and ruthless family antagonisms, however, did not often produce wise and statesmanlike sultans. Many sultans were weaklings, drunkards, vicious, and men of little political experience or understanding. Harem intrigue played a great role in the state.

Efficient administration depended upon maintaining the slave system, which excluded born Muslims. But the sons of the slaves *were* all born Muslims. So in practice this rigid exclusion broke down early, and born Muslims, attracted by the possibilities of gain and power, began to be admitted. Since they could not be regarded as slaves, the chief restraints that kept the machine running weakened. Insubordinate soldiers also sped the decay of the state. Turbulent janissaries frequently deposed sultans.

In this society where religion was the only test of nationality, all Orthodox Christians were automatically regarded as Greeks, and lived under the control of the patriarch. This alienated many non-Greek Christians who might otherwise have been loyal subjects.

The Empire

Expansion, to 1566

The core of the Ottoman state was the same as that around which the Byzantine Empire had been built—Asia Minor and the Balkans. From this core before the death of Mohammed II in 1481, the Ottomans expanded across the Danube into modern Romania and seized the Crimea, which became a vassal state under its Tatar rulers. But Ottomans could not take either the great Hungarian fortress of Belgrade, key to central Europe, or the Hospitaler stronghold of Rhodes in

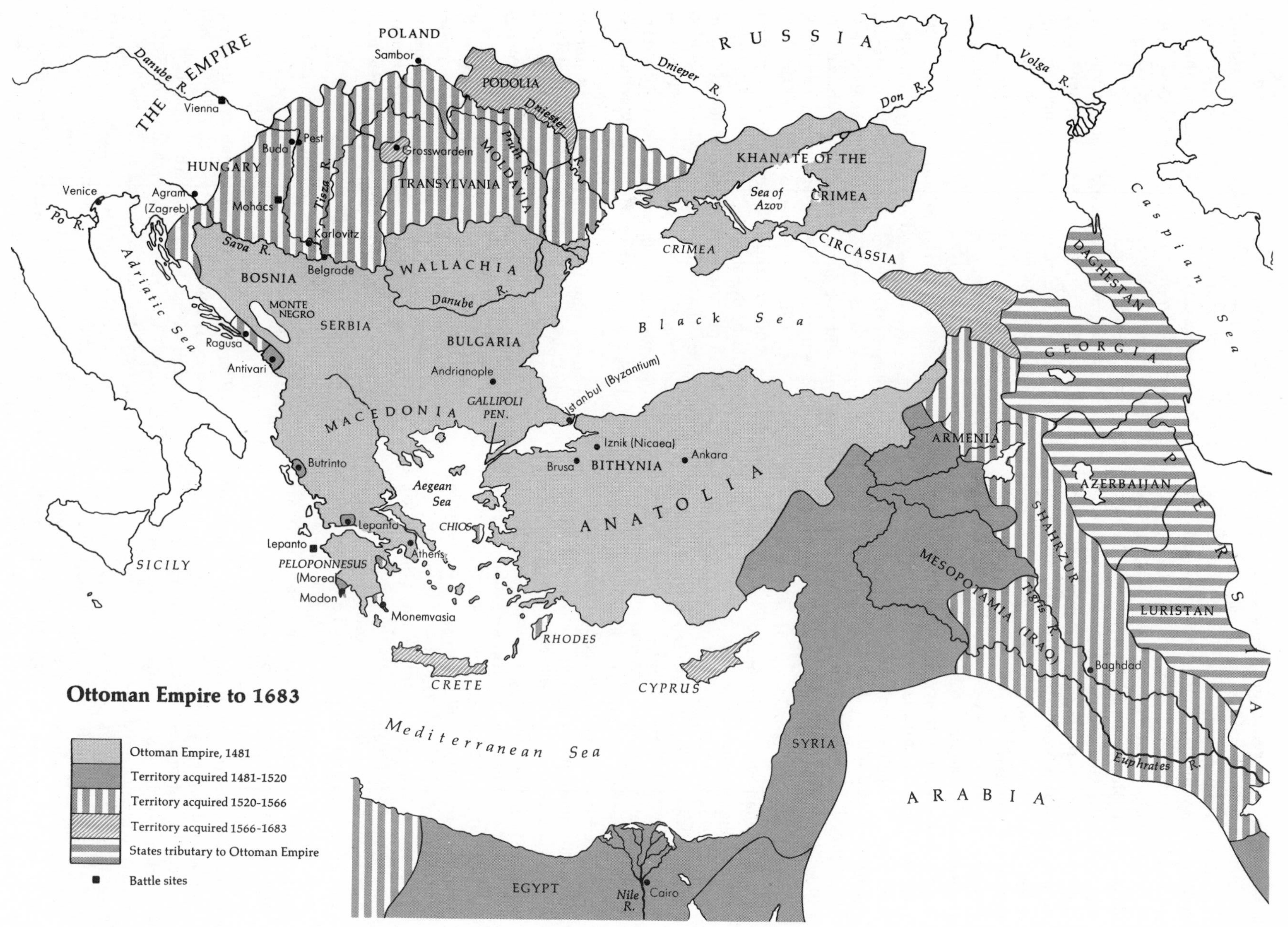
Ottoman Empire to 1683
Ottoman Empire, 1481
Territory acquired 1481-1520
Territory acquired 1520-1566
Territory acquired 1566-1683
States tributary to Ottoman Empire
Battle sites
POLAND
Sambor
THE EMPIRE
Danube R.
Vienna
RUSSIA
Dnieper R.
Don R.
Volga R.
PODOLIA
Dniester R.
Pruth R.
MOLDAVIA
Grosswardein
TRANSYLVANIA
HUNGARY
Buda
Pest
Tisza R.
Mohács
Karlovitz
Venice
Po R.
Agram (Zagreb)
Sava R.
Belgrade
BOSNIA
WALLACHIA
Danube R.
KHANATE OF THE CRIMEA
Sea of Azov
CRIMEA
CIRCASSIA
Caspian Sea
DAGHESTAN
GEORGIA
PERSIA
AZERBAIJAN
LURISTAN
SHAHRZUR
ARMENIA
MESOPOTAMIA (IRAQ)
Tigris R.
Baghdad
Euphrates R.
Adriatic Sea
MONTE NEGRO
SERBIA
Ragusa
Antivari
BULGARIA
Black Sea
Andrianople
Istanbul (Byzantium)
GALLIPOLI PEN.
MACEDONIA
Iznik (Nicaea)
Brusa
BITHYNIA
Ankara
ANATOLIA
Butrinto
Aegean Sea
Lepanto
CHIOS
Athens
PELOPONNESUS (Morea)
Modon
Monemvasia
SICILY
RHODES
CRETE
CYPRUS
Mediterranean Sea
SYRIA
ARABIA
EGYPT
Nile R.
Cairo

the Mediterranean, key to further Mediterranean naval advances.

Sultan Selim I (reigned 1512–1520) nearly doubled the territories of the empire. He defeated the Persians in Asia and in 1517 annexed Egypt. He assumed the duty of protecting Mecca and Medina, and the title of caliph. For the first time, the overwhelming majority of Ottoman subjects was Muslim, mostly Arabs, often more fanatical Muslims than the Turks. The character of Ottoman society was much affected by the change.

Suleiman the Magnificent (reigned 1520–1566) resumed the advance into Europe. He was allied with the French against the Austrians in their dynastic wars (see Chapter 8). In 1521, Suleiman took Belgrade and in 1522 Rhodes, thus removing the two chief obstacles to westward advance. In 1526, at Mohács in Hungary, he defeated the Christian armies, and the Turks entered Buda, the Hungarian capital.

In September 1529, Suleiman besieged Vienna, posing a threat to Christendom greater than any since Leo III and Charles Martel had defeated the Arabs in the early eighth century. But the Ottoman lines of communication were greatly overextended, and Suleiman had to abandon the siege after two weeks. He retained control over parts of Hungary. In North Africa he acquired Algeria, which remained an Ottoman vassal state until the nineteenth century. In Asia he defeated the Persians, annexed modern Iraq, including Baghdad, and secured an outlet on the Persian Gulf.

In 1536, France and the Ottoman Empire concluded a formal treaty, the first of the "capitulations," so called because it was divided into "chapters" not because it was a surrender. It permitted the French to buy and sell throughout the Ottoman dominions on the same basis as any Ottoman subject. They were allowed resident consuls with civil and criminal jurisdiction over Frenchmen in the Ottoman Empire. In Ottoman territory, Frenchmen were to enjoy complete religious liberty and were also granted a protectorate over the Holy Places, the old aim of the Crusades.

The Orthodox church resented these Roman Catholic gains, and the dispute would survive to precipitate the Crimean War in the nineteenth century. These capitulations, whose provisions remind us of Byzantine trade treaties with Venice and Genoa, gave France a better position in the Ottoman Empire than any other European power.

Decline, 1566–1699

After Suleiman, the Ottoman system deteriorated, despite occasional successes. In 1571 a Western league, headed by the pope, won the naval battle of Lepanto but the Ottomans quickly recovered.

The sale of government offices was now a regular practice, and the repeated rebellions of janissaries endangered the sultan's position. Only Western Europe's preoccupation with its own wars saved the Ottoman Empire in the first half of the seventeenth century. What looked like a real revival began with the accession to power of an able family of viziers, the Köprülüs.

The first Köprülü ruthlessly executed 36,000 people in a five-year period (1656–1661), hanged the Greek patriarch for predicting that Christianity would defeat Islam, rebuilt the army and navy, and suppressed revolt. Between 1661 and 1676, the second Köprülü led the Ottoman navy to a triumph in Crete, taken from Venice. The Ottomans temporarily won large areas of the Ukraine from the Russians and Poles. In 1683, the Ottomans for the second time besieged Vienna.

All Europe anxiously awaited the outcome. But again the Ottoman wave was broken and a European alliance began a great counteroffensive. The Austrians drove the Ottomans out of Hungary, and the Venetians seized the Peloponnesus. The Russians now first appeared as effective enemies of the Ottomans. The Köprülüs had galvanized the Ottoman armies into a last successful effort. But the real evils of the Ottoman system remained untouched.

In 1699 an international congress at Karlovitz on the Danube confirmed Ottoman territorial losses. Thereafter, the European powers could stop worrying about the direct Ottoman menace, which had preoccupied them for more than three hundred years. Against their will they came to rely upon Christian Greeks for diplomatic administrators and for commercial and naval skills. The Christian Greeks, with generations of experience, had retained the talents of their Byzantine ancestors.

For Europe, the Ottoman Empire had changed its character. From 1699 on it was no longer a military power but a great landholding power in decline. Who would pick up the pieces of its territory as it fell apart? The states of Europe would spend two and a quarter more centuries—down to 1922—negotiating and often fighting over this "Eastern Question." Having prayed for Ottoman collapse, Europe now struggled—sometimes vainly—to prop up the Ottoman state in order to prevent a major European war over the Ottoman inheritance.

IV RUSSIA FROM THE ELEVENTH TO THE LATE SEVENTEENTH CENTURY

During the eleventh century, the newly christianized society centered on Kiev had frequent contact with the West. The ruling house intermarried with those of Sweden and France, and made alliances with the Holy Roman emperors. Merchants from the West came to Russia. But these flourishing beginnings came to little.

When a Kievan prince died, his sons divided up the land. This soon fragmented the land into petty principalities, which constantly fought among themselves. And this weakened Kievan society in the face of outside dangers.

In the eleventh century, the Turkic tribe of Polovtsy, or Cumans, appeared on the southern steppes. The warring Russian princes made the tragic mistake of hiring bands of Polovtsy. The heroic poem of the Kievan period, the *Song of the Expedition of Igor,* quite comparable with the French *Song of Roland,* scolds the princes for introducing the infidels and creating chaos. Shortly after 1200, the Mongol Tatars conquered the Kievan state permanently. Kiev bequeathed to later Russians the ideal of unity, the common heritage of language, and the Christian faith.

Tatar Conquest and Exploitation

United by Genghis Khan in the early thirteenth century, the nomad Mongol Tatar tribes of central Asia flooded across Russia and into Eastern Europe between 1223 and 1241. Thereafter they withdrew to Sarai at the great bend of the Volga River, in eastern Russia. Sarai became the capital of a new state, the Golden Horde, owing allegiance to the distant Mongol government in Peking.

While they were actually conquering Russia, the Tatars ruthlessly laid waste the land. Once the conquest was finished, however, they were interested in exploiting Russia for tribute in men and money. They did not care about governing Russia directly and left that to the Russian princes. But each Russian prince, on assuming office, had to travel to distant Sarai to do homage. The nearer the lands of a Russian prince lay to Sarai, the heavier the burden and the more humiliating the bondage.

The Western Lands and Novgorod

During the 250 years following the collapse of Kiev, Russian national life continued in four main areas. The southwest, including Kiev itself, became a virtually independent principality. The unruly nobility hampered all efforts of the princes to consolidate their power in the face of pressure from their Polish and Lithuanian neighbors. The northwest, centering around the cities of Polotsk and Smolensk, by the early fourteenth century was subject to the grand duke of Lithuania. Mostly pagan, the Lithuanians at first took over the language and attitudes of their Russian vassals. But in 1386, a dynastic marriage united Lithuania with Poland. The influence of the Polish Roman Catholic Church and nobility became paramount. These two areas were feudal and manorial. As in Western Europe, peasants were restricted in their movements.

Northern Russia, between the Baltic shore and Lake Ilmen, stretched far north and northeast over empty wastes to the Arctic Ocean and Siberia. These lands lay under the dominion of the

Early Russian architecture: the Church of the Savior, Novgorod.

town commonwealth of Novgorod. Long before Kiev collapsed, Novgorod had developed its own tradition of municipal independence. Novgorod traded with the West, especially Germany. Because its soil was infertile, Novgorod depended on the area to the southeast, around Moscow, for grain.

The city council of Novgorod was the ruling force. A few rich merchant families came to control the council and struggled with each other for power. The poor, meantime, might be sold into slavery for debt. They often became brigands. In the fifteenth century, when Poland-Lithuania was at war with the principality of Moscow, the upper classes at Novgorod supported the Poles and Lithuanians, while the lower classes supported Moscow. In 1478 Moscow conquered Novgorod, wiped out the upper classes, and took away the city bell, symbol of independence.

Moscow and the Tatars

When Kiev collapsed, the northeast region—the principality of Moscow—was still newly settled. Agriculturally poorer than the fertile southwest, it was richer than Novgorod and could provide food enough for its people. It also had flourishing forest industries. Here there were neither cities nor nobles. So pioneers turned to the prince for leadership.

This was also the region most exposed to the Tatars. A prince of Moscow won the first Russian victories over the Tatars in 1378 and 1380. In the early fifteenth century, the Golden Horde disintegrated into three Tatar states: one at Kazan on the middle Volga, which blocked the course of the river to Russian trade for another century and a half; a second at Astrakhan at the mouth of the Volga on the Caspian; and a third in the Crimea, which later became a vassal of the Ottoman sultan. The Tatar conquest had a serious retarding effect on Russian civilization, subjecting it to two centuries of cultural stagnation.

A Russian prince and his bodyguard.

During these two centuries, the princes of Moscow gradually assumed leadership. They were shrewd administrators. They married into powerful families and got land by inheritance, by purchase, and by foreclosing mortgages. They established the principle of seniority, so that their domain was not divided among their sons, and the tragedy of Kiev was not repeated. They developed useful relations with their Tatar overlords, who chose them to collect the tribute from neighboring princes and to deliver it to Sarai. After defeating the Tatars, the princes of Moscow could truthfully claim to be the agents of liberation and champions of Russia.

Most important, the princes of Moscow secured the support of the Russian church. In the early fourteenth century the metropolitan archbishop deliberately transferred his see to Moscow and made it the ecclesiastical capital of Russia. When the Muscovite princes went through a temporary period of weakness, the metropolitan administered the principality loyally and effectively until the princely house recovered.

Ivan III of Moscow (reigned 1462–1505) put himself forward as the heir to the princes of Kiev. He made a national and religious appeal by announcing that he intended to regain the ancient Russian lands that had been lost to Catholic Poles and Muslim Tatars. His wars took on the character of a Russian crusade. Many nobles in the western lands came over to him and renounced their loyalties to the Lithuanian-Polish state. In 1492, the Prince of Lithuania was forced to recognize Ivan III as sovereign of "all the Russias."

In 1472, Ivan married the niece of the last Byzantine emperor, Constantine XI. He adopted the Byzantine title of autocrat, used the Byzantine double-headed eagle as his seal, and began to behave like a Byzantine emperor. He sometimes used the title *tsar* (Caesar). He no longer consulted his nobles on matters of state, but reached decisions in solitude. Italian architects built him an enormous palace, the Kremlin, a building set apart, like the one at Byzantium.

From the late fifteenth century on, the tsars acted like autocrats. Unlike the nobles in Western Europe, those of Muscovy did not unite to fight the rising monarchy for their privileges. Instead, they split into various factions, which the monarch could put down one by one. Whereas in the West, the Church was a part of feudal society and jealous of its prerogatives; in Russia it became

The thirteenth-century Kremlin at Pskov.

the ally of the monarchy and a department of state.

Russian churchmen were well aware of Rome's claim to world empire, and they knew that for centuries Constantinople had been "new Rome." After the Ottoman Turks captured Constantinople in 1453, the Russian Church invented a new theory:

> The Church of Old Rome fell because of its heresy; the gates of the Second Rome, Constantinople, have been hewn down by the infidel Turks; but the Church of Moscow, the Church of the New Rome, shines brighter than the Sun in the whole Universe. . . . Two Romes have fallen, but the Third stands fast; a fourth there cannot be.*

* A. J. Toynbee, *Civilization on Trial* (New York, 1948), p. 171.

Between the accession of Ivan III in 1462 and the accession of Peter the Great in 1689, the tsars neutralized the old, established nobility by building up a new class of military service gentry who owed everything to the tsar. Their estates, at first granted only for life in exchange for service, eventually became hereditary. Gradually too, the old nobility was forced to render services in exchange for their estates, which had always been hereditary but for which they had owed no service. By 1609 the two types of noble and the two types of estate had by a gradual process become almost identical. The hereditary nobles often owed service; the military-service nobles often had hereditary land.

This important social process was accompanied by another, which is really the other side of the coin—the growth of serfdom. Economic

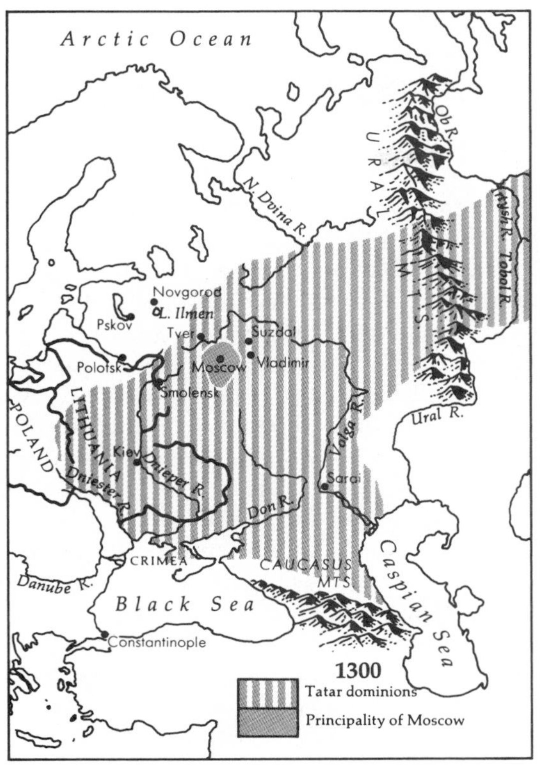

factors and political unrest forced more and more peasants to become dependent on large landowners. A peasant would accept a contract lending him money in exchange for produce and service on the landlord's lands. By the early seventeenth century, it had become customary that the peasant could not leave his plot until he had paid off the loan. Since the debt was usually too big for him to repay, he could in practice never leave.

The process was enormously speeded up when the tsars gave estates to the military service gentry. Without peasant labor the estates had no value. The government therefore helped the new landlords keep their peasants in place. Since the peasants paid most of the taxes, it was more advantageous to keep the peasants where they were. It became harder and harder for a tenant to leave his landlord, until by 1649 the avenues of escape were closed and the peasant was a serf fixed to the soil. The landlord administered justice, had police rights on his estate, and collected the serfs' taxes. He could sell, exchange, or give away his serfs, whose status became hereditary. Autocracy and serfdom were the most characteristic features of Russian society. Their consequences are still visible today.

Ivan the Terrible and the Time of Troubles

Most of the disorders of sixteenth- and seventeenth-century Russia had their origin in the long reign of Ivan IV, the Terrible (1534–1584). Ivan succeeded to the throne as a small child. Rival groups of intriguing nobles made his life wretched. When he was strong enough to assume power, Ivan curbed the greed of the provincial

A contemporary portrait of Ivan the Terrible.

administrators who had oppressed the population. He also convoked the first national assembly *(zemski sobor)*, a consultative body consisting of nobles, clerics, and town representatives, to assist particularly with important questions of war and peace. It was comparable to the assemblies of medieval Western Europe, but under Ivan the *zemski sobor* met only once.

In 1564 Ivan divided Russia in two parts, the *oprichnina*, or "separate realm," which was to belong to him personally, while the rest of Russia was administered as before. His new officers (called *oprichniks*), grimly dressed in black and riding black horses, were symbolized by a dog's head (for vigilance) and a broom (meaning a clean sweep). These forerunners of the secret police waged war on the nobles, confiscating their estates, exiling them, killing them off. By the time of Ivan's death, Russia had fallen into chaos. Pathologically cruel, Ivan had seven wives and murdered his own son in a fit of rage. Yet he extended Russian authority to the east against the Tatars, opening the whole Volga waterway to Russian commerce and making possible expansion further east, into Siberia.

The few foreign observers who knew the Russia of Ivan foresaw collapse. And the tsar himself wrote in his last will: "The body is exhausted, the spirit is ailing, the spiritual and physical wounds multiply, and there is no doctor to cure me"* With the death of his imbecile son, Fyodor (1598), the Moscow dynasty, descended from the Kievan princes, died out. Fyodor's able brother-in-law, Boris Godunov (1598–1605), could not deal with the legacy of disorder, especially after a famine and plague began in 1601. Brigands roamed the countryside. A pretender under Polish protection claimed to be a son of Ivan the Terrible. Russia was launched on the "Time of Troubles" (1603–1613).

Not until it seemed that the Poles, who took Moscow, would impose foreign Catholic rule, was there a national uprising in answer to an appeal from the patriarch. Under the combined command of a butcher and a nobleman, an army of prosperous free farmers from the middle Volga region expelled the Poles in 1613.

The First Romanovs

A *zemski sobor* now elected Michael Romanov tsar. Down to the Russian Revolution of 1917, the Romanovs held the throne. Michael came to power with no limitations placed upon his power by the *zemski sobor*. He was an elected autocrat. For the first ten years of his reign, the *zemski sobor* stayed in continuous session to give the new dynasty the popular support it needed.

But the *zemski sobor* never transformed itself into a parliament like that in England. After 1623 it was summoned only to help declare war or make peace, to approve new taxation, and to approve important new laws. It supported the accession of Michael's son Alexius (1645–1676), and in 1649 it confirmed a major new law code. After 1653 Alexius did not summon it again, nor did his son, Fëdor (1676–1682). Its last meetings were in 1682.

The early Romanovs were neither distinguished nor talented. The ill-defined departments of the central government often had overlapping areas of jurisdiction. Provincial governors milked the long-suffering population. Opposition came from the oppressed and hungry peasantry, who burned manor houses and killed landlords or tax collectors. Such peasant uprisings were almost never directed against the tsar. Indeed a peasant leader would often arouse his followers *in the name* of the tsar, or even pretend to be the tsar.

During the sixteenth and seventeenth centuries, Russian pioneers, in search of furs to sell and new land to settle, led the way in a tremendous expansion of the Russian domain. Russian frontiersmen known as Cossacks (a Tatar word meaning "free adventurer") organized themselves for self-defense against the Tatars. Two Cossack republics arose, one on the Dnieper, the other on the Don, living in a kind of primitive democracy relatively independent of Moscow. As time passed, other Cossack groups formed in the Volga and in the Ural Mountains.

The most dramatic expansion rapidly took the Russians eastward across Siberia to the Pacific. More slowly, because of Tatar, Turkish, and Polish opposition, the Russians also moved southeast toward the Black Sea. Repeatedly Russians and Poles fought over the old west Russian territory of the Ukraine, but by 1682 the Poles were beginning to yield. The Swedes still blocked the Baltic exit into the North Sea. On the southern steppes the Russians struggled against the Crimean Tatars. The Ottomans, overlords of the Tatars, held the key fort of Azov, at the mouth of the Don, controlled the Black Sea, participated in the wars over the Ukraine, and became great enemies of the tsars.

* Quoted by M. T. Florinsky, *Russia: A History and an Interpretation* (New York, 1953), I: 208.

The Church and Foreign Influences

Throughout, the Church remained the partner of the autocracy. The tsar controlled the election of the metropolitan of Moscow, and after 1589 that of the newly proclaimed patriarch of Moscow. Tsar Alexius appointed to the patriarchal throne a cleric named Nikon, whose arrogance aroused protests from both the clergy and the laity.

Nikon advanced the theory that, since the spiritual realm was superior to the temporal, the patriarch was actually superior to the tsar. In the West, as we know, Gregory VII or Innocent III had acted on this belief, but in Byzantium and Russia few churchmen ever dared. In 1666, a church council deposed Nikon, who died a mere monk. Later Peter the Great would abolish the patriarchate because he wished to silence Nikon's claims forever.

By 1500 the Russian monasteries owned more than a third of the land available for cultivation. Opposition to monastic worldliness arose within the Church. Those churchmen who favored monastic poverty also opposed any role for the state in monastic affairs. To preserve its rights to control the monasteries, the government of the tsar therefore had to oppose the reforming movement.

Almost alone, the Church inspired the art and literature of the Muscovite period. Sacred pictures (icons) of a type familiar in Byzantium inspired talented schools of Russian painters. The monks wrote chronicles and theological tracts against both Catholics and Protestants. They wrote in Old Church Slavonic, the language of the liturgy but not of everyday speech. There was no Russian secular learning, no science, no flowering of vernacular literature, no philosophical debate.

Slowly and gradually, during the sixteenth and seventeenth centuries, foreigners and foreign ideas penetrated into Russia. The small group of talented Italians who built the Kremlin in the late fifteenth century had little lasting influence. Ivan IV welcomed English merchants and encouraged them to trade their woolen cloth for Russian timber, rope, pitch, and other naval supplies, which helped build the Elizabethan fleet. The English taught the Russians some industrial techniques and supplied a large number of officers, mostly Scots, for the tsar's armies. In the mid-seventeenth century, the Dutch displaced the English as the leading foreign residents, managing their own glass, paper, and textile factories in Russia.

The foreign quarter of Moscow, always called "the German suburb," grew rapidly. German, Dutch, Danish technicians—bronze founders, textile weavers, clockmakers—received large salaries from the state. Foreign physicians and druggists became fashionable, though the common people thought they were wizards. Foreign merchants enjoyed special privileges, much to the disgust of their native competitors.

A few Russian nobles began to buy books, assemble libraries, and learn Latin, French, or German. Some began to eat salad, to take snuff, and even to converse politely. Some Russians went abroad to travel, and most of these travelers refused to go home again. The lower classes, however, distrusted and hated the foreigners, and jeered at them on the street.

The most dramatic outburst of antiforeign feeling was touched off by learned clerics from the Ukraine and Greece. These churchmen recommended to Patriarch Nikon that the scriptures be corrected in certain places where the texts were unsound. Many Russians were horrified. With their deep regard for the externals, the rite, the magic, they were now told that they were spelling the name of Jesus wrong and using the wrong number of fingers in crossing themselves.

The opponents of change split away from the Church. Some twenty thousand of them burned themselves alive, convinced that the end of the world was at hand, since Moscow, the Third Rome, had become heretical, and there could be no fourth. The survivors mostly became sober, solid citizens, called Old Believers, many of them merchants and well-to-do farmers. Some later Russian governments persecuted them.

Well before the day of Peter the Great, then, the arrival of foreigners and foreign ideas in Russia had split Russian opinion and caused an upheaval in the Russian Church.

READING SUGGESTIONS on The Medieval World: Eastern Europe (Asterisk indicates paperbacks.)

NOTE: *The works by G. Ostrogorsky and A. A. Vasiliev, listed under "The World of Byzantium" in the Reading Suggestions for Chapter 4, are also the best general introductory works for the later years of the Byzantine Empire discussed in this chapter.*

The Crusades

S. Runciman, *A History of the Crusades,* 3 vols. (*Harper Torchbooks). A full-length treatment of the subject, but may be read easily by a beginning student.

H. E. Meyer, *The Crusades,* trans. J. Gillingham (*Oxford). A recent one-volume summary account with a useful bibliography.

K. M. Setton, et al., eds., *A History of the Crusades,* 6 vols. (1969–1979). A collaborative work by many scholars. Uneven, but generally authoritative.

J. Prawer, *The Crusader Kingdom* (1972). A fine study of the Crusader States as European colonies.

A. S. Atiya, *The Crusade in the Later Middle Ages* (1938). Interesting study of the propaganda and the expeditions that marked the decline of the crusading movement.

The following important original sources are easily available in translation:

Fulcher of Chartres, *Chronicle of the First Crusade,* trans. M. E. McGinty (1941).

The Deeds of the Franks and Other Pilgrims to Jerusalem, trans. R. Hill (1962).

Ambroise, *The Crusade of Richard Lion-Heart,* trans. M. J. Hubert and J. L. LaMonte (1941).

William of Tyre, *History of Deeds Done beyond the Sea,* trans. E. A. Babcock and A. C. Krey, 2 vols. (1943). Most important account by the "Latin" archbishop of Tyre in the twelfth century.

An Arab-Syrian Gentleman and Warrior in the Period of the Crusades: Memoirs of Usamah ibn-Munqidh, trans. P. K. Hitti (1929).

Anna Comnena, *Alexiad,* trans. E. A. S. Dawes (1928). The daughter of Emperor Alexius I Comnenus writes an admiring life and history of her father. Of major importance.

John Kinnamos, *Deeds of John and Manuel Comnenus,* trans. C. M. Brand (1976). The first English translation of a major source for the period 1118–1380.

The Final Period of Byzantine History

C. M. Brand, *Byzantium Confronts the West,* 1180–1204 (1968). A detailed study of the final quarter-century before the Fourth Crusade.

Geoffrey de Villehardouin and Jean de Joinville, *Memoirs of the Crusades* (*Penguin). Villehardouin was a leading commander and eyewitness to the Fourth Crusade and capture of Constantinople, Joinville a companion of St. Louis on his later expeditions.

Robert of Clari, *The Conquest of Constantinople,* trans. E. H. McNeal (1936). Another eyewitness account by a Crusader who participated in the capture of Constantinople, but was a humble man, not one of the leaders.

D. M. Nicol, *The Last Centuries of Byzantium* (1972). A good study of the period 1261–1453.

A. Laiou, *Constantinople and the Latins: The Foreign Policy of Andronicus II (1282–1328)* (1972). Fine detailed study of foreign policy during the late period of weakness. The same author's *Peasant Society in the Late Byzantine Empire* (1977) is a highly original study of peasant life.

J. W. Barker, *Manuel II Palaeologus, 1391–1425* (1969). Good study of an emperor in the period of decline.

J. Gill, *The Council of Florence* (1959). A thorough study of the temporary reunion between the churches.

S. Runciman, *The Fall of Constantinople* (1965). A well-written account of the final catastrophe of 1453.

The Ottoman Turks

S. Shaw, *History of the Ottoman Empire and Modern Turkey* (*2 vols. Cambridge). Volume I is a useful introductory textbook on the period that concerns us here.

S. Vryonis, *The Decline of Medieval Hellenism in Asia Minor and the Process of Islamization from the Eleventh through the Fifteenth Century* (1971). The title well describes the subject of this learned and valuable work.

C. Cahen, *Pre-Ottoman Turkey* (1968). By a leading authority. The only book in English on the subject.

N. Itzkowitz, *The Ottoman Empire and Islamic Tradition* (*Knopf). Excellent brief introduction covering the period down to the end of the eighteenth century.

H. Inalcik, *The Ottoman Empire: The Classical Age, 1300–1600* (1973). Though lacking in interpretation and difficult to read, this is nonetheless a significant work by the chief Turkish scholarly authority on the subject.

P. Wittek, *The Rise of the Ottoman Empire* (1958). A good short study, controversial in outlook.

H. A. R. Gibb and H. Bowen, *Islamic Society and the West,* Vol I, Parts 1 and 2 (1950, 1956). A survey of Ottoman institutions.

D. M. Vaughan, *Europe and the Turk: A Pattern of Alliances, 1350–1700* (1954). A useful summary of the diplomatic relationships between the Ottoman Empire and Europe.

The Life and Letters of Ogier Ghiselin de Busbecq (1881). Four remarkable letters by the Hapsburg ambassador to the court of Suleiman the Magnificent, an important source of Ottoman history.

Russia from the Eleventh to the Late Seventeenth Century

M. Florinsky, *Russia: A History and Interpretation,* Vol. I (1953). A solid and reliable textbook.

G. Vernadsky, *Kievan Russia* (1948) and *The Mongols and Russia* (1953), Vols. II and III of The Yale History of Russia. Authoritative and complete.

G. P. Fedotov, *The Russian Religious Mind,* 2 vols. (1946, 1966). Intellectually very demanding, a most original work.

The Russian Primary Chronicle, trans. S. H. Cross and O. Sherbowitz-Wetzor (1954). Our oldest source for early Russian history.

W. K. Medlin, *Moscow and East Rome* (1952). Interesting study of the ideological importance of Byzantium to the Russians.

J. L. Fennell, *Ivan the Great of Moscow* (1961). A useful study.

The Correspondence between Prince A. M. Kurbsky and Tsar Ivan IV of Russia (1955) and *Kurbsky's History of Ivan IV* (1965), ed. J. L. I. Fennell. Regarded as our best sources on Ivan the Terrible's political ideas until the book by E. Keenan, *The Kurbskii-Groznyi Apocrypha* (1971), which argues that they are later forgeries. The question is probably still not definitively settled.

Giles Fletcher, *Of the Russe Commonwealth,* ed. R. Pipes and J. Fine (1966). The account of an English traveler to Moscow in 1591. Very important and interesting.

M. S. Anderson, *Britain's Discovery of Russia, 1553–1815* (1958). Useful account of the early adventures of the English in Russia, who were among the more important Westerners there.

CHAPTER SEVEN

Transition To A New World: Late Middle Ages And Renaissance

The transition from the medieval to the modern world begins in the West with the fourteenth and fifteenth centuries. Everywhere we find the hastening growth of a materialistic spirit. In France and the Low Countries, in Germany, and in England, the prevailing mood was one of depression and uncertainty, as old institutions decayed and people became unsure and pessimistic about the future. By contrast, in Italy—where feudalism and manorialism had never gained so strong a hold—the exuberant life of the city-states produced a spirit very like that of the greatest days of ancient Greece. Here, in spite of the cynicism and brutality of politics, the mood was one of optimism. Italy gave civilization a new impetus that would inspire the regions north of the Alps.

We begin with the economy and with society: depression, plague, and agricultural decline accompanied commercial advances. As the hired mercenary replaced the feudal noble in the battlefield, the rich townsman gradually inherited his economic influence. We continue with politics: in France, England, and Spain, the centralized new national monarchies triumphed. In Germany, particularism developed still further. In Italy, the towns became the centers of the national life. We conclude with the Renaissance, the unparalleled flowering of literature and learning, of painting, sculpture, and the other arts, beginning in Italy but soon spreading northward.

I THE ECONOMY AND SOCIETY OF THE FOURTEENTH AND FIFTEENTH CENTURIES

Depression in the West

Just as the population growth of the eleventh century helped to advance the European economy (see Chapter 5), so a population decline in the fourteenth and fifteenth centuries helped to shrink both the supply of labor and the market for products. Large-scale warfare caused most regimes to debase their coinage, leading to inflation and wild price fluctuation. Everywhere except in Italy the optimism of the thirteenth century shifted to a mood of deepening pessimism in the fourteenth and fifteenth. Nobody really understood what was going on, uneasiness prevailed, and many people tried to pretend that no change was taking place.

Money came to be the basis for social relationships more than it had been. For the peasant in good times, the gain was great: it was more agreeable to pay cash than to owe physical labor. But in hard times, when he had no cash, his loss was great. The security of serfdom, the inherited right to work and live on certain land and to eat its produce, had diminished, sometimes to the vanishing point. Often the peasants would simply move off the land and try to sell their labor in the towns. Since the price of farm products fell off while the prices of other commodities rose, the landowner was caught in a squeeze.

The Black Death (bubonic plague) of 1348–49 and subsequent plagues speeded these tendencies. Disease wiped out a fifth to a third of the population, especially in thickly settled regions. Having suddenly become scarce, manpower grew expensive. Peasants found they could force the landlords to commute for cash the services they still owed. The landlords clung to whatever services they could collect and sought the help of governments in keeping the wages down. In France, in England, in Florence, there were wild outbreaks of social unrest.

In towns, it was the same. Guilds refused to admit new members. Employers and city governments fought to keep wages down. Not until the later fifteenth century did things gradually improve. In France and England and in much of western Germany, serfdom was nearing an end, though in eastern Germany the landlords frequently attempted to enforce their old rights. In Russia, as we have seen (Chapter 6), the bonds of serfdom were actually tightening.

Commercial and Industrial Innovation

The Hanse, Venice, Genoa

During the long depression and slow recovery, we find much new experimentation in commercial methods and organization. The Hanseatic League, an association (Hanse) of north German seaport trading towns, began by occasionally consulting among themselves and ended by organizing a real federation in the fourteenth century. The cities of Lübeck, Bremen, Hamburg, and Wisby (on the island of Gotland in the Baltic) joined with the German traders abroad in Novgorod, London, Venice, and Bruges to protect and increase their business. They put down piracy and brigands; tried to secure monopolies in fish, timber, amber, furs, and metals; assessed themselves for common expenses; and fought and won an occasional war. Only the shift of trade routes to the Atlantic after 1500 hurt Hanseatic prosperity.

In the Mediterranean, Venice remained a main marketplace for the spices, silk, sugar, and cotton of the East, and the woolen cloth of the West. In the huge government-operated shipyard, the Arsenal, shipbuilders improved the traditional long, narrow, oar-propelled galley into a faster and more capacious merchant ship. Four galleys a year sailed to Flanders, four to Beirut in Syria, three to the Black Sea, where the Genoese were still dominant, and about three dozen to other major ports of the Mediterranean. The Venetian colonial empire still included Dalmatia as well as the Greek islands and seaports seized after the Fourth Crusade (above, Chapter 6). The Venetian Flanders service (begun in 1317), calling also in London and Southampton, was the first regular all-water ship line between Italy and northwestern Europe. The Venetians had their own ambassador in London, a step soon to be copied by other states.

Silkworkers. Illustrations from an Italian manuscript of 1487.

Genoa was Venice's great rival. Benedetto Zaccaria, a Genoese, in the 1340s obtained from the Byzantine emperor concessions of alum, a chemical essential in the manufacture of woolens. He built his own fleet to transport alum to the woolen factories in the Low Countries, established a company town with medical services and a population of three thousand at the alum mines in Asia Minor, and in Italy organized a woolen-manufacturing plant of his own. He then obtained a second monopoly, the mastic plant (a luxury useful in perfume and chewed like a gum), which grew on the island of Chios. Zaccaria kept prices high by limiting the supply. He became so influential that his son married into the imperial house at Constantinople.

The manufacture of woolen cloth in the towns of Flanders and North Italy was the largest industry of western Europe. In Florence 30,000 workmen produced 100,000 pieces of cloth a year for their bosses, about 200 "masters" of the guild. The poorest workmen, the "Ciompi," actually staged a revolution in 1378. Western Europe was still in a preindustrial phase because there had been no large-scale development of machinery. But capitalism was well launched.

Capitalism

Bankers and Merchant Princes

Hanseatic, Venetian, and Genoese merchants built up their capital in cash and in goods. They used credit on a large scale. They went in for long-range planning. They took heavy risks. They went all out for profits. They counted their labor as part of their costs. Of course, medieval factories were not comparable in technology with those of later centuries. But equally capitalist economic attitudes and methods are fully recognizable.

Credit came then, as now, from bankers, but the risks were larger then and the profits also. Florentine bankers charged 266 percent annual interest on a loan they thought to be really risky. In 1420, an effort to cut interest rates to a maximum of 20 percent proved a failure, all this at a time when the Church still regarded the loan of money at interest as the sin of usury.

Contrary to widespread belief, the Jews did not dominate the field of banking. They were prominent in Spain, from which they were expelled in 1492. The Templars were the leading bankers until they were destroyed by Philip the Fair (see Chapter 5). Then came the Italians, called "Lombards," (though many came from Tuscany). Florentines managed papal finances, seeing to it that income from distant lands flowed safely into Rome. The Bardi and Peruzzi families financed both sides in the Hundred Years' War and went bankrupt when Edward III of England defaulted on his debts in the 1340s. The Medici, who began in the wool business and then added silk and spices to their interests, had branches of their bank in sixteen cities in Italy and abroad. In Genoa, the Bank of St. George (founded 1407) took over much of the Mediterranean business of Spanish Jews. In Barcelona, in London, everywhere in cities, men in the profession of making money, bred upon money, won wealth, power and influence.

An Italian bank at the end of the fourteenth century.

Jacques Coeur (1395–1456) of Bourges obtained the favor of the French crown. He ran a fleet of trading vessels to the Levant, became the director of the royal mint, and financed the last campaigns of the Hundred Years' War. He built up a business empire of textile workshops and mines, bought landed estates from impoverished nobles, loaned money to half the dignitaries of France, and arranged noble marriages for his middle-class relatives. But too many people owed him too much money. He was disgraced on a fake charge.

In Germany the Fugger family of Augsburg began as linen weavers and in the late 1400s became bankers for the popes and Hapsburgs. Soon they had mining concessions scattered throughout central Europe and made a colossal fortune. It was not until 1607, after Philip II of Spain defaulted on his debts that the Fuggers were ruined. Meanwhile they showed the modern spirit of social service, building for the deserving poor of Augsburg a garden village called the Fuggerei.

The New Materialism

The Impact on Feudalism

The business class, the bourgeoisie, began to assume an ever greater role, not only in the economy but in political life. They governed Venice, Florence, and the Hanseatic towns. Elsewhere they financed those who wielded power. By the fifteenth century, the French and English monasteries depended on them. Their money enabled them to become the patrons of writers and artists. Their materialism also pervaded the Church, and many popes were indistinguishable from the secular magnates of the day in their attitudes toward money, power, and the arts.

In the upper levels of the feudal world, the new materialism often destroyed old established attitudes and relationships. Some nobles lost all but the name of noble, as their manors could no longer support them. Their descendants found their pockets empty, their status gone, but did not understand what had hit them. Even those who kept their wealth in the new monarchies had to put their obligations to the monarch ahead of their duties to any other suzerain. So did their vassals.

Cash also transformed warfare. In the wars of the fourteenth and fifteenth centuries, rulers could no longer rely on the feudal levy, which a vassel was obliged to fight for a limited time only and with only miscellaneous equipment. War now required professional troops who would fight on indefinitely and could be properly trained and equipped. Regularly now, vassals paid money to their overlord instead of fighting for him. Kings and great lords alike recuited their forces in this way.

This military system is sometimes called *bastard feudalism.* Both in France and in England, in the fifteenth century, rival parties of nobles with private armies fought for the control of the central government. The standards of chivalrous conduct that had softened the harshness of earlier feudal periods became corrupt or disappeared. New knightly orders were founded in the fourteenth and fifteenth centuries: the Garter in England, the Golden Fleece in Burgundy. But they were now only exclusive clubs.

The Impact on the Church

Snatched off to Avignon in 1305, the papacy remained there under seven successive popes down to 1377. Away from Rome, the popes were cut off from the ancient source of their spiritual authority. In their magnificent palace at Avignon with their showy court, their smoothy functioning diplomatic service and bureaucracy dedicated to collecting money, they too were deeply affected by the materialism of the time.

From 1378 to 1409 there were two rival popes, one at Rome and one at Avignon, and in 1409 a third was elected. In this "Great Schism," the rulers of Europe decided which pope they preferred on the basis of their national interest. The French supported the Avignonese; the English, naturally enough, the Roman.

To combat this scandal, the Church summoned a series of councils. At Constance (1414–1417) the unity of the papacy was restored. Martin V (1417–1431) returned to Rome. Inside the Church many now urged that the popes yield their autocratic power and act as constitutional monarchs, with the councils serving as a kind of parliament. But the restored popes fought this "Conciliar Movement," maintaining their autocracy. Often cultivated and able, the popes of the late fifteenth century were also usually corrupt, cynical, and ruthless—for example, the notorious Alexander VI Borgia (reigned 1492–1503).

In this period, naturally, the decay of the papacy and the wealth of the clergy aroused more protests then ever. Echoing the Waldensians (see Chapter 5), John Wycliffe (d. 1384) in England and John Hus (1369–1415), an anti-German Czech, strove for reform. In England, Parliament took measures against legal appeals to the Avignonese popes, instruments of the French. John Wycliffe, an Oxford scholar, demanded a church without property, in the spirit of the early Christians. Hus was treacherously executed by the Council of Constance. His Czech followers went underground. Girolamo Savonarola (1452–1498), a Florentine Dominican, led a puritanical reform movement against the vices of the age, calling Alexander VI a devil and a monster. For a brief period (1497–1498) he virtually ruled Florence, but he too was executed.

II THE MAKING OF THE NEW MONARCHIES: FRANCE, ENGLAND, SPAIN

The Hundred Years' War

Round I

In 1328, the direct line of French Capetian kings ran out. Philip VI (1328–1350), a nephew of Philip the Fair (see Chapter 5), became king. But Edward III of England (1327–1377) was, through his mother, Philip the Fair's grandson. He claimed the French throne. The French lawyers rejected the claim, citing a sixth-century Frankish law that said no woman could inherit land. So Edward III's mother, by this Salic law, had no rights to France to pass on to him.

Edward III took this decision as the pretext for war. But there were other good reasons for the French and English to fight. England still held the rich French province of Aquitaine, and the French kings constantly encroached there upon the rights of their vassal, the king of England. The English wanted to get back all that John had lost to Philip Augustus (see Chapter 5).

England and France were also at odds in Flanders. In a local quarrel, the French king was backing his vassal, the count, and many of the wealthy wool merchants, while the English were backing other merchants and most of the workers. In the wool trade England exported raw wool to Flanders and imported finished cloth. Edward could cut off supplies and cause unemployment in Flanders. But this deprived him of the export and import taxes and hurt his pocketbook. Jacob van Artevelde, leader of the pro-English party, rose against the French, organized his own government, and recognized Edward III as king of France in exchange for military help and the promise of a steady flow of wool.

In response to Flemish pressure, Edward launched what proved to be the Hundred Years' War (1338–1453). The English won the major battles, and at times controlled most of France. But the French developed a standing army supported by a system of direct taxation. They eventually expelled the English and unified France under a strong national monarchy supported by the middle classes.

The English invaded France in 1345, and by effective use of the longbow, defeated the French at Crécy (1346) and took Calais. After an eight-year truce, marked by the ravages of the Black Death (1348–49), the English repeated their success at Poitiers (1356), this time taking prisoner King John of France (reigned 1350–1364). John's son, the future Charles V, the Wise (reigned 1364–1380), became regent.

The defeats brought bitter criticism of the French monarchy. The Estates-General (see Chapter 5) insisted not only on specifying what sort of taxes might be levied (sales tax and salt tax), but also on having their own men collect them. For the first time they scheduled future meetings "to discuss the state of the realm." They also demanded that the regent Charles accept as his advisers a committee of their members. Etienne Marcel, a Parisian bourgeois who was leader of the Estates, led a revolution in Paris and forced Charles to yield in 1357.

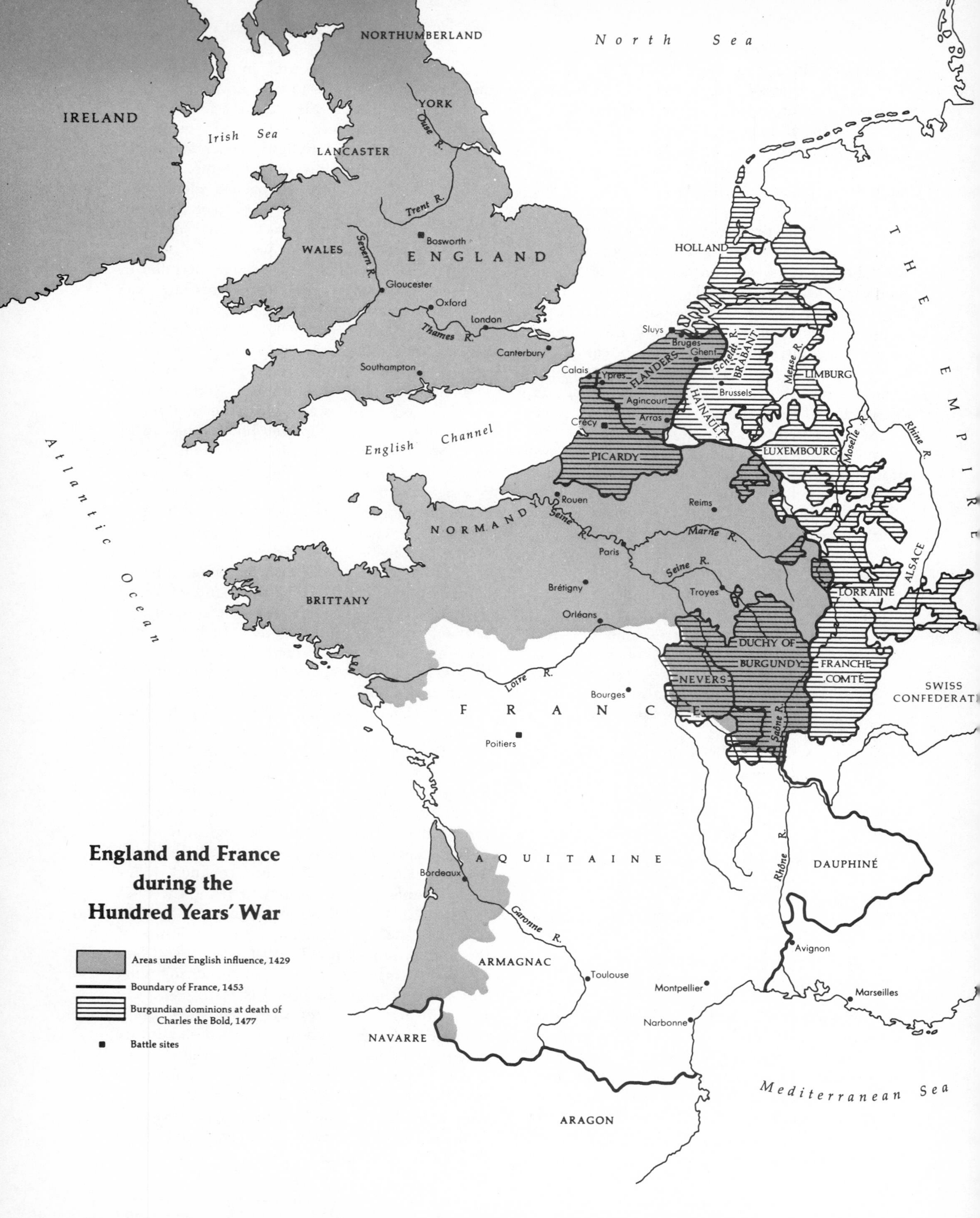

England and France during the Hundred Years' War
Areas under English influence, 1429
Boundary of France, 1453
Burgundian dominions at death of Charles the Bold, 1477
Battle sites
IRELAND
NORTHUMBERLAND
North Sea
YORK
Ouse R.
Irish Sea
LANCASTER
Trent R.
Bosworth
WALES
ENGLAND
Severn R.
Gloucester
Oxford
London
Thames R.
Canterbury
Southampton
HOLLAND
Sluys
Bruges
Ghent
Scheldt R.
BRABANT
Meuse R.
LIMBURG
Calais
Ypres
FLANDERS
Brussels
HAINAULT
Agincourt
Arras
Crécy
English Channel
Atlantic Ocean
PICARDY
LUXEMBOURG
Moselle R.
Rhine R.
THE EMPIRE
Rouen
Reims
NORMANDY
Seine R.
Marne R.
Paris
ALSACE
Seine R.
Brétigny
Troyes
LORRAINE
BRITTANY
Orléans
DUCHY OF BURGUNDY
FRANCHE COMTÉ
NEVERS
Loire R.
SWISS CONFEDERATI
Bourges
FRANCE
Poitiers
Saône R.
Rhône R.
AQUITAINE
DAUPHINÉ
Bordeaux
Garonne R.
Avignon
ARMAGNAC
Toulouse
Montpellier
Marseilles
Narbonne
NAVARRE
Mediterranean Sea
ARAGON

THE RENAISSANCE

Donatello's statue and the four following color plates may suggest the extraordinary range and innovativeness of Renaissance art. Although three of the works illustrate traditional religious subjects, all three break with medieval artistic conventions in their treatment. Donatello's John the Baptist can function as a freestanding work rather than as a small part of a larger architectural ensemble, which had been characteristic of medieval sculpture. Giotto's *Lamentation* and Michelangelo's *David and Goliath,* while they are units in a whole series of paintings, show how Renaissance artists applied new techniques to heighten dramatic effect—*chiaroscuro* in the case of Giotto, and oil paints in that of Michelangelo.

Leonardo's portrait of Ginevra de' Benci marks a still greater departure from earlier artistic norms: the subject is secular, and both the lady's hair and the foliage of the background are painted with the meticulous care of a great scientist. Finally, the hardworking peasants in Brueghel's *Harvesters* show that the commissions of Renaissance artists were not limited to grand biblical themes or to the glorification of well-to-do patrons.

Saint John the Baptist, by Donatello.
European Art Color, Peter Adelberg, N.Y.C.

The Lamentation, by Giotto: detail.
Scrovegni Chapel, Padua. Scala.

Ginevra de' Benci, by Leonardo da Vinci.
National Gallery of Art, Washington. The Granger Collection.

Pendentive, west wall, the Sistine Chapel: David and Goliath, by Michelangelo.
European Art Color, Peter Adelberg, New York City.

The Harvesters, by Pieter Brueghel the Elder: detail.
The Metropolitan Museum of Art, Rogers Fund, 1919.

THE SEVENTEENTH

In contrast to Donatello's John the Baptist, whose saintly quality is emphasized by his emaciated body and crude garments, Bernini's St. Sebastian is a martyr in his physical prime. Fashioned when the sculptor was still in his teens and influenced by Michelangelo, it is a rather mild example of the melodramatic qualities that earned seventeenth-century art the label of *baroque*, a word derived from the term for a large irregular pearl. The exaggerations of baroque art have led some critics to compare it unfavorably with the classical restraint of Renaissance art, citing particularly some of Bernini's later sculptures and the two extravagant constructions—the baldachin and "St. Peter's chair"—that he designed for the interior of St. Peter's in Rome.

Yet Bernini himself continued the Renaissance tradition of versatility in a distinguished career as sculptor, architect, and urban planner. And, as the paintings in the two succeeding plates show, baroque masters could be as subtle as their Renaissance predecessors. Velasquez, the court painter of the Spanish Hapsburgs, made the princess Maria Theresa (the future queen of Louis XIV) look reasonably regal without concealing her ugly thick Hapsburg lips. The Dutch Rembrandt, who shared his countrymen's fascination with light, imparted a golden glow to many of his paintings including the portrait of his son.

Saint Sebastian, by Gianorenzo Bernini.
European Art Color, Peter Adelberg, N.Y.C.

The Infanta Maria Theresa, by Diego Velasquez.
The Metropolitan Museum of Art, the Jules S. Bache Collection, 1949.

The Artist's Son, Titus, by Rembrandt.
The Metropolitan Museum of Art, bequest of Benjamin Altman, 1913.

Marcel then allied himself with a violent peasant uprising, the *Jacquerie* (from the popular name for a peasant, Jacques Bonhomme, "James Goodfellow"), which broke out in 1358. Charles's forces put down the Jacquerie, and Marcel was killed.

The Estates had won a round but had not forced the king to agree to accept their advice in the future. The members of the three estates—clergy, nobles, townsmen—mistrusted one another. Members of a single estate were divided by conflicting regional interests. Thus the French Estates-General did not make themselves a true French counterpart of the English Parliament.

In 1360, by the Treaty of Brétigny, Edward III renounced his claim to the French throne, but only in exchange for all southwestern France plus Calais. The treaty, however, never really went into effect, since the French did not pay the huge ranson required for King John, who died in captivity (1364). By the time Charles V died (1380), the French had ejected the English from all except a string of seaports including Bordeaux and Calais. For the first time since 1340, French ships could sail the Channel and raid the English coast. Charles V also succeeded in getting the Estates to agree that the existing taxes would be permanent.

Round II

But Charles VI (reigned 1380–1422) went insane. A struggle broke out between his brother, the duke of Orléans, and his uncle, the duke of Burgundy. When the Burgundians murdered the duke of Orléans, the quarrel became a civil war. The English backed the Burgundians, who controlled the north and east of France, against the French royal party, who controlled the south and west.

Henry V of England (reigned 1413–1422) won the battle of Agincourt (1415) and reconquered Normandy. The English reached the peak of their success in the Treaty of Troyes (1420), whereby Charles VI adopted Henry V as his heir and as his regent during his lifetime. Henry married Charles's daughter, and retained all his conquests north of the Loire until he should inherit the whole of France on the death of Charles VI. This fantastic settlement would have ended French national sovereignty.

But Charles VI's son, Charles VII, backed by the rival faction, ruled south of the Loire. And when both Henry V and Charles VI died in 1422, the miracle of Joan of Arc saved France. Saints and angels told this visionary peasant girl that she must bring Charles VII to be crowned at Reims. She reflected the deep patriotism of the French. Inspired by her presence, French troops defeated the English and Charles was crowned. Joan was captured by the Burgundians, sold to the English, turned over to the French Inquisition, and burned as a witch at Rouen (1431). The papacy itself reversed the verdict against her in 1456 and made her a saint in 1920.

Her cause triumphed despite her own martyrdom. In 1435, Charles VII made a separate peace with the Burgundians. Without the Burgundian alliance, the English could not win, and Paris fell to the French (1436). France still suffered from the pillaging by private companies of soldiers in the countryside and from the unruliness of factions among the nobles.

Charles VII, however, won from the Estates (1439) the right to have an army and to levy a tax (the *taille*) directly on individuals. He got money also from Jacques Coeur and chose as his closest advisers members of the bourgeoisie. With his new army Charles retook Normandy and Aquitaine. When the Hundred Years' War finally ended in 1453, only Calais remained in English hands.

France: Louis XI

Charles's son was Louis XI (reigned 1461–1483), plainly dressed, crafty, penny-pinching, hard-working, a constant traveler about his kingdom, inquisitive and cautious, accessible and ruthless. He put the seal on the work that his father's bureaucrats had accomplished. Disillusioned with the quarreling nobles, Louis XI trusted only bourgeois advisers whom he could control. He kept the army in fighting trim, but hated the thought of risking it in war.

His great problem was Burgundy, which now included the Low Countries as well as Burgundy itself. Rich and populous, this sprawling realm threatened to turn into a "middle kingdom" between France and the Holy Roman Empire. Louis XI hired Swiss troops, who defeated the Burgundian duke, Charles the Bold (1477). France annexed Burgundy.

Charles's daughter, Mary, inherited the Low Countries; they were her dowry when she married Maximilian of Hapsburg, who later became Holy Roman Emperor. Burgundian ambition and hostility to France were now united to the empire, and in subsequent generations would make much trouble for Louis XI's successors. But Louis himself had consolidated French territory and given it a strong central administration.

Manuscript illumination shows victims of the Black Death being burned in mass graves at Tournai, Belgium, in 1349.

England

Edward II and Edward III

English internal development moved along different lines. Under the weak and inept Edward II (1307–1327), dominated by his favorites and his French queen, the barons revolted again (1311), as they had under his grandfather Henry III. They established as the real rulers of England twenty-one Lords Ordainers, who had to assent to all appointments and to any declarations of war. But the barons were as selfish and as grasping as the king's bureaucrats had been. Edward II was eventually murdered.

Edward III (reigned 1327–1377) needed a constant supply of money to fight the French. Parliament voted it, though objecting to all other royal forms of money-raising. By the middle of the fourteenth century, the knights of the shire and the burgesses regularly met together, apart from the great lords and clergy. This process is the origin of the House of Commons. A similar coalescence of higher clergy and earls and barons, is the origin of the House of Lords. By the end of the fourteenth century, the knights and burgesses chose a chairman to conduct their meeting and report their deliberations to the king: the Speaker of the House of Commons.

Because the king so often asked them for money, the Commons gradually began to feel that he must do so, that they might withhold the money unless certain conditions were fulfilled, and that they might sometimes say how it should be spent and later check to see if it had been. The British tradition that money bills originate in the Commons had its foundation here.

Knights and burgesses collected all their individual petitions and combined them into one all-purpose document. This they sent to the Lords for approval. The Lords would then forward it to the king. This practice foreshadows the House of Commons' later right to pass laws.

The Commons now began to charge royal officials with misconduct—to "impeach" them—and the Lords would acquit or condemn the accused. Such actions usually meant that one faction of the powerful Lords had become influential enough to persuade a majority of Commons to help them ruin individual members of an opposing faction.

The Black Death of 1348–1349 killed almost half the population. A terrible shortage of manpower resulted. Crops rotted in the fields and good land dropped out of cultivation. The agricultural laborers of England quickly realized their suddenly increased bargaining power. After they broke the bonds of serfdom, they flocked to the towns.

In 1351 Parliament passed the Statute of Laborers, an attempt to fix wages and prices as they had been before the plague, to prevent workmen from quitting, and to force the unemployed to accept work at the old rates. To enforce the Statute of Laborers, Edward III appointed the first justices of the peace, chosen from the gentry in each shire. They received no pay, but served from a sense of duty or a wish for prestige. Down almost to our own times, the justices of the peace dominated English rural life.

Richard II

But the Statute of Laborers failed, and under Richard II (reigned 1377–1399) English peasant discontent exploded as it had in the Jacquerie. The crown imposed a poll tax (head tax) on every person over fifteen. The rich scarcely noticed it but the poor bitterly resented it. In 1381, the peasants revolted, burned manor records to destroy evidence of their servile obligations, and marched on London. They demanded the end of serfdom. They also demanded confiscation of clerical wealth, showing how widely Wycliffe's ideas had spread among the lower classes. In London, Richard II, who was fifteen years old, interviewed the peasants' leaders and promised to fulfill their demands. But the revolt was harshly suppressed. Had it been economically possible to restore serfdom, the authorities would have done so.

During these years the English language triumphed over Norman French and Latin. It became the language of the courts (1352), was taught in the schools (1375), and was used to open Parliament (1399). Love for a native language was always and everywhere a fundamental part of quickening national feeling.

The great nobles conspired and quarrelled. Each had his private mercenary army. Although the practice, known as *livery and maintenance,* was forbidden by statute in 1390, it continued to flourish. During every interlude in the Hundred Years' War, these mercenaries came back from France to England and continued to plunder.

The king's uncles, the dukes of Lancaster, York, and Gloucester, each had his own private army. Gloucester defeated Richard himself in 1388. In 1397 Richard arrested Gloucester, packed Parliament with his own supporters, and pushed through severe antitreason laws, many of them retroactive. He seized the Lancastrian estates. This royal absolutism precipitated a revolution. The heir to the House of Lancaster returned from exile abroad, and deposed Richard, succeeding him as King Henry IV (reigned 1399–1413).

Lancaster and York

Both Henry IV and the rival nobles now realized that they needed Parliament, the king to help him levy taxes and pass laws, the nobles to prevent any repetition of Richard II's tyrannical behavior. But Henry V (reigned 1413–1422), the victor in France, died young, and Henry VI (reigned 1422–1461) became king as a baby and later was mentally unstable. Disaster followed.

While England was losing in France, the rival forces of Lancaster and York continued to

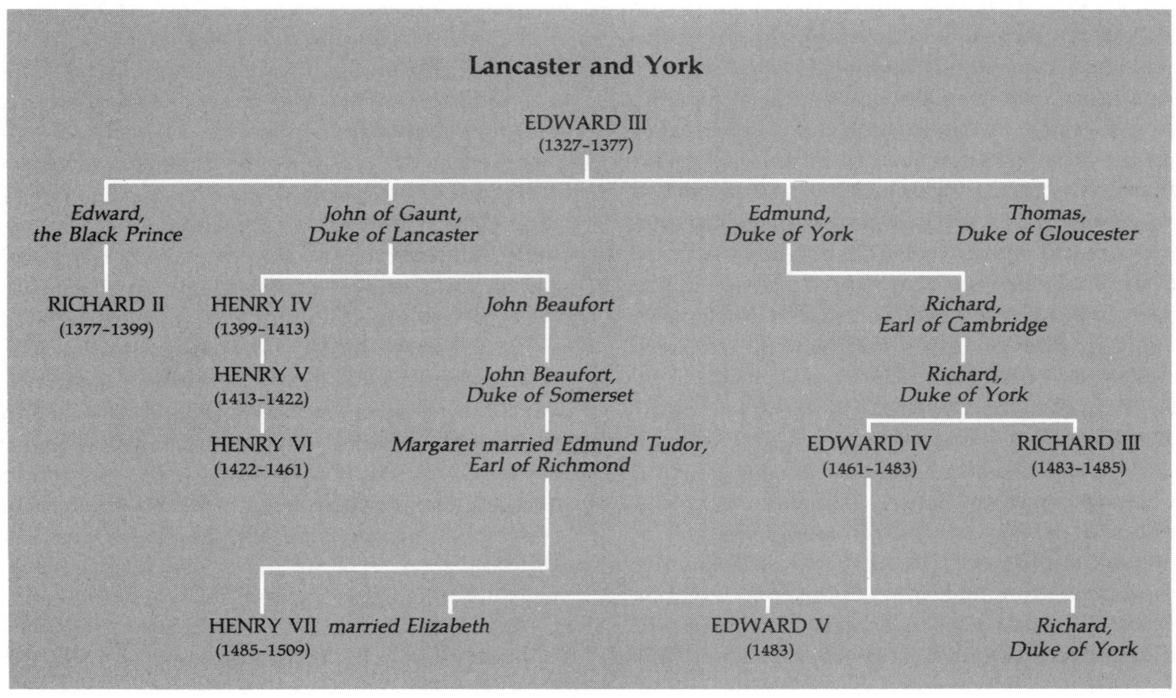

fight at home. These quarrels led directly to the dreary Wars of the Roses (1455–1485), named long afterwards, because of the legend that the red rose was the badge of the House of Lancaster, the white rose that of the House of York. The nobles and their private armies slaughtered each other in droves for three decades.

Parliament became the tool of one or the other faction. The throne repeatedly changed hands: in 1461, the Yorkists installed Edward IV (1461–1483), who eventually killed Henry VI. Richard III (1483–1485), last of the Yorkist kings, may or may not have murdered his two nephews, the "little princes of the Tower." In 1485, on Bosworth Field, Richard III was defeated and killed by Henry Tudor, an illegitimate Lancastrian, who married a Yorkist princess and ruled as Henry VII (1478–1509). This ended the Wars of the Roses at last.

Henry VII

England now had a tough, new-style monarch. Henry VII forbade livery and maintenance. Private armies disappeared. He appointed a special administrative court within the king's council, the Court of Star Chamber (so called from the stars painted on the ceiling of the room in which it met), which bypassed the procedures of the common law, including trial by jury. Star Chamber procedure could easily become tyrannical, trampling on the rights of defendants. Its worst period did not come until the seventeenth century, however (see Chapter 9). Under Henry VII it struck down local privileges, local resistance, local abuses.

Henry and his self-made middle-class officials, whom he rewarded with lands confiscated from the Yorkists, managed to double the royal revenue. When high churchmen were summoned to make payments to the king, the richly dressed were told they could obviously afford to pay heavily, and the poorly dressed that, since they were economical, they too could obviously make a large contribution. In exchange for the valuable trading privileges enjoyed by foreign merchants, Henry's bureaucrats secured comparable advantages for English traders abroad, especially in Italy. Henry VII had the support of the growing middle classes. Like Louis XI in France, he restored the prestige of the monarchy and made it the rallying point of English national feeling.

Henry VII managed his finances so well between 1497 and 1505 that he had to summon Parliament only once, in 1504. When it did not give him all the money he wanted, he did not press the issue. Not even the Tudors could change the unique English tradition that the monarch could not levy taxes or make law without consulting Lords and Commons. Nor did they wish to.

Spain

Despite their troubles, both France and England had long been national states with established centralized monarchies. By contrast, Spain, as a result of its history, had no national identity until the fifteenth century. The gradual reconquest of the peninsula from the Muslims has often been compared to a Crusade that lasted more than five centuries. Yet the little Christian states in the north often put more energy into fighting each other. By the middle of the fifteenth century, the Muslims were restricted to the kingdom of Granada in the south. But there were three separate and often mutually hostile Christian kingdoms.

Castile, in the center of the peninsula, had won some of the major victories over the Muslims. But its kings shared their authority with the *Mesta,* a powerful organization of sheep ranchers. The nobles and the towns were also independent-minded. Castile had its *Cortes,* with all three estates represented, as in Parliament or the French Estates General. Castile's former western province, Portugal, had become independent in 1179. It looked out to the Atlantic and to commerce and exploration overseas.

Aragon, in the northeast, comprised both backward inland mountain areas and the vigorous commercial towns of Catalonia, especially Barcelona. With a long tradition of trade and conquest in the Mediterranean, Aragon had ruled Sicily since 1282 and took Naples in 1435. At home, the Catalans wanted to govern themselves and made trouble for the king of Aragon in his Cortes.

When Ferdinand, heir to Aragon, married Isabella, heiress to Castile (1469), the dynastic alliance united the two largest states. But the two did not even speak the same language (Catalan still thrives today in Catalonia), and royal power was weak in both. Ferdinand looked outward to the Mediterranean and was relatively tolerant in his religious attitudes, while Isabella focused her attention on Castile and was fanatically pious. She summoned the Cortes only when she could not avoid it, and gave large powers to her own appointed council. She allied herself with the

Forcible baptism of the Moors of Granada: from the reredos of the cathedral of Granada.

towns, using their militias as troops rather than relying on feudal levies from the nobles.

Ferdinand and Isabella made a firm alliance with the Church. Her chief minister was Cardinal Ximenes, archbishop of Toledo, who helped reform the Church itself. In 1478, the Inquisition was imported into Spain. It served as an instrument of Isabella's aims: Spanish unity and universal Catholicism. Jews and Muslims, who had long enjoyed toleration and had become prosperous, were its first targets. In 1492 Jews were offered the choice between baptism and exile. In the same year, Granada fell and the last Muslim foothold in Spain was eliminated. Ten years later, the remaining Muslim residents of Spain were offered the same choice as the Jews.

To avoid exile, many Jews and Muslims became nominal Christians, conforming outwardly to escape the harsh punishments of the Inquisition, but inwardly loyal to their old faiths. Many others did go into exile, and cost Spain some of its ablest and most productive people. The year 1492, which marks the fall of Granada and the onset of persecution, also marks the first Atlantic voyage of Isabella's admiral, Christopher Columbus. The Spanish monarchy and its future colonial empire already bore the stamp of the bigotry that would prove both a strength and a weakness in later generations.

III PARTICULARISM

Germany

In Germany, no new-style monarch made his appearance. Rudolf of Hapsburg (reigned 1273–1291), the first emperor after the Interregnum (1254–1273; see Chapter 5), came of a family of lesser nobles whose estates lay mostly in Switzerland. All he wanted was to enlarge his family holdings and to make the German monarchy hereditary in the Hapsburg family. He acquired Austria, and his descendants ruled at Vienna until 1918.

To gain French good will, Rudolf allowed them to occupy his westernmost lands east of the Rhône River. They also got a foothold in Lorraine. This angered the western German magnates, notably the rich and powerful archbishops of the Rhine valley, who were anti-French and anti-Hapsburg.

Power in the German lands continued to lie in the hands of the many territorial princes, while the central government remained weak. As we have seen, this was "particularism." The office of emperor sometimes went to a Hapsburg, sometimes to other noble houses. The only reason to seek election as emperor was to use the office to add to your lands. So the monarchy became just another territorial princedom. In 1356 the system was recognized by the emperor Charles IV in a proclamation called the "Golden Bull."

The Golden Bull declared that the emperor was to be elected by seven German "electoral princes," and needed no confirmation by the pope. Thereafter, the seven electors were the archbishops of Mainz, Trier, and Cologne, the count palatine of the Rhine, the duke of Saxony, the margrave of Brandenburg, and the king of Bohemia. Each had full rights of coinage in his own territory, and there would be no appeal from the decisions of his law courts.

Within each of the many German principalities, the prince faced the threat of the nobility. These now included ministeriales (see Chapter 5), who had acquired lands, feudal rights, and titles. Within each German state, the prince had to face in miniature the same problem from the knights, towns, and clergy—the "estates"—that the kings of France and England faced. This meant increasing disorder. Urban-rural antagonism increased, robber barons infested the roads, and local wars became common.

But in the decades after 1400, the princes combatted the estates by following the rule that their eldest sons would succeed them ("primogeniture") so that their territories would remain undivided. They appealed increasingly to Roman

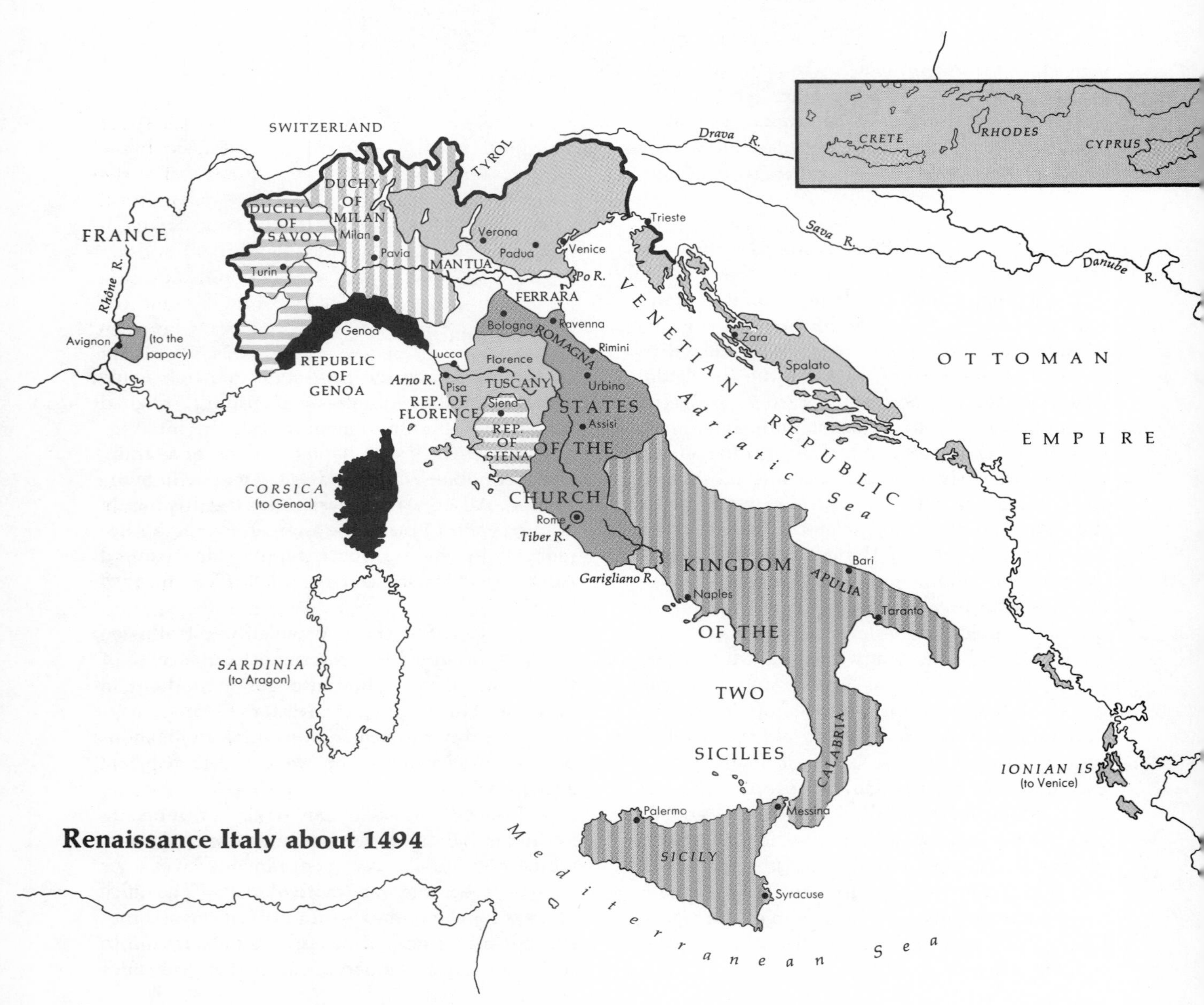

Renaissance Italy about 1494

law, which supported their claims to absolute control over public rights and offices. Gunpowder and artillery, now coming into use, made it impossible for a rebellious vassal to rely on his castle walls to protect him against his prince's new cannon. By the end of the fifteenth century, the German princes had achieved, inside their individual principalities, orderly finance, indivisible hereditary domains, and taxation granted by the estates. Cooperation with the estates had replaced hostility.

The empire as such had become meaningless. It had lost control over the western lands gained by the French and over Switzerland. In 1291 the Swiss had revolted, and thereafter formed a confederation of small local governments (cantons) with a weak central authority. In 1438 the title of emperor passed permanently to the House of Hapsburg. A little over half a century later, Maximilian (reigned 1493–1519) reestablished strong Hapsburg rule in Austria and its dependencies. He also arranged a dazzling series of dynastic marriages for his children and grandchildren. His grandson, Charles V, would rule half of Europe. But there was no mighty German national sentiment associated with the monarchy as there was in France and England.

Italy

In northern Italy, the struggle between popes and emperors had promoted the growth of communes, or city-states, much like those of ancient Greece. In the twelfth and thirteenth centuries, the communes were republics dominated by a few nobles and rich businessmen. Within the ruling group in each town, the pro-papal Guelf faction struggled against the pro-imperial Ghibelline faction. Smaller businessmen and artisans fought their own fight against the ruling oligarchy as a whole.

Like the Greek city-states, too, those of late medieval northern Italy mostly passed from oligarchy to despotism. Sometimes a despot seized power. Sometimes the struggling factions in the town invited him in. Often he was a *condottiere,* captain of the mercenary troops hired to fight the city-state's enemies.

By contrast, southern Italy, including Sicily, had experienced Byzantine, Muslim, Norman, Hohenstaufen, and Angevin domination during the course of the Middle Ages. Sicily passed to Aragon in 1282, Naples in 1435. "The Kingdom of the Two Sicilies," as the region was called, never recovered its earlier prosperity or cultural leadership.

Drawing of a condottiere by Leonardo da Vinci

The pope, Alexander VI (1492–1503), of the Borgia family, stopped at nothing to break the power of Roman princely families and of the lords of central Italy. He reasserted papal political supremacy in the papal lands. Pope Julius II (1503–1513) actually commanded papal troops on the battlefield. But papal power would soon suffer severe blows. Italy itself would become the battleground in a long series of wars between France and the Hapsburgs. And abroad, the first Protestants would challenge and often overthrow papal influence (see Chapter 8).

Milan, Florence, Venice

Among the northern city-states, Milan was strategically located in the fertile Lombard plain and was the meeting place of the routes over the Alps from the north; it manufactured the best velvets and the best armor in Europe. In 1277 the Milanese republic gave way to the despotism of the Visconti family. They took over Genoa and intermarried with the royal houses of England and France; by 1400 they dominated northern Italy.

Francesco Sforza, husband of the illegitimate daughter of the last Visconti, made himself duke of Milan in 1450. For another half-century Sforzas governed Milan and made it a center of art and learning, but by 1500 their rule was broken by the French (see p. 258).

Midway between Milan and Rome, Florence prospered and struggled. The rich merchants and bankers were mainly Guelfs, the older nobility with estates in the environs and great palaces in town mostly Ghibelline. A bloody seesaw

View of Florence at the end of the fifteenth century.

struggle raged through most of the thirteenth century. But prosperity grew, and the gold florin (minted first in 1252) replaced the Byzantine gold nomisma as standard coinage in Europe.

By 1282, the Guelfs had placed political power in the hands of the seven major guilds, including banking and wool-making. A law of 1293 closed off the last possibility of noble participation in government. The dominant Guelfs themselves now split, and continuing factional strife claimed many victims. Among them was the poet Dante (1265–1321), who was permanently exiled from his beloved city.

Terra-cotta bust of Lorenzo de' Medici by Verrocchio.

The politically unprivileged sought to make Florence more democratic. But the lesser guilds, with lower-middle-class membership, would never ally themselves with the poor workmen against the entrenched oligarchy. After the serious uprising of the Ciompi in 1378, the ruling oligarchy returned to power (1382–1434). They bought the towns of Pisa and Leghorn and so obtained access to the sea. In 1434 Florence too got its despot, Cosimo de' Medici, whose family had large woolen and banking interests, but who was a champion of the poor.

Between 1434 and 1494, the Medici ran Florence, introducing a progressive income tax to lighten the burden of the poor. Cosimo's grandson, Lorenzo de' Medici (reigned 1469–1492), earned his name "the Magnificent" by his lavish patronage of all the arts and by his charm, tolerance, intelligence, and wisdom. In 1474 the Pazzi family, rivals to the Medici, obtained the valuable concession of receivers of papal revenues, and in 1478 the Pazzi tried to assassinate Lorenzo. The Medici took savage revenge against the Pazzi. The pope excommunicated Lorenzo and put Florence under an interdict. After Lorenzo's death in 1492, economic decline set in, speeded by French invasions. Twice the Medici returned to power, but by the sixteenth century Florence had become a petty state.

Third of the great north-Italian states, Venice was governed by a doge, appointed after 1171 by an elected assembly of 480 members, which became the Great Council. In 1297, the members of the Council restricted future membership to the descendants of those who had served during the preceding four years, plus certain other families. These names were listed in the "Golden Book," and all others were permanently excluded from the government. A rebellion in 1310 led to the creation of an inner Council of Ten, especially charged with maintaining security.

The doge now became a chiefly ceremonial figure. Every year, for example, he performed the "marriage of the sea" by throwing a ring into the Adriatic, symbolizing the maritime source of Venice's wealth and power. Despite the tight control of the great families and their ruthlessness, Venice enjoyed great stability. Money poured in. No despots overthrew the oligarchy. Only outsiders made trouble.

The Lessons of Despotism: Machiavelli

In the hard-boiled age of Louis XI of France and Henry VII of England, the Venetian oligarchs and Italian despots served as models for statesmanship. The Venetian diplomatic service, with its shrewd ambassadors sending detailed reports from abroad, soon had its imitators. The Italian despots were the first to rely on mercenary troops. The balance of power precariously maintained in the peninsula by the Italians served as a model for the new European monarchies.

Italy was in a real sense the "school of Europe" in statesmanship. Yet the Italian states could not unite in the face of a foreign threat. The French invasion of 1494 ushered in a new period of French, Spanish, and Hapsburg competition in the disunited peninsula.

Summing up the lessons that long observation of Italian political behavior had taught him, Niccolo Machiavelli (1469–1527), a Florentine diplomat, wrote his book, *The Prince* (1514). For him men were ungrateful, talkative, untrustworthy, "anxious to avoid danger and covetous of gain," and he advised a prince "not to keep faith when by so doing it would be against his interest." Princes should be deceitful and unscrupulous like the successful ones he had observed in Italy.

Was Machiavelli perhaps being satirical and might he mean the opposite of what he said? It seems improbable. What he wanted was to expel the French, Spanish, and Hapsburg intruders and to unify Italy. He was ready to sanction any means to gain that end.

In a second work, *The Discourses* (on the Roman historian Livy; see Chapter 3), Machiavelli

The young Machiavelli.

reflected on the larger problem of building a lasting government. For this purpose he urged not a single all-powerful prince but magistrates elected by the people. They would be more prudent and stable than any prince.

The seeming contradiction between *The Discourses* and *The Prince* is the result of differing subject matter. In *The Discourses* Machiavelli was discussing the Romans with their republican civic virtue, in *The Prince*, the modern Italians who had, he was convinced, lost theirs. For this Machiavelli blamed the Church: not merely the worldly papacy, but Christianity itself. By preaching humility and contempt for this world, and by focusing on the City of God, Christian thinkers had made men less well prepared to fight, work, and die for their country here on earth.

In defending secularism and power politics, Machiavelli was preaching what others had already practiced. Louis XI, Henry VII, Ferdinand of Aragon, and the successful German princes and Italian despots were all Machiavellians in action before Machiavelli himself set down the theories. Machiavellianism was the political essence of the age.

IV THE RENAISSANCE: LITERATURE AND LEARNING

The Meaning of "Renaissance"

Renaissance means "rebirth." When used to describe the extraordinary flowering of letters and the arts that began in fourteenth-century Italy and gradually spread to the other countries of Europe, it means a rebirth of ancient Greek and Roman culture and an abandonment of everything medieval. But even in the Middle Ages, the West had recovered many classical authors. Aquinas had incorporated Aristotle into the Christian *Summa*. In fact, people speak of earlier "Renaissances": the "Carolingian Renaissance," the "Renaissance of the Twelfth Century," and even tenth- and eleventh-century renaissances. But of course, the whole medieval period was not merely a series of rebirths culminating in a great rebirth.

Renaissance is a useful name for the culture of a period in which the world was growing less medieval and more modern. It was a movement away from piety, caste consciousness, and otherworldliness, and toward skepticism, individualism, and materialism. Not all scholars or artists of the Renaissance suddenly lost a medieval outlook or suddenly adopted a modern one. But most moved away from the older standards and toward the newer ones.

Some men moved fast and far along all these lines; other men far on some lines and not at all on others. Now it was art for art's sake, politics for politics' sake, science for science's sake. Men were now writing, painting, studying, and engaging in politics not primarily as a means of glorifying God or attaining salvation hereafter.

The Vernacular Triumphs: Dante

Latin remained the language of the Church and the international language of scholars. Classical scholarship flourished and extended rapidly to Greek as well as Latin writings. But at the same time, the vernacular tongues of Europe, whose progress we have been watching throughout the Middle Ages, now came into general literary use. When Italian, with Dante, won general acceptance in Italy at the end of the thirteenth century and the beginning of the fourteenth, this in itself was symbolic of the transition to a new age.

And Dante—whose *Divine Comedy* (pp. 165–166) was the greatest of all medieval works of literature—we may also call the first of the Renaissance men. Sometimes he wrote in Latin: in his *De Monarchia (On Monarchy)* for example, he longed for the restoration of the medieval empire that had forever disappeared. In *De vulgari eloquentia (On the Common Speech),* he stoutly defended, in Latin, the use of vernacular Italian. And in the *Divine Comedy* he practiced what he preached and wrote in Italian.

Humanism and Dante's Successors in Italian Literature

In Italian universities the students called their law teachers by a slang word, *legista,* or *jurista*—the "law guy," one might translate it. *Humanista* was their word for the teachers of grammar, rhetoric, and the other humane studies—the "humanities guy." And the learned men of the new period called themselves humanists, often exhibiting a passionate new devotion for the classics. Humanists rediscovered lost texts such as Tacitus and Lucretius. They copied and recopied texts already known, so that knowledge of the texts spread far beyond a narrow circle.

Greek had a real revival. Despite many contacts between Europe and Byzantium, almost nobody in the West before the late fourteenth century knew Greek or cared about Greek literature. Earlier Latin translations of Greek had often come from an intermediate Arabic version and consisted largely of medical, scientific, and philosophical texts.

The generation of humanists that immediately followed Dante was headed by Petrarch (Francesco Petrarca, 1304–1374). Petrarch collected and copied manuscripts, discovered some lost letters of Cicero, and even wrote letters of his own to Cicero and other ancient writers. Imitating Vergil, he composed a Latin epic to celebrate Scipio Africanus, conqueror of the Carthaginians. He tried hard to learn Greek and employed a teacher, but to his sorrow never mastered the language.

A true Renaissance individualist, Petrarch longed to be remembered after his death. It would

Portrait of Dante attributed to the school of Giotto.

have surprised and hurt him that we remember best, not the Latin works that he himself valued most, but the Italian sonnets (little songs) he wrote in honor of his beloved Laura. These charming verses gave definitive form to the Italian sonnet: fourteen lines, divided into a group of eight and a group of six, each group with its own rhyme scheme. Petrarch admired the beauties of this world, as most Renaissance men did. But in many ways he remained a man of the Middle Ages, turning for inspiration as much to Saint Augustine's *Confessions* as to Cicero. Like many humanists, he felt that the scholastic philosophers had missed the spirit of Christianity in their concern for the detail of controversy.

Petrarch's pupil, Boccaccio (1313–1375), discovered a lost manuscript of Tacitus, succeeded in learning Greek, and taught at the University of Florence. When the Florentines wanted to find a man who had mastered Dante's *Divine Comedy* and could give public lectures on it, they selected Boccaccio. He started life as apprentice in his father's banking business, but detested the sharp practices he saw, and scorned the pious pretensions of the hypocritical rich.

In Italian he wrote *The Decameron,* a series of stories told during ten days by a company of ten lively young people fleeing Florence to escape the Black Death of 1348. They tell of wronged husbands and clever, adulterous wives, cheating merchants and frivolous youths, lustful priests and cynical apprentices, a convincingly sinful cast of characters treated with an earthy lightheartedness. Boccaccio did not invent all the *Decameron* stories. Often he took an old off-color story that everybody knew and gave it literary form.

The Scholars

In the years immediately after Boccaccio's death, the Greek revival in Italy reached its height, stimulated by Greeks from Byzantium. Manuel Chrysoloras came to the West in the late fourteenth century to get help for the Byzantines against the Ottoman Turks. Between 1396 and 1400 he lectured in Florence and Milan on Greek literature and the proper methods of translating it into Latin. George Gemistos Plethon, a scientist and student of Plato, attended the Church Council of Florence in 1437, and encouraged the teaching of Greek in the universities. Homer and the other Greek poets now were translated into Latin, as were philosophers other than Aristotle, notably Plato and the Platonists.

In 1462, Cosimo de' Medici founded the Platonic Academy in Florence, a center for advanced study in Platonism, where he subsidized the researches of a small circle of scholars. Here Marsiglio Ficino (1433–1499) translated Plato and taught Platonism. In the teachings of the Neoplatonists of the third century A.D. and later, Ficino and his school found something very like Christian mysticism. They broadened their approach to philosophy and religion to include those whom the Neoplatonists had revered, Pythagoras and his followers, and the often semimythical "Wise Men" of the ancient Near East.

Ficino's pupil, the brilliant and short-lived Pico della Mirandola (1463–1494), knew Hebrew and Arabic as well as Greek, and studied Jewish allegory, Arab philosophy, and medieval scholasticism. Pico hoped by examining the varied beliefs and ideas of the past to find a set of keys to human nature and the universe, the common denominator of faith.

But the humanists were more than scholars. They wrote voluminous letters, speeches, poems, and treatises on grammar and rhetoric, history, politics, education, and religion. They proclaimed an ideal of eloquence, convinced that classical models were the best. Some scorned the learning of their medieval predecessors, but others continued to study medieval scholastic thought.

By the mid-fifteenth century, many lawyers and doctors and other professional men were also humanists. Only a few humanists were "freelance" writers. Most were teachers or secretaries to princes or city governments. Whatever their profession, they prided themselves on writing correct Latin letters and speeches.

Lorenzo Valla (ca. 1405–1457) tackled biblical scholarship with the methods of the new scholarship. He translated Herodotus and Thucydides, wrote a handbook on Latin style, and a history of the reign of Ferdinand of Aragon. Valla was learned and courageous, and also petty and vindictive. He enjoyed the favorite contemporary game of trading insults with his fellow humanists.

It was Valla who proved in 1440 that the Donation of Constantine (see Chapter 4) was a forgery. He showed that the Latin of the document could not possibly be as early as the time of Constantine. Also, Valla said, the Donation referred to Constantinople as a "patriarchate," when in fact, in 314, the supposed date of the document, it was "not yet a Christian city, nor named Constantinople, nor founded, nor planned."

Any medieval pope would have condemned Valla as a heretic for thus exposing the falseness of the basis for papal claims to temporal supremacy. But the Renaissance pope not only made no effort to punish Valla but commissioned him to translate Thucydides.

Humanism Crosses the Alps

Italian humanists soon took their new attitudes and skills northward out of Italy. They came as diplomats, as visiting lecturers, and even on business. In the less urbanized, less Roman, more "Gothic" north, intellectuals, leading churchmen, nobles, kings, and princes eagerly accepted humanistic attitudes.

Conrad Celtis (1459–1508) wrote verses begging Apollo, master of the Muses and god of the sun, to leave Italy and come to Germany, where he was badly needed. Johannes Reuchlin (1455–1522), who launched a revival of Hebrew letters, was attacked for it by anti-Semites. The episode gave rise to vigorous humanistic defenses of Reuchlin, and a controversy that in many ways foreshadowed the Protestant Reformation soon to begin in Germany.

The flowering of French humanism began when King Francis I (1515–1547) caught the enthusiasm for the classics. Guillaume Budé, a learned scholar, played a major role in the revival of Greek. Under his prodding, Francis founded a great library and college where Greek was taught as well as Latin and French. Lefèvre d' Étaples (1455–1536), studied the Greek church fathers and had much in common with Frenchmen who later turned to religious reform.

Englishmen who had studied in Florence brought the new humanistic learning home about 1500, by launching new programs of study at Oxford. One of them, William Grocyn, became the teacher of the "Prince of Humanists," Desiderius Erasmus (1466–1536), a Dutchman. Erasmus studied, taught, and lived at Oxford, Cambridge, and Paris, in Italy, Germany, and Switzerland. He published a scholarly edition of the Greek New Testament. He carried on a prodigious correspondence in Latin. But Erasmus poked fun at the "knowledge factories" of the grammarians and at the mutual admiration society of his fellow humanists, who were "scratching each other's itch." Erasmus satirized any group or class that he found inflated by a sense of its own importance. But he was no cynic. He believed that we must cherish particularly the few outstanding individuals who have led great and good lives. Christ heads his list of great men. Cicero and Socrates rank very high. Plato's account of the death of Socrates moved Erasmus so deeply that he almost cried out, "Pray for us, Saint Socrates."

So Erasmus joined love of the classics with respect for Christian values. He had little use for the finespun arguments of scholasticism, advocating what he called his "philosophy of Christ," the application, in the most humane spirit, of the doctrines of charity and love taught by Jesus. Yet though Erasmus always considered himself a loyal son of the Church, he unintentionally helped undermine the universality of Catholicism. His edition of the Greek New Testament raised doubts about the correctness of the standard Latin text, and therefore about past Catholic commentaries on the Bible. He attacked the corruption of the clergy, emphasizing the wide gap between the Church's ideals and clerical behavior. Said a contemporary wit, "Where Erasmus laid eggs, Luther hatched the chicks." Erasmus lived to see the chicks hatch. (see Chapter 8).

Science and Medicine

During the fourteenth, fifteenth, and sixteenth centuries, scientists absorbed, enlarged, and modified the knowledge handed down to them from the Middle Ages and antiquity. Aristotelian studies continued to be pursued vigorously at Paris and Padua. The humanists made the first Latin translations of the Greeks Galen, Ptolemy, and Archimedes.

Hans Holbein the Younger's portrait of Erasmus.

But the humanists tended to worship classical antiquity. What use trying to improve, for instance, on the medicine taught by Galen (second century A.D.)? He said that blood moved from one side of the heart to the other by passing through invisible pores in the thick wall of tissue that divides the heart. Galen was wrong: It actually gets from one side to the other by circulating through the body and lungs. But the weight of Galen's authority kept Leonardo da Vinci (1452–1519) from discovering the truth. Leonardo's studies led him to the brink, but he backed away, certain that Galen must have been right. Not until the seventeenth century, when the ancients could safely be doubted, did Harvey discover the truth about blood circulation.

As a scientist, Leonardo took notes in a hit-or-miss fashion, without the modern scientist's concern for the systematic cataloging of observations or for the publication of findings and speculations. Yet he sketched plans for lathes, pumps, war machines, flying machines, and many other contraptions, not all of them workable, to be sure, but all highly imaginative. He did not always bow before established authority, as he did before Galen. His geological studies convinced him that the earth was far older than the men of his time thought it to be. The Po River, he estimated, must have been flowing for about 200,000 years to wash down the sediments that form its alluvial plain.

The University of Padua maintained a lively tradition of medical inquiry that eventually led to the seventeenth-century triumphs of the experimental method. A Belgian named Vesalius (1514–1564), who taught at Padua, rejected Galen's notion of invisible pores in the wall of tissue within the heart because he could not find such pores. But he left the true answer for Harvey to discover.

Astronomy

In 1543, a Polish cleric named Copernicus, who had studied at Padua, launched modern astronomical studies with his book, *Concerning the Revolutions of Heavenly Bodies.* He attacked the generally accepted hypothesis that the earth was the center of the universe, a view held by Ptolemy and all ancient astronomers Copernicus now argued that the sun, not the earth, was the center of our universe.

The older view had maintained that around the stationary earth there revolved some eighty separate transparent spheres, containing the heavenly bodies, each moving on an invisible circular path. Scientists before the time of Copernicus had trouble making this theory agree with the observable movements of heavenly bodies. Copernicus used these earlier observations and his own computations to overthrow the tradition.

Once Copernicus had reversed the roles of the sun and the earth, his universe retained many Ptolemaic characteristics. Its heavens were still filled with spheres revolving along their invisible orbits. Only they now moved about a stationary sun, instead of a stationary earth. Copernicus dedicated his book to the pope, but many Christians were deeply troubled by the disappearance of the earth-centered and human-centered universe. Copernicus had begun a revolution in astronomy that Galileo and Newton would continue.

Technology

The most important Renaissance contribution to technology was printing. The revolution in book production began in the fourteenth century, when Europeans first imported paper from China and found it cheaper than the lambskin or sheepskin previously used. Next, engravers made woodcuts or copper plates that could produce many copies of the same drawing. Then sentences were added to the cuts or plates.

Finally, almost certainly in the German Rhineland during the 1440s, movable type was devised. Each piece of type was a small engraving on metal. It could be combined with other pieces to form words, sentences, or a whole page, and then salvaged to be used again. The great Bible of Johann Gutenberg of Mainz (1456) is not only technically perfect without a single error, but one of the most beautiful books ever produced.

By 1500, Italy alone had seventy-three presses employing movable type. The Aldine Press in Venice (founded by Aldus Manutius, 1450–1515), sold at reasonable prices scholarly editions of the classics printed in beautiful type reportedly copied from the handwriting of Petrarch. Everywhere the printing press for the first time made classical and vernacular literature available to large numbers of people who could never have afforded manuscripts. For education, for the rapid transmittal and spread of news, for propaganda, for all aspects of later human life, printing proved a revolutionary advance.

Europeans first used gun powder—brought from China—in the later campaigns of the Hundred Years' War. Gun and cannon doomed both the feudal knight and the feudal castle. At sea, important aids to navigation came into general use, particularly the magnetic compass and more accurate charts. By the end of the fifteenth century, Europeans for the first time were equipped for world discovery.

V THE RENAISSANCE: THE ARTS

Main Characteristics of Renaissance Art

Renaissance artists shared fully in the age's enthusiasm for classical antiquity and its growing secularism. Many possessed sheer genius. The medieval subordination of sculpture and painting to architecture ceased. The individual statue or picture emerged as an independent work of art. In building, the fashion changed from the soaring Gothic to adaptations of the ancient Roman temple. Reflecting the new wealth and materialism, palaces and private residences began to rival churches in magnificence. Individual artists sometimes reveled in an artistic self-assertion that was quite unmedieval. Statesmen and rich private citizens joined the Church as patrons of artists. Portraits of their patrons and pagan gods and goddesses now shared the limelight as subjects with the traditional Christian saints.

The artists of the Renaissance showed extraordinary versatility. Leonardo was a painter and sculptor, musician and physicist, anatomist and geologist, inventor and city planner. Michelangelo was an architect, sculptor, and painter. In the arts the Renaissance was more than a rebirth. Though often inspired by ancient subjects, its masterpieces are not copies or imitations but display a breathtaking vitality and beauty of their own.

Painting

Giotto and His Successors

Before 1300, Italian painters were greatly influenced by Byzantine art. Often splendid in color and drawing, their pictures also seem two-dimensional. Giotto (ca. 1270–1337), though still admiring the Byzantine tradition, made painting more lifelike and less austere. In Giotto's *Return of Joachim to the Sheepfold,* the dog greets his returning

Giotto's "Return of Joachim to the Sheepfold."

master with his right forepaw raised in welcome. In *The Lamentation,* the angels flying above the dead Christ beat their wings in a transport of sorrow, echoing the intense grief of the human mourners below. By varying the brightness of his colors and introducing new contrasts of light and shade, by studying perspective and foreshortening, Giotto gave his paintings an unmedieval three-dimensional lifelike quality.

Giotto was no medieval craftsman, content to work anonymously. He wanted to be famous, and he was, not only for his artistic accomplishments but for his verses and witty remarks. He made a fortune as an artist and got still richer in business, lending money, running a debt-collection service, and renting looms to poor woolen-weavers. Roman cardinals, the king of Naples, the guilds and millionaires of Florence all were his patrons.

Indeed, such patronage alone made the Renaissance arts possible. In Florence, the government, the wealthy magnates, and the churches and monasteries all engaged in a campaign for civic beauty. Lorenzo the Magnificent subsidized the painter Botticelli as well as the humanists of the Platonic Academy. The Sforza Duke of Milan employed Leonardo da Vinci as his minister of fine arts and later, director of public works. Leonardo found new patrons in the pope and the French kings Louis XII and Francis I. The popes, who employed Leonardo, Botticelli, Michelangelo, and many others, intended to make Rome the artistic capital of the world.

Even when the subject of a painting was sacred, painters often introduced a secular note. Painters would put into a religious scene a portrait of the patron who had commissioned it, often kneeling reverently, but with the satisfied look on his face of a man who had made his pile.

Following many of Giotto's new techniques and perfecting others of his own, Masaccio (1401–ca. 1428) was influenced by the anatomical realism employed by sculptors. His Adam and Eve expelled from Eden look thoroughly ashamed of themselves.

Botticelli (1445–1510), a master of both drawing and color, showed great delicacy in his treatment of pagan themes. In his *Primavera*—a

Giotto's "The Lamentation."

pagan allegory of spring—Mercury, the Three Graces, a surprisingly wistful Venus, the goddess Flora, bedecked with flowers, and Spring herself are all youthful, slender, almost dainty, with an air of otherworldly sweetness. They are partly nude and not at all fleshly. Botticelli was a friend of Pico della Mirandola, and his paintings often suggest lofty Platonic aspiration. But to the puritanical Savonarola, nude pictures were wicked, and Botticelli yielded and threw some of his paintings on Savonarola's bonfire.

Leonardo, Michelangelo, Titian

Leonardo da Vinci was so busy with his scientific activities and his innumerable services for his patrons that he completed few pictures. Some are badly damaged, notably *The Last Supper,* a wall painting in the dining-hall of a monastery in Milan. By arranging the apostles in four groups of three men each around the central figure of Christ, Leonardo made *The Last Supper* in part an exercise in artistic geometry. Earlier painters had usually shown the solemn yet peaceful moment of the final communion, and had suggested the coming treachery of Judas by placing him in isolation from the others. Not Leonardo. He chose the tense moment when Christ announced the coming betrayal, and he placed Judas among the apostles. Facial and bodily expression conveys Judas's guilt and the apostles' consternation. Possibly the most famous single painting in the world is Leonardo's portrait of *Mona Lisa* with her mysterious smile. Many prefer his charcoal sketch of the *Virgin and Child with Saints.* Leonardo's superb talent and his extraordinary range of interests are best seen in his drawings and notebooks. The drawings include every sort of sketch, from preliminary work through realistic human embryos and fanciful war machines to mere doodles.

From an intensive study of human anatomy, Leonardo drew up rules for indicating the actions of human muscles and for establishing the proportions between the parts of the human body. He combined a zeal for scientific precision with a fondness for the grotesque. He often sketched deformed people and those suffering intense strain.

Masaccio's "The Expulsion from Paradise."

Grotesque faces: a drawing from the notebooks of Leonardo.

Botticelli's "Primavera."

God: detail from The Creation of Adam, from Michelangelo's ceiling for the Sistine Chapel.

Titian's portrait of Emperor Charles V.

While Leonardo got on well with his patrons, Michelangelo Buonarroti (1475–1564) quarreled repeatedly with Pope Julius II (reigned 1503–1513), who commissioned a fresco for the ceiling of the Sistine Chapel in the Vatican. The ceiling is approximately fourteen by forty yards, and Michelangelo covered it with 343 separate figures. He did the job in four years, assisted only by a plasterer and a color mixer. He painted lying uncomfortably on his back atop a scaffolding, sometimes not even coming down to sleep at night. No wonder the pope had to beg him to finish the work.

As subject matter, Michelangelo chose Genesis: the creation of sun and moon, God hovering over the waters, the creation of Adam and of Eve, the eating of the forbidden fruit, and the expulsion from Paradise. In this vast gallery of nudes in all types of poses, Michelangelo summed up all that Renaissance art had learned about perspective, anatomy, and motion. The Sistine ceiling also comes close to summarizing the Western world's concepts of God. No medieval artist would have thought of representing the deity so directly, but Michelangelo painted God repeatedly, draped in a mantle, an ever-changing patriarch. Hovering over the waters, he is benign. Giving life to the motionless Adam or directing Eve to arise, he is gently commanding. Creating the sun and moon, he is the all-powerful deity, formidable and urgent as a whirlwind.

Both Michelangelo and Leonardo had received their artistic training in Florence. Their contemporary, Titian (1477–1576), a Venetian, enjoyed almost unbroken professional success for eighty years and produced an average of one picture a month. He painted frescoes for the headquarters of the German merchant colony in Venice, portraits of rich merchants, altarpieces and madonnas for churches and monasteries, and a huge battle scene for the palace of the doge. The despots of Italy and the kings and princes of Europe competed for his services. Titian used rich, intense colors, particularly reds and purples. His portraits, both elegant and revealing of character, are a true gallery of his most prominent contemporaries.

Northern European Painting

The fame and influence of the Italian painters helped to stimulate northern European artists. The northern Renaissance, however, also grew out of native traditions of Gothic art passed down from the Middle Ages, now freshly influenced by the Italian genius. It centered in southern Germany and in the Low Countries. Its leading artists were two Germans, Albrecht Dürer (1471–1528) and Hans Holbein (ca. 1497–1543), and Pieter Brueghel the Elder (ca. 1520–1569), who was born near Brussels. Dürer received commissions from the emperor Maximilian. Armed with an introduction from Erasmus, Holbein moved to England, where humanists, aristocrats, and the court of King Henry VIII all became his patrons. Brueghel painted for the merchants of Antwerp and Brussels.

Dürer, who spent some time in Italy, was in many ways the Leonardo of Germany. His realistic yet compassionate portrait of his aged and homely mother might almost have come from Leonardo's sketchbook. He collected monkeys

Dürer's engraving "Knight, Death, and Devil."

Pieter Brueghel the Elder's "The Triumph of Death."

Renaissance equestrian statue of condottieri; Donatello's of Gattamelata.

Verrocchio's of Colleoni Renaissance equestrian statue.

Statue of the emperor Marcus Aurelius in the Piazza del Campidoglio—Roman model used for the Renaissance equestrian statues.

and other tropical specimens, painted the Virgin in the unusual pose of a *Madonna with Many Animals,* and wrote treatises on perspective and human proportions. By sensitive use of line and shading, Dürer revolutionized the techniques of copper engraving and woodcuts. These innovations permitted the reproduction of drawings in many copies, enabling an artist to illustrate a whole edition prepared by the new process of printing. They brought Dürer closer than any Italian painter to a rapidly expanding public of readers. In a series of sixteen woodcuts, he depicted the Four Horsemen and the other grim marvels of the Apocalypse.

Brueghel delighted in scenes of earthy peasant life—weddings, dances, festivals, skating parties, and activities on the farm. Brueghel's *The Triumph of Death* is a nightmarish landscape; and his bizarre *Battle of the Angels and the Demons* is full of "things," like monsters in our own science fiction, flying oysters, vegetables with wings, shields battling on their own. Most of these fantasies were intended to teach moral lessons. In this, as in their grotesque qualities, they illustrate the medieval aspects of Renaissance men.

Sculpture

Renaissance painting owed much of its three-dimensional qualities to the painters' knowledge of sculpture. Giotto, Leonardo, and Michelangelo were sculptors. Donatello (ca.1386–1466), a Florentine, produced an equestrian statue of the soldier of fortune *(condottiere),* Gattamelata, now in Padua. Inspired by the Roman equestrian portrait of Marcus Aurelius, and cast in bronze, not carved in stone, its theme, treatment, and technique are all typical of the Renaissance. Donatello's huge bronze statue of David was the first sculptured male nude in more than a thousand years. David is a handsome young man, not at all a divinely inspired giantkiller. In his statue of Mary Magdalen, Donatello made his subject all skin and bone, lank hair, and tattered clothing. Somehow she is still a saint.

In the next generation, Donatello's self-conscious rival, Verrocchio (1435–1488), another Florentine, deliberately chose the same or similar subjects: a David, a saint (Thomas, who had doubted Christ), and a condottiere: Colleoni, whose arrogant figure on horseback dominates the square before the Church of Saint John and Saint Paul (Zanipolo) in Venice. Verrocchio was for fourteen years the teacher of Leonardo.

Donatello's statue of Mary Magdalen.

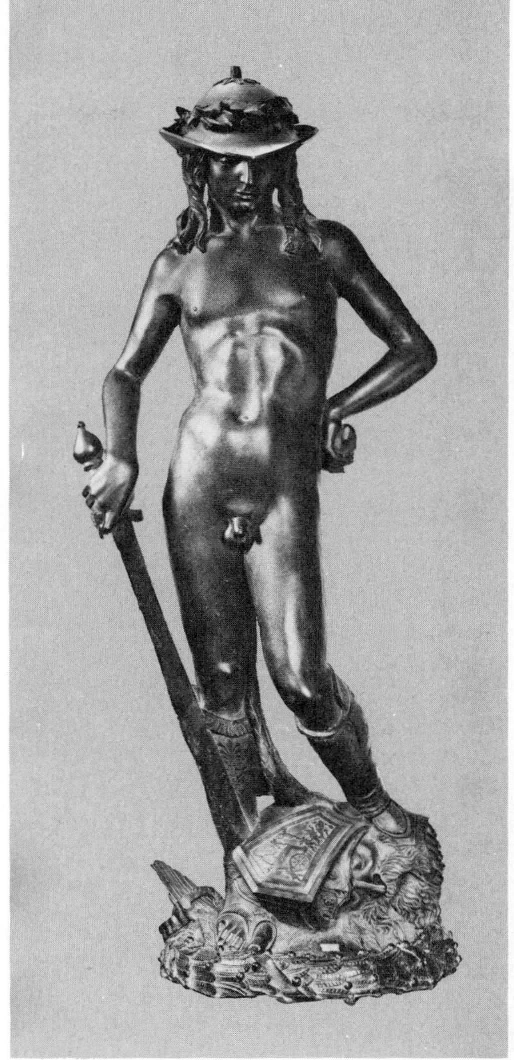
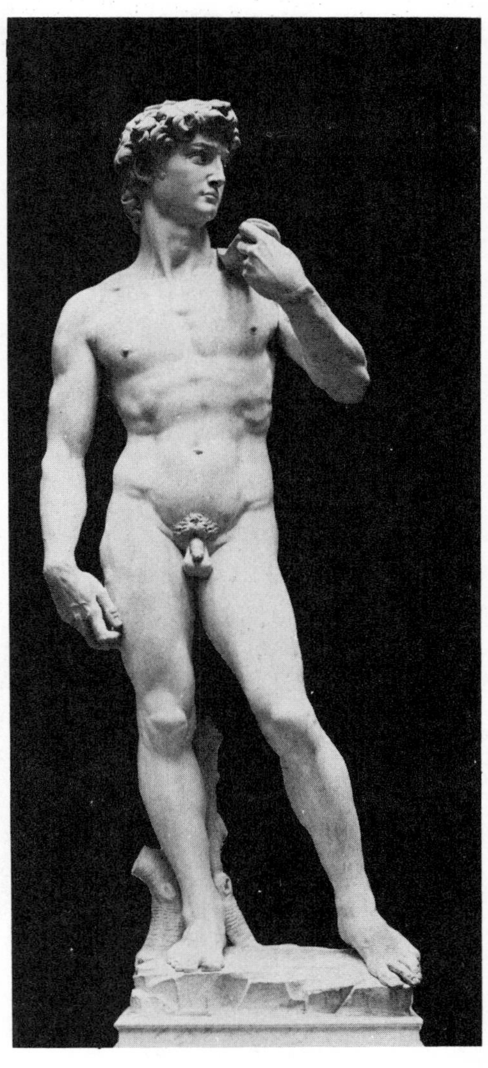

Three Renaissance statues of David. From left to right, by Berrocchio, Donatello, and Michelangelo.

Michelangelo, however, was the greatest sculptor since the Age of Pericles, possibly of all time. Early in his career, he produced his renowned colossal statue of David. Years later in his career, he carved the figures of Dawn, Day, Dusk, and Night to adorn the Medici tombs in Florence. The figures recline on sloping cornices yet do not seem about to slide off; they are relaxed but have enormous latent power. In portraying the Virgin grieving over the dead Christ—the *Pietà*—Michelangelo brilliantly solved the difficult technical problem of posing a seated woman with a corpse lying across her lap. The face of Mary is sorrowful yet composed, and younger than that of the dead Christ. She is the eternal Virgin, Michelangelo explained, and so is always youthful and does not grieve in the manner of an earthly mother.

Benvenuto Cellini (1500–1571) lacked Michelangelo's genius, but also showed great versatility. The popes, King Francis I of France and the Medici duke of Tuscany, all acted as his patrons. An engraver and goldsmith who made lavish creations in precious metals and jewels, Cellini became a sculptor on a larger scale only in middle age. He then surprised his public by producing the bronze statue of Perseus holding the snaky head of Medusa, which is still one of the memorable sights of Florence. Cellini wrote a most readable autobiography, full of vitality, breathing self-confidence and a love of high living, and revealing much about art.

Cellini's statue of Perseus.

Architecture

In 1546, at the age of seventy, the unbelievable Michelangelo agreed to be the chief architect of St. Peter's, the new cathedral in Rome. He died in 1564, long before it was completed in 1626, and others altered many of his details. But the great dome and the basic Greek-cross ground plan with four equal arms were his. Michelangelo's dome rises 435 feet above the floor. Its great height is fully justified by the immense building underneath. Whereas the pointed arches and high-flung vaults of medieval churches sometimes create an impression of nervousness and strain, St. Peter's—with its round arches, heavier walls, and stout columns—is a model of Renaissance symmetry.

Coming rather late in the Renaissance, St. Peter's illustrates long-standing Renaissance architectural practices. Architects had long been studying, adapting, and copying the ruins of ancient buildings that crowded Rome and other Ital-

The dome of St. Peter's, Rome, by Michelangelo.

Palladio's Palazzo Chiericati, Vicenza.

Brunelleschi's dome for the cathedral of Florence.

Palazzo Farnese, Rome.

ian cities. Brunelleschi (1377?–1446) had been the pioneer. His monumental dome for the cathedral of Florence was an engineering masterpiece. Michelangelo had seen it daily in his native city.

Renaissance architects learned from Pythagoras' and Plato's writings on geometry, available now as the result of the humanists' labors. Greek concepts of perfect ideas and perfect geometric forms became influential once more. Palladio (1518–1580), the foremost architectural theorist of his age, praised the Greek-cross plan for churches because of its symbolic values. If the apses (at the ends of the four arms) were rounded, and if the spaces between the arms were filled with rounded chapels, then the whole structure became an almost perfect circle. And the circle, according to Palladio, "demonstrates extremely well the unity, the infinite essence, the uniformity, and the justice of God."* The circle thus represents a shift in emphasis away from the medieval Latin-cross floor plan, whose crucifix shape proclaimed Christ's sacrifice.

* R. Wittkower, *The Architectural Principles of the Age of Humanism* (London, 1949), p. 21.

The lavish private residences built during the Renaissance celebrated success in business or politics. Moreover, the growth of effective government meant that a man's home could be a showplace and no longer had to be, quite literally, his castle. Elaborate villas now ornamented the countryside. In the cities rose the *palazzo,* or palace, often now a private townhouse that combined business offices and residential apartments. Rome and Florence were dotted with them. In Venice they lined the Grand Canal from one end to the other. The usual palazzo was three-storied and rectangular, with its windows arranged in symmetrical rows. It became standard practice to ornament the first floor with Doric columns, the second with Ionic, and the third with Corinthian, thus using all three classical "orders" of capitals one above the other.

The fame of Italian builders soon spread throughout Europe, even to distant Moscow, where, as we saw, Italian experts supervised the remodeling of the Kremlin for Ivan III. Most countries did not copy the Italian style outright, but grafted it onto older native architecture. The resulting compound produced some very striking buildings, particularly the great sixteenth-century châteaux of central France, which gracefully combine elements taken from the Gothic church, the feudal castle, and the Italian palace.

Music

In music the Renaissance did not make a sharp break with the recent past as in the plastic arts, but more readily accepted the legacy it had received from the Middle Ages. Medieval sacred music had achieved complex and elaborate combinations of form, line, and decoration. In the late Middle Ages, the center of music was northern France and the Low Countries.

By the fifteenth century, French and Flemish musicians were journeying to Italy. Here mutual influence developed. The northerners took up the simple tunes of folk songs and dances. The Italians added a strain of Gothic complexity to their austere plainsong. The end product was the sacred music of the Italian Renaissance composer Palestrina (ca. 1525–1594), intricate in the northern manner and devout in the Italian.

In music, too, Renaissance secularism and individualism appeared. The Flemings based their Masses on popular tunes. Renaissance music was no longer anonymous. The day of the celebrated individual composer had arrived. Composers and performers developed or imported a variety of new instruments—the violin, double bass, and harpsichord; the organ, with its keyboards, pipes, and stops; the kettledrum, which was adopted from the Polish army; and the lute, which had originally been developed in medieval Persia and reached Italy by way of Muslim Spain.

The retinue of musicians became a fixture of Renaissance court life. In German towns "mastersingers" organized choral groups. But the mastersingers were directly in the tradition of the thirteenth-century minnesinger, and princely patronage of music went back at least to the twelfth-century court of Eleanor of Aquitaine and its chivalric troubadors.

The Renaissance Ideal: Castiglione

No one individual, nor one single masterpiece of art or literature can fully represent the value and ideals of the Renaissance. Yet a book published in 1528, *The Courtier* by Baldassare Castiglione (1478–1529), comes close. Like a medieval man, Castiglione believed the profession of arms to be the proper one for a gentleman. But he recommended a quite unmedieval moderation and balance, and a humane and literary education in Latin and Greek. His ideal courtier was to be a "universal man" like Leonardo. At the same time, Castiglione was reviving the old classical ideal of the well-rounded individual—"the sound mind in the sound body"—and anticipating modern champions of the humanities and a liberal education.

Castiglione praised beauty, God's physical world, man—a little world in himself—and art. "The world," he says, is praised when one acclaims "the beautiful heaven, beautiful earth, beautiful sea, beautiful river, beautiful woods, trees, gardens, beautiful cities, beautiful churches, houses, armies. Indeed the good and the beautiful are in a way the same thing."* A medieval man might also have coupled the good and the beautiful, but he would have stressed the good and the ways in which God led man to righteousness. Medieval man's vision centered on God's world. The Renaissance man, for whom Castiglione so eloquently speaks, had a vision not only of God's world but also of nature's world and man's world.

* *The Courtier,* T. Hoby translation modernized (1907), pp. 348.

READING SUGGESTIONS on Transition to a New World: Late Middle Ages and Renaissance (Asterisks indicate paperback.)

General Works

R. E. Lerner, *The Age of Adversity: The Fourteenth Century* (*Cornell); and M. Aston, *The Fifteenth Century: The Prospect of Europe* (*Harcourt). These two books may be read together for a good general view of the period.

W. K. Ferguson, *Europe in Transition, 1300–1520* (1963). More detailed than the above.

D. Hay, *Europe in the Fourteenth and Fifteenth Centuries* (Holt). Excellent treatment of social, economic, and political history, with a good bibliography.

J. Huizinga, *The Waning of the Middle Ages* (*Anchor). A famous work that recreates the atmosphere of the whole period; emphasizes France and the Low Countries.

E. P. Cheyney, *The Dawn of a New Era, 1250–1453* (*Harper Torchbooks); and M. P. Gilmore, *The World of Humanism, 1453–1517* (*Harper Torchbooks). Two consecutive volumes in a very useful series.

P. Ziegler, *The Black Death* (*Penguin). Vividly detailed account of the plague.

W. W. Bowsky, ed., *The Black Death: A Turning Point in History* (*Holt). Various modern scholars' views on the subject, conveniently collected.

J. R. Major, *The Age of Renaissance and Reformation* (*Lippincott); and E. F. Rice, Jr., *The Foundations of Early Modern Europe, 1460–1559* (*Norton). Up-to-date general introductory volumes.

Economics and Society

W. K. Ferguson, *The Renaissance* (*Holt). A short survey stressing the economic and social background.

M. Beard, *A History of Business,* 2 vols. (*Ann Arbor). Includes good discussions of individual Renaissance millionaires.

A. V. O. von Martin, *Sociology of the Renaissance* (*Harper Torchbooks). Italian society in the fourteenth and fifteenth centuries.

F. C. Lane, *Venice: A Maritime Republic* (*Johns Hopkins). Fine introductory study by a noted economic historian.

R. de Roover, *The Rise and Decline of the Medici Bank, 1397–1494* (*Norton). Profits and dangers of high finance in Florence.

S. Thrupp, *The Merchant Class of Medieval London* (*Ann Arbor). Mostly dealing with the period after 1300.

The New Monarchies

A. J. Slavin, *The "New Monarchies" and Representative Assemblies* (*Heath). How new were the "new monarchies"? Much useful discussion.

G. Mattingly, *Renaissance Diplomacy* (*Penguin). Shows how many modern practices began in this period.

E. Perroy, *The Hundred Years' War* (*Capricorn). Standard work on the war and at the same time a good survey of French history in the fourteenth and fifteenth centuries.

M. McKisack, *The Fourteenth Century* (1959); and E. F. Jacob, *The Fifteenth Century* (1961). Two more fine volumes in The Oxford History of England.

A. R. Myers, *England in the Late Middle Ages* (*Penguin). A far shorter but still useful discussion of the subject matter of the above two detailed volumes.

P. S. Lewis, *Later Medieval France: The Polity* (1968); and P. M. Kendall, *Louis XI* (1971). By far the best treatments available in English.

R. L. Storey, *The Reign of Henry VII* (1968). Disputes some of the traditional ideas about Henry VII's personality and policies.

S. B. Chrimes, *English Constitutional History* (*Oxford). Useful handbook.

J. H. Elliott, *Imperial Spain, 1469–1716* (*Mentor). A fine introductory survey, very learned and with a good bibliography.

Particularism: Germany and Italy (See also the books listed in previous chapters.)

F. L. Carsten, *Princes and Parliaments in Germany from the Fifteenth to the Eighteenth Century)* (1968). Good discussion of individual German states.

H. Baron, *The Crisis of the Early Italian Renaissance* (*Princeton). Learned work with an emphasis on politics.

D. Muir, *A History of Milan under the Visconti* (1924). Still a useful work.

G. A. Brucker, *Renaissance Florence* (*Wiley). An introductory textbook.

M. B. Becker, *Florence in Transition,* 2 vols. (1967–1968). A full-length study of the fourteenth century.

C. M. Ady, *Lorenzo de' Medici and Renaissance Italy* (*Collier). Brief, readable account.

W. J. Bouwsma, *Venice and the Defense of Republican Liberty* (1968). A very important monographic study; not for beginners.

F. Chabod, *Machiavelli and the Renaissance* (*Harper Torchbooks); and H. Butterfield, *The Statecraft of Machiavelli* (*Collier). The first is more sympathetic to Machiavelli, the second far more critical. Both may be usefully contrasted with the more straightforward J. R. Hale, *Machiavelli and Renaissance Italy* (*Harper Torchbooks).

G. Mollat, *The Popes at Avignon, 1305–1378* (*Harper Torchbooks). The "Babylonian Captivity" of the popes.

Renaissance Civilization

D. Hay, *The Renaissance in Its Historical Background* (*Cambridge). Good study by a leading modern authority on Italy.

J. H. Plumb, *The Italian Renaissance* (*Harper Torchbooks). A useful survey.

B. Mattingly, et al., *Renaissance Profiles* (*Harper Torchbooks). Sketches of individual personalities, including leading humanists.

J. Burckhardt, *The Civilization of the Renaissance in Italy,* 2 vols. (*Harper Torchbooks). A famous classic, arguing that the Renaissance was revolutionary.

P. O. Kristeller, *Renaissance Thought,* 2 vols. (*Harper Torchbooks). By the greatest single contemporary authority. Not for beginners.

G. Holmes, *The Florentine Enlightenment, 1400–1450* (*Penguin). Humanists and their obsession with the classics: a fine study.

M. P. Gilmore, *Humanists and Jurists* (1963). Six essays, especially instructive on Erasmus.

J. Huizinga, *Erasmus and the Age of the Reformation* (*Harper Torchbooks). The best single work on Erasmus by a distinguished Dutch scholar.

M. Boas, *The Scientific Renaissance, 1450–1630* (*Harper Torchbooks). A helpful, detailed account.

A. C. Crombie, *Medieval and Early Modern Science,* 2 vols. (1963). Volume II deals with the Renaissance period.

G. Sarton, *The History of Science and the New Humanism* (*Indiana). By a great master of the history of science.

E. Garin, *Science and Civic Life in the Italian Renaissance* (*Anchor). By a leading Italian scholar.

The Arts

C. Gilbert, *History of Renaissance Art throughout Europe* (1973). Comprehensive and well illustrated.

M. Levey, *The Early Renaissance* (*Penguin). A good introduction.

H. Wolfflin, *The Art of the Italian Renaissance* (*Schocken). Influential and original treatment; not easy reading.

E. Panofsky, *The Renaissance and Renascences in Western Art* (*Harper Torchbooks); and *Studies in Iconology: Humanistic Themes in the Renaissance* (*Harper Torchbooks). Stimulating studies by a leading scholar.

K. M. Clark, *Leonardo da Vinci* (*Penguin). A well-written and valuable introduction.

E. Panofsky, *The Life and Art of Albrecht Dürer* (*Princeton). The best work on the subject.

R. Wittkower, *Architectural Principles in the Age of Humanism* (*Norton). The relationship between intellectual advance and buildings.

B. Lowery, *Renaissance Architecture* (*Braziller).

G. Reese, *Music in the Renaissance* (1954). A thorough study.

Sources

J. Froissart, *Chronicles* (*Dutton).

W. L. Gundersheimer, ed., *The Italian Renaissance* (*Prentice-Hall); and L. Spitz, ed., *The Northern Renaissance* (*Prentice-Hall). Good collections of sources with crisp introductory comments and useful bibliographies.

B. Castiglione, *The Book of the Courtier* (*Anchor).

J. B. Ross and M. M. McLaughlin, eds., *The Portable Renaissance Reader* (*Viking).

E. Cassirer et al., *The Renaissance Philosophy of Man* (*Phoenix).

Erasmus, *The Praise of Folly* (*Princeton).

Machiavelli, *The Prince* and *The Discourses* (*Modern Library).

P. Taylor, ed., *The Notebooks of Leonardo da Vinci: A New Selection* (*Mentor).

S. Putnam, ed., *The Portable Rabelais* (*Viking).

CHAPTER EIGHT

Transition To A New World:

Religious Upheaval, Expansion Overseas, Dynastic Conflict

In this chapter we approach our own modern world. The unity of medieval Catholicism is shattered. European nations discover and conquer whole new worlds across the seas. And one great European power—Spain—almost succeeds in dominating the rest. But the others discover a means to prevent this from happening by acting together.

First we discuss the Protestant Reformation, still often called by Catholics the Protestant Revolt. We deal with its various leaders—Luther, Zwingli, Calvin, King Henry VIII of England—and the combination of religious and political motives that led to the replacement of a single church by many. Because the subject comes closer to most of us than, say, feudalism, it still arouses partisanship in our own day. The Catholic Church had its own reformation alongside and in response to the Protestant movement.

Next we turn to the familiar but still dramatic first chapter in the history of European exploration and discovery, overseas conquest and commerce. We shall see how Portugal and Spain build the first empires in the new worlds of

America and Asia, and begin to be challenged by later-comers, the Dutch, English, and French. And finally, we shall observe the new monarchies—Spain, France, and England, as well as the decentralized empire of the Germanies—evolving into recognizably modern nations. As the Spaniards try to assert their predominance the other new monarchies will find a diplomatic and military answer to the threat by achieving a *balance of power* that no single nation may be allowed to upset. Except for the earliest explorations, which belong to the late 1400s, all of these momentous events took place in the sixteenth century.

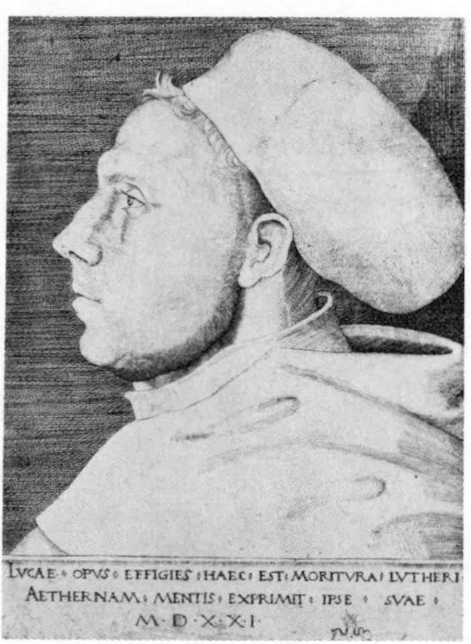

Martin Luther: engraving by Lucas Cranach the Elder.

I The Protestant and Catholic Reformations

Luther

Luther's Revolt

On October 31, 1517, Martin Luther (1483–1546) nailed a document called the Ninety-five Theses to the door of the court church at Wittenberg in Saxony. The action touched off what proved to be a major social, economic, and intellectual revolution. Neither Luther nor other later Protestant leaders like Calvin intended such a revolution. They conceived of themselves not as starting *new* churches but as reforming the Church and returning to the true *old* Church.

Repeatedly, as we know, the medieval Catholic Church had faced and absorbed reform movements: Cluniac, Cistercian, Franciscan. In the fourteenth and fifteenth centuries Wycliffe and Hus threatened to create separate churches. The Conciliar Movement, in the early fifteenth century had challenged papal authority, though its effort to subordinate the pope to a general council had failed.

But Luther's action led to the organization of a separate church. Within a generation after 1517, dozens of other Protestant sects came into existence. Today we take this existence of many Christian churches for granted, but in the sixteenth century this departure from medieval religious unity was a real revolution.

Son of a German peasant who became a miner and eventually a prosperous investor in mining enterprises, Luther studied law in his youth. In 1505, at the age of twenty-two, he was terrified by a thunderstorm. He prayed to Saint Anne for help and promised to become a monk. In the monastery he underwent a major personal crisis: he was sure he was a lost soul without hope of salvation. He submitted to monastic discipline and made a pilgrimage to Rome in 1510. But none of his good works (deeds) freed him from the gnawing fear that he could not win God's grace. He was sure he was going to hell.

Modern psychoanalysts recognize in Luther's agony a case of what they call "identity crisis." Only by studying the Epistles of St. Paul and the writing of St. Augustine did Luther find an answer. The only way he could be saved was to have faith that God would save him. The Roman church had of course always taught the necessity of faith for salvation, "justification by faith," but good deeds were also necessary. What was new about Luther was his emphasis on justification by *faith alone.*

Luther then began to question actions of the contemporary church that in his view were abuses tending to corrupt or weaken faith. He wrote up his questions in Latin in the form of the Ninety-five Theses, a challenge to debate, drafted in the manner of the medieval Scholastics.

Luther's particular target was what he called the "sale" of indulgences by a Dominican named Tetzel who was traveling around Germany raising money for the papacy for the rebuilding of St. Peter's. The theory of indulgences calls for an explanation. Only God could forgive sins. Nobody claimed that any "indulgence" could procure forgiveness. But repentant sinners had to do penance on earth and suffer punishment after death in purgatory in order to be qualified for heaven. The theory of indulgences concerned the remission of such punishment.

The Church said that Christ, the Virgin, and the Saints had performed so many good works they they had accumulated a surplus, a Treasury of Merit. A priest could draw on this heavenly Treasury on behalf of an applicant. This was an indulgence and could remit penance on earth and part or all of the punishment in purgatory. Such an indulgence was "granted" by the priest. Any gift of money contributed by the recipient was a freewill offering. But Luther said that Tetzel was *selling* indulgences.

To the man in the street it seemed as though a sinner could obtain *not only* remission of punishment *but also* forgiveness of sin, if only he secured enough indulgences, and that this depended on his money gifts to Tetzel. In the Ninety-five Theses, Luther objected vehemently both to Tetzel's perversion of indulgences and to the whole doctrine behind them. He thus minimized the importance of good works at a moment when many ordinary believers were trying to increase their stock of such works by drawing on the Treasury of Merit.

Christian theory insisted on the need for *both* faith and good works. Luther's emphasis on faith drove his papal opponents into a corresponding emphasis on works. This in turn drove him, in moments of excitement, to deny the value of good works and to insist on faith alone. Since "works" included all earthly ecclesiastical organization, priests included, Luther was soon denying that priests are necessary. He formed the priesthood of all believers; in popular terms, "every man his own priest."

Pope Leo X (1513–1521) was alarmed by the financial implications of Luther's actions and by the critical importance of the issue Luther raised. Between 1517 and 1520 Luther defied the Pope. In debate he said that popes and councils were not necessarily authoritative, and defended certain views of Hus that the Council of Constance had declared heretical. In 1520, in his *Appeal to the Christian Nobility of the German Nation,* Luther called the term "spiritual estate," as used to describe the clergy, a "lie," and declared that "all Christians are truly of the spiritual estate, and there is no difference among them save of office."

When Leo X issued a bull condemning Luther's teaching, Luther burnt it. In 1520 he was excommunicated, and the emperor Charles V and the imperial assembly at Worms solemnly declared him an outlaw. Once again he was asked whether he would recant. His reply contained his most famous words:

> Unless I am convinced of error by the testimony of Scripture I cannot and will not recant anything, for to act against our conscience is neither safe for us, nor open to us.
>
> *Hier stehe ich. Ich kann nicht anders. Got helff mir. Amen.* [On this I take my stand. I cannot act differently. God help me. Amen.]*

Excommunication and outlawry did not prevent Luther from gathering a substantial following and becoming a national hero. He had the protection of the ruler of his own German state, the elector Frederick the Wise of Saxony, and soon secured the backing of other princes. In the next few years he translated the Bible into vigorous and effective German, and remodeled the Saxon church according to his own views. His revolt was a success.

The Reasons for Luther's Success

The Catholic Church that Luther attacked had come under the influence of the new wealth of the Renaissance and the new worldly fashions. The popes had been drawn into Italian politics. The Rome Luther visited in his youth was full of intrigue, display, and corruption. Some part of Luther's success lay in the fact that he was reasserting the primacy of the spirit over materialism.

Then too, in the name of good Germans, Luther was attacking the practices of Italians and Italianate Germans. Not only was Tetzel performing morally outrageous acts, he was raising money to enrich Italy:

> For Rome is the greatest thief and robber that has ever appeared on earth, or ever will. . . . We Germans were born to be masters, and we have been compelled to bow the head beneath the yoke. . . . It is time the glorious Teutonic people should cease to be the puppet of the Roman pontiff.*

A good many German princes liked the sound of this patriotic note. They followed Luther because they stood to gain by cutting off the flow of German money to Italy and by confiscating Church property, especially monastic property, which was not needed for the Lutheran church.

* *Documents of the Christian Church,* ed. H. Bettenson (New York, 1947), p. 285.

* *Ibid.,* pp. 278–79.

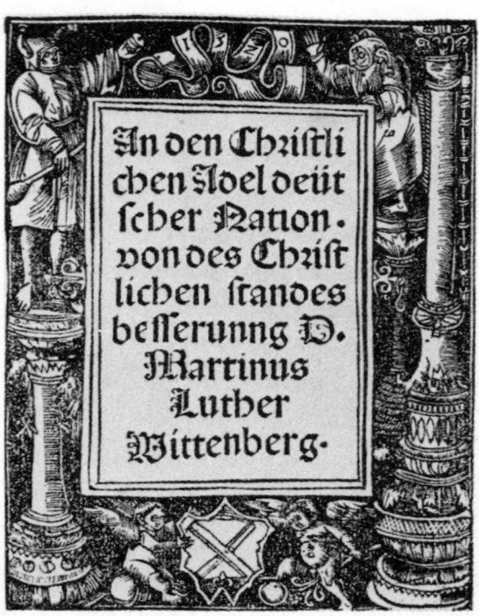

An den Christli
chen Adel deüt
scher Nation.
von des Christ
lichen standes
besserung D.
Martinus
Luther
Wittenberg.

Title page of Luther's "Appeal to the Christian Nobility of the German Nation."

Moreover, Luther gave them a new weapon in their eternal struggle against their feudal overlord, the emperor.

Luther's personal energy, courage, and intelligence were of major importance. He wrote his best-selling revolutionary pamphlets in the vernacular German, not the academic Latin. Luther's German Bible became one of the bases of modern literary German. The Lord's Prayer in his sonorous German, and his great hymns, notably "A Mighty Fortress is Our God," enabled a German to feel that the service in a Lutheran church belonged to him personally. Luther's marriage to a former nun and his raising of a large family dramatized the break with Rome.

The forces that opposed Luther were relatively weak. The top levels of the Catholic bureaucracy, with Pope Leo X as their willing instrument, found negotiation unthinkable. But many moderate Catholics were anxious to compromise and avert a schism. Erasmus, for example, who remained a Catholic, recognized how much the papacy was hated in Germany, acknowledged the need for reform, and said of Luther, "God has given us a radical physician." Once Leo X had excommunicated Luther in 1520, however, the way to compromise was probably blocked, for Luther's associates could have been won away from him only by concessions that no pope could have made.

Politically the Catholic opposition was led by Emperor Charles V (1519–1556). His father's parents had been the Hapsburg emperor Maximilian and Mary of Burgundy. His mother's were Ferdinand and Isabella. No wonder this series of marriages inspired the Latin verse, "Let others wage wars; thou, happy Austria, marry." Charles V inherited the Hapsburgs' lands in Austria and elsewhere and their claim to the title of emperor, the Low Countries, Spain and the Spanish overseas empire, and parts of Italy. He held the biggest European state since Charlemagne. Luther's princely German supporters threatened his hold over Germany. Moreover, Charles was a devout Catholic. In the 1520s he decided to fight the Lutherans, and he had to spend the rest of his reign fighting them.

War and Rebellion in the 1520s

Charles V entrusted the government of the Germans to his younger brother Ferdinand, who formed alliances with Bavaria and other Catholic German states against the Lutheran states. These alliances led directly to the religious wars of the next few generations. These in turn would lead to a permanent division of Germany into, roughly, a Protestant north and east and a Catholic south and west. Since the Hapsburgs also had to fight against the Ottoman Turks and the French, they could not steadily concentrate on defeating the Lutherans in Germany.

German knights backed Luther. Some of them held castles and small estates direct from the emperor, others were vassals of some greater lord. Under the leadership of Ulrich von Hutten and Franz von Sickingen, they were defeated in the "Knights War" (1522).

Even more destructive was the Peasants' Rebellion of 1524–1525. Like the French Jacquerie in 1358, or the English peasant uprising in 1381, the German peasants now rose against the remaining burdens of the manorial system. With-

Woodcut from a Lutheran attack against the Peasants' Rebellion, 1525.

out competent military commanders they were ruthlessly suppressed. The rebellion centered in the southwest, where the peasants had already begun to emancipate themselves and wanted to finish the process.

Much as Wycliffe had influenced the English peasants, Luther's preaching stirred those in Germany. The German peasants now had educated leaders with a revolutionary program of their own: the "Twelve Articles." They demanded that each parish should choose its own priest. Tithes and taxes should be lowered. The peasants should have the right to take game and firewood from the forests. All this sounds reasonable enough. But Luther himself denounced the peasant rebels as "murderous thieving hordes."

In 1531, Lutheran princes and cities formed the Schmalkaldic League against Charles V. In 1547 Charles defeated the League, using Spanish troops, but he could not really take advantage of his victory. It would have made him too powerful to suit even the pope and the Catholic German princes. As we shall see, it would have upset the European balance of power. So, as his reign drew to an end, Charles V was forced to accept compromise. The Peace of Augsburg (1555) left the Lutherans in power in all German states where the prince was a Lutheran (see p. 259).

Luther once said, "The princes of the world are gods, the common people are Satan." This political conservatism not only helped his movement succeed, but is consistent with his spiritual position. If the visible external world is subordinate to the invisible spiritual world, the best anyone can hope for here on earth is that good order be maintained. Kings, princes, authority, custom, law: all existing institutions are preferable to discussion and dissension.

The princes of northern Germany and the Scandinavian kingdoms of course agreed. They hastened the process of converting as many of their subjects as possible to Lutheranism and expelling the rest. By the mid-sixteenth century, Lutheranism had become the state religion of these regions. It was often the docile instrument of political rulers.

In organizing his own church, Luther showed the same conservatism. The logical extreme of the priesthood of all believers is no church at all, or as many churches as there are individual human beings. In Saxony, reformers influenced by Luther tried out these anarchical concepts before Luther himself and the moderates intervened.

Luther's new church often simply took over the existing church buildings. It did have priests; but they were free to marry, a sign that they had no more sacramental powers than other men. The Lutherans retained two of the seven sacraments: baptism and the Eucharist, both specifically mentioned in the Bible. But even these were deprived of their miraculous quality. Veneration of saints and relics, fasts, pilgrimages, monastic orders—all vanished. Yet the forms of worship retained much that had been traditional. To Luther this new church was not merely an alternative to the Church of Rome, it was the *one true Church,* a return to Christianity as it had been before Rome had corrupted it.

Zwingli

Only a year after Luther nailed his theses to the door at Wittenberg, a Swiss priest named Ulrich Zwingli (1484–1531), a humanist trained in the tradition of Erasmus, launched a quieter reform in Zurich. Like Luther, Zwingli objected to the idea that priests had miraculous powers not possessed by laymen. He believed that the social conscience of enlightened people led by good pastors would achieve a common discipline that would promote righteous living. Like Luther, Zwingli opposed priestly celibacy, fasts, monasticism, confession, and indulgences. He thought the appeal to saints and the use of incense, candles, and images were "superstition." He began the process of making the church building an almost undecorated hall, of making the service a sermon and responsive reading, and of abolishing the Catholic liturgy.

Zwingli differed with Luther and both differed with the Catholics over the Eucharist. The Catholics believed that the bread and wine, through the miracle of the Mass at communion, became in *substance* the body and blood of Christ, although their chemical makeup—their "accidents"—remained unchanged. Luther denied the miracle of the Mass and believed in "consubstantiation": that the body and blood were somehow *present* in the bread and wine. Zwingli believed what has become the usual Protestant doctrine: that the bread and wine merely *symbolized* the body and blood.

No "Zwinglian" organized church emerged from his ideas or activities, but Zwingli won over the government of Zurich and most of its citizens. Many of the other German-speaking towns of Switzerland became Protestant. But the Catholic cantons went to war against the Protestants, and

Zurich at the time of Zwingli: panel painting by Hans Leu the Elder.

Zwingli was killed in 1531. Though the individual Swiss cantons were allowed to choose their form of worship thereafter, Protestant leadership had suffered a severe blow.

Calvin

It recovered a decade later, when John Calvin (1509–1564) took power in Geneva. French-born and Paris-educated, Calvin was a classicist and lawyer, converted from Catholicism by his reading of Erasmus and Luther. He took refuge in the Swiss town of Basel and there published his *Institutes of the Christian Religion* (1536), a complete summary of his theological and moral views and a work of great influence in spreading Protestant thought.

Both Calvin and Luther rejected good works as a way to salvation. But, where Luther emphasized the view that man could achieve salvation through faith, Calvin said that man cannot save himself by faith, or by anything else. God alone can save. From the beginning, God had predetermined—predestined—who among the human race would be saved and who eternally damned.

God had chosen very few, his "elect," for salvation. Nobody not "elect" could attain it. Nor was there any way for people to know certainly whether they were among the elect. Of course, they could be sure, if they led a life contrary to Christian morality, that they were damned. But no matter how moral a life they led they could never be sure that they were saved. Just possibly they might be among the elect. This was the only crumb of comfort Calvin's system held out.

Calvinist Practice

Stern logic, rigorous morality, an Old Testament conception of God, and emphasis on the strict observance of commandments characterized Calvinist views and Calvinist behavior. The French-speaking city of Geneva asked Calvin in 1541 to help it rebel against its Catholic bishop and the count of Savoy. From 1541 until his death twenty-three years later, Calvin was the supreme ruler of the city.

Geneva became a "theocracy," literally a government by God. The church governed all aspects of the citizen's life. Protestant refugees from other parts of Europe came to learn from Calvin. John Knox (1505–1572) took Calvinism back to Scotland. Others took it to Holland, to France, to England, whence it crossed the Atlantic to Massachusetts, and to Hungary and Poland.

In the Low Countries, Calvinism became the symbol of Dutch nationalism against the Spanish rule of Charles V's heir, Philip II (1556–1598), In France, Calvinist ideas led to the foundation of churches called "Huguenot" (perhaps from the German word *Eidgenosse,* "covenanted"), chiefly in the old southwestern strongholds of the Albigensian heresy (see Chapter 5). Here, as elsewhere in Europe, the Protestants would have to fight

Two views of John Calvin. By an unknown painter, 1534. Caricature by Giuseppe Arcimboldo, 1566.

not for toleration but for survival. Few men of the time could even imagine subjects of the same ruler peacefully practicing different religions.

Where the Calvinists controlled an area, they censored, interfered, and punished. They were petty tyrants, denying people much of their privacy, pleasure, and individualism. They were sure they were God's agents, doing God's work. These firm believers in the inability of human efforts to change anything were the most ardent workers for change in human behavior.

Calvinists believed that music, dancing, gambling, fine clothes, drinking, and the theater were inventions of Satan. Sexual intercourse, they said, had as its sole purpose the perpetuation of the race. Their outlook is called Puritanism. Within each person the struggle raged between the temptations of the world and his or her "Puritan conscience." In his dealings with others, the Puritan tried not only to coerce but also to convert. We shall encounter Puritanism again in sixteenth- and seventeenth-century England.

The English Reformation

Henry VIII

In England, the signal for religious overturn was very different from Luther's Ninety-five Theses. Henry VIII (reigned 1509–1547), the second Tudor king, wanted a male heir, and his wife, Catherine of Aragon, aunt of the emperor Charles V, had not produced one. His legal case for separation was thin: Catherine had been married first to his deceased brother, Arthur, and Henry now "discovered" after twenty years of marriage that canon law forbade marriage with a deceased

Catherine of Aragon and Anne Boleyn.

brother's widow. Henry had published an attack on Lutheran ideas, for which the pope had declared him "Defender of the Faith." So he tried hard to obtain an annulment from the pope. But the pope was unwilling to risk offending Charles V, whose troops were in control of Rome at the time (1527).

In 1533, the obliging archbishop of Canterbury, Thomas Cranmer, pronounced the marriage annulled, and Henry married Anne Boleyn. The pope excommunicated Henry and declared the annulment invalid. Henry broke relations with the papacy. By Henry's Act of Supremacy (1534), he became "supreme head" of the Church of England.

In these drastic actions, Henry had the support of Parliament, which voted the Act of Supremacy. This proves beyond doubt that more than the king's private life was involved. Had it not been for a long-standing and deep-rooted antipapal and anticlerical feeling in England, Henry could not have acted as he did. The ideas of Luther and other Protestants had won much sympathy among the English. Others, like Thomas More (1478–1535), author of *Utopia,* favored reform only within the Church. More was beheaded by Henry VIII for opposing the Act of Supremacy and was later made a Catholic saint.

One target of the English anti-Catholics was the monasteries, many of them wealthy and corrupt. Henry abolished them and confiscated their property. This won the favor of the nobles and gentry, to whom—at a price—Henry passed on the loot. The confiscation and redistribution of monastic properties amounted to a social and economic revolution. Those who got rich by it were bound more closely to their benefactor, the king.

Yet Henry considered himself a Catholic, not a Protestant. In his eyes the Church of England remained a Catholic body. Except for the abolition of monasteries and the break with Rome, Henry was determined to make no change. His behavior outraged two sorts of opponents. Catholics, of course, felt that Henry had gone much too far. Militant Protestants felt that he had not gone nearly far enough.

English Protestants wanted priests to marry and the service to be in English. They wanted to abolish confession spoken privately into the ear of a priest ("auricular" confession) and the invocation of saints. But Parliament, many of whose members had profited by the distribution of monastic wealth, did what Henry wanted. In 1539 it passed the Six Articles, reaffirming clerical celibacy, confession, and four other important Catholic points of doctrine and ritual, and making their denial heresy. But Protestant sentiment could not be disposed of so easily.

Religion and the Later Tudors

Under Henry's son, Edward VI (1547–1553), the government became more strongly Protestant. The Six Articles were repealed in 1547. In 1549 Parliament passed an act requiring uniformity of church services, and introduced an official prayer book. Cranmer, archbishop of Canterbury and a convinced Protestant (he had married), published the Forty-two Articles of Religion in 1551.

But when Edward VI died, the crown passed to his half-sister, the Catholic Mary Tudor (1553–1558), daughter of Henry VIII by Catherine of Aragon. A plot to put her Protestant cousin, Lady Jane Grey, on the throne failed, and Mary as queen tried to restore Catholicism.

When she announced her intention of marrying the very Catholic Prince Philip of Spain, who was, however, to be without power in England, a rebellion broke out. Mary suppressed it and married Philip. A Catholic became archbishop of Canterbury, and Cranmer was burned at the stake. Perhaps three hundred Protestants lost their lives in Mary's persecutions. She has gone into history as "Bloody Mary."

When Mary Tudor died in 1558, her half-sister Elizabeth, daughter of Henry VIII by Anne Boleyn, succeeded her as queen (reigned 1558–1603). Elizabeth I was a Protestant. Soon after her accession, all of Mary's Catholic legislation was repealed and all of Henry VIII's laws regarding the Church were reenacted.

In 1563 Parliament adopted the Thirty-nine Articles, modified from Cranmer's Forty-two of 1551. The Articles rejected clerical celibacy, auricular confession, papal supremacy, and the use of Latin. They required that the laity receive communion in both wine and bread, whereas the Catholic Church gave only the bread. They rejected Catholic doctrine on the Eucharist, but also the Zwinglian idea that Christ's presence in the bread and wine was merely symbolism. The members of the Church of England (Anglican) would receive the Eucharist as the body and blood of Christ. The Articles avoided any wholly clear statement on Lutheran doctrines. Ever since, the Thirty-nine Articles of 1563 and the Elizabethan prayer book have remained the essential documents of the Anglican faith.

Elizabeth was faced by Catholic opposition, both within England and abroad, from Spaniards and Scots in particular. More serious was the continued opposition of Protestants who wanted to purify the Church of England of what they considered papist survivals.

Some of these Puritans were moderates, who were willing to retain bishops if the ritual were simplified. Some were Presbyterians, who accepted Calvinist theology and wanted to abolish bishops and substitute synods of elders (presbyters) as the government of the church. Some were radicals—called Brownists after their leader Robert Browne—who wanted each congregation to be an independent body, and who anticipated the later Congregationalists and Independents. Elizabeth persecuted only Catholics at one extreme and Brownists at the other.

Ever since, the Church of England has reflected the wide range of religious sentiment in the country. It has always had "High Church" communicants who think of themselves as Catholics, and more Protestant "Low Church" communicants. It retains a modified form of the Catholic hierarchy, with archbishops and bishops. Of course it does not recognize papal authority. Its clergy may marry. Moderation—of ritual, hierarchy, discipline—has been its outstanding characteristic. But it has also had many people who stress evangelical piety, social service, the supreme importance of the Bible, and even Luther's teaching that salvation depends upon faith alone.

The Radical Left: Anabaptists and Unitarians

Among those in Germany touched by Luther's teachings were some who took quite literally his doctrine of justification by faith alone. Since good works did not help achieve salvation, could not believers act as they pleased? Since each believer was to find in his own conscience God's universal law, these people rejected all written law. They were called Antinomians (from the Greek "against law"). They did not believe in class distinctions or in private property. If they took several wives, it was clear that God wanted them to, since they wanted to.

In 1534–1535 a group of these radicals under the leadership of a Dutch tailor, John of Leiden, took control of the city of Münster in western Germany, where John was crowned as "King David" and kept a kind of harem in attendance. They were put down by force, and John was killed.

These radicals believed that the Catholic sacrament of baptism for infants was invalid, since no infant could "understand" the significance of the act. By "understanding" they did not mean an intellectual process but emotional or instinctive comprehension and participation. Therefore they baptized again anybody who joined them. As an adult, he was now for the first time able to "understand" what he was doing, and this kind of baptism alone had validity.

They were called Anabaptists (from the Greek for "baptizing again"). Later generations were not baptized until they came of age, and so they were "Baptists," no longer Anabaptists. Most Anabaptists were not fanatics like the followers of John of Leiden. They established communities and lived as they thought the early Christians had lived—working, sharing, and praying together.

The variety of beliefs and practices among the Anabaptists arose in part because many very earnest and ignorant people were for the first time reading the Bible. In certain books of the Old Testament and in the Book of Revelation they could find almost anything they were looking for. Some broke sharply with the old forms of worship. Their congregations no longer remained quiet in church, but shouted or danced. All sang hymns with great fervor. The sermon became very important and was often highly charged emotionally with hopes of heaven and fears of hell. Some of the sects expected the Second Coming of Christ immediately. Some shared their property among themselves and so were communists of a sort.

Distrusting the state, refusing to take oaths, coming mostly from the poorest classes, occasionally extremists like those at Münster, the Anabaptists became the objects of persecution, which made no distinction between the brave decent Christians and the wild ones. Their sense of community, their asceticism, their sober, industrious behavior have outlived the excesses of the more eccentric, and can be seen today among Baptists, Quakers, Mennonites, Moravians, and others.

Close to the Anabaptists, too, was one other sort of Protestant, the Unitarians, who denied the Trinity and the full divinity of Christ. The Spanish mystic Michael Servetus (1511–1553) stressed the humanity of Christ without depriving him of his divine attributes altogether. He hoped thereby to make it easier for individual human beings to feel a sense of mystic identification with Christ and thus achieve salvation.

Both Catholics and Protestants found these views alarming. Calvin had Servetus burnt at the stake in Geneva in 1553 for heresy. Another Unitarian, however, the Italian Socinus (Fausto Sozzini, 1539–1604) preached successfully among Poles and Hungarians. Present-day Unitarians in England and the United States are not the direct heirs of the mystic tradition of Servetus. Touched by the later rationalism of the eighteenth-century Enlightenment, they believe that Christ was not divine, but an inspired human being.

Protestant Attributes

From Henry VIII (who never thought of himself as a Protestant) through Luther, Zwingli, and Calvin to John of Leiden and Servetus is a broad spectrum indeed. What did these Protestants have in common? All repudiated the claim of the Roman Catholic Church to be supreme. Each was convinced that his own church was the true successor of Christ and the Apostles. Even the Antinomians, who believed that each man carried the truth in his own bosom, went on to say that if the obstacles to truth could be swept away, each man would find the *same* truth in his own bosom.

Some Protestants were prepared to convert humanity gradually by educating every human being in the correctness of their own beliefs. Others could not wait. Calvin, having been persecuted himself, persecuted Servetus. Religious tolerance and the peaceful coexistence of many churches—concepts that we today take for granted—were almost unknown in the sixteenth and seventeenth centuries.

All Protestants reduced the ritual and other external manifestations of belief. The seven sacraments of the Catholic Church were diminished, often to only two—baptism and the Eucharist. Various sects differed widely in their views on the meaning of the sacraments. "Papist" practices like the veneration of saints, the saying of rosaries, and the making of pilgrimages disappeared among all Protestants. The more radical banished music and painting and greatly simplified chuch architecture and decoration. All Protestants appealed from an established order to a "higher law," so echoing Luther's appeal from works to faith. All had at least a tinge of individualism, which they bequeathed to the modern world.

Protestantism and Progress

Some have argued that there was something fundamentally "modern" and "progressive" about Protestantism. They contrast the predominantly Protestant countries of the modern English-speaking world and Northern Europe, generally prosperous and democratic, with Catholic nations, which they regard as poorer, less stable, less advanced. Where they find a Catholic nation that has some "Protestant" qualities, such as France, they attribute this to the presence of a strong anticlerical tradition.

Yet at the time of the Reformation, neither Catholics nor Protestants believed that life on earth was improving or should improve. Protestants were not rationalists: Luther threw his ink bottle at the devil. They were just as intolerant as the Catholics and, like them, believed in rank and status. Lutheranism and Anglicanism were hierarchical and conservative. Calvinism was deeply undemocratic in its view of the small number of the elect, and authoritarian in its theocracy. Only the radicals voiced demands for political and social equality, and many of them were less concerned with this world than with the next.

Protestantism did, however, challenge authority and start all sorts of men, many of them in humble circumstances, thinking about fundamental problems. And Protestant moral ideas fitted in with the strengthening of a commercial middle class. Max Weber, a twentieth-century German sociologist, argued that Protestant ethics were closely related to the capitalist spirit that animated the middle classes who would lay the foundations of modern Western democracy.

Capital accumulation means that profits are "plowed back" into the business. If plowing back reduces the costs of production, still more capital accumulates. In its simplest terms this means hard work and no play all along the line, especially at the top.

Now the Calvinists certainly preached that the devil lies in wait for idle hands, and that work keeps a man from temptation to run after women, or play silly games, or drink, or do many other things unpleasing to God. Moreover they regarded work in itself as a tribute pleasing to the Lord. Luther, too, glorified work, and affirmed the dignity of every human calling, however humble. Contrast the contempt that the medieval upper classes felt for work in the fields or the counting house.

The Calvinists, in particular, also frowned upon the fine arts, the theater, expensive clothing, and beautiful "useless" objects in general: all of these interfere with capital accumulation. The Calvinist countries had a maximum number of working days in the year. They kept the Sabbath rigorously, but eliminated religious holidays, sometimes even Christmas. The Scots, the Dutch, the Swiss, the New England Yankees—all of them with a strong Calvinist background—have long had a popular reputation for thrift, diligence, and driving a hard bargain. Many Protestant theologians rejected the Catholic view that all interest was usury, and the medieval idea of a "just price" (see p. 140), in favor of something much closer to our modern notions of free competition in the market, where God would certainly take care of his own.

Finally, Max Weber argues, the Calvinist focus on the other world as the supreme goal, but one that could never be certain for any individual, helped shield the newly rich Calvinist from the temptation to squander his money and imitate a free-spending, loose-living aristocrat. If he did this, he could be pretty sure he was not of the elect. So the faith itself tended to give cohesion to the middle class. Family fortunes founded on hard work and maintained by reinvestment tended to hold together for several generations.

Yet there are also good arguments against Max Weber. Banking began before the time of Luther in Catholic countries such as Italy, southern Germany, and Belgium, which Protestants never won over. The Genoese Mediterranean traders of the fourteenth century like Zaccaria (Chapter 6) were Catholic capitalists. Furthermore, Protestant areas within a mixed Catholic-Protestant country are often less advanced than Catholic areas. Natural resources are fundamental. If Italy had turned Calvinist, the conversion still would not have given Italy coal and iron. Yet, it does seem that the "Protestant ethic" gave a push to the economic development of the Protestant regions, and helped to start the West on its modern path.

The Catholic Reformation

At first, the Catholic authorities tried to deal with the Reformation by suppressing it. But the Protestant movement itself had begun within the Church, and many Catholics who were not dissatisfied enough to leave the Church still wanted reform within it. The sixteenth century saw a revival of mysticism and popular participation in religion. These diverse forces produced the Catholic Reformation. It failed to restore the medieval unity of Christendom, but it did preserve and reinvigorate Catholic beliefs and practice.

Monarchs helped the Church. The Hapsburgs, both German and Spanish, gave the Catholic movement support. The French king helped keep France Catholic, and in the seventeenth century (see Chapter 9) France would witness a great Catholic revival. Once again, a series of new monastic orders revived the old ideals of austerity and social service. While the struggle with Luther was still young, a group at Rome founded the Oratory of Divine Love, dedicated to the deepening of spiritual experience. The Oratory inspired the foundation of the Theatines, an order designed particularly to advance the education of the clergy. In the 1520s too, the Capuchins (hooded friars) appeared to lead the Franciscan order back to Francis's own ideals.

Best known of the new orders was the Society of Jesus, founded in 1540 by the Spaniard Ignatius Loyola (1491–1556). Loyola, who had been a soldier, intended the Jesuits to be an army for the Church. His *Spiritual Exercises* emphasized absolute obedience to higher authority but displayed a realistic estimate of what can be expected of ordinary human beings.

Always the center of controversy, the Jesuits have been accused of a willingness to use any tactics to win. This is a slander: the Jesuits have always emphasized the hold that moral decency has on human beings. In many parts of Europe they strove to win back souls lost to the Protestants. They moved with European explorers to India, China, Japan, North America, to win new lands and new converts. They were preachers, teachers, social workers, martyrs, and were always disciplined.

In its struggle with Protestantism, the Church also used the Inquisition. This tribunal

Ignatius Loyola: the only authentic portrait of the saint, by Claudio Coello.

began during the Albigensian Crusade of the early thirteenth century (see Chapter 5), and was imported to Spain by Isabella as a weapon against Jews and Muslims (see Chapter 7). The Inquisition tortured and killed Protestants in the Low Countries, but failed as a weapon against Protestantism. It was most active in regions where Protestantism was never a threat (Italy, Spain).

Catholics did not yield to doctrinal pressure from Protestants. The Lutheran theory of the "priesthood of all believers" hardened Catholic insistence on the unique powers of the ordained priest. The Church reaffirmed even its views on indulgences.

The Council of Trent, called by Pope Paul III in 1545 and meeting on and off for twenty years, reaffirmed all seven sacraments, transubstantiation, the necessity of both faith and works, and the authority of both the Bible and unwritten tradition. It also forbade individuals to interpret scripture contrary to the teaching of the Church. Even liberal Catholics have always felt that the Council was a mere instrument of the popes and the Jesuits.

The Council of Trent and the reforming popes of the later sixteenth century did enforce the kind of reform that the Cluniacs had put through five centuries earlier: priestly celibacy, the end of simony, and improved training for priests. The Council also founded the *Index,* a list of books that Catholics must not read because of peril to their faith. It included the writings of anticlericals like Machiavelli and Boccaccio, as well as those of heretics and Protestants. It was regularly brought up to date. Civil authorities in Catholic countries often enforced the censorship it dictated. By the 1570s the papacy had ceased to be the corrupt center that Luther and others had attacked, nor did it ever again become so.

Divided Christendom

Once the Catholic Reformation had been launched, the Protestants gained little more territory. By the end of the sixteenth century, the lines between areas predominantly Catholic and areas predominantly Protestant ran much as they do now. England, Scotland, Holland, northern and eastern Germany (with a southern projection in Württemberg and Switzerland), and Scandinavia were predominantly Protestant. Ireland, Belgium, southern Germany and the Rhine valley, the Hapsburg lands, Poland, Italy, and the Iberian peninsula were predominantly Catholic. But there were Catholic minorities in England, Scotland, and Holland. There were Protestant minorities in Ireland, France, and some of the Hapsburg lands. And the two faiths interpenetrated most confusedly in greatly divided Germany.

To some degree the religious differences contributed to the growth of national patriotism. Where a specific form of religion became identified with a given country, religious feeling and patriotic feeling reinforced each other. Since Elizabeth I, England—despite its Catholic minority—has taken pride in being a Protestant nation. In struggles for independence, Protestantism heightened Dutch resistance to the Spaniards; Catholicism, Irish resistance to the English. In the great wars to which we turn below, religion and politics were both at issue. So was the competition for overseas trade and empire.

II THE FIRST OVERSEAS EMPIRES

In the mid-fifteenth century, Europeans began the explorations that within 250 years would reveal almost the whole world to them. For the first time—except for a few half-legendary Viking voyages—Westerners crossed the oceans, traveled far beyond the orbits of the only two other societies—the Byzantine and the Muslim—that they knew so far, and discovered new races, creeds, and cultures.

The Europeans were superior in military strength to the peoples they met, and so were able to extend their influence around the world. They had guns; but non-Europeans could quickly acquire these and did. More important, Europeans combined their technological superiority with superior political and military organization. No Asian nation could meet them on their own terms until Japan became a modern nation in our own century.

Why did this great movement begin just when it did? There were technological reasons. During the fifteenth century, the magnetic compass that makes navigation possible even when the sun and stars are hidden became standard ship's equipment. Shipbuilders were building longer and narrower vessels, better adapted to ocean voyages.

There were economic and political reasons. The Italian domination of the Mediterranean-Near East trade routes was strengthened by new agreements with the Ottomans. So the Western states were tempted to try the Atlantic instead.

And the new scientific investigating spirit impelled men to explore. Columbus deliberately set out across the unknown ocean to prove his theory that because the world is round, one could travel westward from Europe and eventually reach Asia.

The Portuguese

East by Sea to the Indies

The first great pioneer in exploration was Prince Henry of Portugal (1394–1460), "the Navigator." Deeply religious, he wanted to convert to Christianity the peoples of Asia, already known in the West through the reports of medieval overland travelers like Marco Polo the Venetian (ca. 1264–ca. 1324).

Europeans believed that many Asians were already Christian. The belief was based partly on fact. There were *some* Asian Christians, descendants of refugees from Byzantine theological controversies (see Chapter 4). But Henry the Navigator, like many Europeans, believed the myth that far off in Asia was a great Christian king, Prester (priest) John, who needed only to be brought into touch with Rome. Henry also wanted to promote Portuguese commerce and national power. He carefully planned his expeditions, and his ships had the best instruments available.

The Portuguese had already discovered the Atlantic islands—the Azores, Madeira, and the Canaries. Sailing southward along the west coast of Africa, they hoped to sail around Africa. By 1472 they had rounded the West African bulge and were appalled to discover that the coastline turned south once more. But in 1488, Bartholomew Diaz, blown far south in a storm, rounded the Cape of Good Hope.

In 1497, Vasco da Gama followed him, worked his way north along the east coast of Africa and came to Arab traders who knew how to sail across the Indian Ocean to India. Ten months and fourteen days out from Lisbon, da Gama reached the Indian coast. The Portuguese had an ocean route to the East.

On the next great voyage toward India in 1500, Pedro Cabral—no longer feeling the need to cling to the west African coast—stayed out in the Atlantic after rounding the western African bulge, and was blown so far west that he actually landed in Brazil. Perhaps this was not really an accident. By 1500, the Spanish too had made many voyages and the Portuguese knew all about them. In 1493, after Columbus' first voyage, Pope Alexander VI granted to Spain all lands south and west of a north-south line drawn in the Atlantic between the Azores and the Cape Verde Islands. In 1494, the Portuguese, by treaty with Spain, succeeded in having this line moved 370 leagues further west. So Brazil fell into the sphere of the Portuguese, who may have known about it all along but only announced their landing there after Cabral's voyage. These events determined that Brazil would be Portuguese, while all the rest of Latin America would be Spanish.

But the main Portuguese push was toward India and the Far East. They set up a string of fortified trading posts along the Indian coast and took control of the Indian Ocean from the Muslims. Goa, on the west coast of India, became the capital of the Portuguese holdings (it was not lost until 1962). By 1557, the Portuguese had a base in China at Macao near Canton, which they own today. They landed in Japan in 1542 or 1543, introduced firearms, and opened trade relations. Portugal had assembled a colonial empire.

Africa, India, and China

The Africa the Portuguese explored was hot, poor, and thinly populated. The coastal stations they and later European voyagers established carried on a flourishing slave trade, as did the Arabs in northern and northwestern Africa. The Africans of the West African bulge had been in touch with North African Muslim traders, who had introduced Islam and had come to Timbuktu on the upper Niger to acquire gold and slaves. In our own day when the states of Ghana and Mali became independent, they took the names of black empires that had ruled over these West African regions in the European Middle Ages.

The central and southern African tribes were largely still in a Stone Age culture. Africa was less attractive commercially to the Portuguese than India, China, and much of southeast Asia. Here there was a large population, great wealth accumulated in a few hands, and many luxuries like silks and spices.

India, known only vaguely to the West during the Middle Ages through the intermediary of the Arabs, proved to have very few Christian inhabitants. Most Indians belonged to faiths unknown to the Portuguese. India was also politically disunited. In the north, still unpenetrated by Europeans, Turkish Muslim invaders, wrongly called Mogul (from *Mongol*), were imposing their rule. In the south the local rulers fought each other in bitter rivalry. Some tribesmen in the south were at the Stone Age level. In the Indus and Ganges valleys there was a wealthy Hindu society.

For the Hindus, birth determined status. This was *caste.* There were more than a thousand castes. At the bottom were the "Untouchables." At the top, the two ruling castes were the *Brahmins,* or priests, and the *Kshatriya,* or warriors. Marriage between castes and all social mobility were in theory impossible. The Brahmins presided over a faith that preached the evils of fleshly life and the attainment of salvation by ascetic denial, striving toward a mystical union with the perfect. A sinful life on earth led to reincarnation in a lower animal form; a virtuous life to reincarnation in a higher form. However, the population also believed in many gods and goddesses.

In the sixth century B.C., Gautama Buddha had led a movement against these corruptions. Buddhism, one of the great religions of the world, accepts the Brahmin concept that the world of the flesh is bad. But for salvation ("nirvana") Buddhism prescribed a life of charity and good works, ascetic but not withdrawn.

In India Buddhism died out, but it spread far and wide in Asia. In China and Japan, Mahayana Buddhism ("Great Vehicle") prevailed, emphasizing that Buddha wished to make nirvana available to everyone. In southeast Asia and Ceylon, Hinayana Buddhism ("Lesser Vehicle") emphasized detachment from the world—especially for monks—and relied more heavily on ritual. An offshoot from this is Zen Buddhism, a stoic form of the faith that became popular in Japan.

Chinese civilization first arose in the Yellow and Yangtze river valleys several thousand years before Christ. The nomads of Asia harassed the Chinese, who in the third century B.C. built the famous Great Wall against them. Often the nomads broke through and conquered the Chinese, but the Chinese absorbed each wave of invaders and transformed them into Chinese.

Less than a century after the Portuguese arrived in Macao, the last nomad invasion occurred. The Manchus came down from the north and in 1644 established their own dynasty in Peking which held power until 1911. They too were speedily made over into Chinese.

Well before this, Chinese culture had gradually spread southward and eastward to the region of Canton, to Korea, and across the sea to Japan. The communal village organization, characterized by strong family ties, dominated Chinese society almost without change until the Communist takeover of 1949–1950.

China was always ruled by an emperor, the "Son of Heaven," with his bureaucracy of intel-

The Great Wall of China, built in the third century B.C.

lectuals, the mandarins, selected by examinations in classic Chinese literature and philosophy. In theory open to anybody with talent, the mandarin class in fact required so expensive a preliminary education that very few poor men's sons could ever rise into it. Worldly and realistic, with little mysticism or interest in an afterlife, the Chinese, it has been said, never had a religion.

Confucianism, a code of manners and morals that prescribed temperance, decorum, obedience to the wise and good, governed the behavior of the ruling classes. The Chinese would resist westernization more than any other people. They were always sure that they were superior to the rest of the human race. In the arts—painting, ceramics, and beautiful penmanship—they were quite right in their conviction.

The Portuguese Empire

The new Portuguese Empire, founded in these lands so strange to Europeans, was a trading empire, not an empire of settlement. Along the coasts of Africa, India, and China, the Portuguese established a series of posts, or "factories." They raised the Portuguese flag as a sign that they had annexed these places to Portugal. They offered the inhabitants cheap mass-produced guns, knives, and cloth. In return they got gold and silver when they could, spices, silks and other luxuries, and cotton and slaves.

Later colonizing powers followed their example: the mother country produced the manufactured goods, the colonies the raw materials. Foreigners were excluded. These policies derived from an economic theory called *mercantilism* discussed below.

Few troops were needed to keep the "natives" under control and hold off rival European powers. But the Portuguese needed and built a large and powerful navy to fight off pirates subsidized by their rivals. In their colonial outposts only a few Portuguese settled. They did not rule the inhabitants directly, but allowed the former rulers to do so. A few natives learned Portuguese, but the masses hardly noticed the Westerners.

But, like the other colonial powers later, the Portuguese did try to convert the natives to Christianity. Christian missionaries worked hard and devotedly. Some of the Jesuits in China believed that a reconciliation between Christianity and Confucianism was just around the corner. Often the missionaries tried to protect the natives against exploitation by the traders. But they made few converts in the vast populations of India and China.

In the next century the Portuguese would lose ground to the French, Dutch, and English, who possessed more advanced industrial and banking techniques. But they held their 800,000 square miles of Africa—Angola and Mozambique—well into the 1970s, long after other colonial empires had vanished. In the epic, *Lusiads* (1572), the poet Camoëns tells the dramatic tale of Portuguese overseas expansion.

The Spaniards

West by Sea to the Indies

Spain followed Portugal closely in exploring and colonizing. Ferdinand and Isabella commissioned Columbus (1451–1506) in the hope of catching up. Genoese-born, self-educated in navigation and geography, Columbus, like many others, thought it possible to reach the Far East by sailing west.

Ancient Greek geographers believed the earth was round, and the belief revived during the Renaissance. Toscanelli had published a map at Florence in 1474, and Behaim, one at Nuremberg in 1492 showing the earth as a globe. Of course neither map showed the Americas, and the combined Atlantic and Pacific were much narrower than they really are. But Columbus's ingenuity and persistence in sailing west so as to go east were all his own. Ferdinand and Isabella commissioned him not only to reach the Indies but to discover and secure for Spain new islands and territories.

Columbus did not reach the Indies, but found a new world. On October 12, 1492, after a voyage of a little more than two months with three small ships, he made a landfall on one of the Bahama Islands and continued on to discover the islands of Cuba and Santo Domingo (Hispaniola). On his second voyage, in 1493, with seventeen ships and fifteen hundred colonists, he explored farther in the Caribbean and took the first step toward building the Spanish Empire in America.

On his third voyage, in 1498–1500, he reached the north coast of South America but was sent home a prisoner after difficulties with the royal governor. He was released on his return to Spain, and in 1502–1504 made a fourth and final voyage, reaching the mainland of what is now Honduras. He died in Spain in 1506. He never knew he had landed not in Asia but on two new continents. Both were named America after Amerigo Vespucci, another Italian in Spanish service.

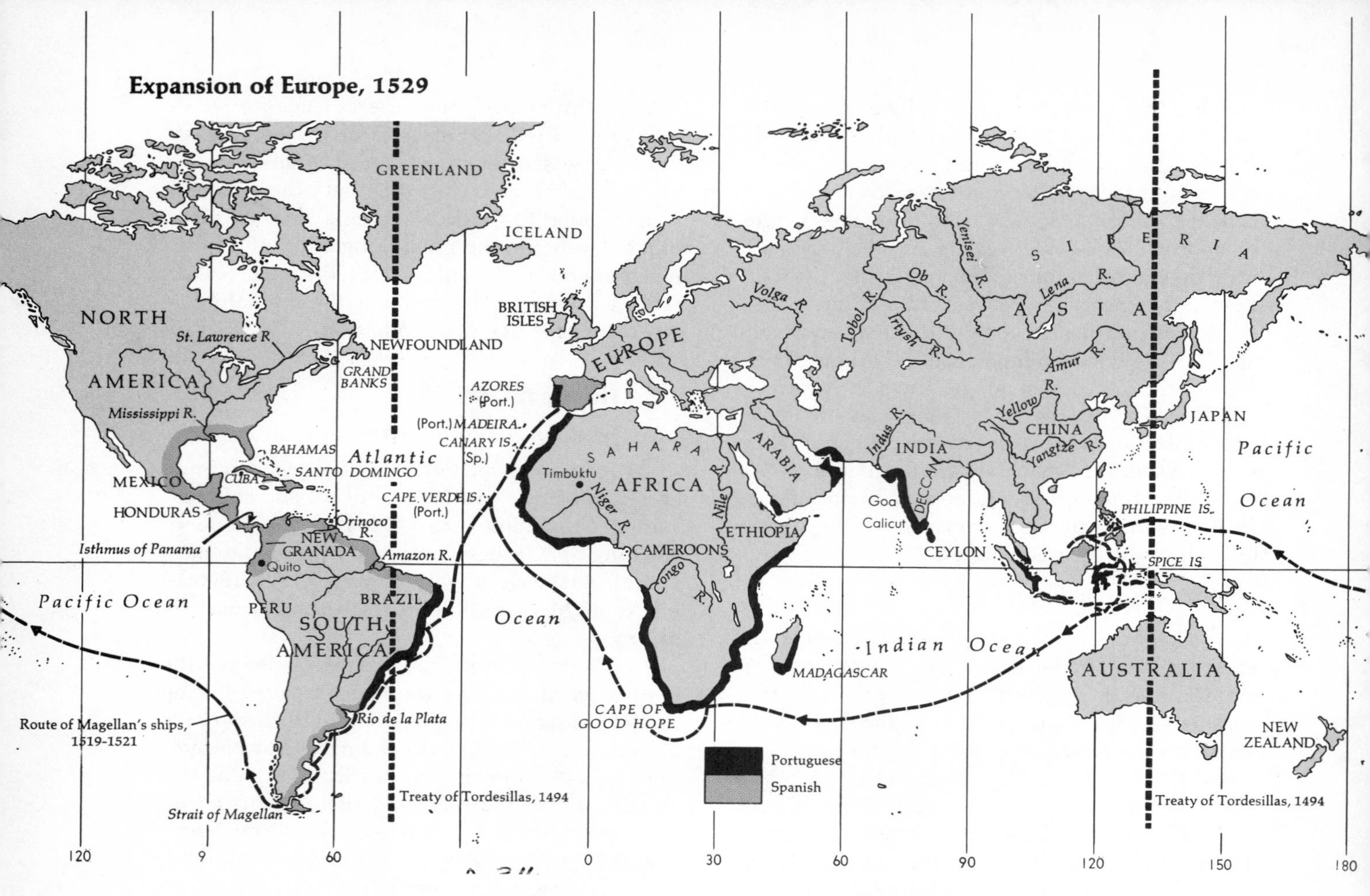

During the next few years, many other explorers discovered that America was a solid barrier. In 1513 Balboa saw the limitless Pacific from the Isthmus of Panama. Was there any water route *through* the barrier and into the Pacific? All the promising openings—Chesapeake, Delaware, Hudson, St. Lawrence—proved to be nothing but river mouths.

Of course, there *were* ways through. The Northwest Passage was usually ice-choked and was not actually found until the 1850s by the Englishman Sir John Franklin, who died in the Arctic wastes. The Southwest Passage, however, around the southernmost tip of South America, was found by Ferdinand Magellan. Between 1519 and 1522, Magellan, a Portuguese in the service of Spain, made an extraordinary voyage through the strait that still bears his name, into and across the Pacific, and all the way to the Philippines, where he was killed. But one of his captains sailed on across the Indian Ocean and home around the Cape of Good Hope. The voyagers had sailed round the world for the first time. The Philippine landing brought Spain into the Far East.

In the Americas, Spanish *conquistadores* were explorers, soldiers, and administrators. They conquered two highly civilized empires. Hernando Cortes took over the Aztec Empire of Mexico (1519) and Francisco Pizarro the Inca Empire of Peru (1531–1533).

Other Spanish conquistadores opened up other regions of the vast and strange New World: Quesada, what is now Colombia; Ponce de Leon, Florida; Coronado, de Soto, and Cabeza de Vaca, the southwestern portions of the United States; Mendoza, the La Plata region of Argentina and Uruguay; Valdivia, Chile; Alvarado, Guatemala. Although millions of people of Indian stock survive in Central and South America today, the structure of the Aztec and Incan civilizations—unlike that of China or India—disintegrated or disappeared before the often brutal conquest of the Spaniards.

The Latin Empires of the New World

Before the end of the sixteenth century the Spaniards and, in Brazil, the Portuguese had completed the foundation of the first colonial empires of settlement. But only in the La Plata region and in central Chile did a European population replace the natives. Elsewhere a crust of Spanish or Portuguese settlers formed at the top of society. Their European language became the language of culture. From the union of Europeans and natives arose a class called *mestizos,* mixed bloods. In many areas the Indians maintained their stock and their old ways of life. But in the Caribbean the Indians were exterminated, and in Brazil they proved inadequate as a labor force. In both cases large-scale importation of black slaves from Africa added another element to the racial mixture.

The geography of South and Central America determined their regional development. The great chain of the Andes, crossed only with great difficulty through high mountain passes, separated Argentina from Chile. The Andes and the great tropical rain forests of the Amazon Basin divided the colonies of La Plata from those of Peru and Colombia (New Granada). Other mountains split Central America into small regions. Even had Brazil been settled by Spaniards, it would almost surely have remained separate because of the difficulty of communications.

Two viceroys governed the American colonies for Spain; one in Peru, with his capital at Lima, and the other in "New Spain," with his capital at Mexico City. The viceroy at Lima ruled over all of Spanish South America except Venezuela. The viceroy at Mexico City ruled all the mainland north of Panama, the West Indies, Venezuela, and—far across the Pacific—the Philippines! In each capital, and also in other centers, there were advisory councils, *audiencias,* that also operated as courts.

This regime seems highly centralized, but in view of the vast areas and the varied peoples under its control, it could not be absolute in practice. The citizens were consulted in assemblies, and before long the colonial bureaucracy was largely managed by *colonials*—Spaniards born overseas who had never seen Spain. It was impossible for the mother country to prevent the growth of local industry and keep the colonies fully dependent on Spain. In time, local officials even connived at local trade with other Europeans: English, Dutch, and French.

By the sixteenth century, the Spaniards were interested chiefly in mining and exporting to Spain the rich and easily accessible deposits of gold and silver in Mexico and Peru. The crown got one fifth of all metals mined. Except for jewelry and other crafts, the precious metals were doing the Indians no good. But, as it turned out, they did the Spaniards little good either, since Spain spent huge sums to finance a vain bid for European supremacy.

By the seventeenth century sugar, tobacco, chocolate, cotton, and hides were flowing from the Americas to Europe in exchange for manufactured goods. The chief beneficiaries of this trade were the *Creoles* (Americans born of European stock) and the mestizos, not the Indians.

All over Latin America the Indians fell to the bottom of the social system. Especially in the Caribbean, but to a degree everywhere, the

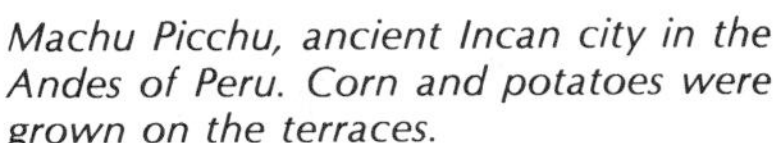

Machu Picchu, ancient Incan city in the Andes of Peru. Corn and potatoes were grown on the terraces.

initial Spanish policy of using native labor proved disastrous to the Indians, who died in droves from diseases to which they had no immunity. Tragedy also marked the installation of the *encomienda,* a semimanorial system of forced labor, and the efforts to regiment Indian labor on plantations. Most Spanish colonists were ruthless with the Indians.

The record of contact between whites and nonwhites everywhere in the world, however, was marked by harshness and brutality. The Spaniards were perhaps no worse than other conquerors, and they did occasionally make an effort to lessen the cruelties. In 1542 they forbade the enslavement of the Indians. They passed other laws, often flouted, but designed to protect the Indian population. The humanitarian bishop of Chiapas in Mexico, Bartholomew de las Casas (1474–1566), "Father of the Indians," wrote on their behalf.

Everywhere in New Spain missionaries were active. Unlike the Asian or African masses, the Indians were converted to Catholicism. In Paraguay the Jesuits set up among the Guarani Indians a benevolent despotism, a utopia of good order, good habits, and eternal childhood. On the northern fringes of the Spanish Empire, where it would later meet the Anglo-Saxons, a long line of missions in California and the American southwest marked the frontier.

In contrast to the Spanish settlements, the Portuguese in Brazil were far less urbanized. No color line was drawn when the black slaves were imported, and the races became more thoroughly mixed in Brazil than in any Spanish colony except Cuba. The Dutch, French, and British all tried to get chunks of Brazil away from the Portuguese, and the three northern South American states of Surinam (Dutch Guiana), French Guiana, and Guyana (formerly British Guiana) still survive as evidence of this effort.

Competition Begins

Portugal and Spain were the only two European countries to found colonial empires during the sixteenth century. France and England were just beginning their explorations and did not enter the competition in earnest until the seventeenth century. Verrazzano, an Italian in French service, in 1524 explored the North American coast in what is now Canada. Between 1534 and 1541 Jacques Cartier several times sailed into the St. Lawrence River, proceeding as far as the site of Montreal. But the French did not immediately follow up these efforts by settlement.

Nor were the English any quicker to pursue the opportunities in North America, although their agents, the Italians John and Sebastian Cabot, in 1497 and 1498 touched on Nova Scotia, Newfoundland, and the American coast as far south as Delaware. Instead, the English began some six decades later to challenge the Spaniards to the south. In the 1560s, John Hawkins made three voyages into Spanish territory to sell slaves. His nephew Francis Drake attacked Spanish shipping on his celebrated trip around the world (1577–1580)—the first by an Englishman—when he landed in California and claimed it for England under the name of New Albion.

The pace now quickened, as Martin Frobisher explored Labrador and the regions to the north and west. Sir Humphrey Gilbert (1583) claimed Newfoundland for England, and other English explorers began to search for the Northwest Passage. In 1584, Sir Walter Raleigh tried to found a settlement on Roanoke Island (North Carolina), but neither his colonists nor a second group sent out in 1587 survived. All these efforts only faintly foreshadowed the large-scale English seventeenth-century settlements in North America.

III THE NEW MONARCHIES AND THE WARS OF THE SIXTEENTH CENTURY

By the end of the fifteenth century, the centralized Spanish, French, and English "new monarchies" dominated Western Europe. In Central Europe, Germany—the Holy Roman Empire—had no comparable internal unity. Yet under the Hapsburgs the empire, too, entered into competition for supremacy. Italy, with its city-states, attracted outsiders by its riches and its civilization.

Between the Hapsburg lands and the French lay a zone of fragmentation, the pieces of the former Burgundian dukedom. Out of this zone have come the modern nations of Holland, Belgium, Luxembourg, and Switzerland. To the east, lay the feudalized Catholic kingdom of Poland. Beyond it, Muscovite Russia had asserted its supremacy over vast lands. To the southeast, the Ottoman Turks had captured the Balkans, and were threatening Italy and Central Europe.

One after another, Western monarchies tried to dominate the entire western portion of the continent. In the sixteenth century, Spain, from the mid-1600s to 1815, France, in the twentieth century, Germany, tried to weaken and control the others. Each time, the threatened states eventually made alliances against the threat and restored the balance. Each time, England supported or led the coalition against the aggressor. No state, then, succeeded for long in upsetting this "balance of power."

During the sixteenth century, Spain, France, and England all had central foreign offices, paid professional armies, and paid professional diplomats and spies. All had paid professional civilian bureaucrats, a central financial system with some control over taxation, and a central legal system that tried to render uniform justice.

In all, the monarch inherited the throne, and passed it on to his nearest heir. Everywhere he claimed the right to make final decisions and overshadowed the traditional assembly—Spanish Cortes, French Estates-General, English Parliament. But everywhere poor communications limited royal absolutism. Everywhere, too, medieval local privileges and local ways of life survived.

Spain

Charles V and Philip II

Spain was the first power to try to upset the balance of power. In Spain, the Hapsburg Emperor Charles V was King Charles I (reigned 1516–1556). He and his son, Philip II (1556–1598) ruled during most of the century. Brought up in the Low Countries, Charles came to Spain as a stranger who hardly spoke the language. His advisors came from Flanders and thought Spain was an old-fashioned, divided, slow-moving country.

When Charles became Holy Roman Emperor in 1519, he left Spain. Angry that an absentee king was spending Spanish money and using Spanish troops abroad, a group of Spanish cities revolted in 1520. The rebels, called *Comuneros,* included both nobles hostile to the king and members of the lower classes with strong radical aims. The upper-class rebels were frightened by the radicalism of the lower and the revolt was put down in 1521. Thereafter, Charles simply tried not to antagonize the Spaniards.

Marble bust of Philip II, from the workshop of Leone Leoni.

Philip II, on the other hand, was profoundly Spanish in character and attitudes. Self-denying and hard-working, he was a fanatical Catholic. He founded a new system of consultative councils, all manned by nobles, with a council of state at the top. But he himself made all decisions. His personal secretaries and the local authorities—not noble—put them into effect.

Especially in Castile, Philip reduced the power of the Cortes almost to nothing. Nobles and priests no longer could attend, since they paid no taxes, and the delegates from the towns could do little by themselves. Philip thought he did not need to ask the Cortes for money because he was so rich. He received the tax of one-fifth on the cargoes from the New World. Money came in from his own royal estates, from the sale of offices and titles, and even from a royal percentage of the profits of the sale of papal dispensations, not unlike indulgences. He spent it all on foreign wars, and left Spain almost bankrupt in 1598.

His vast domains—Spain, the Low Countries, lands in Italy, the overseas empire in America and the Philippines (named after Philip himself)—had no common organs of consultation. The richest of his subjects were tax exempt. There was no trained civil service. Graft and inefficiency prevailed.

Spanish Regionalism and Mercantilism

Spanish regionalism (see Chapter 7) was extreme. The separate provinces often levied customs dues on each other's goods. The northern provinces that the Muslims had never conquered had many ancient privileges, the *fueros.* Aragon had its own chief justice, the *justicia major,* appointed by the king for life.

If Charles V and Philip II had spent their money in uniting and developing Spain, they might have done wonders. Spain had great agricultural and mineral resources. With its head start on overseas imperial development and its flourishing navy and merchant marine, it had a tremendous opportunity. Instead, the kings spent their gold trying to dominate Europe and to wipe out Protestantism. They had to pay their infantry

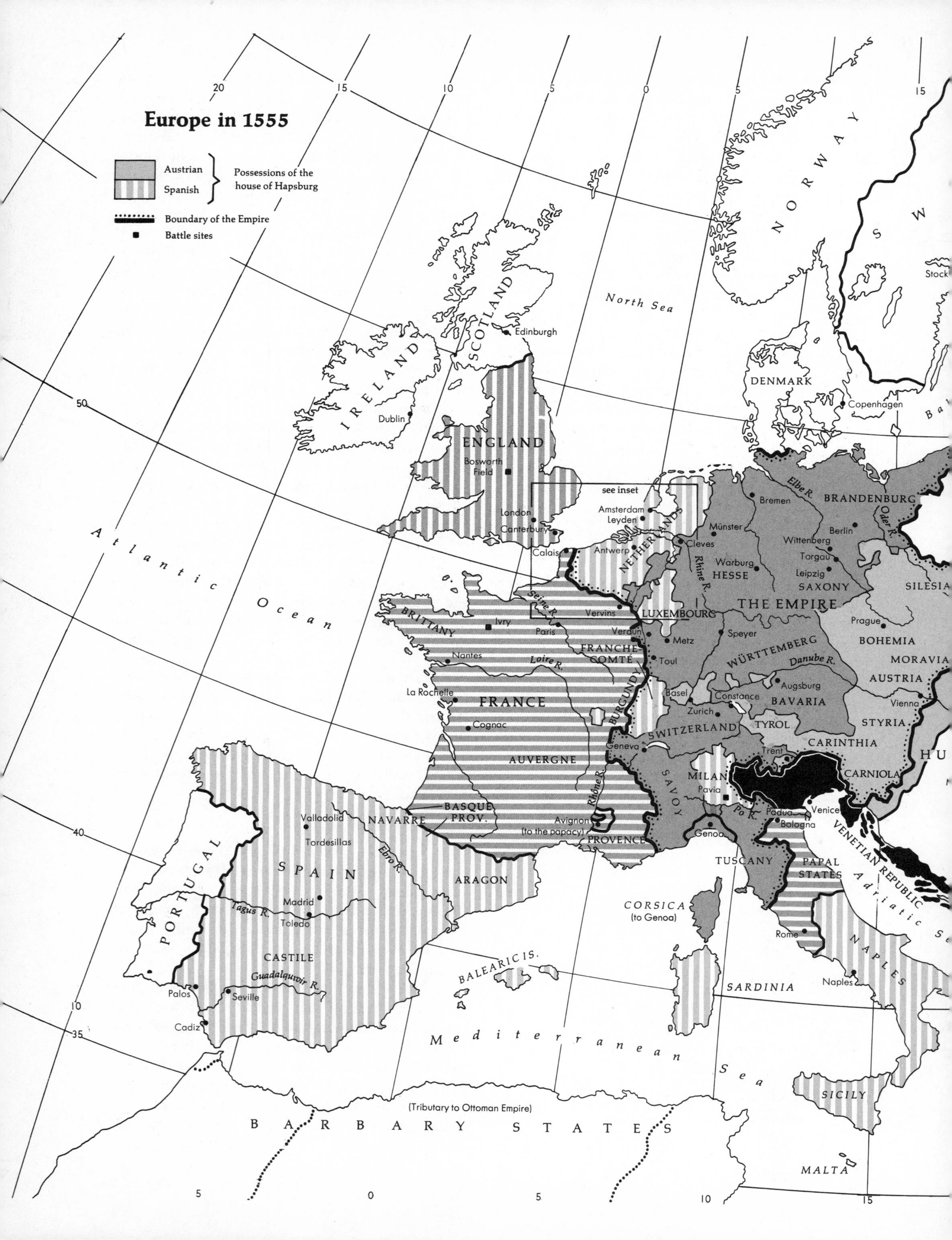

Europe in 1555
Austrian
Spanish
Possessions of the house of Hapsburg
Boundary of the Empire
Battle sites
North Sea
Atlantic Ocean
NORWAY
DENMARK
Copenhagen
SCOTLAND
Edinburgh
IRELAND
Dublin
ENGLAND
Bosworth Field
London
Canterbury
Calais
see inset
Amsterdam
Leyden
Antwerp
NETHERLANDS
Cleves
Münster
Bremen
BRANDENBURG
Elbe R.
Oder R.
Berlin
Wittenberg
Torgau
Leipzig
SAXONY
Warburg
HESSE
Rhine R.
SILESIA
THE EMPIRE
LUXEMBOURG
Vervins
Seine R.
BRITTANY
Ivry
Paris
Verdun
Metz
Toul
Speyer
Prague
BOHEMIA
MORAVIA
AUSTRIA
Vienna
WÜRTTEMBERG
Danube R.
Augsburg
BAVARIA
FRANCHE-COMTÉ
Nantes
Loire R.
La Rochelle
FRANCE
Cognac
BURGUNDY
Basel
Constance
Zurich
SWITZERLAND
TYROL
STYRIA
CARINTHIA
Trent
Geneva
AUVERGNE
SAVOY
MILAN
Pavia
CARNIOLA
Rhône R.
Po R.
Padua
Venice
Bologna
VENETIAN REPUBLIC
BASQUE PROV.
NAVARRE
Avignon (to the papacy)
PROVENCE
Genoa
Valladolid
Tordesillas
Ebro R.
PORTUGAL
SPAIN
ARAGON
TUSCANY
PAPAL STATES
Adriatic Sea
Madrid
Toledo
Tagus R.
CORSICA (to Genoa)
Rome
NAPLES
CASTILE
Guadalquivir R.
BALEARIC IS.
Palos
Seville
Cadiz
SARDINIA
Naples
Mediterranean Sea
SICILY
(Tributary to Ottoman Empire)
BARBARY STATES
MALTA

ENGLAND
North Sea
Amsterdam
Leyden
Utrecht
London
Canterbury
Armada sea fight
Bruges
Antwerp
Calais
FLANDERS
Boulogne
Guinegate
Scheldt R.
ARTOIS
NETHERLANDS
Cambray
Cateau-Cambrésis
FRANCE
TEUTONIC ORDER
Volga R.
Moscow
Oka R.
W. Dvina R.
R U S S I A
Ural R.
PRUSSIA
LITHUANIA
Don R.
Volga R.
LAND
Kiev
UKRAINE
KHANATE
Dnieper R.
OF THE
Dniester R.
CRIMEA
Caspian Sea
TRANSYLVANIA
MOLDAVIA
WALLACHIA
Belgrade
Danube R.
Black Sea
OTTOMAN EMPIRE
MONTE-NEGRO
Constantinople
Salonika
Aegean Sea
Tigris R.
Lepanto
Athens
Euphrates R.
PELOPONNESUS
(to Venice)
RHODES
CRETE
CYPRUS
(to Venice)

forces, the best in Europe. And the money spent on war did not boost Spain's own industrial development. It passed into the hands of foreign bankers and merchants to pay for the manufactured goods needed by the Spanish colonies.

The dominant economic theory of the period—mercantilism—dictated that the mother country should do the manufacturing and the colonies should produce raw materials and buy the finished goods. So Spain forbade the colonies to engage in manufacturing. But, instead of developing its own industry, Spain bought goods abroad. This helped the industries of other states. The Spanish government controlled all enterprise by licensing every export and import to and from the colonies.

In general, the Spanish retained a medieval contempt for business. They preferred war, politics, religion, art, or living like an *hidalgo,* a nobleman (*hijo de algo,* "son of somebody"). Spaniards had too many holidays, took too long a daily nap *(siesta).* There were too many soldiers, priests, monks—all of them unproductive economically. The "capitalist spirit" could not take root in Spain. In the sixteenth century, economic opportunity beckoned and was rebuffed. It never could be recaptured.

Spanish Literature and Painting

Yet the sixteenth-century man could not see all this. Instead, he saw the richest of states, with the best of armies and a magnificent literature and art. Spanish culture reflects a spirit strange to those who know only the books and paintings of other countries: a serious, passionate, unsmiling spirit, fascinated with death and all the details of death, preoccupied with honor and "face," agonized and pious, intensely proud.

Ignatius Loyola the Jesuit represents this Spanish spirit. So do Saint Theresa of Avila (1515–1582), the ascetic and mystical girl who reorganized the Carmelite nunneries and wrote her autobiography, and Saint John of the Cross (1542–1581), her disciple. They did not withdraw from the world of the senses like the ascetics of the early Church, but fought against and almost overcame the necessity of living in the flesh.

In a different way, Miguel de Cervantes (1547–1616) also carries the mark of this Spanish spirit. In his novel, *Don Quixote* (1605), he tells of a gentle elderly knight, half crazed by reading romances of chivalry. Gently Cervantes satirizes the old-fashioned concepts of chivalric behavior, while recognizing that there was something magnificent about self-denial and protecting the innocent that later generations had lost. Speaking for earthy common sense is Don Quixote's devoted squire, Sancho Panza, who shares the loony adventures of his master, but protects him from their worst consequences.

El Greco's "Fray Felix Hortensio Paravicino."

The Spanish spirit was caught also by a painter, El Greco (1541–1614), not a Spaniard at all but a Greek, born Domenico Theotokopouli on the island of Crete and trained both in the Byzantine tradition of the Aegean world and at the school of Titian in Venice. He settled at Toledo in 1575 and lived there the rest of his life. His long, thin personages often turn their eyes upward in piety or simulated piety. His greyish flesh tones contrast with the brilliant colors of landscape and dress. His canvases suggest the Spanish combination of energy and otherworldliness that fostered the Inquisition and built and wasted the first European overseas empire.

France

The Italian Adventure of Charles VIII and Louis XII

Secure at home after the economical reign of Louis XI (see Chapter 7), his two successors, Charles VIII (1483–1498) and Louis XII (1498–1515) embarked on aggressive adventures in Italy. Each had a dynastic claim as an excuse, Charles to Naples and Louis to Milan. Each began with success, Charles taking Naples in 1495, Louis taking Milan in 1499. But each time a league of powers drove the French out. The balance of power thwarted the French, whose Italian wars were only the prelude to the new struggle against the Hapsburgs.

Francis I and the Hapsburg-Valois Wars

The Hapsburg-Valois Wars began under Francis I (reigned 1515–1547), a model Renaissance despot at home in the age of Machiavelli. In 1521, he went to war against Charles V, whose great territorial holdings surrounded France, and whose armies captured Francis in battle in 1525. Charles kept Francis in prison until he signed a treaty giving up French territorial claims in Italy and Burgundy. Francis broke his word; and when the war resumed, Charles V's armies, who had not been paid, ravaged Rome, committing dreadful atrocities. Charles and Francis made peace in 1529 (Cambrai), and the next year Charles became emperor.

Although Francis had been obliged to renounce his Italian claims, he went to war against Charles twice more over Milan. When Charles invaded southern France (1530–1538), Francis allied himself with Suleiman the Magnificent, the Ottoman sultan, who attacked the imperial forces in the Mediterranean and in Hungary. This Catholic-Muslim alliance was a perfectly Machiavellian action. Francis won valuable commercial concessions from the Turks (see Chapter 6). In 1542 the French let the Ottoman fleet use French naval bases. Francis also took as an ally a Protestant German prince who was in rebellion against Charles.

The Second Round: Augsburg and Cateau-Cambrésis

When this war ended in 1544, Charles turned his full strength against the German Protestants. But Francis's son, King Henry II of France (reigned 1547–1559), so effectively helped the Protestants that Charles had to accept the compromise religious Peace of Augsburg (1555). By its terms any Protestant territory could remain Protestant. The principle was called *cuius regio, eius religio,* "Whoever is the ruler of an area may require that it follow his religion." If the elector of Saxony is Lutheran (as he was), Saxony is Lutheran; if the duke of Bavaria is Catholic (as he was), Bavaria is Catholic. The peace said nothing about what should happen to the property of Catholic bishops or abbots who were converted to Protestantism. Also, it made provision for no religion except Catholicism and Lutheranism.

Charles V abdicated in 1556 and spent the last two years of his life in a monastery. His Austrian territories and the title of emperor passed to his brother, Ferdinand. Spain and the rest of the Hapsburg lands went to his son, Philip II. Philip II and Henry II fought the final round in the long struggle begun by their fathers. It ended in 1559 with the Treaty of Cateau-Cambrésis, under which the French won some minor territorial gains. Notable was Calais, the last English possession in France, taken from England, which had been fighting on the Spanish side. Henry died the same year.

Henry II's widow, the Florentine Catholic Catherine de' Medici, greatly influenced her three sons, Francis II (reigned 1559–1560), Charles IX (reigned 1560–1574), and Henry III (reigned 1574–1589). Under these monarchs, the powerful Protestant (Huguenot) minority fought a terrible series of internal religious wars against the dominant Catholic majority that convulsed French society.

The French Wars of Religion

Protestantism in France made a great appeal to the nobles, almost half of whom were Huguenots at the peak of the movement. It also appealed to the middle classes in the towns. It affected the peasantry much less. Regionally, it was strong in the south but scarcely penetrated Brittany, Normandy, or the region of Paris.

For the nobility, conversion to Protestantism was not only a matter of conscience and conviction. It gave them a chance to challenge the centralizing Catholic monarchy and its agents. The French kings had asserted their rights over the French church. Francis I even won from the papacy the right to choose bishops and abbots (1516). Conversion to Protestantism could have brought the kings no more. So, unlike the German princes, they were not tempted to convert.

Between 1562 and 1589 there were no fewer than eight religious wars. In the Saint Bartholomew's Day massacre (1572), thousands of Protestants in Paris and the provinces were dragged from their beds and murdered. The noble house of Guise assumed the command of a Catholic League, while a Huguenot prince, Henry of Navarre, the nearest male heir of the childless King Henry III, took command of the Protestants.

The likelihood that a Protestant would become king caused the Catholic League to redouble its efforts. The Catholics negotiated with Spain, the Protestants with England. The Catholics planned to put on the throne the uncle of Henry of Navarre, not only a Catholic but a cardinal. This prospect horrified public opinion generally.

After fierce fighting and a series of murders, Henry of Navarre—still a Protestant—became king as Henry IV (reigned 1589–1610), first of the House of Bourbon. He defeated the Catholics

Henry IV (Henry of Navarre).

and besieged Paris. He was persuaded that if he himself should accept Catholicism, he could at least obtain toleration for the Huguenots. In 1593 he became Catholic and in 1594 the city surrendered.

In 1598 Henry IV issued the Edict of Nantes, giving the Huguenots a measure of toleration unequaled in any other Catholic country. Citizens of certain cities and towns, and nobles having the old feudal judicial rights, might exercise their religion freely. Public worship by Huguenots was forbidden in and around Paris and in all archiepiscopal and episcopal cities. Such religious concessions alone would probably not have been enough to end the war. But the Huguenots also obtained fortified towns in southwest France where they were strongest, notably the port and fortress of La Rochelle. So they won recognition as a political party in arms, entitled to defend itself. The Edict of Nantes brought religious peace to France.

For almost forty years, France had been torn by war. The men who worked hardest to make peace were moderate Catholics. Michel de l'Hospital (1507–1573) believed that it was un-Christian to try to impose religious conformity by force, although he could not believe that men of different faiths could live peacefully together. He appealed to Protestant and Catholic to submerge their differences in their common Christianity. Jean Bodin (d. 1596) similarly longed for a strong centralized monarchy tempered by the limitations imposed by history and tradition, and thought that the quarreling factions should submerge their differences in loyalty to the French crown. These men and many who shared their views were known as *politiques,* political moralists.

The French Renaissance

Despite the almost constant warfare, sixteenth-century France experienced a cultural renaissance, largely under Italian influence. The French humanist François Rabelais (1494–1553), who began life as a monk, studied the classics, practiced and taught medicine, and created two of the greatest comic figures in literary history, the giant Gargantua and his son Pantagruel. Gargantua helps to found a wonderful unmonastic monastery, the Abbey of Thélème, whose motto is "Do What You Like." Its happy inmates get up and go to bed when they wish and drink and work and sleep whenever they feel like it, and do anything else they please.

Exuberant, fleshly, optimistic, Rabelais is often obscene. His language comes pouring out in a torrent of synonyms, full of energy, sometimes tiring to read. But he recommends self-indulgence. With true humanist zeal, Gargantua wants Pantagruel to learn everything—Arabic, Latin, Hebrew, Greek, all the arts and all the sciences.

Typical of another strain in humanism was Michel de Montaigne (1533–1592). He invented the essay as a literary form, and gave it the name. He wrote about a hundred essays, discussing some of Cicero's favorite subjects like friendship and old age. In a time of brutal intolerance, he taught decency and live-and-let-live. The dry-as-dust lack of originality of the late humanists greatly annoyed him. He wanted free interplay between teacher and student.

Perhaps the single most characteristic monument of the Renaissance in France was the great château. The grim fortress of medieval days was now transformed into a residential palace, often charmingly domesticated, retaining its thick walls and its towers, which now served a decorative rather than a defensive purpose. Many châteaux were built in the peaceful valley of the Loire. Two of the most celebrated are Chambord, built by Francis I, and Chenonceaux, built on a bridge

The Château of Chambord, built by Francis I in the Loire Valley.

over a small river, which Henry II gave to his aging but still beautiful mistress, Diane de Poitiers, and which Catherine de' Medici took from Diane after Henry's death.

In sculpture, Jean Goujon returned to the classical nude as the inspiration for his statues—of Diane de Poitiers as well as of anonymous nymphs. In painting, the French had no artists of the stature of the great Italians and Spaniards of the sixteenth century. However, they did produce a school of portraitists, including Clouet and Fouquet, who left sensitive and realistic likenesses of the men and women of the court.

As a center for the court, Francis remodeled the Louvre, the royal residence in Paris. He employed both Leonardo da Vinci and Benvenuto Cellini. Catherine de' Medici imported new Italian influences. In behavior as well as in decoration, the French court followed Italian precedents.

England

The Tudor Monarchy of Henry VIII and Elizabeth I

Henry VIII (reigned 1509–1547), the instigator of the Anglican Reformation, was a fat man, lavishly bejeweled, with shrewd little eyes staring out of his broad face fringed with beard, his velvet hat on one side. Six times married, self-willed, intelligent, and personally extravagant, he was economical where it counted.

While the Spanish royal house squandered its wealth in war, Henry contented himself with much cheaper pleasures. He never risked big English armies on the Continent, but intervened inexpensively to maintain the balance of power when necessary. Using the proceeds of confiscated monastic properties (see p. 244), he created a whole new class of loyal nobles. He strengthened the central administration and maintained supervision of the justices of the peace, who continued to be the keystone of English local government (see Chapter 5).

Henry's parliaments granted him what he wanted. The Tudor House of Lords had a safe majority of Henry's newly ennobled men, who, like the bishops of the new church (after 1534), owed their place in the House to him. As for the House of Commons, a small minority of the people chose these knights of the shire and burgesses of the towns. In the countryside, only freeholders voted, not the majority of the residents, who were tenant farmers or agricultural workers. The country gentlemen and squires chose their representatives from among themselves. In the towns, too, the franchise was usually a narrow one.

Yet the very combination of knights of the shire and burgesses meeting together made the Tudor House of Commons unique among contemporary European assemblies, since the third estate on the Continent usually represented townsmen only. In England, too, unlike the Continent, only the eldest sons of noblemen, who actually inherited the title, could sit in the House of Lords. The younger ones were eligible to sit in the House of Commons and had to seek representation there. Finally, the English Parliament,

Queen Elizabeth I: "The Rainbow Portrait."

unlike continental assemblies, had during the Middle Ages acquired the right to legislate, especially on money.

Why did the Tudor parliaments not quarrel with the monarch, as the Stuart parliaments would do in the seventeenth century? In part because they owed the king so much gratitude. In part, too, because the Tudor monarchs, Henry VIII and Elizabeth I particularly, were persuasive and popular, symbolizing in their own glittering persons the national sense of patriotism and of hostility to Spain and the Roman Church.

We have already seen Elizabeth I (reigned 1558–1603) completing the establishment of the Church of England. Elizabeth's name has become a synonym for the flowering of English achievement and self-confidence in every field of endeavor. Her people loved her more than did those who knew her best. Proud, cool, and remarkably intelligent, she loved flattery but never let it lead her astray when important matters were at stake. She more than held her own among her contemporaries as a Machiavellian statesman. She never married, and in her early years she played off foreign and domestic suitors against each other with excellent results. Under her able ministers Burleigh and Walsingham, she maintained and heightened the administrative efficiency of her government.

The Spanish and Mary, Queen of Scots

Elizabeth's chief problem was the hostility of Philip II, who had been married to her Catholic half-sister Mary. Philip resented both the very existence of a Protestant England and the beginnings of English penetration into the Spanish New World. Had he been able to concentrate on England, especially early in Elizabeth's reign, her position would have been precarious. But first he hoped to marry Elizabeth, then he hoped to capitalize on her fears that the French would succeed in backing Mary, Queen of Scots, against her, then he was delayed by a great Dutch revolt.

Mary Stuart, Queen of Scots, great-granddaughter of Henry VII and heiress to Scotland, was a Catholic and half a Guise. She lived in France, while her mother acted as regent for her in Scotland. She married the short-lived King Francis II of France (reigned 1559–1560) and took the title of Queen of England as well as Queen of Scots. Since Catholics regarded Elizabeth as illegitimate, Mary might have given Elizabeth a very anxious time if she had been able to combine Scottish with French support.

But in 1555, the Calvinist John Knox returned to Scotland from Geneva and found the country ready for his preaching. The Scots had come to associate Catholicism with the hated French. In 1557 Scottish nobles signed the first agreement (covenant) to defend Protestantism. In 1559 they revolted against Mary's mother, Mary of Guise; and in 1560 Elizabeth helped them oust the French troops.

So when Mary Stuart returned to Scotland in 1561, after the death of Francis II, she found a Presbyterian church, the authority of which resided in the elders of each congregation, who could not be easily dominated by a monarch. Mary's reckless love affairs, punctuated with murder and scandal, made her extremely unpopular.

In 1568 a revolution forced her to take refuge in England. Elizabeth put her under house arrest and had her executed in 1587 for involvement in an alleged plot. Mary left behind an infant son, later James I of England (and VI of Scotland), whose father was Mary's second husband, Lord Darnley.

The Dutch Revolt and the Armada

When Philip II came to power in 1556, it was bad news for the Dutch Protestants, whose privileges had been safe under Charles V. Philip tried to curb feudal and municipal liberties of the Netherlands. He sent Spanish garrisons and tried to enforce edicts against heretics. This effort to enforce Spanish mercantilist policies threatened to stifle Dutch trade.

The battle between the English fleet and the Spanish armada, 1588.

Political, religious, and economic tensions prompted all classes of the Dutch to revolt. Philip sent the ruthless duke of Alba against them. Even the Catholic southern provinces (modern Belgium) joined the northern Protestant ones (Holland) in revolt. In 1578 Philip compromised and won back the southern provinces by political concessions. They have remained basically Catholic ever since.

But Philip could not bring himself to make the religious concessions that alone would have calmed the Dutch. In 1581 they declared themselves independent of Spain. The assassination of the prince of Orange, William the Silent (1584), gave them a national Protestant martyr and strengthened their determination.

At this point Queen Elizabeth came to their aid. She had always sympathized with the Dutch, but had so far hesitated to take on the powerful Spaniards, fearing that the French Catholic party and the Spaniards might unite against her. But a series of crude Spanish plots against Elizabeth's life and throne had aroused public opinion. In 1585 she sent troops to Holland. After she executed Mary Queen of Scots (1587), Philip declared open war.

The great fleet (Armada) that Philip sent out in 1588 was defeated in the English Channel by a lighter, skillfully maneuvered English fleet. A storm ("the Protestant wind") north of Scotland scattered and destroyed what was left of the Spaniards. With this battle, Spain's predominance in Europe began to fade. English might at sea was established. And the Dutch were well on their way to independence, which was virtually achieved in 1609.

Ireland

Elizabeth's last years were marked by a great crisis in Ireland. Henry VIII had put the Irish Parliament completely under English control. His Act of Supremacy, combined with the decision (1542) that the king of England was also king of Ireland, required the Catholic Irish to acknowledge the English monarch as head of the Church. In Ireland most of the Norman and English settlers had been assimilated to Irish ways, spoke the native Irish Gaelic, and remained Catholic. Chieftains regarded themselves as local kings, commanded the loyalty of their followers in war, and were still incited to battle by a professional class of bards. Ireland had only a few Protestant English inhabitants settled near Dublin. Thus the insurrection of 1597 led by "the O'Neill," whom Elizabeth had made earl of Tyrone, was a serious affair. It was not suppressed until 1601, and the Irish Question in its various phases has remained to trouble English governments into our own day.

READING SUGGESTIONS on Transition to a New World: Religious Upheaval, Expansion Overseas, Dynastic Conflict (Asterisks indicate paperback.)

The Protestant Reformation: General Accounts

O. Chadwick, *The Reformation* (*Penguin). Excellent introductory survey.

E. H. Harbison, *The Age of Reformation* (*Cornell). Brief, perceptive, summary study.

R. H. Bainton, *The Reformation of the Sixteenth Century* (*Beacon). Excellent introduction by a Protestant scholar.

G. R. Elton, *Reformation Europe, 1517–1559* (*Harper Torchbooks). Limited to the European continent, but very good. Summarizes the views of the far more detailed *New Cambridge Modern History,* Vol. II, which Elton edited.

A. G. Dickens, *Reformation and Society in Sixteenth-Century Europe* (*Holt). Well-illustrated single-volume survey.

H. J. Grimm, *The Reformation Era,* 2nd ed. (1973). A sound textbook.

Protestant Leaders and Movements

R. H. Bainton, *Here I Stand: A Biography of Martin Luther* (*Mentor). Sympathetic, scholarly, readable.

E. Erikson, *Young Man Luther* (*Norton). A noted psychoanalyst and psychoanalytical theorist explains Luther's "identity crisis."

E. G. Schwiebert, *Luther and His Times* (1952). Strongly Lutheran in outlook; especially good on the setting and impact of Luther's revolt.

J. Courvoisier, *Zwingli: A Reformed Theologian* (*John Knox). The best single study of this important and often neglected leader.

G. Harkness, *John Calvin: The Man and His Ethics* (*Apex). A good brief introduction.

F. Wendel, *Calvin: The Origins and Development of His Religious Thought* (1963). Full study of Calvinist ideas in their setting by a French scholar.

W. Walker, *John Calvin: The Organizer of Reformed Protestantism* (*Schocken). A good biography.

J. T. McNeill, *The History and Character of Calvinism* (*Oxford). An excellent recent study of the Calvinist movement.

J. J. Scarisbrick, *Henry VIII* (*California). The best single biography.

A. G. Dickens, *The English Reformation* (*Schocken). Comes down to 1559 and includes an excellent bibliography.

G. H. Williams, *The Radical Reformation* (1962). Very full study of the Anabaptists and other radical Protestant sects.

F. H. Littell, *The Anabaptist View of the Church* (1952). Useful brief account.

M. Weber, *The Protestant Ethic and the Spirit of Capitalism* (*Scribners). The first formulation of the controversial theory of the close connection between Protestant religion and economic advance.

R. H. Tawney, *Religion and the Rise of Capitalism* (*Mentor). Stands Weber on his head by emphasizing economic motivation.

E. Troeltsch, *Protestantism and Progress* (*Beacon). A leading religious philosopher discusses the question.

The Catholic Reformation

H. Daniel-Rops, *The Catholic Reformation,* 2 vols. (*Image). A fine, detailed account by a French Catholic scholar.

A. G. Dickens, *The Counter-Reformation* (*Holt). An Anglican writes a comprehensive study of the subject.

R. Fülop-Miller, *Jesuits: A History of the Society of Jesus* (*Capricorn), by a Catholic; and H. Boehmer, *The Jesuits,* trans. P. Strodach (1928), by a Protestant.

The Fist Overseas Empires

J. H. Parry, *The Age of Reconnaissance* (*Mentor), and *The Establishment of the European Hegemony, 1415–1715: Trade and Expansion in the Age of the Renaissance* (*Harper Torchbooks). Excellent introductions by a leading expert.

C. E. Nowell, *The Great Discoveries and the First Colonial Empires* (*Cornell). A useful short survey.

B. Penrose, *Travel and Discovery in the Renaissance 1420–1620* (*Atheneum). Very useful; includes accounts of voyages not easily available elsewhere.

C. R. Boxer, *Four Centuries of Portuguese Expansion* (*California). By the world's leading authority on the Portuguese overseas empire.

S. E. Morison, *Christopher Columbus, Mariner* (*Mentor). A brief version of the author's much longer classic, *Admiral of the Ocean Sea,* 2 vols. (1942).

C. H. Haring, *The Spanish Empire in America* (*Harcourt). Standard brief treatment.

L. B. Hanke, *The Spanish Struggle for Justice in the Conquest of America* (*Little, Brown). A subject often slighted or ignored and yet of great importance.

W. H. Prescott, *The Portable Prescott* (*Viking). Gives useful selections from this great American pioneer scholar's famous works, *The Conquest of Mexico* (*Modern Library) and *The Conquest of Peru* (*Dolphin).

H. Labouret, *Africa before the White Man* (1963); B. Davidson, *Africa in History* (1969). Good introductory volumes.

R. Oliver and J. D. Page, *A Short History of Africa* (*Penguin). Very brief on the period in this chapter.

D. F. Lach, *China in the Eyes of Europe: The Sixteenth Century* (*Phoenix), and the same author's parallel works (*all Phoenix) on India, Japan, and Southeast Asia.

K. S. Latourette, *China* (*Spectrum). Good introduction.

A. S. Basham, *The Wonder That Was India* (*Evergreen). India before the Muslim invasions.

R. E. Poppino, *Brazil: The Land and People* (*Oxford). Social and economic study.

The New Monarchies and the Wars of the Sixteenth Century (See also the lists for Chapters 7 and 9)

M. R. O'Connell, *The Counter-Reformation, 1559–1610* (*Harper Torchbooks). Useful study with a good bibliography.

K. Brandi, *The Emperor Charles V* (*Humanities). A good biography.

C. Petrie, *Philip II of Spain* (1963). A useful biographical study.

J. Lynch, *Spain under the Hapsburgs* (1964). Volume I treats the sixteenth century.

R. T. Davies, *The Golden Century of Spain* (*Harper Torchbooks). For the general reader.

J. E. Neale, *The Age of Catherine de' Medici* (*Harper Torchbooks). Short and clear introduction to a complex and tormented period.

Q. Hurst, *Henry of Navarre* (1938). A solid biography.

C. Read, *The Tudors* (*Norton). Good very brief introduction. See also the same author's *The Government of England under Elizabeth* (*Virginia).

S. T. Bindoff, *Tudor England* (*Penguin). An overall introduction, solid and reliable.

G. R. Elton, *The Tudor Revolution in Government* (*Cambridge). Breaks new ground in its study of the bureaucracy.

L. B. Smith, *Henry VIII: The Mask of Royalty* (*Sentry). Interesting psychological study, for the more adventurous reader than Scarisbrick's book (see above).

W. MacCaffrey, *The Shaping of the Elizabethan Regime* (*Princeton). A fine study of Queen Elizabeth I's early years on the throne.

G. Mattingly, *The Armada* (*Sentry). A truly splendid historical work.

P. Geyl, *The Revolt of the Netherlands, 1555–1609* (*Barnes and Noble). By a distinguished Dutch historian who lamented the fact that the Flemings and Dutch were separated.

C. V. Wedgwood, *William the Silent* (*Norton). Fine study of the Dutch national hero.

CHAPTER NINE

The Seventeenth Century: War, Politics, And Empire

In this chapter we deal with the 1600s and the first few years of the 1700s. Modern complexity has set in. Within each state domestic issues are closely related to foreign issues. Political issues and religious issues are so intertwined that matters which at first seem political prove to have important religious implications, and the other way around. Economic and social values become tangled up with politics and religion.

We have already seen, for example, that the French nobles who turned to Calvinism did so in part to defend their traditional privileges against the encroachments of the king. Queen Elizabeth helped the Dutch against the Spaniards partly because the Dutch were fellow Protestants but more because of Philip II's threat to herself. The Catholic Reformation failed to win back some areas of Europe because Hapsburgs headed the Catholic cause, and many powerful Catholics who otherwise would have helped Rome did not want to help the Hapsburgs. The papacy itself was determined to avoid Hapsburg domination.

The Peace of Augsburg of 1555, the triumph of Henry IV in France, and the execution of Mary

Queen of Scots all contributed to the containment of Hapsburg power. But in 1598, when the Hapsburg Philip II died in his colossal monastic palace of the Escorial in the bleak hills near Madrid with an open coffin standing at his order beside his bed, and a skull grinning at him beneath a golden crown, all these related problems remained unsettled.

We turn first to the continental political and religious struggle known as the Thirty Years' War (1618–1648). It had an earlier background in the Low Countries, Spain, and Germany. It convulsed the German lands and ended in the Peace of Westphalia (1648).

England's part in the Thirty Years' War was small, because the Stuart monarchy, new in 1603, created so tense a situation at home that it led to the Civil War, which lasted from 1642 to 1649. The king was executed and a republic established for eleven years. Even after the Stuarts were restored in 1660, the mingled religious and political issues remained unsettled until a new overturn in 1688. To this revolution and its aftermath we devote the second part of this chapter. It was of the utmost importance for future American attitudes toward government.

In the third section we examine the political, religious, and economic developments in France throughout the century. After the 1640s, King Louis XIV personifies the country. Crown and governmental machinery, economic policy, religious issues, and especially Louis's efforts to dominate Europe all pass in review.

And in the final portion we turn to the imperial developments of the century—the growth of English and French overseas empires in America, Asia, and Africa, and their involvement in the affairs of the mother countries. Here and from now on our view must be not merely continental but global.

I THE THIRTY YEARS' WAR

The Dutch and Spanish Background

After the Dutch had won the truce of 1609 with Spain and so achieved independence, they took a leading part in European affairs. Each of the seven "United Provinces" of the Dutch Republic preserved its local traditions of government and sent delegates (the *Hooge Moogende,* High Mightinesses) to the Estates-General, which was more like a diplomatic congress than a central legislature. Each province elected its own chief executive, the *Stadholder,* but often several of them elected the same man. After the truce of 1609, Maurice, prince of Orange, son of William the Silent, was chosen Stadholder by five of the seven.

Religious differences also divided the Dutch nation. There was a large Catholic minority. The Protestant majority was split between orthodox Calvinists and moderates called Arminians (after Arminius, a Dutch theologian). Arminians believed that people's behavior in this life might change God's original intentions about their salvation hereafter. So for them, predestination was not unchangeable.

The Dutch were the world's best businessmen. By the early seventeenth century they controlled most of the coastwise shipping of Europe. They went into the wine business in France and into the fishing grounds of the Arctic. In 1602 they organized the Dutch East India Company and soon launched other ventures overseas.

The Bank of Amsterdam (1609) minted its own florins, which became standard in Europe. Its services to its depositors were so much in demand that Amsterdam became the financial capital of Europe. The Dutch invented life insurance and made it a big business. Diamond-cutting, shipbuilding, gin-distilling, and tulip-growing all made the Dutch provinces rich and famous. Their opulent middle-class way of life is mirrored in the domestic scenes and lifelike portraits of Hals, Vermeer, and Rembrandt.

No wonder Philip II's Hapsburg successors in Spain dreamed of reconquering the United Provinces. Although, as we have seen (Chapter 8), Spanish strength was declining by the seventeenth century, Spain still had the wealth of the Americas, the military manpower of north Italy, and the loyalty of the Catholic Belgian provinces.

After the Dutch revolt, the Spaniards wanted to stabilize a line of communications between their Italian and Belgian lands, so that they could move men and money over the Alps and down the Rhine. This route crossed the lands of some rulers who were friendly to the Hapsburgs and others who were hostile. The Dutch worked hard to deny this communication line to the Spaniards. So did the French, who were still working to break Hapsburg encirclement of France.

The German Background

Geographically, of course, Germany was the key. By the early seventeenth century, it had be-

The emperor Rudolf II, king of Bohemia 1575–1611, shown with the electors on a Bohemian enameled glass beaker.

come a truly fantastic conglomeration of states. Some of the German principalities had been divided and subdivided until an "independent" princeling might rule over only a village or a few hundred acres of forest. Free cities acknowledged no authority but the emperor. Some of them held vast lands outside their walls, others not. The Church governed certain cities and regions which also varied greatly in size. There were more than two thousand governing authorities. Since many of the smaller ones combined or reached understandings locally, this number can be reduced to perhaps three hundred.

Particularly influential were the seven electors, who chose each new emperor. One elector, the king of Bohemia, was in practice always a Hapsburg, so that the imperial family always had at least one vote at election time. Three electors were Catholic—the archbishops of Mainz, Trier, and Cologne. The electors of Saxony and Brandenburg were Lutheran. The elector of the Palatinate, with his capital at Heidelberg, was a Calvinist. His lands, in a rich vineyard area along the Rhine, blocked the Hapsburg communication line to the Low Countries. Some princes who were not electors were very powerful anyhow, especially the Catholic duke of Bavaria.

All this naturally weakened the central institutions of the empire. The imperial diet, consisting in theory of all the independent German rulers, always quarreled when it met. Some princes refused to accept its decisions. The emperor had to try to rule by decree and pressure.

So Germany had no machinery to deal with

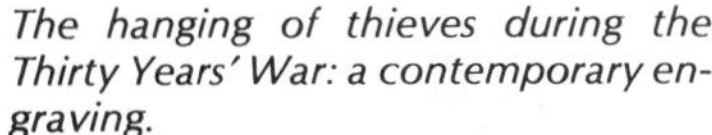

The hanging of thieves during the Thirty Years' War: a contemporary engraving.

the religious difficulties arising from the Peace of Augsburg of 1555 (see p. 259). This peace had not even recognized Calvinism. But after 1555 Calvinism spread rapidly both in Lutheran and in Catholic areas. Where a prince was suddenly converted, all his subjects either had to follow his lead or be persecuted. This led to riots and disorder. In 1600 the Calvinist princes formed the Calvinist Protestant Union, in 1609 the Catholics the Catholic League under Maximilian of Bavaria.

War broke out in Germany in 1618. It lasted for thirty years, drew in all the important states of western Europe, and devastated and depopulated Germany. Its grim progress is best understood if one divides the thirty long years into a Bohemian period (1618–1625), a Danish period (1625–1629), a Swedish period (1629–1635), and a Swedish and French period (1635–1648).

Count Wallenstein: a portrait by Van Dyck.

The Bohemian Period, 1618–1625

Among the seven electorates the kingdom of Bohemia, as the only one held by a Catholic layman, assumed special importance. Since the other three Catholic electorates were always held by archbishops, Bohemia offered the only hope for the Protestants ever to get a majority of four of the seven electoral votes. So, Frederick of the Palatinate, head of the Protestant League in 1618, had his eye on Bohemia. Moreover, in German-dominated Bohemia, the native Czechs expressed their national antagonism to Germans by following the religious teachings of John Hus (p. 207), which included the practice of giving both wine and bread to the laity in communion *(utraquism).*

With the emperor Matthias (reigned 1612–1619) both old and childless, and Ferdinand of Hapsburg, a strong Catholic, slated to become king of Bohemia and emperor, Protestants took alarm, despite Ferdinand's promise that they would have freedom of worship. In 1618, the arrest of some Protestants touched off a revolt in Prague. Two Catholic imperial governors were thrown out of a window into a courtyard seventy feet below, and were saved only by landing in a pile of dung.

The Czechs offered the kingship of Bohemia to Frederick of the Palatinate, who went to Prague. But he left his Rhineland holdings, so coveted by Spain, without adequate defenses, and the Spaniards occupied them. Everywhere in the empire, Catholics rallied against the rebellion. Ferdinand of Hapsburg was duly chosen emperor (1619), and Maximilian of Bavaria, head of the Catholic League, defeated the Czechs (1620). Maximilian got Frederick's electoral post for Bavaria. In Bohemia, Ferdinand took a fierce revenge against utraquists and Calvinists, sparing Lutherans because of obligations to the Lutheran princes. Frederick of the Palatinate fled Bohemia.

But the continued Spanish occupation of the Palatinate frightened the Protestant Dutch and Danes, as well as the Catholic French, who faced a new Hapsburg encirclement. Cardinal Richelieu, emerging as chief minister of King Louis XIII (reigned 1610–1643), was ready to join the Protestant rulers of Europe, including the English, against the growth of Hapsburg power. Even the pope looked understandingly on the growth of this French-Protestant coalition, fearing unchecked Hapsburg preponderance. New Catholic victories over Frederick of the Palatinate (1625), and Ferdinand's transfer of Frederick's lands to Maximilian of Bavaria gave still more urgency to the anti-Hapsburg cause.

The Danish Period, 1625–1629

For the next four years, however, only Christian IV of Denmark (1588–1648) bore the burden of the Protestant struggle. It proved too much for him, since he was opposed not only by Maximilian's Catholic League, but by the private Catholic armies of Count Wallenstein. A convert to Catholicism, Wallenstein bought up a quarter of the lands of Bohemia after Ferdinand had defeated the Czechs, and was now dreaming of converting Germany into a new-model monarchy. The Catholic forces defeated the Danes and moved into Denmark. Christian IV promised in the Treaty of Lübeck (1629) never again to interfere in Germany.

The victorious emperor Ferdinand celebrated his triumph by the Edict of Restitution (1629). It reaffirmed the Peace of Augsburg of 1555, still making no provision for Calvinists. And it turned back to Catholics all Church property that had passed to the Lutherans since 1551. Throughout northern and western Germany many Lutherans were dispossessed, and boundaries were changed. By his behavior Ferdinand showed that the Hapsburgs were ruthless to defeated enemies and that the Protestants had nothing to hope for. From then on it became the chief Protestant goal to overthrow the Edict of Restitution.

The victory still further enriched Wallenstein, who planned to open the Baltic to the Spaniards and let them attack the Dutch from the rear. Wallenstein's ambitions and independence led Ferdinand to dismiss him. But the Catholic armies now had to face Swedish armed intervention.

The Swedish Period, 1630–1635

King Gustavus Adolphus of Sweden (reigned 1611–1632), a first-rate administrator and general, had checked his own nobility at home and defeated the Russians and Poles abroad. He was a devout Lutheran himself and tolerant to Calvinists. With an efficient army, subsidized by Richelieu, Gustavus now joined the German Protestant forces of the electors of Saxony and Brandenburg. The terrible sack of Magdeburg by the Catholics in 1631, followed by a massacre of 20,000 Protestants, galvanized the Protestant resistance.

The Protestant counteroffensive of 1631 and 1632 not only recovered northern Germany but captured much of the southern Catholic territory as well. Prague fell to the Saxons, fighting for Frederick of the Palatinate. Gustavus Adolphus took Mainz and Frankfort. At Lützen he defeated Wallenstein, who had returned to Ferdinand's service, but Gustavus Adolphus himself was killed in the battle (1632). He had planned to become emperor and to reorganize Germany, uniting Lutheran and Calvinist churches.

Famine and plague ravaged the war-stricken lands of Germany. But fighting continued, as Gustavus Adolphus' chancellor, Oxenstierna, became chief of the Protestant cause. Wallenstein's power was diminishing, as Ferdinand suspected him of treachery, and in 1634 he was murdered by an assassin, whom Ferdinand rewarded. In the same year, Ferdinand won a victory at Nordlingen. This meant that Swedish influence lessened and French increased. Richelieu wanted the war to continue in order to further France's territorial ambitions in the Rhineland.

The Swedish and French Period, 1635–1648

In the final phase of the Thirty Years' War, the Protestant cause was dependent upon a French Catholic cardinal. Protestant commanders had to promise that after the war Catholics would not be persecuted in Germany. The religious character of the conflict became less important and the dynastic character more important. In both Hapsburg and Bourbon armies, mercenaries from every nation in Europe took service, switching sides when they thought it advantageous, taking their women and children with them everywhere.

By abandoning the Edict of Restitution at last in 1635, Emperor Ferdinand was able to make a separate peace with most of the Lutheran princes. Richelieu himself had to declare war on Spain to keep the war going. French, Swedes, and a few Calvinist princes struggled on in Germany against the Hapsburgs. The four years between 1639 and 1643 saw the destruction of Spanish hopes. The Dutch defeated the Spanish fleet at sea. Portugal, annexed by Philip II in 1580, revolted in 1640. The French won the battle of Rocroy (1643), and the ambitions of Charles V and Philip II were ended forever.

French policies continued unaltered after the deaths of Richelieu (1642) and King Louis XIII (1643). Negotiations for peace began in 1643 and took five years to complete, as fighting continued sporadically. The issues were many and complex. The Dutch made a separate peace with Spain. And finally on October 24, 1648, the Peace of Westphalia, the first major international settlement of modern times, brought the wretched war to an end at last.

The Peace of Westphalia: Impact of the War

The peace extended the principles of the Peace of Augsburg to Calvinists as well as Lutherans and Catholics. For the status of Church prop-

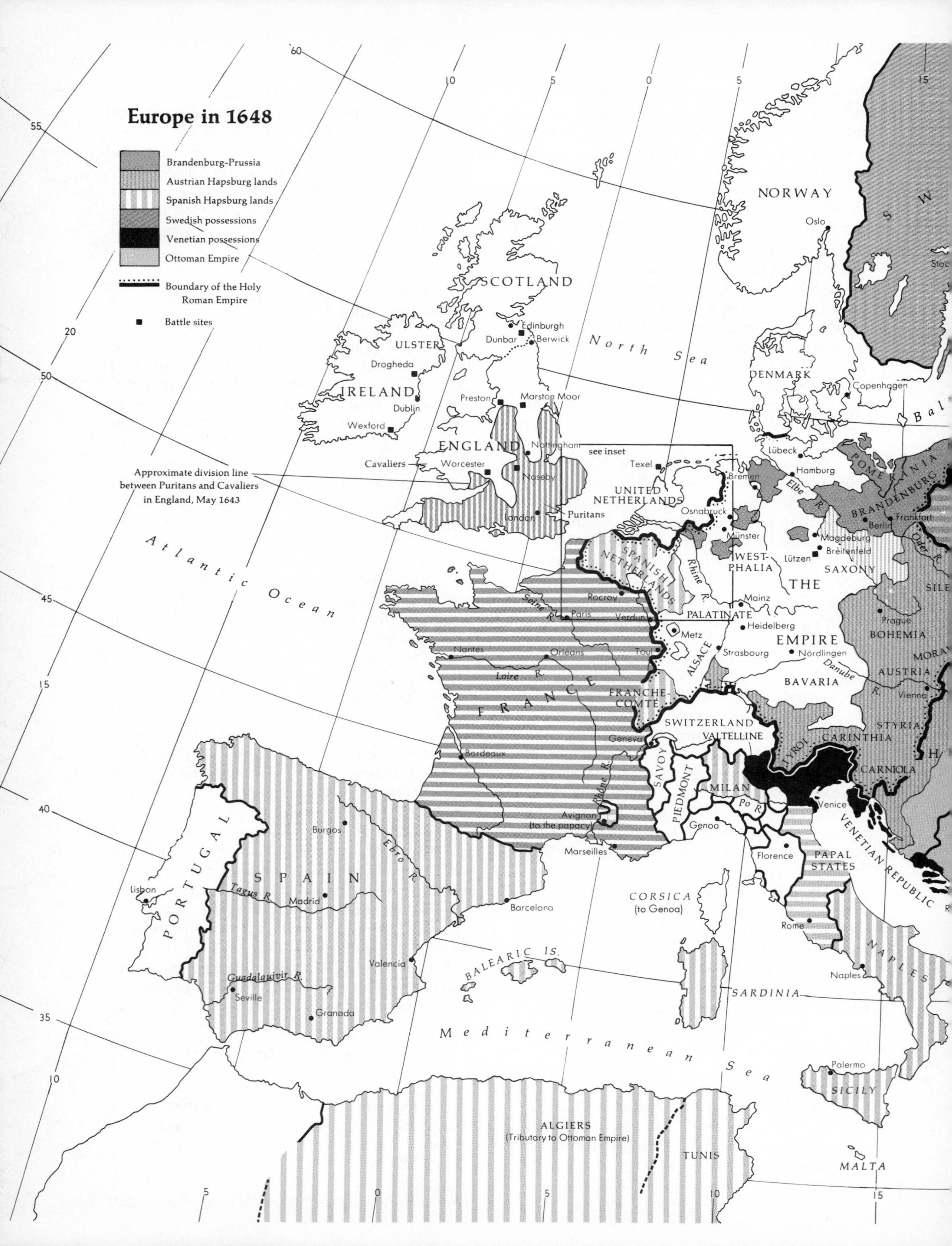

Europe in 1648
Brandenburg-Prussia
Austrian Hapsburg lands
Spanish Hapsburg lands
Swedish possessions
Venetian possessions
Ottoman Empire
Boundary of the Holy Roman Empire
Battle sites
Approximate division line between Puritans and Cavaliers in England, May 1643
SCOTLAND
ULSTER
IRELAND
ENGLAND
Edinburgh
Dunbar
Berwick
Drogheda
Dublin
Wexford
Preston
Marston Moor
Nottingham
Cavaliers
Worcester
Naseby
London
Puritans
see inset
NORWAY
Oslo
DENMARK
Copenhagen
North Sea
Atlantic Ocean
UNITED NETHERLANDS
Texel
SPANISH NETHERLANDS
Lübeck
Hamburg
Bremen
POMERANIA
BRANDENBURG
Berlin
Frankfort
Osnabruck
Münster
WESTPHALIA
Magdeburg
Breitenfeld
Lützen
SAXONY
THE EMPIRE
Mainz
PALATINATE
Heidelberg
Rocroy
Paris
Verdun
Metz
Toul
ALSACE
Strasbourg
Nördlingen
BAVARIA
Prague
BOHEMIA
AUSTRIA
Vienna
STYRIA
CARINTHIA
CARNIOLA
TYROL
Elbe R.
Oder R.
Rhine R.
Seine R.
Loire R.
Danube R.
Rhône R.
Po R.
Ebro R.
Tagus R.
Guadalquivir R.
FRANCE
Nantes
Orléans
Bordeaux
FRANCHE-COMTÉ
SWITZERLAND
VALTELLINE
Geneva
SAVOY
PIEDMONT
MILAN
Genoa
Venice
Avignon (to the papacy)
Marseilles
Florence
PAPAL STATES
VENETIAN REPUBLIC
Rome
NAPLES
Naples
PORTUGAL
Lisbon
SPAIN
Burgos
Madrid
Barcelona
Valencia
Seville
Granada
CORSICA (to Genoa)
BALEARIC IS.
SARDINIA
Mediterranean Sea
Palermo
SICILY
MALTA
ALGIERS (Tributary to Ottoman Empire)
TUNIS

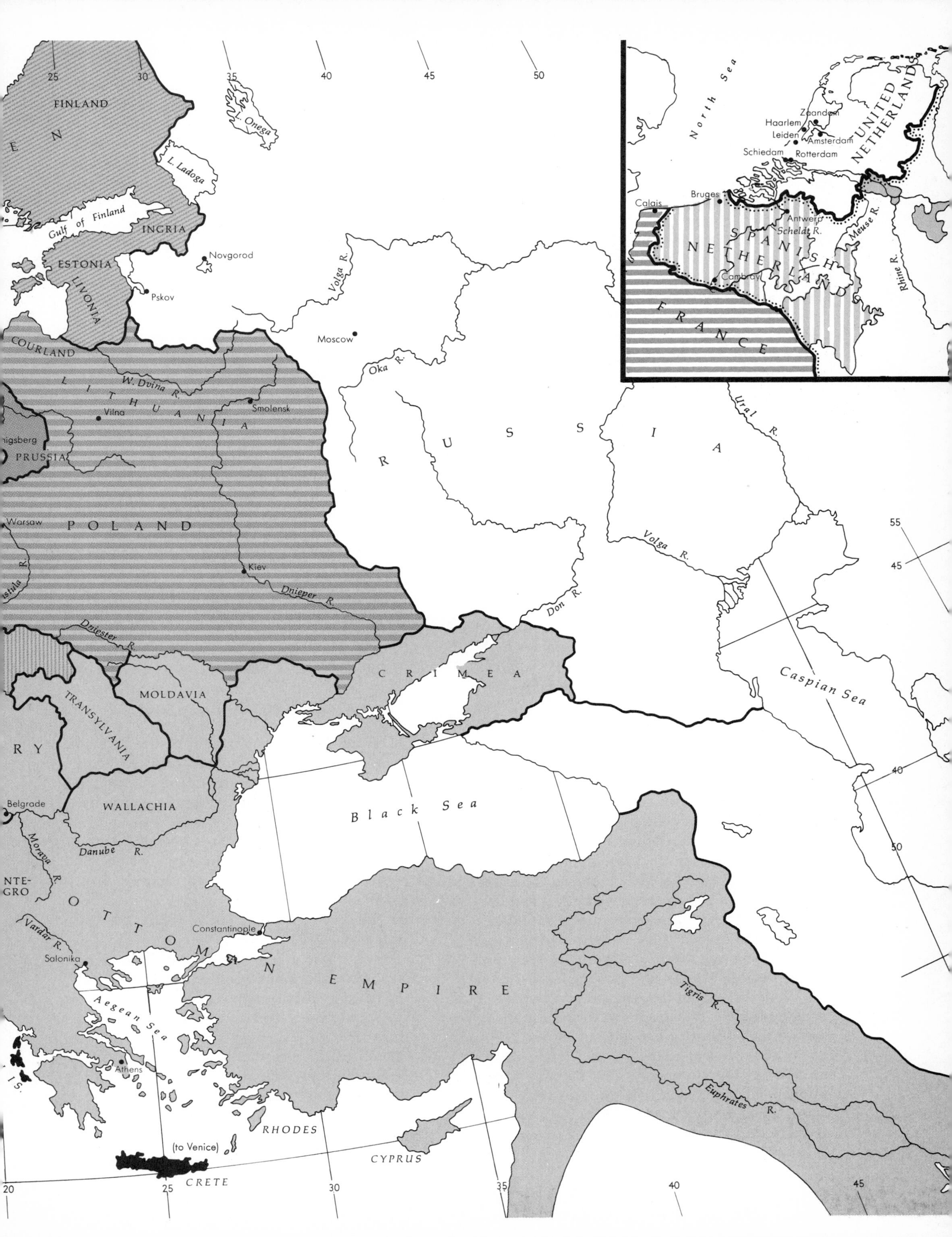

FINLAND
L. Onega
L. Ladoga
Gulf of Finland
INGRIA
ESTONIA
LIVONIA
Novgorod
Pskov
COURLAND
LITHUANIA
W. Dvina R.
Vilna
Smolensk
PRUSSIA
POLAND
Warsaw
Kiev
Dnieper R.
Dniester R.
MOLDAVIA
TRANSYLVANIA
WALLACHIA
Belgrade
Danube R.
Morava R.
OTTOMAN EMPIRE
Vardar R.
Salonika
Constantinople
Aegean Sea
Athens
RHODES
(to Venice)
CRETE
CYPRUS
CRIMEA
Black Sea
Moscow
Oka R.
Volga R.
RUSSIA
Don R.
Ural R.
Caspian Sea
Tigris R.
Euphrates R.
North Sea
UNITED NETHERLANDS
Zaandam
Haarlem
Leiden
Amsterdam
Schiedam
Rotterdam
Bruges
Calais
Antwerp
Scheldt R.
SPANISH NETHERLANDS
Cambray
Meuse R.
Rhine R.
FRANCE

erty, the year 1624 was chosen as the normal year, far better for the Protestants than the Edict of Restitution. States forcibly converted to Catholicism during the war won the right to revert to Protestantism. But there was still no toleration for Protestants in the Hapsburg lands.

Territorially, France secured Alsace and three important frontier fortress towns. Sweden received most of the Baltic shore of Germany, a large cash indemnity with which to pay the huge armies still mobilized, and three votes in the German Diet.

The family of Maximilian of Bavaria kept the electorate of the Palatinate and a part of its territory. The rest was returned to the son of Frederick, who was restored as an elector, thus raising the total number of electors to eight. The many individual German states secured the right to conduct their own foreign affairs, making treaties among themselves and with foreign powers if these were not directed against the emperor. The Dutch and Swiss republics were recognized as independent.

Despite the peace, the danger was great that fighting would resume. Sweden had 100,000 soldiers in Germany, mostly mercenaries whose whole life was war. A similar problem of demobilization and resettlement faced the imperial authorities. Many soldiers hired themselves out to any ruler who would pay them. Some simply became brigands. Moreover, since the treaty did not provide a means for enforcing the new religious property settlement, any attempt to recover lost property might provoke a new fight. The huge amount of money to be paid the Swedes gave rise to such bitterness that this too endangered the peace.

For more than two centuries after 1648, the Thirty Years' War was blamed for everything that later went wrong in Germany. We now know that the figures given in contemporary sources are inflated and unreliable. Sometimes the number of villages allegedly destroyed in a given district was larger than the whole number of villages that had ever existed there. Economic decline in Germany was not wholly due to the war, but had begun well before the war opened in 1618.

Nonetheless, contemporaries everywhere in Germany felt the catastrophe to have been overwhelming. The population fell from about 21 million in 1618 to less than 13½ million in 1648. Individuals suffered terribly. The war was partly responsible for the long delay in achieving German national unity, for the German yearning for authority and eagerness to obey, and even for a kind of national inferiority complex. But how much these later developments can be blamed on the Thirty Years' War remains debatable.

After it was over, the nobility often succeeded in forcing the peasants back onto the soil by denying them the right to leave their villages or to engage in home industry. Politically the main change was probably the shrinking of the power of the empire. The recognition that individual German states could, in effect, conduct their own foreign policies limited direct Hapsburg power to Hapsburg lands. Bavaria, Saxony, and especially Brandenburg-Prussia would now be able to emerge as powers in Germany.

Non-Austrian Germans always afterwards hated the Hapsburgs for having fought a terrible war chiefly to protect family interests. German particularism received yet another long lease on life.

All these issues remained to cause more European wars. Nobody liked the Peace of Westphalia. The pope denounced it. Many Protestants felt betrayed by its provisions. Its only merit was that it ended the fighting in a war that had become intolerable.

II REVOLUTION AND SETTLEMENT IN ENGLAND

Background: The First Stuarts

During the Thirty Years' War, the English went through a major domestic crisis of their own, which continued almost to the end of the seventeenth century. Trouble began under James I, son of Mary Stuart, Queen of Scots, and continued under his son Charles I in a prolonged civil war. In 1649 Charles was beheaded. Thereafter, for eleven years, England was a republic until 1660, when Charles's son, Charles II, was restored. The Stuart family got a second chance and threw it away.

James I was a Scot, a foreigner with none of Elizabeth's enormous popularity. He believed that he ruled by divine right. Kings, he said, were God's "vice-gerents* on earth, and so adorned and furnished with some sparkles of the Divinitie." James went on repeating his opinions insistently and boringly. His son, Charles I, was personally far more attractive, but neither Stuart

* The word is "gerents" meaning "managers," not "regents."

understood the kind of compromises the Tudor monarchs had made in order to keep their Parliaments contented.

Like other contemporary European monarchs, James and Charles worked to make the royal administration strong. But unlike the continental rulers, they found themselves infringing on what the gentry in Parliament and in the countryside felt to be their established rights. The kings also tried to force submission to the Church of England, alienating those Protestants who could not accept the Church. So political and religious questions were knit together.

Worse still for the monarchy: both the king's political and his religious policies angered the same group of important people. Since the English king was obliged to ask Parliament for funds, quarrels over money proved critical. Also, Charles lacked a bureaucracy of the kind that ruled France. The unpaid English justices of the peace rendered justice in the parishes, administered poor relief, and indeed managed the administration in the countryside. The knights of the shires and burgesses who made up the House of Commons came from the same class of gentry. Many of them were "Puritans," English Calvinists. Finally Parliament grew suspicious that the king was pro-Spanish and pro-Catholic, and no longer trusted him on issues of foreign policy.

Both parties to the quarrel were trying to make revolutionary changes in the traditional system. The crown was trying to make England more like a continental divine-right monarchy, in which the king was the earthly representative of God. The idea, as old as the Roman Empire, was strongly revived in the sixteenth and seventeenth centuries. It was completely different from the Tudor compromise in which a strong monarch worked with and through his Parliament and satisfied the goals of the gentry and commercial classes.

On the other hand, the parliamentarians who revolted against the Stuarts were trying to secure for Parliament final authority in the execution of policy as well as in the making of law. This was something equally new, not only for England but for the Western world as a whole.

The Reign of James I

All the issues began to ripen during the reign of James I (1603–1625). James once said about the House of Commons, "I am surprised that my ancestors should ever have permitted such an institution to come into existence. I am a stranger, and found it here when I arrived, so that I am obliged to put up with what I cannot get rid of."

Portrait of James I by Daniel Mytens, 1621.

When the Commons objected to James's insistence on certain legal but out-of-date royal rights, he acted as though they were personally insulting him. He tried to develop sources of income outside parliamentary control. Parliament insisted on the principle that it had to approve any new methods of raising revenue. When Parliament did not pass a law he wanted, he would try to get the courts to declare the measure legal.

One case, seemingly on a small point, illustrates the question of principle: John Bate, a merchant, refused to pay duty on imported currants. The judges ruled that there was no parliamentary authority for James to levy these customs duties, but that nonetheless he had the right to levy them. In a matter concerning the common good, they ruled, the king had absolute power, and all foreign affairs, including foreign trade, fell within this category.

So James's officials joyfully began to levy sales taxes without parliamentary authority, and when Parliament showed alarm at the possibility that James might make himself financially independent, he tried to forbid discussion of the question. Finally, James dissolved his first Parliament, which had sat from 1604 to 1611. Another met briefly in 1614, but thereafter none was elected until 1621. To raise money in these years, the king relied partly on "benevolences," supposedly free gifts granted by the subject to the monarch when he asked for them, but often in fact extracted under pressure.

James also behaved as if Parliament had no legitimate concern in foreign affairs. For years, in the face of the popular hatred for Spain, he tried to arrange a Spanish royal marriage for his son Charles. In 1621 when Parliament petitioned James to go to war with Spain instead and marry Charles to a Protestant, he threatened to punish the "insolent behavior" of anybody who continued to discuss the question. The members admitted that the king alone had the right to make war and peace and to arrange for the marriage of his son, but said that they wished to call his attention to the European situation as they saw it. James answered that this was merely a way of concealing their real intention to usurp royal prerogative.

The House of Commons then presented the Great Protestation (1621), which denied the king's right to imprison its members at will, and asserted their right to discuss and resolve any question concerning the state. James dismissed Parliament and imprisoned three of its leaders. In fact, James was right in alleging that the Commons were making a new claim, but the unpopularity of his Spanish policy made their protest a popular one. And James himself threw his case away in 1624, when—the Spanish match having fallen through—he summoned Parliament, gave it a complete report on foreign affairs, and asked its advice on the very same questions he had been ready to punish them for discussing.

In religion James was determined to enforce conformity to the Church of England. He rejected a moderate appeal presented by Puritans inside the Church: to relax or make optional certain requirements of the ritual. This probably reflected the majority sentiment in the House of Commons, but James told the Puritan leaders (1604) that he would make them conform or harry them out of the land.

James summed up his view as "no bishop, no king," stressing his belief that each depended on the other. The bishops did depend on the king for their continued support against the Puritans and he did depend on them to preach his views of divine right and to urge obedience to the royal will. One great service was rendered the English-speaking world by James's love of uniformity: between 1604 and 1611 a commission of forty-seven scholars prepared the King James version of the Bible, a major influence in the shaping of literary English.

Charles I and Parliament

Charles I (1625–1649) shared his father's theories of monarchy. He wrote less about it but acted on it even more vigorously. His first Parliament voted him only a fraction of what he asked for and needed for wars against Spain and France. Charles raised money by forced loans, always unpopular, and arrested some who refused to contribute. The courts upheld the legality of both loans and arrests.

In 1628 both houses of Parliament produced the Petition of Right. This document listed Charles's infringements of ancient statutes. It demanded no royal taxes without the consent of Parliament, no billeting of troops in private houses, no imprisonment without a charge or legal protection. The king assented. But by his assent, he later said, he had meant only to affirm previously existing rights, not to grant any new ones. Nor was his assent to the petition a law. Indeed, after Parliament had voted the subsidies he asked for, he went right on collecting customs duties that Parliament had not voted. Parliament protested.

Sir John Eliot, leader of the House of Commons, attacked Charles's religious policies. Eliot denounced the bishops as unfit to interpret the Thirty-nine Articles (see p. 244). So Eliot was in effect claiming for Parliament the right to determine the religion of England. Amid protests, Charles dissolved Parliament in 1629 and had Eliot and others arrested; Eliot died in prison, the first martyr in the parliamentary cause.

For the next eleven years (1629–1640) Charles governed without a Parliament. He totally failed to sense the rising popular support for the views of Eliot and the Puritans. To him any subject who did not adhere to the Church of England was disloyal. The whole duty of a loyal subject consisted in obeying king and bishop. Like James, he referred questions of legality to the courts, but if the judges did not say what he wanted to hear, they were dismissed and replaced by judges who would.

To save money and postpone indefinitely the recall of Parliament, Charles made peace with France and Spain. He revived obsolete medieval (but perfectly legal) ways to collect money. He forced all those who owned land worth forty

Van Dyck's portrait of Charles I hunting, ca. 1635.

pounds a year and who had not been knighted to pay large fines. He said that large areas now in private hands were in fact royal forest, and collected fines from their owners. He enforced feudal wardships.

All this aroused the wealthy against him. He also regularly collected from all of England a tax called ship money, which had been traditionally levied only on coastal towns to pay for defensive ships. John Hampden, a rich gentleman from Buckinghamshire, an inland county, refused to pay it and lost his case (1637). But the case dramatized the issue, since the judges who found for the king echoed the divine-right theory. They said that the king was *lex loquens,* the law itself speaking.

Charles's unpopularity grew as his archbishop of Canterbury, William Laud, drove the Puritans from their pulpits and censored all but approved books on religious subjects. The Puritans denounced the established ritual as "popish" and contrary to the Bible, and gave their resistance the color of martyrdom.

In Scotland, by reannexing in 1625 all the Church and crown land that had fallen into private hands since 1542, Charles enraged all Scotch nobles who had acquired the land in the interim. English and Scots often disliked each other, the English thinking of the Scots as barbarous and greedy, the Scots of the English as too rich for their own good and inclined to "popery." Unable as usual to judge public opinion, Charles decided in 1637 to impose a Book of Common Prayer on the Scots. They rose in their wrath, as if "the Mass in Latin had been presented."

In March 1638, the Presbyterians of Scotland banded together in a Solemn League and Covenant (its members were called Covenanters) to defend their faith. In November, a general assembly—despite royal objections—abolished bishops and prescribed a definitive ritual for the Scottish Kirk (church).

The Covenant united almost all Scots, who insisted all along that they were undertaking nothing against Charles as their king. But it was impossible to do away with bishops and still uphold Charles as king. Charles went to war in Scotland (1639). Immediately the question arose: how could he pay for the war? In 1640 Charles summoned Parliament once more.

Reforms of the Long Parliament

The Short Parliament of 1640 would vote no money until the piled-up grievances of almost forty years were settled. Charles refused all compromise and dissolved it. But a defeat in Scotland forced him to promise to buy off the Scots, and since he could not find the money, he had to summon another Parliament. This was the Long Parliament, which sat for twenty years, 1640–1660.

It began by arresting the most powerful royal favorite, Thomas Wentworth, earl of Strafford. Strafford was tried for high treason without a verdict being reached. But Charles eventually sacrificed him to the passions of the public and let him be executed. Archbishop Laud also was imprisoned and later executed.

Parliament now passed the Triennial Act, providing machinery for summoning Parliament if the king did not summon it himself within three years after a dissolution. It also passed a revolutionary act making it illegal for Charles to dissolve the present Parliament without its own consent. It abolished the Court of Star Chamber (see p. 212), reversed the judgment against Hampden in the ship money case, abolished ship money, reverted to the forest boundaries of 1623, and declared it illegal to require anybody to become a knight. Charles assented to all of these antiroyal measures, gritting his teeth. Many suspected that he was only waiting for a favorable moment to repeal them.

The Long Parliament, however, could not agree on Church affairs. The House of Lords would not accept a bill excluding bishops from their house, largely because they resented the Commons' interference. A "root and branch" bill abolishing bishops altogether had passionate defenders and a good many lukewarm opponents. The Commons favored, but the Lords did not, various regulations of ritual and Sabbath observance. The extreme radicalism of some of the Puritans began to produce a reaction among the milder ones.

The king's position was improving, when it was damaged by an Irish Catholic revolt that began in October 1641 with the massacre of some thirty thousand Protestants who had been settled in Ulster by James I. Parliament suspected that Charles had encouraged the Irish rebels. It refused to entrust to royal command an army to put down the revolt, and threatened to take the appointment of officers into its own hands. Finally, Parliament produced a monster list of grievances, the Grand Remonstrance, and so advertised its anger to the public. It began to discuss the appointment of a "lord general" who would have power to raise and pay troops. It talked of impeaching the queen (the French princess Henrietta Maria) on suspicion of instigating the Irish rebellion.

Charles unwisely tried to arrest five leading members of the Commons for treason and for complicity with the Scots. He took the unprecedented step of entering Parliament with a group of armed men, but found that the five had fled. They returned to Parliament in triumph (January 1642). Charles consented to a bill removing bishops from any temporal position and depriving them of any private law court. But he refused Parliament's "Nineteen Propositions" (June 1642), demanding the right to veto appointments to the great offices of state, to approve the education and marriages of the royal children, to consent to all appointments of new peers, and to dictate further reform of the Church.

England was now dividing into two camps and heading into civil war. Leadership of the Commons passed to the Independents, who were Brownists, or extreme Calvinists (see p. 245). Around Charles there gathered a party loyal to the Church and to him, including members of both houses. When Parliament announced that the cost of its own military operations would be borne by its opponents, many who had been neutral joined the king. For Charles money continued to be the problem: he depended on gifts from rich individuals. The north and west of England were largely royalist, the richer and more populous south and east, including London, largely parliamentarian.

In recent years, English historians have argued heatedly over the economic motives of the parliamentary side. Much of the writing has tended to reflect the individual author's political position on twentieth-century questions in England. Those who favor the present-day Labour party have argued that the Puritans of the Civil War included the most enterprising, advanced, and successful members of the gentry. Present-day Tories have answered that the gentry who backed the Puritans were actually those on the way down in the economic competition and unable to face inflation, the enclosure of lands for sheepraising and other economic threats. Neutral scholars enjoy the argument, but accuse both sides of oversimplification. Economic motives alone, they argue, did not determine allegiance in the English Civil War any more than they have in any other complex political and social and religious struggle.

Civil War, 1642–1649

In the Civil War the early advantage lay with the king. But he could not win a quick decisive victory, and this cost him the war in the end. He made peace with the Irish rebels in 1643, intending to use Irish Catholic forces in England. This increased the fear of "popery" that all along had driven neutrals toward Parliament, which now reached a "Solemn League and Covenant" with the anti-Catholic Scots.

This brought Scottish forces into England against Charles, in exchange for a promise to make English and Irish religion as nearly like Scottish Presbyterianism as possible. Parliament won the battle of Marston Moor (1644) largely owing to specially trained cavalry led by Oliver Cromwell, one of the radical Puritan gentry. Soon afterwards, Cromwell reorganized the parliamentary forces into the "New Model" army. At Naseby (1645) his Roundheads (so termed from their close-cropped hair) decisively defeated the Cavaliers (royalists).

In 1646 Charles surrendered to the Scots and stalled for time by launching prolonged negotiations with them and with Parliament. Dissension now developed among his opponents. The army, representing the radical, Independent (Congregationalist) wing of Puritanism, quarreled with the moderate Presbyterian leadership of Parliament that had begun the Civil War. The Independent members (about sixty) and the speakers of both houses fled London and joined the army, which marched on London and forcibly restored them to their places. Even more radical than Cromwell and the Independents was one faction in the army called Levellers. They advocated a universal franchise and relief from social and economic grievances.

In December 1647, the king secretly agreed with the Scots to establish Presbyterianism in England for three years and to suppress the Independents. Parliament thereupon renounced its allegiance to the king, and a "second" Civil War began. The Presbyterians, who had formerly supported Parliament, now joined the royalists and the Scots against the army. Most Englishmen, however, seem to have remained neutral.

In August 1648, Cromwell thoroughly defeated the Scots at Preston Pans and ended the second Civil War. The army seized Charles. Colonel Pride, acting for the army, excluded 140 Presbyterian members from Parliament in "Pride's Purge," leaving only about 60 Independents as members. The "Rump" as this much reduced body was called, created a special court to try the king. In January 1649, Charles was tried, condemned, and executed. The killers of the king believed that they were acting as agents of God. But the execution aroused genuine horror in England and abroad.

The Commonwealth and Protectorate

The Rump now abolished the monarchy and the House of Lords. England became a republic, called the Commonwealth (1649–1653), ruled by a Commons comprising only about one tenth the original membership of the Long Parliament. This minority regime depended for support on the radical army of Cromwell, who was the dominant personality of the republican experiment.

Cromwell himself with the utmost ruthlessness began the reconquest of rebellious Ireland (1649–1650). Next he turned to the Scots, who supported Charles I's son, Charles II. Cromwell defeated them, and Charles fled to France in disguise.

The Navigation Act of 1651 forbade the importation of goods into England or the colonies except in English ships or in ships of the country producing the goods. The Dutch carrying trade was so damaged that they went to war. Cromwell won.

But England itself remained Cromwell's greatest problem. Government by Rump and army aroused much bitter opposition. To grant

The House of Commons as shown on the Great Seal of England used by the Commonwealth, 1651.

an amnesty to the royalists and to enact conciliatory reforms seemed impossible in the face of parliamentary opposition. Under pressure the Rump did fix a date for new elections, but its members voted to keep their own seats in the new Parliament and to accept or reject all other representatives.

Discarding the last pretensions to be acting legally, Cromwell and his musketeers dissolved the Rump (1653), thus earning the eternal hatred of the extreme republicans. Then the army itself elected a Parliament of members nominated by Congregational ministers in each county.

After a few months, the members of this new Parliament resigned their powers to Cromwell, who became Lord Protector of England, thus inaugurating the second phase of the republican experiment—the Protectorate (1653–1660). It had a written constitution, the Instrument of Government, drawn up by some of the army officers. The Instrument restricted voting to those with an estate worth two hundred pounds, so the new Parliament proved to be an upper-class body. It proved so uncooperative that Cromwell—who believed that only a military dictatorship could govern England properly—dissolved it in 1654.

After a royalist uprising in 1653, Cromwell ordered Catholic priests exiled, forbade Anglicans to preach, and divided England into eleven military districts. In each, the major-general in command collected the taxes, policed his district, and served as censor of public morals. Many popular sports were prohibited. Alehouses, gambling dens, and brothels were closed or regulated severely. The theater was forbidden.

The English hated this Puritan regime and its attempts to impose Calvinist morality by force. The revulsion of opinion was evident in the parliamentary election of 1656. Even when the army had purged members of whom it did not approve, those who were left still produced the "Humble Petition and Advice," revising the Instrument of Government in the direction of traditional English monarchy. It asked Cromwell to become king (he refused), gave the House of Commons the right to exclude any elected member, and created a second house to be nominated by Cromwell. Though Cromwell accepted some of the amendments, he dissolved this Parliament too (1657).

Cromwell died September 3, 1658, and was succeeded as lord protector by his son, Richard, who proved unable to reorganize the army and weed out the most fanatical extremists. The army forced Richard to recall the Rump and resign (May 1659). As tension grew between the army officers and the Rump, royalist activity increased. In October, General Lambert expelled the Rump and set up a Committee of Safety to govern England.

But a popular reaction soon set in against the assumption of such a major political role by the military. General George Monck (or Monk), a leading Cromwellian officer who had always upheld the principles of military obedience to properly constituted civil authority, emerged as the decisive figure in ending the political turbulence. In December 1659, the army gave in and restored the Rump for the third time. Monck allowed the surviving members excluded by Pride's Purge to take their old places.

The partially reconstituted Long Parliament prepared to restore the monarchy as the only barrier to chaos. At Monck's suggestion, the exiled Charles II issued the Declaration of Breda, promising a free pardon, confirmation of all land sales during the Civil Wars, payment of the soldiers' back pay, and liberty of conscience. Charles added, however, that on each point he would be bound by what Parliament wanted. A new Parliament, chosen in free election, summoned the king home in a burst of enthusiasm. On May 29, 1660, Charles II (reigned 1660–1685) arrived in London.

The English Revolution in Review

Revolutionary changes had occurred in England since 1642. Divine-right monarchy had been challenged, and a constitutional and representative government set up, based on a legislature backed by politically active private citizens. Though the Stuarts were restored, no English king ever again could hope to rule without a Parliament or to reinstate the Court of Star Chamber or to take ship money, benevolences, and other controversial taxes. Parliament thenceforward retained its critical weapon: ultimate control of the public purse by periodic grants of taxes.

Moreover, minority groups had gone much further toward political and social democracy. The Levellers put forward a program (later carried by emigrants to the American colonies) that favored universal suffrage, progressive taxation, separation of church and state, and protection of the individual against arbitrary arrest. A more extreme group called the Diggers actually dug up public lands near London and began planting vegetables in a kind of communistic enterprise. They were driven off, but not before they had got their ideas into circulation. The Fifth Monarchy men, the Millenarians, and a dozen other radical sects preached the Second Coming of Christ and the achievement of some kind of utopia on earth.

During the English struggles the Puritans urged freedom of speech and of the press, although when they came to power they often failed to practice what they had preached. Another basic liberal idea to emerge from the Civil War was religious toleration. Some of the Puritans believed that compulsion should not be exercised to secure conformity, and at least one sect held that religious toleration was a positive good.

The Quakers—more properly, the Religious Society of Friends—led by George Fox (1624–1691), were Puritans of the Puritans. They rejected all worldly show: for example, they regarded the polite form "you" as hypocritical, and so addressed everyone as "thou" or "thee." They took so seriously the basic Protestant doctrine of the priesthood of all believers that they had no ordained ministry and encouraged any worshiper to speak out in meeting if he felt the spirit move him. The Friends were—and still are today—pacifists, who opposed all use of force and would have no part in war.

The Restoration

Although many of the ideas advanced during the civil wars were much too revolutionary to win easy acceptance, the Restoration settlement showed a high degree of political tolerance. Except for a few revolutionaries, including the surviving judges who had condemned Charles I to death, Parliament pardoned all those who had been involved in the Civil War or the republican regimes. It made every effort to injure as few people as possible in settling the claims of royalists and churchmen to their former lands.

Political forbearance was not matched in religious matters. Though personally rather disposed to toleration, Charles II governed a country where very few people were yet ready to accept it. Parliament enacted many acts aimed at the Puritans but hitting at Catholics also. Bishops were restored. The Corporation Act (1661) required all magistrates to take the sacraments according to the Church of England. The Act of Uniformity (1662) required clergymen and teachers to subscribe to the Book of Common Prayer; those who refused were known as Nonconformists or Dissenters. The Conventicle Act (1664) limited to five the number of persons allowed to attend a Nonconformist meeting in a private household. The Five Mile Act (1665) forbade those who had not accepted the Act of Uniformity to come within five miles of any town unless they swore a special oath.

Much of this was impossible to enforce. It placed the Dissenters under disabilities but did not cause them great suffering. The Test Act (1673) required that all officeholders take communion in the Church of England and renounce transubstantiation (the Catholic doctrine of the Eucharist). One way around this was "occasional conformity," whereby a Dissenter whose conscience was not too strict might worship as a Presbyterian or Congregationalist most of the time, but take Anglican communion occasionally. Another way, common after 1689, was to allow Dissenters to hold office, and each year pass a special bill legalizing their acts.

The revulsion against Puritanism carried over into all aspects of the Restoration period. The Commonwealth and Protectorate had forbidden all theatrical performances. Restoration England thoroughly enjoyed them, the more indecent the better. Charles II himself and his court led cheerfully immoral lives.

Everywhere in Europe there was a trend back toward Catholicism. In Sweden, for instance, Gustavus Adolphus' own daughter, Christina, abdicated and became a Catholic (1654). Charles II sympathized with Catholicism and in 1672 tried but failed to free both Catholics and Dissenters from restrictions.

Charles greatly admired the flourishing monarchy of Louis XIV across the Channel. Without the knowledge of Parliament, he made a secret treaty with Louis (1670) and promised, in exchange for an annual subsidy, to support the French in their wars and to become a Catholic as soon as he could. His brother James, duke of York and heir to the throne, openly practiced Catholicism.

English popular suspicion of the Roman Church, however, was still strong. In the late 1670s a series of disclosures about alleged "popish" plots to murder the king and restore Catholicism aroused great popular excitement. One faction in Parliament wanted to exclude the Catholic and pro-French James from the succession.

These were called *Whigs,* a Scotch variant of "wigs." They included many well-to-do urban merchants and certain very powerful peers, who hoped to enhance their own political influence if the monarchy should be weakened. Supporting Charles and the succession of James were the landed gentry, lesser lords and country gentlemen who had been pro-Stuart all along and who suspected the newly rich townsmen. They were called *Tories,* a Gaelic term for "robber."

James II and the Glorious Revolution

James II (reigned 1685–1688) alienated even the Tories. He put down an ineffectual effort of a bastard son of Charles II, the duke of Monmouth, to invade England (1685), and sent a brutal judge to try and punish those suspected of sympathizing with Monmouth. Disregarding the laws, James appointed Catholics to high office. His Declaration of Liberty of Conscience (1687), extending religious toleration, was issued without parliamentary approval or support.

When a son was born to James (June 1688) and the prospect of a Catholic dynasty loomed, seven Whig and Tory leaders offered the throne jointly to James's daughter Mary, a Protestant, and to her husband, William of Orange. Stadholder since 1673 of six of the seven Dutch provinces, William was a vigorous enemy of Louis XIV. When William landed in England (November 1688), James fled to France. Elections were held. The throne was formally offered to William and Mary. They ruled as William III (1689–1702) and Mary II (1689–1694).

The invitation to them was accompanied by the Declaration of Rights, summing up what had been won in the long struggle with the Stuarts. Parliament alone makes or suspends laws.

Seventeenth-century Dutch engraving: fireworks in London celebrating the coronation of King William III and Queen Mary II.

The king cannot tax without Parliament. Freedom of election, freedom of debate, freedom of petition, frequent elections, no trial without jury, no excessive bail: all these William and Mary accepted as the rights of Englishmen. Parliament made them into laws as the Bill of Rights (1689), adding that in the future no Catholic could become king of England. A Toleration Act (1689) allowed Dissenters to practice their religion freely but excluded them from public office.

The sum total of the almost bloodless events of 1688–1689 is called the Glorious Revolution. In 1690 at the battle of the Boyne in Ireland, William secured it by defeating James II with his army of Irish Catholic rebels and French troops.

After the Glorious Revolution three major steps still lay ahead before England could become a full parliamentary democracy. First: the cabinet system, whereby a committee of the majority party would manage affairs of state would take shape in the eighteenth and early nineteenth centuries. Second: universal suffrage and payment of salaries to members of the Commons was gradually achieved during the nineteenth and early twentieth centuries. Third: curbs on the power of the Lords to veto legislation did not begin before our own twentieth century.

William and Mary were childless, and Mary's sister Anne, who succeeded as queen from 1702 to 1714, had no living children. Parliament, fearing that James II's son, the Catholic "James III," would try to seize the throne, settled the succession upon the descendants of Sophia, granddaughter of James I, twelfth child of Frederick of the Palatinate (see p. 268), wife of the elector of Hanover. When Anne died in 1714, Sophia's son George, elector of Hanover, became king of England as George I, and his descendants have sat on the throne ever since. By excluding the elder Catholic line of succession, Parliament had shown who really made the kings of England.

There remained the danger that the Scots might prefer a Stuart monarch to a Hanoverian. But under Anne, in 1707, the old problem of Anglo-Scottish union was worked out. Scotland accepted the Protestant succession, would send its own members to both houses of Parliament, and would join its cross of Saint Andrew with the English cross of Saint George on one flag, the Union Jack—symbol of Great Britain. Despite two efforts (1715 and 1745) of the Catholic Stuarts to rouse the old Scotch loyalties, Protestantism was too strong. And despite Scottish nationalism, revived in our own day, the Union of 1707 still holds.

The lot of the Irish was far harsher. After his victories in the Boyne and at Aughrim (1691), William III agreed to the generous Treaty of Limerick, but Parliament never ratified it. Penal laws imposed galling disabilities on the Catholics. Irish trade was stifled by mercantilist regulation. Irish misery was so acute that the Anglican Jonathan Swift made with bitter irony his famous "modest proposal" that they solve their economic problems by selling their babies to be eaten.

III DIVINE-RIGHT MONARCHY IN FRANCE

Henry IV, Richelieu, and Mazarin

The real danger that a Hapsburg combination—Spanish and Austrian—would upset the balance of power was dead after Rocroy (1643; see p. 269). But by repeatedly leading the other powers in checking any Hapsburg threat, France prepared to make its own bid for European supremacy. At home, France recovered quickly from the wounds of the sixteenth-century religious wars (see Chapter 8). Henry IV (reigned 1589–1610), dashing and popular, took a real interest in the popular welfare. His economic experts reclaimed marshes for farmland, encouraged the luxury crafts of Paris, and planted thousands of mulberry trees to feed silkworms and nurture a silk industry. They built the canals, roads, and bridges that made the French communications system the best in Europe.

Faced with a deficit, Henry IV found an efficient finance minister in Sully (1560–1641), who gradually brought income up and expenditure down until they balanced. Monarch and minister even toyed with an advanced idea for a general European international Christian republic that would include everybody but the Hapsburgs. This "grand design" obviously was conceived in the interest of France, but it also was an ancestor of future leagues of nations.

Assassinated in 1610 by a madman, Henry IV was succeeded by his nine-year-old son, Louis XIII (reigned 1610–1643). His mother Marie de' Medici became regent and her favorites almost undid what Henry IV had accomplished. But in 1624 Richelieu became the king's chief minister. We have already seen him allying France with the Protestants during the Thirty Years' War. Ev-

Triple portrait of Richelieu by Philippe de Champaigne.

erywhere the interests of the state *(raison d'état)* governed his policy.

Richelieu subsidized Lutherans and Calvinists in Germany. But in France he felt that the Edict of Nantes (see p. 260) had given too many privileges to the Huguenots. The hundred-odd fortified towns in Huguenot hands seemed potential centers of disorder and a threat to his program of increased royal centralization. Foreseeing punitive measures against them, the Huguenots rebelled. Richelieu's forces had trouble taking their key port of La Rochelle (1628), largely because he had no navy.

Over the next decade, Richelieu built French Atlantic and Mediterranean fleets. He tried to curb the French nobility by ordering some of their chateaux destroyed and by forbidding their favorite pastime of dueling. But he by no means succeeded in taming them completely. He did successfully transfer responsibility for local administration from the nobles to royal officials, the *intendants,* who obtained greatly increased power to assess and collect taxes.

Without Richelieu, later French greatness under Louis XIV would have been unthinkable. He left little place for government by discussion. Except for a few highly trained professional bureaucrats, the middle classes took little part in government. He handpicked and trained his immediate successor, the Italian-born Cardinal Mazarin, who inherited an efficient centralized administration.

Succeeding to power in 1642, Mazarin soon faced the crisis caused by the death of Louis XIII (1643), whose heir, Louis XIV (1643–1715), was only five years old. Mazarin's foreign birth, his failure to pay the interest on government debts, and his amassing of a huge personal fortune antagonized the French nobility.

The nobility consisted not only of the descendants of the feudal aristocracy—the nobility of the sword *(noblesse d' épée)*—but also of those who had been given titles because of their services as judges or administrators—the nobility of the robe *(noblesse de robe).* The old nobility of the sword hated Mazarin partly for snobbish reasons, partly for keeping them out of power; the newer nobility of the robe worried about his fast-and-loose ways with money.

This discontent and the ambitions of rival cliques of nobles led to the complex disturbances known as the Fronde, 1648–1653 (the name refers to a slingshot used by Parisian children to throw mud at passersby). In the end, Mazarin defeated both old and new nobles. He maintained himself in power until he died in 1661. By then Louis XIV was twenty-three and ready for personal rule in the fullest sense of divine-right absolutism.

Louis XIV: Le Grand Monarque

It is not James I—despite all his theorizing on the subject—nor even Philip II of Spain whom we think of as *the* divine-right monarch, but Louis XIV. Of course, he is supposed to have summed it all up by saying, "L'état, c'est moi" (I am the State). God had from the beginning destined this descendant of Hugh Capet for the throne of France. To challenge his right to it was to challenge the structure of God's universe.

Louis was able to act as a divine-right monarch partly because of the revival of the concept from Roman law that God directs the affairs of states through his chosen agents. Moreover, the French monarchy had for centuries combatted the old deep provincial loyalty—to Normandy, Brittany, Burgundy—and emphasized instead a loyalty to France.

Louis XIV.

The subjects of the French crown spoke several different languages or, at least, dialects. They had no common educational system, or press, or political life. What they had in common was the king, a symbol of common "Frenchness," who collected taxes and raised armies. Frenchmen had to feel that he had a right to do these things, and was doing it *for* them, not just *to* them.

Of course, Louis lacked the physical means for controlling all the actions of all his subjects. Indeed no ruler was ever absolute in this sense until the days of the twentieth-century dictatorships, with all their totalitarian techniques of propaganda, surveillance, and terror. Medieval local survivals in language, law, customs, weights and measures all stood in the way of real uniformity in France. Louis could not ride roughshod over city corporations that appealed to their ancient charters granting them immunities, or over guilds that could show a privileged status that they had "always" possessed. He could not force nobles and clergy to conform completely.

He did, however, deprive the nobles of their political function, and left them only their social and economic privileges and their military careers. Louis XI had begun to tame them in the fifteenth century. Henry IV's victory in the religious wars was a defeat for them. So was Richelieu's increased use of nonnobles as intendants, judges, and local officials. Louis XIV finished the job.

The French Church, too, had gradually come under the control of the crown. Under Louis XIV it was "Gallican"—that is to say, national, though of course Catholic. His bishops supported the monarchy. But the French clergy were not subject to royal taxation. Of their own free will

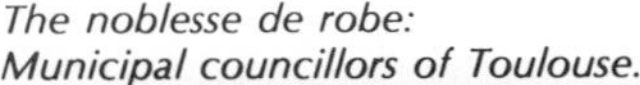

The noblesse de robe: Municipal councillors of Toulouse.

in their own assembly they voted gifts of money to the king.

Louis abolished the religious toleration that Richelieu had left the Huguenots after taking away their fortresses and political privileges. In 1685 he revoked the Edict of Nantes. Fifty thousand Protestant families fled abroad. In Prussia, some of the exiles found a place in the military services, and their descendants fought against the French in the wars of the nineteenth and twentieth centuries. In Holland, England, North America, and South Africa the talents and skills of these refugees greatly strengthened the lands that received them. Some Huguenots remained in France, where they had to worship secretly.

Within the Catholic Church itself, Louis had to deal with enthusiastic mystics (Madame Guyon and the Quietists) and with puritanical Jansenists, named after Cornelius Jansen, bishop of Ypres in the early seventeenth century. The Jansenists, who virtually agreed with Calvin on predestination, questioned the authority of both pope and king, since both were mere men. Their most distinguished spokesman was the scientist and philosopher Pascal (see Chapter 10). Though Louis contained the threat that they posed to uniformity, he did not succeed in suppressing them.

Intent on his own glory, Louis worked hard and in his youth played hard. In middle age, after his Spanish queen's death, he contracted a morganatic marriage with Mme. de Maintenon, former governess of his illegitimate children. She was a devout Catholic, and it seems certain that she influenced Louis's decision to revoke the Edict of Nantes.

Louis installed the French court at Versailles, where he built a splendid palace on the site of a former hunting lodge. Almost half a mile long, the main buildings at Versailles housed a court of ten thousand tame nobles and their families, followers, and servants.

So completely did Louis make Versailles the center of French social life that everything else in Europe seemed provincial. The proper standard

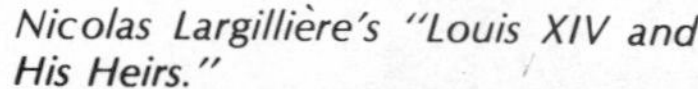

Nicolas Largillière's "Louis XIV and His Heirs."

of sophisticated behavior for all Europe was set here: how to dress, how to speak French, what to read, what sort of story to tell, how far to go in gossip, what games to play, what food to eat at what times of day, what music to listen to, and what dances to dance. At every European court and in every nobleman's private house, the master and mistress would ask what Versailles did and imitate it.

Here Louis met with his ministers, the heads of departments like those in any modern state: war, finance, foreign policy, interior. They were directly responsible to him and not to any legislative body. Indeed, the Estates-General never met at all during Louis's entire reign of seventy-two years. From the top, the chain of command went down through the intendants, in charge of the *généralités,* or large province-sized administrative units, to smaller regional units, and then to the towns and villages. Even Louis could exercise only a general supervision.

His subjects had to fill out all sorts of official forms. Many thousands of them remain today duly filed in the French local archives. As members of the noblesse de robe, the intendants transmitted their titles and rank to their heirs and so formed a new kind of privileged corporation. They got more power than the theory of royal absolutism ideally would have allowed and so asserted provincial initiative against the monarchy.

The judges of the high courts of appeal, too, could not be removed by the king and therefore exercised considerable independence. These courts were the *parlements,* of which the Parlement of Paris enjoyed the widest jurisdiction and the most prestige. The parlements had to register each royal edict. But they claimed the right to refuse if they thought an edict violated the law of the land. Louis intimidated the Parlement of Paris by summoning the judges before him in a formal session *(lit de justice,* "bed of justice") and commanding them to register a royal edict. The claim that the parlements might throw out a royal edict, however, remained to plague his successors.

Mercantilism and Colbert: Economic Policy under Louis XIV

The economic policies of Louis XIV's government reflected mercantilist theories and practices. Mercantilists believed that hard money, gold and silver, was the basic wealth. Therefore, the state should try to get as much of it as possible and to arrange that more should come in than go out. It should maintain this "favorable balance of trade" by encouraging exports (which bring in cash from abroad) perhaps by bounties, and discouraging imports (which cause cash to flow out) perhaps by tariffs. Carried to its extreme, this would be absurd, since gold and silver were of no use to the state except as media of exchange.

But the mercantilists were not absurd. They were trying to make their own state as self-sustaining as they could. National production, they argued, should provide the necessities of life for the population and the sinews of war for the armed forces. They favored rigorous planning and control, sweeping away the traditional ways of manor and guild and the medieval notion of the just price. Instead, mercantilists favored directing the economy by subsidies, grants of monopolies, government participation in industry, encouragement of research, and imposition of tariffs.

As we have seen in the case of Spain, they viewed the overseas colonies of the mother country as a source of necessary raw materials. Possession of these made it unnecessary to import from rival states and encouraged manufacturing at home. Therefore, the colonies must be strongly governed and their economies directed as the mother country saw fit.

Louis XIV's finance minister, Jean Baptiste Colbert (1619–1683), was a thorough-going mercantilist. He exercised more influence over the king than any other royal servant. Colbert supported new inventions, improvements in ship building, technological education, the settlement of foreign experts in France, and the founding of new industries. This was the first major experiment in a modern controlled economy, and the result was prosperity.

In Colbert's time nobody had yet put forward the rival theory of free trade *(laissez-faire),* which would leave businessmen alone, arguing that the mere removal of regulations enables the individual entrepreneur and therefore the whole economy to enrich itself still further. So we cannot say whether France would have been richer under laissez-faire.

Colbert's system gave France the economic leadership of Europe. During the eighteenth century, France would lose this lead. England would adopt new methods of power machinery and large-scale production of inexpensive goods, while the French would cling to small-scale production of a large variety of products, chiefly luxuries and consumer goods. England also had more easily exploitable resources, like coal, iron, and water power, and so would get a head start in modern industrialization. Very important too were the expensive wars of Louis XIV. They built up a burden of debt that depressed the economy in the latter part of his reign and even after his death.

The Wars of Louis XIV

As the real victor in the Thirty Years' War, France had defeated the Hapsburgs and got new territory cheaply. Louis XIV set out to expand still farther. France took the Hapsburgs' place as the threat to the European balance of power. Louis wanted to push French boundaries east to the Rhine, annexing the Spanish Netherlands (Belgium) and the Franche Comté (Free County of Burgundy). As time went on, he hoped also to secure Spain and the Spanish Empire. He also wanted to assert the predominance of France in every part of the globe and in every area of human life.

Louis had agents in India, in Canada, in Holland, and on the Rhine. He regarded it as natural and proper that French culture, French taste in the arts, French social ways should influence all of Europe. To an astonishing degree they did. But when other European rulers felt France was too threatening, they united against Louis XIV.

A legal quibble gave Louis the excuse for his first war, the War of Devolution (1667–1668). When he had married the daughter of Philip IV of Spain, his wife had renounced her right to inherit her father's lands. But her dowry had not been paid, and Louis claimed that this voided her renunciation. After the death of Philip IV (1665), Louis claimed that his queen ought to inherit the Spanish Low Countries by virtue of an old Flemish law of "devolution."

The threat to Belgium aroused the Dutch, who made an alliance with England and Sweden against France, thus joining their old enemies, the Spaniards, in supporting the balance of power. Louis made peace at Aix-la-Chapelle in 1668, collecting twelve fortified Flemish towns.

Furious at the Dutch, Louis bought off Charles II by a secret treaty in 1670 (see p. 279) and also made a treaty with the Swedes. Then he began his second war, the Dutch War (1672–1678), quickly occupying large areas of southern Holland. Six of the seven Dutch provinces elected William of Orange stadholder and decided that the office should be hereditary in his family. William allied himself with both Spanish and Austrian Hapsburgs and prevented a decisive French victory. At the Peace of Nijmegen (1678–1679), the Dutch lost no territory but had to promise future neutrality. Spain gave Louis the Franche Comté and some towns in the Spanish Netherlands.

The superb French armed forces now dominated Europe. On the eastern frontiers, special French courts ("chambers of reunion") decreed annexations of still other areas that could be shown to have belonged at any time to any of the territories newly acquired by France. Louis's armies would then proceed to take over these too. In this way France "reunited" Strasbourg (1681) and Luxembourg, all of Lorraine (1683), and the Rhineland bishopric of Trier (1684). These French aggressions in time of peace met with no resistance. Europe was busy with the Ottoman siege of Vienna (1683) and its aftermath (see Chapter 7).

Louis now put in a farfetched claim to the lands of the Palatinate and insisted on pushing his own candidate for the archbishopric of Cologne (1688). The revocation of the Edict of Nantes (1685) had distressed the Protestants of Europe. Sweden, the Palatinate, Saxony, Bavaria, the Austrian and Spanish Hapsburgs, together with William of Orange, who was soon to be king of England, formed the League of Augsburg against Louis XIV. In the War of the League of Augsburg (1688–1697), Louis was defeated, and by the Treaty of Ryswick (1697) had to give up much of the land "reunited" since Nijmegen, including Lorraine.

The War of the Spanish Succession

But within four years Louis embarked on his last and most adventurous war. When Louis's brother-in-law, the Hapsburg king of Spain, Charles II (1665–1700), died childless, his will left all the vast Spanish possessions in Europe and overseas to his great-nephew, the grandson of Louis XIV, Philip of Anjou. Louis could not resist the temptation. He proclaimed his grandson King Philip V of Spain. At once, England, Holland, the Empire, and the German states, which had been trying to avert this overwhelming addition to Bourbon strength, formed a new grand alliance against the French.

The War of the Spanish Succession (1701–1713) was fought in Italy and overseas, and especially in the Low Countries. The allies gradually wore down the French. Queen Anne's great general, John Churchill, duke of Marlborough and ancestor of Winston Churchill, won battles at Blenheim (1704), Ramillies (1706), Oudenarde (1708), and Malplaquet (1709). Malplaquet alone cost the victorious allies twenty thousand casualties, which in those days seemed "butchery" to the people of England.

In 1711 the threat arose that the new Hapsburg emperor might inherit all the Spanish possessions. This would have recreated the old empire of Charles V. Once more, the balance of power would be upset by the Hapsburgs. The English feared this as much as a French victory. Negotiations for peace began, culminating in the Treaty of Utrecht (1713), a major event in the diplomatic and territorial history of Europe.

Philip V was accepted as king of Spain, but Louis XIV promised that the crowns of France and Spain would never be united. He recognized the Protestant succession in England. In America, France gave up Newfoundland, Acadia (Nova Scotia), and the Hudson's Bay territory to England, but retained Quebec and Louisiana. From Spain the English obtained Gibraltar, which they still hold. Because the Austrian Hapsburgs lost their claim to the Spanish throne, they received the former Spanish Netherlands (Belgium). The duke of Savoy, a great general, eventually got Sardinia in 1720. As kings of Sardinia, the dukes of Savoy would later unite the rest of Italy into a kingdom. The elector of Brandenburg was recognized as "king in Prussia."

Utrecht was on the whole a moderate and sensible peace. Yet it did not end overseas rivalry between the French and English. It did not really protect the Dutch, satisfy the Hapsburgs, or settle the tangled affairs of Italy. French aggression was halted, but only temporarily, for it would be resumed at the end of the century under the impulse of the great Revolution (see Chapter 12).

The wars of Louis XIV, however, despite their great cost in human life and in treasure, and despite the popular hatred aroused by the French in their drive into Dutch and German territories, were less savage than the Thirty Years' War or the wars of nationalism and revolution that would follow after 1789. Religion played a minor role. Although Louis regarded himself as a Catholic champion, and William of Orange was hailed as a Protestant one, hundreds of thousands of Catholics were lined up against Louis on the "Protestant" side. Louis's aggressions were not religious or political crusades. His wars were more measured and "classical," as befitted le Grand Monarque.

IV EUROPE OVERSEAS

At Utrecht, we saw, Nova Scotia and Newfoundland changed hands as well as Gibraltar. Indeed, the last war of Louis XIV was almost a world war, fought not only to maintain the balance of power in Europe but to gain advantages and resources overseas. The increased concern with the world beyond Europe resulted from the faster pace of colonialism in the seventeenth century, when the English, French, and Dutch all joined the ranks of empire builders.

The Thirteen Colonies

The English got their first two permanent footholds in North America at Jamestown in Virginia (1607) and at Plymouth in Massachusetts (1620). At first similar to Spanish or Portuguese trading posts, these were established by English trading companies which vainly hoped to find gold and silver as the Spaniards had. Both settlements barely managed to survive the early years of hardship. Then the sparse Indian population was gradually replaced by immigrants of English stock.

Tobacco and the resourcefulness of Captain John Smith saved Virginia. Furs, codfish, and Calvinist toughness saved Massachusetts. Both gradually built up an agricultural economy and traded with the mother country. Neither received more than a few tens of thousands of immigrants from abroad, but the population grew steadily.

In 1664 the English defeated the Dutch in a round of the warfare for economic advantage. They took over New Amsterdam, founded in 1626, which became New York. Its important Dutch families—Stuyvesant, Schuyler, Roosevelt—would supply some leading participants in American development. In 1655 the Dutch had already eliminated the Swedish settlement at Fort Christina on the Delaware, and here, too, the English now ousted the Dutch. Pennsylvania, chartered in 1681 to the wealthy English Quaker William Penn, filled the vacuum left by the expulsion of the Swedes and the Dutch from the Delaware.

By the early eighteenth century, the English settlements formed a continuous string of thirteen colonies from Maine to Georgia. The new settlers came from all strata of English life except the very top. New England was for the most part

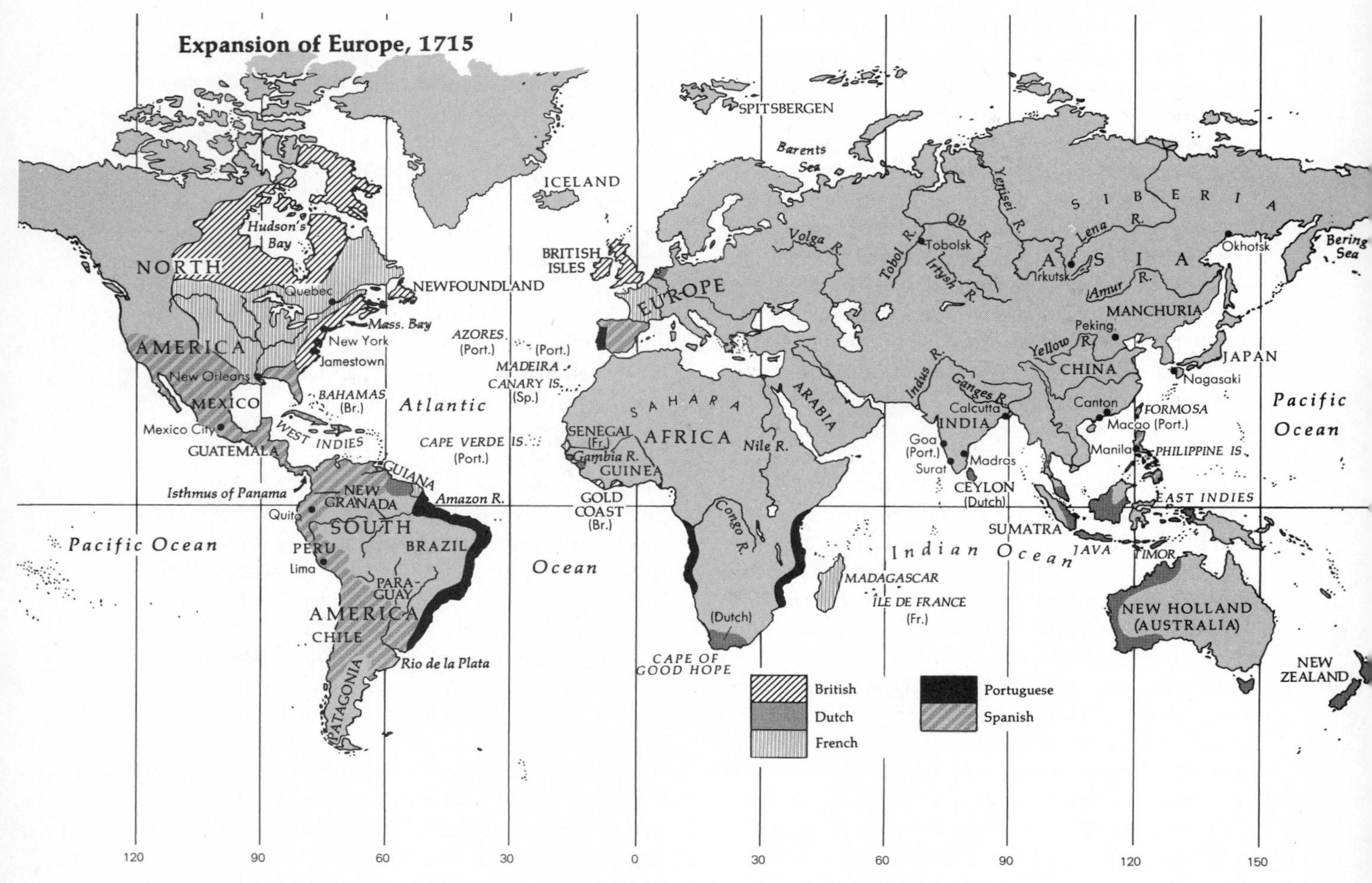

Expansion of Europe, 1715

settled by Calvinist Independents (Congregationalists), who believed in local self-government, and who set up their own Puritan state church, like Calvin's in Geneva or Cromwell's in England. Yet "heresy" appeared from the start, as Baptists, Quakers, and even Anglicans came to New England.

The southern colonies, especially tidewater Virginia, were settled for the most part by Anglicans, comfortable with the social distinctions and the large landholdings of rural England. The Church of England became the established church in Virginia. Yet in the Piedmont section of Virginia and the Carolinas, there were small farmers—"Scotch-Irish" Presbyterians and Germans from Pennsylvania. Geography and climate played their part, making the South the land of one-crop plantations producing tobacco, rice, or indigo, while New England and the Middle Colonies went in for small farming, fishing, and small-scale industry and commerce.

Maryland was founded partly to give refuge to Catholics. Rhode Island was founded by Roger Williams and others unwilling to conform to the orthodoxy of Massachusetts. Pennsylvania was founded by Quakers who believed in the separation of church and state. Such variety lay at the base of the religious freedom later prescribed in the Constitution of the United States. During the eighteenth century, it came to be recognized that people should be free to belong to any church or even to no church at all.

The colonists, as men of the seventeenth century, accepted class distinctions as a matter of course. Yet the seeds of democracy were present. There was no titled colonial nobility. The egalitarianism of the frontier and the career open to talent in the town balanced the privileged gentry in the coastal cities and in the Hudson Valley. Each colony had some sort of legislative body. Government by discussion was firmly planted from the beginning.

The crown was represented in most colonies by a royal governor. But the English government, in the instability of the Civil War, Cromwellian rule, Restoration, and Glorious Revolution, exerted no continuing bureaucratic or absolute rule over the colonies, as the Spaniards and French did over theirs. The English royal governors bickered with the colonial assemblies and often lost. Local government—in village and town and county—fostered wide popular participation. The English common law, which provided for trial by jury and lacked bureaucratic administrative regulation, perpetuated a very different tradition from that of the Spanish or French.

New France

To the north of the thirteen colonies, in the region around the Bay of Fundy and in the St. Lawrence Basin, New France for a century and a half posed a serious threat to the English North American colonies. The St. Lawrence and the Great Lakes gave the French easy access to the heart of the continent, whereas the Appalachians stood between the English and the Mississippi.

The French were also impelled westward by the fur trade. Furs are goods of very great value and comparatively little bulk, easily carried in canoes and small boats. Led by the Jesuits, the Catholic French were far more eager to convert the American Indians than were the Protestant English. The priest as well as the trapper led the push westward. In North America, the French were also moved to advance by the conscious imperial policy of the Bourbon monarchs.

The result was that the French, not the English, explored the interior of the continent. The names and accomplishments of the French explorers, missionaries, and traders—Marquette, Joliet, La Salle, Frontenac, Cadillac, Iberville—are a part of our American heritage. By the early eighteenth century, the French had built up a line of isolated trading posts—with miles of empty space between, thinly populated by Indians—which encircled the English colonies on the Atlantic coast.

From Quebec, one line of outposts led westward. From Mobile and New Orleans, in a colony founded at the beginning of the eighteenth century and named Louisiana after Louis XIV, other lines led northward up the Mississippi to join with those from Canada and Illinois.

But there were too few Frenchmen to contain the English. The French loss of Newfoundland, Acadia, and Hudson's Bay to England in the Utrecht settlement reflected their weakness. Theirs was a trading empire with military ambitions. Only in Quebec did it become a true colony of settlement. The Huguenot French, who might have come to settle as did the Puritans, were deliberately excluded by a royal policy determined to uphold the Catholic faith in New France.

The Indies, West and East; Africa

The French, Dutch, and English intruded upon the pioneer Spanish and Portuguese throughout the overseas empires. They broke the Spanish hold over the Caribbean and ultimately made that sea of many islands a kaleidoscope of colonial jurisdictions and a center of continuing naval wars and piracy. The West Indies were then one of the great prizes of imperialism. The cheap black slave labor that had replaced the exterminated Indians raised the staple tropical crops—tobacco, fruits, coffee, and, most important, cane sugar.

In India, the Mogul Empire proved strong enough to confine the Europeans chiefly to the coastal fringes. Gradually the French and English nibbled away at the Portuguese holdings. The English defeated a Portuguese fleet in 1612 and got trading rights at Surat on the west coast of India. The Mogul emperor, Aurangzeb, tried vainly to exclude them in 1685. In 1690 the English founded Calcutta in Bengal in eastern India.

The French got footholds on the southern coast near Madras at Pondichéry and soon had established other stations. Early in the eighteenth century, the stage was set in India as in North America for a decisive struggle between France and Britain. Both countries operated in India, as they had initially in North America, by means of chartered trading companies, the English East India Company and the French Compagnie des Indes Orientales. The home governments backed the companies when it came to annexing bits of land around the trading posts. Gradually both England and France became involved in Indian politics and wars. But neither country made an effort to found a New England or a New France in the East.

The Dutch, who operated the most profitable of all the East India companies, bypassed India but drove the Portuguese from the nearby island of Ceylon. In the East Indies proper, they built Batavia (from the Latin name for Holland) on the island of Java and founded an empire in Indonesia which they held until after World War II.

The island in Nagasaki harbor to which the Dutch were confined, 1699.

When the Dutch reached Japan in 1609, the Japanese rulers were already suspicious of Christian penetration and irritated at the bickerings between Portuguese Jesuits and Spanish Franciscans. Gradually the Japanese expelled all Christians. In 1641 only the Dutch alone were left, confined to an island in Nagasaki harbor. Japan remained sealed off from the West until the American Commodore Perry arrived in 1853, more than two centuries later.

In Africa, the Dutch took over the Cape of Good Hope from the Portuguese in 1652 and settled there—the ancestors of today's Afrikaners in South Africa. The French, too, were moving into Africa, first into Senegal on the west coast (1626). In the Indian Ocean, Louis XIV annexed the large island of Madagascar in 1686, and in 1715 the French took the island of Mauritius from the Dutch, rechristening it the Île de France.

The British broke into the competition by securing a foothold at the mouth of the Gambia River in West Africa (1662) and later added other acquisitions at French and Dutch expense. Thus a map of Africa and adjacent waters in the eighteenth century shows a series of coastal stations controlled by European states. Until the nineteenth century the interior remained untouched, except by slavers and native traders.

The Balance Sheet of Imperialism

Seen in terms of economics, the expansion of Europe in early modern times was by no means pure "exploitation" and "plundering." There was robbery, just as there was murder and enslavement. In dealing with the American Indians, the Europeans often gave far too little in exchange for land and goods of great value. The Indians sold the island of Manhattan to the Dutch for $24.00 worth of trinkets.

And the almost universally applied mercantilist policy kept money and manufacturing in the hands of the home country. It limited the colonies to the production of raw materials, a role that tended to keep even colonies of settlement economically dependent. Yet the expansion of Europe did add to the goods available to non-Europeans. Although few Europeans settled in India or Africa, their wares, and especially their weapons, gradually began the process of Europeanizing the rest of the world. By the eighteenth century this process was only beginning. The improvements in public health that Europeans would later discover and bring to the East were still unknown. But in America especially there were signs of the westernization to come.

The West in its turn was greatly affected

by the world overseas. The long list of items from the colonies included foodstuffs, utensils, and gadgets like pipes for smoking, hammocks and pajamas, and style of architecture and painting like bungalows and Japanese prints. Some novelties caught on more quickly than others. Tobacco, brought into Spain in the mid-sixteenth century as a soothing drug, had established itself by the seventeenth century as essential to the peace of mind of many European males. Potatoes, on the other hand, though highly nourishing and cheaper to grow than the staple breadstuffs, did not immediately catch on in Europe.

Among Westerners, knowledge of non-European beliefs and institutions eventually penetrated to the level of popular culture, where it is marked by a host of words—*powwow, kowtow, tabu, totem.* At the highest level of cultural interchange, that of religion and ethical ideas, however, the West imported little. The first impression of Westerners, not only when they met the relatively primitive cultures of the Americas, but even when they met the ancient cultures of the East, was that they had nothing to learn from them.

In time the West would learn to respect the other worldliness of Hinduism and the dignity and simplicity of primitive peoples. But for the most part what struck the first generations of Europeans—when they bothered to think about anything but money-making and empire-building—was the poverty, dirt, and superstition they found in India and China, the low material standards of primitive peoples, the heathenness of the heathens.

But even then exposure to these very different cultures acted as a stimulus in the West. It increased the fund of the marvelous, the incredible. The early accounts of the New World are full of giants and pygmies, El Dorados with gold-paved streets, fountains of eternal youth, fantastic plants and animals. The literary and artistic imagination revelled in all this, from the island of Shakespeare's *Tempest* to the Xanadu of Coleridge's *Kubla Khan,* two hundred years later.

Science, too, was stimulated. A dip into any of the early collections of voyages gives an impression of the realistic sense and careful observations of European travelers rather than of their credulity and exaggerations. Here is the modern science of geography already well on the way to maturity, and here too are contributions to the modern social sciences of anthropology, comparative government, and economics.

The effects of expansion were harsh and unsettling as well as stimulating. The great new supplies of gold and silver from the Americas pushed European prices up. This inflation accompanied, perhaps indeed "caused" or at least helped, general economic expansion. In this process, the merchants and financiers gained. People on fixed incomes suffered. The income of wage earners and peasants increased but usually not as fast as prices.

The Beginnings of One World

By the early eighteenth century the interior of Africa and our Pacific Northwest were still blank spots on the map. Yet it was already clear that only one system of international politics existed in the world. From now on, all general European wars tended to be world wars, fought on all the seas and all the continents. By the eighteenth century the world was already one world.

Of course, no common authority of any kind could reach all men. There were pockets of isolated peoples. And the masses of the world, even in Europe, remained ignorant of, and uninterested in, what went on in the heads and hearts of people elsewhere. But already Western goods had penetrated almost everywhere. Already an educated minority was growing up: professional geographers, journalists, diplomatists, men of business, specialists who had to deal with the problems of remote places and even of the world as a whole.

READING SUGGESTIONS on The Seventeenth Century: War, Politics, and Empire
(Asterisks indicate paperback.)

General Treatments

C. J. Friedrich, *The Age of the Baroque, 1610–1660;* F. L. Nussbaum, *The Triumph of Science and Reason, 1660–1685;* and J. B. Wolf, *The Emergence of the Great Powers, 1685–1715* (*all Harper Torchbooks). Three consecutive volumes in the Harper Rise of Modern Europe series, with good bibliographies. The first is particularly original in its treatment.

G. N. Clark, *The Seventeenth Century* (*Galaxy); and D. Ogg, *Europe in the Seventeenth Century* (*Collier). Two briefer treatments.

R. S. Dunn, *The Age of Religious Wars, 1559–1689* (*Norton). A valuable survey.

M. Ashley, *The Golden Century* (1969). The entire century in perspective.

A. Vagts, *A History of Militarism* (*Free Press); and E. M. Earle, *Makers of Modern Strategy* (*Athenaeum). Both include good treatments of seventeenth-century warfare.

E. F. Heckscher, *Mercantilism,* 2 vols. (1955). Standard advanced work by a distinguished Swedish economist. Controversial and not for beginners.

T. Aston, ed., *Crisis in Europe, 1560–1660.* The essays examine the upheaval of the century and include some very distinguished historical writing.

The Thirty Years' War and Germany

C. V. Wedgwood, *The Thirty Years' War* (*Anchor). Good full-length treatment, perhaps underemphasizing the destructiveness of the conflict.

S. H. Steinberg, *The "Thirty Years' War" and the Conflict for European Hegemony* (*Norton). Shorter than Miss Wedgwood's masterly book.

G. Pagès, *The Thirty Years' War* (*Harper Torchbooks). Heavily diplomatic in its emphasis, not so recent as the two books listed above.

T. K. Rabb, ed., *The Thirty Years' War* (*Heath). Collected modern essays on the war's motives and impact.

M. Roberts, *Gustavus Adolphus,* 2 vols. (1953, 1958). A solid, detailed biography.

H. Holborn, *History of Modern Germany,* 2 vols. (1959, 1963). Volume I includes the Thirty Years' War.

Revolution and Settlement in England

M. Ashley, *England in the Seventeenth Century* (*Penguin); and C. Hill, *The Century of Revolution, 1603–1714* (*Norton). Two surveys by well-known scholars, the latter a Marxist.

G. Davies, *The Early Stuarts, 1603–1660* (1949); and G. N. Clark, *The Later Stuarts, 1660–1714* (1949). Two good but more detailed volumes in The Oxford History of England.

W. Notestein, *The English People on the Eve of Colonization, 1603–1660* (*Harper Torchbooks). A fine brief account of the earlier period from the social historian's point of view.

D. H. Wilson, *King James Sixth and First* (*Galaxy). Good study of the first Stuart.

C. V. Wedgwood, *The King's Peace 1637–1641* (1955); *The King's War, 1641–1647* (1959); and *A Coffin for King Charles* (1964). *The* detailed study of the entire English Civil War.

L. Stone, *The Causes of the English Revolution, 1529–1642* (*Harper Torchbooks). Modern interpretations of the key event.

C. Hibbert, *Charles I* (1968). Useful biography.

C. V. Wedgwood, *Oliver Cromwell,* (1973). By the same specialist we have cited so often above.

C. Hill, *God's Englishman* (*Harper Torchbooks). Authoritative study, strongly pro-Cromwellian in tone. M. R. Ashley, *Oliver Cromwell and the Puritan Revolution* (*Collier). A more conventional but reliable brief work.

S. R. Gardiner, *The First Two Stuarts and the Puritan Revolution* (*Apollo). A textbook first published just over a century ago. Gives a good example of the work of the learned author of a multivolume history of seventeenth-century England.

J. H. Hexter, *Reappraisals in History* (*Harper Torchbooks). The controversy over the role of the gentry, masterfully summarized.

L. Stone, *The Crisis of the Aristocracy, 1558–1641* (*Oxford), and *Social Change and Revolution in England, 1540–1640* (*Barnes and Noble). Two fundamental, more detailed studies of the same subject.

C. Hill, *The World Turned Upside Down* (*Compass). The "far-out" radicals of the English Revolution and their ideas.

M. Walzer, *The Revolution of the Saints* (*Athenaeum). Another sympathetic account of the extreme radicals.

W. Haller, *The Rise of Puritanism* (*Harper Torchbooks). By a leading authority on the religion and politics of the Puritans.

G. Davies, *The Restoration of Charles II, 1658–1689* (1955). Good detailed study.

F. C. Turner, *James II* (1948). Makes the best possible case for James.

G. M. Trevelyan, *The English Revolution, 1688–1689* (*Galaxy). The Glorious Revolution as seen by a master historian.

G. M. Straka, ed., *The Revolution of 1688* (*Heath). A collection of modern studies on the subject.

S. B. Baxter, *William III and the Defense of European Liberty* (1966). A sympathetic account.

J. T. Tanner, *English Constitutional Conflicts of the Seventeenth Century* (*Cambridge). Extremely useful and comprehensive work.

Divine-Right Monarchy in France

G. R. R. Treasure, *Seventeenth-Century France* (1966). Clearly written and detailed survey.

J. D. Lough, *An Introduction to Seventeenth-Century France* (*McKay). Primarily designed for the student of literature, but useful for anybody interested in the subject.

A. Guérard, *France in the Classical Age: Life and Death of an Ideal* (*Harper Torchbooks). An original interpretation of the period.

C. V. Wedgwood, *Richelieu and the French Monarchy* (*Collier); and M. Ashley, *Louis XIV and the Greatness of France* (*Free Press). Good brief introductions.

J. B. Wolf, *Louis XIV* (*Norton). A detailed political biography.

P. Goubert, *Louis XIV and Twenty Million Frenchmen* (*Vintage). The king and his subjects.

W. H. Lewis, *The Splendid Century* (*Morrow). Social France under Louis XIV.

W. F. Church, ed., *The Greatness of Louis XIV* (*Heath), a collection of modern scholarly studies; and *The Impact of Absolutism in France* (*Wiley), source materials and commentaries on the Age of Richelieu and Louis XIV.

C. W. Cole, *Colbert and a Century of French Mercantilism,* 2 vols. (1939). A standard work.

Europe Overseas

J. B. Brebner, *The Explorers of North America, 1492–1806* (*Meridian). Good brief survey.

D. J. Boorstin, *Americans: The Colonial Experience* (*Vintage). A short introduction.

C. M. Andrews, *The Colonial Period of American History,* 3 vols. (*Yale). A detailed treatment.

L. B. Wright, *Cultural Life of the American Colonies, 1607–1783* (*Harper Torchbooks). An excellent study.

J. H. Elliott, *The Old World and the New, 1492–1650* (*Cambridge). The impact of the New World on the Old.

G. M. Wrong, *The Rise and Fall of New France,* 2 vols. (1928). Solid study by a Canadian scholar.

S. E. Morison, ed., *The Parkman Reader* (1955). Selections from Parkman's many volume classic history, *France and England in North America.*

C. R. Boxer, *The Dutch Seaborne Empire, 1600–1800* (1965). By a leading authority.

B. H. M. Vlekke, *Nusantara: A History of Indonesia* (1959). Where the Dutch founded their most important colony.

CHAPTER TEN

The Great Modern Revolution Begins

Twice in human history a chain of developments has enabled civilization to make a great leap forward. About 10,000 years ago people began to grow the food they consumed rather than to depend upon hunting and wild crops. Then, hundreds or even thousands could settle in one community and begin to trade with other settlements. These advances led to the formation of governments and to the evolution of the written languages needed by merchants and officials in their expanding activities. Together, these achievements constituted the Neolithic Revolution.

No advances of comparable significance were made until the beginning of the scientific revolution less than five hundred years ago. The rapid progress in astronomy, physics, and mathematics during the sixteenth and seventeenth centuries awakened new interest in the forces of nature. Thinkers turned away from traditional religious teachings to explore nature on their own. Their studies led many intellectuals to champion the new ideas for the improvement of humanity known as the Enlightenment. The Enlightenment, in turn, set the stage for the dramatic innovations that would begin to transform the economy and politics of the West during the last quarter of the eighteenth century.

I. THE SCIENTIFIC REVOLUTION

The scientific trailblazers of the 1600s relied both on their own insights and on the development of new instruments and techniques. The new approach was defended most forcefully by the English politician and intellectual Francis Bacon (1561–1626), who insisted on the systematic accumulation of data. The empirical method—the careful observation of experience—would enable the human mind to understand nature. Bacon asserted that valid conclusions about natural events could be reached only through the process of *induction,* proceeding from the evidence of details to a general conclusion. Bacon's faith in empiricism and induction departed sharply from the widespread acceptance of *deduction,* which proceeded from the general to the particular. Bacon deplored the continued reliance upon views of the universe many centuries old, particularly those of Aristotle (4th century B.C.) and Ptolemy (2nd century A.D.). Bacon's great Italian contemporary, Galileo, ridiculed the blind acceptance of ancient authority and thereby came into conflict with the teachings of the Catholic Church.

Galileo (1564–1642) and other scientists devised new instruments that made possible more exact measurements of the natural world. These in turn promoted the inductive approach to science. By putting two lenses together, an experiment probably originated by Dutch glassmakers, scientists obtained greater magnification of the natural phenomena they were studying. Galileo applied the new technique to devise a telescope that revealed new details about heavenly bodies. The Dutchman Van Leeuwenhoek (1632–1723), using the same method, made a microscope that enabled him to discover tiny organisms hitherto unknown—red blood cells, bacteria, protozoa, and spermatozoa. Working from the experiments of Galileo, other technicians developed the thermometer and the barometer. Employing the barometer a Frenchman, Blaise Pascal (1623–1662), proved that what we term "air pressure" diminished as altitude increased, and he went on to explode the old adage, "Nature abhors a vacuum," by showing that a vacuum is possible.

King Charles II of England roared with laughter on being told that members of his Royal Society were weighing the air. Nevertheless, the Royal Society for Improving Natural Knowledge, founded in 1662, and the French Academy of Sciences, founded in 1666, were important promoters of scientific investigation. In characteristic English fashion, the Royal Society was a private undertaking, though with a royal charter. Its French counterpart, sponsored by Colbert for the greater glory of Louis XIV, was a government institution whose fellows received salaries along with instructions to avoid discussion of religion and politics. Meantime, two important societies had already appeared in Italy: in Florence an academy to promote experimentation, and in Rome the Academy of the Lynx-Eyed (the lynx is a wildcat with acute eyesight).

Through the formal correspondence of their secretaries and informal letters between members, these institutions fostered the growth of an international scientific community. They admitted as members both professional men and inquisitive aristocrats. Among the aristocrats was Robert Boyle (1627–1691), the son of an Irish earl, who discovered the law of physics that bears his name. Boyle's Law states that under compression the volume of a gas is inversely proportional to the amount of pressure.

Although many scientific works were published in Latin, they were often translated into the vernacular to reach a wider public. The basic language for scientific computation, however, was mathematics. This branch of knowledge was benefiting from a series of innovations that made it possible to perform traditional calculations more quickly and to make new ones never before possible. In 1585 Simon Stevin, who came from the Low Countries, published a book with a wonderfully explicit title: *The Decimal, Teaching with Unheard-of Ease How to Perform All Calculations . . . by Whole Numbers without Fractions.* In 1614 John Napier of Scotland devised another mathematical shortcut with his *Marvelous Rule of Logarithms,* which simplified the processes of multiplying, dividing, and finding square roots. The French mathematician and philosopher, René Descartes (1596–1650), invented analytical geometry, which brought geometry and algebra together. His "Cartesian coordinates" made it possible to solve an algebraic equation by plotting it on a graph.

The most brilliant mathematical achievement of the century was the devising of ways to deal with such uncertain quantities as variables and probabilities. Pascal contributed his studies of games of chance, and Dutch insurance brokers drew up the first actuarial tables predicting the life expectancy of their clients. Then Isaac Newton (1642–1727) and the German philosopher Leibniz (1646–1716), apparently quite independently of each other, invented the calculus. This new mathematical tool, together with Cartesian geometry, enabled Newton to make the calculations supporting his revolutionary hypotheses in astronomy and physics.

Astronomy and Physics

In astronomy the heliocentric theory of Copernicus (see Chapter 7) had raised many difficulties. Subsequent observations had failed to confirm his belief that the planets revolved about the sun in circular paths. The German astronomer, Kepler (1571–1630), opened the way to a resolution by proving mathematically that planetary orbits were elliptical. Then Galileo's telescope revealed spots on the sun, rings around Saturn, and moonlike satellites around Jupiter. This evidence of "corruption in high places" led Galileo to publish a book in 1632 defending the heliocentric concept and ridiculing supporters of the geocentric theory. Traditionalists in the Church thereupon brought Galileo before the Inquisition, which placed his book on the *Index* of prohibited works. He was subjected to a kind of house arrest and forced to make a public recantation of his unorthodox views. However, Galileo is reported to have had the last word: "and yet it does move"—the Earth is not stationary, as the Church insists, but behaves as the other planets do.

An even more celebrated story recounts how Galileo dropped balls of different weights from the Leaning Tower of Pisa to test Aristotle's theory that objects fall with velocities proportional to their weight. Although the story may be untrue, Galileo did in fact prove Aristotle wrong. His studies of the motion of projectiles, of pendulums, and of falling and rolling bodies helped to establish the concepts of acceleration and inertia, which were later refined by Newton.

Isaac Newton (1642–1727) made many of his most exciting discoveries when he was still a student at Cambridge University. When a severe outbreak of plague forced the university to close in 1665, he returned home; there, according to the well-known tale, he observed an apple falling to the ground in his family's orchard. Wondering why the apple fell as it did, he found the answer in the force of gravity, which attracted the apple to the vastly larger earth. Later he drew up laws of motion, arguing that the force of gravity operated throughout the universe in a more complex fashion. He concluded that it was mutual attraction that caused the planets to move in orbit around the sun, and satellites, such as the earth's moon, to move in orbit around the planets. In mathematical terms Newton stated the force of gravity as directly proportional to the masses of two bodies attracted one to the other, and inversely proportional to the squares of the distance between them. Put very simply, his laws of motion argued that bodies were not in effect "self-starters" but moved in response to forces imposed upon them.

Newton waited until 1687 to publish his theories in *The Mathematical Principles of Natural Philosophy,* better known by its Latin title, *Principia Mathematica.* Newton also contributed to the development of optics by using a prism to separate the rays of sunlight into the colors of the spectrum. He demonstrated that objects themselves have no intrinsic color; rather, the color of an object depends on what light it absorbs and reflects. In contrast to Galileo, Newton gained full recognition for his achievements from the "establishment" of his own day. He was awarded a professorship at Cambridge University, the presidency of the Royal Society, a knighthood with the title of "Sir Isaac," and the well-paid post of Master of the Mint. But even Newton was not quite the model scientist, for he put consider-

Newton.

able energy into the pseudoscience of alchemy and unscientific efforts to determine the precise dates of events related in the Bible.

During the eighteenth century, physicists and astronomers consolidated the great advances made in the seventeenth. The versatile Benjamin Franklin (1706–1790) helped found the American Philosophical Society in Philadelphia, which still exists today. He demonstrated the identical nature of lightning and electricity by obtaining an electrical charge from a key attached to the string of a kite he sent aloft during a thunderstorm. The experiment aroused much interest in Europe and was repeated at Versailles for the instruction of the French royal family. The "Newton of France," the Marquis de Laplace (1749–1827), rounded out Sir Isaac's investigation of celestial mechanics, as Newton's theories were termed, and described the movements of the solar system in mathematical formulas and theorems.

Geology, Physiology, Biology, and Chemistry

The mechanistic views of the physicists and astronomers spread to other fields of science. In geology the English physician William Gilbert (1540–1603) published in 1600 a study of magnetism suggesting that the earth itself was a giant magnet. In physiology another Englishman, William Harvey (1578–1657), physician to King Charles I, argued that the human heart was a pump that drove the blood through a single circulatory system. He thus challenged the idea handed down from Galen in the second century A.D. that the arteries and the veins were two entirely separate systems. Harvey's challenge was confirmed when a microscope revealed that tiny blood vessels called capillaries linked the arteries to the veins. In biology proper, progress advanced with the careful collection of specimens and the classification of plants and animals according to genus and species. This classification, still employed today, was perfected by the Swedish botanist Carolus Linnaeus (1707–1778), who followed the old custom of Latinizing his Swedish name (Carl von Linné).

Modern chemical analysis came of age when the Scottish professor, Joseph Black (1728–1799), exploded the theory that the air was composed of a single element by proving that it contained several different gases. Continuing the study of gases, the Frenchman Antoine Lavoisier (1743–1794) demonstrated that water was formed by a union of hydrogen and oxygen, the familiar H_2O. Lavoisier also contended that all substances were made up of certain basic chemical elements, of which he identified twenty-three.

World Machine and Rationalism

These scientific advances had a revolutionary effect beyond the realm of science proper. They exalted rationalism (reliance on reason) and innovation at the expense of religious belief and old established authority. The new mechanistic interpretation of the universe transformed the concept of God from an incomprehensible creator and judge to the chief architect of a world machine. Humans could grasp the operations of that machine if they applied their reasoning faculty, as Newton had demonstrated. The new view of humanity stressed the mechanical aspects of the human body—the heart was seen to be a sort of pump, the arm a lever.

A century earlier the materialism and rationalism promoted by the scientific revolution had found a most articulate spokesman in the Frenchman René Descartes. When he was a young man, as his *Discourse on Method* (1637) relates, he resolved to mistrust all authorities, theological and intellectual. His skepticism swept everything aside until he concluded that there was just one thing he could *not* doubt: his own existence. The self engaged in the processes of thinking and doubting must be real—"I think, therefore I am" (in Latin, *Cogito ergo sum*). Descartes then reconstructed the world until he arrived at God, whom he viewed not as a patriarch but as a master of geometry whose mathematical order-

Descartes: portrait by Frans Hals.

liness foreshadowed the great engineer of the Newtonian world machine. But where Newton would proceed inductively by drawing on the data compiled by the observations and experiments of earlier scientists, Descartes proceeded deductively, deriving both the universe and God from himself in the act of thinking.

The world that Descartes reconstructed proved to be two separate worlds—one composed of mind and soul, the other of body and matter. Descartes himself claimed competence only in dealing with the material world, yet the way in which he dealt with it suggested that only the world of science and reason counted. He even boasted that if given matter and space, he could construct the universe itself.

Not all the contributors to the new age of science abandoned traditional religious concerns. Pascal, the great mathematician and experimenter, was also an eloquent spokesman for the Jansenists, a puritanical sect of French Catholics who accepted the belief in predestination taught by Cornelius Jansen, a Dutch theologian (see Chapter 9). Repelled by the idea that God was merely a master engineer, Pascal sought the Lord of Abraham and the Old Testament prophets. And one night in November 1654 he had a mystical experience during which he felt with absolute certainty the presence of God and Christ.

Baruch Spinoza (1632–1677), a Dutch Jew, tried to reconcile the God of science and the God of Scripture. He constructed a system of ethical axioms as logical as a series of mathematical propositions. He also attempted to reunite the two separate worlds of Descartes by linking matter with mind and body with soul. Spinoza concluded that God was present everywhere and in everything—an acceptance of pantheism that horrified many of his contemporaries. His fellow Jews ostracized him, Christians shunned him as an atheist, and intellectuals deplored his rejection of rationalism and materialism.

II THE ECONOMIC REVOLUTIONS

Matching the scientific revolution in importance were the advances in commerce, agriculture, and industry that together constitute the great modern economic revolutions. They began earlier, in the late Middle Ages, but proceeded more slowly with many ups and downs. There were no dramatic breakthroughs comparable to those of Galileo and Newton until the industrial revolution "took off" in late eighteenth-century Britain. By then commerce and agriculture had already made many significant advances.

Commerce

The oldest component of the economic revolution was commerce, which included many of the activities Americans call "business." Banking, accounting, and insurance had all become prominent factors in urban Europe during the fourteenth and fifteenth centuries. The sixteenth added the institution of the regulated trading company, which pooled the resources of individual merchants to make long and risky voyages. It became a more tightly organized association with the development of the joint-stock company, in which many individuals bought shares but left management in the hands of a few specialists.

Earlier chapters have noted how some governments brought commerce under strict controls in order to advance national self-interest—the policy known as mercantilism. The most prominent examples were the Spain of Philip II and his successors, and the France of Louis XIV and Colbert. The do's and dont's of mercantilism, however, seldom solved the complex economic problems that confronted Europe in the seventeenth century. The huge imports of gold and silver from the New World caused prices to rise rapidly, which in turn increased the difficulties stemming from inflation. Then, during the 1600s, the population of European states either ceased to grow or actually declined as the result of a series of unfavorable factors—prolonged warfare, crop failures, famine, very high death rates among the young, and epidemics of bubonic plague. In 1665 an outbreak of plague in England is estimated to have killed 100,000 in London and its environs—twenty percent of the area's population. The calamities of the seventeenth century rivaled those of the fourteenth.

Despite a prolonged depression and other woes, the 1600s scored important advances in commerce. The newly independent Dutch republic became "the schoolmaster of Europe," thanks to the leadership of Dutch merchant vessels in seaborne trade, of Dutch brokers in life insurance, and of the Bank of Amsterdam in international finance. But the republic, which was a very small state, became exhausted by its wars against the

France of Louis XIV. By the early eighteenth century, economic leadership passed to Britain and France.

At the same time, the long depression of the seventeenth century ended. Renewed growth in population caused a rising demand for food and goods, which in turn stimulated maritime trade. Many ports enjoyed great prosperity—London, Bristol, and Liverpool in England; Nantes, Bordeaux, and Marseilles in France; Hamburg in Germany; and in Italy Leghorn, the admirably managed free port of the Grand Duchy of Tuscany. As the growth of trade increased the demand for insurance of ships and cargoes, insurance brokers in early eighteenth century London gathered at Edward Lloyd's coffee house in Lombard Street to discuss business, news, and politics. Thus was born Lloyd's of London, the firm that developed the standard policy for marine insurance and published *Lloyd's List,* the first detailed shipping newspaper.

Improved charts and a greater number of lighthouses and buoys made navigation safer. And so did two new instruments: the sextant, an elaboration of the telescope that showed the altitude of the sun at noon, and the chronometer, a timepiece unaffected by the motion of a ship. The sextant determined the ship's latitude, its position measured by degrees north or south of the equator. Longitude was determined by the difference between local time aboard ship calculated by the sextant, and Greenwich Mean Time, the hours and minutes on the zero meridian at Greenwich near London registered by the chronometer. East of Greenwich local time was faster, and to the west it was slower.

Advances in land transport came more slowly. Except in France, which continued Henry IV's example of building good highways, "roads" were often mere paths or trails. The shipment of goods was slow, costly, and unsafe until the construction of turnpikes and new canals gradually improved the situation after 1750. Business was also handicapped by the restrictive practices of guilds and by the enormous variety of coins, weights and measures, and local tolls. Baden, one of the smaller German states, had 112 separate measures for length, 65 for dry goods, 123 for liquids, and 163 for cereals, and 80 different pound weights! A merchant who shipped 60 planks down the Elbe River from Dresden to Hamburg had to pay so many tolls to the towns and principalities along the way that only 6 of the 60 would reach Hamburg.

The vigorous survival of local vested interests revealed the limitations of mercantilism, which in theory required the regulation of trade at the national level. But no eighteenth-century government had the number of officials needed for effective regulation. Austria, Prussia, and some other German states tried to assimilate mercantilism into the more systematic policy of *cameralism* (from the Latin *camera,* chamber, in this instance a council dealing with expenditures and income). The cameralists devoted their main effort to the management of state budgets and the increase of revenues. Other European states relied heavily on private companies and individuals to execute national policies. The English and Dutch East India Companies exercised not only a trading monopoly in their colonial preserves but also virtual sovereign powers, including the right to maintain soldiers and conduct diplomacy. On the whole, private initiative did more than sluggish governments to advance the commercial revolution.

The Mississippi and South Sea Bubbles

In the years after 1715, when almost every state in Europe staggered under the debts piled up during the recent wars, France and Britain both turned to the private sector. To meet the large annual interest on bonds and other obligations, they transferred the management of state debts to joint-stock companies. They awarded trading concessions to the companies which, it was hoped, would prove so lucrative that the companies' profits would easily cover the interest due on government bonds.

In France the Duke of Orléans, regent for the boy king Louis XV, allowed his crony John Law (1671–1729) to try out his "system." The system of this Scottish adventurer and mathematical wizard was mercantilist but with a difference. Where orthodox mercantilism measured the worth of a state by the amount of silver and gold it possessed, Law claimed that the limited supply of precious metals made it difficult to increase the coins in circulation and therefore difficult to promote business. Law's solution was to issue paper money, backed by the nation's wealth in land and in trade. The amount of paper in circulation would be increased or decreased according to the needs of the business community. A new central bank established by Law, following the practice of the Bank of Amsterdam, issued paper notes of stable value. Business activity at once increased.

Law then set up the Mississippi Company,

which monopolized commerce with the Louisiana colony and soon absorbed the other French colonial trading companies. Law's system reached to almost every corner of the French economy, as the Mississippi Company took over the government's debt. When it agreed to accept government bonds in partial payment for shares of its stock, the bondholders responded with enthusiasm, for their bonds had fallen to 20 percent of their face value. To obtain working capital, however, the company had to sell additional shares of stock, and Law painted the company's prospects in vivid colors to attract cash purchasers. Investors, large and small, caught the fever of speculation, and by the close of 1719 Mississippi stock was selling for forty times its par value. Cautious investors began to sell their shares, receiving payment in banknotes, which they took to Law's bank for redemption into specie. The Mississippi Bubble burst when the bank used up its reserves of gold and silver and suspended specie payments in February 1720. Law, whose talents might have revitalized the French economy had he used them more discreetly, fled from France.

In England, meanwhile, the South Sea Company had paid the government an exorbitant sum for the privilege of managing the debt. The company's resources consisted mainly of the right to furnish slaves to Spain's American colonies under the Asiento agreement of 1713 between Britain and Spain. The South Sea Company, like the Mississippi, invited government creditors to exchange their bonds for stock. To make the stock more attractive, the directors of the company bought and sold shares in secret and permitted new investors to obtain stock with a down payment of only 10 percent in cash. They also circulated reports of forthcoming and immensely profitable voyages by the company's ships. Like Law, the South Sea directors created a speculative boom, in which South Sea shares, with a par value of £100, sold for £129 in January of 1720, and for £1,050 in June. The bubble then burst, and by September the company's shares had fallen to £150. Parliament ordered an investigation and

London during the South Sea Bubble: a Hogarth engraving. The sign above the door at the upper left reads "Raffleing for Husbands with Lottery Fortunes—in Here."

seized properties of the directors to protect the company's creditors. Many reputations were ruined or tarnished, and the future development of stock companies was impeded by the new requirement that they buy costly charters.

The Mississippi and South Sea Bubbles were acute examples of the economic growing pains affecting the states of Europe as they groped for solutions to baffling financial problems. The end results were not always unfortunate. Voltaire, who was a very successful and not very scrupulous speculator, observed that Law's "imaginary system gave birth to a real commerce," and released French business from the torpor created by the defeats of Louis XIV. The Mississippi Company, reorganized after 1720, consistently made a handsome profit. In England, the political overturn after the South Sea Bubble brought to power the Whig leader Robert Walpole with a program of honoring the debt as a *national* debt. This was a novel concept and a great advance in fiscal morality, for most states still treated their debts as the personal obligations of the monarch, to be repaid or repudiated as he saw fit.

The Agricultural Revolution

The second force modernizing the economy, the revolution in agriculture, centered on improvements that enabled fewer farmers to produce more crops. The Dutch Republic and its southern neighbor, the Spanish Netherlands (Austrian after 1713), pioneered in the culture of new crops—the potato, the turnip, and clover. Turnips furnished feed for livestock over the winter, thus eliminating the traditional slaughter of stock in the autumn. Clover, by fixing nitrogen in the soil, increased the fertility of the land and eliminated the need to let fields lie fallow every second or third year.

In England the new crops were introduced during the seventeenth century and vigorously publicized by "improving landlords" in the eighteenth. Charles Townsend (1674–1738), nicknamed "Turnip," promoted a four-year crop rotation, planting a field to turnips, then barley, then clover, then wheat. Jethro Tull (1674–1741) was impressed by the high yields obtained in small French vineyards and truck gardens where seeds were planted individually and each plant cultivated by a hoe. In *The Horse Hoeing Husbandry* he informed his countrymen how he adapted French methods to larger English fields. Instead of the wasteful practice of scattering seed broadcast, he planted it deep in regular rows by using a horse-drawn "drill," and he cultivated crops with a horse-drawn hoe.

For such improvements to be efficient, large farms were required on land that was not subdivided into long narrow plots or used in common with neighboring farmers. Improving landlords therefore sought to fence off common lands as their private property; thus enclosures, which in Tudor times had served to enlarge sheep pastures, now increased the amount of crop land. The enclosure movement reached a peak in the last decades of the eighteenth century and the first of the nineteenth, as Parliament passed hundreds of separate acts that affected several million acres. Rural England began to assume its modern aspect of large fields fenced by hedgerows, and an important transition had occurred from the nearly self-sufficient manor of the Middle Ages to the capitalist farm that produced a specialized crop.

Enclosures enabled England to feed a growing population, but they also caused widespread social misery. In eighteenth-century England, as in ancient Greece and Rome, the development of capitalistic estates ruined many yeomen. These small farmers could not get along without rights to use common land, nor could they afford to buy tools, install fences, and become improving farmers themselves. Many of them reluctantly became hired hands on big farms or sought work in the rapidly growing towns.

The Industrial Revolution Begins

By increasing productivity and releasing workers for jobs off the farm, the agricultural revolution assisted the industrial revolution. But industry also required capital to finance buildings and equipment, raw materials, and markets for its manufactures. The colonies helped to provide the last two items, and merchants who traded overseas supplied part of the capital. Thus the commercial revolution assisted industrial growth.

In textiles, the making of yarn and cloth had long been under the "domestic system." Spinners and weavers worked at home on simple wheels and looms, often as laborers for a middleman who furnished materials and sold the finished yarn and cloth. In some industries which also depended on hand processes, many laborers were assembled in a single large workshop. The industrial revolution made the domestic system obsolete and converted the large workshop into a factory. Machines replaced the spinning wheel, the loom, and other simple hand tools; and water or steam replaced human and animal muscle as the source of power. Because power-driven machines were often cumbersome and complicated, sizable factories were needed to house them.

By 1789, these revolutionary changes had affected only a few industries—mining, metallurgy, and textiles. Coal-mining was already a big business, mainly because of the demand for coke by iron smelters. Smelters had formerly used charcoal to convert ore into iron, but as more and more English forests were cut down charcoal became so scarce and expensive that it constituted 80 percent of the cost of producing iron. Raw coal could not serve as smelter fuel because the chemicals it contained would make the iron brittle. Then in the eighteenth century the Darby family of Shropshire discovered how to remove the chemical impurities by an oven process that converted coal into coke.

The revolution in textiles centered on the cheaper production of cotton cloth. The flying shuttle, a device first applied to the hand loom in England (1733), enabled a single weaver to do work that had previously required the services of two. Looms equipped with the flying shuttle used up the supply of hand-spun thread so fast that the London Society for the Encouragement of Arts, Manufactures, and Commerce offered a prize for improving the spinning process. It was won in 1764 by James Hargreaves for his "spinning jenny," a series of spinning wheels geared together to make eight threads simultaneously. Soon the jenny was adapted to water power and its output grew to a hundred or more threads at once. The eventual release of industry from dependence on unreliable water power was foreshadowed in the 1760s when the Scotsman James Watt introduced the steam engine.

But large-scale production of Watt's engine was delayed for a generation by the difficulties of making the precisely fitting parts it required. And, although Britain had nearly 150 cotton mills by 1789, woolens and dozens of other basic commodities continued to be made by hand. Full industrial development depended on skilled labor forces using precision technology and also on the extension of canals and the building of railroads to make possible the cheap shipment of heavy freight. While the eighteenth century took many of the initial steps in the industrial revolution, it remained for the next century to apply them on a truly revolutionary scale.

III THE ENLIGHTENMENT

The *Encyclopédie* and the *Philosophes*

The new industrial machines and the details of their operation were illustrated in elaborate plates that filled eleven of the thirty-three volumes comprising the French *Encyclopédie.* This ambitious publishing venture, which began in 1751 took three decades to complete. It was committed to ending the superstition, intolerance, and inequality in existing society, and to instructing its readers in the wonders of science and the virtues of nature. Its editor, Denis Diderot (1713–1784), was a prominent spokesman for the Enlightenment who devoted many years of fourteen-hour working days to a crusade on behalf of reason and progress.

Among the 160 contributors to the *Encyclopédie* were many leading figures of the Enlightenment—Voltaire, Montesquieu, Rousseau, Condorcet, Quesnay, and Turgot. They were called *philosophes* (French for "philosophers"), although few of them were philosophers in the scholarly sense. They were critics, publicists, economists, political scientists, and champions of projects for the improvement of mankind. What linked many of them together was the conviction that human reason could cure people of past ills and enable them to discover the natural laws regulating human existence, thereby assuring humanity's

Smelting copper: an engraving from Diderot's "Encyclopédie."

progress toward perpetual peace and a utopian society.

Not all the philosophes were so optimistic, however. Voltaire devoted his most famous tale, *Candide,* to ridiculing the idea that all was for the best in the best of all possible worlds. Nevertheless, the mainstream of the Enlightenment was optimistic. A famous example is the American Declaration of Independence, which listed the pursuit of happiness as a fundamental human right along with life and liberty. The idea that a human being could pursue and perhaps achieve happiness was indeed a revolutionary departure from the traditional Christian belief that happiness could be found only in heaven. Still more optimistic was Condorcet's *Progress of the Human Mind,* written, ironically, when the author was in hiding from the French Revolution's Reign of Terror. "Nature has placed no bounds on the perfecting of the human faculties," Condorcet concluded, "and the progress of this perfectibility is limited only by the duration of the globe on which nature has placed us."*

The philosophes' belief in human potential derived in part from Descartes, who had deduced a whole philosophy from the fact that he reasoned at all. And it derived still more from John Locke (1632–1704), who eloquently defended England's Glorious Revolution in two works published in 1690. *The Second Treatise of Government* argued that a government must respect human life, liberty, and property. When it fails to do so, as it did under James II, then the overthrow of the monarch is justified. The *Essay Concerning Human Understanding* strengthened Locke's case against the defenders of absolute monarchy. The *Essay* ridiculed their argument that the inclination to submit to authority was present in human beings from birth. Locke denied the existence of innate ideas and compared the mind of the newborn to a blank slate, which would later acquire knowledge from experience. Locke's reliance on empiricism and his common sense place him among the rationalists. Although he acknowledged that human reason cannot account for everything in the universe, "the candle that is set up in us shines bright enough for all our purposes."

The philosophes also hailed Newton's discoveries as revelations of ultimate truth. By claiming that the forces of gravitation held the universe together, for instance, Newton made the universe make sense. The philosophes then dramatically asserted that laws of comparable importance could be discovered to govern all phases of human activity. They claimed to be the Newtons of statecraft, justice, and economics.

* Condorcet, *Esquisse d'un tableau historique des progrès de l'esprit humain* (Paris, n.d.), p. 5. Our translation.

The Physiocrats and Adam Smith

Foremost among these "Newtons of the social sciences" were the French *Physiocrats* (believers in the rule of nature) and Adam Smith. The leading Physiocrat was the versatile François Quesnay (1694–1774), biologist, surgeon, and personal physician to King Louis XV and his mistress, Madame de Pompadour, herself a patroness of the philosophes. In articles Quesnay wrote for the *Encyclopédie,* he claimed that the natural laws of economics prove that "land is the only source of wealth, and that agriculture increases wealth.* The mercantilists, therefore, were mistaken in attaching so much importance to the accumulation of money. They tried to regulate commerce, when they should have freed it from controls; they made goods more expensive by levying tariffs and other indirect taxes, when they should have collected only a single direct tax on the net income from land. "Laissez faire, laissez passer" (let do, let pass), the Physiocrats urged, let nature take its course.

Adam Smith.

* From E. Daire, ed., *Physiocrates* (Paris, 1846), I:82. Our translation.

The most famous statement of laissez-faire economic doctrine was made by the Scottish professor Adam Smith in *The Wealth of Nations* (1776). Smith, too, attacked mercantilist attempts to protect industries by high tariffs:

> It is the maxim of every prudent master of a family never to attempt to make at home what it will cost him more to make than to buy. The tailor does not attempt to make his own shoes, but buys them of the shoemaker. The shoemaker does not attempt to make his own clothes, but employs a tailor. . . . What is prudence in the conduct of every private family, can scarce be folly in that of a great kingdom. If a foreign country can supply us with a commodity cheaper than we ourselves can make it, better buy it of them. . . .*

Like the Physiocrats, Adam Smith attributed the wealth of nations to the production of goods, but, unlike them, he argued that production depended upon the labor of farmers, craftsmen, and millhands. Again like the Physiocrats, he minimized the role of the state, claiming that men freely competing to seek their own wealth would enrich the whole of society. It was as if they were being guided by "an invisible hand"—that is, by nature. Smith advised governments to limit their role to providing defense, a police force, and little else.

The mercantilists had placed the state above the individual and expected ceaseless trade warfare among nations. Adam Smith and the Physiocrats proclaimed that both the economic liberty of the individual and free trade among nations were natural laws. Their program of laissez-faire marked a revolutionary change in economic thought. But economic practice was slow to change, and the great powers continued to follow mercantilist policies. In the 1770s Turgot, the chief minister of the French government, tried in vain to free farming and business from the restrictions of mercantilism by applying physiocratic teachings. The Physiocrats overlooked what many other philosophes also neglected: the difficulty of adjusting the simple and reasonable dictates of natural law to the complications of politics and to the irrational side of human nature.

Justice and Education

Letting nature take its course was also the Enlightenment's prescription for improving law and justice. The philosophes were horrified by the unjust and antiquated laws, the cumbersome legal procedures, and the frequent recourse to torture and capital punishment. New lawgivers were needed to simplify legal codes, and a new science was needed to make punishments both humane and effective.

The new science, which laid the foundations for modern sociology, was projected by the Italian philosophe, Cesare Beccaria (1738–1794). His *Essay on Crimes and Punishments* (1764) formulated three basic laws of justice, which are good examples of the Enlightenment's effort to express nature's truths. First, punishments should aim to "prevent the criminal from doing further injury, and to prevent others from committing the like offense. Such punishments ought to be chosen, as will make the most lasting impressions on the minds of others, with the least torment to the body of the criminal." Second, justice should act swiftly, "because the smaller the time between the punishment and the crime, the stronger and more lasting will be the association of the ideas of *Crime* and *Punishment.*" Third: "Crimes are more effectively prevented by the *certainty* than by the *severity* of the punishment. The certainty of a small punishment will make a stronger impression than the fear of one more severe."*

In education, as in justice, the philosophes found that existing institutions failed the tests of reason and natural law. They deplored the control of education by the churches and the stress placed on theology, ancient history, and the Greek and Latin languages. They demanded greater emphasis on science, modern history, and modern languages.

In primary education the most sweeping revisions were advanced by Jean-Jacques Rousseau (1712–1778). Rousseau rebelled against the strict traditions of Calvinist Geneva, his birthplace, and against the intensely bookish studies forced upon him as a boy. The result was *Émile* (1762), half treatise and half novel, with two heroes—Émile the pupil, and Rousseau himself the teacher. The training he prescribed was a total departure from eighteenth-century practice: "Life is the trade I would teach him. When he leaves me, he will be neither a magistrate, a soldier, nor a priest; he will be a man."* He did not discipline Émile or force him to read at an early age. Émile observed the world of nature at first hand, not from books; he learned farming by working in the

* *The Wealth of Nations,* Book IV, Ch. 2.

* From *Essay on Crimes and Punishments,* Chs. 12, 19, 27.

* *Émile* (New York: Everyman's Library, 1911), p. 9.

fields and geography by finding his way in the woods. And when, in his teens, he was finally taught to read, his first assignment was Defoe's *Robinson Crusoe* (1719), in Rousseau's view, "the best treatise on an education according to nature."

Deism and Atheism

Defenders of the Enlightenment campaigned against the role of the clergy in education, particularly the Jesuits, the symbol of militant Catholicism. A campaign for the dissolution of the Society of Jesus won the backing of Catholic monarchs who were angry over Jesuit interference in politics. In the 1760s the Jesuits were expelled from Portugal, France, and even Spain, the homeland of Loyola. The pope dissolved the order in 1773; it would be revived forty years later in a different political and intellectual climate.

On the positive side, the religious program of the Enlightenment was marked by the cultivation of "deism," which had emerged in the seventeenth-century England of Civil War and Newtonian science. Deists like John Locke sought to settle religious strife by reason rather than by resort to arms. All men, they argued, can agree on a few broad religious principles and tolerate any remaining differences. The deists accepted God as the creator of the universe, but they doubted that he was concerned with the daily activities of people or would respond to prayer or bestow grace. Deists attacked as irrational the doctrines associated with the Trinity, the Virgin Birth, and the Eucharist.

The leading exponent of deism in France was Voltaire (1694–1778), who published a stream of letters, plays, tales, epics, histories, and essays. Clear, witty, and sometimes satirical, his writings were enormously popular, especially when they were printed under an assumed name or outside France to evade censorship. Voltaire's histories stressed economics and culture in addition to the conventional concern with war and politics. He also made his French readers aware of the contributions of Locke, Newton, Shakespeare, and other Englishmen. As a young man he had spent three years of exile in England after he had criticized the French government and offended a member of the privileged nobility. Voltaire was enormously impressed by British tolerance:

> If there were just one religion in England, despotism would threaten; if there were two, they would cut each other's throats; but there are thirty religions, and they live together peacefully and happily.*

Voltaire carried on a lifelong crusade for tolerance. His most famous "case" was that of Jean Calas, a Protestant merchant of Toulouse, executed for allegedly murdering his son to prevent his conversion to Catholicism. Voltaire discovered that the case against Calas was based on rumor and that the court condemning him had acted out of anti-Protestant hysteria. And so Voltaire campaigned for three years until the original verdict was reversed and the name of Calas cleared.

The existence of evil, of an injustice like that suffered by Calas, confronted the Enlightenment with a major problem. Few of the philosophes accepted the Christian teaching that evil arose from the original sin of Adam and Eve. If God is purely benevolent, they asked, why then does evil so often prevail in the world he created? They rejected the pessimistic answer provided a century earlier by Thomas Hobbes in *Leviathan,*

Jean Antoine Houdon's bust of Voltaire, 1781.

* *Lettres Philosophiques,* No. 6. Our translation.

published in 1651 and much influenced by England's Civil War. Unless men accept an all-powerful authority, Hobbes argued, the state of nature will become a state of war; men will prey on their fellows and human life will become "solitary, poor, nasty, brutish, short." At the other extreme, many philosophes could not accept the jaunty assertion of Alexander Pope, an English contemporary of Voltaire, that this was the best of all possible worlds:

All Nature is but Art, unknown to thee;
All chance, direction which thou canst not see;
All discord, harmony not understood;
All partial evil, universal good:
And, spite of Pride, in erring Reason's spite,
One truth is clear, Whatever is, is right.

In *Candide* Voltaire satirized the disasters abounding in the best of all possible worlds, an argument made more telling because there had recently been a real disaster, the earthquake, tidal wave, and fire that engulfed Lisbon, the Portuguese capital, on November 1, 1755, and killed some 60,000 people.

Deism enabled Voltaire to reconcile a perfect God and an imperfect world by comparing God to a watchmaker who fashioned a delicate mechanism but assumed no responsibility for its operation once it started to run. Voltaire argued, however, that since only intellectuals were likely to accept deism, the great majority required a more exacting faith. "Man has always needed a brake," he observed, and he built a fine church for the tenants on his estate.

Some philosophes, however, argued that human beings did not require the external brake of religion because their very nature would act as an inner brake. La Mettrie (1709–1751), a French physician, published a book entitled *L' Homme Machine (Man a Machine),* which contended that all the inhabitants of the world, both human and animal, are self-regulating mechanisms made from one universal substance and behaving as their natures compel them to behave. D'Holbach (1723–1789), a German baron residing in Paris, argued that "The virtuous man is one who has been taught by correct ideas that his self-interest or happiness lies in acting in a way that others are forced . . . to approve out of their own self-interest."* D'Holbach was the most outspoken atheist of the Enlightenment. He dismissed God as a "phantom of the imagination," whose existence was denied by the shortcomings and miseries of the world. Such radical doctrines attracted few followers in France, which was not yet prepared to dispense entirely with traditional religion.

* *Systèm de la Nature,* trans. L. G. Crocker, ed., in *The Age of Enlightenment* (New York, 1969), pp. 160–61.

Political Thought

"In politics as in religion toleration is a necessity," said Voltaire. Tolerant Britain was his utopia, and he paid its unwritten constitution the most flattering compliment of an enlightened age by claiming that it "might have been invented by Locke, Newton, or Archimedes." A more detailed analysis of British political virtues was drawn up by Montesquieu (1689–1755), an aristocratic French lawyer and philosopher. In *The Spirit of the Laws* (1748), he asserted that no one system of government suited all countries because of their wide differences in climate, resources, and traditions. Republics were best suited to small and barren countries, limited monarchies to the middle-sized and more prosperous, and despotisms to vast empires. Accordingly, middle-sized and prosperous Britain was quite properly a monarchy limited by aristocracy. The hereditary nobility sat in the House of Lords, and the elected representatives, constituting a nobility of talent, sat in the House of Commons. All this seemed admirable to Montesquieu, who thought the masses "extremely unfit" for government. He found another reason for the political superiority of Britain in the play of checks and balances. In Parliament, Lords and Commons checked one another; in the government as a

Montesquieu: bust by Lemoyne.

whole, a balance was maintained by the separation of powers, legislative, executive, and judicial.

For Americans, Montesquieu and Locke were the most important thinkers of the Enlightenment and their ideas were reflected in the constitution of the new republic. For Europeans, the most important thinker was Rousseau, who inspired the radicals of the French Revolution. Rousseau's ideas proceeded from a sweeping generalization typical of the age: Whereas nature dignifies humanity, civilization corrupts it; humanity would be corrupted less if civilized institutions followed nature more closely. This theme lay at the heart of the educational reform proposed in *Émile.* In an earlier work, the *Discourse on the Origin of the Inequality of Mankind* (1755), Rousseau attributed the vices of civilization to private property:

> The first man who, having enclosed a piece of ground, bethought himself of saying, "This is mine," and found people simple enough to believe him, was the real founder of civil society. From how many crimes, wars, and murders, might not anyone have saved mankind, by pulling up the stakes and crying to his fellows: "Beware of listening to this imposter; you are undone if you once forget that the fruits of the earth belong to us all, and the earth itself to nobody."*

To protect private property men accepted laws and governors:

> They had too many disputes among themselves to do without arbitrators, and too much ambition and avarice to go long without masters. All ran headlong to their chains in hopes of securing their liberty. . . .†

Government was evil, Rousseau concluded, but a necessary evil. In *The Social Contract* (1762), he sought to make the necessity less evil by reconciling the liberty of the individual and the institution of government. This he proposed to accomplish through a revolutionary version of the contract theory of government. From the Middle Ages to John Locke, contracts had hinged on an agreement between the people to be governed and their governor or governors. In contrast to this political contract, Rousseau recommended a *social contract,* in which a whole society agrees to be ruled by its general will. "Each individual," Rousseau explained, "may have a particular will contrary or dissimilar to the general will which he has as a citizen."‡ If the individual insists on putting self-interest above the interest of the community, he must be made to honor the general will. "This means nothing less than that he will be forced to be free."§ Thus the general will has a moral quality, for it represents what is *best* for the whole community, what the community *ought* to do.

Everyone must participate in formulating the general will, according to Rousseau. Executing the general will once it has been formulated, however, could rest with a smaller group. Like Montesquieu, Rousseau believed that the number of governors should vary inversely with the size and resources of the state—monarchy for the large wealthy state, aristocracy for the state of middling size and wealth, and democracy for the small and poor. Rousseau doubted, however, that any state was suited for the absolute form of democracy in which the people themselves executed the laws: "Were there a people of gods, their government would be democratic. So perfect a government is not for men."‖

Almost every radical political doctrine advanced during the two centuries since Rousseau's death has owed something to him. Socialists justify collectivism by citing his attacks on private property and his insistence that "the fruits of the earth belong to us all." Patriots and nationalists hail him for exalting "the dear love of country" and pleading in the final chapter of *The Social Contract* for the establishment of a "civil religion" that would free the state from competing with the Church for the allegiance of citizens.

Rousseau's "civil religion" and "general will" have also been interpreted as totalitarian concepts. Hostile critics see him as a man who worshiped the state and paved the way both for the French Revolution's Reign of Terror and the dictatorships of the twentieth century. This authoritarian interpretation, however, neglects both the strongly idealistic and democratic tone of Rousseau's writings and his personal hostility toward absolutist governments. It seems probable that by the general will Rousseau was simply trying to describe how a good citizen participated in decision-making and then accepted the final outcome. The process was rather like achieving "consensus" or determining the "sense of the meeting," and the concept of the general will attempts to explain the psychology of obedience

* *The Social Contract and Discourses* (New York: Everyman's Library, 1913), p. 192.

† Ibid., p. 205.

‡ Ibid., p. 15.

§ Ibid., p. 15.

‖ Ibid., p. 56.

to man-made laws. Finally, Rousseau's declaration—"Were there a people of gods, their government would be democratic"—has stirred champions of democracy ever since the French Revolution to find ways to make people more godlike. *Émile* showed how education could help, and the *Social Contract* implied that citizens might one day follow the general will naturally and would no longer have to be "forced to be free."

Enlightened Despotism

Some of the philosophes, however, sought a political alternative that could operate more readily within existing monarchical institutions. This was enlightened despotism, for which a hereditary monarchy seemed ideally suited. The monarch, as co-owner of all the territories under his rule, was in the unique position of having his personal interests coincide with the national welfare. Both aristocratic and democratic governments, on the other hand, suffered from a conflict of interests between the ruler's selfish concerns and the well-being of the nation. Only a king could follow the example of the reforming tyrants of ancient Greece and Renaissance Italy and permit the laws of nature to replace the hodgepodge of man-made laws that frustrated progress.

Thus it is scarcely surprising that in the eighteenth century self-proclaimed "enlightened" or "benevolent" despots occupied many thrones. They could claim to be the champions of reason and nature while pressing the age-old fight to make royal authority more absolute. What is more surprising, perhaps, is that some of the despots proved to be genuinely enlightened rulers, as the next chapter will show.

Critics of the Enlightenment

Most of the philosophes expected people to accept reason when it was pointed out to them and to give up the habits of centuries and to behave according to natural law. But people would not always accept reason and would cling to irrational customs and unnatural traditions. The French historian and philosopher, Mably (1709–1785), got at the central problem when he inquired: "Is society, then, a branch of physics?" The philosophes and their followers did indeed try to extend the mathematical methods used in the physical sciences to the unpredictable activities of humanity. The Physiocrats, for example, tried to reduce human economic activities to a few simple laws.

Hume, Rousseau & Kant

But not all the philosophes agreed that society was a branch of physics. David Hume (1711–1776), a brilliant Scot, while sharing the Enlightenment's criticism of existing institutions, was skeptical that anything could be achieved by appeals to nature and reason. Human conduct, he asserted, could not be analyzed "in the same manner that we discover by reason the truths of geometry or algebra."

> The ultimate ends of human actions can never be accounted for by *reason,* but recommend themselves entirely to the sentiments and affections of mankind, without any dependance on the intellectual faculties. Ask a man *why he uses exercise:* he will answer, *because he desires to keep his health.* If you then enquire, *why he desires health,* he will reply, *because sickness is painful.* If you push your enquiries farther, and desire a reason *why he hates pain,* it is impossible he can ever give any.*

The problems that troubled Hume also disturbed two of his contemporaries, Rousseau and Kant. Rousseau coupled a passionate defense of nature and natural law with a warning against relying on reason. "Too often does reason deceive us," he wrote in *Émile.* "But conscience never deceives us, . . . he who obeys his conscience is following nature and need not fear that he will go astray."†

Immanuel Kant (1724–1804), professor of philosophy at the University of Königsberg in East Prussia, advanced a similar argument in Platonic terms. While supporting many of the doctrines of the Enlightenment, Kant also believed in a higher reality rather resembling the Ideas of Plato. He called the eternal truths of the higher realm *noumena* (the Greek term for "things thought") in contrast to the *phenomena* (observations through the senses) of the material world. Knowledge of the world of noumena, Kant believed, reached men through reason—not the reason of common sense, however, but that of intuition. The highest expression of Kant's reason was the *categorical imperative,* the moral law within, the conscience implanted in man by God. When an individual confronted an ethical choice, he must follow the course that would serve as a universal precedent, not just the most expedient solution to his own dilemma.

* *An Enquiry Concerning the Principles of Morals,* ed. L.A. Selby-Bigge (Oxford, 1902), p. 293.

† (New York: Everyman's Library, 1911), pp. 249–50.

Pietists and Methodists

Other reactions against the rationalism of the Enlightenment came from the churches, especially those involved in the Protestant evangelical revival. The revival began with the German Pietists, who were the spiritual heirs of the sixteenth-century Anabaptists. Deploring the deists' stress on natural law and the growing formalism of the Lutheran establishment, they turned to the "evangel," the good news of Christ's teachings. They asserted that faith came from the heart, not the head, and that God was far more than the creator of the world machine. One Pietist leader was a German noble, Count Zinzendorf (1700–1760), who founded the Moravian Brethren and set up a model community based on Christian principles. Moravian emigrants to America planted a colony at Bethlehem, Pennsylvania, helping to give the "Pennsylvania Dutch" their reputation for thrift, hard work, and strict living.

In Britain the example of Zinzendorf and other Pietists inspired John Wesley (1703–1791), an Anglican priest who felt his own faith evaporating after the failure of his two-year ministry in the backward colony of Georgia (1736–1737). Pietism enabled Wesley to recover his faith through inner conviction. For more than fifty years he labored tirelessly to share his discovery, preaching in churches, in the fields, at the shafts of coal mines, and even in jails. He was such a charismatic preacher that crowds who came to scoff remained to pray. When he died, his movement had enrolled more than a hundred thousand adherents, termed Methodists because of their methodical devotion to piety and plain living. Though Wesley always considered himself a good Anglican, the Methodists eventually set up their separate nonconformist chapels ("Church" was reserved for members of the Church of England).

John Wesley in 1788.

The new sect won its following almost entirely from among the lower and middle classes, among people who were seeking the religious excitement and consolation that neither deism nor the austere formalism of the Church of England could provide. The Methodists had in full measure the Puritan conscience of the nonconformists. They agitated against drunkenness, against the trade in slaves, and against the barbarous treatment of prisoners, the insane, and the sick. Wesley opened dispensaries for the poor in London and Bristol and established schools for coal-miners' children. Where the philosophes argued for public reform, the Methodists favored private charity. And where the philosophes sought to attack the *causes* of social evils, the Methodists, while accepting evil as part of God's plan, yet sought to ease its *effects.* On the practical level, the skepticism of the philosophes and the faith of the Methodists contributed to the long process of improving the institutions of society.

IV LITERATURE AND THE ARTS

Literature and the arts also shared in the great modern revolution. The seventeenth and eighteenth centuries witnessed the birth of the novel, the opera, the symphony, and other new media of expression. Writers and painters helped lower rigid social barriers by choosing more subjects from the middle and lower ranks of society. Yet a striking characteristic of these centuries was the extent to which Paris and Versailles served as the arbiters of taste and fashion for most of Europe. Although French military glory had lost its luster by the time Louis XIV died in 1715, Europeans still looked to France for guidance in how to behave at court, what clothes to wear, what to eat and drink, what diversions to pursue and dances to favor, and what books to read, plays to see, and music to hear.

French cultural imperialism depended on the fact that nearly everywhere on the Continent sovereigns, aristocrats, and intellectuals used

An illustration from Abraham Bosse's "Le Palais Royal" (1640) gives a picture of French fashions and taste.

French in preference to their native tongue. German, for example, came close to vanishing as the language of educated Germans, and it was ironic that one of the major heroes of German nationalism, King Frederick the Great of Prussia, habitually spoke and wrote in French. Although English suffered no such eclipse in its home islands, it did not begin to compete with French for international status until the heyday of British imperialism in the Victorian age. Even Shakespeare was as yet little appreciated beyond the English-speaking world because of the difficulty of translating his exuberant language into French. In the fine arts, however, many of the leading innovators were not French but Dutch, English, Spanish, and Italian. And while the greatest monument of neoclassical architecture was Versailles, many of the best examples of the more innovative baroque and rococo styles were to be found in Rome, Germany, Portugal, and even overseas, in Mexico and Peru. France was not an oasis in the midst of a cultural desert but the acknowledged capital of a vigorous culture that had flourishing outposts elsewhere in Europe and in the New World.

Literature

Just as Louis XIV and his predecessors imposed greater discipline on French politics, the classical writers of the seventeenth century disciplined the French language and French literature. They insisted on the observance of more rules, on the authority of models from classical antiquity, and on a more select vocabulary. Early in the 1600s the example of the new refinement was set by the marquise de Rambouillet, an aristocratic lady who held a *salon* (literally, a reception room) in her Paris town house. Later, proper behavior was standardized by the court ceremonial at Versailles and proper vocabulary by the great dictionary of the French language compiled by the experts of the Academy founded by Richelieu. Exaggerated notions of propriety outlawed from polite usage the French equivalents of *spit, vomit,* and dozens of other plain-spoken words. The result was a widening gap between classical French and the coarser language of the majority of French people.

The linguistic purge of the seventeenth century also brought important benefits, for without its discipline French could not have won its unique reputation for clarity and elegance. The great playwrights, Corneille (1606–1684) and Racine (1639–1699), obeyed all the do's and don'ts of classicism. These included the "unities" of Aristotle's *Poetics* which limited the actions of a drama to one place, one twenty-four-hour span of time, and one topic. Within this rigid form Corneille and Racine created moving portraits of

Painting of a Molière farce, with Molière himself shown at the far left.

individuals upholding exalted ideals of honor or crushed by overwhelming emotions. In psychological insights their classical tragedies rank with those of the ancient Greeks.

As a writer of comedies Molière (1622–1673), the other master dramatist of the age, was under less pressure to follow classical rules. He was able to create a gallery of characters who were at the same time distinct individuals and examples of social types. The gallery included the hypocrite *(Tartuffe)*, the miser *(L'Avare)*, the newly rich and self-important *(Le Bourgeois Gentilhomme)*, and the pedantic ladies of the *salons (Les Précieuses Ridicules)*. Like all good satires, those of Molière have more than a touch of moralizing. A more cynical evaluation of human nature appeared in the *Maxims* of La Rochefoucauld (1613–1680), which he phrased in prose of classic purity. Here are two of them: "We generally give praise only in order to gain it for ourselves." "We always find something not altogether displeasing in the misfortunes of our friends."*

Seventeenth-century English literature also had its cynics, notably Wycherley, Vanbrugh, Congreve, and the other playwrights who wrote the witty, bawdy, and disillusioned Restoration comedies. They reflected the violent swing in the pendulum of public taste after the restoration of Charles II against the moralistic Puritans, who had closed the theaters as dens of sinfulness. One Puritan, however, John Milton (1608–1674), who was the secretary of Oliver Cromwell, produced a truly major work of literature—*Paradise Lost*, the only English epic in the grand manner that still attracts many readers. Milton's complex style of writing and his profound belief in Christian humanism made him the last great figure of the English Renaissance rather than a pioneer of English classicism.

To attain classical status the English language needed to standardize its chaotic spelling and restrict the elaborate flourishes and flights of rhetoric favored by Shakespeare and other writers in the age of Elizabeth I and James I. Under the influence of John Dryden (1631–1700), English began to model itself on French, adopting its straightforward word order, its relatively brief sentences, and its concern for polish, neatness, and clarity. English letters then entered the Augustan Age, which lasted through the first half of the eighteenth century, when Britain boasted a group of talents comparable to those of Vergil, Horace, and Ovid in the days of Rome's Emperor Augustus. Addison and Steele made the *Tatler* and

* *The Maxims of La Rochefoucauld*, trans. F. G. Stevens (London, 1939), pp. 49, 173.

Spectator vehicles for popularizing serious intellectual discussion, and Alexander Pope cast his philosophical and satirical essays in the poetic style of rhymed couplets. The greatest writer of the age was Jonathan Swift (1667–1745), author of the corrosive satire, *Gulliver's Travels,* whose pessimism and convictions about human depravity went far beyond the moderation of the classical spirit.

As the eighteenth century advanced, literature in the classical style lost ground to less inhibited and more emotional writings. In England, particularly, the simplification of the language enlarged the market for fiction. Two very early examples were by Daniel Defoe—*Robinson Crusoe* (1719) and *Moll Flanders* (1722), both novels, though masquerading as autobiographies, and both far removed from the refinements of classicism. In 1749 the London magistrate, Henry Fielding, published the first great social novel, *Tom Jones,* which portrayed very realistically both the toughs from London slums and the hard-riding hard-drinking squires of the countryside.

Fielding's contemporary, Samuel Richardson, a printer by trade, wrote three gigantic sentimental novels in the form of letters by the main characters. In *Clarissa Harlowe* (1748), 2,400 pages of small print record the misfortunes of the heroine, whose suitor was a scoundrel and whose greedy relatives were scheming to get hold of her valuable property. Although Richardson was prone to excess emotionalism and preachiness, his description of the struggles of passion and conscience carried such conviction that he won a large middle-class reading public for the novel of "sensibility."

In France the leading novel of sensibility was Rousseau's lengthy account of a conflict between love and duty, *La Nouvelle Héloïse* (1761). Because of the strict sexual morality preached (but not always practiced) by Rousseau, the new Eloise, unlike her medieval namesake in the affair with Abelard, died in time to avoid adultery. The retreat from classicism was also marked on the French stage by the popularity of "tearful comedies," a blend of laughter, pathos, and melodrama.

In Germany the dramas of Lessing (1729–1781) combined the middle-class appeal of Richardson with a moderation and tolerance more in tune with the classical spirit. In his romantic comedy, *Minna von Barnhelm,* the lively heroine pits her feminine values and charm against a Prussian officer in a fashion quite contrary to the stereotype of German militarism. In the 1770s young German writers were associated in the movement called *Sturm und Drang* ("Storm and Stress") that focused on yearning, despair, and self-pity. Its great landmark was the short novel, *The Sorrows of Young Werther,* by the youthful Goethe (1749–1832). This lugubrious tale of a young tutor who falls in love with the mother of his pupils was immensely popular. Napoleon claimed to have read it seven times and wept when the hero shoots himself because the woman he loves is already married.

Architecture

The great palace that Louis XIV built at Versailles is an admirable introduction to the artistic styles competing in the seventeenth and eighteenth centuries. The exterior of the palace, with its emphasis on symmetry and its columns, followed the classical models of Renaissance builders. Neoclassicism extended to the gardens, with their geometrical layout, straight avenues, and carefully clipped trees and shrubs; only the fountains provided a touch of exuberance. Inside the palace, however, exuberance was everywhere—in the dramatic Hall of Mirrors (they created an illusion of great width); the majestic Staircase of the Ambassadors, designed to remind diplomats that the Grand Monarque was unique; and the acres of ceilings painted with smiling cherubs.

The theatricality and lavish embellishments inside Versailles were hallmarks of the style called *baroque,* a term derived from the Portuguese *barroco* (an irregular pearl). Baroque architects placed great emphasis on the vertical line and curves, and on striking effects to assert a building's dominance. A moderate example of baroque, still under classical restraints, is St. Paul's Cathedral in London, designed by Christopher Wren to replace a structure destroyed in the Great Fire of 1666. Even today, when London has a fair quota of skyscrapers, Wren's huge structure still dominates the City, the mile-square financial district. Examples of uninhibited baroque may be found in sites as far apart as Austria and Mexico and, above all, in Rome. Many of the Roman baroque monuments were the work of Bernini (1598–1680), who created the great open spaces and curving colonnades of St. Peter's Square as a most impressive entrance to the imposing basilica designed by Michelangelo. More grandiose than anything on the exterior of St. Peter's is Bernini's baldachin, a canopy over the main altar as high as an eight-story building and supported

Versailles.

by immense twisted columns of bronze, at once massive and restless.

In the early eighteenth century the baroque style evolved into the *rococo,* a term derived from the French word for seashells. Often employing a shell motif in its intricate ornamentation, rococo was lighter and more elegant than baroque, depending less on mass to create an effect and more on graceful lines and elaborate decoration. Some of the smaller European palaces and hunting lodges are charming examples of this style. So are the delicate chairs, tables, and other furniture called Louis Quinze (XV). Rococo taste for the dainty and exotic made Chinese objects extremely popular: scenic wallpaper, painted scrolls, delicate porcelains, and the other decorative items known collectively as *chinoiserie.* An eighteenth-century garden often boasted a pagoda, while the gardens themselves began to exchange the severely formal landscaping of Louis XIV for the more natural look of the English garden.

During the second half of the century, rococo was eclipsed by a neoclassical revival resulting from the discovery of the well-preserved remains of Roman Pompeii, destroyed by the eruption of Vesuvius in A.D. 79. In Paris classical models were used for the strikingly well-proportioned buildings flanking the Place de la Concorde (then called the Place Louis XV). In Britain the Adam brothers adapted Roman models most skillfully to design some of the most elegant townhouses and country mansions ever built. In Virginia, George Washington's residence at Mt. Vernon was a modest example of the neoclassical style still flourishing in America today under the labels of "colonial" or "Georgian."

Painting

A baroque combination of the theatrical and the otherworldly had characterized the paintings of El Greco in late sixteenth-century Spain. Velázquez, the outstanding painter of seventeenth-century Spain, returned to the secular and realistic traditions of Renaissance art. He executed forty faithful portraits of the homely Hapsburg

St. Paul's Cathedral, London.

king, Philip IV, and some marvelous pictures of the royal children and court dwarfs. By painting what the eye sees at a glance, rather than all the details, Velázquez created what has been termed "optical realism."

In the Low Countries, the center of northern European painting in the 1600s, some artists also achieved optical realism in such themes as the painter at work in his studio and the well-to-do businessman and his household. But at least one operated in a thoroughly baroque manner and made painting a big business. Rubens (1577–1640) received handsome commissions from French and English royalty, ran a studio with two hundred students, and executed personally at least part of the brushwork on two thousand canvases, many of them very large. Rembrandt (1606–1669) displayed a more subtle baroque quality in his effort to involve the viewer directly in the action depicted. In successive sketches for *"Ecce Homo,"* when Pilate has the crowd choose between Christ and Barabbas, Rembrandt progressively eliminated the crowd, so that the beholder comes to realize that he is one of the multitude choosing to release Barabbas. Rembrandt, who was a devout member of the Mennonite sect of Anabaptists, is the only great Protestant religious painter, an exception to the Protestant shunning of the visual arts.

In the eighteenth century, painting, too, evolved from the baroque to the rococo. Two French artists, Watteau (1684–1721) and Fragonard (1732–1806), often painted the flirtatious pampered favorites of the court. In England Sir Joshua Reynolds (1723–1792), the president of the Royal Academy, and his talented contemporaries—Romney, Gainsborough and Lawrence—produced handsome portraits of aristocrats and such prominent figures as the actress Mrs. Siddons. The leading innovator was William Hogarth (1697–1764), who accomplished in art what Defoe, Richardson, and Fielding achieved in the novel. Instead of catering to a few wealthy patrons, Hogarth won a mass market for the engravings he turned out in thousands of copies—"Gin Lane," "Marriage à la Mode," "The Rake's Progress," and other graphic sermons on the vices to be found at every level of British life.

Bernini's baldachin in St. Peter's, Rome.

Rubens' "Maria dé' Medici, Queen of France, Landing in Marseilles."

Rococo architecture: the Amalienburg hunting pavilion at Nymphenburg, near Munich.

Velázquez "The Maids of Honor."

Rembrandt's "The Descent from the Cross."

Fragonard's "The New Model."

Reynolds' "Mrs. Siddons as the Tragic Muse."

Music

The seventeenth and eighteenth centuries were the formative period of classical music, when the opera and oratorio, the sonata, concerto, and symphony all made their debut. The first innovators were Italian, followed by Germans, Austrians, and English. In Venice Monteverdi (1567–1643) composed the first important operas, a baroque fusion of music and theater which became so popular that the city soon had sixteen opera houses. Later, operas degenerated into ramshackle vehicles in which "stars" could show off their vocal prowess. The stars themselves provided the final touch of unreality, since male roles were sung by women and female by *castrati* (male sopranos). From Italy Louis XIV imported Lully (1632–1687), musician, dancer, speculator, and politician who vied with Molière for the upper hand in directing the cultural life of the court.

Many techniques of baroque music were brought to perfection early in the next century by a German choirmaster, Johann Sebastian Bach (1685–1750). For the organ Bach developed the fugue, an intricate adaptation of the round in which each voice begins the theme in turn while the other voices repeat and elaborate it. For small orchestras he composed the Brandenburg Concertos, in which successive instruments are given the chance to demonstrate their charms. And for

Hogarth's "The Orgy": a scene from "The Rake's Progress."

choirs and solo voices he composed the Mass in B minor and two moving reenactments of the Passion of Christ, according to the gospels of Matthew and John.

In contrast to Bach's quiet provincial life was the stormy international career of his countryman, Handel (1685–1759). After study in Italy, Handel passed most of his adult years in England attempting to run an opera company. Although he wrote more than forty operas himself, he is best known for the *Messiah* and other sacred works arranged for large choruses and directed to a mass audience. These oratorios were an elaboration on the earlier and simpler Italian oratorios, designed for the tiny prayer chapels called oratories.

Although Bach and Handel composed many instrumental suites and concertos, it was not until the second half of the eighteenth century that orchestral music came to the fore. New instruments appeared, notably the piano, which had a much greater range than its ancestor, the harpsichord. New forms of instrumental music appeared, developed in particular by the Austrian Haydn (1732–1809). He wrote many piano pieces in sonata form, in which two contrasting themes are stated, developed, interwoven, repeated, and finally resolved in a *coda* ("tail" in Italian). For orchestras Haydn grafted the sonata onto the Italian operatic overture to comprise the first movement of the symphony. At the same time, opera itself was making a revolutionary advance, thanks to another German composer, Gluck (1714–1787), who devised well-constructed musical dramas based on the heroes and heroines of classical mythology.

The concerto, symphony, and opera all reached a climax in the works of the Austrian, Mozart (1756–1791), a child prodigy whose versatility multiplied until he died at thirty-five, a debt-ridden pauper. Mozart added new solo instruments for concertos, such as the French horn and the bassoon. He carried one tradition of Italian comic opera to new heights with the lighthearted *Così Fan Tutte* ("Thus Do All Women"); *The Marriage of Figaro,* based on the great hit of the Paris theater in the 1780s, in which the valet outwits and outsings his noble employers; and *Don Giovanni,* a "black comedy" about the havoc wrought by Don Juan on earth before his descent to hell. The ballroom scene in *Don Giovanni* was both a tour de force and a social commentary, as three different tunes were played simultaneously for three different dances—a minuet for the aristocracy, a country dance for the middle class, and for the lower orders a waltz, then not yet accepted as appropriate for polite society.

Indications were multiplying in the eighteenth century that Europe was on the brink of a social revolution. Writers, artists, and musicians no longer had to depend almost entirely on the patronage of the powerful, the well-born, and the rich. In England the growing middle class bought the prints of Hogarth, the novels of Defoe, Fielding, and Richardson, and attended orchestral performances conducted by Haydn. It was symptomatic that Haydn exchanged the patronage of the immensely wealthy Hungarian family of Esterhazy for a successful independent venture with the popular concert audiences of London. Thus, a lively interest in culture was evident among the bourgeoisie when the French began their turbulent experiment with democracy in 1789.

READING SUGGESTIONS on The Great Modern Revolution Begins
(Asterisks indicate paperback.)

General Surveys of the Seventeenth and Eighteenth Centuries

M. Ashley, *A History of Europe, 1648–1815* (*Prentice-Hall); M. S. Anderson, *Europe in the Eighteenth Century,* 2nd. ed. (*Longmans); R. J. White, *Europe in the Eighteenth Century* (*St. Martin's); L. Krieger, *Kings and Philosophers, 1689–1789* (*Norton). Introductory accounts designed for college classes.

The New Cambridge Modern History, Vols. IV–VII (Cambridge). Wide-ranging essays by many scholars covering the period from 1609 to 1763; uneven in quality but often dealing with topics and countries neglected in briefer surveys.

The Scientific Revolution

H. F. Kearney, *Science and Change* (*McGraw-Hill). A many-sided introduction.

H. Butterfield, *The Origins of Modern Science* (*Free Press). A lively and controversial interpretation minimizing the contributions of scientists before Galileo, notably Copernicus.

A. N. Whitehead, *Science and the Modern World* (*Free Press). An incisive critique of the implications of the scientific revolution by a celebrated English philosopher of the early twentieth century.

Martha Ornstein, *The Role of Scientific Societies in the 17th Century* (Arno, 1975). Reprint of a standard study of these important institutions.

J. E. King, *Science and Rationalism in the Administration of Louis XIV* (Johns Hopkins, 1949). Evaluation of the impact on France.

E. A. Burtt, *Metaphysical Foundations of Modern Physical Science* (Humanities, 1967). Reprint of an older study of the links between philosophy and science.

F. H. Anderson, *Francis Bacon: His Career and Thought* (Greenwood, 1978). An informative study of the celebrated English defender of inductive science; first published in 1962.

G. de Santillana, *The Crime of Galileo* (*University of Chicago). An assessment of the famous Italian scientist and the difficulties resulting from his innovative views.

F. Grayeff, *Descartes* (*British Book Centre). An assessment of the equally famous French mathematician and philosopher.

E. Mortimer, *Blaise Pascal* (Greenwood, 1976). Reprint of an older sympathetic study of a remarkable man.

F. Manuel, *A Portrait of Isaac Newton* (*New Republic); and E. Andrade, *Sir Isaac Newton* (Sharon Hill). Reprints of two informative studies of another remarkable man.

The Economic Revolutions

C. M. Cipolla, ed., *Fontana Economic History* (*Watts). Volume II of this introductory study covers the sixteenth and seventeenth centuries, and Volume III the industrial revolution.

S. B. Clough and R. T. Rapp, *European Economic History,* 3rd ed. (McGraw-Hill, 1975). Informative general textbook.

The Cambridge Economic History of Europe, Vols. V and VI. (Cambridge). More advanced scholarly essays by many experts.

T. S. Ashton, *An Economic History of England: The Eighteenth Century.* (*Methuen). A lucid introduction by an expert.

A. Redford, *Economic History of England, 1760–1860.* Another study of the leading innovator in economic revolution.

P. Deane, *The First Industrial Revolution,* 2nd ed. (*Cambridge). Up-to-date study of the British economy from 1750 to 1850, based on lectures to undergraduates at Cambridge University.

The Enlightenment and the Philosophes

P. Gay, *The Enlightenment: An Interpretation,* 2 vols. (*Norton). Comprehensive scholarly survey with extensive bibliographies. Gay has also published several other works on the Enlightenment.

I. Berlin, *The Age of Enlightenment: The Eighteenth Century Philosophers* (*Mentor). A lucid introduction.

N. Hampson, *The Enlightenment* (*Penguin). Another helpful introduction to eighteenth-century thought.

E. Cassirer, *The Philosophy of the Enlightenment* (*Princeton). Important study of the main principles of eighteenth-century thought.

C. Becker, *The Heavenly City of the Eighteenth-Century Philosophers* (*Yale). Delightful essays seeking to prove that the philosophes were less modern in their outlook than is generally believed.

R. Anchor, *The Enlightenment* (*University of California). A stimulating interpretation linking intellectual and social history.

L. Crocker, *An Age of Crisis* (John Hopkins, 1959). Study of the attitudes of eighteenth-century French thinkers toward humanity and the world.

D. Mornet, *French Thought in the Eighteenth Century* (Shoestring, 1969). English translation of an important older study by a French scholar.

C. Frankel, *The Faith of Reason* (Octagon, 1969). Reprint of an older study on the idea of progress in the French Enlightenment.

L. Bredvold, *The Brave New World of the Enlightenment* (University of Michigan, 1961). Highly critical assessment.

R. Darnton, *The Business of Enlightenment* (Harvard University, Belknap Press, 1979). A history of the trials of publishing the *Encyclopédie,* the great vehicle of enlightened ideas.

A. M. Wilson, *Diderot* (Oxford, 1972). The definitive biography of the influential editor of the *Encyclopédie.*

N. Torrey, *The Spirit of Voltaire* (Russell, 1968). Reprint of an older study of the celebrated defender of enlightened ideas.

B. R. Redman, *The Portable Voltaire* (*Penguin). A good sampler of his writings, with an introduction assessing the man himself.

L. Crocker, *J.-J. Rousseau,* 2 vols. (Macmillan, 1968, 1973). A detailed biographical study of this controversial figure. For other assessments, see G. Havens, *J.-J. Rousseau* (Twayne, 1978); A. Cobban, *Rousseau and the Modern State* (*Allen & Unwin); J. Talmon, *The Origins of Totalitarian Democracy* (*Norton); and E. Cassirer, *The Question of J.-J. Rousseau* (*Indiana University). Useful editions of Rousseau's key writings are *The Social Contract and the Discourses* (*Dutton) and *Émile,* in a new translation by A. Bloom (*Basic Books).

Literature and the Arts

F. Artz, *From the Renaissance to Romanticism: Trends in Style in Art, Literature and Music* (*University of Chicago). A helpful introduction.

B. Willey, *The Seventeenth-Century Background* and *The Eighteenth-Century Background* (Columbia). Widely used studies of the relationship between English literature and the broader intellectual and cultural world.

W. P. Ker, *The Eighteenth Century* (Porter, 1978). Reprint of a useful survey.

A. R. Pugh, *From Montaigne to Chateaubriand* (*Humanities). Introduction to prose literature in France during the seventeenth and eighteenth centuries.

J. S. Held and D. Posner, *Seventeenth- and Eighteenth-Century Art* (Prentice-Hall, 1972). An informative comprehensive survey.

S. Faniel, ed., *French Art of the Eighteenth Century* (Simon and Schuster, 1957). Valuable for its coverage of the minor arts.

M. Bukofser, *Music in the Baroque Era* (*Norton, 1947). A survey down to 1750.

C. Rosen, *The Classical Style* (*Norton). Evaluates the contributions of Mozart, Haydn, and Beethoven.

Index